HEADPRESS GUIDE TO THE COUNTERCULTURE

A SOURCEBOOK FOR MODERN READERS

EDITORS

TEMPLE DRAKE & DAVID KEREKES

WRITERS

K A BEER · ANTON BLACK · BEN BLACKSHAW
TOM BRINKMANN · MIKITA BROTTMAN
JAN R BRUUN · MICHAEL CARLSON
JOHN CARTER · RICK CAVENEY
SIMON COLLINS · MARK FARRELLY
DAVID GREENALL · MARTIN JONES
DAVID KEREKES · JAMES MARRIOTT
PHIL DALGARNO · PAN PANTZIARKA · RIK RAWLING
ROBERT ROSEN · JACK SARGEANT
STEPHEN SENNITT · SARAH TURNER
JOE SCOTT WILSON · WILL YOUDS

critical vision — an imprint of headpress

A Critical Vision Book
Published in 2004
by Headpress

Headpress/Critical Vision
PO Box 26
Manchester
M26 1PQ
Great Britain

[**tel**] +44 (0)161 796 1935
[**fax**] +44 (0)161 796 9703
[**email**] info.headpress@zen.co.uk
[**web**] www.headpress.com

British Library Cataloguing in Publication Data
A catalogue record for this book is available from the British Library

ISBN 1-900486-35-0

HEADPRESS GUIDE TO THE COUNTER CULTURE
A Sourcebook for Modern Readers
Text copyright © Respective contributors
This volume copyright © 2004 Headpress
Layout & design: Walt Meaties
World Rights Reserved

Front cover images are details from the following book/zine sleeves (clockwise from top left): *The Killer* (Savoy 2002), *Japan In Bondage* (Artware 1997), *Ultra Violent 3* (UV Magazine 2001), *Careful 3* (Omniumgatherun Press 2003)

Images are reproduced in this book as historical illustrations to the text, and grateful acknowledgement is made to the respective studios and distributors.

All rights reserved. No part of this book may be reproduced or utilised in any form, by any means, including electronic, mechanical and photocopying, or in any information storage or retrieval system, without prior permission in writing from the publishers.

www.headpress.com

CONTENTS

Introduction	4
PERIODICALS	6
ART & GRAPHIC NOVELS	43
Daniel Clowes 81	
Roy Stuart 85	
Crumbs 86	
FILM	89
Italian Horror 127	
MUSIC	129
GRAB BAG NON FICTION	149
Barroom Transcripts 218	
Stewart Home 219	
Machine Dreamers 221	
Bukowski 222	
FICTION	225
Savoy 248	
Contributor Notes	254
Index	256

INTRODUCTION

Counter culture. A catchall expression for the alternative or underground society that the hippies were hoping to create in the late sixties, a society removed from that of the mainstream with its own set of values.

This book doesn't attempt to chart a timeline of the counter culture, rather it free-falls through it by way of the vast assortment of publications which exist as an adjunct to the mainstream press, or which promote themes and ideas that may be defined as pop culture, alternative, underground or subversive.

Guide to the Counter Culture is a book of reviews. Independent to one another these reviews are an informed and fascinating look at a tiny fraction of the material bubbling beneath the surface of popular culture; taken collectively they trace the underground through its printed legacy.

The majority of publications in this book were printed — or have seen a reprint — in the last decade. It is a guidebook firmly and unashamedly entrenched in contemporary society, offering a comparative review of modern pop culture but without losing sight of its heritage.

If this book is something of an eclectic mix, it is because there exists no clear signposts. By including arguably borderline works, ones that can perhaps be assigned to genre and *oeuvre*, *Guide to the Counter Culture* is contributing to the ebb and flow of its ill-defined boundaries.

That is the nature of the transmogrifying beast.

In these pages you will find coverage of Beat authors alongside S&M erotica, luminary artists alongside the production-line superheroes of DC and Marvel, hand produced booklets of severely limited numbers alongside full colour oversize coffee table tomes, tie-in books on Hollywood blockbusters alongside biographies of no-budget renegade filmmakers.

Readers will note that there aren't any specific discourses on the grandmasters and major shakers of counter cultural writing. (An obit for William S Burroughs was scheduled to appear but we ran out of room.) Indeed there aren't any specific discourses on anything. *Guide to the Counter Culture* instead acknowledges that counter-literature took a major turn with the publication of Amok's *Apocalypse Culture* in 1987, a compendium that brought together essays on all manner of disparate, dangerous and plain weird ideas. This type of material certainly wasn't invented with the publication of *Apocalypse Culture*; rather the book pulled it all together in the right place at the right time, giving a focus and direction to the cultural shift hanging in the air.

Apocalypse Culture was the tip sheet for a diseased world. With it came the celebration of the serial killer, unrepentant necrophiles and marginalia slipping into a wider consciousness. A small, but influencing flurry of like-minded titles soon appeared courtesy of new independent publishing houses. Amongst these were titles like *Pranks!* (RE/Search), *The Manson File* (Amok) and *Rants and Incendiary Tracts* (Amok/Loompanics). Book catalogues from left-field publishers and distributors became defining works in their own right, most notably *Amok: Fourth Dispatch* and the *Loompanics Unlimited: Main Catalogue*.

The first issue of *Headpress* journal appeared in 1991, carrying the subtitle "Bizarre culture, deviant conceptions, cinematic extremes". Unlike the above publications, which all heralded from the US, *Headpress* was UK based. Whilst often promoting darker cultural ideas, the debut issue also carried an article by co-editor David Kerekes that pondered the state of post *Apocalypse* literature and its increasingly familiar figureheads, lamenting on the fact that the dark milieu was already out of steam and moving in circles.

Thankfully the counter culture can't stay put for long. Assimilated into the mainstream — which often remains oblivious to all but the most prurient aspects — its roots have been forced to stray further into the cracks and crannies of popular society.

And so low art and high art meet in the middle, where disposable culture is big money and major publishing houses can apply an academic veneer to subjects that once fell way below the critical radar.

With the exception of two reviews (*The Complete Crumb Comics* and *Headpress 23*) all the material in this book originally appeared in *Headpress 13* through to *24*. The former was the first edition on which Kerekes acted as sole editor/publisher and the latter happened to be most recent when the wheels began to roll on *Guide to the Counter Culture*.

All the reviews have been updated for inclusion in this book, with added notes on any significant developments since the material first appeared.

Finally, a big thank you to the reviewers whose writing has graced the pages of *Headpress* (and now this book). It wouldn't have been possible without you. Really.

David Kerekes & Temple Drake
Manchester, England
April 12, 2004

PUBLISHER'S NOTE

While every effort has been made to check the infomation listed in this book and bring it up-to-date, by the time *Guide to the Counter Culture* reaches you some things may have changed. Check first with the relevent publisher that items are still available (mentioning, of course, that you read about them here). If using snail mail be sure to include an SAE or IRC.

Guide to the Counter Culture is not an endorsement of the subject matter of any book or organisation that comes under discussion. In presenting this information, Headpress/Critical Vision are not giving you — the reader — legal, financial, medical, or any other type of advice, and cannot accept responsibility for any loss or damage through use of this book.

SUBMIT TO US

If you would like to send material for review either online [**w**] www.headpress.com, in the pages of *Headpress* or in a future edition of this book, send it to us at Headpress, 40 Rossall Avenue, Radcliffe, Manchester, M26 1JD, United Kingdom. Include on a separate sheet of paper the following details: title / page count / release date / your contact details and email address (as you would like them to appear) / web site / price / postage.

ZINES & PERIODICALS

79 REASONS WHY HITCHHIKING SUCKS
$1.00 (include something for p&p) / Andrea Wyckoff, PO Box 19554, Portland, OR 97280, USA

ALTERNATIVE CINEMA
Alternative Cinema, PO Box 132, Butler, New Jersey 07405 USA / www.alterntivecinema.com / Please make checks payable to Alternative Cinema Inc.

AZRAEL PROJECT NEWSLETTER
40pp / Westgate Press, 5219 Magazine St., New Orleans, LA 70115, USA / www.westgatenecromantic.com

BAD PILLS
£8 / $6.66 / 60pp / Europe: J R Bruun, Munkebekken 257, 1061 Oslo, Norway / http://home.online.no/~janbruun/ / USA: Mike Hunt Comix, PO Box 6366 Chicago, IL 60680, USA / www.mikehuntsonfire.com

BANAL PROBE
$1.50 / 26pp / Alaina Duro, PO Box 4333, Austin, TX 78765, USA / www.mindspring.com/~lainie/oyster.htm / oysterpubs@mindspring.com

BEEF TORPEDO
20 single-side, photocopied pages, US

---

79 REASONS WHY HITCHHIKING SUCKS
Andrea Wyckoff

Two female friends decide to go off on a hitchhiking tour across the US. After travelling from Portland, OR, down to Los Angeles and over to Colorado, they give up and head back home.

This slim booklet — its pages printed on different coloured paper stock — offers an annotated insight into what caused Andrea Wyckoff and her pal to change their minds. In other words, seventy-nine reasons why they think hitchhiking sucks. Reason No 1 is having to

> … listen to people go off on their life stories, like how their wife left them, how they lost their virginity in college to some redhead, and how they think the government sucks.

The booklet is divided into equally short and concise hitchhiking insights, running through a whole bunch of vaguely humorous non-events and dippy on-the-road characters. There are two photo montages (one of which constitutes the cover), offering the opportunity to try and match a blurry Polaroid to relevant folk mentioned in the text. Unfortunately the guy who makes up Reason No 49 — the Cub scout dad — isn't one of them. He lectured the girls on "how bears are attracted to the scent of a girl 'at that time of the month'".

Pity the whole bum trip is over all too quickly. [David Kerekes]

ALTERNATIVE CINEMA 8

Admittedly, we didn't hold out much hope for *Alternative Cinema*, an independent film review zine edited by king of video swill himself, J R Bookwalter (*The Dead Next Door*, *Ozone*). But actually sitting down and perusing the thing we were pleasantly surprised. While it *is* a rather lavish springboard for Bookwalter's own productions (his latest, *The Sandman*, takes pride of place on the cover and grabs a two-page review in this issue), it doesn't necessarily think they're any good (his *Humanoids From Atlantis* "stinks"). *Alternative Cinema* covers a lot of other stuff too, such as the current state of porn in the USA, the trials and tribulations of shooting a low-budget production for Todd Tjersland (*Legion of the Night* — "Always be prepared for the worst. I mean, the absolute *worse* you could possibly imagine."), and of course carries reviews for films by every clod that managed to operate a camera with the lens cap off. This is the "Your Movies… Our Opinions" section, the backbone of the mag, devoting twenty-plus pages to the likes of Tim Ritter's *Creep* ("… features a performance by Tom Karr, the producer of *Deranged*…") and Gary Whitson's *Zombie Holocaust* ("… a number of mud-wrestling and wet T-shirt scenes…"). You know some of these must be *seriously* bad when they're listed, not in the main reviews section, but under the sub-header "Camcorders Should *Still* Be Illegal!" A great source for movies you'd rather read about than actually sit through, and competently written (unlike, say, *Draculina*). [David Kerekes]

Update *Alternative Cinema* is still going — issue 21 is in full colour and features Misty Mundae on the cover. The cost is now $5 + p&p, although there is a reduction in price if you subscribe.

AZRAEL PROJECT NEWSLETTER VOL 6 NO 1

The purpose of the New Orleans-based Azrael Project is "to put forth the word of the Angel of Death and thereby conquer fear through understanding", "to view the world through neither side of eternity, but rather from the threshold between the dimensions of space and time", and "to reconcile Life with Death, rekindle precarnate memory, and replace fear with love". To this end, under management of Leilah Wendell, Azrael put out a small, quarterly forty-page booklet full of all things necromantic, including over-written Gothic poetry, Anne Rice-style ramblings, necrophile erotica, true-life accounts of near-death experiences, personal encounters with the Angel of Death, and the 'Necronet' — a listing page to match-up like-minded goths and ghouls. If you're not put off by the overly adjectival short stories about entropy and stagnation, and you're heavily into vampires, dark erotica and the 'left hand path', this is something nice for you to flick through after the sun goes down. [Mikita Brottman]

Update With Vol 6 No 2, the newsletter folded. The editorial states, however, that "periodic updates and other mailings" will be forthcoming. And there's more than enough stuff on the Project's website listed above to keep you happy in the meantime.

BAD PILLS

Sverre H Kristensen was a Norwegian comic artist who died from a long and painful illness back in 1997. While one might suggest this accounts for some of the venom in his work, it was Kristensen's employment as a designer of cute animals for a children's clothing manufacturer during the nineties that undoubtedly shaped it. Kristensen's drawings are almost Disneyesque in their execution: simple, well-rounded, effervescent and pleasing to behold. As with most all his work, the characters in *Bad Pills* look every bit like they belong in an infant's toy box, except that the strips themselves are full of misdeeds and embittered rants, with graphic depictions of drug abuse and violence. In one story, Prison Toons, a cop on drugs shoots a black guy dead mistaking a sandwich the victim is eating for a gun. To avoid the paperwork, he then makes a 'nigger sandwich' and eats the evidence. Another strip, Daisy Brown, has the unfortunate girl of the title dying from AIDS after being raped by her father. She goes to heaven, only to become a sexual victim of Jesus.

Not really an indictment of our terrible modern times, I rather suspect Kristensen had no point to make whatsoever. *Bad Pills* is hard work — an exercise in vitriol from start to finish. [David Kerekes]

Update Sverre H Kristensen's obituary can be found in *Headpress 17*.

BANAL PROBE 13
The Rectal Thermometer of a Dying Planet

Banal Probe is a family-happy fanzine edited by Alaina K Duro, with layout by husband Steve, and lots of references to the baby. This in itself is a bit off-putting, the contents are similarly worthy but not especially interesting — non-fiction accounts of encounters on the social margins. This issue features a description of a true-life combat scene in Vietnam, somebody's experience trying to get their stuff back from a dump in Marietta, Georgia, and somebody else's experience having sex with an older woman who was still bleeding from a recent hysterectomy. Most of the accounts, however — which range from a couple of paragraphs to a number of pages — are memoirs of parents, recently-dead friends and neighbours, and the wonder of children, rather than more interesting encounters with strangers. Many of these tales of life-changing moments are by Alaina K herself. Uplifting accounts of daily blessings for eco-friendly alternative-types who like to 'experience'. [Mikita Brottman]

Update From the website: "bAnal Probe No 15 is currently available for $2. Back issues are also available. Submissions of a true-story nature are always welcome." So if you've bonked anyone post-hysterectomy lately, let them now.

BEEF TORPEDO 9

These are strange days indeed when this little bugger can pop through your letterbox unsolicited, draped in anonymity. Beyond the golden buns of the college jock on the front cover, *Beef Torpedo* is nothing more than a poorly produced advertisement feature/confessional for gay men devoted to mutual masturbation and DIY. With a very brief appreciation of Tom of Finland (including four illustrations from *The Rope*), a full-frontal shot of porn stars Chris Lord and Tom Chase, this is basically a two-article zine. And a surprisingly tame one at that. The first article

BIZARRISM
$5 / 40pp / 1999 / Chris Mikul, P.O. Box K546, Haymarket, NSW 1240, Australia / cathob@wr.com.au

BLOODSONGS
£2.95 / 64pp / BBR, PO Box 625, Sheffield, S1 3GY, UK / www.bbr-online.com

BLUE BLOOD
$7.95 / 2625 Piedmont Road, Suite 56-332, Atlanta, GA 30324, USA / www.blueblood.net

BOMBA MOVIES
31pp / £1.95 / J.Marriott, Flat 8, 21 Victoria Square, Bristol, Clifton, BS8 4ES, UK

BOOK HAPPY
$5 / 34pp / Donna Kossy, PO Box 86663, Portland, OR 97286, USA / dkossy@book-happy.com / www.book-happy.com

---

deals with a visit to a Philadelphia jack-off club called Philly Jacks, a venue I gather is a regular haunt of the editor (check out the website at [w] www.philadelphiajacks.com), and the second article deals with a visit to a $28 a night gay guest house in Atlantic City.

Editor "Bob" begins with his discovery of Ocean House, a fifteen-room men only hotel while browsing the classified section of the *Philadelphia Gay News*. Subsequent investigation reveals the hotel management considers clothing 'optional' on the premises, and warns that self-gratification in a room with the door open "may be seen as invitation for anyone else to participate". As you would expect, "Bob" just can't wait to pay a visit. The funny thing is, his entire stay proves a total disappointment. The place is run down, sandwiched between derelict buildings, the fifty-year-old owner wears only boxer shorts and sandals and — tragically — our editor is the one and only guest! So it's DIY by circumstance for the time being, until, that is, he's caught in the act by the owner who gets spattered with sperm ("Bob" certainly isn't choosy).

After a certain amount of digression regarding various pornographic videos, "Bob" makes his exit only to discover a handsome young man has just checked-in. Sod's law! Despite the veritable orgy that never was, I get the feeling that at least some satisfaction was granted and, without a tendency to exaggerate about his sexual exploits, I believe every word.

And just in case you wanted to know a little more about the elusive "Bob", he gives us a simple tracing of his modest erection on page three ("What I lack in length I make up for in thickness"). It must have been tempting to stretch the truth somewhat with this one, after all, who's gonna find out? In an age where size matters, I'm touched by such honesty. [David Greenall]

Update No trace of this one, but unbelievably, the url for Philly Jacks still works. Maybe you could ask them if they know where "Bob" is.

BIZARRISM 7
Chris Mikul's chronicle of kooks and charlatans makes a fascinating read, with articles on the anatomy of conspiracy theory, the great rip-off of the sea-monkeys, Donald Cammell and *Performance* and the first in a series on 'My Favourite Dictators' (No 1: Ceausescu). Equally entertaining are the book reviews and illustrations, also by Mikul (check out his crazed comic-strip adaptation of AG Major's 1915 poem "The Idiot Boy"). Dann Lennard has an illuminating piece on the Von Erich pro-wrestling family dynasty ("an obsessive father who guided five sons into wrestling only to see four of them die through drugs and/or suicide"), and there's an interesting article by James Cockington on pervy Australian sculptor Lyall Randolph. But the bulk of the work is Mikul's, which happily gives the magazine a nice coherence and unity of tone and style. Mikul has a connoisseur's eye for the uncanny coincidences and freakish details of these bizarre, neglected and not-so-charmed lives, which makes this bi-monthly publication a genuinely compelling read. [Mikita Brottman]

Update Bizarrism No 8 is now available, featuring evil clowns, transvestite murder and Chairman Mao (My Favourite Dictator No 2). A *Bizarrism* book is published by Headpress.

BLOODSONGS 8

A magazine devoted to all aspects of the macabre... coming at macabre from a Ronnie James Dio angle, y'understand. And, wouldn't you just know it, the ex-Sabbath frontman is interviewed; so are King Diamond, a "Danish-bred Heavy metal group". Apparently, *Bloodsongs* has gone through a change of publisher and had a year's hiatus between the last issue and this, and while it's a bit too much 'leather wristbands' for my sensitive tastes, solace may be found in Kyla Ward's piece on horror fiction for kiddies (*à la* the Goosebumps series). [David Kerekes]

Update Issues 8 & 9, produced by the original Australian editor before he suspended production of the magazine, are still available from BBR. *Bloodsongs* is now put out by Implosion Publishing in the US.

BLUE BLOOD 7

This is a little surprising. It looks like any one of a number of glossy horror and 'vampire chic' magazines currently in vogue, most of which seem to be emanating from the US and Australia. Well, while the calibre of the writing is on a par with those publications — "I've just never been that big a fan of torture murders (although I know some of you are,) [sic] but I've always wanted to try cannibalism" — its content is decidedly more risqué, with *Hustler*-type photo spreads — but switching the sexy secretary scenario for shaved-blonde-piece-with-fangs and her curiously coiffured boyfriend. It ends with him being butt-fucked with a strap-on. Another spread features two lesbians, playing with a bag of anal love toys against a tropical backdrop, and getting covered in mud/shit.

So long as you don't stray into the text, you might get a rise out of it.

Blue Blood — a non-humour magazine that has on its cover 'The Trade Mag of Cool'. [David Kerekes]

Update Old issues of *Blue Blood* are available at the above website, otherwise it is now an online mag.

BOMBA MOVIES 6

This sleazy little item has been around for quite a while now, but times have changed and *Bomba Movies* now costs £1.95 more than it used to. With early issues bearing a resemblance to those great American zines of the eighties such as *Gore Gazette* and *Subhuman*, cut and paste production has made way for professional composition of image and text and glossy paper. But do not for one minute think that this means the Bomba boys have traded in their damaged brains for more sensible models. *Bomba Movies* is still a riot, it's just easier to read now.

This issue is an all review issue, twenty-nine in all. A typical Bomba movie being crammed full of strong violence, gore, and hardcore sex. *Emanuelle in America*, *Porno Holocaust*, *Entrails of a Virgin*, *The Killing of America*. Just don't mention horror-comedy, *Bomba Movies* hates these with a vengeance (so do I). Some of the reviews are updated reprints from earlier issues, but even if you have all these, don't let this put you off, it's worth buying just for the amazing (unrelated) stills and illustrations that accompany the reviews.

But the real fun to be found here is in the writing style, vulgar without being juvenile. And it's not for the uninitiated, if you have never seen a porno video featuring Peter North then I am afraid you will not fully appreciate the review of *Entrails of a Virgin*!

Bomba Movies is required reading for all (I steal the following quote from the *Bomba* review of Joe D'Amato's *Porno Holocaust*: "junk movie fans in search of that ultimate fix of mayhem, mutilation and glistening twats". [David Greenall]

Update Copies of *Bomba Movies* are still available. Send an A4 SAE with a couple of stamps to the above address.

BOOK HAPPY 1, 2, 3, 4

Give praise to all the powers of Heaven & Hell for the materialisation of this amazing little zine! A much-needed review of strange, out of print, off-the-beaten-path books and all things pulp. If you have an inquiring mind, and are not afraid of where it might lead you, this zine is for you. Likewise if you enjoy finding unwanted books in the trash, or find very peripheral pseudo science and theory your cup of tea, Ms Kossy (famed for her excellent zine and book, *Kooks*) has served it up again in assembling this menagerie of writers and connoisseurs of unusual pulp. It's refreshing in these days of zine proliferation — where you can pick out any ten and read reviews of the same newest "cutting edge" books — to have a publication with hindsight and foresight enough to forego all that and go for the throat. The articles and reviews in *Book Happy* are a combination of precise criticism, wry and insightful humour and just plain interesting information for the basic bibliophile. Pick a review, any review — *A Strange Manuscript Found in a Copper Cylinder* (1888), for example, in issue No 2, an early social commentary

BRUTARIAN
$2.95 / 84pp / PO Box 210, Accokeek, MD 20607, USA / www.brutarian.com

BUKOWSKI ZINE
£2.50 / 40pp / PO Box 11271, Wood Green, London, N22 4BF / www.members.aol.com/sbaker1357

CAREFUL
£1.25 & £2 / 28pp & 36pp / Omnium Gatherum Press, 5c Whitehall Court, Retford, Notts, DN22 6JQ UK / www.altarimage.co.uk/careful

CARPE NOCTEM
$5.00 / 80pp / 260 S Woodruff Avenue Ste, 105, Idaho Falls ID 83401, USA / www.bbr-online.com

disguised as a fantasy novel. We get a review, a reproduction of the cover of the original book (published anonymously and posthumously) and a sample of one of the engravings from the original edition. Also a synopsis of the book and its publishing history, with a few notes on its Canadian author, James De Mille (d 1880), and his other works. The coverboy for issue No 3 is one Casimir Zwerko, a son of Polish immigrants who seems to have been a bachelor recluse of some sort, whose legacy is an attic filled with thousands of strange books, tabloids, pamphlets, magazines and personal manuscripts of a pornographic nature. This attic treasure is discovered by a student who rents the attic room for next to nothing and discovers the pulp treasure. The student hips the author of the article, who she knows to be a lover of strange and curious books, to the incredible find in the attic. The rest of the article is about the rescuing of these things and the loss of the ones left behind. It all makes for a most Lovecraftian little adventure, minus the cosmic entities. A pulp addict's dream come true! Issue No 4 leads off with an editorial about the pitfalls of eBay — the online auction site where you can find almost anything, including strange books, some cheap, some not so. I myself have acquired this bad habit, only with magazines, not so much books — yet. The problem with my addiction is I don't stop with $5 bids. The issue is rounded out with diverse articles such as 'The Epidemic of Bad Drug Books', an article on Tom Sharpe, 'master of black humour', collecting books on UFO contactees, 'Lurid Pamphlets In Merrie Olde England' and much more. All issues are heavily illustrated with reproductions of book covers as well as diagrams and illustrations from within their covers. This zine will be well loved by anyone who loves books, and drooled upon by those who love sacred and profane esoterica. My one concern is the day all these books are brought to light and there will be no more to find; when there will be twenty people bidding on each title on eBay, because they will all have become 'highly collectable' and — *gulp!* — fashionable! So go quietly and send for *Book Happy* but don't show or tell too many people… sshhh! [Tom Brinkmann]

Update Well bless her cotton socks; we are relieved to have discovered that Donna has not abandoned her quest for printed treasures and the latest issue of *Book Happy* is No 7. There is now a website which includes a weird book catalogue, ordering facilities and an excellent list of weird books links. Enjoy.

BRUTARIAN 35
Now that the essential ingredients of 'low brow' or 'trash' culture (as it likes to refer to itself as) have been appropriated by the mainstream, what's left for those who want to feel like they're 'out on the edge'? Either you admit that there is no edge and shamelessly and happily indulge your interests or start immersing yourself further into the nether-regions of Western culture where you are inevitably left with C90s of bad noise made by ugly men in their bedrooms and zines praising Ted Bundy for being a real man.

Brutarian is one of those rare titles that remains outside the mainstream — partly down to production values — but can still provide a thrill for the curious who don't feel their nuts are being cupped by *FHM* skim-jobs on hot rods or Mexican wrestlers. Editor Don Salemi has managed to keep it and his enthusiasm truckin' down the highway for thirty-five issues which is as solid testament as any to his steely-eyed resolve and unwavering commitment to things that excite and interest him.

On the surface it seems to be predictable enough — Mitch O'Connell cover and interview, Nick Zedd interview (yes, for the thousand, millionth time), obscure horror films — but what saves the title is the healthy attitude and sense of humour displayed by the contributors. The whole exercise buzzes with enthusiasm and a sense of play that make just about everything else look like a list of guests at a funeral. It starts off with an amusingly irreverent Letters Page that features mail from the likes of Mike Tyson, Ariel Sharon, The Pope and George W Bush. From then on you've got a gist of the tone but it's not all superficial humour — the Mitch O'Connell interviewer actually gets the man to talk about his work and his techniques and doesn't just riff on about 'martini's and floozies and kitsch'. There's a totally unexpected and insightful interview with fifties Country singer Wanda Jackson and an interesting discussion of the snuff issue that comes to pretty much the same conclusions as Messrs Kerekes & Slater did in *Killing For Culture*. Interspersed are cartoons and artwork that are *not* shit, which is an amazing feat in this day and age, and pages and pages of reviews. In amongst the inevitable coverage of no-hoper punk albums there's plenty of column inches given to smart assessments of Santana remixes by Bill Laswell, Impulse's recent re-issue of Coltrane's last ever gig, Feral House's *Voluptuous Panic*, a Henry Darger collection, a reissue of Lautremont's *Maldoror* and even Dean R Fucking Koontz! For what is seemingly a 'trash' magazine I came away buzzing with new ideas and new things to seek out. I know the purpose of most modern magazines is partly to act as a kind of catalogue but at least *Brutarian* has the taste to feature things that the genuinely engaged and curious reader would want to know about. There's something for everyone here and fans of *Headpress* could *not* go wrong in making the effort to get a copy. Fuck it, make it a subscription. [Rik Rawling]

Update As of writing *Brutarian Quarterly* is now up to No 39.

BUKOWSKI ZINE 4

The Bukowski scene really seems to be thriving since the death of the grizzle-faced old lush, who appears to be gaining the status of a sordid guru for a new generation of European neophytes. For new followers of this alcoholic idol, Rikki Hollywood's *Bukowski Zine* offers a wide and interesting selection of cartoons, comic strips, reviews of Bukowski movies, reviews of other Bukowski fanzines and a guide to all the hard-living drunkard's books and poems. Most interesting, perhaps, is the brief analysis of the 'Beat' and 'Meat' writers and the pages devoted to work of other members of the 'Meat School' — Harry Crews, Jack Black, Edward Bunker and Hubert Selby Jr. [Mikita Brottman]

CAREFUL 1 & 2

Some of the names involved with *Careful* will be familiar to regular readers of *Headpress*, so don't expect it to be a regular comic book. The debut number was a courageous but naturally tentative and faltering step, with both comics and text-based pieces, and showcasing the oddball talents of Martin Jones and artist Oliver Tomlinson in the strip Everything Becomes Nothing. If you want a foothold, think of Edward Gorey if he had ever got to work for D C Thompson. For issue No 2 some of the more raw aspects of artwork have been ditched, the balance is more in favour of comic strips, and the whole thing has a more sure-footing. Here Jones and Tomlinson offer us Goodbye To The Cancer Ward, a kind of observation on the futility of sexual fantasy — hey, I'll be the first to hold my hand up if I'm way off the mark — as well as the more openly satirical It's An Odd Boy Who Doesn't Like Sport (my favourite piece this issue). Elsewhere, Rik Rawling pays homage to *2000AD*'s D R & Quinch, and a crazed fan emails his plans to abduct Christina Ricci. It would be remiss of me not to acknowledge the contribution of Darren Jones, whose fine pen-and-ink work we could well do more of. All in all *Careful* promises to evolve into something truly fresh and majestic. [Joe Scott Wilson]

Update Careful No 4 is now out. Also available from the same publisher is Rik Rawling's *Shock Beef*, limited to fifty numbered copies only.

CARPE NOCTEM 13

With a title that (I presume) means bats that seize the pleasure of the moment, this could be nothing else but a Goth magazine. Glossy and well-produced, *Carpe Noctem* if fodder only for those children of the night still trapped within the black-eyed, black-nail-varnished, lager and black drinking Gothic Rock days of

CHAOTIC ORDER
£2 / 3-issue sub £5 / 40pp / Chaotic Order, 15 Digby Close, Doddington Park, Lincoln, LN6 3 PZ, UK / atrocity-367@fsmail.net

COP PORN
$5 / 84pp / 1573 N. Milwaukee Ave #481, Chicago, Il 60622, USA

DAINTY VISCERA
United Federation of Contempt 1998 / address & price unknown

DELIRIUM
56pp / www.mediapublications.co.uk

DERRIERE
£3.99 / Gold Star Publications Ltd / www.gold-star-publications.com

the mid 1980s. I am amazed there is so much interest in this stuff, I thought this lot had died off with the *Batcave* and the Virgin Prunes! But no, the entire magazine is crammed with advertisements from companies flogging black vampire fetish clothing, skulls and bones jewellery, Gothic CDs and 'accessories'. Maybe I am out of touch, or just too old, but this stuff really bores the pants off me! Music reviews and fiction aside (I am not even attempting to read the fiction!), there are a few... well... three points of interest here. The centre pages, which are irritatingly inserted upside down, deal with the oriental art of foot binding. This beautifully designed colour insert deserves a better afterlife. As does a pretty good article on the artistry and manufacture of gravestones. But best of all is the cringe-inducing 'Cinematic Autopsy: The Artistry of the Giallo Film'. Dario Argento's anus must be clean enough to eat your dinner off after this sycophantic scrawl. *Opera* is described as "a stunning display of camera pyrotechnics and fluid motion utilised within the fabric of a seductive mystery" and "truly inspired". But I am saving the best bit till last. Lamberto Bava is "every bit the film-maker his father was". Need I say more? [David Greenall]

Update Carpe Noctem is up to issue 16 and this and other issues can be found at BBR.

CHAOTIC ORDER 7

Chaotic Order is an A5 zine published on a (theoretically) bi-monthly basis which dabbles in much the same sort of dodgy extreme/exploitation culture as *Headpress*, though admittedly in a less in-depth way. This issue features interviews with Richo Johnson of *Grim Humour* and *Adverse Effect*, industrial band Leech Woman, a sort of FAQ piece on power electronics band Whitehouse (largely culled from the Susan Lawly website), a piece on 'Xenomorph-osis' by Cinema of Transgression veteran Nick Zedd, a profile of Nick Zedd's old mucker Kembra Pfahler, articles on Mondo movies and necrophilia, and a pretty terse and opinionated review section. There is also a quite gratuitously revolting and not very good short story called 'Assault' by 'Mr E' — I guess this sort of goes with the territory — and some not very literate poems and other bits and pieces.

Overall, production values are reasonably good, though some more time spent with the spellchecker wouldn't go amiss, and there are a couple of bits of white-on-black text that I couldn't read at all. Like all the best zines though, there is a very personal flavour and distinctive editorial voice to *Chaotic Order*, which you may find either endearing or irritating.

One final point: the editor of *Chaotic Order* is named Bob Smith. I was watching Russ Meyer's *Faster, Pussycat! Kill! Kill!* last night, and seventy-three minutes into the film the name 'Bob Smith' is clearly visible on Tura Satana's licence plate. Coincidence or something more sinister? I think we should be told. [Simon Collins]

Update Chaotic Order is now up to issue 15, and I am now a regular contributor — which I wasn't when I wrote this review

COP PORN
Lively Essays for the
New Police State
Dan Kelly

Dan Kelly writes concise essays in a pleasing style. This collection of essays by Kelly — culled from a variety of publications printed over the years — covers an enormously broad array of subjects. Everything, in fact, from the Art and Practice of Cadaver Display, to the Physical Properties of the Stigmata. Elsewhere, he provides a historical discourse on the eating of one's dog and a Top Ten of White Supremacist book titles (*Hollywood Reds Have Acquired Strange Protectors* by Myron Fagan is at the bottom of the list). The articles average about two pages apiece. [David Kerekes]

DAINTY VISCERA
VOL 4 NO 6

Ah, America. Land of the free, home of the brave. Home, too, of the First Amendment, guaranteeing freedom of speech, and leaving people more or less able to publish what they like (Mike Diana notwithstanding). Hence the existence of Loompanics Unlimited, *ANSWER Me!* magazine, and Paladin Press, crazed survivalist purveyors of such 'information-only' gems as *Ragnar's Guide to Home and Recreational Use of High Explosives* (I'm not making this up!). Hence, too, *Dainty Viscera*. This small-format B&W zine contains, amongst other things, an interesting interview with Jim Blanchard, *ANSWER Me!* cover artist and inker of Peter Bagge's *Hate!* comic in its latter-day, much-unloved colour incarnation. Also a strange piece of fiction (?) entitled 'The Feraliminal Lycanthropizer'. So far, so uncontroversial. The First Amendment-stretching doozy of this issue, however, is a two-page article at the back by one 'Bob Arson' (any relation to Bob Violence from *American Flagg*!?), called 'Butchering the Human Carcass for Human Consumption'. This is an informative and technical piece about, well, killing and eating people, illustrated textbook-style by Sergio Posada. The tone is largely dry and non-judgemental, although not entirely devoid of a certain lip-smacking relish:

> We personally prefer firm Caucasian females in their early twenties. These are 'ripe'. But tastes vary, and it is a very large herd.

Not having even killed, much less, eaten anyone myself (though don't think I haven't been tempted), I can't really judge the quality of the advice offered on skinning and butchering, but it all seems pretty sensible. Believe me, I'm more than happy to be wrong about this! Serving suggestions are largely absent, apart from some tips on what to avoid:

> In the female the breast is composed largely of glands and fatty tissue, and despite it's [sic] appetising appearance is rather inedible.

So, essential reading for all you budding Geins, Dahmers, Nilsens and Albert Fishes out there? Well, there's a snag. *Dainty Viscera* bears neither a price nor a contact address, contenting itself with the helpful suggestion that you, "… send a SSAE to a random address anywhere in the USA and we'll get back to you in a flash". And trust me, gentle readers of *Headpress*, when I assure you that it is for the benefit of your immortal souls that things should be left thus. [Simon Collins]

Update Good luck.

DELIRIUM 4
The Essential Reference Guide to Delirious Cinema

With issue 4, this entertaining investigation into Italian cinema reaches the year 1981. Twelve months of celluloid horror, crime and filth culminating in a myriad of familiar and not-so-familiar titles. Here you will find the likes of Lucio Fulci's *Black Cat*, Umberto Lenzi's *Cannibal Ferox* (incidentally, the shot of Zora Kerowa, her breasts skewered with meat hooks, has recently been seen in newsgroup smut pages under the posting 'hookbabe'), Alan Birkinshaw's *Horror Safari*, Ovidio Assonitis' *Madhouse*, and not least, Lee Castle's *Watch Out For Those Two… Nymphomaniacs* (not its actual title, but the one we like best). Comprehensive production notes are followed by a synopsis and one or two informed reviews. Also included in this issue are interviews with directors Luigi Cozzi, Antonio Margheriti, Michele Soavi, and Joe D'Amato, with a couple of filmographies thrown in for good measure. Here's the kind of devotion to detail and retentiveness that a major publishing house would scoff at. Excellent. [David Kerekes]

Update There is a site at [w] www.deliriummag.com which covers the same ground as the above, but confusingly states that *Delirium* magazine in print form ended with No 3.

DERRIERE 39

Seems like every product these days is the 'New' version — 'New, Fresher' or 'New, Whiter' — and porn is no exception. Always adaptable and aware of the need to 'keep up' with public tastes, porn is often a more reliable indicator of cultural trends

DESIRE DIRECT
£4 or 6 issues for £10 / 138pp / Moondance Media Ltd, 192 Clapham High St, London SW4 7UD

DRACULINA
$7 / Draculina, PO Box 587, Glen Carbon, Il 62034, USA / www.draculina.com

THE EROTIC REVIEW
£2.50 / 48pp / Vestry Rd, Sevenoaks, Kent TN14 5XA, UK / www.theeroticreview.com

than many a survey.

Which brings us to *Derriere* — or rather 'New' *Derriere* and, for once, the change is noticeable. I've monitored the progress of this magazine on and off over the years and for all those put off by the consistent appearance of sub-*Razzle* swamp donkeys, I'm happy to report that all that has changed. A quick flick through this issue is enough to make the heart sing and the juices flow. These girls are all lookers and more than willing to go down on all fours and pull their arse cheeks apart so we the Readers can get a gynaecological close-up view of their rectums. Because, in case the title is too subtle (and judging by the content perhaps 'Count My Rings' would be more appropriate) *Derriere* is designed specifically for the growing army of anal maniacs out there. Quite what has made anal sex so popular — it was taboo subject matter until very recently in Britain — is open to many theories, none of which are relevant here. What does seem apparent is that despite the cover price being a full £1.50 higher than the ubiquitous Paul Raymond titles, *Derriere* is a big seller, with new copies flying out the door of the newsagent that I frequent.

With a gloss card cover and top notch paper throughout, *Derriere* doesn't shirk on the production values, and the photo scenarios don't seem as stilted as those featured in the likes of *Men Only*. There's little in the way of Readers' Letters but what there is gets right down to the butt-slammin' action. Invariably these are two-guys/one-girl orientated, with the first guy permanently wedged in the eager lady's mouth, while the other stud drills away at her arse. The pop shot is always delivered over her 'gaping hole', but doing little to quench her seemingly insatiable thirst for semen... These stories are absolutely pared to the bone; Olympic fit with not a trace of fat, serving only to get the reader's blood racing before he (or she) embarks on his (or her) journey through the photo spreads. For me this issue peaks early with the first guy/girl scene ('Indecent Proposal') in which a really attractive and stacked brunette with a wide, firm rear, has donned stockings and PVC to cavort with some rent-a-stud (who's head hair is jet black but, curiously, whose pubes are blonde — an intriguing inversion of the usual Collar & Cuffs mismatch). As you'd expect in magazines of this price range, there are no insertion shots (which, to be honest, would destroy a lot of the fantasy aspect for many readers), but our boy's bacon torpedo is at full stretch and often seen poised precariously at the gates of her pussy/arse.

Further in (the mag, that is) we get 'Virgin Fresh' where a girl I recognise from many a *Mensworld* shoot is sporting glasses, pigtails and posing arse in the air in what looks like a young girl's bedroom, complete with teddy bears and fluffy white rug. She's got a great body but the paedophilic aspect leaves me cold. The two-girl session ('Bottom Dwellers') is a must for blonde fans everywhere but not pubic hair fans, as both ladies sport the dreaded 'racing stripe'.

As is so often the case, the last quarter of *Derriere* is taken up with ads for phone sex, videos, sex toys and other Gold Star publications. It's interesting to note that the photos that accompany the phone line ads here don't feature any of the inept censorship of the Paul Raymond mags, where mention of anal sex is still avoided.

But the real connoisseur won't give a fuck about that, he (or she) will have flipped right back to the hot brunette photos — revelling in the knowledge that, yes, this is the new Derriere. [Rik Rawling]

Update The new *new Derriere* now costs £6.99.

DESIRE DIRECT

While you could probably beat your meat to it, this isn't really a porn mag as such. The Readers' Letters seem a little fabricated, true, but cover such topics as a girl getting her boyfriend to go with another man. That doesn't happen in porn mags. There's also an article on the pleasures of chubby-chasing (complete with beached-whale photos), which you don't get in porn mags — not many porn mags anyway. No, *Desire Direct* is for singles and couples with an interest in sex and the erotic, hence articles on cyberporn, readers' porny poems (including, somewhat incongruously, 'Working Girl' the melancholy tale of a junkie prostitute who tops herself), David Flint on Michael Ninn, Tuppy Owens on honeypot-holing (that's fisting to you), a shit heap of contacts and a shit heap of ads. One of the ads is for Fiona Cooper's videos — she's got a better class of model these days. Some of the writing is a little prosaic, but I like this magazine; it has joyful, non-exploitative attitude towards its subject matter. [Anton Black]

DIABOLIK 1

Diabolik is devoted to "il cinema fantastico Italiano"; the debut number carries pieces on the music of Goblin, a guide to Italian Apocalypse movies (part one), Spaghetti Westerns, interviews with Dario Argento and Michele Soavi, and a spot of 'nunsploitation'. It will be interesting to see how *Diabolik* progresses, because, as the contents of No 1 would indicate, the world of Italian cinema devotee-ism can be very familiar indeed. It is for this reason that the most entertaining moments come via Ian McCulloch, as he talks of his short but colourful acting career, from TV's cult series *Survivors*, to starring in the seminal chunk-blowers *Zombie Flesh-Eaters*, *Contamination* and *Zombie Holocaust*.

Q: *How did you feel about* Zombie Flesh-Eaters? *Did you like the film?*
A: *(Pause) No, not really. It's a very silly and horrible film.*

[David Kerekes]

Update Diabolik No 2 can be found at [w] www.midnight-media.demon.co.uk

DRACULINA 29–33

Draculina has an identity problem. Is it a horror comic, showcasing a rather poor comic strip about a sexy female vampire? This would be a waste, as there seems like there should be a niche for a magazine devoted to contemporary schlock horror and thrillers, featuring photo spreads from imaginative B-movies and enthusiastic pictorials of naked stars. Or is it historical? The high point of these five issues is a feature in No 29 by editor Hugh Gallagher, chronicling the deaths and lives of porn suicide Savannah and perennial problem starlet Margaux Hemingway.

On the other hand, Gallagher's similar feature on seventies B-queen Claudia Jennings in No 31 adds little that is not already available to her film legend, or to the details of her highway crash-style death. Even the pix are uninspired.

There are signs that Gallagher is tempted to take *Draculina* down the soft-focus silicone path that *Scream Queens* and *Femme Fatales* have already staked out (so to speak). This would be a mistake. The positive side of *Draculina* is its raunchiness, its authenticity, and its real position outside the commercial mainstream.

Thus it's a little surprising that the main feature in the so-called Special Vampire Issue (No 33), which otherwise offers nice pieces on the remarkable Sasha Graham and talented Tina Krause, is an interview with Annie Sprinkle that strives for a sort of mainstream respectability, rather than delving at long and degrading depth into the pre-performance art phase of her career. This is the sort of stuff that would be better left to magazines like *Gauntlet*...

Update Draculina is up to issue 46 and now costs $7.

THE EROTIC REVIEW

This key player in the increasing gentrification of porn — or 'erotica', as I'm sure they prefer to think of themselves — is on the up and up, changing from a quarterly to a monthly, adding more pages and getting 'raunchier' (they promise), and enjoying critical praise from the mainstream press. Nevertheless, I will not be renewing my subscription, which has just run out, and here's why.

I originally subscribed in response to a special offer whereby you got a free sub if you bought the *EPS* catalogue for £5 (more on the catalogue later). As soon as I saw the mag, I

FEAR AND LOATHING
£1 / 32pp / Andy P, PO Box 11605, London E11 1XA / andyfnl@dircon.co.uk

FEBRUARY 24
20pp, £1.20, payable: Douglas Baptie; Top Flat, 1 Ancrum Court, Hawick, TD9 7DB, Scotland

FLESH & BLOOD
FAB Press, 7 Farleigh, Ramsden Road, Godalming, Surrey, GU7 1QE / fax: +44 (0)1483 527424 / info@fabpress.com / www.fabpress.com

knew it was not for me. The adverts it contained were a dead give-away. Dear oh dear! Paunch concealers, baldness remedies, impotence cures... Without wishing to brag, I felt the advertisers were missing their target market with me. I may be a degenerate, but I'm not such a decrepit degenerate as that (yet)!

Nor was the editorial content much more beguiling. *The Erotic Review* has made much of their use of big-name writers, and indeed there are many (Arnold Wesker, Simon Raven, Philip Hensher, Michael Bywater, Susan Crosland, Martin Amis, Auberon Waugh — a veritable plethora of the great and not-so-good). But this is not necessarily a guarantee of steaminess. If you want to know about Naim Attallah's interest in knickers, or the intimate ins and outs, so to speak, of Peter Stringfellow's fantasies (he wants to exile himself in a tropical hotel with twenty-five young girls to dance attendance on him for the rest of his life — the annoying thing is, he fuckin' can!) then, mister, you're a sadder perv than I'll ever be.

Visually, the mag resembles *The Spectator*, but with more tits (and I don't mean Roger Scruton and David Starkey!). The pictures are consistently more interesting than the text, but it just isn't enough. *The Erotic Review* bills itself as "the fastest-growing magazine in the UK", and I have no reason to suppose that this isn't true, but it's certainly never caused any fast growth in my underpants. Not even a little bit. It's aimed fairly and squarely at the sort of crusty old twat whose idea of a sexual fantasy is some posh Sloaney bird wearing jodhpurs and pearls eating oysters in Paris, so unless you're a Young Conservative (the last one in captivity?) or over fifty, forget it. Though if you have a randy old uncle, a gift subscription might be just the ticket for Christmas.

The Erotic Print Society catalogue is an entirely different proposition. Now in its third edition, and niftily presented in a dinky A6 format with glossy paper and full colour throughout, the 108-page catalogue is jam-packed with trouser-arousing imagery of excellent stuff that you probably can't afford, but is nice to look at anyway, and at a fiver is a bargain purchase — for the price of a couple of issues of *Razzle*, you could show a bit of class about being an unrepentant filth-hound. Or you could wait for another promotional offer and get some crap magazines as well. [Simon Collins]

FEAR AND LOATHING 53 & 54
For many years now Andy Pearson (or "Pigswill" to give him his 'punk zine writer' name) has been putting this little mag out, and for many years now it's changed nary a jot. For your pound you will get details of where Andy's been, what friends he's met, what bands he's seen, reviews of the records he's bought... you get Andy's diary, basically. His taste has stood still too, scared to move lest any musical development of the past decade might catch his eye. The cut 'n' paste layout and dodgy printing should give it away... that's right, Andy likes Punk, and if you don't like Punk — well then mister, don't read his magazine. He spends most editorials bellyaching about the fact that over the past twenty years punk has been watered down and co-opted by market forces and is now a style choice rather than a state of mind. Fair enough, but the only

person who hasn't actually noticed this blatant axiom by now is the only person who might actually *need* to read *FnL*...

Andy clearly sees himself as Hunter S Thompson with a Ramones collection, but unfortunately neither his prose nor his life is that interesting. Andy probably means well (though an acquaintance of his tells me he's a tight git) but his writing style dies on the page. Take his review of *Magnolia*: "The movie is pretty good. I really enjoyed it. The only problem is I didn't realise how long it was — three hours!"

Is this all he has to say about one of the most complex, emotionally wrenching American films of the past ten years? That it's too long? His music reviews are similarly lamebrained — either "it's punk and it rocks!" or, "It's lame indie shite!" He's enthusiastic to be sure and *Fear and Loathing* features the odd subject of note (The Residents, Penelope Houston, Mick Mercer), but his writing lacks any real flair or passion. He harks on about a past now long dead, oblivious to the fact that a live DJ set by the likes of Billy Nasty or Laurent Garnier — in the appropriate atmosphere and with the appropriate medication — is harder, more intense and more relevant than any of the twentieth generation punk dolts he worships. As a primer for culture beyond the mainstream this rag might lead some sixteen year old Limp Bizkit fan in a positive direction, but it serves little other purpose. [Anton Black]

FEBRUARY 24 NO 18

This is the *Lost Highway* special of the long-running *Twin Peaks* fanzine... *Lost Highway*, of course, being David Lynch's new movie. No superficial unrelated nonsense here, this is pure fan-focus. The movie hasn't been seen yet in this country, but catch the low-down on box-office returns in the US (not good), previews and reviews of the movie that have turned up on the box and in print, Lynch's promotional appearances ("It looks as tho' he's having a good time but he occasionally looks uncomfortable and calls [Jay] Leno a 'funny guy' in much the same manner as you would to a boor in a pub..."), and a lively letters page that suggests the rather lack lustre *Millennium* might be the "last post-*Peaks* show". Unlike many of the publications that pass for fanzines, *February 24* isn't simply a cut and paste job, reproducing articles to have appeared elsewhere in the mainstream, there's actually someone behind it, writing it. Obsessive to the point of intrigue. [David Kerekes]

Update *Lost Highway* has of course since been released in the UK. Can no longer find a trace of this zine anywhere but in the meantime *Wrapped in Plastic* fanzine is up to No 66, and includes a look at the Japanese *Twin Peaks* board game — anyone for donuts? [w] www.wrappedinplastic.com

FLESH & BLOOD 9 & 10
Cinema and Video for Adults

Harvey Fenton and Bill Lustig are interviewing Jesús Franco on the nature of sex and eroticism in his films. "Do you prefer the erotic approach?" they ask. Franco replies: "I prefer what the story asks you for." A great answer, but for anyone who's sat through a half dozen of the exploitation-maestro's works, patently not an accurate one. 'Story' is the least of Franco's worries. However, he does have an interesting perspective on what differentiates a sex film from an erotic film... it's all in the positioning: "If you shoot a scene with the camera above it is erotic," muses Franco, "but you do the same thing with close-ups... it's porno."

So we arrive at *Flesh & Blood* No 9, wherein Fred Williamson discusses his career in blaxploitation, the folk behind *Razor Blade Smile* say hello, and the British horror filmography reaches the year 1984... that's right, the year of *Suffer Little Children*, an amateur direct-to-video effort that somehow got national distribution and made the press after police impounded the master-tapes. An action motivated, it would appear, by the simple fact the film was made by students at a drama school, utilised teenage students from said drama school, and had for a title *Suffer Little Children*. Result: horror beyond believe... in as much as acting and technical competence go, anyway. For the media and the cops, however, it all pointed to child abuse... probably. Nigel Burrell offers hitherto unknown facts in the case while Stephen Thrower presents a detailed synopsis and review.

Moving on... The meat of *Flesh & Blood* No 10 is a special report from the Fant-Asia festival in Canada, including conversations with the directors of several of the festival's highlights. These include Nacho Cerdá, whose *Aftermath* ("in essence a half-hour in an autopsy room with a necrophiliac pathologist") is described as "gut-wrenchingly violating and relentlessly subversive"; Todd Morris and Deborah Twiss, the folk behind the low-budget 'man-hating' *A Gun For Jennifer* (which has a scene wherein hecklers at a

FUCK
$5 / 32pp / Dr Randall Phillip, PO Box 2217, Phila., PA 19103, USA

GAUNTLET
£6.99 & £5.99 / 112pp & 88pp / 309 Powell Rd Springfield PA 19064 USA / www.gauntletpress.com

Go-Go club get the tables turned on them, and reamed with a pool cue); and Jim Van Bebber, whose almost legendary *Charlie's Family* (nine years in the making and still not finished!) got an airing in the form of a work-print. Those familiar with *FAB* will know of the quality of reportage to expect. Issue 10 even carries a review of *Sleepwalker*, possibly "the most obscure horror film ever made in Britain". Directed by Saxon Logan in 1984, *Sleepwalker* received — as far as anyone can determine — a single, isolated promotional screening back in 1985. Kim Newman was there taking notes. Intended to play at the bottom end of a double-bill, at fifty minutes *Sleepwalker* was a film of the type that wasn't quite a movie and not really a short film. Such films had a hiatus (perhaps that's too grand a word for it) in the eighties. Newman's piece makes reference to another example: *The Orchard End Murder* (which supported *Dead and Buried* on its theatrical release in Britain). This I saw. It had a scene — the only scene I can remember with any clarity — where the naked body of a young woman buried in a shallow grave in an orchard, has one of her blue-coloured breasts exposed courtesy of the prevailing winds. I don't remember it as a black comedy, more a very haunting, curious piece of filmmaking. [David Kerekes]

Update Following issue No 10, the format switched from a magazine to a book format (*Flesh & Blood Book 1*). In 2003 came the *Flesh & Blood Compendium!*, a 455-page celebration of the first ten years. *Charlie's Family* got its official world premiere at the 2003 Fright Fest in London. It's a mess of a film. The full story about *Sleepwalker* can be found in *Creeping Flesh Vol 1*, from Headpress.

FUCK 11
I wonder how many printers initially turned this job down? Business must be *real* slack for the company who took it on. Maybe it wasn't a company at all, and editor Randall Phillip stole his way into a print shop after dark and rolled the presses himself. The paper stock doesn't match, but that's gonna be the least of your worries. *Fuck* is probably the most disorientating publication you'll ever lay eyes on in your life. That's disorientating as opposed to disgusting — for while *Fuck* is certainly vile, it's because it's playing a game of vileness, deliberately breaking all notions of good taste, decency and morality. You're not *supposed* to like it or agree with it — *Fuck* exists to antagonise you. It parades death images, disfigured children and photos of abuse victims like pin-ups, and intersperses them with cut-and-paste genitalia and stupid comments. The text consists of expletives and vitriolic rants. Phillip isn't interested in making a point or yielding information — if any of his pieces appear to be doing so, it's a chink in the armour, and he's quick to retaliate with some intolerable nonsense. In the piece 'Unmentionable Acts', for instance, Phillip relates an incident in which somebody — "probably a disgruntled customer" — has left a box of child pornography outside a bookstore. He takes the box inside to show his friends who work there and they panic, lock the doors, debate on who would do leave such a thing. Phillip doesn't care, he just wants to see what all the fuss is about. But looking at the magazines he becomes bored — they are mean-

ingless to him. Whether he likes it or not, Phillip exhibits a fragment of humanity in the tale. By way of compensation, the story has to conclude on a note of hyper-nastiness: Phillip suggests that on his way home, he beats and kills a child.

Fuck isn't satire, *Fuck* doesn't allow the reader the comfort of such disciplined notions as satire.

Defend it? I fuckin' hate it. [David Kerekes]

Update A subsequent issue of *Fuck* arrived with what appeared to be flakes of human excrement inside — not Randall Phillip's specific response to the above, it transpires, but a piece of general mailshot cheekiness which apparently landed him in trouble with the US authorities. *Fuck* was nowhere to be found on the Internet, save for ancient "you have been warned" reviews.

GAUNTLET 13

New digest format and with fewer illustrations... What on first glance might appear a step-backwards for the thought-provoking *Gauntlet*, fortunately isn't reflected in the quality of articles within. The major stories for No 12 concern both Recovered Memory syndrome and the suppression of Hemp (Woody Harrelson, Hollywood star and environmentalist, got busted after putting four hemp seeds into the ground in an act of civil disobedience.) Also featured is an interview with Jim Goad, and a look at the furore and hypocrisy in the wake of *ANSWER Me!* No 4, the 'rape' issue. Why should a so-called 'anti-censorship' bookstore refuse to stock the magazine but happily carry *The SCUM Manifesto*, which, as Goad points out, was "written by a woman who actually *did* shoot a man, who actually, *seriously*, with no hint of satire, [say] that men should be castrated and their entire generation exterminated".

The cover story for *Gauntlet* No 13 is the book that was at the centre of a case where a Motown Music sound engineer hired a hit man to murder his ex-wife and child. The ugly deed over, the hit man collected his money, and both men were caught, tried and found guilty. Crime doesn't pay. Not even if you claim to have followed the twenty-seven steps suggested by Rex Feral in his book *Hit Man: A Technical Manual for Independent Contractors* for your nefarious deed. Paladin Press, publisher of *Hit Man* and other similar-minded practical 'guides', were drawn into the trial. The article discusses the court case, the book itself, and the very precarious moral ground on which it exists. Another literary-based furore comes in a piece detailing Jim Hogshire's altercation with fellow scribe and people's champion Bob Black. Black was kicked out of the Hogshire home in the middle of the night at gunpoint (after using Mrs Hogshire as a shield), and the following day was refused an interview he had scheduled with Mike Hoy, president of Loompanics and publisher of both men's books. Black returned home and informed police that Hogshire was running a 'drug lab' in his apartment. Hogshire was arrested. Loompanics ceased printing Black's books and remaindered the rest, donating proceeds to Hogshire's defence fund... [David Kerekes]

GAUNTLET 18

The theme of this issue is 'The Feminine Mystique' and it seems to mark a continuing change of attitude for *Gauntlet*, which for a while stuck sharp teeth into censorship issues, but recently has been more like a toothless puppy gnawing at the boner of the sex industry. The centrepiece of this issue is Justice Howard's photo-essay on 'fiery feminists'. As a photographer, Howard's idea of fiery is that 'girl power' kind of pose where an open mouthed snarl or kung-fu style fist is supposed to signify some kind of liberation. It winds up being about as emotionally involving as a Spice Girl photo shoot, with Tammy Balinewski and Julie Strain seemingly competing to see who can look more like a topless Emma Peel who's just eaten a giant chilli pepper. Howard also provides the single most boring photo of Nina Hartley's elysian backside I've ever seen. Talk about achieving the impossible!

I'm not as convinced as Justice that tattoos across the biceps or body-piercing automatically convey any sort of authenticity, whether fiery or feminist. Sporty Spice can get three new face studs and two new tattoos (as she did, apparently, for her new album) but that doesn't turn her into either a singer or a feminist, just a consumer of ink and metal grabbing at the pocket-money of impressionable pre-teens. It doesn't help that Howard can't write (sample: "both books, signed copies all, grace my coffeetable"), but she and the magazine are caught in the same dilemma, trying to create a self-justifying rationale for work that flies (if not anything else) in the face of the philosophies they claim to espouse. Stripper Jessica Haskin's sophomoric 'attack' on suburban life, which lists "thou shalt not get a tattoo" as one of the Ten Commandments of Suburbia tells you less about the suburbs than mainstream movies like

GLOBAL TAPESTRY
£2.40 / 52pp / ISSN 0141-1241 / payable DA&R Cunliffe; Spring Bank, Longsight Rd, Copster Green, Blackburn, Lancs, BB1 9EU, UK

GOD IS HAPPY!
ALL ABOUT FUCKIN'
UGLY CUNT FUCK
Josh Simmons, 3065 Chartres St., New Orleans, LA 70117, USA / www.knownothingfamily.org / christmuffins@hotmail.com

HAIR TO STAY
$9 / 96pp / Winter Publishing / PO Box 80667, Dartmouth, MA 02748, USA / www.hairtostay.com

HAPPYLAND
$3 & $5 / Happyland, 141 29th Street, Apt. 2F, Brooklyn, NY 11232, USA / HappylandUSA@hotmail.com

The Ice Storm or *American Beauty*, and winds up feeling more conformist than the culture it attacks. Even better (or worse), Athena Douris details her attempt to produce a feminist porn mag that would humiliate men. She's now writing a monthly lesbian sex column for *FHM*. Reading *FHM* is indeed pretty humiliating, but it takes a special kind of disassociation to write a sex column for them with a feminist straight face!

In the same way that these theoretical feminists wind up producing the same sort of sex stuff as the most unliberated men, *Gauntlet* itself appears to have 'marked' for the sex industry, and it's starting to bear the same relationship to sexual reality that wrestling magazines do to their sport. Mimi Miyagi's 'I'm a Cyber Feminist' is a simple two-page plug for her various money-making enterprises. In the end, as it were, that's what it's all about. Money talks and bullshit walks. Susan Bremner, who writes to "educate and promote a non-stereotypical view of women in the stripping industry" dances once a week to support herself while she "strategizes and implements my new entrepreneurial endeavours". Stripping may have liberated her from her own sexual hang-ups, but her livelihood still depends on exploiting the hang-ups of its audience. Will Bremner educate herself right out of a job? Will *Gauntlet* 'educate' the marks out of giving her dollar bills? On the positive side there is an update on the *Hitman* and *Natural Born Killer* cases, keeping in vague touch with the censorship issues, and Nina Hartley offers a hopeful sounding column that pleads for understanding and tolerance. Tolerance is one thing, but creating something worth the reader's interest is another. Even with Nina on board. [Michael Carlson]

Update I may have slighted Justice Howard. Her photos seem to have been a major influence on the fiery feminism of *Charlie's Angels II*, whose Hollywood heroines appear to have studied the poses and the attitude. Whooooo! Art imitates life imitates…huh? A recent issue of *Gauntlet* was No 21 (2001), though there has undoubtedly been more (distibution in the UK appears to have nose-dived with the change in binding). This was an independent films special which included interviews with Troma's Lloyd Kaufman, and directors Fred Olen Ray and Jon Keeyes.

GLOBAL TAPESTRY JOURNAL 23
An A4-sized literary mag based in Blackburn, *Global Tapestry* features interviews, non-fiction pieces, and the usual glut of personal-themed, first-person free verse. As usual with these small-circulation mags, it's hard to imagine who would subscribe to it except the writers themselves (the standard of individual pieces varies tremendously). Highlights include an interview with William Burroughs from 1970, and an interview with Quentin Crisp conducted not long before he died in 1999. [Mikita Brottman]

GOD IS HAPPY! ALL ABOUT FUCKIN' UGLY CUNT FUCK
These three independently produced dinky comic books showcase the artistic talents of one Josh Simmons. I suspect that *God is Happy* (12pp) is the earliest of the comics, given the obsessive detail in the art work and the fact that the whole thing has

been trimmed to size using hand scissors. It is a psychedelic manifestation of the familiar Jack T Chick school of Bible Bashing. But here the morality has been replaced with the promise that you, the reader, are happy. The penmanship is pretty amazing.

Different in tone and artistic style is Simmons' *Ugly Cunt Fuck* (24pp), which features several short tales, each with a sentiment as mindless as *God Is Happy* — except that here it's taken to a different extreme. Everybody in *Ugly Cunt Fuck* hates one another (and themselves), and the stories are a relentless, vitriolic preamble with beatings, rape, torture, murder and suicide. The panels are very bold with plenty of black, and the overall look is akin to a more harder-edged Chester Brown.

The final comic, *All About Fuckin'* (44pp), is different again, in that the panels comprise of staged photographs with crude pen-and-ink drawings on top. The stories are a rather extreme interpretation of — don't blow a fuse trying to figure it out — fuck-scenarios, with women getting it on with Lovecraftian like creatures in several of the strips, and what appears to be an act of genuine bestiality between a man and a dog in another. While *All About Fuckin'* may be lacking the penmanship of the former two titles, I'm very much intrigued as to what Simmons could possibly do next. [David Kerekes]

Update The listed website and email are kaput. Good luck trying to find this stuff and let this be a warning to anyone who sends stuff to *Headpress* for review — include an *address*. Simmons now does strips for *Cinema Sewer*.

HAIR TO STAY 1
"The World's *Only* Magazine For Lovers Of Natural, Hairy Women" the subtitle of this publication proudly proclaims. And it could be true, but then my search for the hirsute has never been a wildly comprehensive one.

In here you will discover women with hairy navels ('treasure trail' I believe is the terminology), women with hairy legs, even women with hairy *chests* (don't get too carried away now, we're not talking *forests*...). There are plenty of snaps too of women, hands above their heads, revealing their unshaven armpits. As with all minority interests, *Hair To Stay* might appear odd to the casual reader. Many of you, for instance, would have to look long and hard at the photo of a girl's face on page seventy-three, before the 'penny drops'. Why — her eyebrows meet in the middle. And that is as innocuous as this whole fetish malarkey can be — necrophilia at one end of the scale and eyebrows at the other. The casual reader might also be surprised at the sheer scale of a hitherto 'unknown' subculture. *Hair To Stay* rounds up many hirsute-related videos, contains readers letters, and some fiction. The videos are rated on hair-factor (more interesting than at first it might appear), and are all essentially home-made jobs catering for the hairy market. Articles include one man's ruminations on hairy women in Hollywood, which deliberates over the mini-trend for hair in mainstream movies. This apparently started sometime around *Irreconcilable Differences*, in which a young Sharon Stone displayed in one scene, "nicely hairy underarms". Patricia Arquette followed suit several years later, in *Flirting With Disaster*, and had a male co-star lick her hairy armpits. (I'd divulge more furry film facts, but the excursion ends prematurely.)

Most of the reader comments in *Hair To Stay* are of the complimentary type, thanking the publishers for filling a void, but there are some which border on the psychotic. One reader, for instance, has assured himself that men who don't like hairy women are paedophiles, and that women with hairy legs have less chance of being brutally raped or killed. "After a while all shaved legs start to look alike (shaved)," ruminates the embittered one. "They all begin to look like aliens from outer space to me." Why does it come as no surprise that this particular reader admits to being 'lonely'... Also included are warnings of scams taking place on the hair fetish scene ("This man was sending out photographs, taken by William, claiming they were of himself but he was calling himself female.")

The 'natural look' is the key here. Along with the hirsute, *Hair To Stay* is fully supportive of silicone-free breasts, naturism and DIY porn. They're also pretty big on bigger European ladies. Entertaining whatever your persuasion. [David Kerekes]

Update Hair to Stay is still around and is still just as entertaining — "see Hirsute Sandra shave her legs!"; issue 1 now costs a whopping $40, and the website also sells hairy mousepads.

HAPPYLAND 9, 10, 11
This primitive photocopied zine gets my vote for the best marketing campaign since September 11: the cover of issue No 9 states "If you don't read this zine *it means the terrorists have won*!!!'

Imagine if you can *Sleazoid Express* but with a bad attitude and

HEAD MAGAZINE
£4 / 136pp / Head magazine, BM Uplift, London, WC1N 3XX / www.headmag.com

HEALTER SKELTER
£4.50 / 56pp / Mondo Bizarro Press 1999 / via Alessandrini 7, 40126 Bologna, Italy / www.mondobizarro.net

HOOVER HOG
80pp; Richard (Chip) Smith, PO Box 7511, Cross Lanes, WV 25356-0511, USA

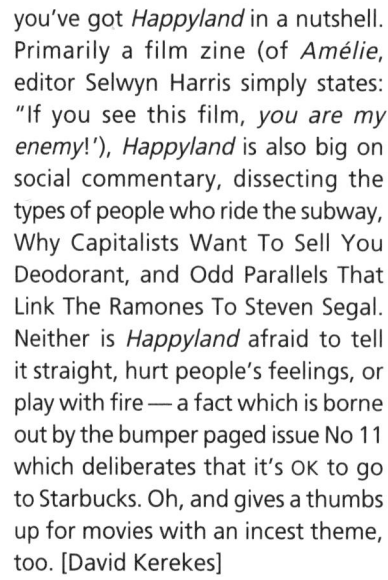

you've got *Happyland* in a nutshell. Primarily a film zine (of *Amélie*, editor Selwyn Harris simply states: "If you see this film, *you are my enemy*!'), *Happyland* is also big on social commentary, dissecting the types of people who ride the subway, Why Capitalists Want To Sell You Deodorant, and Odd Parallels That Link The Ramones To Steven Segal. Neither is *Happyland* afraid to tell it straight, hurt people's feelings, or play with fire — a fact which is borne out by the bumper paged issue No 11 which deliberates that it's OK to go to Starbucks. Oh, and gives a thumbs up for movies with an incest theme, too. [David Kerekes]

Update We found the following on a message board: "After an eight-year break, Selwyn Harris published three enormous issues of *Happyland* in the wake of 9/11 (anticipating a full-on, three-dimensional realisation of *After the Fall of New York*, et al), but he has since re-retired." So I guess that means *Happyland* is no more. For now.

HEAD MAGAZINE 8
Healing

Head magazine is a great big thick, professionally-produced black-and-white New Age periodical from BM Uplift, crammed full with articles and information on Gaia, anarchy, social subversion, 'guerrilla mobility', class war, Shiatsu, mantric prayers, crystals, magic and alchemy. There's also a section of CD, video and small press reviews. The writing is concise and professional but not without a sense of irony, and the articles present an interesting mixture of the serious/academic and the creative/personal. High points in this issue are an essay on the truth about the pet food industry (pet food contains "the rendered remains of cats and dogs"), an interview with "medical clairvoyant" Caroline Myss entitled 'Illness as a Disorder of Power', and a transcript of Howard Marks' application for the position of Drug Czar, given at Frome One World Festival. Low points include a piece about trees in Japan that "synchronise electrical biorhythms", and some blarney about loving your periods (especially the kind of dark, clotted menstrual blood that's apparently "full of life, full of magic, full of potential"). Basically, this is a very carefully crafted New Age journal, almost encyclopaedic in its coverage, with a nicely balanced variety of articles on all aspects of alternative culture in the nineties. [Mikita Brottman]

Update The Head Magazine website now redirects to a [w] www.pronoia.net but there's no mention of the magazine. You'll know whether you're interested in following this up or not.

HEALTER SKELTER
Mondo Xtremo

The fact that editor Alex Papa has chosen to name his magazine after the words scrawled in blood on the wall of the LaBianca residence in August 1969 — keeping the original misspelling intact — highlights two issues. The first, that this is a magazine with a distinctly Manson-esque theme to it, and the second, that there are healing aspects to all forms of destruction — the too-often ignored truth of 'regeneration through violence'. This is a zine of superior quality. Glossy pages and dynamic graphics are matched by English/Italian text in flawless translation — a rare virtue in most Eurozines. This 'Mondo Xtremo' issue features a series of intelligent interviews with some of the most interesting and exciting people in the worlds of radical publishing, nihilistic crime, avant-garde film-making and underground art. Manson-themed interviews include face-to-face chats with original Family member Sandra Good and Manson groupies George Stimson and Michael Moynihan. Other interviewees include Jim Goad of ANSWER Me!, Norwegian underground guru Jan R Bruun, John Pirog, editor of The Necroerotic, Jörg Buttgereit, cult Mondo directors Angelo and Alfredo Castiglioni, and — to cap it all off — a great article on Headpress and an interview with our very own David Kerekes. A truly exciting magazine, professionally and thoughtfully produced. [Mikita Brottman]

HOG 3

Dear oh dear. Hog is a comic featuring sex, violence, sexual violence and violent sex in a manner so shameless that to call it 'gratuitous' would be redundant. The perpetrators — Rik Rawling, Jim Boswell, and Chuck U Farley (yeah, right!) — seem hellbent on wallowing (like, er, hogs) in the PC flak their smutty rag would certainly attract if it fell into the hands of right-thinking folk, but I ain't gonna give them the satisfaction. I mean, when they describe themselves as 'guilty parties' and put Yorkshire Ripper photofits in place of author photos, what's the point?

Hog contains three stories, 'Dial M for Motherfucker', The Bitch in 'Pump Action' (no, really), and 'Slutfreak'. Rik Rawling draws better than the other two, though all the women who appear (and there are many) are so obviously cribbed from porn mags that it's amazing they can be made to walk and talk, rather than just crawl round on all fours with their tongues lolling out. It's difficult to see any redeeming value anywhere in the whole mucky mess — the interruption of the action in 'Slutfreak' by a pair of critics arguing about the meaning and worth of it all indicates that Rik Rawling is not devoid of a sense of irony, yet it can't deflect completely the very reasonable accusations of misogyny, immaturity etc that could be levelled at Hog.

Listen — you know better than I do whether you're gonna find an endless parade of chicks with big tits and bigger sidearms fucking, sucking and blowing heads off entertaining (you sick puppies), but be warned. Anybody less jaded than a big Chinese jade necklace (eg your mum) is liable to find this stuff seriously offensive. Hog is reprehensible… but (sorta) fun. [Simon Collins]

Update You can find out more about Rik Rawling at [w] www.rikrawling.co.uk

HOOVER HOG 2
A Review of Dangerous Ideas

Here I was expecting the usual 'dangerous ideas' — deviant sexuality, serial killers, porn, the stuff that Headpress readers lap up — but I was quite surprised by what this deceptively low-rent magazine contains. Race, Holocaust revisionism, paedophilia, abortion… Material that really is taboo now that sexuality has moved centre stage. And, I'll admit it, this is one magazine that has left me feeling very disturbed. The lead article looks at the thorny issue of race and IQ, surveying the current state of the (non-) debate. With the establishment consensus eschewing any semblance of discussion, and with officially sanctioned 'anti-racism' the order of the day, anyone daring to ask too many questions risks being labelled a racist. I have to admit that reading this material left me feeling extremely uncomfortable, and the conclusions it draws are not the ones that I want to be drawn. However that's clearly the intention, because debate is surely what is missing, particularly in the US (where the magazine originates). Nobody disputes racial differences in IQ, what is in dispute is the cause. It's that same old nature versus nurture argument, and in this case Chip Smith of Hoover Hog comes down on the nature side of the fence. I would still disagree with him, but he points out enough facts to give plenty of pause for thought. In the end though, and despite the persistence of differences in IQ scores between blacks and whites, I would ask why IQ scores continue to rise. If intelligence is hereditary, why is it that scores — for black and whites — are increasing? Oh, and in case you think this magazine's full of Aryan's bragging about how smart they are, the article gleefully points out that Ashkenazy Jews are way ahead of the 'master race'. Still, the whole issue of race and anti-racism is in need of being questioned. Calling everyone who questions the current orthodoxy 'racist' is certainly only going to create more racists — including such militant anti-racists as Anti-Fascist Action in the UK. Just as disturbing to read is Jewish Holocaust revisionist David Cole. To date I've always assumed that Holocaust revisionists were right-wing apologists for National Socialism (as a good percentage of them are), however to read left-wing revisionists is distinctly unsettling. I don't have the knowledge or the expertise to com-

L'HORREUR EST HUMAINE
8 Euros / 124pp & 60pp / 26, rue du Tapis Vent, 79500, Melle, France

IMPLOSION
£2.50 / 64pp / Distributed in the UK by BBR, PO Box 625, Sheffield, S1 3GY, UK / www.bbr-online.com

INFILTRATION
$1 / 28pp / PO Box 13, Station E, Toronto, Canada, M6H 4E1 / www.infiltration.org

IS IT... UNCUT?
£6.95 / 56pp / Midnight Media, PO Box 211, Huntingdon, PE29 2WD / paul@midnight-media.demon.co.uk / www.midnight-media.demon.co.uk

LIFE SUCKS DIE
www.lifesucksdie.com

---

ment one way or another, but the questions that David Cole asks can't be dismissed easily. Other articles include anti-abortionism from an atheist libertarian perspective and a look at male attraction to adolescent females. But to be honest the other articles are more intriguing, at least to this reader.

This really is a review of ideas, and the fact that it's caused me to question so many assumptions is testament both to the quality of writing and research, and also to the fact that honest debate on many of these issues is clearly lacking elsewhere. The fact that many of the positions adopted here are 'right-wing' makes life more difficult for libertarians and egalitarians, but somehow labels like 'left' and 'right' don't have much meaning here. If you want an interesting and challenging read then this is highly recommended. [Pan Pantziarka]

L'HORREUR EST HUMAINE 3 & 4
This is the kind of curious publication that can only exist on the continent — an independently produced zine compiling a variety of art. Not having seen issues one or two of L'Horreur est humaine (edited by Sylvain Gérand), I can't say how they compare or whether there is a theme running throughout, but No 4 is presented as a fake medical dictionary (in that all the entries and ailments are fictitious), while No 3 is comprised almost entirely of drawings and comic strips. Despite the fact that I really like the idea of a fake medical dictionary, I actually prefer the text-free latter — primarily because my French isn't good enough to sustain my interest in the wordy No 4 (the text of which looks to have been printed at the wrong resolution anyway), but also because the selection of drawings in No 4 are, by comparison, much more fragmented and less satisfying. Like I said, a curious thing. [David Kerekes]

IMPLOSION 7
A Journal of the Bizarre and Eccentric
From the publishers of *Bloodsongs*. Same mag, different name. An interview with the Misfits, an interview with photography-artist J K Potter, and, if the aforementioned don't tweak any buttons, the following alone warrants your buying *Implosions* No 7: on the road with G G Allin... Sure, sure, who cares, but author Joe Coughlin's attention to detail, his obsession with getting the facts right, and his non-hysterical approach to the punk rocker some called crazy and Satanic, are most rewarding.

As GG paced around, I felt like I was looking at either The Last Free Man or someone more trapped than any of us... GG was all movement and animal grace... the music started... Right away, I saw a girl unconscious, her friends pulling her away by the feet. A crying teenager ran for the door with his hand on his face, blood streaming through his fingers. I thought about bolting, but couldn't look away...

[David Kerekes]

Update BBR has a link to [w] www.implosion-mag.com although it now appears to be a porn site rather than anything to do with this publication. Still, you might find something interesting...

INFILTRATION 9, 11 & 12
The zine about going places you're not supposed to go

This zine is for the — literally — underground, possibly even the chthonic. Subversion in an exploratory vein. Who knows, in the future these small thin tomes of *Infiltration* may be requisite reading! Parisian Catacombs, The Botanic Gardens of Subterranean Glasgow, Storm Drains, Chicago Tunnel Company — these are some of the themes and articles you are likely to come across. Even if you're not one of the cave/tunnel/drain world underground, this is informative, fascinating stuff. For some reason J G Ballard comes to mind… The main article in No 12 on Toronto's Union Station is fairly typical: it reads like the instructions on how to navigate through some labyrinthine video or computer game. Encounters with tunnels of opaque air, metal staircases leading to crawlspaces, hallways leading nowhere, disassembled escalators, hot metal ladders and staircases in steam tunnels etc. But instead of some virtual bullshit, these guys are breathing the dust, sweating through the steam tunnels, smelling the stench of dead vermin, and interacting with (and avoiding) security guards and employees. In these days of high tech surveillance and terrorist paranoia (not to mention in some places, submachine-gun toting security) your curiosity quotient has to be high to explore some of this territory. Looking at the Manhattan skyline I've often wondered what must be underneath it all, besides the "mole people". With all manner of tunnels below tunnels below even more tunnels, what holds up all the weight? Hollow earth theory?

The back cover of No 11 even has a glossary of 'Drainspeak' and inside an interview with one of "the most active members of the Australian draining syndicate known as the Cave Clan". Down Under indeed! Each issue is heavily illustrated with photos from the explorations. There are numerous web sites for those who seek these activities also. So send in your mined and minted metal or postal equivalent to the address above and go underground, way underground. [Tom Brinkmann]

Update As of writing the latest Infiltration is No 21 and "offers an in-depth case study of how the nut that is the University of Toronto was cracked". Whatever. Back issues are $3 each, or $40 for the lot (1–20).

IS IT… UNCUT? 10

One of my favourite film review zines of recent years, *Is it… Uncut?* runs informed appraisals of obscure DVD and video releases from around the world. The fact that it's published in the censorious UK (its title being something of an in-joke), *Is it… Uncut?* has a healthy tendency to compare and contrast the various prints available of the films it discusses — though thankfully never quite in the retentive frame-counting manner of, say, *Video Watchdog*. Films covered in issue No 10 include Joaquin Romero Marchent's *Cut-throats 9* (described as "the ultimate Gore Western"), Irv Berwick's *Hitch Hike To Hell* ("ineptly produced in most departments"), Jack Woods' *Equinox* ("animated beasties chasing slender 60s bimbos"), and H Tjut Djalil's *Misteri Janda Kembang*, an Indonesian horror film that is said to contain "several gleefully non-PC scenes' (in which men begin to exhibit "ridiculous 'gay' mannerisms"). All this and an interview with Camille (*I Spit on your Grave*) Keaton go to make *Is it… Uncut?* essential for dedicated fans of low-brow movie entertainment. As with most publications from Midnight Media, quality is also very high. [David Kerekes]

Update Now up to No 15, with two special editions collecting material from early out of print issues, one obscurity to recently come under scrutiny is Michael Skaife's 1971 *Graveyard of Horror*, which "sports lots of camera shots from the waist down" and "has the distinction of not being liked by the majority of reviewers".

LIFE SUCKS DIE 3

This is, without doubt, the most moronic magazine to cross the portals of Pantziarka mansions in years. *Life Sucks Die* purports to be an underground hip hop magazine, though I find it hard to believe that this is really representative of US hip hop culture in general. Here you can read incisive rants such as "You want anarchy? Okay, I'm going to burn your parents house down then, smarty pants, how's that for anarchy?", which eventually reaches the inevitable (and tedious) conclusion "Yeah, Karl Marks-A-Lot, tell me when your graffiti revolution starts so I can move to Afghanistan or Rwanda, please!" Deep stuff, eh? On the same page you can read the words to the rap 'Illegal Aliens' by the Convicts, which is basically a long and pathetic racist chant against Hispanics/Iranians/Koreans/Nigerians and others. It just serves to prove that black racists are just as moronic as white ones, and it leaves me wondering why the white editors would chose to include such drivel in their magazine.

Other highlights include an inter-

MALEFACT
$5 / 64pp & 68pp / Send a SASE/IRC to PO Box 20175, Seattle, WA, 98102-1175, USA

MANSPLAT
Free! / Hairball Press, 2318 2nd Avenue, Suite 591, Seattle WA98121, USA / mansplat@beer.com / http://home.earthlink.net/~mansplat/

MORBID CURIOSITIES
£4.95 / $6 / 112pp / BBR, PO Box 625, Sheffield, S1 3GY, UK

NAMELESS AEONS
Logos Press 1999

view with "blood sucking freaks Ink and Dagger", a band from Philadelphia. I was kept awake reading this only because I was trying to work out who was the most stupid — the band or the interviewer. In the end I figured it was a draw as nobody had the remotest bit of intelligence or originality. A big chunk of the magazine consists of collages of graffiti tags interspersed with bits of porno magazines — and the porno pictures were way more interesting then the graffiti.

I could go on, it's so easy, but I've already devoted more time and energy than this dross merits. It's hard to believe that anyone would really pay for shit like this. Avoid it like the plague, it doesn't deserve to make it to No 4. [Pan Pantziarka]

Update Sorry, but *Life Sucks Die* did not cease and desist, in fact it is up to No 8 and even has a spivvy website to boot.

MALEFACT 3 & 4
One of the more pleasing art showcases, *Malefact* is a kind of *Raw* for the terminally apocalyptic. Running down the list of contributors ought to give clear indication of the type of subject matter on offer here: Miguel Angel Martin, Mike Diana, Nick Bougas, Trevor Brown, Sverre Kristensen, to name but a few. And if it still isn't clear, how about serial killers on the job, huge ejaculating schlongs, and torture? Some of it is in comic strip, some of it big and bulbous full-page splashes. The artists in No 4 have an even greater obsession with cartoon shit cakes. [David Kerekes]

Update Got as far as No 9. Editor Tom Crites' website can be found at [w] http://home.earthlink.net/~tmcrites/

MANSPLAT 15
"Bathroom Litter-ature for Men... but Chicks Can Read It Too!" is the tag line and based on that alone you could be forgiven for thinking that this cheaply printed tabloid paper is nothing but a low-rent *Loaded*. And you would be wrong.

Loaded is shite whereas *Mansplat* — despite sharing the same obsessions with beer, tits, farts and 'trash culture' — is actually pretty funny. If I were twenty-years-old I would probably think it was hilarious but a page full of listings for different types of fart or coolest cars on TV is as lazy as it gets. However, a surreal and sardonic streak of wit runs through the *Mansplat* collective and is best expressed through items like the 'Shat in The Hat' column where the worlds of William Shatner (in Captain Kirk mode) and Dr Seuss are intertwined with amusing consequences. Elsewhere there's 'Horror Movie Chicks We Wanna Do It With', 'Nixon — What A Dick' and the intriguing 'Perfect Woman' ("Would you like to watch me go down on my girlfriend", "I'm bored, let's shave my pussy") but the winner, the page you'll most want to photocopy and post to your friends comprises Ron Jeremy Bumper Stickers ("Ron Does It Deeper"), lovingly illustrated with images of the man who physically and spiritually most resembles the *Mansplat* mentality. As it's published infrequently the occasional dose of this nonsense is welcome but repeat readings may have you longing for some Kafka. [Rik Rawling]

Update Mansplat is sadly no more, and the above urls ain't working. This may or may not have something to do with the fact that editor Jeff Gilbert went to court in 2000 to try and wrestle the domain name "mansplat.com" from one of those serial domain name registering types who claimed to be a fan of the magazine before offering to sell it to him for $5000. Who the fuck was he kidding? That much money would feed *Headpress* for ten years! And this was a *free* magazine. If anyone knows anyone at Clausen Enterprises, go and kick them from us.

MORBID CURIOSITIES 5
This is a very *small-press* type of small-press publication. Personal and conversational, it is solely devoted to weird experiences as related to the editor. Subject matter is what can loosely be labelled counter-cultural, pertaining as it does to sex, death, medical marginalia and the like. Some of the more intriguing features deal with an American in Old Compton Street as the bomb went off, LA's Museum of Death (which sounds well worth a visit and can be found at 6340 Hollywood Blvd), spending the night in a coffin for a dare, starring in porn, appearing in grade-z movie *Warrior Princess* and funny UFO pranks.

At its best, *Morbid Curiosities* is like a particularly interesting pub anecdote. However, it is written by Americans, which means that some contributors are inclined to 'process' their 'issues', whine on about imagined victimisation (some punky middle-class students visit a small Texas town and get stared at — well, boo fucking hoo), and revel masochistically in how taking enough drugs to raise the Titanic turned out to be a life-enhancing experience. Perhaps the worst offender is some dopey white witch wannabe who curses an ex-boyfriend with urine, bones, and stuff — she later learns that "he's done crack rock several times". Well then, that must be the curse in action. It couldn't be to do with any natural fuckwit proclivities on his part, could it? There's also a piece (Why We're Like This) that assumes a big group-hug mateyness on the part of everyone who might have an interest in such matters as those covered in this mag. It's a rather shallow premise upon which to base an identity — after all, these things are only interests and should not be used to define one's whole character. *Morbid Curiosities* may be callow but it is often interesting and has a likeable earnestness about it. [Anton Black]

NAMELESS AEONS
Peter Smith with a foreword by Kenneth Grant

Iä! Iä! Cthulhu fhtagn!

In this, the latest pamphlet I've seen from Logos Press, an attempt is made to explicate the works of 'weirdists' H P Lovecraft, Clark Ashton Smith, Arthur Machen and Bulwer Lytton in terms of practically applicable occult content. The essays are short — none is much over ten pages long — and of those concerning Lovecraft and Clark Ashton Smith much of the content is taken up with autobiographical details. As a general overview of occult interpretations of the writers' works, it's interesting and concise, but anyone wanting actual spells and practical applications will have to look elsewhere. There's an introduction by Kenneth Grant, who's clearly been a major influence on the author — possibly too much of an influence, as Grant's Typhonian tradition isn't the only way to interpret Lovecraft.

The quality of the essays is a little variable. The only downside to those on Lovecraft and Clark Ashton Smith is that they're too short, but some of the later pieces overstay their welcome. The author operates from the basic premise that the creatures referred to in the stories of the weirdists actually exist — no ifs or buts. I can appreciate the use of Cthulhu-related worship in a personal occult system — as is pointed out in the literature of the Esoteric Order of Dagon, while their members "do not believe in the absolute existence of the deities which are portrayed in the Cthulhu Mythos", they find the iconography of Lovecraft's work to be a useful paradigm for gaining access to deeper, non-rational areas of the subconscious". But here Smith really does seem to believe in their existence, which has had the unfortunate effect of short-circuiting all of his scepticism, so that he throws all kinds of apparently unrelated weirdness into his essays in the service of some demented grand unified theory. One of the essays here, 'The Negative Ones', contains one of the wildest pieces of dream analysis I've ever seen. The following sentence should give you an idea of the breathless and awestruck tone:

> And was the unknown power behind this manifestation nothing less than the foreshadowing of the aeonic succession of Horus himself — in his incarnation as Hoor-Paar-Kraat, the black god of silence, the post-nuclear avatar of a coming era of global devastation and the resultant evolutionary mutation of the entire human race?

That said, this makes an excellent introduction to occult readings

NETWORK NEWS
£1.50 / 24pp and 28pp / N Ayers, Earthly Delights, PO Box 2, Lostwithiel, Cornwall, PL22 0YY, UK

NOX
59pp / Logos Press 1998

ONE SUMMER DAY
MAMA SNAKE
ANGELS IN DISTRESS
Chris Campbell, 4100 Lake Washington Blvd, N. #B202, Renton, WA 98056, USA

ONGAKU OTAKU
£4.95 / $5.95 / 130pp / BBR, PO Box 625, Sheffield, S1 3GY, UK

of the weirdists, and if some of the other pieces seem a bit nutty, what do you expect from a small press occult publisher? [James Marriott]

Update Logos Press is no more and a reality TV show could probably be made of a person's gargantuan efforts to track this stuff down but don't let that put you off.

NETWORK NEWS
13 Secret Power of Music
14 Total Eclipse

Boycott consensus reality with this essential journal of guerrilla sign ontology.

Having, by a strange coincidence, actually visited Lostwithiel, I can testify to the appropriateness of something this weird and marginal coming from somewhere that remote! This is a quarterly newsletter produced by the ambient/industrial band Nocturnal Emissions. These two issues, though, contain little in the way of 'news', being instead given over to an ongoing fictional narrative set in the crusty eco-squat scene of London and elsewhere, involving cults, sacred architecture, free festivals, stone circles, witches' flying ointment, sex magick, performance art (that old urban legend about the self-amputating performance artist John Fare gets a fresh airing), Semtex, civil disorder, Throbbing Gristle and a load of other cool stuff, illustrated with bizarre photographs and interspersed with shameless product placement for Nocturnal Emissions recordings and merchandise.

There is a touch of the Stewart Homes and Iain Sinclairs about all this, with conspiratorial talk of the occult power behind the establishment and so on, but what I was most reminded of was the 'Fear Machine' storyline that ran in DC's *Hellblazer* comic these many years ago.

Allusion could no longer help herself. "Oh it's so sexy when you talk about Stonehenge. Tell us about the 70s, tell us about the 80s, tell us about Wally Hope, tell us about archaeology, tell us about psychogeography — it makes me go all moist."

Well, I can't say I feel *that* enthusiastic about it myself, but I was reasonably entertained. This is very much a personal project — how much you like it will depend on how attuned to the author's preoccupations you are. At least there is a discernible level of irony present — it's always reassuring when someone writing about this kind of heady stuff doesn't appear to take it all completely seriously. [Simon Collins]

NOX: THE BLACK BOOK 1
Infernal Texts
Ed. Stephen Sennitt

This is "the first in a series of three volumes transgressing the definitions of modern occultism", and it makes for fairly entertaining reading. It's a cheaply produced pamphlet that appears to contain instructions for rituals such as a Satanic mass, a ritual of destruction and the "rite of nine angles", supposedly the "central mystery of alchemy". I haven't tried any of them out so can't vouch for how well they work — in any case some of them are 'bare bones' rituals and you'll have to go elsewhere for the incantations to make them complete. Other pieces in this grab-bag collection include rants about Lovecraft and Atlantis and an intriguing exploration of the demons of one's own psyche.

While some of the information here strikes me as being fairly sound in its own way — rituals of deprogramming and derangement of the senses for personal 'development' — when it comes to a textual analysis of Lovecraft, taking his fictions as factual accounts, or numerological analyses of the geometry of pyramids, it's difficult to take it as seriously. At least this is still fun, though, especially considered as fiction. Less entertaining is the undercurrent of fascism running through a lot of this, as it does through a good deal of occult/new age material:

> Radio Werewolf is opposed to the general decadence of contemporary youth-culture; a sewer of mind-numbing drugs, primitive African rhythms, the unbalanced encouragement of androgyny and homosexuality, the blurring and muddying of racial and cultural boundaries. Radio Werewolf stands as the standard-bearer of a new kind of youth — orderly, disciplined, drug-free, proud and re-awakened to their pagan heritage; the cadres of the Radio Werewolf Youth Party.

I've always thought mind-numbing drugs and primitive African rhythms go pretty well together. Not a good candidate for the Radio Werewolf Youth Party, then... [James Marriott]

Update Logos Press is no more but anyone with an interest in Lovecraft should be able to point you in the right direction.

ONE SUMMER DAY
MAMA SNAKE 2 & 4
ANGELS IN DISTRESS 1

Chris Campbell contributes a strip and several spot illustrations to the debut issue of *Angels In Distress*, a collaboration venture with Greg Goodsell. Those who recall the film zine *Subhuman* should be familiar with the name Goodsell, one of the mainstay writers of that classy publication. However, judging by the self-importance lauded upon himself in this most recent outing, Greg must have taken a knock on the head in the interim. Sure, Goodsell's film flotsam sensibilities are still attuned, with coverage of Al Adamson and the likes of *The Adjuster* and *Hollywood Meatcleaver Massacre*, but that hardly warrants celebrity status ("... I had achieved name recognition and value to the point where people asked me for autographs at Fangoria Conventions..." Greg decides in his editorial). Goodsell is a fine writer to be sure, funny, with some interesting off-kilter observations on tired movies, but when the essence of self-righteousness creeps in — as it does here — you really feel it's time to rediscover the Rubik's cube and do something useful with your time. As for Campbell, it must have been hell working in the shadow of such an awesome presence. [David Kerekes]

ONGAKU OTAKU

Having read William Gibson's novel *Idoru*, about a Japanese virtual pop star, I can reveal to you that 'otaku' means something like 'geeky obsessive fan-boy'. As for 'ongaku', that means 'music'. So if you were to guess that *Ongaku Otaku* meant something like 'music fans', you wouldn't be far off the mark, would you? Thus, you will be unsurprised to hear that *Ongaku Otaku* contains lots of stuff about Japanese music — its unique selling point, however, is that it's written in English and aimed at Western consumers of what can often seem like the impenetrably difficult and obscure Japanese music scene. This is a substantial, square-bound, large-format magazine with a more expansive approach to layout than the traditionally crammed format of music zines. Nevertheless, there's plenty of meaty content, including a Japanese tour diary from Scot Jenerik of The Haters (the only non-Japanese act to be featured) and interviews with DemiSemiQuaver, Billy?, Jack or Jive, Kazumoto Endo, Little Fujiko, Depth, Ningen Isu (these names must mean something to someone out there), and last but not least K K Null, awesomely noisy solo guitarist and sometime member of Alternative Tentacles band Zeni Gava, whom I saw supporting Alice Donut at a pub gig a few years back. They startled the audience by announcing that they were a non-smoking band and asking everyone to refrain from smoking near the stage, but then redeemed themselves by delivering a blistering set. There are also a number of pieces on non-musical topics — two intriguing articles about Japanese dolls, including one about the creepy-sounding Ningyo Osame doll cremation ceremonies that take place at temples, a comparison test of different flavours of gum, book reviews, a manga strip and a guide to cool shops and clubs in Tokyo. But the emphasis is still very much on music, and *Ongaku Otaku* is rounded out with a solid forty pages of reviews. Some of these bands are well-known in the West, but for others you'd be hard

PAPERBACK DUNGEON
24pp / Available for SAE with two first class stamps and age statement from: J Marriott, Flat 8, 21 Victoria Square, Cliffton, Bristol BS8 4ES, UK (please do not put Paperback Dungeon on envelope)

PORCO MONDO
£3.95 / 40pp

PROHIBITED MATTER
[No details available]

put to find another source of info in English. [Simon Collins]

PAPERBACK DUNGEON

Paperbacks weren't always an expensive commodity. Back in the seventies, publishers like NEL and Futura (but mainly NEL), were pumping out pulp novels and decidedly curious factual paperbacks for little more than the price of a school dinner. It was always a mystery how the latter ever managed to generate mass interest, dealing, as they invariably did, with end of the world scenarios, black holes, second sight, vampires and other off-kilter subjects.

The fiction titles were a different story — a good deal ended up in the schoolyard, with the authors of choice tending to be James Herbert or Guy N Smith (moving further north of England, I am reliably informed it was Sven Hassel and his WWII tales). Common to them all was the purple prose; long descriptions of steamy sex and brutal violence.

It is difficult to envisage James Herbert's *The Fog* ever making it into W H Smith nowadays. Indeed it's probably amazing that it ever made it onto the high street *back then*, given the twisted and relentless nature of its set-pieces. The book simply doesn't let up for a moment, and while the accolades bestowed on Herbert as an author have increased over the years, he has never tried to emulate the accelerated sex and violence of *The Fog*.

But the book was a bestseller, as indeed were many of the other pulp paperbacks of the day. And it is in homage to them that we come to *Paperback Dungeon*, a free — yes, free — zine from editor Justin Bomba's stable of publications. There are overviews of pulp authors Guy N Smith and Sven Hassel, as well as articles on popular genres such as the Frankenstein Monster revival and the Kung Fu series of books from the seventies. Also from the same era is the inflammatory 'plantation-ploitation' novel (*Black Stud* or *Slave's Revenge* anyone?), which gets an all-too brief 'appreciation' here of under two pages. *Paperback Dungeon* is rounded out with reviews of several tawdry novels, including Pierce Nace's *Eat Them Alive*, Mark Ronson's *Ogre*, and ME Knerr's *Sasquatch*. (Pseudonyms anyone?) It's far more entertaining reading *about* this stuff now than it is reading the stuff itself. [David Kerekes]

PORCO MONDO
European Erotic Entertainment

This purports to be a debut issue, but I wouldn't cancel the milk in anticipation of the subsequent number. I'd *like* to see more, but not necessarily because *Porco Mondo* has a finger on the pulse of the European sex industry. My reasons for taking a liking to the thing are rather more left-field than that. For one, the films under review tend to be a decade out of date; secondly, there is a good degree of laughable English-as-a-second-language writing (the first line of text in the magazine is "The art name of this Italian actress doesn't want to remind the notorious Lucrezia, sister of Cesare Borgia Duke of Valentino, she who poisoned her lovers by order of her brother."); thirdly, the veil of secrecy which cloaks the editor and publisher gives *Porco Mondo* the feel of a leaked MI5 document; and fourthly — the best part — I don't believe for a nanosecond that the selection of titles under review is a fair representation of European porn movies... are mainstream audiences *so* obsessed with bestiality!? I think not, Mr Dan — reviewer of most titles in *Porco Mondo* — Pydynkowski! Let's see: horse or dog fucking footage appears in almost fifty percent of Italian porn movies if this seemingly random selection of reviews is anything to go by. Dan feigns disgust whilst describing in detail scenes of women masturbating horses and going at it with German Shepherds. His writing is pedestrian, sometimes funny (funny in that it's pedestrian), but he has an exuberance for his subject matter. Take the following, from Dan's review of *La Donna Delle Bestie* [d: Salvo E Martin]:

Despite being almost humorous watching a mutt screw a female 'doggie' style, it gets nasty when the dog is held on its back so one of the women can ride him. The disgusting nature of these clips has an erotic effect on the blonde watching them, as she quickly begins masturbating (cue to close-up of her eyes and her vagina).

Also featured are interviews with porn stars Luana Borgia ("the art name of this Italian actress...") and the late-Moana Pozzi. But it's Dan who really saves the day. If not for his wild and wanton coverage of the more esoteric European sex movies, *Mondo Porco* would have to be relegated to the bin marked 'Get a fucking Seeing-Eye Dog for the Proof Reader and Typesetter — Quick'. The magazine is nicely produced, with more than its fair share of colour, and covers interesting ground, but it's all very nearly to no avail simply because no one down the line has stopped to actually read and check the thing before going to press. [David Kerekes]

Update There have been no further issues of *Porco Mondo* to date, although there is an Italian porn website [**w**] www.porcomondo.ws which may or may not be related.

PROHIBITED MATTER 5

This zine from Australia deals in crime, sci-fi and horror fiction — subjects lending themselves nicely to editor Rod Marsden's sense of psycho-sexual excess. Don't worry too much about characterisation here, it's left by the wayside in lieu of long, descriptive passages detailing mutilation (of the female). A good case in point is 'Sociopath' one of Marsden's own contributions to issue 5. The tale — a virtual précis of John Fowles' *The Collector*, but with more murders — concerns one Peter Mantis, a bitter and twisted bachelor of fifteen years, whose job as photographer of models lands him in the company of young, career-minded girls. As can be expected, all of womankind is scum and forced to atone for their sins. Mantis drives his victims to his secluded shack and tortures them to death. Jenny, tied to a cross and stripped of her clothing, is despatched thus:

Without warning he thrust the apple up her vagina until bleeding was evident. A great tremor shook her young frame, a gust of air escaped her contracting lungs and then a moan which evolved into a wail echoed off the brick walls. He shoved a ball gag in her mouth and left her to suffer.
He returned after an hour with a jug of water with which to revive her and three apples. The water slapped against her face and brought a new tremor to her fragile body. There was little movement, however, as the apples were crowded in and, after the third, profuse bleeding indicating oncoming death. The fourth apple took the place of the now broken ball gag. He sawed up her expanding and badly slit vagina with a threaded needle and shaved the triangle of hair which was now blood smeared...

More girls follow — fanciful descriptions of subjugation, youthful beauty, and death being the whole purpose of the story. In S Carter's 'Blaspheron', a schoolboy is punished for drawing lewd pictures in class. Later, at dinnertime, he happens upon the eponymous title creature, a "seductive siren and a beast of prey", who assists him in his revenge: with Blaspheron at his side, the boy fucks, buggers and generally defiles and mutilates his class teacher and the school principle, a satanic orgy that ultimately stretches to include all the other pupils in his class.

All of this is suitably distracting in a mindless, cod de Sade kind of way. Despite the misogynist excess of most of the material here — which gives *Prohibited Matter* the appearance of a masturbation fantasy by the local misfit — at least it can't be described as being *dull*. The tales that *do* forsake the 'horror-torture' format, however, *are* maudlin. Take for instance, Pauline Scarf's 'His Shining Armour', with Sir Tristan Osborne and company legging it around the countryside exchanging dialogue straight out of *Captain Pugwash*... [David Kerekes]

PSYCHEDELIC NAZIS
20pp / Rosa Schlüpfer, PO Box 3344, Norman Park 4170, Brisbane, Queensland, Australia

RAG 3
$3.50 / 32pp / Fall 2000 / PO Box 248, Campbell Hall, NY 10916, USA / www.ragcooperative.com

THE RANDY REVIEWER
$4 / 20pp / Jabberwocky Graphix, PO Box 165246, Irving, TX 75016, USA / jabberwocky2000@hotmail.com

REEL WILD CINEMA
A$3 / 32pp / J Harrison, 2 Glenbrae Court, Berwick, Victoria, Australia 3806 / www.hippocketsleaze.freewebspace.com

HIP POCKET SLEAZE
A$2 / 26pp / J Harrison, 2 Glenbrae Court, Berwick, Victoria, Australia 3806

SHAG STAMP
£1.50 / 52pp / Mohawk Beaver, Poste Restante, N rrebro Postkontor, 2200 K benhavn N, Denmark

SHOCK CINEMA
c/o Steve Puchalski, PO Box 518, Peter Stuyvesant Station, New York, NY 10009, USA / www.members.aol.com/shockcin/

SICK PUPPY COMIX
$5 / 56pp / Rabid Publishing, PO Box 93, Paddington, NSW 2021, Australia / www.sickpuppycomix.com

PSYCHEDELIC NAZIS
Rosa Schlüpfer specialises in extremely limited, low-budget zines dedicated to Nazi iconography. The latest, *Psychedelic Nazis*, does nothing to deflect criticism — which would surely range across the board if ever the mag managed anything like a decent print-run. As with *Nazi Frauleins*, *Hollywood-SS* and *Hitler's Panties* before it, *Psychedelic Nazis* presents fascistic imagery in a fetishistic and not always flattering light. Here, the juxtaposition is Nazis and Hippies. "Could there be two more diametrically opposed ideals?" asks Schlüpfer in the introduction. "Is there any greater disparity than the personalities of John Lennon and Heinrich Himmler?" In suggesting that there isn't, Schlüpfer proceeds to contextualise symbols adopted by both the Aryan Nations and the youth movement of the sixties. These include the VW badge (the Beetle being a car beloved by both Nazis and Hippies), the Life rune (or peace symbol), the 'Swastika' on the forehead of Manson, the Arriflex camera used for Nazi propaganda and Rock festivals, musicians dressed as storm-troopers, and so on. There isn't much reading to be had, and I doubt the intention here is a serious investigation, but it's outrageous and in full-colour. [David Kerekes]

Update Rosa Schlüpfer was interviewed in *Headpress 21*.

RAG 3
A Women's Source for Progressive Thought
Rag is a magazine published by a women's co-operative in New York that features non-fiction articles dealing with women's issues in contemporary society, especially parenting. This issue deals with urban living, single motherhood, Tracy Chapman, queer marriages and the precarious balance between parenthood and independent work. Most interesting is an article by a woman whose husband, 'The King,' doesn't give her enough 'bare-assed fucking', so she's resorted to masturbating with a shower massager. This magazine is an honest and forthright mouthpiece and information source for women living alternative lifestyles, but I doubt it would interest too many readers of *Headpress*. [Mikita Brottman]

THE RANDY REVIEWER 10
Brad W Foster is making a conscientious effort to chronicle and review every smutty comicbook that he can lay his hands on. The result is *The Randy Reviewer*, an on-going series comprising in the main of the kind of titles that rarely make it to British shores, i.e., full-on, hot'n'torrid hardcore pummelling. The reviews are lengthy (the *Ramba* series gets close on four pages) and while Brad knows good inking from bad, he doesn't get precious about it. Virtually every title is accompanied by sample artwork. Most of this is of a high standard, and realistic in nature (when Ramba suffers from looking 'ugly' in some poorly executed panels, Brad accuses the artist of 'erotic comic sin #1'). Not so realistic is Ted Nomura's *No-No UFO* (Ted draws like a girl). *The Randy Reviewer* is an original, enlightening and welcome idea. [David Kerekes]

Update The Randy Reviewer appears to have made it to at least issue 13. There's no website as such, but copies are still available from the above address.

REEL WILD CINEMA 5

HIP POCKET SLEAZE 2

Two Australian fanzines from the cut-and-paste school. The first costs more and looks like shit, shoot the cover artist! Anyone old enough to remember the boom in horror fanzines during the late eighties will think they have fallen through a time warp. *Reel Wild Cinema* is basically a review zine, detailing anything from Fulci to Hong Kong Cinema, classic B's to video slashers. Strangely, it reads like a UK-based zine, with articles on David Lynch at the Edinburgh Film Festival and many references to UK video censorship. It's all too familiar. Publisher John Harrison should concentrate more on his other zine *Hip Pocket Sleaze*, a much more mature-looking publication dipping its dirty fingers into the world of trashy pulp-fiction novels and art work. This has at least some constructed direction to it and looks good, an antipodean *Sheer Filth* if you will. Dedicated to reviewing printed material, *Hip Pocket Sleaze* concentrates on the likes of Eric Stanton, Herschel Gordon Lewis (his film novelisations) and artist Dave Burke. At only $2, I shouldn't moan! [David Greenall]

Update Editor John Harrison has recently completed a *Hip Pocket Sleaze* book, containing many reviews and interviews, to be published by Headpress in 2005.

SHAG STAMP 8

This slim little fanzine is the work of one Jane S, sex worker, performer and wanderer around Europe. She writes about the different places she's visited, the places she's stripped or danced or stayed. There are interesting snippets of conversations and some thoughtful pieces on sexuality, sexism, Annie Sprinkle and the life of a sex worker. Some of the pieces seemed to meander, such as the reminiscence of Glastonbury and Jane's attraction to a bloke called Nick, but on the whole I like the unassuming, unpretentious nature of this. And some of her observations about life, politics and places are spot on. [Pan Pantziarka]

SHOCK CINEMA 8

This is one of the healthiest film review zines going. *Shock Cinema* — like *Psychotronic* — is one of those rare beasts that is able to cover the most diverse material and by so doing imbue it with a common underlying thread. Movies as diametrically opposed to one another as *Expresso Bongo* (yes, the old Cliff Richard thing) and *Rapeman* are 'Shock Cinema' movies, simply because they're here, reviewed in *Shock Cinema*. That might sound like a rather obvious argument, but it's a point of fact that simply doesn't carry for the majority of review zines on the market. For them, the films remain as their genre defines them: musical, manga, horror, thriller, etc. Anyway, *Shock Cinema*... The latest issue covers big budgeters like the Ringo Starr western *Blindman*; independents like J R Bookwalter's *The Sandman*; and obscurities like Werner Herzog's documentary on televangelist Dr Gene Scott, *God's Angry Man*. ("Even when he gets the dough, he *still* screams that his lazy, cheap viewers didn't cough it up quickly enough.") Do yourself a favour, get a copy now. [David Kerekes]

Update Shock Cinema is still going strong. The format remains the same, except that colour has been added to the cover and interviews with cult personalities are now also featured alongside the reviews (which remain as varied as ever; *Jim the World's Greatest*, anyone? Or *Staircase*, "a sad gay story" starring Rex Harrison and Richard Burton?). Issue 23 carries dialogues with actors Fred Ward (*The Right Stuff, Tremors*), Bill McKinney (*Deliverance, The Gauntlet*) and David Carradine (*Kung Fu, Death Race 2000*), plus producer/musical director Igo Kantor (*Head, Kingdom of the Spiders*).

SICK PUPPY COMIX 11

This treads a similar path to *Malefact*, in as much as it features good artwork and questionable subject matter. *Sick Puppy* is also predominantly comic strips as opposed to single-panel sketches — so that's another difference. Some of the work is pretty funny (like 'Tom Cruise is not Gay', wherein the diminutive actor has sex with women, picks up female hookers, and beats the shit out of queers to try and dispel the rumours), while most all of it is sex-obsessed: many of the strips conclude with women drenched in sticky ejaculate, courtesy of some big bad mean motherfuckin' man wearing leather and tattoos. Or a horse. The creamed women either love it in a subservient way, or are forced to endure it. Actually I'm lying — only ten out of the thirteen strips end like that (eleven if you include the cover). That's a lie too; you don't think I'd sit here counting cum-covered comic strips, do you? [Joe Scott Wilson]

Update The Sick Puppy Comix website announces issue No 13, "available end of April, 2002". However it would appear that the creator of *Sick Puppy* and *Atomiser* has found God (we're not kidding) and is therefore unable to publish such material any more. You can

SOMETHING WEIRD VIDEO BLUE-BOOK
£6.99 / 138pp / Something Weird / www.somethingweird.com

SWEET SMELL OF SICK SEX
$10 / 88pp / Sophie Cossette, PO Box 41, Place du Parc, Montreal, Quebec, Canada, H2W 2M9 / requin@hotmail.com

TALES FROM THE IDIOT BOX
darrenarnold@laposte.net

Ad mat from *Something Weird Video Blue-Book 1*.

read about his conversion at [w] http://atomiser.blogspot.com/

SOMETHING WEIRD VIDEO BLUE-BOOK I

Essentially this is a catalogue advertising blue movies from the seventies. To leave it there would do the volume a great disservice (and make for a rather dull review): *Blue-Book* is a labour of love, a wealth of 'lost information' and fascinating firsthand account articles. Indeed, the sales pitch and order forms will be largely inconsequential to British readers (who might not trust hardcore to make it through Customs) but that doesn't make *Blue-Book* any less entertaining or important to aficionados of obscure skin flicks. Obscure?! For crying out loud, *Sex Psycho* — that's obscure! A triple-XXX 'horror comedy' from 1971 (by Walt Davis, he of *Evil Come, Evil Go* fame), *Sex Psycho* managed one disastrous preview screening in the early seventies, and that was it… until now. One scene features a gory machete attack on a couple of queers while they're having anal sex. Another scene has a woman giving head, who then gets a fright and accidentally bites off and chokes on her lover's member.

All of the films offered in the catalogue are given a level-headed review, along with credit details (when known), cross-referencing and some juicy snippet. For instance, Instant Sexual Arousal features…

two couples (including the guy who gets his leg chopped off in I Drink Your Blood*) demonstrate positions in this phoney 'educational' loop.*

Many of the films are loops and appear to have been made for a specific theatre, hence distribution prior to *Blue-Book* has been nil. Most originate in the days before hardcore went 'legit' with *Deep Throat*. An article by Eric Shaefer, which opens the magazine, gives an insight into 'storefront theatres': lofts or basements converted into 'mini-cinemas'. The Dragon Art Theatre was one such venue. A bunch of their 16mm sex flicks are offered here for sale as double-bills. They include: *69 Minutes* (which opens with a supermarket heist and a dude who says, "Seeing you waste the motherfucker like that makes my cock hard!"); *World of Peeping Toms* (a roving camera crew speak to prowlers who are peering through windows and watching couples having sex. "How long have you been peeping?" they ask one degenerate); *Hitler's Harlots* (concerns an Ilsa-esque kommandant and her 'ape-like' assistant, who gets a victim to gobble him while threatening to use her breasts as lamp shades); *Bat Pussy* (when Dora Dildo's "twat begins to twitch" she knows that a crime is being committed, dons her green tights, cape, and T-shirt with actual Batman insignia, and rushes to the scene on one of those big rubber Hoppity Hop balloons); and *Tunga, God of Love & Lust* (whose budget doesn't extend to a prop revolver, henceforth a gun used in a hold-up is actually a hand drill painted black)…

Other articles include David Friedman tracing the rise and fall of the Pussycat Theatre chain; Michael Copner on his stint as a projectionist at Seattle's Dirty Bird, which claimed to show twenty-four-hour-a-day "highly experimental art films" and in whose gloomy auditorium, once or twice a year, a customer "would close his eyes for the last time"; Charles Kilgore recalls the 'white coaters' or 'fuckumentaries', early hardcore masquerading as educational films; 42nd Street Pete takes a stroll across Times Square in its sleazy heyday, and talks of a projectionist who would splice a few minutes of gay porn into the straight smut film playing just to get a kick out of the reaction from the bemused audience; and Dwight Pangborn on seventies gay theatres and some of their more colourful clientele, such as the 'creepy old fart' in The Kings who would crawl beneath the seats in the dark and latch onto people's legs. Excellent all. But, still, they pale next to Johnny Legend's personal reminiscence 'The Legend of Porn'. A delirious tirade of famous names, bum deals, sexual conquests, made and unmade smut films (which Legend has had some hand in) and his walking into the AIP offices only to discover that the studio's famed series of literary adaptations were based on a pile of *Classics Illustrated* comics! The piece concludes with a story of how Legend was forced to cut Alex de Rezny's *Long Jeane Silver* on account of one scene that freaked out every audience who saw the film… Silver, who boasted a real-life 'penis-shaped stump' where her leg should be, picks up a gay guy and proceeds to stick her truncated limb into his poop shoot, deeper and deeper and deeper and… The 'missing' reel still rests in Legend's garage. [David Kerekes]

Update Blue Book 2 Sloppy Seconds! has since been published. Equally as important a time capsule as the first edition, though somewhat slimmer, all-new material in *Sloppy Seconds!* includes features on the Unsung Gals of Porno, Philadelphia X, Vanessa del Rio, and of course plenty of film loops you're never going to have heard of before.

SWEET SMELL OF SICK SEX 2

Sweet Sophie — who would think you'd have such a filthy mind? Absolutely anything goes in Sophie's gag cartoons and comic strips, and this giant collection of material doesn't skimp on the cum quota as stars from stage and screen rub schlongs alongside royalty and Presidents. Kurt Cobain holds a pistol to his head while porking Courtney. "C'mon Kurt," she hollers, "do me a big favour and blow your brains out already! I can't wait to go from grunge to Gucci!" Also included in *Sweet Smell* No 2 are features on a great-looking Canadian crime tabloid from the Fifties called *Allo Police* (which often ran lurid sketches on its covers when lurid crime scene photographs weren't available) and the supposedly true tale of two murderous madams from Mexico, as recounted by Ramona, "slave-whore" and "lone syphilitic survivor"…

Oh! I couldn't stop myself. I kept licking and sucking on her cunt even though I knew it was riddled with the deadly curse of syphilis… Yeah, I buried myself in Ilena's stinky snatch and I truly relished each new droplet of her death-drenched cream on my lips.

There's even a sensitive illustration by Sophie running alongside.

Danny Hellman, Al Goldstein, The Cramps and Phil Liberbaum number among the interviewers and interviewees also featured in *Sweet Smell* No 2. [David Kerekes]

Update No response from our email to Sophie. Maybe Courtney got to her first.

TALES FROM THE IDIOT BOX 1 & 2

This Xeroxed and stapled fanzine from Queensland is dedicated to Australian cinema of any genre. It's a basic affair that would have looked amateur ten years ago. Dated by design, each issue contains fifty brief reviews and a handful of actor and director profiles. Of the reviews, most are scribed by editor Darren Arnold with a few culled from the likes of *Headpress* and *Samhain*.

Its intentions may be well-meaning, but *Tales from the Idiot Box*

THIRD EYE
£2.50 / 48pp

TRASH CITY
£2 / 108pp / PO Box 13653, Scottsdale, Arizona, AZ 85267, USA / www.trashcity.org

TWOBLUE COUPLES
£3.50; Galaxy Publications Ltd, PO Box 312, Witham, Essex CM8 3SZ, UK / www.galaxy.co.uk

ULTRA FLESH
£10.99 / 94pp / 1998

ULTRA VIOLENT
$4.95 / 72pp / UV Magaine, PO Box 110117, Palm Bay, FL, 32911-0117, USA / info@uvmagazine / www.uvmagazine.com

UNRATED
£4.95 / 42pp / Unrated Press, 142 Hounslow Road, Feltham, Middlesex, TW14 0BA, UK / carl@unrated.co.uk / www.unrated.co.uk

Viva La Muerte (Long Live Death), reviewed in *Ultra Violent 5*, an obscure 1971 film which will enlighten, depress and more than likely confuse viewers.

(named after David Caesar's 1996 heist film *Idiot Box*) suffers one major flaw: a lack of information! The profile and filmography of Peter Weir for instance takes up less than half an A4 page. Poor design and photocopying I can forgive, but if the text contains nothing you can't find in your average film guide then why bother. The whole thing smells of teenage film-fan vanity.

Stick with the seventh edition of the *Time Out Film Guide* which reviews 114 more Australian films than these two publications. [David Greenall]

THIRD EYE 5
Mark Coulson, editor of this small format, B&W review of "sex and violence in the media", seems to be suffering from a bout of deep-rooted angst; in the editorial for *Third Eye* No 5, he laments the fact that the current issue is almost a year late, adding that the New Year makes him feel "it might be time for a change… or even an end", and asks himself whether *Third Eye* "is worth carrying on". Not an auspicious editorial for the New Year, which is a shame, because this magazine's got some good stuff in it — notably, a piece by Keith Breese on Renatto Polselli, another by Anthony Wright on sex and violence in art-house cinema, and an article by Richard King on the inseparability of sex and violence in the contemporary horror film. The "gore-drenched, sex-filled film reviews" are equally honest and unpretentious. On the down side, however, take a close look at the seemingly incompatible and random fillers (Jayne Mansfield, Tabatha Cash, Ashlyn Gere and Anna Nicole Smith in one brief, arbitrary 'girlie gallery'), and the amateurish spelling mistakes, and you start to understand what Coulson's getting so depressed about. [Mikita Brottman]

Update No luck here so it seems like Mr Coulson did meet some sort of end.

TRASH CITY 18/19
Twenty months since the last edition, the eclectic film zine *Trash City* makes a welcome (double issue) return. Eclectic film zine because, if anything, films almost seem an afterthought. Editor Jim McLennan goes on holiday to Greece. A search for local sleazy video and comics shops is quickly aborted because the signs prove too difficult to follow. The most exciting thing that happens is while awaiting the flight home, an ice cream vendor at the airport serves up two ice creams and only charges for one. What's more, he does it deliberately and gives a thumbs up! Other articles include a look at 'new lad' magazines *GQ*, *Maxim*, *Loaded*, *FHM* and *Arena*, complete with a comparatives table. There's more intrepid reporting from pubs around the capitol that feature strippers. And Rik Rawling investigates telephone sex lines ("Nature demands that men empty their bollocks on a fairly regular basis"), narrowing the phenomena down to two basic types: 'Raunch' and 'Rip off', the rule of thumb being that the more the ad promises, the less you'll get. He's been investigating for quite a while, too, and discusses the changing face (ear?) of phone sex lines, and his most unsettling telephone encounter (it involves giggling girls and the dwarf from *Twin Peaks*)… Lots more like-minded reportage throughout, *Trash City* is ace. [David Kerekes]

Update Trash City is still ace but now costs £5 or $5. There are heaps of online reviews and you can even get some *Trash City* apparel.

TWOBLUE COUPLES VOL 3 NO 2

Little more than a 'Now That's What I Call Porn', this bi-monthly mag is made up of photosets that, to this seasoned eye, look swiped from the files of other titles like *Cheri*, *High Society* and *Fox*. This means that most of the girls are your generic Yank porn babes but, compared to the boilers you usually find in other Galaxy titles, this is most welcome.

To be fair this particular issue is class all the way — Page Three regular Karen White appears in a lively spit-dribbling dyke session with another blonde and, in one full page shot, has her arse cheeks splayed by her bleached buddy to reveal an invitingly gaping ring. Despite her impossibly cute, pixie-like nose our Karen is well stacked and I'm suddenly looking at her in a new light. Elsewhere there's splayed labia aplenty from what looks like two brunette twins, a lively threesome in a shower stall and a girl/guy session featuring whipped cream dribbled from bell-end to chin and even a precariously placed strawberry! Only the horrific Reader's Wives and Reader's Boners' (!?!) shots bring a jarring note of reality to the proceedings and the full page cartoons are some of the worst I've ever seen outside of a Student Rag Mag.

It's nowhere near 'hardcore' and not even up to speed with *Cheri* (which still doesn't show penetration but has recently featured 'cumshot aftermath' shots) but is a long way from the quite tame porn mags of ten years ago.

I flick back to page seven where cute Alex (female, for those suddenly confused) firmly grips a gleaming red erection close to her gaping mouth, looking like she's just found a new religion and I'm suddenly glad that moral standards continue to decline as we head towards the end of the millennium. By December we could have cum shots on the front of *The Star*. [Rik Rawling]

Update No mention of *TwoBlue Couples* on the Galaxy Publications website; they are obviously concentrating on video and the net, including a mind-boggling number of reader's wives pics.

ULTRA FLESH VOL 1
A Connoisseurs [sic] Guide to the Halcyon Days of Pornography

In perfect-bound magazine form, how can this homage to seventies smut fail? It has archival Readers' Wives snaps, reviews of seminal porn films, articles on Linda Lovelace, Gerard Damiano, *Flesh Gordon*, *The Enema Bandit*, and even a crap comic strip (based on Richard Aldrich's film *Ms Magnificent*). The soft-core pictures (erect members have been tactfully removed) and thick, glossy paper make the entire publication look less like a porn mag and more like a theatrical programme. *But what the hey! It's supposed to be the seventies!* There's even a John 'The Wadd' Holmes centrefold, in which the mightily donged actor is dwarfed by the majesty of his surroundings for a change (he's standing in a dramatic, arms-outstretched, Christ-like pose under a waterfall). Lightweight but fun. [Sarah Turner]

Update Ultra Flesh doesn't seem to have made it past Vol 1…

ULTRA VIOLENT 4
Horror & Exploitation Cinema

With a title like *Ultra Violent* you probably have a good idea that this isn't a magazine produced for fans of Hollywood musicals. Instead, the fourth issue of Scott Gabbey's *Ultra Violent* features a bunch of interviews with the likes of filmmakers Olaf Ittenbach (*Premutos*), Roger Watkins (*Last House on Dead End Street*), Jean Rollin (*Living Dead Girl*), Fred Dekker (*Night of the Creeps*), novelist Jack Ketchum (*Off Season*), and choreographer-turned-director Busby Berkeley (*Gold Diggers of 1935*). OK, I was kidding about the last one. [David Kerekes]

Update As of writing, *Ultra Violent* has hit No 5 with No 6 scheduled soon. No 5 features more low-key trash-film faves, such as David (*I Drink Your Blood*) Durston and Jeff (*Squirm*) Lieberman.

UNRATED 1
Cinema of the eXtreme

This is a new publishing venture from Carl T Ford, devoted to critically ig-

VEX
$3.95 / 64pp / www.vexmag.com

VIXXXEN
£3.50 / 64pp

VOLUPTUOUS
The Score Group / 1629 NW 84th Ave, Miami, FL 33029, USA / www.voluptuous.com

WEIRD ZINES
£1.50 (cash only, incs p&p) / 24pp / age statement reqd / do not write 'Weird Zines' on envelope / J Marriott, Flat 8, 21 Victoria Square, Clifton, Bristol BS8 4ES, UK

X THE UNKNOWN
$1.50 / 10 & 16pp/ PO Box 14, Matawan, NJ 07747, USA

nored cinema. Admirable and slick, it has one or two genuine curios up its sleeve, including an interview with Joe Christ (whose name was familiar to the pages of the long-gone *Film Threat Video Guide* and little else) and articles on the likes of Lech Kowalski's *Gringo*, Francis Von Zerneck's *God's Lonely Man* and Lodge Kerrigan's *Clean, Shaven*. Definitely deserves your support for bothering to tread some unlikely ground. [David Kerekes]

VEX 3
A magazine professing to be about "Movies & Whatever". Got to confess that I got a lot of mileage out of this, despite it looking exactly like a multitude of other cheap paper stock, poorly-hacked movie zines. Issue 3 is a special animal issue. We're talking a massive survey of gorilla movies — that's right, ape rapes, monkey men, and mad doctors with monkey pets. From the obvious to the obscure. We're also talking an interview with a zoophile (his favourite Hollywood film is *K-9*, with Jim Belushi). While entertaining, I don't believe a word of it. Not forgetting a guide to doggie movies (from *The Adventures of Milo and Otis* to *Dogs of Hell* — well, it starts off as an A–Z and just kinda gets lost), plus a piece of pro-Christian drivel by a former gorehound zine editor, now born again and warning of the evils of video-trading. And what prompted Nick the Yak to denounce Deodato? One night "a cab driver told me about Jesus Christ on the way home from a screening of *Rocky Horror* (which I saw sixty times!)". A fuckin' *cab driver*! Uh, did I say I liked this...? [David Kerekes]

Update Vex made it to issue 4 in print ('Death On The Set! Over 100 On-Camera Mishaps, Misses, and Murders!') and is now an online magazine.

VIXXXEN 1
The Fanzine of XXX Entertainment in Movies, Videos and Comics

There aren't many zines knocking about that set out to cover the so-called 'adult entertainment' industry in all its forms. (Fewer still make it past the first issue.) Well, here comes *Vixxxen*, a zine devoted to doing just that, edited by Justin Bomba and Steve Midwinter. Presented in a highly readable and entertaining fashion, no way does *Vixxxen* take itself or its subject matter too seriously. The scope of 'adult' matter covered doesn't become tedious because nothing is dwelt on for too long. No author credits are given, either, and the various contributors — such as The Jazz Master (should be Jizz, surely?!), Jarvis Throat and Rabid Shafter — take great pleasure in sharing their love of the genre with us.

Amongst the many and varied delights on offer are an overview of Michael Ninn's *Sex* in contrast to Greg Dark's *New Wave Hookers 4*; an interview with porn performer Jamie Gillis; and a look at the work of Samantha Fox and Ashlyn Gere.

Justin Bomba delivers the two most interesting articles, with his overlook of the world of Eros Comix (with plenty of groovy graphics), and a peek at the odd vision of comic artist Richard Corben. Massive breasts and mighty tools aplenty!

All in all a light-hearted, fun read, recommended to anyone with the slightest interest in the genre. [John Carter]

Update *Vixxxen* 1 and 2 sold well and are now sadly out of print

VOLUPTUOUS
APRIL 1995 & JULY 1996

A magazine for lovers of girls who are 'full of figure'. Not so as to be actually 'fat', just plump or big breasted. OK, fat. "All Stacked! All Natural!" decries the subheading on this Stateside publication, and of the two issues under review here, the models leave a smidgen to be desired by way of 'good-looks'. It's full colour throughout in real cellulite-o-vision with the likes of Chelsea rippling beneath latex ("I didn't think, in my wildest dreams, that these pictures would ever get published"). Cast your vote for the coveted 'Big Breast Challenge'! With each issue readers are encouraged to vote on who has the "best boobs of all-time". The July 96 heat is between Lisa Phillips and Cassandra: the former a caped Elvira-clone (kind of) vs the fretful aunt-type. Yummy. Being US-based, things are that much more raunchy for a softcore mag. Not to mention about as erotic as watching your mother take a shower. Take a look at blonde-haired Rhonda's big fat ass in granny-like pants as she does the vacuum cleaning! Turn over the page and see how she's overcome with excitement, sticking the nozzle of the vacuum on her tummy, pulling a glob of flesh skywards! (Luckily she isn't using a Dyson.) Then she simply *has* to cut holes in the tips of her bra so that her nipples stick through! There are a lot of shots of women eating cream cakes. Rhonda takes a respite by shoving a whole cream slice in her mouth. Later in the mag, Krisztina (from Hungary) poses with a candy covered donut in one hand, a chocolate finger in the other and a whipped cream mountain on her butt. Indeed the photo spread for July features Krisztina with a cake on each knee. Don't know about you, but that never fails to get *me* hot. Hairy girls also appear to be a flabby favourite. But without doubt, my personal moment in *Voluptuous* comes by way of a piece of verbiage: "A Trip To The Gynaecologist With The Ideal Woman!" In answer to a question posed by a "CJ from Sacramento", intrepid columnist Rachel Norman relates her own personal experiences… "the doctor sticks an instrument in the twat area called a 'speculum', which is cold, metal and sorta 'opens wide' for the doctor". [David Kerekes]

Update Voluptuous is still out there, and you can get your "free daily Titfix" at the official *Voluptuous* website.

WEIRD ZINES

Justin Bomba, the man responsible for *Bomba Movies*, the one-shot *Sadomania*, and sundry other small press publications, turns his attentions away from cinema for a moment and toward small press publications that don't encompass music, poetry, politics, riot grrls or fiction. In other words, the kind of zines reviewed in *Factsheet 5* that appealed to Justin Bomba, but were few and far between and took "page upon page to find". Well, you won't get lost with *Weird Zines* — it's only twenty-four pages for a start, and constitutes a diverse collection of cheap'n'cheesy paper oddities, along with their ordering details. Some of this stuff may already be familiar to anyone with their ear to the ground of marginalia, but a lot more won't be. *Sex & Violence* is a zine devoted to obscure B-pictures (some of which might be fictitious) and comics; *Stupor* features interviews with bar-hoppers around Detroit, who drunkenly recount tales of woe and stupidity; *Danzine* is for working girls, with news and advice on things like club conditions, affordable housing in various cities, and bad dates. [David Kerekes]

X: THE UNKNOWN
32, 38/39, 40/41

You know how it is, right? You're innocently watching the skies over Arizona one night, photographing UFOs with a night vision scope, when lo and behold, out of the San Andreas fault leaps a bunch of enraged subterranean Bigfoot creatures who throw rocks at you until you're forced to run for it. Life really *is* a bitch, innit? Of course, the Bigfoots (Bigfeet?) are trying to conceal from you their complicity in the epidemic of alien-inspired cattle mutilations that have occurred in the area — it turns out that the alien 'greys' are transfusing the Bigfoots with blood from the dead cows in order to alter their genetic make-up and make them easier to control. So it's all quite simple, really.

That, at least, is what Lyle Vann, director of the Arizona Bigfoot Center and author of *Mars Needs Bovine!!!* would have us believe in *X: The Unknown* No 32 (edited by Pat O'Donnell). Vann writes in a breathlessly excited style and seems to think that the more words in block capitals and exclamation points he uses, the more credible his assertions will become:

As I gazed behind the brush, my curiosity and bravery was [sic] rewarded. I can claim something that no other person on Earth

YANKEE CLIPPER

$16.95 / 44pp / Suite #293, 61 E. 8th Street, New York, NY 10003, USA / http://members.aol.com/CliptOne/clipper.htm

Betsy has a companion (not pictured) who offers support and endorses the new look wholeheartedly. Yankee Clipper.

can: I witnessed a cattle mutilation unfolding! I SAW IT ALL WITH MY OWN TWO EYES!!

OK, two can play at that game. I AM NOW USING CAPITAL LETTERS! NOTE HOW MUCH MORE AUTHORITATIVE AND WISE THIS REVIEW HAS BECOME!!! Vann pops up again in issue No 40/41, a 'Special Double Sized News Watch Issue' with more of his Bigfoot-watching anecdotes:

> … the female Bigfoot was wearing twigs in her hair like barrettes.

And also in No 38/39 (a double sized 'Exorcism' issue):

> My world became unreal and mysterious the day of October 22, 1994 when I viewed "the message from the ape-man".

It sounds like it's been unreal and mysterious for a lot longer than that, guy!

As you will have gathered by now, X is a *Fortean Times*-style zine about, well, everything. Bigfoot, Nessie, spooks (both the supernatural and CIA-funded varieties), men in black, extraterrestrials, fairies, JFK conspiracies, military cover-ups... *X: The Unknown* is more chokka with all the usual suspects than *The X Files*. What irks me, though, about this broad-spectrum approach is the way you are asked to believe in absolutely any loopy proposition or be seen as a crusty hidebound sceptic. Personally speaking, I'm much more prepared to believe in US military cover-ups and political conspiracies than in underground Bigfoots, and I can't really see why belief in one should imply belief in the other.

And frankly, the daily behaviour of ordinary human beings is so hilarious and strange that I don't feel the need to go out looking for *outré* things to believe in — coping with 'consensual reality' is enough of a struggle.

I did get a few laughs out of these zines, though. Apart from the ever-entertaining Lyle Vann, I particularly enjoyed this gem from 'Symptoms of Demon Possession' by J F Cogan in No 38/39, an article which appears to lay the blame for almost all the woes of humanity on demonic possession:

> …what makes a person risk a prominent career for no good reason at all? The answer may well be intermittent demon possession on a time-share basis.

So that's Bill Clinton off the hook, then.

Journalistic integrity compels me to point out that the back page of No 40/41 contains a rave review of *Headpress 17*, abruptly and bizarrely spliced onto the end of an article on the typology of necrophilia (talk about guilt by association!), so I'm sorry I can't return the compliment, but, to rephrase Dana Scully, "I don't want to believe." [Simon Collins]

YANKEE CLIPPER

"Ahoy Mateys! That's how editor 'Captain Stanley' addresses his readers in this issue of *Yankee Clipper*, a zine devoted to the fetish of bald-headed ladies. That's right, bald-headed ladies. On the cover is an attractive girl posed in front of a waterfall. From one side of her head down to her waist flows her lovely long locks; the other side of her head is completely bald. The blurb beside her queries whether the young lady's scalp is "*Half Full* of hair, or (in fact) *Half Empty?*"

I like to get a piece of card and blank off half the girl's face, down the middle, in order to help determine what kind of mood I'm in: do I find myself going for the wholesome *full* head of hair or the Charlie's Family *empty* look.

(Can never seem to get my head around both at once, though.)

Yankee Clipper provides a glimpse into a whole new world, one which operates under its own agendas. From its pages you will discover what makes one scalp more appealing than the next, the numerous levels upon which the fetish operates, the minutiae that propels the fetishist, recommended reading and viewing materials, and of course further contacts.

Here's a quick look through the forty-four (economically produced) pages: Amongst the letters, one gent decries having to pay his partner to shave her head ("It keeps me broke, but I enjoy my poverty"), and a German reader reminisces on a magazine from a number of years back called *Shaved*.

The first of two major articles is focussed on the Shingled Bob, a short hairstyle popular with women in the twenties and thirties (and is "perhaps the most important hair style of all time"). The second main article is devoted to shaven heads in comics, which laments that the *Archie* humour titles — in spite of being about teenagers and aimed at teenagers — rarely addresses the issue of hairstyles…

How many pubescent Americans fantasized about dramatic makeovers for those smooth raven locks of Veronica's, and the bouncing wavy blonde mane of her friend/antagonist Betty.

In the best fan tradition, much of *Yankee Clipper* is devoted to news and photo clippings, including one full-page reproduction of a Calvin Klein ad for jeans. The good Captain is up-in-arms because the ad crops the top of the model's cranium off. The latter portion of *Yankee Clipper* is given over to video reviews and advertisements for specialist tapes. Amongst them is *Back to School*, which follows Michael Chapman, a travelling barbershop, on his visits to the college towns of Chapel Hill and Greensboro, North Carolina. Here, on the college steps, he snips the hair of female students. The review doesn't state whether he performs the cuts for free, but it seems Chapman is operating without any permission, in public, for the sole purpose of making videos ("events of great daring, always pushing the envelope" states the reviewer).

The subjects in the film talk about their hair, how they usually wear it, and why they have chosen to get it cut. Moving away from the colleges, Chapman takes to cutting hair in a night-club and later, in the street. The review closes on the consideration that "you'll need a rest" after having watched this video.

The critic for this and the other tapes under review is 'Al Opecia',

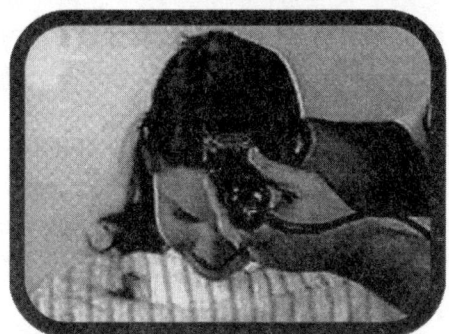

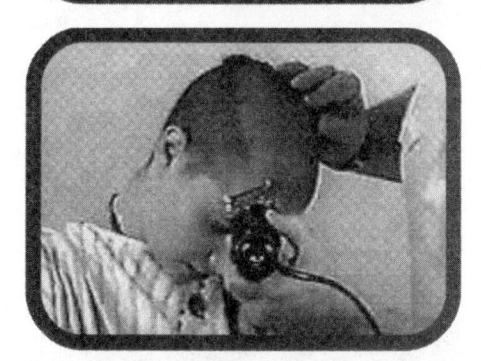

THE 101 BEST GRAPHIC NOVELS
£10.99 / hb / 80pp / ISBN 156163283X / NBM 2001 / www.nbmpublishing.com

2024
$16.95 / hb / 96pp / IBSN 1561632791 / NBM Publishing 2001 / www.nbmpub.com

THE ADVENTURES OF MENG & ECKER
£9.99 / pb / 256pp / ISBN 0861300998 / Savoy / 446 Wilmslow Rd, Withington, Manchester M20 3BW / office@savoy.abel.co.uk

but I suspect that this, along with the majority of names in *Yankee Clipper*, are all pseudonyms for the Cap. And what type of man might the Cap be? Dunno, but under a picture of one *Back to School* student wearing a nose ring, he states haughtily:

The body modification fans of the younger generations enjoy head shaving along with their tattoos and body piercings. They would probably like it more if it hurt like brain surgery.

(Younger generation? If *what* hurt like brain surgery?)

Another video company is LA Smoothies, who specialise in a series of tapes, each devoted to an individual head shave. The women in these tapes are doing it for the money, and it's not without some trepidation that they sit in the barber chair watching their locks fall to the ground. The long-haired April comes close to tears the closer the cut gets. Betsy on the other hand has a companion who offers support and endorses the new look wholeheartedly.

In much the same vein, Close Crops offer Haircut-of-the-Month, a series of videos filmed by Ed and Linda Cookingham in their hair salon.

The emphasis of all the above videos is the slow, deliberate cropping of hair via a sequence of ever-shortening styles. Not all the subjects end up as 'smoothies', but one gets the distinct impression it's a swizz if there isn't at least one smoothie somewhere on a tape. A quite different approach is taken by Q-Ball, where head-shaving is presented in an overtly sexual context. However, it is clear from the review that this particular series comprise less films made by fans than they are films made by someone wishing to grab a slice of the bizarro porn market. The first Q-Ball tape has a naked obese woman getting her head shaved in a scene the reviewer describes as "one of the most unpleasant moments we've witnessed in video history". A marginal improvement is the woman in the sequence that follows: "While she is very attractive, she seems to be quite dumb". Most unforgivable however, is the way the Q-Ball series is made: the head shavings are handled all wrong...

I picked up *Captain Stanley's Yankee Clipper* in New York's now defunct basement store See? Hear! Ted, behind the counter, said that before this particular issue, he'd never seen nor heard of the publication. He thought this odd because Vol 4 No 11 suggests it has been around for quite some time. We deliberated on whether it may have been a debut number using the familiar ploy of masquerading as a long-standing title, but concluded that, hitherto, *Yankee Clipper* had probably only been available by mail order. I was somewhat surprised to later discover that the issue I picked up was actually published in 1997, some four years before it had arrived on this particular newsstand!

The internet was only just being invented in 1997, and a *Yankee Clipper* list of approved websites in this issue takes today's browser to dead ends and redirections. Interested parties, however, might care to try the Short Hair Enthusiasts [w] www.haircut.net which offers a large bunch of links. From here I was able to locate the *Yankee Clipper* homepage (see above), which is less up-to-date than the issue I've just reviewed. [David Kerekes]

ART & GRAPHIC NOVELS

THE 101 BEST GRAPHIC NOVELS
Stephen Weiner

Given that Weiner is only stretching to 101 recommendations you'd think that he'd have at least put a little time aside to write something more than a capsule comment on each. He doesn't and so the 101 best graphic novels ever are relegated to a paltry thirty-eight pages (which includes an illustration on each page). An index, a guide to further reading, a section on (six) novels featuring comic book characters, a preface and — get this! — an introduction entitled 'A Very Short History of Comics and Graphic Novels' help to pad things out to a mightily jaundiced eighty pages in total. The whole thing would have been more suited to an article in a magazine, or a catalogue for public libraries. It surely can be of no interest to comic fans or the casual reader. [Joe Scott Wilson]

2024
Ted Rall

2024, an updating of the immortal *1984*, depicts a future in which the state keeps the population numbed with TV, shopping, pornography and the like. Judging by the introduction (in which the author laments the fact that people are happy to have their freedom taken away in the nebulous interest of national security), the book would appear to have laudable intentions. However, every page drips with just the sort of sneering cynical don't-give-a-fuck-about-anything attitude which *2024* purports to critique; hypocritically, Rall has churned out a product custom-built for the loathsome Gen Xers his book seeks to condemn.

Reprehensible as this may be, the book's worst crime is that it simply isn't any good. It isn't a riff on *1984* but rather the exact same story with silly cosmetic changes. Instead of clocks striking 13, ironically-purchased Texas Instruments watches do so; Winston is not sent to Room 101 but made to watch Channel 101 (which is showing a documentary about rats); instead of loving Big Brother, he loves himself. The lack of subtlety in the writing matches the lack of originality in the concept: "The chain bar-café's beverages were bitter and overpriced, but everyone drank them anyway because they were so popular."

The medium of the graphic novel is no excuse for this sort of lazy corner-cutting. Instead of a coherent narrative or solid characters, Rall randomly throws in supposedly 'cool' elements in an attempt to hold our attention. 'Anarcho-capitalism', 'Neo-postmodernism'… these neologisms mean sod-all since Rall does not see fit to explain them; that would be too much effort (as would a fluent, logical page layout). Consequently, the book is a tedious mess, lacking the thematic unity that is essentially its *raison d'être*. A smart arsed disclaimer ("This work contains numerous errors of omission, extraneous subplots, continuity problems, disjointed narratives…") attempts to brush this off but succeeds only in further annoying the reader. To cap it all off, the drawing style is affectedly amateurish. There is no point in reading this smarmy graphic novel whilst the immortal *1984* remains in print. That sound you can hear is Orwell spinning in his grave. [Anton Black]

THE ADVENTURES OF MENG & ECKER
David Britton & Kris Guidio

Hot on the heels of the Meng & Ecker novel, *Motherfuckers*, the foppish twins are back! Here they resurface in a collection of their comic strip capers from the past decade, with new material thrown in for good measure. More inflammatory than a swastika in Burger King, these are tales that fear neither the wrath of the law nor public indignation. No one is sacred, no one is spared. One might call it satire, but Meng & Ecker don't play by such rules. Real events and imaginary characters are squeezed through a press tarnished with the deeds and misfortunes of publishers, Savoy — their police raids and trials for obscenity. What comes out the other end is an alternate history of life in a northern town. Each story has a tale to tell, but is exquisitely distracted with its abundance of peripheral characters all desperate to get in or off the page. Arthur Askey, the Dark Knight, Will Self, Andrew Lloyd Webber, Tank Girl, the Manchester Police…

In case you need reminding, the first issue of the *Meng & Ecker* comic is banned as obscene in Britain (not subsequent issues, because the wheels of justice have yet to turn that far).

The Adventures of Meng & Ecker means bookstore distribution for *les enfants terrible*. A hard-on in Dillons anybody? [David Kerekes]

ANIMAL MAN
£14.99 / pb / 239pp / ISBN 1840234601 / Titan Books 2002 / titanpress@titanemail.com

ART AT THE TURN OF THE MILLENIUM
£19.99 / pb / 576pp / ISBN 3-8228-7393-4 / Taschen / www.taschen.com

BABY DOLL
£12.95 / pb / 96pp / ISBN 187159278X / Velvet/ Creation Books 1996 / www.creationbooks.com

BATMAN: OTHER REALMS
£12.95 / pb / 134pp / ISBN 1563894203 / DC Comics 1998 / www.dccomics.com

ANIMAL MAN
Grant Morrison et al

A decade after its initial run, Grant Morrison's critically rated fan favourite is back in print. The first thing one notices in the wake of *The Invisibles* and Morrison's current Vertigo series, *The Filth*, is just how dated this looks — especially in the artwork department, though of course this is hardly anyone's fault, merely the fact that comic book design has changed (for better or worse?) so radically over the last ten years. What obviously hasn't changed — only improved — in the intervening years is Grant Morrison's talent for creating dazzling and innovative stories and character situations. More than an inkling of this is apparent in *Animal Man*, though it's noticeable that in comparison to his later work this is predominantly safer stuff, and there's very little here to upset the kiddies, or, indeed, dyed in the wool traditionalists. There are, however, some of the usual clever references we've come to expect from Morrison, not least of which is the agonisingly gory reference to the Road Runner's arch nemesis, Wile Coyote. Interesting, but not an essential part of the Morrison oeuvre. [Stephen Sennitt]

ART AT THE TURN OF THE MILLENIUM
Ed. Burkhard Riemschneider & Uta Grosenick

The best modern art can be summed-up in neat, concise sentences. Rather, that seems to have been the criteria for including the 137 artists who go to make up this book, each being prefaced by an arresting quotation:

An object is capable of creating the place in which it is shown.

My work derives from the snapshot. It is the form of photography that most closely stands for love.

We are sore-eyed scopophiliac oxymorons… We are artists.

'They,' the artists, would appear to be pranksters with funding. Henrik Plenge Jakobsen, for instance, has a 'Laughing Gas Chamber' installation in which two people can sit and get high on laughing gas. His very colourful acrylic painting with the wording 'everything is wrong' looks great and I can see how it is art. I can see how the 'Laughing Gas Chamber' might be art, too, but that brings with it some awkward questions on education, presentation and contextualism. Would it be less artistic if Jakobsen charged people an entry fee into his Laughing Gas Chamber? Or erected it in the street? But it's a funny concept, and I like it. I also like Sharon Lockhart's photographic studies of bored-looking curators overseeing Tokyo's Museum of Contemporary Art; Joachim Koester's boarded-up window installation (which effectively makes the gallery look like it's been closed down); Jeff Wall's 'Sudden Gust of Wind (After Hokusai)' which has figures in a barren landscape surrounded by an unfeasibly large quantity of airborne papers; Cosima Von Bonin's woman with extra long arms (she stands on an elevated plank and still they reach the ground)… You get the picture/installation. [David Kerekes]

BABY DOLL
Peter Whitehead

Pop socks. I originally thought that the clothing worn in this book (though there isn't much of it) exhibited a keen sense of retro chic — until, that is, someone more closely associated with the book's internal workings pointed out that the images are genuinely from a time gone by and, for him at least, those hideously awful seventies fashions killed any erotic potential dead. I have a soft spot for the hideously awful, but my feelings toward this book are mixed.

Baby Doll is a collection of photographs by Peter Whitehead, the guy responsible for *Charlie is my Darling*, the first Rolling Stones film, and various other rock and beat documentaries throughout the sixties. At the tail-end of that decade, Whitehead met and fell in love with Mia Martin, a nineteen-year-old actress. In 1972, armed only with film stock and psychedelic drugs, the two of them slipped away to a château in the south of France. The result is this, a series of intense, surreal and vaguely pornographic studies of Mia.

To maintain a semblance of narrative, the photographs have been arranged for the book into chapters, each chapter having a specific 'feel'. The first chapter is the most sexually explicit and centres on Mia doing pseudo-Carroll Baker impressions on an old iron-frame bed, exposing herself in a manner that most sanitised British top-shelf mags until recently weren't allowed to show. Here we have Mia on her hands and knees, butt forward, fingering herself. Another shot shows her lifting her legs high above her head, genitalia aimed squarely at the camera. The following chapters are not quite so obvious and play around with mirrors, shadows, camera shenanigans, until, finally, by the end of the book, all that's left are portraits of Mia, double-exposed and deliberately blurred.

For a collection of erotic photography, *Baby Doll* goes about its work in a curious way, chiselling away at its own energies. As the book progresses, so deteriorates the sexual *frisson*. Neither is there much warmth in these pictures — Mia seems merely to be going through the motions, acting out someone else's fantasies. If you look into her face, there is little of the 'mischievous spark' that the models of say, Richard Kern or Romain Slocombe, possess. She looks to be having no fun at all. Come the end of *Baby Doll*, the reader feels as though they have been privy to someone's collapsing relationship, listening in on private, desperate snatches of dialogue. It would be nice to think that it was the drugs slowly working their magic, causing each successive image to appear more topsy-turvy than the last, but the book is far too dark for that.

Hell, *dark*? It's almost fucking black.

These photos have never seen publication before. Shortly after they were taken, Mia suffered a nervous and mental breakdown. Here, in *Baby Doll*, the cracks are all too obviously beginning to show. [David Kerekes]

BATMAN: OTHER REALMS
Bo Hampton, Scott Hampton & Mark Kneece

Yet another in a long, long, way too fucking long line of attempts to 're-invent' the Batman character.

Word Up Fellas! Frank Miller's *Dark Knight Returns* still stands as the *ultimate* take on the mythos of the character, and that's because Frank has respect for what has gone before and a clear understanding of the inherent symbolic power — not to mention the cold-light-of-day silliness — of the idea of a man dressed as a bat. The fools involved in the two strips featured in this hastily and lazily assembled collection have presumably read *Dark Knight* but have never tried to take on board many of it's exemplary lessons in how to treat a genre as ludicrous as the superhero. This is most clearly illustrated in the first strip 'Destiny' which, I shit ye not, features the Bat Man of Norse legend! What the fuck?!? At the very least they could've had loads of 'Praise Odin' dialogue and much smiting with huge fuck-off axes but, no, they haven't even got the wits to play it for laughs, which is the *only* way to treat a premise as idiotic as this. Justifying the setting by embroiling the present-day Batman in dirty dealings with evil corporations looking to dump toxic waste in Scandinavian fjords is as lazy as it gets and the rest of the story, what there is of it, is played out in such a pedestrian fashion, with all it's Norse legends reference worn on it's sleeve, that it makes any episode of the *Batman* TV cartoon look like a Thomas Pynchon novel. And barely a wench with ripped bodice in sight. Piss poor.

But, at least the first strip is so ridiculous that you're propelled along by its car crash logic. 'The Sleeping' is as pointless a comic strip as you could possibly imagine. Batman/Bruce Wayne ends up in a coma and the rest of the story is played out in his mind. You would think this would have given any writer/artist the rare opportunity to go whole hog and chuck in all kinds of crazy shit. But no, just lots of moody black ink, a briefly deadly giant eel and

THE BEST OF AMERICAN GIRLIE MAGAZINES
£16.99 / pb / 704pp / ISBN 3822879142 / Taschen 1997 / www.taschen.com

CHEESECAKE!
£19.99 / pb / 768pp / ISBN 382287194X / Taschen 1999 / www.taschen.com

THE CHUCKLING WHATSITS
£11.99 $16.95 / pb / 202pp / ISBN 1560972815 / Fantagraphics Books 1997 / www.fantagraphics.com

CITY OF THE BROKEN DOLLS
£12.95 / pb / 128pp / ISBN 187159281X / Velvet/Creation Books 1996 / www.creationbooks.com

a gut with a beard who looks like everyone's idea of a child molester. Only some dynamic Corben-esque panels featuring Bats twatting a huge demon thing are worth looking at twice. The rest of it is shite.

The comics industry is in decline right now and anyone observing from outside of slavish fandom would not be surprised based on this evidence. *Stop* making comics like this. Go do charity work or get pissed and cruise for chicks instead. The world will be a better place. [Rik Rawling]

THE BEST OF AMERICAN GIRLIE MAGAZINES
Harald Hellman

Robert Harrison was the publisher of the hugely successful scandal sheet *Confidential*. A series of court actions forced him to sell the title in 1958. Before that, back in the 1940s, Harrison was employed to work on *Motion Picture Daily* and *Motion Picture Herald*. At night, when the office was closed, he would stay behind and piece together *Beauty Parade*, his very own girlie magazine. He got found out and was given the boot (one Christmas Eve). Undeterred, Harrison decided to cash-in on the current craze in pin-ups. He commissioned some great artists for covers, hit on the novel idea of putting scantily-clad girls in 'humorous' photo-strips, and came up with a bunch of magazines with titles like *Titter*, *Wink*, *Flirt*, *Whisper* and *Eyeful*. (Sounds like an explosion in a Carry On factory.) 'Girls, Gags & Giggles' was his motto.

Taschen have gone berserk collecting material from each of the above. The result is a book well over two inches thick. As well as full-page reproductions of the covers (the majority of which are in full colour), there are snippets from the pages which lay beneath them: the groan-inducing photo gags, John Willie's *Sweet Gwendoline* in serial form, readers' letters, and actual ads for stag films, fishing bait and dodgy books. (*I Was Hitler's Doctor* sounds like a good read…)

None of the girls in any of Harrison's publications strip down beyond their underwear, and when viewing these pages today, 'sexy' isn't a word that springs readily to mind. Betty Page fans might get a kick out of it (she appears in several spreads), as might fans of lightweight corporal punishment (some photo-strips end with a spanking retribution), but for most, *The Best of American Girlie Magazines* will probably come across as being — that most Mrs Marple of expressions — quaint. [David Kerekes]

CHEESECAKE!
The Rotenberg Collection
Mark Lee Rotenberg

Hot-blooded males in post-war America found their pleasures in new-fangled girlie magazines like *Titter* and *Wink*. While the models in these publications didn't reveal everything or indeed much of anything at all, readers could find more obliging lassies via the coy classified ads elsewhere in the magazines.

Glossy B&W photos measuring four by five inches were typically available in sets of ten or twelve. Known as 'strip sets' these showed some lass getting her kit off, but so as not to draw too much undue attention were promoted using carefully selected wording like 'French' and 'art photos'.

These once filthy photographs are regarded today as kitsch. This book is a collection of a *lot* of them.

Although some of the models are professional, the majority are amateurs and wear uncomfortable smiles or appear mortified at the sudden realisation of what it is they're doing.

Like the models, the photographers are largely unknown. Their 'studio' might comprise a thinly disguised bedroom, bathroom, kitchen, office or cheap motel room. Into these come whatever props are close at hand — evidentally a half-hearted attempt to bring to each set a theme or novelty (The Wild West, Down a Mineshaft, Voodoo Queen, Puzzled By Cooking Utensils, and so on).

The result is a delirious catalogue of women caught in peculiar and unflattering poses, like mid leap with a skipping rope (ripples of fat rising), telephone cords wrapped around the neck, adjusting the knobs of an electrical gadget wearing fishnets and fag in hand, strained looks on rocky seashores and even tits caught in mangle!

Cheesecake! comes with a good informative introduction and, yes, a bundle of cheap laughs — unless of course you spot your mum. [David Kerekes]

Update Taschen liked this review, from *Headpress 19*, using a quote from it for their catalogue but miscrediting the source. Buggers.

THE CHUCKLING WHATSITS
Richard Sala

From the consistently excellent Fantagraphics stable, *The Chuckling Whatsit* is Richard Sala's fifth book, though it's the first work by him that I've seen.

A fresh-faced, naïve young reporter named Broom is unwittingly drawn into the investigation of a spate of murders of astrologers, which seem to be connected to the crimes committed some fifteen years earlier by the 'Gull Street Ghoul'. Along the way to the truth, he crosses paths with a bewildering array of supporting characters, all of whom have their own vested interests in the stuff he's digging up. The eponymous Whatsit is an evil-looking fetish doll with a noose around its neck. As the plot gathers momentum, fresh revelations are thrust upon Broom willy-nilly, but the last snooper to fish in these murky waters — another reporter named Cyril Root — wound up stabbed by the Gull Street Ghoul Mark II, along with all the stargazing buddies in whom he'd confided!

Critical plaudits for Sala — quoted on the back cover of *The Chuckling Whatsit* — mention the film noir ambience, but I discern rather earlier visual influences at work, especially German Expressionist cinema. The book's climatic denouement takes place in a burning windmill, like that of James Whale's 1931 classic *Frankenstein* (itself heavily influenced by Expressionism); the wraithlike Celeste resembles Carol Borland in Tod Browning's *Mark of the Vampire*; and the catsuit-wearing, mask-toting, roof-hopping Phoebe Duprey is a dead ringer for Irma Vep, heroine of the 1915 French serial *Les Vampires*. Broom himself is an insufficiently embittered and world-weary protagonist to be truly 'noir' — more Tintin than Philip Marlowe!

The sinuous, hatched pen and ink work, with heavy areas of black, looks like woodcuts in general, and in particular like the Belgian artist Frans Masereel's famous 'novel without words' *Passionate Journey*, with its lonely, distorted figures scurrying through stormy landscapes.

None of this, however, is to denigrate Sala's work — it simply shows that he's seen and enjoyed a lot of the same films, books and comics as me. *The Chuckling Whatsit* is quirky, funny, spooky and groovy. I liked it a lot, and it made me want to see more of Sala's work. [Simon Collins]

CITY OF THE BROKEN DOLLS
A Medical Art Diary, Tokyo 1993–96
Romain Slocombe

What would it be like if this book fell open and you knew nothing of its background? Confronted, say, by the picture of a girl in a night dress with both arms heavily bandaged, wearing an orthopaedic collar and a couple of sticking plasters on her face? On the facing page there's a picture of train doors. Quite inconspicuous. You would think that perhaps the girl was famous. Or the photograph was by a rock star's wife or something. Maybe you would even think she was sexy: She has a pretty face; her knees are showing; through the night-dress you can follow the shape of her breasts. But not sexy because she is 'damaged', though. In bandages.

That's how this book works. It draws you in, slowly. Manipulates your concept of erotica. Initially, it was a little disappointing for me to learn that the majority of girls in here are models, and the scenes staged. I thought that Romain Slocombe was some guy who spent his days dashing in and out of Tokyo streets and hospital wards snapping his camera. But then that would be a certifiably mad thing to do. With staged sets

THE COLLECTED CHECKERED DEMON
$19.95 / pb / 248pp / ISBN 0867193840 / Knockabout Comics 1998 / available from Last Gasp, 777 Florida Street, San Francisco, California 94110 / www.lastgasp.com

COLLECTED PALESTINE
$24.95 / pb / 286pp / ISBN 156097432X / Fantagraphics 2002 / www.fantagraphics.com

THE COMPLETE CANNON
£19.95 / pb / 132pp / ISBN 1560974257 / Fantagraphics 2001 / www.fantagraphics.com

COMPLETELY MAD
208pp / hb / ISBN 0316738913 / Little Brown / www.littlebrown.co.uk

The Checkered Demon in 'The Hog Ridin' Fools' (*Zap Comix* No 2). © S Clay Wilson

and models, you have an 'excuse'.

Another minor disappointment is the fact that *City of the Broken Dolls* is part of an erotic imprint series. It kind of gives the game away. I suspect that Mr Slocombe feels a little the same way, too. With regard his previous book, titled simply *Broken Dolls*, he is quoted as saying that he'd be delighted if, by mistake, a medical bookshop placed it among other surgical or orthopaedic books.

The point I'm trying to make is that much of the book's potency is drained by the fact that the book is presented as erotic. The majority of photographs contained in it are not overtly sexual. Indeed, the most sexually explicit shot — that of a girl in a sling gnawing on the end of a giant dildo — is effectively the 'weak link' in the book. Generally, we see the girls sitting on their bed, a little coy, contemplative, dishevelled, or in the street, seemingly glad to be out again in the sunshine after a little convalescing. The bandages become a second underwear.

But then again, if *City* wasn't presented as erotic, it is unlikely that it would be presented at all. (Who would publish it and why?) For that reason alone, we ought to be thankful that it's here, now. Slocombe has assembled one of the most thrilling, bizarre and kinky photograph albums of our time. What's more, it's available over-the-counter in Britain, despite the inevitable minor flurry of tabloid chest-beating that followed its publication. [David Kerekes]

THE COLLECTED CHECKERED DEMON VOLUME ONE
S Clay Wilson
Believe it or not, this is the first major retrospective of Underground Comix's most controversial and uncompromising figure. We've had Crumb up to here; Robert Williams, Gilbert Shelton, even Spain's Agitprop *Trashman* has been collected, so this bumper grimoire of Wilson's demonic drawings is more than welcome...

The Checkered Demon, deranged delinquent that he is, first featured way back in 1967 in Wilson's self-published *Grist* before his 'public' debut in the Crumb-edited *Zap* No 2 the following year. *The Collected Checkered Demon* follows the course of his 'progression' from atrocity to atrocity in chronological order, featuring all his appearances in *Zap* through to the notorious 'banned in the UK' issue of *Weirdo* No 17, and beyond. On the way we take in all the demented sexual perversions and apocalyptic landscapes of surrealistic nightmare (this is not more hyperbole, I promise you!). With tales like 'Thumb and Tongue Tales' and 'The Swap', and incredibly detailed drawings with titles such as, 'Spoonful of Maggots', 'Toast to the Severed Head' and 'Baby Sitting The Little Carnivorous Cyclops Child'. First announced (to my baited breath!) in a S Clay Wilson issue of *The Comics Journal* three years ago, finally the ultimate Wilson tome has arrived. I can only say that while the waiting has seemed eternities, it's been worth it! Buy this *now*! [Stephen Sennitt]

COLLECTED PALESTINE
Joe Sacco
Here's the hefty re-release of the 'Landmark Work of Comics Journalism'. So now all those non-fan boy types who lament the lack of serious themes in the comic genre can hold something up as a standard.

Personally, they're welcome to it; I much prefer *Biffo the Bear*, or even, at gunpoint, Garth... gulp... Ennis. [Stephen Sennitt]

THE COMPLETE CANNON
Wallace Wood

This book is one of those slightly irritating items which are too massively-formatted for comfortable reading. Aside from this, I can't think of one other complaint, and challenge anyone to read the sexy exploits of Wally Wood's super-spy, Cannon, without 100 percent enjoyment! And, of course, the artwork is superb; in fact it's beyond comparison, as Wood was without doubt the *absolute master* of this type of straight-ahead, gutsy comic strip action art, being technically leagues ahead of anyone else in his day, and certainly several million more leagues ahead of what passes for action artists in comics today. There is a great introduction by Wood fan Jeff Gelb, and an appended photo of Wally looking drunk and weird in his lonely bedsit studio in Syracuse New York, circa 1980. [Stephen Sennitt]

COMPLETELY MAD
A History of the Comic Book and Magazine
Maria Reidelbach

The origins of *Mad* lie in the comics panic of the 1950s, following Dr Wertham and colleagues' condemnation of most all dramatic comic books for their supposed detrimental effect on young readers. The innovative publishing house EC were responsible for several of these 'objectionable' titles (*Tales from the Crypt*, *Vault of Horror*, etc). However, another EC title, the humour comic *Mad*, was also coming under fire.

EC initially tried to resist the encroaching Comics Code by launching some very curious, non violent, non-genre publications. They weren't a success. Before long, with EC very much in debt and the Code effectively having wiped out their entire catalogue, all that was left at EC was *Mad*. The publishing house took a gamble, borrowed money, and concentrated all their efforts on this one remaining title. Switching from a comic to a magazine format, EC were able to steer *Mad* around the stifling confines of the Comics Code, and *Mad* grew from strength to strength. In instigating the comics clampdown, Wertham *et al* had inadvertently created an even greater 'menace' for young minds: the totally irreverent *Mad*.

Maria Reidelbach has had full access to the *Mad* back catalogue and files, interviewing along the way virtually everyone on or associated with the team, including the late Bill Gaines. But don't think of this as a cosy PR job; we get to hear of money disputes, petty grievances, and Gaines' tough contractual obligations. Reidelbach is a devoted fan but her literary judgement isn't clouded by the fact.

Completely Mad is a gorgeous looking book, too, in full colour throughout. Included are plenty of illustrations taken from the pages of *Mad*, as well as thumbnail reproductions of each and every cover. One chapter deals with the history of Alfred E Newman, the grinning, slightly unsettling masthead who has graced most every *Mad* cover since 1955. The kid's actual origins are vague, but Reidelbach traces him

DC VS MARVEL
£10.99 / pb / 200pp / ISBN 1852867507 / Titan Books 1996 / titanpress@titanemail.com

DIGITAL BEAUTIES
£20 / pb / 575pp / ISBN 3822816280 / Taschen 2001 / www.taschen.com

DUH
£6.99 $9.95 / pb / 96pp / ISBN 1560974168 / Fantagraphics Books 2001 / www.fantagraphics.com

ENCYCLOPAEDIA ANATOMICA
£16.99 / hb / 704pp / ISBN 3822876135 / Taschen 2000 / www.taschen.com

back, via a plethora of old advertisements and photographs, to at least the turn of the century and quite possibly beyond. Other chapters chronicle the development of the magazine, putting it into social and political perspective.

Many people regard the early issues of *Mad* as the best. I'm not so sure about this. Those early issues tend to be overly satirical in content and, as with much satire, a little stale when viewed many years later. (Though a couple of the digs, like the attack on the KKK, still carry a punch.) My own favourite *Mad* memories are locked in the period when I used to read the comic most regularly, when I was aged between eleven and fifteen. It used to make me laugh out loud. In one particularly memorable issue from this era, *Mad* addressed a great niggling question of young TV viewers everywhere: in *Star Trek*, what would happen to a person in the transporter if the transporter suddenly had a hiccup. The answer? They would materialise with one hand sticking out of their ear and no belly.

According to Reidelbach's book, that *Star Trek* spoof originally appeared in *Mad* No 115. Even today, I cannot see Shatner-era *Star Trek* without thinking of *Mad*'s spoof, 'Star Blecch'.

Whether a fan or not, *Completely Mad* stands as a brilliant insight into a publishing and cultural phenomenon. [David Kerekes]

DC VS MARVEL
Marz, David, Jurgens, Castellini, Rubinstein, Neary, et al
"The epic mini-series they said would never happen!" I'm going to assume "they" are not the desperate parasites at Marvel and DC who saw a perfectly good opportunity to rake in some cash quick. The comics industry is in steady decline and the fuckers involved are so clueless as to what to do about it that they respond with this kind of speedball logic.

Maybe I'm just too old to get it? Maybe if I was younger I would have shit blood to get my hands on this? Maybe. But just flicking through the pages I'm overwhelmed by the chloroformic stench of cynicism that this venture reeks of. It's the equivalent of taking not one but two cars full of crack into a New Orleans welfare project. I know how easy it is to pick on superhero comics but this is total and utter bollocks — with obligatory workman-like artjob throughout, big 'star' fight-scenes every two pages and a breathless fear of having the target audience's attention span distracted for a split second. Lots of rippling chest muscles, gritted teeth, furrowed brows and not one fucking idea what to do with the mess they've created, as Superman kicks the Hulk's ass and Shazam leathers a faggoty looking Thor. It could have gone into high gear when Elektra faced up to Catwoman but apart from some coy 'up' shots of Catwoman's taut purple ass it fails to live up to its potential.

I cannot report on any aspect of the script because it is *impossible* to read. It comes laden with the baggage of fifty years' worth of character detail and not one shred of humour, making it nothing more than *Eastenders* on steroids.

To add insult to injury there are Writer & Artist profiles at the back, where a brain-numbing clumsiness with self-deprecating humour and 'zany' wit is evinced. They are not writing *Seinfeld*. They are not even writing *Oh, Dr Beeching*! They are writing comics. Superhero comics. It's probably better than sucking cock in the subway toilets to make enough change for a Big Mac meal, but not by much. [Rik Rawling]

DIGITAL BEAUTIES
Julius Wiedemann

It's strange how these digital beauties — two and three dimensional computer-generated models — can be as sexually appealing as their 'real life' counterparts. Sometimes more so. This might be due to the novelty factor, though I suspect it has more to do with the fact that virtual reality is creating its own race and creed: digital beauties might look human but they're *of themselves*, they exist on a different plain (the downloadable porno plain of the www), and trigger strange new receptors in our brain… That said, I'm a little disappointed that the ninety-odd artists featured here — great technicians for the most part — don't do more with their craft. Why not give their models a little something extra, something their flesh and blood sisters don't have or can't do? Indeed, one of the most fascinating images in the book is by Thierry Rousseau, who makes the limbs of his particular digital dolls slightly disproportionate, i.e. unnaturally long legs. Rousseau consciously uses a 'wrong' perspective to bring emotion to his pictures. (It's hardly a new idea, but it still works.) More discretely 'wrong' is Alcu M Baptistao's incredible Kaya — a model in close-up, whose imperfection is that she looks too real, too detailed, too perfect.

A good deal of the work featured in *Digital Beauties* is from Japan. Perhaps this has something to do with the way the occidental face has been assimilated and recast by manga animators — doe-eyed and innocent, but looking not quite any race on Earth? [David Kerekes]

DUH: UNDERWORLD 4
Kaz

This is a collection of Kaz' syndicated newspaper strip *Underworld*, but don't be fooled — Garfield this ain't. The format is deceptively simple — B&W line artwork, four frames to the page, one gag per page, no continuing narratives, but gradually a devastatingly twisted worldview is revealed. Kaz' strips abound in perverted elves, runaway penises, dysfunctional families and one or two recurring characters. Creep Rat and Snuff provide a consistently sleazy double act — wearing nappies whilst chugging beers to save having to get up to piss, washing their underwear by chewing it, doing questionable drugs. A recurrent theme is the loss of childhood innocence: a teddy bear winks to the reader as he's hugged to a girl's substantial bosom, cute woodland creatures smoke dope, babies score breast milk off lactating hookers, and so on. Through all of this float reminders of classic comics from happier, more innocent times — Nancy, Little Nemo, Krazy Kat, early Disney — though there's also a strong influence from the sixties underground comix of Robert Crumb and others. The humour of the individual strips is, it has to be said, rather hit and miss, though their cumulative effect is great.

Part of the limitation of the one-page strip format is that it demands a good gag in the final frame of each and every strip, and sometimes in *Duh* the punchline just isn't there.

My favourite strips in the book are the sudden, audacious flights of fancy like Superbillies, 'common hillbillies transformed by atomic moonshine into lazy superbeings,' and best of all, the Grim Chicken Reaper — a skull-faced, cowled chicken with a scythe walks into a house, sees a roast chicken on the table and says, 'Too late'. Now, the Grim Chicken Reaper is funny in the first panel, just because it looks funny, but then it gets *even funnier* in the last panel with the punchline. If *Underworld* could sustain this level of wit, it would be a classic. As it is, though, it's still pretty good. Free samples of the bizarre mindset of Kaz can be enjoyed at [w] www.fantagraphics.com and [w] www.kazunderworld.com — the latter has a large archive of strips, a new one each week, and also features an amusing section of hate mail sent to the *Arizona Republic* protesting Kaz' cartoons. [Simon Collins]

ENCYCLOPAEDIA ANATOMICA

Taschen's excellent series continues with a mesmerizing and horrifying addition to their chunky A5-sized collection. From medieval times onward the art of the waxworker has been a poor relative to practitioners in the 'elevated' sculptural media of stone and bronze, never afforded the respect that the considerable craft required to successfully work it deserves. But, as Georges Didi-Huberman observes in one of the several introductions to this collection of full-colour photographs, wax is the material of all resemblances, and its virtues are so remarkable that it was often attributed with magical properties. *Encyclopaedia Anatomica* makes this immediately apparent with around 1,500 studies of the human body from the Museo

THE EXIT COLLECTION
$60 / pb / 384pp / ISBN 0966134001 / Tacit 1998 / 1341 W. Fullerton Ave, suite 182, Chicago, IL 60614-2134, USA

EXQUISITE MAYHEM
£40 / hb / 487pp / ISBN 3822859060 / Taschen 2001 / www.taschen.com

Battling Girls — "the world's most erotic spectacle!" Photo by Theo Ehret. *Exquisite Mayhem* © Taschen

La Specola in Florence, the cream of sixteenth- and seventeenth-century wax-artists working when medicine was starting to take a serious interest in the mechanisms of the body.

Everything from the brain to the metatarsals, the viscera to the voicebox, is depicted, often with such astonishing accuracy and clarity (or as far as I can tell, not having a pass to the Royal College of Surgeons) that you might think you are looking at real dissections. The full-figure studies of flayed men reclining — as if in some tortural ecstasy — on silk cushions, or the advanced representation of a young woman with her removable skin and organs, are especially hypnotic. (I still can't look at some of the pictures without wincing and flicking the page. The final section on reproduction is a particular challenge.) It is one of the central mysteries why when we look at the insides of our own bodies we confront horror and beauty in such close proximity.

Taschen are to be recognised for bringing such an important collection to a wider audience. If a criticism can be levelled it's the lack of size for such detailed images. There's a fair amount of white border on each page and, even taking into account the A5 size of the book, the images could have been ten, maybe even twenty percent larger. On the whole, though, this is a definite must if you have any interest at all in anatomy or curious museums and collections. [Jerry Glover]

THE EXIT COLLECTION
Ed. George Petros

Exit was a 'zine' produced in the eighties under the guidance of George Petros and — for the first three issues — Feral House's Adam Parfrey. The publication gave voice to many of the key artistic figures to emerge from the dirty underbelly of the underground subculture: John Aes-Nihil, Kim Seltzer, Jim Blanchard, Richard Kern, G G Allin, Nick Zedd, Nick Bougas, Lung Leg, Boyd Rice, various members of Cop Shoot Cop, Genesis P Orridge, etc. All of whom contributed work to what Petros describes in his introduction as the magazine of "Outlaw Liberal Fascist Sci Fi Pop Art". Now, some four years since the last issue of *Exit*, Tacit have published this collection — which includes work from all six issues as well as unpublished material — in a lavishly produced 384-page book.

Exit was predominately a graphic and visual publication, and the book includes the large, symmetrical contstructivist-manga of J G Thirlwell, which, with its harsh chiaroscuro, looks as powerful as the quasi-industrial propaganda on which it is at least partly based. Also included is Joe Coleman's beautiful *The Dance of Death*, some great pictures by Steven Cerio, and some Mark Mothersbaugh strips. R N Taylor includes detailed pictorial anthropological and artistic histories of both the swastika, and the pentagram, tracing their usage across cultures and continents. John Aes-Nihil co-ordinates a series of Charles Manson and Fredrich Nietzsche quotes, each of which is suitably (mis-)interpreted by an artist. On a literary front, contributions come from Henry Rollins' *Love Life*, and Lydia Lunch's *Meltdown: The Gun Is Loaded*, whilst non-fiction is provided in Adam Parfrey's *Eugenics: The Orphaned Science* (a version of which was published in *Apocalypse Culture*), and Carlo McCormick's *L(aw), S(cience), D(isorder)*.

This collection is an insight into the early work of some of today's underground luminaries, and contains several interesting pieces. For the archivist, or enthusiast, it is a valuable source. It should be noted, however, that it does represent only a small selection of many of these artists' work, which, in most cases, has progressed since first contributing to *Exit*. [Jack Sargeant]

EXQUISITE MAYHEM
The Spectacular & Erotic World of Wrestling by Theo Ehret
Ed. Cameron Jamie & Mike Kelley

German-born Theo Ehret moved to Los Angeles in 1953 and ten years later opened a photographic studio. His first commissioned work was taking publicity shots of boxers at the nearby Olympic Auditorium. He had no interest in the sport itself, and to Ehret taking pictures of boxers "was just a job". When it came to pro wrestling, his next stint as a photographer for the Olympic, he was no more sympathetic — indeed he regarded this particular sport as "comical". However, Ehret was the consummate professional, studying a wrestler in order to anticipate his moves on the day of a ringside shoot, or putting himself in the line of a barrage of missiles from the audience. (At Mexican wrestling matches the missiles were frequently paper cups full of piss.) Later on, Ehret was asked to create and photograph sleazy scenarios for the covers of *Detective* and *True Crime*. In a not-so-roundabout way this led to work on *Battling Girls* magazine and apartment wrestling erotica — invariably two bikini-clad women wrestling in an apartment.

Exquisite Mayhem is a stunning book and, like its subject matter, it is larger than life. An oversized hardback (weighing an unwieldy four kilos), it showcases the best of Ehret's photographic work in the fields of pro wrestling, apartment wrestling, foxy boxing, mud wrestling, crime magazines, and hitherto unpublished nude battling gals — the kind of exciting subject matter that most jobbing photographers would give their right arm for. Ehret captures the moment in his stark B&W images and the result is positively electric. Dipping into the wealth of pro wrestling snaps, for instance, we have the imposing figure of Andre the Giant wading through his fans, The Gorgeous One (not really, girls) getting his hair done at a salon, midget wrestlers, Raul Reyes and Don Carson being forcibly ejected from the ring and tumbling headlong into the audience, blood drenched unknowns, battle royals with fifteen or so fighters in the ring at once, the masked Destroyer chomping on a cigar, Fred Blassie biting John Tolos' forehead, the aesthetically pleasing form of The Sheik, Giant Baba and a referee entangled in the ropes, and so on.

In an interview conducted by the book's co-editor Cameron Jamie, Ehret maintains that he had no personal interest in the subject matter, other than it brought his family a much-needed income. But this makes the case of the nude battling girls all the more curious: by Ehret's own admission these particular photos — because of their explicit nature — could never appear in the wrestling girls magazines, and have instead been sitting all these years in the photographer's office. So why bother taking them in the first place?

FANTASY WORLDS
£24.99 / hb / 340pp / ISBN 3822871907 / Taschen 1999 / www.taschen.com

BUILDING A NEW MILLENNIUM
£19.99 / hb / 553pp / ISBN 3822863904 / Taschen 1999 / www.taschen.com

FEAR OF COMICS
£9.99 $12.95 / pb / 120pp / ISBN 1560973838 / Fantagraphics Books 2001 / 7653 / www.fantagraphics.com

FETISH
£50 / hb / 223pp / ISBN 1858686741 / Carlton Books / www.carlton.com

Like Ehret, I too have no interest whatsoever in the world of wrestling (unless it's girls), but I enjoyed *Exquisite Mayhem* enormously. A bloody treasure. [David Kerekes]

FANTASY WORLDS
Deidi von Schaewen & John Maizels

BUILDING A NEW MILLENNIUM
Philip Jodidio

Large, beautiful and crammed with glossy photographs, *Fantasy Worlds* pays tribute to the creators of fantasy architecture and their alternative and eccentric worlds. But don't let the word 'architecture' put you off. Anyone with even the remotest interest in art, interior or garden design, sculpture, madness, inspiration and obsession will find the book fascinating. Though *Fantasy Worlds* includes certain classics of off-the-wall architecture — such as the Sedlec Ossuary in the Czech Republic or the Tarot garden in Tuscany — this book is at its best when delving into personal and domestic madness. People decorating every free surface in their house with broken pots, for instance; entire house façades covered in retrieved junk; the Watford Shell Garden with its stuffed toys encased in concrete and shells... These are quite rightly as prominent within *Fantasy Worlds* as professionally created large-scale works of religious grandeur.

From Europe through the East to America, each fantasy is different, and each is inspired. 'The Garden of Eden' is set in the garden of a log cabin home and consists of large sculptures in concrete tree shapes, representing the creator's political and religious beliefs. Stranger still is the fact that their creator, Samuel Perry Dinsmoor (1843–1932), not only married a twenty-one-year-old at the age of eighty-nine, but also lies buried in a glass-topped coffin in the garden's very own mausoleum.

As wonderfully colourful as the *Fantasy Worlds* creations are the glimpses of the creative, scavenging, recycling and obsessive single-minded visionaries who brought them to life.

Another Taschen architecture book, *Building a New Millennium* is sure to have Prince Charles quaking in his boots at the "daring innovation in space, light and form" which will seemingly shape the buildings of the future. Many new structures are photographed, notably the 'Pharmacy' Restaurant designed by Damien Hirst and Mike Rundell in which the pharmacy theme is explored in the pill-shaped chairs, the cold, sterile atmosphere and the pharmaceutical product in glass cabinets lining the walls. Also included is the Eden Project in St Austell, Cornwall — a huge "showcase for global biodiversity". *Building a New Millennium* represents a cleaner, more organised and more modern view of built structures than does *Fantasy Worlds* and therefore will likely have less general appeal. [Sarah Turner]

FEAR OF COMICS
Gilbert Hernandez

Holy shit. There is no way to deliver an adequate and coherent review of this book. It would be easier to try and fuck fog. Even Fantagraphics start their blurb on the rear cover with the warning: 'Be afraid. Be *very* afraid.' My initial impression was that this could only be the product of someone in a mental institution. It holds that potent charge of total mindfuck that you get from Daniel Johnston albums or the paintings of Henry Darger and the fact that it comes from one of 'alt.comics' more accomplished writers and artists makes it all the more surprising and intriguing.

Gilbert Hernandez, together with his brother Jaime, started *Love & Rockets* back in the mid eighties and proceeded to become the darlings of the new comics-reading intelligentsia — the types who (quite rightly) decried the likes of Marvel and DC for continuing to spew out shit and desperately wanted all comics creators to follow the examples of these new blazing talents. *Love & Rockets* was initially a breath of fresh air but readers gradually abandoned the title as the Hernandez Brothers lost their inspiration and in 1996 it unceremoniously folded.

Gilbert had always been the more unpredictable of the two. While Jaime played with his post-punk pseudo-lesbian soap opera, Gilbert immersed himself in the strange locale of Palomar (a long and complex saga that drew comparisons to Borges and the 'magical realists') and even took time out to do the *Birdland* series for Eros Comix — a totally wigged-out porno fantasy shedding new light on that which festers in the limbic core of his strange brain. But even that mad carnival of sperm and surrealism could not ever hope to compare with this collection of utterly fucking bizarre material that hurtles way beyond Dada into some nether-region of the imagination never previously charted in a comic book format. Where do I even begin? How about with the Contents Page? Here's just a few titles: 'Return of the Tzik', 'Drink, Fucker!', 'Wobbly Buttocks Frenzy', 'The Shit Eaters', 'She Sleeps With Anybody But Me'.

Already there's a big red neon flashing in your mind and once you're into the first strip 'All With A Big Hello' that neon sign explodes into a supernova spiralling out into infinity. A woman in a fifties style superhero outfit and a crescent moon on her head is on stage singing. She leaves the theatre to loud applause and gets into a car. The car takes her up into the woods above the city. Out of the woods stumbles a 'thing' best described as something out of Dr Seuss meets Charles Burns on a dark night. Next panel we see the woman half-in, half-out of her costume with the thing giving her one from behind while a crowd of other 'things' watch on from the shadows. Suddenly both characters undergo some kind of metamorphosis and in the very next panel the things are seen putting a cloak over the shoulders of a young, well-hung male human. They wave him goodbye and... well, I won't spoil the ending but it's like an episode of *The Twilight Zone*, filtered through the Phantom Tollbooth, left to fester in a Freudian swamp and then dredged up and wiped off. It's just so fucking... strange that it leaves you disturbed and exhilarated at the same time. This makes it great art but I'll be fucked if I can explain any of it.

The rest of the book is similar in tone — stark B&W artwork, a skilful use of subtly different drawing styles and a riotous assembly of freaks. It's all reminiscent in tone of some of Dan Clowes' more impenetrable short strips (which Fantagraphics have noted and clearly packaged the book to look like a Clowes collection) but they all go way beyond anything even he's attempted. Childhood fetishes for gonks and masturbation fantasies over cartoon characters are allowed to blur while the 'rules' of narrative are torn up and fed to the dog. Flying women, pop-art drunks, existential jack-in-the-boxes, poisonous slugs, screaming ghosts, and, inevitably, the end of the world. The result is the best comics I've seen in years and a source of inspiration and enquiry that I'll be dipping into for years to come. Just don't expect to 'get' any of it as that's not really the point. Be more concerned if you do 'get' any of it.

It seems obvious that Hernandez was tired of the constraints of the medium and just let his imagination go wild across the page, confident its own deranged logic would see him through. This approach is in keeping with the best examples of the Underground comics of the late sixties and it would be nice to see a similar wave of experimentation triggered amongst young artists by this book. Far too many of the next generation of comics writers and artists have their eyes on the movie deal and 'franchises' which is only going to contribute to the death of the medium. We need more shameless experimentation like this to remind us of the joy of submitting to our imaginations. That's how we got to the moon in the first place so what are we doing rooting in the gutter for other people's scraps? It's time to evolve, and mutate and the less we recognise what we become, the better that is for us all. [Rik Rawling]

FETISH
Masterpieces of
Erotic Fantasy Photography
Ed. Tony Mitchell
This is basically an updated and glossier version of Jurgen Boedt's

GENERATION FETISH
$37.95 / hb / 368pp / ISBN 3980587681 / Goliath 2001 / www.goliathclub.com

GHASTLY TERROR!
£13.95 / pb / 224pp / ISBN 1900486075 / Critical Vision 1999 / www.headpress.com

HARD BOILED
£11.99 / pb / 136pp / ISBN 1840237511 / Titan Books / titanpress@titanemail.com

Panels from 'A Death for a Death', one of the early comic titles covered in *Ghastly Terror!*

Secret Fetish Photo Anthology, edited by Tony Mitchell of *Skin Two* fame. Like the original, it aims to showcase work by the best photographers working in the fetish scene. However, unlike the original, the production values match those of *Skin Two* magazine — good quality paper, good use of colour, excellent design and generally stylishly done.

The introduction by Mitchell attempts to set the scene a bit, but to be honest it's the pictures which are going to sell the book. As one would expect, all of the well-known fetish photographers are here, from Bob Carlos Clark through Trevor Watson to Doris Kloster. Lesser known names include Nic Marchant and Sandra Jensen, both of whom may be known to regular readers of Nexus paperbacks.

Many of the images may well be familiar to regular readers of the pervy press, though there are enough new names involved to keep things interesting. For me, the pictures by Housk Randall-Godard, Jo Hammer, Herbert Hesselman, Giles Berquet and the batch of Chris Bell classics stood out from all the rest.

If there's a criticism of the collection it's one that is generic to all coffee-table photo anthologies — the images are divorced from their context. Collected here in one place these 200-odd pictures soon lose their power to shock or arouse. The pictures risk becoming sexless, divorced as they are from the fantasies which inspire them. Part of the problem is that publishers shy away from the implications. Tony Mitchell probably convinced Carlton Books that this was merely just another fashion book, albeit a slightly risqué one. What no mainstream publisher has dared to do yet is to marry a set of fetish photographs with a set of erotic fantasies or short stories. Come on — somebody, somewhere must be willing to put together the stories of Maria Del Rey, Penny Birch, Jean Aveline *et al* with a set of illustrative photographs? [Pan Pantziarka]

GENERATION FETISH
Lee Higgs
A heavy photographic tome depicting numerous 'cute'/'very cute' femmes tied, bound, gagged, and strapped in the usual mix of leather, rubbery and hose. Aesthetically the cunt-purples and pinks of the cross-processed photographs, the occasional use of lenses to distort perspectives, and the photographic technique is fine, but do we really need another book of goth/fetish chicks tied up? Especially because there's so little else going on in these pictures, nothing either glorifying or subverting the representation of the fetish (*à la* Kern or Araki — both of whom have been able to engage with and depart from the predictability of 'the scene' in order to explore their own specific interests with incredible results). For example, I would like to see the women actually looking embarrassed or ashamed or pained to have their bodies distorted by bondage and gags — if my nipples were in a clamp it would hurt — I wouldn't be thinking about my fucking eye-liner. The quasi-moral tongue clicking of the S&M scene aside (safe words, rules for play etc) submission is about power-games, but too often now it appears as if the emphasis is on fetish fashion. The book even features an introduction by Gisele Turner that non-ironically compares the "cool, fresh" models and photos as being analogous to

MTV, in my world that isn't a compliment, but it shows how mainstream this kind of scene is now. If this book is about creating/pandering to sexual fantasy then I want to see the more contentious zones of S&M explored rather than the hipster angle. [Jack Sargeant]

GHASTLY TERROR!
The Horrible Story of the Horror Comics
Stephen Sennitt

The world of the illustrated comic can be a troubling one. And often for all the wrong reasons, conjuring images of an overly moral universe, of caped superheroes and flashy villains, set loose in some juvenile morality play.

But back in the seventies, some of us were infected by darker, more ambivalent material. To our peers, gorged on the above banality, such reading seemed deviant, even dangerous. We were viewed as 'Midwich Cookoos', sullen fanatics, seeking out these large B&W horror magazines from the States. Early exposure to this unusual brand of highly literate, visionary horror, has led to life-long changes of attitude, habit, even outlook.

Such was the power of those early Warren titles, *Creepy* and *Eerie*. And, most remarkable of all, the phenomenon that was Skywald's *Nightmare*, *Psycho* and *Scream* — the inspired work of editor 'Archaic Al' Hewetson and his 'Horror-Mood' team of artists and writers.

Ghastly Terror! navigates a long-awaited journey down the dark, rotting highways and by-ways of the horror comic field. It is so refreshing to find a volume rich with the unbridled, but critical enthusiasms of a true aficionado. There is a wealth of detail and handsome illustration here to delight the connoisseur, but this opus is not so dense as to exclude the first time adventurer. Indeed, like the very best of the comic titles themselves, the author acts as your host, welcoming and beckoning with a warm, tattered grip that will cut you to the bone.

Stephen Sennitt has done us all a great service. He strikes out boldly from the well documented history of the William Gaines EC titles, into a nefarious labyrinth of pre-code horror from the fifties, rarely documented until now. We enter a printed universe gone mad, a delirium of sewer-living monsters, of ultra-violent, grotesque sadism, each horror admirably rushing to top the last in terms of bloody excess.

If Skywald represent the horror comics field in its highest form — as convincingly argued by the author — it becomes no less a pleasure to peer into the sixties sepulchre of the obscure Eerie Publications, whose weird titles achieved some new 'bottom-of-the-bloody-barrel' nadir. Their vivid cover art alone seems a triumph of vicious, absurd lunacy.

In all, this is an invaluable work which serves to resurrect the masters of the genre for fresh appraisal — those great writers and artists, by whose example we are given proof that contemporary imaginations are slack, tired and formulaic. Hell, this book could even herald some bloody, dark renaissance! Let's hope so! [Mark Farrelly]

Update Skywald is the subject of a book published by Headpress in 2004, *The Complete Illustrated History of the Skywald Horror-Mood*, edited by the late, great 'Archaic Al' Hewetson himself.

HARD BOILED
Frank Miller, Geof Darrow & Claude Legris

First published in 1990 this three-book series was met with one huge, collective jaw-hanging-in-disbelief. Ten years later it still stands as the ultimate comic. Not from a writer's point of view, seeing as the script is little more than a frail skeleton of intentionally exaggerated pulp fiction clichés, but from the point of view that it's the comic book artjob of the century. There are many great artists out there but none could ever hope to match the deranged intensity and obsession to detail that Geof Darrow brings to every single page of this book. You could study the panels for the rest of your life and you would never pick up on everything that he puts in there. It is fucking unbeliev-

HIGH ART
£20 / pb / 176pp / ISBN 1860742564 / Sanctuary Publishing 1999 / 45 Sinclair Rd, London, W14 0NS / www.sanctuarygroup.com

FUCKED UP & PHOTOCOPIED
$25 / hb / 240pp / ISBN 1584230002 / Gingko Press 1999 / www.gingkopress.com

HÔPITAL BRUT
£13.50 / cheques payable to Mark Pawson, PO box 664, London E3 4QR / www.mpawson.demon.co.uk / www.lederniercri.org

G Liani art from Horrogasmo.

able and no amount of hyperbole can do it justice. Page three of Book One has Nixon — the psychotic cyborg protagonist — dripping blood, encrusted with broken glass and on fire, stood against a wall covered with graffiti and blood splatters. Then you turn the page and get a double spread of Nixon being charged at by a car sporting double belt-feed machine guns, surrounded by dozens of dead hoodlums and auto wrecks. The car smashes through a wall and into a club where naked couples are fucking on a stage while women wielding chainsaws walk amongst them hacking off limbs! Darrow draws every person clearly, every facial expression, every fold of clothing, every piece of litter, every brick in the smashed wall. At this point you realise that you are in the hands of a total madman and that nothing is ever going to be the same again. And this is all just in the first seven pages! How could it get any crazier?

Well it does. Book Two features a forty-one page fight/chase scene that almost defies description. Mass freeway pile-ups, killer grannies, innocent bystanders slaughtered, SWAT teams leathered, ambulances launched through supermarket walls — the succession of events is relentless in its escalation of violence and absurdity. It is our world gone totally haywire; a gleeful celebration of pop culture out of control and teetering on the brink of destruction.

Book Three features the now fleshless robot Nixon fending off the advances of a female droid in a scrapyard. The backdrop is an intensely detailed pile of household detritus and junk. You see this same pile of junk for nine pages, shifting slightly in point-of-view each time.

Arguably Darrow could have just drawn it once and photocopied it before dropping the characters in on top. But he didn't! He re-drew the same junk nine times on nine full page panels! That's dedication. That's intensity. These young guns who come along talking about how art should be like Chinese cooking — "if it takes longer than five minutes it's ruined" — are obviously talking shit. If you are going to blow minds, then *this* is how you do it.

On initial publication *Hard Boiled* was met with enthusiastic fanboy cheers and howls of derision from those who felt it signified a new low point in comics. The fact that it is a pastiche of the 'One Guy Kicks All Ass' action films was wasted and there seemed to be no understanding or respect for the sheer labour that Darrow put into each and every page. Comics as a medium needed this book. It needed someone who was willing to go totally over the top and raise the bar. It still serves today as a great example of why comics aren't just films on paper, because this is, and always will be, unfilmable. There will *never* be the budget or the SFX to do this justice. It stands alone as a work of demented genius in a field that boasts few others. [Rik Rawling]

HIGH ART
A History of the
Psychedelic Poster
Ted Owen & Denise Dickson

FUCKED UP &
PHOTOCOPIED
Instant Art of the
Punk Rock Movement
Bryan Ray Turcotte and
Christopher T Miller

These two books should reside next

to each other on one's bookshelf. Invaluable collections of paper ephemera, from the psychedelic posters of the sixties, through the flyers of the late seventies and early eighties punk/hardcore scene of certain cities, and the musical denizens thereof. Essential for anyone interested in the paper trail left by the youth culture of the late twentieth century.

High Art will warm the heart of the most wizened aficionado of psychedelic posters and art. The posters reproduced (all in colour and many full page) range from the Art Nouveau influences of Jan Troop, Beardsley, Klimt etc to their sixties' counterparts who took it even further in the direction of Surrealism and Symbolism. The text is well written and informative and even covers such topics as the artwork on sheets of blotter acid. It is mind blowing and it is a trip!

Starting with the earliest work of the nuclei of San Fran artists Wes Wilson, Alton Kelly, Stanley Mouse, Rick Griffin and Victor Moscoso (all of whom have biographical sections) and the hot house of the Avalon and Fillmore Auditoriums and the Haight, an historic overview of origins is given. Individual artists and poster companies are profiled throughout. Lesser known artists and their work are all represented. The book is basically in three parts, the first concerning the US, the second the UK (which covers *OZ* magazine, the UFO Club and Big O Poster company, also with individual artists profiled) and the third, a chapter on the 'New Wave' of poster/flyer artists such as Frank Kozik, Alan Forbes and the 'Coop', amongst others. The Appendix is about collecting the posters themselves, if one has enough time and money to pursue such a hobby. If not, this book is the next best thing and well worth the price.

Fucked Up & Photocopied is a 180-degree turn in the direction of the punk/hardcore scene and the multitude of 'instant art' flyers it spawned, some of which are as crude as it gets and others coming close to their sixties forerunners in innovation and talent. Fleeting, ephemeral, timeless, surreal street trash that covered the telephone poles, walls and gutters across the US. This book is page after page of full color flyer reproductions, the chapters breaking them down by cities and sections of the country. Some of the flyers would not be of much interest by themselves, but they have been arranged and juxtaposed, many to a page with added background graphics and text to make a most aesthetic whole. This paper stew of images is full of meaty chunks of higher interest, swimming in the lesser momentary endeavours of the time. Such artists as the always enigmatic and always interesting Raymond Pettibon(e) of Black Flag flyer fame, someone who went by the name 'Pushead', and some early Kozik are here, along with the unknown and anonymous. Some of the bands heavily represented by these flyers are Dead Kennedys, Black Flag, Weirdos, X, Misfits, Fear and Circle Jerks. A lot of the images are bizarre and extreme, as per the music they advertise.

The youth cultures that these two books encapsulate seem at once very different and closely linked. The psychedelic posters taking time, thought and care to create and print, were made to be looked at over and over again, at length. The flyers of the punk/hardcore scene were, in many cases, literally 'instant art', quickly done and cheaply printed (or Xeroxed), and more often than not, black ink on colored paper, made to be handed out, tacked up and thrown in the street. But where *High Art* and *Fucked Up & Photocopied* come together is in the combination of the newly aquired freedom of youth in the later half of the twentieth century, and the technology to express it. [Tom Brinkmann]

HÔPITAL BRUT 2/3

I first met Mark Pawson at the London Small Press Book Fair a couple of years ago. Standing out from the other stalls selling self-published poetry and lower-end fanzines, he stocked a variety of eye-catching material, including garish Panter-style French comics, printed in a variety of weird formats and looking unlike anything I'd ever seen before. I asked him about them and was stunned by the price — they don't come cheap. But he explained that they were really a labour of love, coming in print runs of 100–150, and with an attention to detail almost unheard of in anything so resolutely uncommercial. I bought some. And then more. Mark runs a mail-order service, selling cool toys, good fanzines (*Anxiety Culture* etc), weird books — from SubGenius to Jim Goad, copy culture artefacts, handmade books — and these French comics, published in Marseilles by Le Dernier Cri.

Le Dernier Cri is a loose-knit collective of comic artists who grew out of the Paris punk scene of the early eighties. They moved to Marseilles a few years ago and publish principally material by their members: Yves Blanquet (who has had material published in Fantagraphics' *Zero Zero*), Bruno Richard, Caroline Sury and Pakito Bolino, to name a few.

HORRORGASMO
$19 / pb / 72pp / ISBN 8887581002 / Mondo Bizarro Press 1999 / via Alessandrini 7, 40126 Bologna, Italy / www.mondobizarro.net

HORROR OF THE 20TH CENTURY
$60 / hb / 256pp / ISBN 1888054425 / Collectors Press 2000 / Collectors Press Inc, PO Box 230986, Portland, OR 97281, USA / www.collectorspress.com

COMIC BOOK CULTURE
$49.95 / hb / 208pp / ISBN 1888054387 / Collectors Press 2000 / Collectors Press Inc, PO Box 230986, Portland, OR 97281, USA / www.collectorspress.com

They've also published work by Gary Panter and Mike Diana, which should give you some idea of where they're coming from. Ratty, fucked-up lines and extreme, offensive imagery beautifully presented, usually silk-screened, in Day-Glo colours on thick, high-quality paper. This kind of attention to detail given to this kind of material seems a peculiarly European sub-genre of comics. In Lambiek, Amsterdam's premier comics shop, last year, I saw a load of silk-screened comics, and not much of it by Le Dernier Cri. There was even a huge, beautifully produced A3 book of silk-screened comic art by our very own Savage Pencil — going for about £100.

Le Dernier Cri stuff is cheaper than that, although some of their comics go for £25. *Hôpital Brut*, the most recent Dernier Cri effort that I've come across, is a good introduction to what they do, being two thick A4 comic magazines featuring all the regulars. Mark had a couple of them seized by Customs, who probably objected to, among other things, the ridiculously offensive blood, guts and porn photo-comic about the death of our beloved Princess. The layout and presentation is amazing — foldouts, all sizes of pages, every space filled with bizarre illustrations — and the content no less so. It seems that every imaginable graphics style is represented here, with an emphasis on the extreme — Romain Slocombe's illustrative work wouldn't look out of place here, and there's a clear embrace of things Japanese throughout. There are also text pieces on a variety of themes, from art brut (Dubuffet's term for the work of self-taught artists, particularly the institutionalised) to interviews with artists, via pieces on the Angoulême comics festival. I can't really recommend this — and other Dernier Cri products — enough. In a world in which fewer and fewer worthwhile comics seem to be made, there's at least one source of quality material left. If you want to have a look, Mark Pawson, as well as running a mail-order service, has a stall at Camden market, which is well worth a visit anyway. [James Marriott]

Update Issues 2 and 3 of *Hôpital Brut* are now sold out but importer Mark Pawson writes that issues 5 and 6 of Le Dernier Cri's flagship magazine is now available in a monolithic two volume, 276-page monster-sized issue for £30 inc p+p in the UK. Pawson's website is worth checking out too, with a great collection of indescribable stuff and T-shirts for sale.

HORRORGASMO
Psychotic Art for New Mutants

Visionary, profane, disturbing, depraved. Now while I enthusiastically welcome any kind of book that promotes the work of unknown artists who specialise in 'unusual' art I can't help feeling that warnings of "Open at your own risk!" went out with *Tales from the Crypt*.

Or maybe I'm just jaded. After years of drawing my own similarly 'difficult' material and exposing myself to the work of many, many others I am now totally desensitised to what must be for some, *genuinely* shocking images. Having said that, this *is* a limited edition release (of 999 copies) that you'll never see in Waterstone's and will only be sought out by those punters who groove on pictures of crucified mutant foetuses, angels pissing on a vomiting clown or a dildo-wielding nun menaced by a

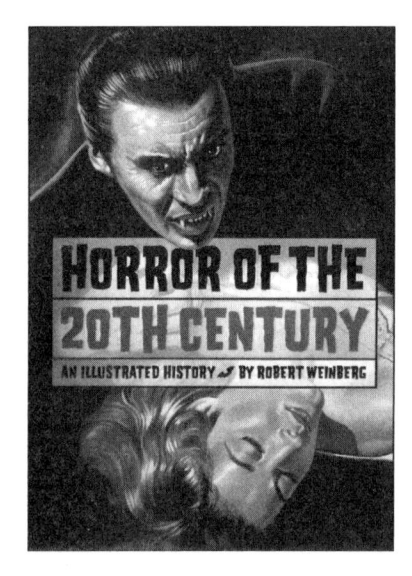

Lovecraftian sex god in a cell full of bleeding walls, so I think such "we're so bad" warnings are redundant.

Reservations on the packaging aside, this is a *good* collection featuring artists from the Italian 'underground' comics scene who all owe a debt to Charles Burns.

Stefano Zattera has the most humorous approach and blends Bettie Page and Bob Dobbs in with his own creation 'Cowgirl' — a Fresian spotted fuckbunny who shoots satanic sheriffs and lassos mustang penises.

Gianmaria Liani is the man working closest to my own tastes. With a crisp, confident line he details the adventures of stacked horror momma Betty Sue — an ageing, sperm-slurping, fur-slippered murderess — and her mad family. His style is like Jamie Hewlett raised in a dark cellar on a diet of The Cramps and phallic hot dogs wrapped in pages torn from lingerie catalogues. Stockings, porno heels, fuck-off bulldogs and ripped flesh aplenty, his images bristle with potential *lustmord* and black as arseholes humour.

'Spiderjack' has a more idiosyncratic style that echoes early Ted McKeever, Peter Kuper, Mike Diana and, in particular, Chester Brown. Except those guys, even at the zenith of their weirdness, never drew vaginal third-eyes, crucified batwing punks with syringe-pierced boners in Take That T-shirts or detachable ray gun cocks that blast holes in the cheeks of famine-victim fellatists. The *only* response is a bemused admiration for someone's willingness to open up *that* far.

But, just when you think it's peaked, in comes 'Dast' to take the doors off completely.

I don't even know where to *start* with this guy. His favoured subject matter is S&M nuclear families and religious iconography, played out by encephalic dominatrixes and skeletal junkies sporting anaconda cocks that spurt seminal napalm. Whilst possibly the least competent artist in the collection, the intensity and sheer fucking *strangeness* of his vision stays with you longer than the rest. The other three guys are 'only' artists but Dast really does seem like the asylum-bound nut that most decent people would dismiss the contributors as being.

Ultimately I think this book is long overdue. Art like this has been too long buried in obscure, small print-run magazines and deserves a much wider audience. For every vacuous Dave McKean book cover there should be a Dast two-headed mutant cocksucker special alongside to provide that all important yin/yang balance that keeps the universe ticking.

Horrorgasmo does the job it was designed for. More of the same, please. [Rik Rawling]

Update Published by Mondo Bizarro, it seems that particular name (and URL) has since been acquired by a rock band.

HORROR OF THE 20TH CENTURY
An Illustrated History
Robert Weinberg

COMIC BOOK CULTURE
An Illustrated History
Ron Goulart

Collectors Press publish high quality, oversize picture books. Of particular interest to us here is the recent *Horror of the 20th Century* (which is a companion volume to *Fantasy of the 20th Century*) and the slightly less recent *Comic Book Culture*. Both are written by authors knowledgeable in their respective fields, but it is no insult to suggest that the real attraction here is not the text, but the rare illustrations which feature throughout the books, printed full-colour in stunning clarity on quality stock.

Horror of the 20th Century opens with a chapter on Dark Roots — acknowledging Horace Walpole's 1765 *The Castle of Otranto* to be the first horror novel — before moving on to chapters which cover antiquarian ghosts, Hollywood, horror comics, pulp paperbacks and magazines, before culminating in the modern horror boom and subsequent slump. It is in these latter pages that the book — for this reader — falls down. It seems a precious waste of space to devote full-pages to videobox art for *Friday The 13th Part VI*, *Scream*, and the cover of a *Buffy the Vampire Slayer* tie-in novel (tellingly, one of the poorest reproductions in the book). Maybe in generations to come these contemporary artifacts will be as scarce, as colourful and as sought after as their horror peerage, but I somehow doubt it. Moving on to that peerage — the book's strongest points — we have some beautifully rendered art for the covers of *Strange Tales*, *Weird Tales*, *Horror Stories* and the like. Many of these covers fixated on (surprise) semi-naked women being menaced by mad scientists or drooling idiots. *Horror Stories* from October 1935 is a personal favourite: A suave devilish gent with a huge grin oversees the unholy wedding of a beautiful unwilling bride to a happy mutant midget. Conducting the service is a priest — not only is he held at gunpoint, but he has a noose around his neck and is wearing a blindfold (with a book in his hands nonetheless)!

HOW TO DRAW AND SELL COMIC STRIPS
£9.99 / pb / 144pp / ISBN 1852868996 / Titan Books / titanpress@titanemail.com

It might not be very practical to drive, but oh, what fun! Cover for an issue of Horror Stories (1939). Taken from Horror of the 20th Century.

As if all of that wasn't an exciting enough combination, there's a guy with a revolver in the background threatening to upset the whole ungodly mess. (In order to fit him in, he is painted in a manner that suggests he might be descending the stairwell headfirst on his belly.)

Other illustrations are more simplistic or have been rendered by less competent artists, but the end result is quite often equally as eye-catching. Take for instance the cover for the 1944 collection of Lovecraft tales, *The Weird Shadow Over Innsmouth*, which features a giant humanoid silhouette striding through a small townscape, or the blood-red-and-lime-green cover for the 1935 anthology *Grim Death* (reproduced on page three).

It's also interesting to see how cover art has changed with the tastes of the decade: art of the thirties and forties leaned toward the glamorous and realistic, while art of the fifties and sixties relied more on abstract form and colour, even incorporating typography into the designs. The seventies and eighties saw a kind of Pre-Raphaelite return to realism, with the finely detailed, anatomically perfect creations of artists like Frank Frazetta and Boris Vellejo. Present art relies heavily on photo manipulation.

No such modern rubbish in Ron Goulart's *Comic Book Culture*; this title is devoted to the Golden Age of comic books, an era which ranged from the middle 1930s to the late 1940s. Goulart offers a basic price guide to each of the titles reproduced, and rightly suggests — given the high asking price for many of these early comics — for those who 'simply want to enjoy old covers, our book is a much more economical solution'. Again, as with *Horror of the 20th Century*, the presentation and quality is top-notch. The comic covers themselves mirror the fact that this was a brand new medium, with many artists coming over from newspaper work to earn a few extra bucks. Characters are stilted, and often have a pistol — or space age laser — to fire. Quite often the anatomies depicted will slip into a meaningless jumble of disproportionate lines, particularly if some feat of exertion is being depicted (like Hercules throwing over a train load of bad guys on the cover of *Hit Comics*, September 1941).

Not all of the comics from the Golden Age feature superheroes, but it's the superhero and action comic that proves the more collectible; they certainly have the best covers. *Funny Pages* from November 1939 is reputed to have the first cover drawn by a woman — Jane Mills, under the pseudonym Tarpé Mills — which shows a jungle woman being manhandled by a gorilla while guy in a pith helmet films from a distance (hang on a minute: isn't Tarzan's mate called Jane, like the artist? Mmm…). One of the most accomplished female artists, Ramona Patenaude, specialised in drawing the Blue Beetle. Her covers for *Mystery Men Comics* and *The Blue Beetle* are all part of a slight variation on the same scenario, in which women, bound, about to be tortured (on a waterwheel, a pyre, over a cauldron, by a clawed hand, a red-hot poker) are saved at the eleventh hour by the distinguished masked man.

Nazis and the Japanese are often the featured villains of the early superhero comics (even before America joined the war). The Hangman manages to thwart both enemy forces at once on the cover of his self-titled comic from Summer 1942. ('Nazis and Japs, you rats! Beware! The Hangman is everywhere!'). Even earlier and weirder yet, is *Daredevil Battles Hitler* (July 1941) which has on its cover various superheroes attacking Der Fürher's oversized head (one superdude is firing miniature aeroplanes from a cannon).

The medium was also generating the likes of Jack Kirby and Bill Everett, artists who quickly got to grips with the comics form and the possibilities it presented. They are covered here in chapters devoted to The Old Masters.

Comic Book Culture covers a more innocent age, before archival storage bags and political correctness were invented, where bad guys could be identified by their swastika armbands, and the words 'Death Drill' etched onto the side of an object created an unlikely instrument of destruction. [David Kerekes]

HOW TO DRAW AND SELL COMIC STRIPS
Alan McKenzie

This is a book on How to Draw Comics for people who've never seen a comic. Which begs the question — if you've never really looked at comics before why would you suddenly want to draw them? It's like never listening to rock music but wanting to be in a band. And so from this flawed premise, Alan McKenzie attempts to fashion the definitive guide to that most maligned of mediums. And fails.

A bit of background first: Alan McKenzie used to work in some editorial capacity at *2000AD*, until he left/got ousted in one of their increasingly Premier League-like management reshuffles. He did *not* work there when the comic was any good. For the first three years or so *2000AD* was great — a mutant mishmash of ideas ripped-off from American movies and the warped imaginations of genuine talents like Pat Mills, Kevin O'Neill and John Wagner. Eventually the bubble burst and the title began its inexorable slide into the sewer of quality that it inhabits at present. McKenzie has no innocent part in the story of its demise — under his captaincy it plumbed new depths of banality and crassness, employing on the way some of the *shittest* artists ever to waste tree pulp. His choice of what to publish was a fair indication of his 'taste' and this is reflected in his choice of examples chosen to illustrate the book. He couldn't hope to do a realistic overview of comics without at least touching on the work of Will Eisner or Moebius, but often sidelines their seminal contributions to the medium in favour of twats like Rob Liefeld which, to me, is like placing a pint of Newcastle Brown next to a jam jar of wino piss.

The majority of *How to Draw and Sell Comics* is taken up with step-by-step tips on how to create from scratch an actual comic strip, with entire chapters devoted to script writing (entire *pages* devoted to 'What is a story'!), composition, pencilling and inking, lettering and colouring. Each separate 'discipline' is reasonably well covered with side-bar comments that so consist-

ICON
£25 / hb / 163pp / ISBN 1887424415 / Underwood Books 1998 / www.underwoodbooks.com

PULP ART
$14.99 / hb / 188pp / ISBN 0517200589 / Gramercy Books 1997 / Random House Value Publications / www.randomhouse.com

JACK COLE AND PLASTIC MAN
$19.95 / pb / 145pp / ISBN 0811831795 / Chronicle Books 2001 / www.chroniclebooks.com

JIMMY CORRIGAN
£18 / hb / 384pp / ISBN 0375404538 / Fantagraphics Books 2001 / www.fantagraphics.com

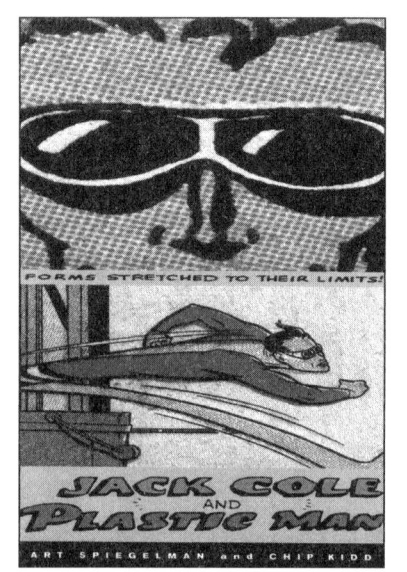

ently state the obvious that I had to wonder if this was some attempt at irony. *"A radio is a useful source of inspiration for artists but it can be distracting for writers."* He's obviously a fan of the production-line approach to comics which, while certainly ensuring that titles meet deadlines, often leads to a piss-weak diluted quality.

Throughout, there is artwork from Steve Parkhouse — one of the best cartoonists around. His energetic linework kept me turning the pages long after I had given up on the author having anything of interest to say. My main problem with the book is that McKenzie's approach is so anal it removes all the potential joy to be had from working in the medium. But then, his advice is aimed at the eventual 'journeyman' artists and writers who clog up the comic shop shelves every week offering nothing new whatsoever — in which case, he's probably written a masterpiece. He just seems to have no *joy* for comics, there's not one trace of enthusiasm in any of this book's 144 pages, and producing what is the equivalent of a Department of Transport Major Roadworks pamphlet is not going to bring to the medium any of the fresh and exciting creators that it desperately needs. Fortunately, these wild-eyed crazy innovators will continue to learn their craft their own way and bring us visions far removed from the tedious mainstream that Alan McKenzie is so fond of. [Rik Rawling]

ICON
Frank Frazetta

PULP ART
Robert Lesser

If we accept that fantasy fans are life's seven-stone weaklings, used to having sand kicked in their faces while they sit on the beach engrossed by Robert Heinlein or William Gibson, then Frank Frazetta's art is designed to conjure up the very Charles Atlas figures that, as the old ads in the comics said, "made a man out of Mac." In Frazetta's imagination, the world is filled with men whose muscles were Hoganic centuries before anyone discovered steroids. His women are beyond pneumatic: tautly muscled themselves, with feline faces that alternate innocence with seduction, and breasts that would get them talk shows on Channel 5 the first time they were bared.

Frazetta was already a legend in the world of comics when his covers for Lancer Books' reprinting of the Conan stories shot him into prominence in the slightly more mainstream world of SF. A generation of fantasy fans created by Tolkien in the mid sixties went looking for something else to read, and Frazetta's Conan was what drew their eyes. Frazetta had a way of anchoring his larger than life figures in a very real sort of action — movement that we can recognise, that must owe something to a sportsman's past. What *Icon* demonstrates so well, however, is the wide range of Frazetta's talent, and the way he was almost always working, often anonymously, at the higher-paying ends of the market: as an 'assistant' to Al Capp on 'L'il Abner', or with Will Elder on Playboy's 'Little Annie Fanny' for example. Looking at L'il Abner's Schwarzeneggarian physique, or the dangerous curves of Daisy Mae you see his dynamism busting out of the page the same way Moonbeam McSwine busts out of her scant clothing.

The relatively small number of actual comic books he drew, for EC and others, have, by their very rarity, helped contribute to his legend, as have the occasional high-profile mainstream advertising and magazine work. The influence of talented graphic artists like Roy Krenkel, Al Williamson, and Wally Wood is apparent. But one of the beauties of *Icon* is the reprinting of some of his SF covers from *Weird Science Fantasy* and *Famous Funnies*, and seeing how he raised the artistic bar for himself with his covers for paperback books and for the Warren magazines (*Creepy*, *Eerie*, *Blazing Combat* and *Vampirella*). The reproduction of these covers is wonderful, usually a full page with a smaller, related piece of art decorating the brief explanation. The sometimes impressionistic colouring in the background helps set the mood for Frazetta's best work, contrasting with the obvious energy in the foreground: when he calms the action in the foreground, as in 'The Moon's Rapture', which closes out the book, the effect is stunning.

Some more of the background to Frazetta's work can be gleaned from another impressive volume, Robert Lesser's *Pulp Art*. This is a collection of cover art from the pulp magazines, which flourished in the thirties and forties, and is also reproduced to a high standard. They are quick to trace the influence of the Howard Pyle school of book illustrating, particularly N C Wyeth, which is also quoted as a major influence on the young Frazetta. Looking at J Allen St John's Tarzan book illustrations and his jungle pulp covers gives you a good idea of Frazetta's roots. In fact, Frazetta's first paperback cover, for *Tarzan and the Lost Empire*, looks like a more direct version of St John.

But in a more general sense, what impresses the most about this art is its sheer inventiveness. There are different conventions to each writing genre, and general conventions too, like use of diagonals to attract attention on news-stands, but within those formulae artists like George Rozen (*Shadow Magazine*), Edd Cartier (*Unknown Worlds/Fantasy Fiction*), Rafael DeSoto and many more can create an often surreal tension out of pulp writing.

Lesser's own text for *Pulp Art* is augmented by numerous brief essays, including an effective overview by Roger Reed of Illustration House in New York, an artist's perspective from Jim Steranko, and a short interview with J Allen St John from 1950.

In virtually uniform format, these two books will stand happily side-by-side on the shelves of anyone interested in popular art. Indispensible. [Michael Carlson]

JACK COLE AND PLASTIC MAN
Forms Stretched To Their Limits!
Art Spielgelman & Chip Kidd

Boasting an excellent title and a grand production job (with a cover made of plastic and several old comic strips reprinted on authentic-looking pulp paper stock), this book traces the career of comic artist Jack Cole (1914–1958) and his most famous creation, Plastic Man, a crime fighter with the ability to elongate himself and change shape at will. Cole delighted in the opportunities presented by his tongue-in-cheek protagonist, and took full advantage of the medium, messing about with logic and time lines. Indeed, the stories seemed to be less about bending Plastic Man and more a vessel by which Cole could bend *the rules*. That said, I confess to not being a huge fan of the 'jokey' drawing style on Plastic Man, much preferring Cole's horror and crime strips. Every bit as anarchic, in these comics Cole has bad guys positively drenched in sweat getting up to all manner of lawless mischief, and buxom gals making risqué innuendo. This, together with the mastery of his execution, ensured that Cole's work was singled out during the comics clampdown of the fifties as being a particularly pertinent representation of the rot that was eating the minds of America's youth (he was responsible for the oft seen trauma-to-the-eye comic panel and the infamous strip, 'Murder, Morphine And Me!').

Later on, Cole worked as a cartoonist for *Playboy*. But something was lost in Cole's transition from the relative innocence of his early pen-and-ink comics work — which he now held in little regard — to the maturity in style of his *Playboy* gags. Tragically and without warning, the artist was to take his own life, aged forty-four. *Jack Cole and Plastic Man* is a wonderful and not-before-time homage to one of comicdom's true innovating forces. [David Kerekes]

JIMMY CORRIGAN: THE SMARTEST KID ON EARTH
Chris Ware

This collected edition of Ware's long-running series appeared on the shelves of my local comic shop during the same week as the much-heralded release of *DK2 — The Dark Knight Strikes Back*, a title alleged by many to be the one that will 'save comics'. Save comics from what, you may ask?

JOEL PETER WITKIN
£47.50 / 272pp / hb / ISBN 1881616207 / Scalo Publishing 1995 / www.scalo.com

Well, how about the gradual decline of the medium both in a commercial and artistic sense. Less kids buy comics these days because of the myriad other distractions — PS2, the Internet, football and lest we forget the timeless appeal of easily-plied local slags — so in a climate of diminishing returns the creative geniuses at Marvel, DC, Dark Horse etc etc have circled the wagons and decided to fight to the bitter end with the only weapon they've ever had that proved to be effective — superheroes.

Back in the mid eighties when Miller produced *The Dark Knight Returns*, along with Alan Moore & Dave Gibbons' *Watchmen* there was much talk of these works signifying the 'death of the superhero'.

Other creators like Pat Mills and Kev O'Neill attempted to nail the casket shut on the caped twats for good with overtly cynical creations such as *Marshal Law* where superheroes and 'gifted mutants' were hunted down, got the shit kicked out of them and occasionally slaughtered — a gaudy display of catharsism for Mills and the thousands of readers who responded to it. At the time there was an air of expectation surrounding the medium with much bold experimentation taking place — and, yes, a lot of it was shit, but people were being drawn to the medium for its possibilities and it wasn't too ridiculous to start talking about a 'Rennaisance' for a medium that had been long ago left to stagnate in its own juices.

Unfortunately, greed and stupidity, two of the founding principles of the comics industry, triumphed in the end. The young artists ran for cover in games design or animation and it was left to a hard-core of chinless geeks in Buffy T-shirts to perpetuate the sorry mistakes of the past, in short — more superheroes.

More superpowers. More killer cyborgs. More balloon-titted ninja hacker SWAT bitches.

Cheers fellas.

The only viable alternative to this unmitigated tide of *shit* was the occasional good title published by Fantagraphics Books, comin' atcha from Seattle, USA. They themselves have published some real shit in the past, so much so that the accusations of supporting their vanity projects with sales of the Eros titles started to seem plausible. I've got a lot of their books on my shelf — mostly those by Peter Bagge and Dan Clowes, as most of the other things they insist on publishing just don't appeal.

And, for many years, one of those titles that just didn't appeal was *Jimmy Corrigan: The Smartest Kid on Earth*. I just didn't get what all the fuss was about and eventually dismissed it as the latest bandwagon for the comics snobs to pontificate about as they sneered down on the superhero fans. I even found myself coming down on the side of the geeks for a while, justifying their 'innocent' pleasures and letting them off the hook. But after week upon week of dragging my arse into Forbidden Planet to be assaulted by what was the direct result of their continual indulgence of 'innocent' pleasures (not forgetting the aforementioned greed and stupidity of publishers, distributors and the corporations that own them) I finally cracked. I gave up on comics altogether, only venturing into these spiritual hellholes if Clowes had anything new out. Fuck it, I said. The sooner they flush the toilet the better.

Then someone sent me a copy of *The Imp* — an irregularly published zine, expertly written and designed by Dan Raeburn, that focuses on particular comics creators that take his fancy. Issue three is all about Chris Ware and his comic *Jimmy Corrigan*. Dan had designed the comic along the lines of a 1920s newspaper with an almost pathological attention to detail and this feat alone impressed me to read on.

What he had to say about the *Jimmy Corrigan* saga and Chris Ware's comments on his own work inspired me to seek the title out if it ever got the collected edition it seemed to deserve.

And here it is, winner of a *Guardian* award, all £18 of it. I don't even know where to begin to even explain it, except to say that it's all about Jimmy Corrigan, a middle-aged man living in Chicago. There's no simple way to explain the story because it flits back and forth between past and present (and occasionally the future), sometimes within the space of a page, and relies so much on the relationship between the often sparse word balloons and panels and the specific details of each panel. In the complexity of its structure and the range of themes it explores it almost redefines the term 'post-modern' and makes literary efforts from the likes of Pynchon and DeLillo read like Shaun Hutson in comparison. No, I'm not shitting you, this book is one of *the* great artistic achievements of the twentieth-century. It will fuck with your head and make you think long and hard about yourself more than anything else you will read this year. If nothing else, it will make you realise that most of the 'art' and 'entertainment' you subject yourself to is utterly meaningless shit.

The art and design work is fucking incredible. With a highly stylised clear line style and flat shades of colour and black, each page is absolutely rock solid — nothing is extraneous, no big show-off panels, everything serving the narrative. Multiple POVs and numerous wide shots of the city reveal Ware's firm ability as a draughtsman and while his obvious love of the designs of the early part of the twentieth-century may repel those who demand everything predictably filtered via Photoshop, they help to bolster the impression that this is someone who gives a shit about what he's created. In an age of instant thrills and ideas being more important than ability, a labour of love like this might be seen as an anachronistic indulgence but it's your loss if you think that way. As far as I'm concerned this proves that the best art is produced by a singular vision, someone with something to impart that may be of value to the audience.

All this from just a comic? Yes, why not? Finally, after strong hints from Dan Clowes, Alan Moore and Bill Sienkiewicz, the medium is being dragged kicking and screaming out of its sperm-encrusted adolescent bed and into blazing light of a new dawn. Finally.

Why has it taken so fucking long? Why are we still having to wade knee deep through mounds of shit comics to get to something good? Why is a piece of nostaligic crap like *DK2* being seen in a positive light? The comics medium is at a crossroads now — it can take the familiar and comfortable road of the cape and the smack in the face that will ultimately lead to its doom within ten years, or it can veer off into new territory where there are no signposts, no maps and only one rule of the road:

Don't Be Shit.

The choice is yours. What's it gonna be? [Rik Rawling]

JOEL PETER WITKIN

Headpress readers are probably aware of Mr Witkin's disturbing photography. This book came out with very little fanfare… I think a small mention of it appeared in the *Independent*'s Christmas round-up of books for 1995. By chance, a year later, I came across a copy of the book in the photography section of a well-known book emporium (OK, it was Waterstone's). It was shrink-sealed (naturally) to keep out the idly curious. The book is distributed in Europe by Thames and Hudson, so should still be available to order from good bookshops. Perhaps it would make a nice gift for a 'loved one'.

Says the introductory blurb:

This collection of [Witkin's] works manages to present an almost complete anthology of his oeuvre. Indeed, for the breadth of its offering of photographs both known and unknown, it is the first exhaustive survey of the work this artist has produced up to 1995.

The book includes a worthy essay on Witkin's art (which the general reader will probably skip and come back to later — if at all), some words from Mr Witkin himself and the pictures… The purchaser of the book will probably have their own particular favourites, but a few worthy of a mention are:

'Testicle stretch with the Possibility of A Crushed Face'(1982) — A hooded man gets more than his leg

JUDGE DREDD
GOODNIGHT KISS
£9.99 / pb / 90pp / ISBN 184023346X / Titan Books
2001 / titan-press@titanemail.com

JUDGE DREDD
HELTER SKELTER
£14.99 / hb / 94pp / ISBN 1840233869 / Titan Books
2001 / titan-press@titanemail.com

pulled... (love that title/image!)

'Eunuch' (1983) — A study of a man and a dog... Lassie come home?

'Journeys of the Mask: The History of Commercial Photography In Juarez' (1984) — A reclining woman appears to be inserting her foot up a man... (where the sun don't shine)

'Man Without A Head' (1993) — Probably the most disturbing image in the book: a cadaver sits bolt upright in a chair, wearing only a pair of socks.

To sum up, if you like classy photographs of 'very special people' in strange, surreal tableaux, then I would say buy this book. Fans of pre-op transsexuals (pics of chicks with dicks?) should also have a field day, as they seem to be well represented.

To the Witkin aficionados I would say that the contents of the Scalo book make it a better purchase than the imported Twelve Trees Witkin things. [K A Beer]

Update K A Beer's favourite Witkin picture can be found here at [**w**] www.zonezero.com/exposiciones/fotografos/witkin2

JUDGE DREDD
GOODNIGHT KISS
Garth Ennis et al

JUDGE DREDD
HELTER SKELTER
Garth Ennis et al

Oh no. Not one but two collections of old Judge Dredd comic strips sit before me, like miniature black holes sucking all the positive energy out of myself and the room around me. What have I done to deserve this? Haven't I already made it abundantly clear that this character is now a spent force and utterly irrelevant, except to a few dewy-eyed old school *2000AD* fans who've still got a bit of growing up to do? Conceived as a pastiche of the Dirty Harry ubercop fantasy in the mid seventies by Pat Mills, the character was only effective as a straight man with Mega City One and its bizarre denizens being the real stars. There should have been endless mileage in this approach but, some time during the early nineties, things changed... for the worse.

Goodnight Kiss is a compilation of three loosely-connected stories from those heady days. Comics had been hailed as 'the new rock'n'roll' throughout the late eighties and the medium was still enjoying a boom period which the editors at Fleetway tried to cash in on. Unfortunately they were utterly fucking clueless as to how to go about this and totally oblivious to the fact that their flagship title had actually been in decline (in terms of quality, if not in sales) for at least five years. The new obsession was with painted artwork — triggered by the obvious natural talent of Simon Bisley who's work on *Slaine: The Horned God* had spawned a whole new generation of eager young copyists, each desperate to get some of the fame & fortune that it seemed comics could now bring. No longer a cultural cul-de-sac inhabited by anorak-clad geeks and no-knob fat boys, now you get featured in *The Face* and, let's face it, you *can't* get any more rock'n'roll than that, can you?

As the long-established creative teams like Wagner/Grant and Mills/O'Neill had fucked off to Yankee Land to cop for some of the action Alan Moore was getting, it was left to, shall we say, 'lesser talents' to milk the tit dry and it was these

Art & Graphic Novels

new writers and artists who were the first generation to have grown up influenced by what was now being defined as the *2000AD* 'house style'. Prior to that the writers had been influenced by a diverse range of material — from mad-ass sixties sci-fi to Hollywood's early seventies golden period — and this was reflected in the quality of the scripts. The publishers (Fleetway) were still stuck in the days of Archie the Robot and lantern-jawed Tommys cracking the skulls of the Hun so they really had no idea what kind of new monster they had created. Once the editors and middle-management dickheads got wise on how to 'market' the 'product' it all went down the karzi and never came back. Garth Ennis was part of that new generation of writers trailing in the wake of Wagner, Grant & Mills but clearly had no idea of how to assimilate those influences into something of his own. That's clearly the case here on *Goodknight Kiss* where both stories are dull, predictable and utterly patronising to the readers. Yes *2000AD* has always been full of exploding heads and men screaming "*eeeargh*!" as they die bloodily but it was the bits in-between the gore — y'know, characters, story, atmosphere, stuff like that — that kept the readers coming back. The Marshal, if you care, is a vigilante from the Cursed Earth (the radioactive wasteland that lies beyond the city limits) who is inspired by the Lone Ranger to bring his own brand of vigilante justice to what's already a totalitarian fascist society. He should blend in nicely but, as you might expect, he falls foul of Judge Dredd and, well, just have a guess how it ends.

The art job by Nick Percival is most politely described as 'workman-like'. The guy was clearly young, learning his trade and under pressure to conform to the Bisley style. Doing his best with punishing deadlines, the result is big blobs of acrylic and figurework that recalls Jack Kirby and Frank Miller at their most minimal. Meanwhile, in *Enter: Jonni Kiss*, Greg Staples has totally embraced the Bisley technique to such an extent that it becomes insulting. Biz, as I said, has a natural talent that throbs on the page, while his most accomplished copyists look like they're straining over each panel like constipated pensioners. The story introduces the Heavy Metal Heathcliffe alpha male that is 'Jonni Kiss' who crops up again later in 'Goodnight Kiss' where Nick Percival is back on the art chores and seemingly had more time to spend on each page as there's noticeably more detail and control on display. The villain this time around — Gideon — is a jaw-droppingly obvious rip-off of DC's Spectre, with added steroids. As for the story, well, do you care? Does anyone on this planet give a flying fuck? It's just one long procession of Arnie-film quips and threats, punch ups, gun battles and... yaaaaaaaaaawn. It's shit. It's ordure. It's excrement. It patronises and insults the reader's mental faculties and sloppily assumes that an acquiescence to the dictates of Hollywood crassness is enough to make these stories and the Dredd character resonate in the mind of the target audience. The reason why other characters like Spiderman, Daredevil and even the Silver Surfer have been so popular over the decades is because they were created and developed by writers who cared and understood what they were doing. Bearing in mind the time they were created, perhaps these strips do suffer from a certain inexperience but I'm not feeling charitable so fuck it. They're shit.

Now, if *Goodnight Kiss* suffers somewhat from youthful naivety what excuse can be offered in defence of the turd that is *Helter Skelter*. It's Ennis again at the helm, only this time he's ten years older and now a celebrated author with successful series' like *Preacher* and *Hellblazer* under his belt. He's got the sales to prove his talent and *2000AD* is proud that this writer ("much in demand for his hard-edged, wickedly humorous style") is back to give the fans the one they've been waiting for — which is easily the most asinine and fatuous pieces of in-house nostalgia that these tired and jaded eyes have ever had to witness. *2000AD*, collectively, ran out of ideas long ago and has been regurgitating past glories ever since but this is just taking the piss. 'The very structure of reality has been altered' — a plot device that creaks under the weight of its own obsolescence — allowing Dredd to face off against many of the key villains from his entire twenty-five year history. Does that sound exciting or does that sound like the biggest load of lazy-arsed bollocks you've ever heard? Yup, thought so — big, sweaty, hairy, cheese-encrusted bollocks. Every villain — from Dredd's clone-brother Rico to robot revolutionary Call-Me-Kenneth — is let loose in the streets of Mega City One on the hunt for one Darien Kenzie, the kind of BBC-approved dynamic black female protagonist that is now an essential ingredient of every shit-arsed cyberMatrixRunner sci-fi rip off bag of wank. Dyed hair, special ability, streetwise... you may have seen this before. She holds the secret to why

JUSTICE LEAGUE OF AMERICA
£8.99 / pb / 160pp / ISBN 1840230649 / DC Comics 1998 / www.dccomics.com

LEGS THAT DANCE TO ELMER'S TUNE
300pp / hb / ISBN 3822881880 / Taschen 1998 / www.taschen.com

MALICIOUS RESPLENDENCE
£60 / hb / 282pp / ISBN 1560972785 / Fantagraphics 1998 | £35 / pb / 282pp / ISBN 1560973668 / Fantagraphics 1999 / www.fantagraphics.com

MATTRESS
£19.99 / hb / 112pp / ISBN 3980760286 / Goliath 2002 / www.goliathclub.com

NASTY TALES
£13.95 $19.95 / pb / 191pp / ISBN 190048613X / Critical Vision 2001 / www.headpress.com

all these entities are turning up and in an idiotically blatant reference to *The Terminator* even has Dredd save her ass and utter the line: "Take my hand if you want to live."

Am I honestly supposed to accept this without comment or complaint? I know it's 'only comics' but Come The Fuck On! This kind of stunt cannot be allowed. No amount of post-modern irony can be offered up in his defence. Ennis is utterly shameless in his plundering of the *2000AD* archives and seemingly nothing is sacred — *Flesh*, *Fiends of the Eastern Front*, even *DR & fucking Quinch* are not spared and whilst it gives the Mack Daddy of the medium Carlos Ezquerra a chance to flex his muscles on the visuals it's all so jaw-droppingly shit that you want to burn every copy in a giant pyre that can be seen from outer space.

Comics is a stunted idiot-child medium — that's the main part of its appeal — but most of the writers now working in the medium have basically run out of ideas, run out of enthusiasm and are, for all intents and purposes, redundant.

So, fellas, there are many charitable causes out there that need your help. Go do something worthwhile instead of making bad copies of straight-to-video action bollocks. The world doesn't need your comics. The kids don't want them.

Save some trees. Save Africa. Save your souls. [Rik Rawling]

JUSTICE LEAGUE OF AMERICA
The Nail
Alan Davis and Mark Farmer

JLA! A man has his limits y'know! Fortunately, this is pretty good. An artist working from his own script usually makes for a better comic as it comes closer to a singular vision than a clusterfuck like the JLA's *Strength in Numbers*.

Alan Davis first started in *2000AD* and went on to work with Alan Moore on *DR & Quinch* which still stands today as the Dog's Bollocks. He's now well-entrenched in the US comics scene, working exclusively in superhero comics but I have no problem with this because (a) he's a really good artist and (b) he *loves* superheroes. This makes for good old fashioned rip-roarin' entertainment as the reader regresses to eight-years-old and cheers on the ass kickin' good guys and gals.

The premise of the story is very simple — what if there was no Superman? Jonathan and Martha Kent's truck gets a nail in the tyre so they never drive on further down the road and never come across the fallen meteor with little Kal-El inside. Consequently there is no Clark Kent and superhero history is altered forever. Lex Luthor is mayor of Metropolis, Jimmy Olsen is Deputy and it gets crazier from then on as Davis throws in virtually every DC character and *almost* manages to make it work. Half of the spandex wrapped geeks I didn't recognise but it didn't matter — the whole thing moves at breakneck speed and brims with confidence and Davis displays a keen understanding of the dynamics required and an almost religious respect for the DC Universe.

Of course it all works out well in the end and along the way you get some storming fight scenes, unintentionally hilarious dialogue (Green Lantern: "My ring responds to my willpower.") and cameos by long-lost crazy ass characters like Ragman, Deadman and a Superfly-afro'd Black Lightning. Verve and nostalgia delivered with a truly exemplary art job. Smooth expressive layouts, multiple POV's and impressive detail — all made to look like a piece of piss.

Well worth buying for your kid brother and sneaking a read for yourself. [Rik Rawling]

LEGS THAT DANCE TO ELMER'S TUNE
Elmer Batters

Elmer Batters, according to the introduction in this book, was 'the greatest foot photographer of all time'. The label of being a 'foot man' has a nice, nostalgic ring to it. Batters died in June 1977, aged seventy-seven. Like the nostalgic-sounding accolade awarded him, the photos presented in *Legs That Dance To Elmer's Tune* are a glimpse at a by-gone generation of smut, with buxom gals lounging around the house dressed in traditional black silk stockings, suspenders, panty girdles and slips.

The focus on toes and feet does little for me (other than remind me of the suspect in the Boston Strangler case who got his jollies peeking at girls' feet in a darkened cinema), so it's something of a relief that *Legs That Dance* does indeed tackle a bigger picture, painting with a broader and oft times curious, palette. At least one of the women in the book wears nothing but a Pork Pie hat, while another, elsewhere, poses with a pair of industrial shears. One particularly odd shot shows a lady lying on a kitchen work surface with the top half of her body stuck through a serving hatch…

This is 'cheesecake' erotica. Masses of it. And it comes in a cheesy package, too: instead of the usual plastic shrink-wrapping for protection, *Legs That Dance To Elmer's Tune* is sealed by a stocking, tied at the end. A leggy stroke of marketing genius. [David Kerekes]

MALICIOUS RESPLENDENCE
The Paintings of Robt. Williams
Robert Williams

Self-defined 'lowbrow' artist Robt. Williams has influenced a couple of generations of similar, kitschy, scuzzy artists whilst always remaining several (thousand!) steps ahead — as testified in this present, huge volume which showcases an exhaustive retrospective of the unparalleled artist's work. The whole gamut is covered, ranging from early drawings, paintings and sculpture (how come Robt.'s work in this area looks so much like that of Stanislav Szukalski, who he apparently didn't meet until years later…? Hmmm…) to the hot-rod stuff in conjunction with Ed 'Big Daddy' Roth, Underground comix work for *Zap* and the notorious *Felch*, and, of course, the full scale, brain-rotting canvases, of which there are around 200 full colour plates — the most detailed viewing you will get of Robt.'s work outside a gallery. The production of the volume is stunning; the design exquisite. Fantagraphics should be congratulated on spending so much time and effort in giving this Dalí of the Underground Comix Culture a fitting platform. Resplendent works on a grand scale! [Stephen Sennitt]

MATTRESS
Greg Friedler

A hard back full colour book by Friedler, the photographer behind the naked series (*Naked Los Angeles*, *Naked London* et al) depicting naked women lying on a floral mattress. According to Jordan Schaps' intro the book sees Friedler as a photographer whose work fits into the wider history of the reclining nude in art, but is separate from this because it is "purer" and the photographer is more honest. The reality is that the book consists of pictures of twenty-somethings naked, often pierced, often tattooed, largely trim (of both figure and bush). This book is no more honest than any other, instead it is possibly dishonest because there's no acknowledgement that the photographer is actually foregrounding his taste (even unwillingly) — I mean, there's no fat ugly women here, no hirsute middle aged, saggy breasted grey haired types. That's not to say I want to see a book of unattractive women, but then, I wouldn't evoke terms such as honesty and purity. That quibble aside, the general premise of the book is a good one: cute naked chicks on a dirty mattress, presenting themselves for our delectation. [Jack Sargeant]

NASTY TALES
Sex, Drugs, Rock'n'Roll and Violence in the British Underground
David Huxley

Summer 1978: I was fifteen years old and my heart was palpitating in anticipation of my first visit to London! My sister, Susan, had recently married and moved there, and together we were going to visit Dark They Were And Golden Eyed, a true-to-life comic shop just like they had in America — I couldn't believe it! Just a few weeks earlier I had an inkling of the type of stuff they might sell when I bought a book called *Masters of Comicbook Art*, which had fea-

PUNK STRIPS
£6 $12 / pb / 128pp / ISBN 1899866353 / Slab-O-Concrete Publications 1999

RAW CREATION
£22.95 / pb / 240pp / ISBN 0714840092 / Phaidon 2000 / www.phaidon.com

SCARY!
£9.99 / pb / 96pp / ISBN 1560972742 / Fantagraphics 1997 / www.fantagraphics.com

STRUGGLE
$29.95 / pb / 200pp / ISBN 0867194790 / Last Gasp 2000 / 777 Florida Street, San Francisco CA94110 / www.lastgasp.com

tures on the likes of Richard Corben, Moebius, R Crumb and Victor Moscoso. These lurid and sexy images immediately riveted me, opening up for me a whole new world of insight into the possibilities of the comicbook genre.

The shop certainly didn't disappoint me. Though funds were severely limited, I came away with a copy of *Heavy Metal* (the first I'd ever seen), a Frazetta poster, and several recent editions of *Creepy*. However, the whole time I was in the place, my rather nervous sidelong glance kept returning to the cheap-looking Underground comix which were ruled out-of-bounds (Susan deciding that *Heavy Metal* was "quite adult enough" for me at that time). The titles — *Skull*, *Zap!*, *Slow Death* — glowed intensely in my brain, but also some titles that struck me as *odd* in some way: *Nasty Tales*, *Cozmic Comics*, *Brainstorm*... What was it about them that bothered me? Suddenly, thunderstruck, I realised what it was: they were *British* Undergrounds, and I never thought there were such things!

A few weeks later came the discovery of *Near Myths* No 1. I subscribed immediately and was extremely irritated when copies were rolled up and posted in a cardboard tube! Another discovery was a battered copy of *Graphixus* No 5 on a Doncaster market stall — an issue featuring Brian Bolland's adaptation of Harry Harrison's *The Streets of Askelon*, which I'd read originally in *The Seventh Pan Book of Horror Stories*. Now the ball was rolling good and proper. I sent off for the Forever People Underground list. I scoured everywhere I could think of to get these disreputable items (more difficult for me than you'd imagine: although I was sixteen by now, people took me for a precocious twelve-year-old because I was so small and innocent-looking!). I even wrote to Mal Burns for back issues of *Graphixus*, enclosing several weeks' worth of pocket money, but I never received anything in return.

What's the point of all this reminiscing, you might ask? Simply that it all flooded back to me with the same sense of excitement and, somehow, *involvement*, when I picked up David Huxley's marvellous *Nasty Tales* — the first book to classify and put these now obscure and wonderfully unsavoury British publications into some sort of perspective. In this sense, Huxley has done a great job. *Nasty Tales* is methodical, strategically and logically-planned, and excellently researched. What it suffers from in a little dryness is more than made up for in its evocation of a chaotically exciting period in British publishing history, every bit as distinctive and challenging as the more familiar story of American Undergrounds. Huxley's approach is unsensational and objective, and he divides his subject matter into sections which allow for the optimum use of analysis of these comix' major themes — Sex, Censorship, Drugs, Violence — with more specific subsections. Huxley's book is a long-awaited tribute to a bygone era, which over the years seems to increase in vitality when one compares it to ninety-nine per cent of today's apathetic products. *Nasty Tales* looks set to be the standard text on the British Undergrounds for years to come. [Stephen Sennitt]

PUNK STRIPS
Simon Gane

"Anarcho Terrorist from the *real*

punk underground" — here we fucking go. It would be easy to imagine this work summed up as 'Jamie Hewlett on speed' but 'Jamie Hewlett on White Lightning' might be more appropriate seeing as each page comes reeking of dosser juice.

Not that any of this bollocks does Simon Gane's work justice. While many other fly-by-nights have dipped their toes in the UK zine underground, only to fuck off back to their day jobs as soon as it got cold or graduated to doing shit illos for 'lad's mags', Simon Gane continues to do his thing and do it well. His truly idiosyncratic style — really chunky marker pen line-work, stark spotted blacks and a *Roobarb & Custard* approach to pacing — is just the type of thing advertising twats love to grab hold of and suck dry. Six months of doing ads for mobile phones, club compilation CD covers and *Guardian* feature illos and the guy would suddenly be deemed redundant by our ever more avaricious culture — which isn't going to happen as Simon Gane's political stance, made crystal clear in these strips, means he would probably glass the media twats and then go neck some more rocket fuel cider.

The guy brings a much-needed energy and sense of humour to the 'radical politics' underground. Some of that humour is either as subtle as a sledgehammer or nothing better than a Hale & Pace sketch with piercings — 'Arnie the Anarchist' features a lot, as does 'Sub Vert Man' ("he's been on the cider and he's fuckin' angry!") and the political sophistication they convey is almost non-existent, but it's that total lack of subtlety that engages in more ways than any tedious anarchist pamphlet ever could. Patriotic yobs get beat up, coppers (*the* enemy) get grenades stuck down their throats, insensitive punk boys get routinely leathered by their feisty Tank Girl friends. It's all very much an unfocussed howl of rage at the fucked-up state of England in the nineties and seems the best kind of response to the Paxman-endorsed level of debate that we've become used to. While a lot of it may be pissing in the wind it comes infused with genuine human emotion, missing from most levels of art these days. It's worth a measly £6 for the reminder. [Rik Rawling]

Update Slab-O-Concrete are no more but sister publisher Codex might be able to help.

RAW CREATION
Outsider Art and Beyond
John Maizels

A rather belated paperback release of a book first published in the mid nineties, this is a massive, comprehensive tome that does fair justice to a wide array of 'self-taught' 'folk' artists from the fringes of world culture. Here are paintings, sculptures, statues and whole environments created by the mad, the dangerous, the 'simple-minded' and the simply marginalised. The immense scholarship that has gone into *Raw Creation* is breathtaking; the selection of illustrations (hundreds and hundreds of them) is widely representational; it's difficult to imagine a better introduction to the subject for the general reader. If there has recently been a move away from 'highbrow' art history towards an appreciation (or appropriation) of previously rejected artefacts to form a 'lowbrow' art history (beloved of, say Joe Coleman and that whole *Juxtapoz!* crowd) the artists in *Raw Creation* must represent a refreshingly un-poseuring, no-brow zone, where Art is about Art, and the Cult of the Artist has no place. [Stephen Sennitt]

SCARY!
Theodore Jouflas

This is the most fascinating, shocking, disturbing book I've come across in a long time. A ninety-six-page adult comic strip, it's described as "the bastard offspring of 'fractured fairytales' and the B&W horror movies of the thirties and forties". Deciphering this book is like walking down a grimy funhouse hall of twisted mirrors into the mangled nightmares of some unrepentant psychopath. "A tale of debauchery, crime, neuroses, greed, lust, psychosis, vengeance, love, rage, mystery, comedy and sorrow", runs the blurb — "in short, everything about American life at the end of the millennium that we have come to know and savour". The prose, with its fiendish neologisms, reads like the work of a lobotomised Lewis Carroll; the print looks like the ugly scrawlings of a serial killer. Imagine Picasso dropping acid with Dr Seuss, and you still don't come close to the contorted atrocities of the illustrations. Imagine Lucien Freud and Edward Lear co-hosting a prime-time US talk show, with all its trailer-park mayhem, and you still fall short of the insane fairy tale of a storyline. Jouflas uses his neurotic, emetic beast fables to pick at the grotesque scabs of American television culture, exposing all the filthy infections beneath.

Traumatic, sinister and deviant, *Scary!* is the bedtime story for the apocalypse. [Mikita Brottman]

STRUGGLE
THE ART OF SZUKALSKI

STRUWWELPETER
$24 / pb / 178pp / ISBN 0922915520 / Feral House 1999 / www.feralhouse.com

Ed. Eva Kirsch & Donat Kirsch

I put Rodin in one pocket, Michaelangelo in the other, and I walk towards the sun
— Stanislaw Szukalski

Pretentious? Consider also the introduction to this volume by Leonardo (yes, him) and George DiCaprio where the case is made for Szukalski to be more deserving of the term 'Twentieth-century's greatest artist' in place of the man they refer to as 'Pick Asshole'. They don't have much time for that old mysoginistic paint swabber Pablo and I think they've got a point.

As we lurch dazed and numb into the twenty-first century Picasso's work has finally found its rightful place — in mass-produced prints on sale in Ikea or used as a 'special edition' selling point for hatchbacks. Such a fate will never befall the work of Stanislaw Szukalski.

Until recently the man and his work were almost entirely forgotten by a world more inclined to accept a pile of bricks or a turd in a jar as 'art'. Which would have pissed me off had I been Szukalski because he spent much of his ninety-four years on Asylum Earth rendering some of the most bold and potent artistic statements ever created. Ever. And he knew it! Not only that, the man managed to forge his own unique (to say the least) 'scientific discipline' called Zermatism which requires a book of its own to even begin to explain (see also *Behold! The Protong*, also by Last Gasp).

Born and raised in Poland, Szukalski bounced between his homeland and the USA, finally settling in California when the Nazis started kicking off but he never forgot his roots. Much of his work was rooted in legends and events from Polish history, giving his drawings and sculptures an added resonance beyond their own form and presence. I've never much cared for sculpture in the past, it's always appeared as a form long since adulterated by the trust fund hippies and witless pisstakers — you know what I mean, the fucking bits of cardboard and chicken wire propped in a gallery corner and called 'Untitled No 17', the lumps of slag iron welded into car crash shapes — big wastes of time for all concerned and a depressing distraction from the real possibilities of the form. Szukalski seemingly shut himself away from all that post-war avant garde bollocks and cracked on with his own ideas. He had plenty to keep him occupied after the Nazis had trashed most of the work he produced in Poland, as he set about diligently recreating and improving some of his finer pieces that had been crushed under Das Jackboot — which is surprising as there was much in Szukalski's thrusting Teutonic lines and rampant ubermensch figurework for the likes of Albert Speer and even old Adolf himself to groove on. Szukalski's own fairly extreme and outlandish theories on art, history and culture were sometimes not so far removed from the more wigged-out sci-fi elements of *Mein Kampf* — believing as he did that Anglo-Saxon politicians, fascist Germans and communist Russians (amongst others) were direct descendents of human/ape interbreeding.

Of course, coming from a successful artist (as opposed to a failed one like Hitler) this could easily be interpreted as the more volatile part of his muse and dismissed accordingly but it was notions like this, woven

This is what happens to children who harm poor dumb creatures. Sarita Vendetta's interpretation of 'Cruel Paul' from Struwwelpeter. © Vendetta/Feral House

into his burning commitment to Polish history and his growing fascination with the symbolic imagery of the lost cultures of the Aegean and Meso-American empires that helped him to blossom with confidence as he charged headlong into a thunderously creative period, producing some of the best art in history.

Szukalski didn't work from life study, allowing his interpretations on the physical form to run rampant. Human figures featured prominently in his major works: writhing torsos, muscles rippling like a Terminator, sinews caught forever in rigid torment, surrounded by such potent archetypes as the soaring eagle, the sun, the eye, the dragon. His pantheon and whole stylistic approach reminds me of no-one but Jack Kirby with his New Gods and his cosmic vision that was too large for comics. Rooted in the 'Fine' arts Szukalski wasn't constrained by rigid formats or narratives, freeing him to go hog wild on mind-boggling works like the 'Rooster of Gaul' and the awesome 'Katyn'. Exquisitely detailed, every atom loaded with meaning and fashioned by an intellect that had something to say beyond "it doesn't have to mean anything. It's an installation."

Szukalski's art exposes with blinding sun-going-nova clarity the absolute paucity of imagination and talent in the likes of Emin and Hirst. Visions such as his are deeply unfashionable in these woeful times simply because they dare to stand for something but long after Emin's tent — and sweaty old Pablo's dove of peace Ikea prints — end up flapping in the breeze in some seagull shit-splattered landfill the ever-grasping claw that is Szukalski's 'Struggle' will forever be reaching out into the ether where the Mystery will always hide. [Rik Rawling]

STRUWWELPETER
Fearful Stories & Vile Pictures To Instruct Good Little Folks
Heinrich Hoffmann

In the autumn of 1844, a respectable bourgeois doctor in Frankfurt named Heinrich Hoffmann went shopping for a picture book to give to his three-year-old son Carl for Christmas, but he was disappointed by what was on offer — all the children's books available seemed too sentimental, preachy and didactic. So he sat down to write and illustrate his own, and the result, *Struwwelpeter*, was published to great acclaim in 1845. Although out of fashion now, it has been one of the world's most perennially popular children's books, and a constant source of fascination to psychiatrists.

For what makes *Struwwelpeter* remarkable is the high level of sadistic violence displayed in both pictures and text. As the psychoanalyst Wilhelm Stekel dolefully observed in his classic monograph *Sadism and Masochism* (and he had *Struwwelpeter* specifically in mind): "It seems to give adults satisfaction to tell children cruel and gruesome stories."

In a typical poem (the stories are all written in doggerel), a child commits some offence, frequently trivial,

SUPERGIRL
£9.99 / pb / 223pp / ISBN 1852869607 / Titan Books
1998 / titanpress@titanemail.com

SUPERMAN
£6.99 / pb / 55pp / ISBN 1840233842 / Titan Books
2001 / titanpress@titanemail.com

TALES OF TERROR!
£29.99 / 296pp / ISBN 1560974036 / Fantagraphics
2000 / www.fantagraphics.com

for which a hideous and completely disproportionate retribution is exacted from them. Thus, Romping Polly plays a little more boisterously than a good girl ought, after being warned against it by her aunt. She promptly breaks her leg, and is crippled for life. Augustus refuses to eat soup, and starves to death in an improbable five days. Pauline plays with matches, watched by her horrified pussy-cats, Minz and Maunz — predictably, she catches light and is incinerated. In a delicious last image, the cats are seen quenching her ashes with a flood of tears. Cruel Paul is a seriously disturbed child. He tortures and mutilates any animal he can lay his hands on. Yet his punishment is no worse than that of the lesser transgressors.

Most memorably and terrifyingly, perhaps, young Conrad is warned against sucking his thumb. Of course, he does so, and in comes a "long, red-legged scissor-man"...

Snip! Snap! Snip! The scissors go;
And Conrad cries out — Oh! Oh! Oh!
Snip! Snap! Snip! They go so fast
That both his thumbs are off at last.

Are you beginning to see why followers of Freud groove on *Struwwelpeter* so much? There is no hint of the sickly Christian piety so prevalent in most nineteenth-century children's literature — the peremptory way in which hubris is punished is more akin to Greek tragedy than anything else. I was unsurprised to learn that Hoffmann went on to found a lunatic asylum — whether he himself was aware of it or not, the stories in *Struwwelpeter* seethe with neurotic fantasy. The title-poem itself, 'Struwwelpeter' or 'Shock-Headed Peter', is rather different. There is no narrative of crime and punishment here, only an extraordinary iconic image of a boy in a medieval-style tunic with wildly tangled hair and enormous talon-like fingernails, looking like a poster boy for extreme yoga.

Hoffmann's own illustrations for *Struwwelpeter* are naïvely charming in their folksy Teutonic nineteenth-century way, but are admittedly rather crude. Feral House's beautifully-designed deluxe reissue, however, boasts not only a facsimile of a 1915 American translation, complete with the original illustrations, but also modern illustrator Sarita Vendetta's B&W takes on some fifteen of the poems, and a full-colour plate of her fetishistic vision of the Scissor-Man, capering about in rubber with his thighs stuck full of pins and needles, with a jar full of severed thumbs on the floor behind him, and a naked child in a cage behind that. "Warning! This children's book is not for children!" screams the back cover of the book, and whilst many modern parents would doubt the pedagogical wisdom of giving any child a copy of *Struwwelpeter* to mull over, Vendetta's pictures are the main reason for this admonition. In a painstakingly pointillist pen-and-ink style, she lays bare the outrageous psychopathology of the poems, with their undercurrents of abjection, castration and trauma, in a series of vivid tableaux of child abuse. Like Paula Rego and Angela Carter, Vendetta is evidently fascinated by the repressed content of much children's literature, and like Trevor Brown (of Whitehouse cover art infamy), she excels at rendering images of children in pain. These pictures will give a lot of *adults*, let alone children, nightmares!

Also lurking beneath the tastefully spot-laminated cover of Feral House's *Struwwelpeter* are an informative introduction by Jack Zipes, professor of German and expert on children's literature, a foreword from Adam Parfrey, and a facsimile of an historical curiosity called 'Struwwelhitler', a British propaganda parody from World War II depicting prominent Nazis as naughty children. This book reaffirms my opinion of Feral House as being one of the most exciting and innovative publishers currently active, and is highly recommended. [Simon Collins]

SUPERGIRL
Peter David, Gary Frank, Cam Smith et al

I could never figure it, but when the world is under threat in comicbooks, why does the responsibility to try and save it invariably fall squarely on the shoulders of the superhero or superheroine whose name is plastered across the front cover? Why don't all the superheroes just band together... or easier still, why doesn't Superman just take over and do it all himself with one giant super-punch?

I guess it boils down to comic publishers' licence or something.

I don't claim to know how many riot grrrllls read Supergirl, but I can wager there's an awful lot of teenage boys who do.

This is supposedly a 'new dawn' for Supergirl, and I have to confess I rather enjoyed it. The main thrust is that a group of Satanic individuals are about to unleash demonic forces and destroy the planet, unless something major comes down and stops them. Into the equation comes an unstable Supergirl, who has psychological problems in that she is now part Linda Danvers, a girl who once fell under the influence of the diabolic group and committed a murder for kicks. The tale concludes as one might expect it to — with a climatic battle between Supergirl and evil. But there's a lot of interesting stuff leading up to that, with Supergirl turning super-bad (replete with leather pants and cut-off 'S' top), half of the city's inhabitants slipping down the evolutionary ladder, organised religion getting a slap in the face, Superman making a brief God-like appearance — all of which is handled with a viciousness and a degree of blood-letting not normally associated with the Super family... Heck, who am I kidding? Supergirl — she's a looker all right. [David Kerekes]

SUPERMAN
Whatever Happened to the Man of Tomorrow?
Alan Moore & Curt Swan

Whatever Happened to the Man of Tomorrow? closes the book on the Superman saga (or one of them, or maybe none at all) when the Man of Steel ultimately breaks his vow never to kill a foe in anger — an action he finds impossible to live with.

As someone who reads very little by way of new-fangled comicbooks — though hardly ignorant of them — I wouldn't say that this is the 'perfect jumping-on point for new readers', as claim the publishers. It's another confusion in the Death of Superman grab bag, serving only to stir the convoluting waters yet further. Writer Alan Moore's opening statement — that "this is an imaginary story... aren't they all?" — may seem innocuous enough and place the yarn within a fairy tale context, but at the same time it does convey a certain reticence at the whole commercial business that sees not only one Superman of late, but several, each with their own comic.

What I do like about this tale, however, is that it addresses some gaping illogicalities in the superhero universe, no less the curious Bizarro, the anti-Superman from a world diametrically opposed to (Superman's) Earth: Bizarro's world is square not round; to do badly at school is to succeed; when things are messed up they are going well, and so on. Bizarro has only ever been played out in the past as a well-meaning nuisance to Superman, and the whole maddening fantasy of a world opposite to this one generally slips by as a lightweight sub-plot. Here, however, Bizarro suddenly comes to grips with the whole anti-Superman schtick — if Bizarro really is anti-everything that Superman is, then it stands to reason he should be hurting people as opposed to protecting them. Furthermore, if Superman is alive, then in order to be the 'perfect imperfect duplicate', Bizarro has to be dead. It's all over for Bizarro by page six. Pity, but inevitable. [Joe Scott Wilson]

TALES OF TERROR!
The EC Companion
Fred von Bernewitz & Grant Geissman

Just what the world needs, another EC comics checklist and cover gallery. At least that's what I thought when I clapped eyes on this oversized hardback of 296 pages. But then, once under its covers, I was surprised to discover that *Tales of Terror!* is co-authored by Fred von Bernewitz, who had published *The Complete EC Checklist* way back in 1955 (fifty mimeographed copies only). EC's own Bill Gaines found

TEMPLE OF BLASPHEMY

$45 / pb / 148pp / ISBN 8887581037 / Mondo Bizarro Press / Piazza San Martino 3/d, 40126 Bologna, Italy / www.mondobizzarro.net

ULTRA-GASH INFERNO

£11.95 / pb / 222pp / ISBN 1840680393 / Creation Books 2001 / www.creationbooks.com

A 1950s and 1960s superstar (we're not kidding): William M Gaines. Tales of Terror! © William M Gaines Agent Inc

the *Checklist* indispensable, and helped Von Bernewitz — "one of the founding members of first-generation EC fandom" — in amending and updating the information it contained for subsequent editions. The most substantial part of *Tales of Terror!* is devoted, naturally, to a checklist of all titles published by EC (together with colour cover repros), starting with *Picture Stories from the Bible* in 1942, running through the crime, horror, sci-fi, war and humour titles, to conclude with the Balantine EC reprint books in the mid sixties. On top of this are articles and interviews, including a transcript of Bill Gaines' 1954 Senate Sub-Committee Testimony, where, as a voluntary witness, Gaines tried to champion comics in the face of the witch hunt that Dr Fredric Wertham had helped to instigate.

He started off well, but as his Dexedrine-based prescription diet medication wore off, Gaines began to lose focus, and didn't come out of the hearing at all well. Indeed, given that the hearing was widely reported and even televised, he found himself suddenly the face and name of the 'enemy'. Shortly after, EC were amongst many comic publishers forced to fold their horror and crime titles (though unlike Gaines and EC, not many had run inflammatory editorials stating "the group most anxious to destroy comics are the communists!"). EC struggled to keep their head above water with the short-lived New Direction comics (bizarre, more mature comics such as *MD* and *Psychoanalysis*) and their Picto-Fiction line (text-based story magazines with spot illustrations), before hitting pay dirt with *Mad*.

Also included in *Tales of Terror!* are interviews with the late Gaines, Russ Cochran (whose reprints have enabled EC to reach a new generation of fans), artists Al Feldstein and Shelly Moldoff, co-author Von Bernewitz and others. *Tales of Terror!* is a lovely piece of work and one that sits nicely with Grant Geissman's *Collectibly Mad*. [Joe Scott Wilson]

TEMPLE OF BLASPHEMY
The Black & White Artwork of Trevor Brown

For those who don't know: Trevor Brown is an Englishman living in Japan, a self-propelled exile brought on by the total lack of a home market for his 'transgressive' (to say the least) artwork and his inclination for Japanese females. A long-time contributor of artwork to the Susan Lawly label (home of Whitehouse), he specialises in airbrushed paintings of dolls and young girls where he toys with a personal aesthetic that could be construed as 'paedophilic'. He denies any overt intent in that direction but lovingly rendered paintings of bruised and cut doll-girls with lizards scooting off up their snatches and obviously pre-teen punkettes squatting to piss into gleaming white toilet bowls offer little in the way of a defence to the 'moral majority'. However, Trevor Brown is an intelligent man who has long since tired of the 'child porn art' debate that surrounds his work. Many of his fans and customers are female, drawn to the same often surreal expressions of sexuality and iconography that neither they nor the artist themselves can fully explain.

Along with the paintings, which make up the majority of his output and income, he also produces B&W artwork using Radiograph pens. This is the medium with which he first chose to express his ideas in the eighties, in booklets such as *Graphic Autopsy*, *Necro Porno* and, inevitably, *Graphic Autopsy 2*. *Temple of Blasphemy* collects all his output from that period to the present in one volume, enhanced by enviably slick production values. The early work now looks quite amateurish and seems deliberately intent on shock value: cut-up images, laid out like comic-strip panels, juxtapose Himmler with babies on respirators, young girls bound and gagged with splayed vaginas sporting gaping cyclopean eyes. Myra Hindley. Son of Sam. Intravenous drips. Car wrecks. You can spot the influences and from today's perspective it all looks a bit like the empty magazine of a gun, the 'shock bullets' having long since been spent by lesser triggermen. But, this is where Brown was learning, developing his technique and exploring his own aesthetic sensibilities. The drawing style is sparse, one thickness of line throughout and flat blacks for shading. Occasional use of zip-a-tone and splashes of blood red add little to the overall effect which is as grim as an ambulance parked on Saddleworth Moor.

Brown's move to Japan had an obvious impact on his work — suddenly it's Oriental girls sporting the bruises and the bandages. Inspired by the extreme pornography of the Far East, his images become full of Kinbaku rope bondage scenes and depictions of truly unpleasant degradation: shit, piss and menstrual blood sluicing across the pages.

Here his drawing style is more fluid but still obviously reliant upon detailed photo-reference to capture the looks of jaded pain and the 'glib smiles' that Brown claims to find so appealing. Sparse medical dungeons are the backdrop for the perversions — white tile, chairs and a cloying astringent stench to mask the bodily discharges. Whether this is the man's sexual inclination or his response to the libidinal underbelly of an almost alien society is a moot point; the fact remains that these images, more than the later works featuring close-ups of cocks pissing into women's mouths and bandaged Japanese girls slurping custard-like ropes of semen, are the ones that fix their crampons in your mind. The best image of the entire collection is Brown's famous 'Black Eye Madonna', a fine drawing of the popular female songstress from her early puppy fat 'Into The Groove' years sporting a bleeding shiner — which, in itself, renders Peter Sotos' fatuous introduction utterly redundant.

As all the images are obviously culled from photos, the question that begs is: Why bother? The images already exist in one form and even reduced to a B&W assimilation it is still essentially the same image. Perhaps the purpose lies in the fact that Brown has taken the time and effort required to render the original source image in its new form? Perhaps if the viewer spends as long looking at the finished image as Trevor Brown did creating it then the essential truth of its appeal and intent will become apparent? Perhaps.

Ultimately, this is a unique (in every sense) collection detailing one man's ongoing obsessions, which is valid in itself, but it's difficult to say just how many other people it would appeal to. And best of luck to anyone trying to sneak a copy past our boys at HM Customs. They will be all over this like flies on shit. [Rik Rawling]

ULTRA-GASH INFERNO
Suehiro Maruo
As the proud possessor of Brenda Love's invaluable book *The Encyclopedia of Unusual Sexual Practices*, I'm able to tell you that oculolinctus is a sexual act consisting of licking the eyeballs of one's partner. Strangely enough, I'd, erm, come across oculolinctus before:

XXXOOO VOLUME 1
£11.95 / pb / 60pp / ISBN 1889539007 / Gates of Heck 1997 / www.gatesofheck.com

CARICATURE
£29.99 / hb / 104pp / ISBN 1560973293 / Fantagraphics Books 1998 / www.fantagraphics.com

It is a recurring motif in the work of Suehiro Maruo, maestro of the 'ero-guro' (erotic-grotesque) style of Japanese manga comic. I'd assumed that this was a personal idiosyncrasy of Maruo's, too weird and disgusting to have a name…

I'd previously encountered Suehiro Maruo's work in the form of Blast Book's English translation of his graphic (and how!) novel *Mr Arashi's Amazing Freak Show*, in which a young girl runs away with the circus and wishes she hadn't after being subjected to certain — shall we say — *indignities*, and also in the booklet art for John Zorn's *Naked City* CD.

Ultra-Gash Inferno, a collection of nine short strips created over the past ten years, is every bit as intense as the title would suggest, featuring enough piss-drinking, shit-eating, banister-licking (!), mutilation, dismemberment, incest, cannibalism, violent mayhem and all-round perversion to keep the Marquis de Sade happy, as well as lashings of oculolinctus, of course (on pages nine, sixty-one and seventy-eight, eyeball-licking fans!). A panoply of other transgressive influences, both Western and non-Western are on display: Pasolini's *Salò*, Bataille's *Story of the Eye* (an eyeball is inserted into a vulva in a direct homage), the perverse horror tales of cult Japanese author Edogawa Rampo, and David Cronenberg among others. It's a heavy and foetid hell broth of sickness. All this is delineated in a clean-lined, stark, precise pen and ink style which compositionally owes much to the Japanese ukiyo-e woodblock print tradition, and which leaves me torn between admiration for the beautiful artwork and fascinated repulsion for what it delineates. The curious Japanese taboo against explicit depictions of genitalia sometimes leads to bizarre results — legs spread wide to reveal a Barbie-like nothingness — but this enforced reticence doesn't really impede the overwhelming atmosphere of ultraviolence and the old in-out that prevails. The titles of the stories — Putrid Night, Sewer Boy, Shit Soup — pretty much speak for themselves, though the narratives can be hard to follow, partly due to having to read everything 'backwards' i.e. right to left from the back of the book, and partly due to general cultural dissonance. When it is possible to work out what's happening, though, you'll wish you hadn't — it's invariably extremely nasty. [Simon Collins]

XXXOOO VOLUME 1
Love and Kisses from Annie Sprinkle
Annie Sprinkle & Katherine Gates

Here is a collection of thirty Post-Porn postcards by former X-rated movie actress Annie Sprinkle, spanning a twenty-year period. Some of the designs will be familiar to anyone who has followed Annie's career as a 'Pleasure Activist' (more slogans than you can shake a willy at), while other designs are new. "You can help change the world by mailing these to your friends and lovers," encourages Annie in the introduction to this book, whose pages can be pulled out and are suitable for mailing. The images include the classic 'Anatomy of a Pin-Up Model' and 'Bosom Ballet' pieces. Some of the postcards are lovely in a girlie-like way, while others, like 'A Public Cervix Announcement', which offers a gynaecological close-up of Annie, would probably put most

DANIEL CLOWES

CARICATURE
Daniel Clowes

Hailed by many as the only man who can save comix from itself Clowes is a man it's difficult not to admire, if only for his work ethic which is focused on consistent (as opposed to prolific) output and a belief in the viability of comix as a storytelling medium on a par with cinema and the novel. So far, so good, but my problem with Clowes, and his admirers, is that for all his deserved praise, awards and kudos, he does come out with some real shite sometimes.

His ongoing title *Eightball* has evolved over the years from a *Mad*-inspired anthology of decidedly patchy quality to what is now a marketing banner for his latest, longer and more involving stories like 'David Boring'. The major shift in focus and content came with 'Ghost World', his poignant and understated study of two teenage American girls on the cusp of adulthood. This work was a breakthrough for Clowes, allowing him to leave behind annoying and silly shit like 'Zubrick' so he could pour all his attention into the type of work he feels comix should be celebrated for.

Caricature collects nine stories published alongside and after the 'Ghost World' episodes and compared to previous Clowes collections (*Lout Rampage* and *Orgy Bound*), it almost reads like the work of a different artist. His drawing style has matured considerably and he no longer veers between styles and techniques so much.

Clowes has developed a way of depicting America today as a mirror of itself and recent decades past, all perspectives blurring into one another, which, for all his pop-culture references, hints at a timelessness to the stories he's depicting. His twilight cityscapes, windblown streets and empty yards are haunted with potential that, unfortunately, is only occasionally fulfilled.

Of the nine stories collected here only four are really any good, which is not a good score for a book costing over twenty quid. The title story, 'Caricature,' is recognised by some as a modern classic and is certainly one that resonates here the longest. Mal Rosen is an artist working the County Fair circuit, drawing caricatures for $10 a time. Told in the first person, we are privy to Mal's diary entries as he is forced to doubt his place and purpose in the world. He meets Theda, a strange young female who acts as the catalyst for Mal's doubts that his work has any real validity. Clowes manipulates the reader's emotions skilfully so that we feel equal amounts of pity, loathing and despair for the ultimately sad figure of Mal. "I think art is like shitting," says Theda at one point and this becomes the overriding metaphor, particularly during the curious and vacant finale where Mal seems to conquer his doubts, only to see his reflection in the toilet bowl, a caricature of the person he thought he knew.

This strip also gives an ideal opportunity for Clowes to flex his strongest muscle — drawing the faces of ordinary Americans in all their tragic, unadulterated glory.

The strips 'Blue Italian Shit' and 'Like A Weed, Joe' both feature Rodger Young, yet another mask for Clowes to hide behind, as he reels out what must be episodes from his own life, blurred by the screen of fiction. How much of these stories is pure fiction is irrelevant — the tone of these strips is obviously more heartfelt as he recounts younger years living with his grandparents or alone in New York with a succession of surreal and horrific flatmates. It's telling that both strips are rendered in a decidedly more 'cartoonish' style than that employed on 'Caricature'. Rodger Young himself appears as little more than an assembly of dots and slash lines, as if anything approaching a realistic depiction would give the game away completely. There is no real story here and it doesn't really matter. The reader is encouraged to remember similar episodes from their own life and thus the all-important connection with the artist and the 'great insight' into 'their' souls is made. However, it is good to see Clowes stoking the embers of his misanthropy as he lays into the freaks from his past, a trait he may not be too proud of but which certainly helps empower his best work and should be utilised more as far as I'm concerned. Do what you do best, not what it's best to do.

'MCMLXVI' (1966, for the rest of us) is an attempt at laying into the 'scenesters' who've decided America's cultural apotheosis was garage rock, *Batman* with Adam West, Sinatra's 'Rat Pack', trash/sleaze paperbacks, Tiki lounges and 'authentic diners'. We're encouraged to sneer at anyone who's desperately appropriated these totems as part of their 'lifestyle' but it's obvious that Clowes, and no doubt many of his

GHOST WORLD
£12.99 / pb / 106pp / ISBN 1560974397 / Fantagraphics Books / www.fantagraphics.com

LIKE A VELVET GLOVE CAST IN IRON
£12.99 / pb / 142pp / ISBN 1560971169 / Fantagraphics 2000 / www.fantagraphics.com

PUSSEY!
£6.99 / pb / 56pp / ISBN 1560971835 / Fantagraphics Books 1997 / www.fantagraphics.com

Clowes comes up with the title of a future R.E.M. track in this touching moment from *Like A Velvet Glove Cast In Iron*. © Clowes/Fantagraphics Books

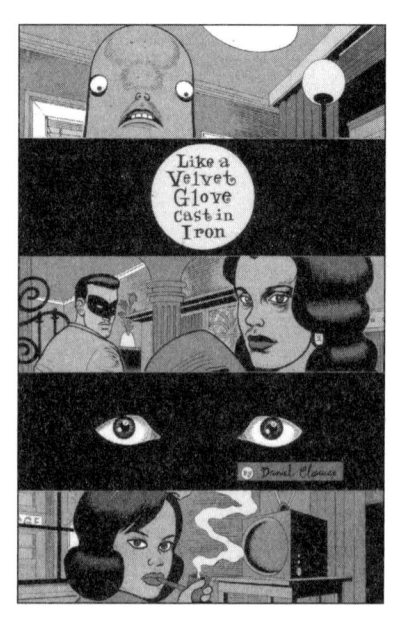

readers, are nuts for this stuff. The references are too accurate, the tone a little strained in its detachment — it's like someone overcompensating their story in an obvious lie. Again, it's a sign that Clowes' best work comes not just from his observations and obvious artistic abilities but also when he injects a little bit of heart and soul.

Which is where the other strips in this collection fall down, and fall down badly.

'Green Eyeliner' is a six-pager originally published in *Esquire* (not that that means shit). Clowes has since claimed that six pages is nowhere near enough space to really do a story justice, but I suppose it's not worth pointing out that this wasn't a problem for him with the early issues of *Eightball* where one- and two-page strips are commonplace. It doesn't excuse a poor strip, focusing on a young vain woman descending into a hollow kind of madness.

'Immortal, Invisible' is about a boy who's a little too old to go out trick-or-treating, a tale that wants to recall the tone of 'Ghost World' but ends up fumbling with the whole 'mask' metaphor and goes nowhere.

'Black Nylon' is a guy in a homemade superhero costume who drifts through a fatuous and unfocussed narrative that seems to have been made up as it went along. If a complete unknown had come up with this strip, *The Comics Journal* would have rained down molten hot turds of contempt upon it. But because it's Clowes it rules, obviously.

These strips that make up the latter half of the book are devoid of something vital — a sense of purpose or even a sense that they have anything to say. Clowes has, throughout his career, made a bad habit of doing strips that many other comic artists would leave as forgotten notes and doodles in their notebooks. This has helped to flesh out a few issues of *Eightball* and add to his image of prolificity but it doesn't really make for an impressive body of work.

Some of Clowes' strips are pure genius, some are total crap. This drunken slew between these two sides of the artistic highway is fascinating and frustrating to follow, but I'd like to hope that one day he will finally crash the car into the ditch marked 'Ghost World, Caricature and Pussey' and not the other — the other really is a dead end. [Rik Rawling]

Update Caricature is available now in paperback at a less frightening cover price.

GHOST WORLD
Daniel Clowes

For those unfamiliar with his work, Clowes originally became popular thanks to his drawing style and design sensibilities appearing alongside the recent 'kitsch' and 'retro' infatuation with 1950s Americana. His character, Lloyd Llewellyn, grooved through a world of Tiki lounges, cocktail bars and sub-Lynchian weirdness for the sake of weirdness. There were occasional flashes of his sardonic wit and jaded misanthropy but it wasn't until he started the ongoing anthology title *Eightball* that he began to develop his strongest abilities — a simple but potent art style and a disturbingly keen insight into people's true feelings and motivations.

In previous book collections — like *Pussey!*, *Like A Velvet Glove Cast In Iron* (the title is a line from *Faster, Pussycat! Kill! Kill!*, trivia fans!) and the best-of-*Eightball* books — it's clear that Clowes has been holding back the sauce, pissing about with pointless one pagers like 'Needledick the Bug Fucker'. But, in getting that shit out of his system, it's clearly allowed him to make Ghost World, his most impressive and, I've got to say, *intelligent* piece of work to date.

The story, such as it is, can be summed up in one sentence: two teenage girls in modern America — Enid and Rebecca — face up to the impending horror of adulthood. That's it, and told like that it sounds no different to so many other books that are doomed to wind up in the Waterstone's sale. What makes this different is the comics medium used, allowing Clowes to turn in a wonderfully sparse art job — an Anywhere USA rendered in B&W, with pale turquoise accent shades that lend an air of deliberate melancholy, and the sheer depth of insight and empathy in his writing. The sense of alienation, of mundane polarisations, is subtly but brilliantly achieved. The girls talk, sit in diners, play pranks on strangers; barely animated but utterly desperate. The target audience — that 'Gen-X Post-Literate' demographic — will probably want to run and hide under the stairs when they see their culture and its flotsam of nostalgic ephemera exposed in such howlingly stark detail. Clowes is never judgmental though; he simply shows what he's seen and lets the reader decide.

There are some disturbingly accurate depictions of everyday losers — minimum wage slaves, nihilistic zine writers, neighbourhood oddballs, even the lonely heart known only as 'Bearded Windbreaker' — but they serve to add what little substance there is to the world of Enid and Rebecca. The title says everything, or, nothing at all. [Rik Rawling]

Update Director Terry Zwigoff turned *Ghost World* into a successful movie in 2001.

LIKE A VELVET GLOVE CAST IN IRON
Daniel Clowes

A re-issue of Clowes' dark, moody tale of sex, love, cults and... er... er... um... aw heck... *mutating synchronicity*, which reads every inch like a waking dream. It's the tale of Clay Loudermilk who one day pops into a run-down adult movie theatre and witnesses a film unlike any other he's ever seen: no sex, no nudity, just weirdness. "I didn't know they made movies like this," he muses, and goes to ask the girl behind the desk whether she knows anything about it. She looks kinda funny, and seems oblivious to his questions, but a small guy suggests Clay checks out the men's room. Normally he wouldn't have gone in there for a million dollars... And so for Clay the journey begins, permeated by strange and vicious people, cryptic clues, and secret societies. It runs anything but smoothly. In fact, some parts are sickening.

Perhaps you're not 'into' comics, but — for 142 pages at least — *Like A Velvet Glove* just might make you change your mind. Forgive it the last chapter and this is a masterwork in which Clowes' artwork is pure and simple and black. [David Kerekes]

PUSSEY!
Daniel Clowes

From the introduction:

Comics — too often they're dismissed as simple-minded irrelevant pabulum for mental defectives...

Anyone who's ever written or drawn comics and harboured dreams of 'making it' in the industry, anyone who reads SFX and would begin hyperventilating if they missed an

ROY STUART
£9.99 / pb / 200pp / ISBN 3822829129 / Taschen 2003 / www.taschen.com

ROY STUART VOL II
£19.99 / hb / 200pp / ISBN 3822868701 / Taschen 1999 / www.taschen.com

A windy day in Roy Stuart*-land.*
© Stuart/Taschen

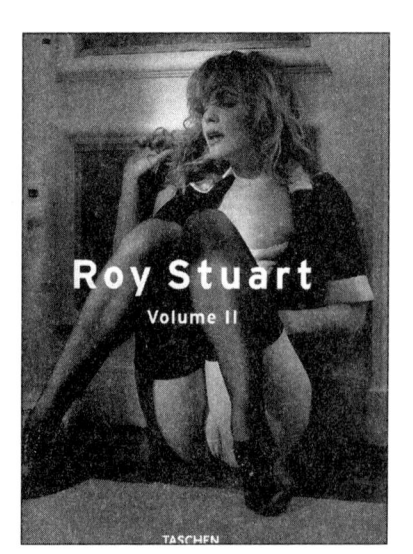

episode of *Buffy the Vampire Slayer*, shit — anyone who grew up reading comics and liking sci-fi, only to find themselves ostracised by the 'normal, sporty' kids will find this book a painful reading experience. Every disappointment, every unrequited dream, every embarrassment is here, rendered with the stark and unflattering line of Daniel Clowes. It is simply a truth too close to the cock-shrivelling reality of it all.

The individual stories originally appeared in the early issues of *Eightball* and were far easier to ingest in small doses. Read as one volume they are simply mind-blowing as Clowes absolutely rips into the comics world, propelling his goofy-toothed, double-chinned nerd-hero through a succession of adventures that pull the whole history of the comics medium under the relentless laser beam of his sensibilities.

As a young boy Pussey (pronounced 'Poo-Say') runs from the disaffection of his family dynamic into the welcoming fantasy-arms of 'Volcano Boy' and his myriad pals.

As a teenager, he stumbles into the world of arcane rituals and sweat-freezing patheticness that is comics fandom. Once he's got his foot on the first rung of the ladder as a professional penciller he becomes a pawn in the game — manipulated by horrific caricatures of established comics 'luminaries' who represent the opposing ends of the comics spectrum — superhero crap or avant-garde bollocks. Eventually he 'makes it', right at the height of the nineties comics 'boom' when distinctly average talents raked in millions and set their jaded eyes on the big movie deal.

Every single aspect of the comics world — from Marvel's well-documented rip-off of its writers and artists over the years to *Raw*'s absurd 'We're so fucking out there' art pranks, from modern art's 'appropriation' of images by Brian Bolland and John Buscema to the current grim and relentless decline of the medium as an artform — is assaulted with absolutely no prisoners taken. Clowes wades in with the facial caricatures, relentless character assassinations (the comic mart dealer in the 'Who Farted?' T-shirt being especially accurate) and truly scathing observations. Not that Clowes actually says anything new about the idiotic machinations that go on in the medium (and the entertainment world at large) but he does manage to distil what have been endless tedious debates in places like *The Comics Journal* down to two or three panels. The reader is never allowed to feel comfortable, as every possible stance is revealed to be as ridiculous and as pathetic as the rest. You never really empathise with Pussey and yet the other characters are so repellent that you are left with little choice. Besides, Pussey is that part in all of us who just wants to be left alone to dream while the world around goes fucking crazy. He embodies our most cherished childhood dreams and our most shameful teenage memories. Lost in a world of cynical manipulators and total bastards he is, at the very least, human.

This book is relentlessly, laugh-out-loud funny throughout, but by the end you come out shell-shocked and sober. It says more about ambition, dreams and the fucked-up world in which we live than any shedful of Booker Prize nominees. And it's only a comic!

Who's going to read crap like that anyway? [Rik Rawling]

ROY STUART

ROY STUART
Jean-Claude Baboulin
While the models depicted in some of Taschen's other photographic books are, shall we say, on the chunky motherly side (I'm thinking *Cheesecake!*, *Elmer Batters* et al), Roy Stuart's preference swings more to the waif-like. Here we have beautiful wretches in petite white pants and blouses, in poses that at times transgress the flimsy divide between softcore and hardcore — I refer specifically to the series of shots showing middle-aged men with their peckers stuck in glory holes, while on the other side of the wall several young things suck at the disembodied hardened members. Stuart also knows that sexiness doesn't have to equate with glamour: his models have a *casual* sexiness about them, as if the camera has captured an unguarded moment: girls in busy open places 'surreptitiously' flash their knickers whilst crouching down to read a map or take a photograph. Some of the shots are more elaborate, with scenarios acted out over several pages: the set titled 'Séance', for instance, would seem to suggest that a spirit enters the body of a beautiful medium in a trance, whereupon the guests strip her naked and engage in somnambulistic sex. A similar theme is at play in 'Initiation', where hooded figures in a dark chamber have sex with glassy-eyed girls.

I've looked through this book two dozen times or more and I still get a kick out of it. One of Taschen's finest. [David Kerekes]

ROY STUART VOL II
Roy Stuart
This second collection of work by photographer Roy Stuart continues exactly where the first left off: with cute models in some playful photo vignettes. 'Emergency Stop' has a blonde caught short and taking a pee in a side-street. Her discarded knickers are picked up by a passer-by who insists on pulling at the freshly relieved babe's skirt. A good karate kick from her stops him in his tracks and she shuts him up by stuffing the undergarment in his mouth. Another vignette, 'No Smoking,' was originally used in *Leg Show* magazine, where it received letters of protest because of its anti-smoking theme (which, incidentally wasn't intended by Stuart). In it a woman taking a crafty drag of a cigarette is confronted by her boss (mother, whatever). A scuffle ensues with knickers aplenty being flashed, and the crafty smoker is left displaying a gob full of crushed and broken cigarettes. 'The Big Surprise' is a little more unusual with its homosexual connotations. A man picks up what he perceives to be a rent boy in a darkened side-street. In a hotel room, some petting takes place, the man receives a blowjob, and finally pulls down the youngster's jeans to reveal... a very female gash. (The deceptively innocent and androgynous model is shown in the photo montage at the front of the book, holding up her ID for the camera.)

Other erotic adventures take on more obvious themes (ballerinas, French maids, lesbian schoolgirls, cellists), with the sole exception being an elegant elderly lady exhibiting what appears to be an aged and stretched caesarean scar — a photograph which is devastatingly out of place amongst the little pants and tight butt cheeks. [David Kerekes]

CRUMBS

AMERICAN SPLENDOR PRESENTS
ROB & HARV'S COMICS
£9.99 / pb / 86pp / ISBN 1568581017 / Four Walls Eight Windows / www.4w8w.com

THE BOOK OF MR NATURAL
£9.99 / pb / 126pp / ISBN 1560971940 / Fantagraphics 1995 / www.fantagraphics.com

THE COMPLETE CRUMB COMICS
$18.95 / pb / 112pp / ISBN 1560974605 / Fantagraphics Books / www.fantagraphics.com

THE LIFE AND TIMES OF R CRUMB
£11.99 / pb / 182pp / ISBN 0312195710 / St Martin's Press 1998 / www.stmartins.com

(L–R) Harvey Pekar, Robert Crumb and Marty Pahls in a panel from the strip 'The Young Crumb Story'. *Bob & Harv's Comics*. © Four Walls Eight Windows Story: Pekar / Art: R Crumb

AMERICAN SPLENDOR PRESENTS ROB & HARV'S COMICS
Harvey Pekar & Robert Crumb

No one should need reminding of who Robert Crumb is, but Harvey Pekar? He's the guy behind the *American Splendor* comicbook, writes it all and has other people illustrate it. Well, this is a collection of strips — written by Pekar; illustrated by Crumb — which have graced two decades of *American Splendor*. (That's something like five issues.) And no mistake, every single panel is a gem. Pekar writes about everyday things, and in Pekar's life that means, essentially, collecting jazz records and going to work. The most exciting it gets is when he receives a rejection slip from *Village Voice*. In 'Standing Behind Old Jewish Ladies in Supermarket Lines', Harvey can't bring himself to short-change the cashier. Edge of the seat stuff! In 'The Kissinger Letter', Harvey relates the time he received a hand-written letter from Henry Kissinger before Kissinger was famous, but threw it away (Pekar's moral: never throw anything away). It's a true talent that can turn the seemingly mundane into gripping, 'what's gonna happen next?' stuff. And Crumb's art is the perfect compliment. The comicbook equivalent of Raymond Carver. [David Kerekes]

Update A couple of very good films based on this material and these lives have appeared in recent years: *Crumb* (1994) and *American Splendor* (2003).

THE BOOK OF MR NATURAL
Profane Tales of that Old Mystic Madcap
Robert Crumb

Mr Natural is a reluctant guru and mystic who seems to be part genuine and part charlatan. His ways are sometimes so deep as to be impenetrable (he goes to sleep with one shoe on his bed), while his 'enlightenment' often has a familiar ring to it ("Get the right tool for the job"). Mr Natural does appear to possess extraordinary abilities and to be operating from a higher plane of existence, but he also has a very human streak; he has a sense of the theatrical (appearing suddenly in a puff of smoke, going "Ta-da-a-a-a!"), and easily tires of the inane demands made on him by his followers to say something profound. For members of the opposite sex, however, his patience lasts a little longer… (I wonder if Mr Natural has a real life counterpart in one-time Beatles spiritual leader, the Maharishi Mahesh Yogi? For all his pontificating, there is no doubt for a moment that Mr Natural grants *his* female followers 'special tuition'.)

Included in this collection are some of the Wise One's best adventures. In some of these adventures nothing very much happens (in the strip 'Mr Natural Does the Dishes', Mr Natural does the dishes), while several others entail him trying to set up Flakey Foont — an unlikely materialistic follower — with a girlfriend. Of course, this wouldn't be Robert Crumb without *some* contentious material, and here the rub is a series of encounters Flakey and Mr Natural have with the Amazonian 'Devil Girl'. It is what feminists like to call 'objectification' — Mr Natural has the ability to render Devil Girl powerless and do with her body whatever he will; in one strip he 'removes' her head and gives the body to Flakey as a present. [David Kerekes]

THE COMPLETE CRUMB COMICS VOL 16
The Mid-1980s
More Years of Valiant Struggle

This ongoing series is testament to the skill and popularity of the former Underground artist. Detailing every aspect of Crumb's work, from childhood sketches onwards, it is a pretty amazing and ambitious document.

The first volume of *The Complete Crumb Comics* appeared back in 1987 and is pretty much for completists only, recalling the hand-produced comic books which Robert created for the amusement of himself and his brothers. It's an interesting time capsule but divulges little of the talent to soon emerge.

Vol 16 is the most recent as of writing and brings us to the mid eighties. Here, amongst other work, is Crumb's meditation on 'The Religious Experience of Philip K Dick'. A BBC arts programme in the eighties, I recall, happened to capture Crumb as he worked on this particular strip. In the programme — possibly *Omnibus* — Crumb, who had yet to relocate from the US to France, came across as pretty isolated and perhaps a little paranoid. 'Philip K Dick' is a departure in style for Crumb, in that it drops the customary crosshatching technique for solid blacks. It is a style he adopted a few times during this period, though the actual nature and content of the 'Philip K Dick' strip remains an anomaly for Crumb.

Also in Vol 16 we have a piece of "hard satire" rejected by the publishers of *Weirdo*. The piece, an ad for missing children which toys with the theme of child abuse, seems particularly harsh. All told, it comes as no great surprise that the mid eighties was a time of profound suicidal depression for the artist.

Sixteen volumes of *The Complete Crumb Comics* span thirty years of creativity; we're probably about halfway through the artist's career now, with much greatness still to come. [David Kerekes]

THE LIFE AND TIMES OF R CRUMB
Comments from Contemporaries
Ed. Monte Beauchamp

An impressive array of hip movers and shakers make up the 'contemporaries' who offer their thoughts, opinions and personal reminiscences on R Crumb, Underground artist extraordinaire. It's a formula Monte Beauchamp utilised to equally good effect in the acclaimed *Blab!*, the first edition of which had comic artists fondly recalling EC comics. For Crumb, however, Beauchamp has been able to recruit such names as Terry Gilliam, Matt Groening, Roger Ebert, and Ralph Steadman, to run alongside the appreciations of these lowly comic artist types. The entries range from a half-page to twenty pages. Don Donahoe recalls his forays into publishing Crumb's early comics, *Zap* and *Mr Natural*, and the pornographic *Snatch Comics*, "distributed in an atmosphere of secrecy and caution." Comic artist Trina Robbins reflects on how seeing the first issue of *Zap* in the sixties was an experience akin to being "born again". Her condemnation of Crumb's later work as being hostile to women earned her ostracism among fellow artists, but she stands by that claim today (she refers to Crumb's early work as "sweet", an acolade which is so limp it sorta necessitates any hostile change Crumb may have exhibited). On the other hand, Steadman reckons Crumb has "never influenced me

MAXON'S POE

$17.95 / 86pp / Cottage Classics / Word Play Inc, 1 Sutter St, San Francisco, CA 94104, USA

ALL I NEED TO KNOW ABOUT FILMMAKING I LEARNED FROM THE TOXIC AVENGER

$13.95 / pb / 336pp / ISBN 0425163571 / Berkley Boulevard 1998 / only available from Troma Studios / www.troma.com

ANTICRISTO

£29.99 / $50 / hb / 318pp / ISBN 1903254027 / FAB Press 2000 / www.fabpress.com

---

in the slightest", while Robert Armstrong, fellow musician in Crumb's band The Cheapsuit Serenaders, provides an insight into an aspect of the artist that is rarely touched upon: "his deep affinity to certain styles of music." Eric Sack, Underground art collector, discusses the rising value of Crumb's original work and laments that certain early pieces can now command prices over $50,000!

One of the most fascinating, less obituary-like, entries comes from Tom Veitch, who tears into Straight Arrow Press — the book publishing arm of *Rolling Stone* — for burning so many comic artists with their book, *A History of Underground Comix*. The author, Mark James Estren, wanted to pay everyone for using their artwork in the heavily illustrated tome (which even today remains one of the few dedicated to the subject), but the publishers refused point blank. Crumb was the exception. As Crumb had invented Underground comics, Straight Arrow Press had to play by his rules or there couldn't be a book. Outside of a few renegades — S Clay Wilson, Greg Irons and Tom Veitch — everyone else, after being plied with free booze at a 'preview party', signed releases for their work. The three protestors were told, in no uncertain terms, "Either you sign or you're out of the history of underground commix". They didn't sign.

The book, *A History of Underground Comics*, was a success and has been reprinted several times over. In it, there are two tiny pieces of art by Greg Irons, which he had failed to copyright (the publishers originally intended to use fifty-seven pages of Irons' work); Veith has one piece; Wilson has several. All lacking a copyright. [David Kerekes]

MAXON'S POE
Seven Stories and Poems by Edgar Allan Poe
Illustrated by Maxon Crumb

Part of a mini-series, it would appear, in which famous artists illustrate classic narratives. There's a volume of S Clay Wilson interpreting tales by Hans Christian Andersen, and this one, *Maxon's Poe*, being a showcase for the artistry skills of Maxon Crumb. Seven well-known works by Edgar Allan Poe provide the subject for ten twisted perspectives — a natural choice, given Maxon's affinity with the innovative author. Back in 1991, Anthony Petkovich's *Liquidator* magazine (the one and only issue) published a piece by Maxon on the nature of epilepsy, bearing the legend 'an update to *The Tell-Tale Heart*...'. Accompanying the piece were a number of Maxon's surreal cubic etchings, which incorporated gibberish languages, characters with distended limbs, and harsh pointy shapes. The drawings suited the discourse perfectly, but remained hard to look at and a little unnerving in themselves. That was the last I saw of Maxon's art until Petkovich's book, *The X Factory*, a full five years later... Here the drawings maintained a surreal edge, but the harshness had been superseded by a bolder, more confident penmanship.

And the confidence has grown, for in *Maxon's Poe* can be found the artist's best work to date.

Everybody is familiar with the seven Poe stories and poems contained herein (abridged by Cottage Classics). They are the hinge by which we can better access Maxon's world, while at the same time keeping one foot in the real world. [David Kerekes]

FILM

ALL I NEED TO KNOW ABOUT FILMMAKING I LEARNED FROM THE TOXIC AVENGER
The Shocking True Story of Troma Studios
Lloyd Kaufman & James Gunn

Troma are the independent film company responsible for dumping such charmless no-budgeters as *Bride of the Killer Nerd* and *Surf Nazis Must Die!* onto the world. Often, the most exciting thing about a Troma movie is its title. They deal almost exclusively in tasteless movies full of juvenile sight gags, shoddy effects, and a cost-cutting veneer that makes the lowliest Monogram picture sparkle in comparison. But the company hit pay dirt with *The Toxic Avenger*, a movie which played up to the 'cheapness' as if it was some kind of artistic statement. It followed the story of a hideously deformed mop-carrying superhero with a no-nonsense ultra-violent attitude towards lawbreakers. Should you be thinking Christopher Reeve and *Superman* right now, well, don't. The Toxic Avenger isn't out to save the world from any single-minded, power crazed megalomaniac — his crooks are smack heads, happy to drive repeatedly over a child for kicks, rape blind girls and shoot guide dogs. As wholesome as that might sound, *The Toxic Avenger* managed to spawn not one, but two sequels, and Toxie himself became a Marvel comicbook hero and a syndicated cartoon character for kids, with his own TV show (for which the name was changed from Toxic Avenger to Toxic *Crusader*, should any little viewers go insane and become demented vigilantes).

One of the co-founders of Troma is Lloyd Kaufman, a roving publicity package with a self-styled 'wacky' personality. One glimpse at *All I Need to Know About Filmmaking*, Kaufman's book on the story of Troma, and you'll want to throw it quickly down again, on account of his big stupid face leering right back from the cover — as it does again several times throughout the book. Bracing yourself against the 'zany' mug shots and silly asides, you might care to delve a little further and decide that the story Kaufman has to tell isn't uninteresting. Indeed, parts of it are very interesting and sometimes quite funny. Read how Kaufman's first big break into film work came via porn movies, notably *A Dirty Western* (thankfully, not in front of the camera), and an early student film of his co-starred Lynn Lowry, the ingenue who was to become a minor cult figure through her appearances in *Shivers*, *The Crazies* and *I Drink Your Blood*.

In a section discussing the making of the film *Troma's War*, Kaufman admits to being genuinely surprised that people were offended at the concept of 'The AIDS Brigade', one of the fighting teams he had scripted, and around whom a 'rape joke' had been constructed.

Troma's War is Kaufman's favourite Troma movie. *Big Gus, What's the Fuss?*, on the other hand, is one that Kaufman would rather forget. Following a conversation with a guy called Ami, who guarantees that his idea for a film will return an original investment ten-times over, Kaufman travelled to Israel to shoot *Big Gus, What's the Fuss?* This supposed 'family film', which, Kaufman recalls, concerned "a pudgy Israeli running from place to place in Tel Aviv", was filmed in both English and Hebrew, and starred people of no acting capability who in real-life refused to communicate with one another. Ami effectively hired himself as co-director but promptly disappeared when the film was over, leaving no trace of the big money backers he promised would be funding the movie. Kaufman and Troma partner Michael Herz were left broke with a film no one wanted. Their only option? To try and rent the Hebrew language print to synagogues around America. Only one synagogue actually took the film, but after screening it refused to pay the $100 rental fee, accusing Kaufman and Herz of being a "disgrace to Jews".

Beneath the kooky façade, Kaufman comes over as though he could be a likeable and conscientious kind of guy. He makes some interesting points as to why mainstream movies like *Forrest Gump* and *Pretty Woman* have a far greater corrupting influence on audiences than *Blood Sucking Freaks* (despite the latter being the one film in the Troma library that Kaufman is queasy about distributing), and he states in writing that a McDonald's restaurant which opened next door to the Troma office brought with it rats. [David Kerekes]

ANTICRISTO
The Bible of Nasty Nun Sinema & Culture
Steve Fentone

Am I dreaming? I could have sworn a big fat book devoted to sexy nuns-on-film arrived on my doorstep... Nothing bad can be said about *AntiCristo*. It's a well-researched, heav-

THE ART OF THE NASTY

£19.99 / pb / 140pp / ISBN 0953454908 / Redemption Books 1999 / Salvation Films, BCM Box 9235, London WC1N / www.salvation-films.com

All Hell breaks loose in *The Convent of Hell*, as featured in *AntiCristo*. © Art/Story: Noe & Barreiro

ily illustrated, great-looking volume aimed — and here's the important bit — squarely at an incredibly select market, with a mere 666 print run in hardback. Talk about specialist, niche and marginalia — I'm having to pinch myself as I write!

The impetus for *AntiCristo* appears to have been Ken Russell's *The Devils,* a film which author Steve Fentone (who also produces the zine dedicated to Mexican wrestling movies, *Panicos!!)* regards as the epitome "of all that is Nasty Nun Sinema". From here an obsession was born.

The main body of *AntiCristo* is comprised of an alphabetic listing of movies whose main focus is nuns. Everything from 'serious' productions (such as Norman Jewison's *Agnes of God)*, through to obscure horror (like Juan Lopez Moctezuma's *Alucarda, Hija de las Tinieblas)*, and the many soft-focus fantasies to have emerged from Europe are covered. Each entry comes with production details, alternate titles, a synopsis and Fentone's comments. Photographs for many of the entries are also included, along with promotional artwork and the occasional photo-strip comic adaptation so popular on the continent. You'll be glad to know that the cloistered life — rather, our wishful interpretation of it — lends itself nicely to porno as well, and Fentone has done a masterful job of weeding out what surely must stand as the bulk of the hardcore nun oeuvre (once again, with plenty of pictures). Strangely, nuns even find a place in Japanese porno with Oriental Sisters lapsing into erotic fevre dreams in *Seijo No Hard-Lez* (1992), and *Seijû Gakuen* (1974), whose scandalous imagery incorporates a novice urinating over an effigy of the crucified Christ.

How's about that, Borowczyk!

A supplementary section deals with movies in which nuns might only play a peripheral role, such as *Airplane!, Cannonball Run II* and *The Magic Christian*. Other sections of the book cover the depiction of nuns on stage, TV (including *The Benny Hill Show* and *Are You Being Served?)*, comics (Noe and Barreiro's fabulously blasphemous *The Convent of Hell)*, pop music (songs about nuns, by nuns, and bands with nuns in their name), multimedia (nunsploitation in the digital age), and ultimately advertising and merchandising (the Fighting Nun glove puppet and a *Flying Nun* lunchbox).

Several printers turned this job down flat. Whatever next? [David Kerekes]

Update Asking publisher Harvey Fenton about getting *AntiCristo* into print, this is what he had to say: "What a nightmare! My fondest memory of that one was a particularly splendid excuse: 'Well, you see, we do print a lot of bibles here…'" Available now in paperback.

THE ART OF THE NASTY
Nigel Wingrove & Marc Morris

Entering a video shop in this day and age is a depressing experience. Blockbuster, the McDonald's of the entertainment industry, is full of multiple copies of identikit Hollywood mindrot. Look hard and you might find a copy of *Nikita* or *Cyrano de Bergerac* lurking in a dusty corner — the tokenistic 'world cinema' section; but you'll have to fight your way through the lobotomised masses staring gormlessly at the covers of *Terminator 2* and *Home Alone* and bothering the staff with their 'I don't know what it's called or who's in it…' queries to get there.

Flashback sixteen years. There are no multiplexes, and the cinemas may be showing *Axe*, *Frauleins in Uniform* or *One on Top of the Other*. In Regent Video, my prepubescent eyes are wide with wonderment. My dad has just bought a video player and we're looking for something to watch on it. Hmmm, *The Blood Spattered Bride*, perhaps? How about *The Headless Eyes*? Maybe *I Spit On Your Grave* or *Zombie Flesh Eaters*? — they must be good, because they've been in the Top Five Most Rented Films for a good few months. Do we plump for Nazis torturing naked women or for psychotics slicing up co-eds? So many films, so little time.

The shop was just down the road from St Marie's RC Church, which I attended every Sunday. I'd end up impaled upon Satan's pitchfork just for thinking about these films, let alone for watching them. What the fuck was all this stuff? *Dracula's Virgin Lovers*? *Werewolf Woman*? *Beast of Blood*? Who made them? Where did they come from? Did the priest know about this? My dad let me see them, and the films themselves were as great as the covers. Even when they were crap they were great. *City of the Living Dead* gave me nightmares, but that was great too. (He wouldn't let me watch *Grange Hill* in case it made me violent, but that's another story…) It's hard to believe now, but in the very early eighties you could barely find a Hollywood movie in a video shop. These places were plastered wall-to-wall with porn, grindhouse trash and Eurosleaze. Hell's bells, it makes me misty-eyed just thinking about it. So please tolerate this self-indulgent interlude; I read *The Art of the Nasty* in a haze of blissful nostalgia.

Produced by Salvation Films' head honcho Nigel Wingrove, the book is fundamentally a coffee-table volume reproducing approximately 350 of the choicest covers from video's golden age in fairly arbitrary categories: 'Official Nasties' (the DPP's thirty-nine prime suspects); 'Nasties On Parole' (*Evil Dead*, *Toolbox Murders* et al, those that the DPP eventually dropped from the list); 'The Ones That Got Away' (nastier than the nasties, but never prosecuted: *Africa Addio*, *Mark of the Devil*); 'Nice And Sleazy Does It' (sexploitation and softcore rather than splatter), and finally 'The Good, The Bad And The Vomit-Inducing' (basically, every sleeve from the Wingrove archive that didn't fit into any of the other categories).

Also provided are capsule notes on each title, with some details on censor cuts and obscure trivia (did you know that *The Burning* marked the debut appearance of Holly Hunter, or that Sandra Bernhardt provided one of the voices for the dubbing of *Shogun Assassin*, or that *Pink Flamingos*, "could be obtained by sending a blank tape and some cash to Palace video and they'd send you the film by return post"?). Also included are sidebars on what was happening in the world beyond your VCR:

> *1982. Neighbourhood Watch introduced. Householders agree to look out for dodgy geezers in their area.*

I'd forgotten what video sleeve designers used to get away with in those happy-go-lucky days, and it's astonishing to witness in the VPRC-ridden 1990s just how gruesome and misogynistic video wrappers used to be: would a film called *Violation of the Bitch*, boasting the tag line, "She asked for it!" get shelf-space today? I think not. And neither do I think we'll be seeing the return of *Blood Vengeance* ("Tortured by his lust for two women!"), its cover proudly depicting a demented George (*Anthropophagous*) Eastman, meat-cleaver raised above head, about to hack up a blood-drenched nubile. Of course, the come-on covers preserved for posterity in this volume were largely what all the furore was about. Video company owners, being one part film distributor to four parts carny barker, knew that to sell any screaming shitflick the only

THE AVENGERS COMPANION
£14.99 / pb / 200pp / ISBN 1852867280 / Titan Books 1997 / titanpress@titanemail.com

BABYLON BLUE
£16.95 / pb / 188pp / ISBN 1840680024 / Creation Books 1999 / www.creationbooks.com

CHRISTOPHER WALKEN
£12.95 / $17.95 / pb / 134pp / ISBN 1871592844 / Creation 2000 / www.creationbooks.com

things you needed were a healthy disregard for Trading Standards practices and plenty of blood, breasts and sharp knives up front and visible. The films themselves were almost an afterthought. Is *Savage Terror* any good? Who the fuck cares? The cover is *great*! It's a huckster tradition as old as Christianity: sucker the rubes by using their own repressed desires against them. If you can get some good controversy going, all the better for sales. If not, invent some.

Such showmanship would eventually backfire: a Go Video promo man anonymously complaining to Mary Whitehouse that *SS Experiment Camp* was obscene may have shifted a shitheap of copies to a suddenly interested populace (who would never have seen the film if not for tabloid outrage), but the snowball effect that such tactics produced would drive his company out of business.

The Art of the Nasty is comprised mostly of visuals, but for your £20 you also get a contextual introduction by Wingrove. Grammatically dubious and a little cursory, this intro places nasty-ism over the backdrop of 1970s Britain: post-hippy, contemporaneous with punk rock, three-day weeks, riots in Brixton and Toxteth, and a world-wide desire on art's part to shock, shock, shock. All of these and more were laid to rest by Margaret Thatcher during her unprecedented stretch as leader of the country; logic went out the window, leaving the UK with the reputation of being the joke of Europe, an anally-retentive Victorian back-alley of a country — a reputation which it enjoys to this day. Your coffee table will look naked without this tome. [Anton Black]

THE AVENGERS COMPANION
Alain Carrazé & Jean-Luc Putheaud

OK I'll admit it. Most tributes (musical, literary or whatever) appeal little to me. They're an odd breed of creativity and frequently reminiscent of music appreciation classes, where the pieces (after dissection to a near molecular level) lose mystery, and you lose interest.

The Avengers Companion could have fallen into this same trap, as much is devoted to synopsising each episode. But it didn't fall. There are loads of good photographs (both B&W and colour), star interviews, plus detailed breakdowns of ten classic episodes. It's possible that die-hards will find no revelations, but for one who knows little but enjoys a lot, there's things to be learnt from looking through this stuff. Like the fact that Honor Blackman was born in 1926 and that Patrick Macnee really did come from an aristocratic background. And there's also more seductive stuff — in the section paying tribute to *Avengers* fashion, the 'feline Mrs Peel' wears a sleeveless body suit with pelvic cut-outs, while holding a tiny gun. Very cute. Homage is paid, quite rightly, primarily to Steed and Peel — theirs was the era of the greatest Avenging.

The Avengers were, and still are worth viewing, but I surprised myself by also enjoying this *Companion*. It's visually attractive, informative and you don't need to be an anorak to appreciate it. Creator of *The Avengers*, Brian Clemens described the series as a "happy pantomime of fast action and good humour", but that owners of a dirty mind would see there were "many more delights to be found". I suspect this universality may also be true of this book. Great for sixties-style Ikea coffee tables, and for nonchalantly flicking through in knee-length boots and a leather mini skirt. I'm game if you are! [Sarah Turner]

BABYLON BLUE
An Illustrated History of Adult Cinema
David Flint

One of the strange things about the "mini-flurry" (as Flint puts it) of books on the adult film industry that came out around this time is that they're actually all quite different — *Pornocopia* is a fairly academic if readable tome dealing with a lot of the moral and legal concepts surrounding porn; *The X Factory* is an enthusiastic book aimed at fans (and you can almost imagine author Anthony Petkovich drooling as he meets the stars of his fantasies, who he describes in unbridled gonzo terms); and this one's an overview and history of the industry itself, right up to the present-day fascination with Ninn-style glossy fetish fashion, with a tone pitched somewhere between the other two. Flint's clearly a fan, but he avoids dealing with the rights and wrongs of porn (possibly feeling that the ground's been covered before, or that he'd be preaching to the converted) and expresses his enthusiasm in a more restrained way than Petkovich, although occasionally passages such as the following slip through:

> ... the most astonishing close-ups and camera angles that you will ever see in any hardcore movie. When the man fucks Gabriella doggie-style, we get two remarkable shots — one from above, and the better of the two from below, offering an ultra-tight close-up of his member slamming into her, and a crystal-clear shot of her asshole. A few moments later, this is bettered by a shot of him shoving his finger up her anus, which fills the whole screen.

Whoa there! Another strange thing about these books, along with a couple of others, is that they're all British. Considering the situation — distribution of hardcore is still illegal in this country — it seems bizarre that there's so much interest here. It's similar to the situation regarding violent films: the fanzine attention paid to 'video nasties' and other restricted films often seems far out of proportion to the actual merit of most of the films themselves, the main point of interest being that these films are banned... but I digress.

Involved in the birth of *Headpress*, David Flint has since written for all sorts of publications, from Harvey Fenton's *Flesh & Blood* to his own *Divinity* and short-lived *Sexadelic*. He's an excellent and highly readable writer, mixing incisive comment with an attention to detail which is comprehensive without quite being obsessive, and an understated humour which is the perfect foil for some of the more ludicrous areas highlighted — such as *Itty Bitty Gang Bang*, a group-sex movie featuring exclusively (you guessed it) dwarves. As far as I'm aware this book was meant to come out a couple of years ago, but publication was postponed due to a police raid on Flint's home, in which his video collection and computer were confiscated; the text of *Babylon Blue* was on the hard drive. The police couldn't charge him and after six months everything was returned.

The focus of the book is well balanced, concentrating on what must be the two key areas of interest in porn history: the seventies golden age and the 'new porn generation' (Andrew Blake, Michael Ninn, Antonio Passolini etc). The interviews featured are with industry heavyweights, concentrating on directors/producers rather than on starlets and 'woodsmen' — namely Passolini, Lindsay Honey (aka Steve Perry aka Ben Dover), Jane Hamilton and David Friedman, all of whom come across as remarkably articulate and interesting individuals, especially Passolini, who turns out to be a big Throbbing Gristle fan. It's telling, too, that Passolini and Ninn were heavily influenced by British fetish fashion in putting together *Sex* and *Latex*, and Passolini regards British kinkiness as the classiest in the world. Reasons to be cheerful... The chapter on 'Fortress Britain' is one of the best pieces I've read on the lame home-grown industry (our classy kinkiness doesn't seem to translate to our movies), and there are a lot of stills and an excellent colour section, albeit no note of the films the latter stills are taken from. In short, the book's superb, and is a must-have item for anyone interested in this kind of material. One minor gripe — the price, which is surely a bit steep. [James Marriott]

Update The law concerning hardcore pornography in Britain has relaxed somewhat since this review was written.

CHRISTOPHER WALKEN
Movie Top Ten
Ed. Jack Hunter

It's been hard to approach Creation's 'Movie Top Ten' series with anything

CINE EAST
£9.95 / pb / 160pp / ISBN 0952926024 / FAB Press 1998 / www.fabpress.com

CINEMA CONTRA CINEMA
£12.99 / $17.95 / hb / 192pp / ISBN 907620750X / Fringecore 1999 / PO Box 165, 2600 Berchem 1, Belgium / www.fringecore.com

THE COMPLETE FRANKIE HOWERD
£15.95 / pb / 240pp / ISBN 1903111080 / Reynolds & Hearn 2001 / www.rhbooks.com

THE DEAD WALK
£11.99 / pb / 160pp / ISBN 095365642X / Noir Publishing 2000 / PO Box 28, Hereford, HR1 1YT / noir@macunlimited.net

DESPERATE VISIONS
£14.95 / pb / 256pp / ISBN 1871592348 / Creation Books 1996 / www.creationbooks.com

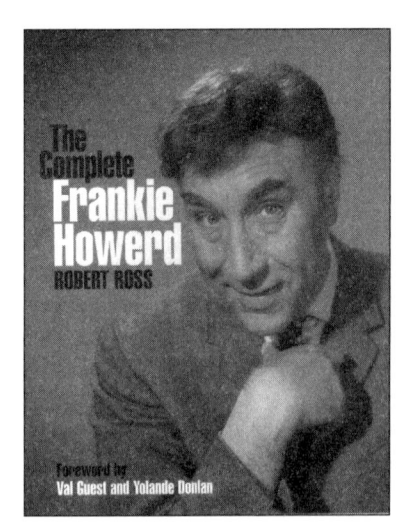

but mild contempt, especially since reading a sneeringly wonderful comment on the series in an edition of the *Midian Mailer*: "Will appeal to readers of *Neon*." In fact, it's a job to think of who would want to return to these titles again and again. The essays in *Christopher Walken: Movie Top Ten* range from nosebleed-inducing film theory to straightforward facts-and-all articles, but, generally, the same conclusions are inevitably reached on the Alien Actor. Walken is, after all, one of that select breed who can light up any old shit by simply doing nothing. The best writings jettison theory-for-theorists: James Marriott's short essay on *The Dead Zone* works as a reintroduction point for both David Cronenberg's and Stephen King's work; David Prothero and Jonathan Wright's essays — on *The Comfort of Strangers* and *Suicide Kings* respectively — balance insight with film history; whilst Richard Goodwin's piece on *Communion* offers a touch of humour in a relatively humourless book. Nice to see underrated straight-to-video flick *The Prophecy* get some recognition as well.

Of course, the problem with any 'best of' is that it creates instant dispute between writer and reader: why is there only a mention of Walken's career-starting turn in *Annie Hall* (a memorable role that acts as the set-up and pay-off to one of the film's best jokes)? And nothing on *Wild Side*, Donald Cammell's final work? Nag, nag, nag. There's a filmography and a good selection of B&W illustrations, but thirteen quid is a lot to ask for that plus ten essays of wildly varying quality.

Perhaps now is the time to kick this series into the exploitation swamp, where an army of cult actors and pin-ups await *their* turn? [Martin Jones]

Update Creation no longer list their Movie Top Ten books on their website. Harvey Keitel was one other Top Ten subject.

CINE EAST
Hong Kong Cinema Through the Looking Glass
Miles Wood

This is a fascinating look at Hong Kong cinema from an Eastern perspective, which escapes the typical concentration on martial arts, gunplay and ghost movies to give an overview of what the industry's really like. There are interviews with twelve prime movers, chosen partly for their importance within the industry (rather than their appeal to the West) and partly because they have not yet had much exposure in English language publications. Which means that unless you're a hardcore fan, most of the names here will probably not be familiar. I've only seen a handful of the movies mentioned in *Cine East*, but didn't find this, or my lack of familiarity with the interviewees, a problem. It's intriguing to get the insiders' view of how their industry works, especially as most of the interviews appear to have been conducted immediately before the 1997 handover. There are also some acute observations on other film industries, particularly Hollywood. All in all, I would have welcomed a longer introductory essay (the introduction is concise, to say the least), an endpiece describing what has happened to the HK film industry since the political handover, and possibly some colour pics. That said, I've yet to see anything bad from FAB. [James Marriott]

CINEMA CONTRA CINEMA
Jack Sargeant

Jack Sargeant writes about the true independents of cinema, for whom budget generally extends no further than the price of raw film stock or videotape. For many of these filmmakers ideas are the impetus, nothing more. Collected together in *Cinema Contra Cinema* (a terribly pretentious title) are some of Jack's most recent articles and interviews concerning the key figures in the underground's latest wave (which could be regarded as an extension of his own *Deathtripping* book — the history of the cinema of transgression). Here you have Eric Brummer talking about set-design ("You can take any space and make Hell out of it by sprinkling body parts all over the place and writing 'Hell' on the wall"); Charles Pinion on the necessity to feed your cast and crew; a discussion of mondo atrocity, *True Gore*; and a host of others. This book is not without its flaws — what is the point of the 'Ten Brief Notes and Observations' piece? — but then I can think of no other writer who's championing new indie filmmakers with the dedication and enthusiasm of Jack Sargeant. [David Kerekes]

THE COMPLETE FRANKIE HOWERD
Robert Ross

With an Introduction by stalwarts of the British film industry, Val Guest and wife, Yolande Donlan, (who say Frankie was their 'chum'), it's difficult to think who could dislike this thoroughly researched and immensely entertaining book. Though there has been a lot of material on old Lurkio over recent years, this has got to be one of the most attractive items to see light. A fantastic addition to the Reynolds & Hearn series of British film books, it should be purchased immediately... Oh, please yourself then, Missus. [Stephen Sennitt]

THE DEAD WALK
Andy Black

Back in the mid 1990s Andy Black edited *Necronomicon*, a Devon-based horror film magazine. Much has changed since then, with the mag going to book format (through a dalliance with Creation Books) and ending up on Black's own imprint, Noir Publishing. *The Dead Walk* is the third title to be released by them, an updated, revised version of an earlier book by Black concentrating on movie zombies. More of a general overview than a detailed examination, it contains chapters on the likes of George Romero and Lucio Fulci, as well as going off down roads less travelled (the sci-fi undead of *Invasion of the Body Snatchers*; the 'social' zombies of *A Clockwork Orange*). Black even manages to shoehorn in references to drug-soaked singer Roky Erickson. Straight after reading the Romero chapter I sat down and rewatched *Day of the Dead*, which must count for something.

Perhaps more importantly, *The Dead Walk* marks a huge leap in design and typesetting standards for Noir Publishing, and also sports a great cover featuring proto-industrial babe Mindy Clarke from *Return of the Living Dead 3*. [Martin Jones]

DESPERATE VISIONS 1: CAMP AMERICA
The Films of John Waters and George & Michael
Jack Stevenson

John Waters is noted as saying that it was abstract colours "jumping around" on the screen that killed the Underground. It's ironic, but to many people the idea of underground cinema *is* colours jumping around. A falsehood. Early underground practitioners had tales to tell and, indeed, aspired to emulate Hollywood mainstream in the telling of them. The most enduring works of 1960s and seventies underground have been those films that adhere to some semblance of plot. It's no coincidence that John Waters — the most popular and bankable director to emerge from this period — always stuck steadfastly to a script and allowed little space for improvisation. Waters in turn acknowledges his debt to the more personalised films of George and Mike Kuchar, who occasionally avoided a script altogether but maintained an informal narrative nonetheless. It is upon these two groups of filmmakers — Waters and the brothers Kuchar — that Jack Stevenson focuses in the first (and to date, only) volume of *Desperate Visions*, the Journal of Alternative Cinema. Stevenson conducted interviews with the principle players throughout the eighties (and which first appeared in *Pandemonium* magazine, now out of print) — a time when Waters was 'breaking through' with *Hairspray* and the Kuchars were... well, keeping a low profile and watching tornadoes, basically. Hence, there is an enthusiasm and a freshness to the conversations, aided immeasurably by Stevenson's refusal to steer matters into cut-and-dry film-related topics. The first section covers Waters — the "sultan of sleaze" — opening with a succinct appraisal of his work ("He was as much a product of his generation as Jerry Garcia but the

DVD DELIRIUM
£14.99 / $19.99 / pb / 639pp / ISBN 1903254043 /
FAB Press 2002 / www.fabpress.com

EROS IN HELL
£14.95 / pb / 228pp / ISBN 1871592933 / Creation Books 1998 / www.creationbooks.com

THE ESSENTIAL MONSTER MOVIE GUIDE
£16.99 / pb / 448pp / ISBN 1852869356 / Titan 1999 / titanpress@titanemail.com

flip side of the coin"), followed by interviews with Waters, Divine, Mink Stole, Mary Vivian Pearce and Miss Jean Hill. (The conversation with Hill — the near-on 400lb black lady who hijacks a crowded bus in *Polyester* and pursues a gang of juvenile delinquents — is conducted shortly after her appearance in *Jumbo*, a porn magazine for "chubby chasers".) The second section of the book is devoted to the Kuchars.

The Kuchar brothers made films on budgets that rarely exceeded the cost of actual film stock and development. Their films have remained for the most part, the preserve of the few. *Hold Me While I'm Naked* and *Sins Of The Fleshapoids*, possibly the best-known Kuchar films, still pale into commercial insignificance next to the works of Waters and Warhol. But the brothers have never sought that kind of exposure anyway. As Stevenson puts it in his essay 'The Day The Bronx Invaded Earth', the brothers, Mike in particular, were never motivated by "careerism". The impact they had on the Underground, however, was such that while the brothers were taking a natural transitory step up from 8mm to 16mm stock, and the better detail and clarity that provided, other filmmakers were moving from 16mm down to 8mm, having 'discovered' that Kuchar intimacy.

Lack of finance didn't mean that spectacle was out, just that it had to be done differently. Although *The Desperate And The Deep* was a drama at sea, it was set at night against a black background so that the only water necessary was cupfuls thrown at the actors intermittently, and a credit sequence shot through an aquarium.

George Kuchar also wrote and starred in Curt McDowell's *Thundercrack!*, "the world's only underground porno horror movie." Shot in stark B&W, this wordy film with its bevy of strange, rasping bisexual characters, was not a hit with the dirty mac brigade — and it was too 'dirty' for a more generalised Art audience. George describes McDowell as being mainly interested in "men's buns", but that he did also like to watch heterosexual couples humping. The one lasting image that George has of Curt McDowell, is, "him one time when we went to the North Country by the beach, and he was standing in a field with flowers with his pecker dangling out." *Thundercrack!*, which has the tag of being "the most walked-out-of movie ever", takes up much of the latter part of the book, in the guise of a very welcome career retrospective of its lead actress Marion Eaton.
[David Kerekes]

DVD DELIRIUM
The International Guide to Weird and Wonderful Films on DVD! Vol 1
Ed. Nathaniel Thompson
Simple ideas often translate into the most enjoyable books. Almost as often, these simple ideas generate unforeseen headaches. A book reviewing DVD films — what could be simpler? Well, if the book is comprised of over 600 pages of fine, eye-wrenching type, you could hazard a guess that it has gone through more than one author and has overshot its scheduled publication date several times over!

In the hands of any less conscientious publisher, the book would have been released on time but invariably half-baked. What we get with *DVD Delirium* is a good general guide to all manner of weird and not-so weird movies as found in the technological quagmire that is the DVD market. The reviews are informed and make for fine reading in themselves, while the DVD details are kept to a useful minimum — discussing picture and sound quality, extras, and pointing the reader in the best direction when there is more than one choice of the same movie available.

Through *DVD Delirium* I have learned that (a) the same extra footage for John Carpenter's *Dark Star* has been utilised by different DVD companies in different ways; (b) some people never learn and insist on forking out hard cash for Jess Franco product in whatever medium happens to come along, and, (c) curiously, nobody really seems to like Norman Jewison's *Rollerball* very much.

As with any expansive work there are going to be idiosyncrasies, but to me it seems odd that *Friday the 13th* parts one to seven are reviewed in *DVD Delirium*, yet none of the *Nightmare on Elm Street* films. Oh, and one solitary concert film — Talking Heads' *Stop Making Sense*. That said, there are hours of entertainment to be had trawling through this book. [David Kerekes]

Update The all-new *DVD Delirium Vol 2* is now available. I didn't know that the German release of *Once Upon A Time In The West*, in a wooden box, comes complete with a harmonica in a leather pouch. *DVD Delirium* — still no *Nightmare* films, but proving an indispensible series nonetheless.

EROS IN HELL
Sex, Blood and Madness in Japanese Cinema
Jack Hunter

Books dedicated to Asian cinema are rife at the moment. Most devote themselves to the subject of latter-day Hong Kong action flicks, or those films which utilise poster art that has cute girls brandishing guns and bum cheeks. The surge of popularity in these types of films means that I, for one, don't want to see them. Fortunately, there is another side to Far Eastern cinema, one that Jack Hunter explores in his book *Eros in Hell*. This is the realm of the New Wave 'pink' films, the underground films and the extreme films — alien landscapes and phantasies, often driven by the equally alien concept of a unison between sex, art, and commerce.

Eros In Hell commences with a history of Pink cinema (the Japanese equivalent of the Blue movie), the first film of which is generally considered to be Tetsuji Takechi's *Daydream* (1964), whose theme of an anaesthetised girl being molested and raped by a dentist caused the Japanese government some embarrassment when released during the Tokyo Olympics. A whole chapter is devoted to an essay by Rosemary Hawley Jarman on *Ai No Corrida* (1976), Nagisa Oshima's landmark film about two enraptured lovers whose increasingly passionate bouts of lovemaking ends with one of them dead. Jarman explains how the director initially intended the film to be hardcore porn, processing it in France so as to avoid the Japanese tradition of exercising images of genitalia. Other chapters move into darker waters, discussing the films of the prolific Hisayasu Sato (who claims he wants to drive his audience mad), the pseudo-snuff of the *Guinea Pig* series, and the appalling sounding *Death Women*, the latest in a long line of Asian 'shockumentaries'. Hunter notes that *Death Women* is comprised of "nothing but real-life studies of dead females... ranging in age from infancy upward". The footage comes from accident scenes, official sources, and actual autopsies (but autopsies in which the deceased can be dressed in pure white cotton panties). *Death Women* is currently up to volume eight as of writing, is believed to be of Taiwan origin, and has editors who remain anonymous.

You need more than one book on Asian cinema. *Eros in Hell* ought to be your other one. [David Kerekes]

THE ESSENTIAL MONSTER MOVIE GUIDE
A Century of Creature Features on Film, TV and Video
Stephen Jones

There have been many encyclopaedias devoted to horror film. This one's a little more genre specific (monsters only) but still manages to turn in a wide selection of foreign-language obscurities, some British obscurities (lacking in most US-centric guides), recent TV series (like *Poltergeist The Legacy* and *Eerie Indiana*) and plenty of movie minutiae. Hardcore porn cash-ins, sitcoms and old cartoon shows also feature. For instance, who's ever heard of the Japanese/US co-production *The King Kong Show*? This mid sixties animated series for children contains characters designed by Jack Davis, and "features the once-mighty sixty-foot ape as a 'loveable' hero who teams up with Professor Bond, his son Bobby and daughter Susan to battle evil scientist Dr Who". While episodes from *The Young Ones* ('Nasty'), *F Troop* ('V is for Vampire') and *The Muppet Show*

FILMBOOK REFERENCE GUIDE
$5 / pb / 187pp / David McDaniel, 5845 Oakland Road, Baltimore, MD 21227, USA

FLESHPOT
£14.95 / pb / 256pp / ISBN 1900486121 / Critical Vision 2000 / www.headpress.com

Bodil Joensen, star of *Animal Lover*, caught in the blinding flash bulb of immortal — if poorly paid — fame. *Fleshpot*

(starring Vincent Price) might seem a little left-field for a monster movie guide, their inclusion does liven up the proceedings. Together with it having rather more credit info than most books of this ilk (seemingly in favour of actual 'comment' at times), *The Essential Monster Movie Guide* is deserving of a place on the cineaste bookshelf. [David Kerekes]

FILMBOOK REFERENCE GUIDE
From Fantasy To Comedy
David McDaniel

Ever wonder if your collection of books on Woody Allen is complete? Or whether you've got every book on the making of *The Exorcist*? Perhaps your shelf devoted to German Expressionist cinema is still missing one elusive university press tome? If it is, you'll know about it courtesy of this little item. *Filmbook Reference Guide* is a wall-to-wall listing of books on film stars, film genres, studios, television shows… all written in that monotonous single-spaced typewriter typeface that so well qualifies a work as being (a) for research purposes only, and (b) a fan-effort. There is no attempt to 'liven-up' the presentation. Works are listed by category, such as Horror, Apes/King Kong, Villains, and so on. These can often be confusing, and works related to a specific subject may not come under the most obvious category, or may be dispersed over several categories throughout the book, i.e., you won't find *Captain Quirk: The Unauthorized Biography of William Shatner* under the *Star Trek* entries, it comes under Personalities — rightfully so, perhaps, but the fact does highlight the book's complete lack of cross-referencing. Indeed, the book lacks a lot of things. I'd like to know how McDaniel acquired his information, for one. A few words as to why he would want to undertake such a project and who it's aimed at wouldn't go amiss, either. The listings themselves are perfunctory: you get the book's title, a subtitle if applicable, the author (or editor), the publisher's name, the year and country of publication. A very primitive coding system is applied in some instances.

However, this isn't to say the book is useless. It's not definitive (such projects never can be), but, with a lot of small press, university press, and religious group publications included, I'd propose it isn't far off. (In The Omen section is a book entitled *The Antichrist: After The Omen*, published by Bible Voice. I wonder what that's about?…) It's also pretty up-to-date, with many 1997 entries [the year in which this review was written]. What's more, for a US book, it does an admirable job in its coverage of British TV shows and personalities. A quick perusal of *Filmbook Reference Guide* will undoubtedly bring to light works that are unfamiliar, and which the reader will be anxious to investigate. For this reviewer it's *London After Midnight: Reconstructed*, a 1985 effort by Philip J Riley and published by an outfit called Cornwall, which — according to McDaniel's coding — presents the complete text of this 'lost' movie in photo-captions. If I ever find it I'll let you know. [David Kerekes]

Update Have no idea how you would track down a copy of this now and I never did find that copy of *London After Midnight: Reconstructed*. According to a recent *Video Watchdog* article, the film itself is unlikely ever to come to light.

FLESHPOT
Cinema's Sexual Myth Makers & Taboo Breakers
Ed. Jack Stevenson

Even now, twenty-seven years later, I can still see myself sitting in the Mini Cinema, on 49th St and 7th Ave, just off Times Square. I was a twenty-one-year-old college senior — a veritable innocent — transfixed by grainy images on a movie screen. I was watching a chubby, though not unattractive, young woman, a 'Danish farm girl' as she'd been described, being fucked by her dog — a collie named Lassie. It was only my third porn flick, but it was definitely the most interesting yet. Unlike *Deep Throat* (which I'd seen a few months earlier and found shocking and bizarre, though hardly erotic) or *It Happened in Hollywood* (which featured a sex scene with Al Goldstein, the obese, barely functioning publisher of *Screw* magazine), *Animal Lover* was real and intimate... too real. The dog and the woman were hot for each other, familiar lovers, fucking with passion, as if there were no camera present. The woman would go on to make love, somewhat less successfully, to her pig and to her horse.

I was sent there to review *Animal Lover* for an underground newspaper, which looked upon the film as little more than a curious cultural artifact. Based on the merits of the dogfuck alone — "the most erotic scene in any of the porn movies I've seen" — my write-up was positive. Reading it today, however, I'm struck only by my naïveté. The review doesn't even come close to capturing the deranged essence of what was really happening in that film.

I hadn't thought much about *Animal Lover* since 1974. It wasn't the sort of thing that often came up in conversation, even in the pornography business, where I toiled as a magazine editor for sixteen years. Bestiality, like kiddy porn and incest, was thought crime, a taboo that, because of a wide array of censorship regulations, had been banished to the depths of my professional consciousness. That's one reason I was so taken by Jack Stevenson's essay 'Dead Famous: the Life and Movies of Cinema's Most Exploited Figure, Bodil Joensen'. Stevenson is an excellent writer, and also the editor of *Fleshpot*. His Bodil Joensen piece tapped into all kinds of long-repressed emotions. For one thing, I had no idea that *Animal Lover* was such a landmark work (to anybody but me), or that the Danish farm girl had done other bestiality films, or that she even had a name. As it turned out, she also had a life, a childhood, a mother and father. And Stevenson has apparently gone to great lengths to unearth the details of that life. What emerges is, essentially, a heartbreaking celebrity biography — the compelling story of an abused, repressed, rebellious woman who is headed only for

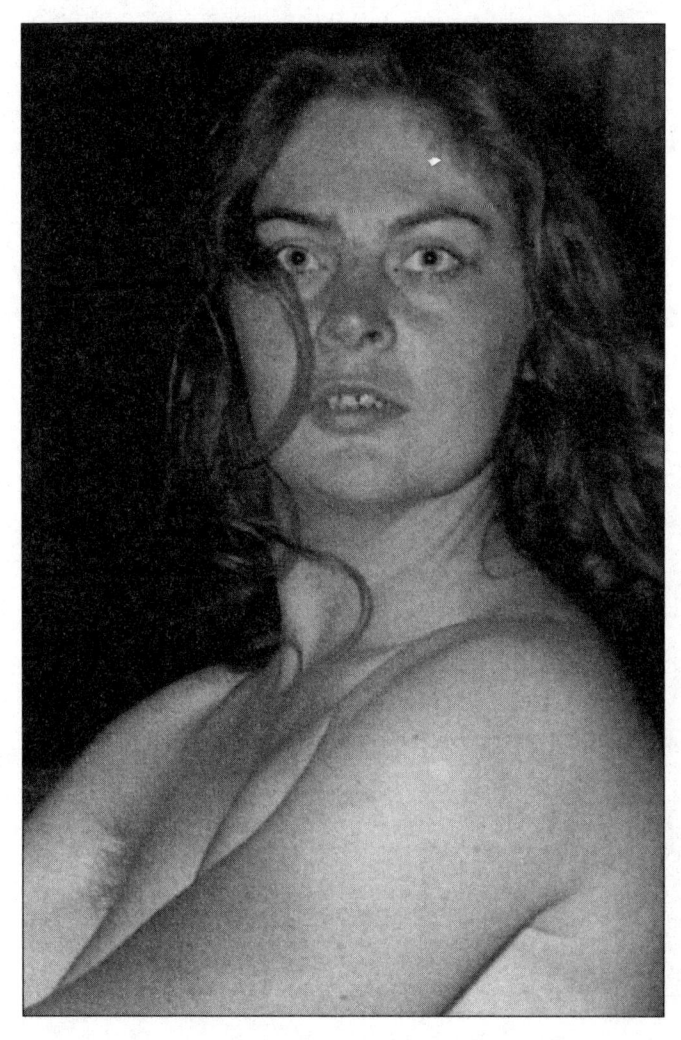

FORMER CHILD STAR
$17.95 / pb / 225pp / ISBN 155022428X / ECW 2000 / www.ecwpress.com

FRAGMENTS OF FEAR
£14.95 / pb / 284pp / ISBN 1871592356 / Creation Books 1996 / www.creationbooks.com

The half-pint cast of *Diff'rent Strokes*: Dana Plato, Gary Coleman and Todd Bridges. *Former Child Stars*

doom and degradation at the outer limits of the porn industry. 'Dead Famous' is one of the numerous high points of this curious work. Based on the highly suggestive cover graphics and the 'Adult Content' warning, one might expect *Fleshpot* to be only a history of porn movies. And in part, it is. Other Stevenson-penned chapters like 'Hardcore Circus', which describes the commotion surrounding a 1998 screening of *Deep Throat* in Norway (attended by its star, the now vehemently anti-porn Linda Lovelace) and 'Blue Movie Notes', which puts in perspective the entire history of modern pornography, were very well done. The information found in 'Blue Movie Notes' on early stag movies and America's first public porno theatres is fascinating, and not easily located in other sources. Stevenson clearly knows his material inside out. He is a porno scholar, and he has put together a densely written work of straight and queer sex-film scholarship — a college textbook, rather than an entertainment, apparently intended for other porno scholars.

Fleshpot's other contributors also know their stuff. But with the exception of David Kerekes' essay on British porn filmmaker John Lindsay, Tons May's interview with erotic actor Udo Kier, and Linda Hedihn's callow but spirited depiction of the scene in Stockholm when gangbang queen Annabel Chong came to visit, the writing tends to be dry, in an academic way that often borders on the unreadable. Also, for many of these writers, English is not their native language, and it shows in the syntactical awkwardness of their prose. I'd have much preferred a book written completely by Stevenson. And I'd have also very much preferred a larger typeface, which could have been easily achieved by eliminating some of the less compelling chapters. The microscopic typeface used was murder on my middle-aged eyes.

Fleshpot ends with a Tijuana Bible, a primitive porno comic from the thirties. In this particular story, a groupie sucks off clarinetist Benny Goodman. It was an intriguing counterpoint to Ken Burns's sanitised documentary *Jazz*, which I'd been watching religiously on public TV here in America, in between bouts of *Fleshpot*. [Robert Rosen]

Update Linda Lovelace died from injuries sustained in a car accident in April 2002; and you can find out more about Jack Stevenson's porno scholar life in his latest book from Headpress, *Land of 1000 Balconies*.

FORMER CHILD STAR
The Story of America's Least Wanted
Joal Ryan

Author Joal Ryan, a journalist who hosts a website on former child stars, traces the behind-the-scenes history of child TV stars from the fifties to the present day. A lot of these are virtual unknowns, especially to British readers (anybody remember Shavar Ross? Johnny Whitaker? Steven Mond?) — and, since these are TV and not movie stars, lots of the greatest child hasbeens are neglected. Emphasis, quite naturally, is on the tragic and talentless trinity that made up the cast of *Diff'rent Strokes* — the Unholy Three of former child stars — with *two* (count 'em) separate chapters on Gary Coleman (whose gargoyle visage also graces the book's cover), not counting the entire chapter devoted to *Diff'rent Strokes* (which, since Dana Plato took her last breath, has been a staple of cable channel Nickelodeon). But that's dead celebrities for you. *Former Child Stars* is sleazy, it's sordid, it's gossipy, and it's in very bad taste. Highly recommended. [Mikita Brottman]

FRAGMENTS OF FEAR
An Illustrated History of British Horror Fillms
Andy Boot

When was the last time you picked up a book devoted to the history of British horror movies? Certainly, there is no shortage of magazine articles and essays on the subject, nor volumes devoted to the illustrious Hammer studios, but British horror *per se*? Surprising as it may be, *Fragments of Fear* — the fifth entry into Creation's ongoing series of film genre studies — is only the second volume ever to devote itself entirely to the subject.* And for those who might be expecting a stiff-upper-lip, critical appraisal, well, thankfully, they'll be disappointed. This is an informal guide, with author Andy Boot reflecting upon little quirks and nuances in a film just as much as who might have directed what and when. For instance, he makes an issue of the frequency with which Boris Karloff lights up in *The Man Who Changed His Mind*, and how Tigon generally had "groovier soundtrack music" than other studios of the day. Chapters are given over to specific studios, such as Amicus, the aforementioned Tigon, Anglo-Amalgamated, Independent Artists, and Hammer. Other chapters focus upon individual decades and that old barnstormer himself, Tod Slaughter, who is credited here as being the first British horror film star.

Fragments of Fear takes as the first British horror a five-minute short by one Dicky Winslow, who, in 1902, cranked his camera toward a theatre company re-enacting *Maria Marten, Or Murder In The Red Barn*. The last entry is 1995's *Shallow Grave*. To give some idea of where Boot's sensibilities lie, en route he determines Cy Roth's *Fire Maidens From Outer Space* to be "possibly the worse British movie ever made", and that Ian Merrick's *The Black Panther*, based on the Leslie Whittle murder case, as the "most horrific". Because Boot has a keen eye for pulp and gothic fiction, his film history unfurls with a pleasing literary counterpoint. He also appears to have a keen musical sense, too, but unfortunately doesn't indulge himself on that particular score nearly as often. (Music on Gary Sherman's *Death Line*, for instance, was supplied in part by Will Malone, "ex-member of psych legends The Smoke and The Orange Bicycle... and a progressive legend with Motherlight". Boot also notes that two of the characters in *Death Line* are listening to "progressive rock legends Secondhand on the record player". That's the kind of info sorely lacking in *Haliwells*...)

Boot almost can't wait to get *A Clockwork Orange* out of the way so that he may tackle the likes of *The Corpse*, starring Michael Gough. Which makes for far more interesting reading — who wants capsule comments on the overly familiar? *Fragments of Fear* wisely plays to more critically maligned fare. Movies discussed with no uncertain relish include obscurities like *The Ghost of Rashomon Hall*, a 1949 picture starring Valentine Dyall (in which pro-

THE HAMMER STORY
£19.99 / pb / 190pp / ISBN 1852868767 / Titan Books / titanpress@titanemail.com

HOLLYWOOD HEX
£14.95 / pb / 201pp / ISBN 1871592852 / Creation Books 1999 / www.creationbooks.com

duction values are so poor that the hall of the title is spelled differently throughout and actors supposedly engaged in background banter in one scene can clearly be heard going "hmmmm, hurummmmm"!), and Michael Armstrong's ugly-hippy horror extravaganza *Haunted House Of Horror.* (Why does Dennis Price play a policeman who walks on and then off again? Because the producers insisted on 'writing in' a part for Boris Karloff, only he couldn't make it...)

Boot admits that he has a preference for productions made prior to and during the early seventies, and it can be no coincidence that with this era the book is at its best. When Boot actually begins to trawl beyond this period, things become a little scattershot. Though *Fragments of Fear* attempts to be a comprehensive study — an appendix offers to cover those titles missed from the main text — omissions become greater and more evident as the years roll on. Not trifling little things, either, but inexcusable stuff like the *whole* of the Norman J Warren catalogue (oh, *Inseminoid* is in there all right, but it isn't credited as being a British film...)! And there are plenty of others. Also, Boot's writing is needlessly repetitive, reiterating points not only on the same page, but often in the same paragraph and occasionally in the same sentence. Which makes for a bit of a slog.

Choice morsels are to be had in this overview, but approach *Fragments of Fear* as a selective history of British horror films and you'll enjoy it a lot more. [David Kerekes]

* The first book was David Pirie's *A Heritage of Horror.*

THE HAMMER STORY

Marcus Hearn & Alan Barnes
Is it not time again for another attempt at resurrecting Hammer? In 1994 Hollywood got serious about a remake of Hammer's *The Quartermass Xperiment* with an estimated budget pushing on for £70 million (the original film came in at 97 pence). More recently *The Devil Rides Out* has been cited as the favourite to launch a battalion of Hammer remakes. But it's a shame that this renewed interest in the British studio is down to the fact that Hollywood fears to take chances on anything new, and Hammer offers a back catalogue of increasingly popular titles ripe for picking. The last thing to emerge from Hammer was in 1984 and the final episode in the *Hammer House of Mystery and Suspense* TV series. Since then, other than two co-productions for TV (*The World of Hammer* series, and *Flesh and Blood*, a documentary), efforts to come up with anything new have been thwarted in every instance. A whole bunch of titles for pictures-never-made punctuate the latter part of the studio's productive years — pre-publicity exists for both *Nessie: Monster from the Past* and *Vampirella*, an adaptation of the Warren comicbook character. Shortly before his death, Hammer head man Michael Carreras claimed that *Vampirella* not getting made was his "greatest disappointment".

Marcus Hearn and Alan Barnes' *The Hammer Story* is possibly the definitive Hammer book. Over-sized, full-colour throughout and printed on quality stock, it makes for an immediate, visually striking impression. But the wealth of rare illustrations and the info-heavy text takes the book far beyond a mere coffee table tome. Indeed there is good reason why the authors have managed to come up with so many choice morsels: this is an *authorised* history of the studio, the first book to which Hammer have given active backing.

We learn that the only scene the BBFC objected to in the script for *The Curse of the Werewolf* was the rape of the servant girl: the half-man half-wolf beggar, determined the BBFC, couldn't have fangs. "You can have fangs or relations with the girl, but not both." As it turned out, however, when the Board got to see a print of the completed film, it was more than fangs in relationships that they objected to. They wanted a whole bunch of scenes cut — including a shot of a flaky nose, a stabbing, dialogue about children born on Christmas Day, Leon's hairy palms, Leon's transformation into a werewolf, and any killings perpetrated by the werewolf — but in the end, settled with chopping just three.

Because of budget restrictions, the entire asylum sets for *Frankenstein and the Monster from Hell* had to be squeezed onto a single stage at MGM-EMI Elstree. Not bad considering the film takes place predominantly within an asylum, adding a nice claustrophobic feel to the proceedings.

Christopher Lee begrudgingly donned his cape again for *Dracula AD 1972*, but categorically refused to utter the lines that reinvented the character as the Devil himself: "I am Dracula, Lord of Darkness, Master of the Walking Dead! I am the Curse, the Apollyon, Angel of the Destroying Furies! I am the Apocalypse!" Originally to be titled *Dracula Today*, authors Hearn and Barnes surmise that *Dracula AD 1972* "was irretrievably undermined by a perspective on youth culture that seemed a good decade behind the times".

A number of scenes intended for *Vampire Circus* had to remain unshot because time ran out on the allotted six-week shooting schedule. Director Robert Young was forced to make do with what he had and cut around the missing material.

Sixty key films are tackled in the book under their own chapters, with other chapters and sidebars devoted to directors, principal actors and actresses, the television shows (including the aborted *Tales of Frankenstein*), genres, and Hammer ephemera. Each page is a veritable treasure trove of images and facts, culled from Hammer's own files and personal correspondence. Superb. But back to those films that never got off the ground... *The Experiment*, *Vlad the Impaler*, *Kali... Bride of Dracula*, the rather wonderful sounding *Chaka Zulu — The Black Napoleon*, *To Kill a Stranger* and *The Savage Jackboot*, a war story whose poster featured Peter Cushing in Gestapo attire wielding a whip. [David Kerekes]

HOLLYWOOD HEX
Mikita Brottman

The ratio for fatalities within the film and TV industry is proportionally greater than that of, say, the police and highway construction industries. The rise in explosive, action-orientated movies in the mid 1980s saw ten fatalities on film sets with complaints of unsafe filming conditions more than doubling. In the midst of all this was *Twilight Zone: The Movie*, an arid cash-in on Rod Serling's influential TV show of the fifties, which has gained notoriety in recent years thanks to the circulation of out-take footage depicting the death of veteran actor Vic Morrow and two young extras. Comprising vignettes by Hollywood's young directorial talent, it was John Landis' tale 'Bill' that met with disaster. Fleeing enemy soldiers and under simulated artillery fire, the story required Morrow's character to rescue two Vietnamese children as around him a village exploded and above a helicopter whirred. The crew was tired from three straight weeks of filming and Landis was under pressure to call it a wrap. With multiple cameras rolling, Morrow started out across a shallow river, plucking the children from the water. The detonation of the first of the explosives created an unexpected dirt-cloud, and the heat was enough to force the nearby camera team backwards, leaving their equipment. The subsequent barrage of explosions occurred directly under the helicopter and knocked it out of the sky.

Shocked and confused, Landis couldn't understand why the helicopter was suddenly in his shot. Seconds later it became clear that Morrow and the children were dead. The footage was confiscated for investigation and used as evidence in a trial that ultimately cleared the director.

The story is a chilling one, and author Mikita Brottman uses it to help construct *Hollywood Hex*, a fascinating account of murder and misadventure in Tinseltown. On this literary death trip are the supposed 'cursed' movies *The Exorcist* and the *Poltergeist* series, around which cast and crew members dropped dead with rumour-inspiring regularity. Also included are the mystical connotations of Brandon Lee's *The Crow*, and the less familiar John Schlesinger film *The Believers*, which has been

HOLLYWOOD RAT RACE
£10 / pb /138pp / ISBN 156858119X / Four Walls Eight Windows 1999 / www.4w8w.com

IF I'M SO FAMOUS, HOW COME NOBODY'S EVER HEARD OF ME?
£11.99 / pb / 223pp / ISBN 0878164758 / Kitchen Sink Press 1996/ www.deniskitchen.com

ILSA CHRONICLES
£10 / $15 / pb / 60pp / Midnight Media 2000 / PO Box 211, Huntingdon, PE18 8WD, England / paul@midnight-media.demon.co.uk / www.midnight-media.demon.co.uk

Of all the publicity material for the *Ilsa* films — most all of it except this particular one being reproduced in *Ilsa Chronicles* — 'Who's That Woman With Hitler?' is the weirdest and most provocative.

adopted by the Mexican Matamoros cult as a 'training model' for initiates (who are required to view the film fourteen times).

Regular readers of *Headpress* and those familiar with Creation's back catalogue will recognise some of the material included in *Hollywood Hex*. Don't be put off, as much fresh ground is covered in what is an unashamedly esoteric film book with a very entertaining premise. [David Kerekes]

HOLLYWOOD RAT RACE
Ed Wood Jr

You must act! You must! You must! You must!

But how?

Ed Wood spent most of the 1960s working on this (previously-unreleased) book in answer to the most potent of all questions posed by young Hollywood hopefuls: "How can I make it in showbiz?" It's an odd concept — Wood advising starlets on how to learn their craft and perfect their art — and remarkably conservative advice from a man whose own career appeared to rely more on charm and cheek than thoroughness and perfection. Wood's reputation as the worst director of all time simply can't be discarded when reading *Hollywood Rat Race*, to the extent that it's impossible to read as the self-help manual Wood had intended. However, as a glimpse into the character of this fascinatingly and obliviously confident man, this book is great. The prose could have been written by a seventeen-year-old, and at times is compellingly banal. He contradicts, illuminates, amuses, and repeats the same advice over and over (don't pay for your own screen test, do get an agent, do get professional photographs printed, don't pay for your screen test...). Not surprisingly, there are frequent references to angora sweaters. Sadly they are mainly worn by starlets. Utterly priceless. [Sarah Turner]

IF I'M SO FAMOUS, HOW COME NOBODY'S EVER HEARD OF ME?
Jewel Shepard

She is sixteen and in Hollywood trying to make it as an actress. She's quite pretty and comes over as fairly bright, but her youthful naivety ensures that she falls into the same traps as countless others before her. OK, so she does eventually make it to the top in the heady world of B-movie starlet-dom, but it really could have been anybody else — Jewel Shepard just happened to have all the right curves and be in the right place at the right time. Her first acting role is a two-line bit-part in *The Junkyard*, a sequel to the original *Gone In Sixty Seconds*, starring Toby Halicki (that's right, *the* Toby Halicki). Her most famous movie probably remains *The Return of the Living Dead*. First, however, she has the soul-destroying day-to-day rigmarole of looking for work, calling agents, posing semi-naked in car magazines, before eventually turning to stripping to pay the rent. This is where the book becomes interesting. Jewel is not particularly enamoured with the business of taking clothes off for strangers for money, but neither does she denigrate the job or come across as superior. (Which might prove difficult anyway, coming after the photo on page 127 in which an almost naked Jewel is seen on all-fours, head bowed in front of a crumpled dollar bill that someone has thrown onto the stage.) Indeed, she relates some great inside stories and her memories are for the most part fond ones. For instance, when stripping, be sure to choose appropriate music as opposed to songs you yourself might like. One of Jewel's 'themes' is the Vietnam War, dressed in fatigues, dancing to White Rabbit. Many dancers simply fall for '"mellow" seventies shit' like Neil Diamond's Forever In Blue Jeans.

In no particular order, here are some other facets of strip life, as related in Jewel's book…

Many clubs would put what are known as 'chuggers' on the bottom of a bill, girls who make up the numbers. These 'strippers' would invariably be alcoholics or drug addicts, not dancers; their idea of dancing would be to stand in the middle of the stage and 'chug' their arms, like a train, in time to the music.

The more money the clubs made, the greedier they got. Sometimes it would develop into shootings on the street, with one club trying to encroach on another's territory.

Management, seemingly oblivious to the fact that most men worked during the day, would set about trying to bolster daytime business. Discounts on hamburgers being the obvious choice…

Witty and articulate, Jewel breaks the B-movie bimbette stereotype. She could have taken the easy route and told an 'everything is wonderful' story of her life. But the most glamorous thing in this tale are the posed photographs. *Glamour?!* It's a story that opens and closes in the Philippines on the set of a Cirio H Santiago women-in-prison movie, fer crying out loud! [David Kerekes]

ILSA CHRONICLES
Darrin Venticinque & Tristan Thompson

Tristan Thompson, in his introduction, asks of *Ilsa She Wolf of the SS*: "A revolutionary piece of filmmaking? Certainly not! This is sheer unadulterated *exploitation*."

Earning the accolade of being perhaps the most repellent film ever committed to celluloid, *She Wolf* follows the exploits of a sadistic, sex-mad female SS officer (called Ilsa) who overseas the experiments conducted on human guinea pigs in Medical Camp 9. Made in 1974, its director was Don Edmonds, and its producer, Dave Friedman, only recently owned up to having any involvement. Given that the illustrious Friedman has put his name to all kinds of dodgy crap over the past several decades (including *Love Camp 7*, an earlier Nazi Camp effort), his use of a *nom de plume* on *She Wolf* can be taken as a mark of the film's overt tastelessness and depravity.

She Wolf has little by way of a plot, but revels in scenes depicting the (beautiful and handsome) prisoners of the camp being tortured: having their toenails removed with pliers; being penetrated with huge, electrically charged dildos (in order to measure female resistance to pain); dipped into scalding hot water; castrated; and infected with new, virulent strains of typhus. The special makeup effects of Joe Blasco are suitably disgusting, and they make for an interesting counterpoint to the film's use of full-frontal nudity and the rampant sexuality of Ilsa her-

**IT CAME FROM
BOB'S BASEMENT**
$24.95 / pb / 144pp / ISBN 0811825728 / Chronicle Books 2000 / www.chroniclebooks.com

JAMES BIDGOOD
£25 / 175pp / ISBN 3822874272 / Taschen 1999 / www.taschen.com

**KEEPING THE
BRITISH END UP**
£15.95 / pb / 239pp / ISBN 1903111218 / Reynolds & Hearn 2001 / 61a Priory Road, Kew Gardens, Richmond, Surrey, TW9 3DH / www.rhbooks.com

MARS ATTACKS!
£17.99 / pb / 158pp / ISBN 0345409981 / Del Rey 1996 / www.randomhouse.com

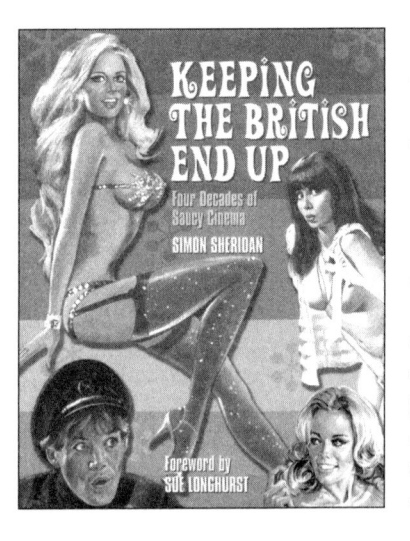

self, who shows as little mercy to her lovers as she does the victims who pass through her laboratory. And it's because of Ilsa — or rather, Dyanne Thorne, the actress who portrays her — that *She Wolf* has managed to elevate itself to being more than just a cinematic anomaly. Unlike most other Nazi Camp films, part of a cycle that quickly dropped from favour in the seventies, *She Wolf* has gained a sizeable cult following and has spawned several sequels (its box office return is estimated to be in excess of $10M). Even though Ilsa is killed at the end of *She Wolf*, Thorne's popularity ensured that she return the following year as harem keeper to a ruthless oil baron in *Ilsa, Harem Keeper of the Oil Shieks*; as a Colonel in charge of a Siberian prison camp in *Ilsa The Tigress of Siberia* (1977); and as *Greta the Mad Butcher* (1977), an unofficial entry in the series in which Thorne plays the brutal doctor of a clinic that supposedly treats sexual deviations in women.

Ilsa Chronicles covers all of these films in-depth and features an interview with Dyanne Thorne. The overall quality and wealth of full-colour illos are impeccible so I'm not sure why Midnight Media adopted a magazine format. *Ilsa Chronicles* would have lent itself nicely to a bound-book treatment. [David Kerekes]

**IT CAME FROM
BOB'S BASEMENT**
Bob Burns with John Michilig
Bob Burns is the high grade junk collector *par excellence*! This is a massive, luxurious book full of photos of monsters from movies and TV representing a lifetime of dedicated hoarding. Burns is the actual owner of such esoteric items

as Lily Munster's dress, a tunic from *The Mole People*, Glenn Strange's Frankenstein boots, the remote mind control creature from *It Conquered the World,* Paul Blaisdell's concept artwork for that awful Tobonga tree creature which featured in *From Hell It Came*, and loads of other items even more mind-blowingly weird! Of special interest to me is the gorilla suit section, which finally puts to rest the notion that I must have dreamed about a Saturday morning show called *Ghostbusters* featuring an aged Forest Tucker, some Hispanic guy in a zoot suit and a moth-eaten 'gorilla' which nobody else ever seems to remember! Thoughroughly good fun and totally edyoocashional. [Stephen Sennitt]

JAMES BIDGOOD
Bruce Benderson
Anyone remember 'The most infamous and Erotic Gay film of all time' shot by 'Anonymous' and featuring the first ejaculation shot to be given an 18 certificate? No? Can't say I'm surprised.

The film in question is *Pink Narcissus*, and the 'Anonymous' no other than Mr James Bidgood.

Bidgood spent six-and-a-half-years (1964–1970) filming this homage to the young male body, only to have his footage taken away from him before he'd finished shooting and — in his own words — "ruined" in the final editing.

The film was finally released in 1971. (A remastered version was released for video in 1994.) Bidgood was furious and disappointed with the end result and refused to allow his name to be connected to the film in any way, hence the 'Anonymous' credit. Then in 1985 after the death of his partner, Bidgood fell into a deep depression and destroyed all his prints and sketches from *Pink Narcissus*.

Luckily he kept the still shots and many of these are included in this volume, along with sessions from his physique photographer days. The detail in his photography is quite astonishing, and obviously a big influence on the likes of Pierre et Gilles. Without the help of digital technology, each set, each costume, each camp scenario is designed to the finest detail and caught on camera in the comfort of his own apartment.

This book takes us through Bidgood's career, notably his work for *The Young Physique*, *Muscleboy*, *Demi-Gods*, *Muscle Teens* and other magazines; his 'off-Broadway' performances and drag performances at the infamous Club 82; his first meeting with the seriously cute Bobby Kendall in 1962 who "Had the look of a deer caught in headlights", and right through the making of *Pink Narcissus*.

Unfortunately, due to his depression, very little new Bidgood work has been realised. But he is presently working on a biographical film, *FAG: The Pretty Good Life of Jimmy Bundle*, the release of which I await with baited breath. [Rick Cavaney]

KEEPING THE BRITISH END UP
Four Decades of Saucy Cinema
Simon Sheridan

Simon Sheridan is the author of *Come Play with Me*, an excellent book about tragic British porn queen Mary Millington published back in 1999. He follows close suit with *Keeping the British End Up*, but broadens the workspace to cover not only Millington's forays into film but everything else in the limp oeuvre of British sex cinema. Between an informative history lesson and a Who's Who of the British sex industry is the meat of the book: a run-down of every sex movie to come out of Britain between the years 1958 and 1983 — the point at which the whole British film industry came to a virtual standstill, thanks in part to government funding being axed.

Accompanying the movie reviews are many pictures indicative of the British sex film: blokes in silly outfits, flashing hairy bottoms and sporting cheeky expressions. Meant to be funny — and perhaps even erotic or sexy! — these pictures come over instead as relentlessly tragic.

The reviews themselves however are pithy, knowledgeable, give cast and credit details, and are peppered with the occasional interview.

The subject of British sex films has been tackled elsewhere, no less by David McGillivray in his book, *Doing Rude Things*, and while Sheridan merely expands on this particular tome, he devotes enough time, space and energy to make *Keeping the British End Up* the last word. (Damn, I didn't manage one smutty innuendo. Must try harder.) [David Kerekes]

MARS ATTACKS!
The Art of the Movie
Karen B Jones

Tim Burton's bio-pic, *Ed Wood*, brought the thrill to cinema-going back for me. I hadn't been that excited in anticipation of a movie for years. When it became clear that it wasn't going to get a major release, and that not even the local rep cinema was going to bother, the must-see factor went up several notches to reach almost sexual pitch. *Ed Wood* — an affectionate and rose-tinted movie about the crown prince of bad movies, who had a love-affair with ladies' underwear, and which was shot in B&W. How would that work? It would work because it was directed by Tim Burton. And when eventually I did get to see it, I wasn't disappointed — grinning like an idiot throughout one of the limited midday screenings at the local Odeon.

A couple of years later and I'm getting that same buzz again in anticipation of *Mars Attacks!*, the new Burton movie.

It's safe to assume that *Mars Attacks!* won't suffer the same, limited-run fate as Burton's earlier film. The lavish, full-colour book before me is testament to that.

Mars Attacks! The Art of the Movie is a chaser for the film to come, with storyboard sketches, photos on-set and behind-the-scenes, special effects work and costume design. Not too stimulating in itself, perhaps, but Karen Jones manages to pull it all off painlessly enough. My favourite chapter is devoted to the history of the 1950s Topps bubblegum cards that inspired the movie. Norm Saunders, one of the two artists involved, was in his sixties when he took to producing the set. Considered unsuitable for children by the press, the cards had to be withdrawn by Topps almost immediately. The funny thing is — particularly when considering their massive international cult status today — the cards were never distributed nationally, they only made it to the East Coast.

Also of interest is the fact that many months of preparation and work went into creating life-size stop-motion Martians for the movie... only for them to be dropped

MOONCHILD
£11.95 / pb / 128pp / ISBN 1840680296 / Creation Books 2002 / www.creationbooks.com

NAKED LENS
£12.95 / pb / ISBN 1871592674 / Creation 1997 / www.creationbooks.com

at the eleventh hour when it was thought that computer-generated animation might be less time consuming. The decision to make *Mars Attacks!* an all-star extravaganza came about because of the disaster movies of the seventies, particularly *The Towering Inferno*, whose 'Robert Wagner in flames' scene is a personal favourite of Burton's. Another favourite and influence, we discover, was the madcap comedy, *It's a Mad Mad Mad Mad World*. I love *Mad Mad World*.

Mars Attacks! I can't wait. [David Kerekes]

Update I thoroughly enjoyed *Mars Attacks!* when eventually it did arrive. But, curiously, as with several of Burton's recent movies, I still came away thinking I would never want to sit through it again.

MOONCHILD: THE FILMS OF KENNETH ANGER
Persistence of Vision Vol I
Ed. Jack Hunter

Kenneth Anger, underground filmmaker, author of *Hollywood Babylon*, occultist and *éminence grise* behind The Rolling Stones in their Sympathy for the Devil phase, Charles Manson associate Bobby Beausoleil and Led Zeppelin's Jimmy Page, is finally accorded some long-overdue critical attention in this new publication from premier alternative film press Creation Books. Editor Jack Hunter's previous books include *Eros in Hell* and *Inside Teradome*, both also from Creation. Other contributors include *Headpress'* own Mikita Brottman (who wrote the introduction), Carel Rewe and Anna Powell.

Anger's considerable reputation as a filmmaker rests on a remarkably slender body of work, the six short films of the so-called *Magick Lantern Cycle* — *Fireworks*, *Eaux d'Artifice*, *Inauguration of the Pleasure Dome*, *Scorpio Rising*, *Invocation of My Demon Brother*, and *Lucifer Rising*. The longest of these, *Inauguration of the Pleasure Dome*, is only about forty minutes, the shortest, *Invocation of My Demon Brother*, a mere eleven minutes... one hell of an eleven minutes, though — a sulphurous phantasmagoria of black magic, swastikas, Hell's Angels, stock footage from the Vietnam war, soon-to-be convicted murderer Bobby Beausoleil, Anton LaVey, The Rolling Stones in Hyde Park, and a truly head-fucking Moog soundtrack by Mick Jagger. This is the scariest of Anger's films by far, but they are all memorable in their own ways. Anger once said, 'Making a movie is casting a spell,' and he has evidently approached the screenings of his films as rituals in themselves, often recutting and augmenting the films so that no one screening is quite like any other. Free of dialogue, packed with occult symbolism, exquisite, decadent and swooningly homoerotic, Anger's films have been deeply influential in their use of colour, rhythmic cutting, montage, postmodern 'appropriation' of stock footage and clips from other films, and their pop soundtracks. This last has caused Anger to be dubbed the 'Godfather of MTV', and certainly some of his films have the vigour and impact of rock videos. *Scorpio Rising* (1963), the prime example of this tendency, was described by Anger as 'Thanatos in chrome and black leather and bursting jeans' and features several of the best pop singles of the early sixties — He's A Rebel, Wipeout, Blue Velvet.

The first section of *Moonchild*, 'Blue Velvet' by Carel Rewe, examines Anger's use of symbolism, both magical and otherwise, with special reference to *Lucifer Rising* and *Scorpio Rising*. The former has had a particularly vexed production history — all the original footage was stolen by Bobby Beausoleil and buried in Death Valley, according to Anger. Beausoleil says Anger destroyed it himself in a fit of pique. Remaking the film took most of the seventies, and the new version features a drugged-out Marianne Faithfull as Lilith, *Performance* co-director Donald Cammell as Osiris and a hypnotic soundtrack composed and recorded by Bobby Beausoleil in prison (this replaced an earlier soundtrack by Jimmy Page). *Scorpio Rising*, meanwhile, is arguably his most successful and complete film, though less overtly magical than some, being chiefly concerned with Anger's taste for rough trade in the form of preening teenage bikers and their gleaming choppers (actually full-dress Harleys, but let's not split hairs).

The second part, Anna Powell's 'A Torch for Lucifer', is more particularly focused on Anger's occultism, in particular on his devotion to Aleister Crowley. Every film in the *Magick Lantern Cycle* except *Eaux d'Artifice* is examined in turn. *Eaux d'Artifice*, incidentally, was filmed in the famous water gardens at Tivoli created by the Cardinal d'Estes, according to Anger, as an ode to watersports:

> the whole garden is actually a private dirty joke... everything is pissing on everything else and it's like inexhaustible piss. There are sphinxes pissing out of their tits, which I think is wonderful.

Moonchild is rounded out with a filmography, a chronology, a bibliography and an index, making it a useful reference volume rather than just a collection of essays. The wide margins created by the unusual square format of the book are also put to good use, being filled with notes, small photos and sidebar articles about such important background figures as Sergei Eisenstein, Maya Deren, Aleister Crowley and Jack Smith, the director of *Flaming Creatures*.

OK, enough praise, here's some moans — the Teutonic cult site used as a location in *Lucifer Rising* is called the 'Exersteine' by one author, the 'Exernsteine' by another, but no one actually gets it right and calls it the Externsteine! Much more seriously, the otherwise detailed and exhaustive filmography by Jack Hunter unaccountably omits a plot synopsis for *Lucifer Rising* — every other film gets one, so surely some mistake? And although *Moonchild* contains a rich array of images from Anger's films, some luxuriantly spread over two full pages, I was a bit sad that the budget didn't stretch to full colour throughout, or a least a colour section. The colour of Anger's films is so opulent, and often so symbolically significant, that B&W stills don't really do them justice. It's worth pointing out, though, that both paper quality and picture resolution is far superior to those found in Creation's 'regular' film titles, which range from indifferent to appalling.

These quibbles aside, I really can't think why anyone with an interest in the enigmatic and fascinating (if undeniably rather sinister) Mr Anger wouldn't want this book. One thing to note, though, is that *Moonchild* is not intended as a biography of Anger — for that, interested parties are referred to *Anger* by Bill Landis (HarperCollins, 1995), which as you might expect is full of scintillating information. For instance, we learn that Anger's real name isn't Anger (duh) but Kenneth Wilbur Anglemeyer — his adoption of the name Anger makes him the spiritual ancestor of Richard Hell, Johnny Rotten and Sid Vicious. He allegedly appeared as the Changeling Prince in Max Reinhardt's 1935 production of *A Midsummer Night's Dream*, though some have cast doubt on this assertion. And he had the word 'lucifer' tattooed right across his chest. Rock and roll! Anger is reportedly not too happy with Landis' unauthorised book, presumably because it contains too much unhappy truth — an ironic position for the author of those masterpieces of muckraking, the *Hollywood Babylon* books, to find himself in. [Simon Collins]

NAKED LENS
Beat Cinema
Jack Sargeant

The notion of Beat cinema, for a lot of people, but me in particular, will be Jack Kerouac set to pictures. Of course, such a notion wouldn't be very accurate. According to Jack Sargeant's book *Naked Lens*, for instance, the parameters of 'Beat' are continually being renegotiated and redefined, aesthetically, philosophically, socio-politically and spiritually. (The parameters don't stop there, either, but there isn't room to list them all.) Indeed, it might be argued that Beat cinema, by its own definitions, covers an awful lot of ground. Ground the size of half the movies ever made. Definitions not withstanding, *Naked Lens* manages to narrow the field somewhat and get a grip — it discusses works

OFFENSIVE FILMS

£44 / $67.95 / hb / 224pp / ISBN 031330033X / Greenwood Press 1997 / www.greenwood.com / Greenwood Publishing Group, 88 Post Road West, Box 5007, Westport, CT 06881-5007, USA / customer-service@greenwood.com

PASS THE MARMALADE

1999 / Contact the author for details: 34 Wild Street, Derby, DE1 1GN, UK / www.british-horror.fsnet.co.uk/index.html

PLANET OF THE APES

$17.95 / pb / 178pp / ISBN 1550224468 / ECW 2001 / www.ecwpress.com

THE PLANET OF THE APES CHRONICLES

£9.99 / $15.95 / pb / 174pp / ISBN 0859653129 / Plexus 2001 / www.plexusbooks.com

PORN KING

$19.95 / pb / 192pp / ISBN 1880047691 / Johnny Wadd Publications 1998 / 8200 Montgomery Blvd. NE Suite 210, Albuquerque, New Mexico USA

such as *Chappaqua* and *Tales of Ordinary Madness*, and interviews people like Allen Ginsberg and Brion Gysin. I may be mistaken, but despite it all, I think Jack sees Kerouac set to pictures, too. [David Kerekes]

OFFENSIVE FILMS
Towards an Anthropology of Cinéma Vomitif
Mikita Brottman

This book sets out to do two things: analyse cinematic forms and traditions through several decades of supposed 'disposable' films, i.e. films which fall outside the canon of most mainstream reference works, and also to show that these films are deserving of critical readings. The movies included in *Offensive Films* were produced foremost as commercial ventures, "designed to stir up cheap publicity by disgusting and exciting the gullible rubes." Don't expect to find experimental art-house films and deliberately resistant films (such as *A Clockwork Orange*) here, instead the book devotes chapters to the likes of *Blood Feast*, *Cannibal Holocaust*, and *Snuff* — several of the author's own self-confessed favourites in the arena of neglected cinema.

Offensive Films doesn't seek to chronicle the history of exploitation cinema. In analysing these key movies, Mikita Brottman comes at the whole genus on a much more guttural level. Literally. "I am interested in films," says Mikita in her introduction, "that can be understood as symptoms of a nervous disorder, revealing themselves to be part of the *unconscious* of mainstream cinema..." This takes the casual gore-hound into some rather unfamiliar territory; the rest of you will relish notions of film being "a kind of carnivalesque folk theatre", as the book prepares to examine, say, the function of laughter in *Death Scenes*.

Fortunately, Mikita suffers no delusions about the makers of these low-budget pictures having some great deep-rooted plan. They wanted to make money, pure and simple. Were William Castle to be told that *The Tingler* had parallels with Tibetan tulpa and African forms of animal double, I'm sure if he thought it'd help to sell two more tickets, he'd happily agree. The ideas in *Offensive Films* aren't presented as intentional motivating forces in the films themselves, but rather, as springboards for investigation and dissection. [David Kerekes]

PASS THE MARMALADE
A Comprehensive Catalogue of British Horror movies
Darrell Buxton

Beneath its cheap'n'cheerful print job exterior (straightforward layout; no images; slide binder spine), *Pass the Marmalade* sets out to document every genre related film production to have emerged from Britain, which it does with a fair quota of curios and surprises. Did you know that eight versions of *Scrooge* have emanated from British shores down the years, or before the end of the 1920s seven versions of *Faust* had been made (one adaptation of which — dated 1898 — is promoted here as possibly the first British horror film*)?

As well as full-length features and shorts (several being independents, distributed by mail-order only), a section entitled 'Problem/Borderline Films' collates those titles about which little is known, which may or may not have had British production involvement, or aren't genre films at all but do have horror references. Hence the inclusion of TV sitcom *Please, Sir!* (because of a brief 'werewolf' gag), *Prehistoric Peeps* (silent fantasy with a giant and an apeman), and *Eskimo Nell* (because of a character supposedly based on Tigon chief Tony Tenser, and a poster for the fictitious movie 'Vampire Vomit' on a wall).

Darrell Buxton makes no apologies for this being a no-nonsense reference tool, but I can't help thinking it would have been that much better with more annotations and some consistency in the write-ups for the entries. Why, for instance, does *A Clockwork Orange* get a comparatively lengthy synopsis and *Shallow Grave* none at all? Nevertheless, a useful source and one that stands for the moment as 'definitive'. [David Kerekes]

* This is in contradiction to Andy Boot's *Fragments of Fear* which credits a 1902 re-enactment of *Maria Marten, Or Murder In The Red Barn*, as the first British horror film.

Update Pass The Marmalade has since transmogrified to the internet, which better suits such a reference work as this. Of the original, self-published hardcopy version, printed in January 1999, Darrell Buxton states that only 100 copies were made available.

PLANET OF THE APES
An Unofficial Companion
David Hofstede

THE PLANET OF THE APES CHRONICLES
Paul A Woods

These two books were redundant the minute Tim Burton's 're-imagining' of the *Planet of the Apes* movie hit the screens. Being unofficial companions, the authors can do no more than speculate on what the multi-million dollar movie might bring to the *Apes* timeline — a facet which dates the books badly. Even more detrimental: the movie turned out to be awful.

It's very plausible that both books have since been swept off bookstore shelves everywhere and pulped for the inevitable *Matrix 2* tie-in, but Paul Woods' effort — *The Planet of the Apes Chronicles* — is probably not really deserving of such a fate. It is certainly the better of the two books, digging deep into the whole *Apes* myth, beginning with an overview of Pierre Boulle's novel on which the series is based (including an interview with Boulle dating back to 1972), and encompassing many intelligent articles and titbits (I didn't know that Rod Serling tried for several years back in the sixties to adapt the book for the screen).

Hofstede's book on the other hand — *An Unofficial Companion* — is completely forgettable. It's written with a profusion of bullet points, a great big type face, and is almost entirely anecdotal, containing chapters with headings like 'Whatever Happened To...' It also has a bunch of photographs of *Apes* superfans standing in their favourite *Apes* locations. [David Kerekes]

PORN KING
The John Holmes Story
John C Holmes, with Laurie Holmes & Fred E Basten

John Holmes falls into the same category as freak shows and movie special effects, in as much as most people would not admit wanting to look at the former, but do, and love the wide-screen spectacle of the latter. But as with the now popular 'freak', Holmes was just human like us all, while at the same time being unlike most. This of course caused his fame and fall. On one level he served as shock value and on another as a tool (pun intended) for many a voyeuristic, vicarious fucking.

The first chapter in *Porn King* gives the story of his days at UCLA as student, art class model and eventually his introduction into the world

THE PSYCHOTRONIC VIDEO GUIDE

£19.99 / pb / 646pp / ISBN 1852867701 / Titan Books 1997 / titanpress@titanemail.com

THE SATANIC SCREEN

£14.95 $19.95 / pb / 246pp / ISBN 1840580431 / Creation Books 2001 / www.creationbooks.com

of stag film loops. In subsequent chapters we learn of his childhood — starting in rural Ohio — his lack of a positive father figure, and his closer relationship to his mother and three siblings. The book, not being an in-depth objective biography, skims over much of his life in the service and at UCLA. It could be termed an insider's overview of the porn industry from the late sixties onward.

According to the book, Holmes wanted to set the record straight and separate fact from fallacy in the last years of his life, which was cut short at age forty-three by his contraction of the HIV/AIDS virus. He does go into more detail and explanation about his involvement in the mysterious bludgeoning deaths of four people on Wonderland Avenue on July 1, 1981. Also his battle with cocaine addiction and finding the love of his life and wife, former porn actress Misty Dawn (Laurie Holmes). In fact, most of the slim book is about the events leading up to the murders and his life thereafter. In an interview for *Hustler* (Vol 9 No 12 June '83), with his then 'autobiographer' Barbara Wilkins, given while incarcerated for 110 days in a LA County jail, he told the same tale of being caught between a wealthy freebasing nightclub owner and a gang of drug-dealing junkies. In the same interview he answers questions about his life in jail which he only mentions in passing in the book.

This is not *Boogie Nights*, a movie whose soundtrack could serve as a late night info-mercial for seventies and eighties wallpaper music. A more 'documentary' film — although certainly not objective — is *Exhausted* (1981), the last movie he made before the murders, which Holmes himself has admitted was made when he was at his lowest point. In it we see an at times jittery, sweating, uneasy Holmes being interviewed by someone off-camera. This is sandwiched between film clips from his movies, 'person on the street' interviews, and behind the scene looks at porno shoots. He went on to make more movies in the eighties, even after he found out about his HIV-positive status, according to Holmes himself. But also making the point that none of the actresses he worked with came down with the disease. He also tried, unsuccessfully at the time, to get mandatory HIV tests for the actors in the porn industry. He and his wife both cast aspersions toward the government as to the source of his getting the disease. Ms Holmes, in the epilogue, sets the rumours straight that her husband did not get the virus from using dirty needles — which makes sense since he talks of freebasing cocaine throughout the book.

Porn King also contains a partial filmography, listing the main body of his work on film and video (1969–1997), a body of work which, according to the blurb on the back cover, contains some 2200-plus productions.

Nobody can really judge whether Holmes is guilty or innocent of the murders, because we were not there and those that were are not talking. But I doubt one person could subdue four others while beating another to death. The man, the myth, the legend — read the book, see the movie. [Tom Brinkmann]

Update This book is now out of print, and both the publishers listed here and on Amazon sound pretty dodgy so your best bet will be a second-hand copy.

THE PSYCHOTRONIC VIDEO GUIDE
Michael J Weldon

It's nothing short of amazing that books consisting solely of capsule movie reviews continue to appear, year-in, year-out. For the most part they say the same thing about exactly the same bunch of movies, devoting so little space to each that the word 'review' is negligible. Michael Weldon must sympathise, for this follow-up to his own seminal *Psychotronic Encyclopedia* goes a different route. It goes by forklift truck too, the thing being so big and fucking heavy. To call *The Psychotronic Video Guide* a review book would be like walking into a Real Ale festival and asking for "a beer". It's more akin to an 'event'. For a start, the scale of the thing is enormous — the definition of what constitutes a Psychotronic Film having gotten pretty flexible of late. Secondly, his 'reviews' aren't necessarily about the film in question but might focus instead upon some half-cocked bit of nonsense.

> Five Came Back (1939)
> Although we never actually see them, this is the first major movie with cannibals, and it's a good one.

A big improvement on the first book is that Weldon tends to devote more space to each film; the downside is that collectors of *Psychotronic Video* magazine might be smitten with a case of *déjà vu*... a lot of this is reworked material from those very pages, though you will not find that mentioned anywhere in the book itself. Still, an absolute goldmine of obscure nuggets, big-budget blockbusters and TV shows and definitely worth the twelve-year wait since *The Psychotronic Encyclopedia of Film* back in 1983. Oh, and the UK edition sports a better cover than the American one. [David Kerekes]

THE SATANIC SCREEN
An Illustrated Guide To The Devil In Cinema
Nikolas Schreck

Nikolas Schreck's history of devilish cinema is the latest tome to add to the distinguished shortlist of really excellent genre books to come out of the alternative press. Along with Stephen Thrower's *Beyond Terror*, Kerekes and Slater's *See No Evil* and Jonathan Rigby's *English Gothic*, *The Satanic Screen* is a thorough, intelligent and well-written work which will endure to become a standard text in its specific field. For the most part resistant to the average occultist's temptation to indulge in purple prose, Schreck's book is pacey, informed and succinct; and despite its surprisingly mutable theme, presents the complex theological and historical ramifications of the satanic archetype with crisp, clear precision in the excellent Introduction.

All this seems light-years away from the garbled naval-gazing which we've come to associate with many other seriously-intentioned cinematic studies. No coma-inducing deconstructionism of the Xavier Mendik school here, the author manages an almost perfect blend in providing both penetrating insight and contentious fun.

The book traces the mass-marketing of diabolism with gusto, beginning with the fascinating story of seventeenth-century magic lantern shows and through the expressionist landscapes of early silent cinema, progressing beyond the 'interim' period of the thirties, forties and fifties to document the satanic cinema boom of the sixties and seventies in depth. On the way, many surprising and obscure films and personalities are unearthed, some of which will be unfamiliar to even the most knowledgeable of film buffs. But don't get the impression that *The Satanic Screen* is elitist in any way — Schreck is just as penetrating in his discussion of familiar milestones such as *Night of the Demon* (1957), *The Devil Rides Out* (1967), *Rosemary's Baby* (1968) and *The Ninth Gate* (1999) as he is in revealing little-known snippets of information on Hans Heinz Ewers, Hans Poelzig, Marjorie Cameron, Kenneth Anger and Anton LaVey. In fact, Schreck's lengthy and sober analysis of *Rosemary's Baby*, as contentious as some may find it to be, seems to me one of the most interesting and thought-provoking pieces I've read on this spooky, rumour-haunted blockbuster. Commendably, the author carries this sceptical and carefully balanced view to every major film under scrutiny — with one exception.

My only real bone of contention arises out of Schreck's surprisingly stock contribution to the recent *Exorcist* backlash. Taking the hackneyed view that Friedkin's *magnum opus* is some sort of sly unofficial advert for the Catholic Church, Schreck really lays into *The Exorcist*, allowing for no other interpretation of the story to contaminate the mind. This is a one-dimensional view which arises from the author's strictly romantic interpretation of the 'real' Devil as some sort of noble, Byronic anti-hero. If allowance is made for other (equally viable) interpretations, *The Exorcist* becomes more understandable — especially in light of it's original creator Peter Blatty's slant that Satan is a

SCREAMS & NIGHTMARES
£16.99 / pb / 191pp / ISBN 1852869343 / Titan Books 1998 / titanpress@titanemail.com

SEE NO EVIL
£15.95 / $25.95 / pb / 416pp / ISBN 1900486105 / Critical Vision 2000 / www.headpress.com

British theatrical poster for *Eaten Alive* — a liable contender for the UK's 'video nasties' list but never included. On the other hand, jungle gut-munchers such as *Cannibal Terror*, *Cannibal Holocaust* and *Cannibal Ferox* did become 'banned' titles. *See No Evil* spirit of spite, pettiness and cowardly malice; a false accuser. In this sense, the Devil's penchant would be to attack the weak and vulnerable — such as Regan MacNeil and her immediate family. Even if this unflattering 'religious' definition of Satan cuts no ice with Schreck, what about the cogent point that nowhere in *The Exorcist* does anyone categorically state that the demon possessing Regan is the *actual Devil himself*! This is merely implied. It's just as easy to read into one of several other contradictory implications that this may be a lesser spirit *masquerading* as the Devil. Another possible error is in viewing 'possession' as a strictly Catholic phenomenon in the first place. As Marc Cramer points out in his definitive Jungian study, *The Devil Within* (W H Allen, 1980) this particular demonic archetype is a worldwide phenomenon which crosses all cultural and religious barriers. Possessed individuals, whether they be in China, Africa or Europe, tend to manifest the exact same antisocial and vomitous symptoms in attacking the sacred cows of their specific cultural and religious environment as lapsed Catholics. It seems this form of 'paranormal illness' (particularly associated with the often-morbid temperament of adolescents in the same way poltergeist attacks are said to manifest) is independent of any specific church or denomination. It is in this sense that *The Exorcist*, like it or not, is in all honesty an *accurate representation* of a frightening, puzzling, and often seemingly absurd incursion into mundane reality.

This one caveat aside, *The Satanic Screen* is recommended as an essential purchase. Anyone, like me, who has wondered what erstwhile lycanthrope Schreck has been up to in the last twelve years or so since he produced the trend-setting *The Manson File* has found their answer. He's been mellowing out and watching films. Here's sound evidence that this is not the waste of time it's cracked up to be. [Stephen Sennitt]

SCREAMS & NIGHTMARES
The Films of Wes Craven
Brian J Robb

At first sight, this looks like just another glossy coffee table book from Titan, but actually turns out to be quite a substantial (200-page) guide to the work of writer, producer and director Wes Craven, including lots of B&W photographs, a full filmography, plus a detailed overview of his many TV projects. The earlier chapters detailing Craven's 'low-budget beginnings' are the most interesting, but then, these low-budget films are themselves far more fascinating than the later 'box-office triumphs'. We learn that Craven is an ex-English teacher with a master's degree in philosophy, who was heavily influenced by childhood fears and experiments with recreational drugs in creating film sequences. Much of the text gives us the film-maker's own words on the subjects of film-making, commercial cinema and violence in the movies. He claims, for example, that he walked out of *Reservoir Dogs* "because I felt at a certain point that the film-maker was just getting off on the violence" — and this from the man who directed *The Last House on the Left* with its protracted rape sequence, and who, in *The Hills Have Eyes*, brought us "the closest the movies have ever come to wasting a baby", according to cult movie reviewer Joe Bob Briggs.

Craven also discusses the fact that people wouldn't leave their children with him after the release of *The Last House on the Left*, mentions the influence on his work of comicbook styles, and notes that at one point he was working on a movie project based on the Jonestown massacre. Robb claims that the success of *A Nightmare on Elm Street* in 1984 "turned Craven's career around", enabling him to make films that were commercially successful, but — I would argue — much less interesting; nothing he's made since 1972 even comes close to the compelling violence of *Last House on the Left*.

Although Robb quotes a fascinating (bad) review of *Elm Street*, which essentially criticises the film for breaking the "implicit contract between a horror film director and his audience that dreams don't kill", the chapters after the one on *Elm Street* — just like the films — get increasingly less interesting. There's a chapter on Robert Englund and the marketing of Freddy Krueger, detailed accounts of the production of each of the *Elm Street* sequels, and some discussion of special effects. Analysis gives way to quotes from *Fangoria* and *Cinefantastique*, along with lots and lots of detailed descriptions, which, while interesting in their way, never seem to address the issues behind Craven's ongoing fascinations with suburbia, the broken family, and children in peril.

Incidentally, as the film posters in this book reminded me, Craven's films always seem to be tagged with some of the best and most original movie marketing slogans of all time: "Don't bury me... I'm not dead!" (*The Serpent and the Rainbow*); "If Nancy doesn't wake up screaming... she won't wake up at all!" (*Elm Street*); "Not recommended for persons over 30" (*Last House on the Left*); "Mari, 17, is dying. Even for her the worst is yet to come!" (*Last House on the Left*); "A nice American family. They didn't want to kill. But they didn't want to die" (*The Hills Have Eyes*); "The lucky ones died first" (*The Hills Have Eyes*), and, for the miserable *Scream 2*, "Someone has carried their love of sequels one step too far". I'll say. [Mikita Brottman]

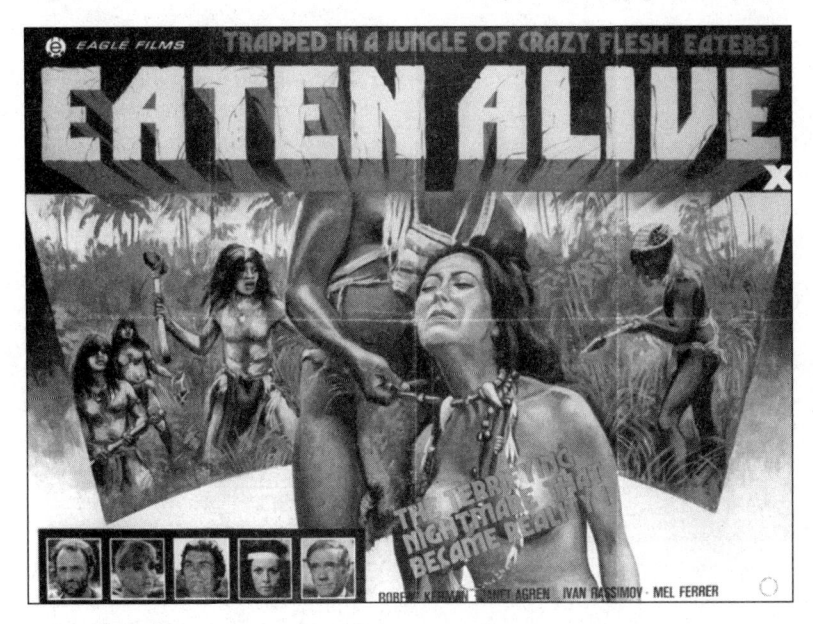

SEE NO EVIL
Banned Films and
Video Controversy
David Kerekes & David Slater

Of the various books that have been published in the last ten years about the campaign against 'video nasties' (including Martin Barker's *The Video Nasties* and Nigel Wingrove and Marc Morris' *The Art of the Nasty*), *See No Evil* is by far the most interesting and comprehensive. Kerekes and Slater's 416-page book is a reference work of sorts — though far more compelling than most similar works — which includes plot synopses and analyses of all the original 'nasties'.

There's also a close analysis of the roles of key figures like David Alton, Mary Whitehouse and James Ferman, as well as a study of the press coverage given to so-called 'copycat' crimes like the Dunblane Massacre and the murder of James Bulger.

One thing I particularly liked about this book was its authors' eye for rare gems and video diamonds in the rough, especially genuinely naff British obscurities, which are treated to a real appreciation of their more endearing qualities. Kerekes and Slater seem to have an almost gleeful affection for the cheap cinematic absurdities and pathetic attempts to shock that were basically a crap attempt to cash in on the whole 'nasty' debate. Consider, for example, this description of Julio Perez Tabernero's 1981 abortion, *Cannibal Terror*:

The jungle soundtrack comprises an unending loop of a single birdcall. The supposed heart of the jungle is a cluster of palm trees some one hundred yards

SEX MURDER ART
£11.95 / pb / 177pp / ISBN 0952328844 / Critical Vision 1998 / www.headpress.com

SEX, STUPIDITY AND GREED
£9.99 / pb / 235pp / ISBN 0965104273 / Juno Books 1998 / 111 Third Ave, #11G, New York, NY 10003, USA / ajuno@junobooks.com

from a busy road with vehicles visible in the distance. Most of the jungle natives are actually Caucasian, wearing body paint and carrying sticks mounted with cheap plastic skulls. Some tribesmen sport Elvis Presley sideburns, or moustaches, and several look every inch like out-of-condition businessmen without their clothes on. Few of them can refrain from laughing when they are supposed to be engaged in a tribal dance (of which there are many), or cannibalising their victims and tugging on raw offal.

Most interesting, however, are the chapters dealing with press hysteria and the many raids that took place on the homes of 'illegal dealers'. In retrospect, the whole bizarre affair seems like the symptom of a kind of ten-year national psychosis, a kind of mass delusion. We laugh at 'primitive' people who believe the soul is captured by the camera, but here was an entire nation of supposedly 'rational' and 'civilised' people gripped by a superstitious terror of reels of magnetic videotape. It's hard to believe how widespread is the belief — even today — that videotapes can contain 'evil', and have the power to transform kids into perverted killers and to release crazed demons upon an unsuspecting populace. And, as the authors remind us, this wasn't just a theoretical issue. People had their houses raided and ransacked and were actually given prison sentences simply because they possessed these 'evil' spools of tape.

Another thing I really enjoyed about this book is the way in which Kerekes and Slater — without being in any way dogmatic or polemical — gradually bring up more and more ridiculous examples of spurious 'links' between 'video nasties' and real-life acts of crime. The result suggests utter madness on a huge scale, a kind of 'folie de nation'. One final example. During a police raid on his home, one gent had the movie *Death Scenes* confiscated, while the book of stills from the film was seen as relatively harmless. This, I think, has some very serious implications about our beliefs in the power of the moving image. If the moving image *doesn't* contain magical powers of persuasion, then the whole debate is irrelevant. If it *does*, then surely the sacrilege is nothing to do with 'video nasties', but that such a powerful and spiritual medium is used to make films like *Patch Adams*. [Mikita Brottman]

SEX MURDER ART
The Films of Jörg Buttgereit
David Kerekes

Given that Jörg Buttgereit has only made a handful of films, it might seem strange that people want to write books about him and his work. But then for those of us in the UK, suffering the harshest censorship laws in Western Europe, read about his films is about the only thing we can do. So far only one of Buttgereit's film is legitimately available on video release in this country — *Der Todesking*, courtesy of Screen Edge.

Sex Murder Art provides a detailed analysis of Buttgereit's films, including excellent synopses, and also a wealth of background material. Kerekes gets to grips not only with the films but also with the disparate (and occasionally desperate) cast and crew. The photographs and graphics in the book serve to give a taste not only of the films but also on the milieu that they traverse.

Why Buttgereit's films — which veer from a haunting *artiness* to crass splatterama — should attract so much controversy is beyond me. His themes of death, decay and sexuality are the stock products of horror cinema, though they seem to lack the exploitational cheap thrills of much of Hollywood's products. The only one of his film's that I've seen is *Der Todesking* (being a law-abiding sort), and I found it intensely moving, lyrical and genuinely disturbing. The film is made up of seven segments — one for each day of the week — in which we are presented with characters who are isolated, alone and apparently ordinary. Each segment ends with a death, and again there are none of the pyrotechnics which we associate with Hollywood. This bleak realism is deliberately thrown back at us on several occasions, forcing us to acknowledge that this is film, breaking up any incipient complicity between the characters on film and those of us watching.

Perhaps it is this handling of death which is the problem. In a western world in which youth is everything, a world in which death is sanitised and hidden away, perhaps an honest mediation on the facts of death is unwelcome. *Der Todesking* opens with a body uncurling from a foetal position until it is flat on its back, dead. The gradual decay and putrefaction of the body through the film is the motif which links together different segments, and it is as haunting an image as any that you'd see on film today.

Sex Murder Art manages to capture all of this, as well as detailing the reactions that Buttgereit's films have managed to garner. And, despite the grim subject matter, the book is an enjoyable read. Highly recommended. [Pan Pantziarka]

Update The 1994 edition of *Sex Murder Art* is sold out, but a greatly revised and updated edition was published in 1998.

SEX, STUPIDITY AND GREED
Inside the American Movie Industry
Ian Grey

A look at the mainstream Hollywood movie biz by someone who much prefers cheap horror movies. The end result, not surprisingly, doesn't come as a huge Tinseltown thumbs-up. Author Ian Grey hasn't set out to systematically attack the movies themselves, or their makers in his book, he takes a hard-line Gonzo approach and goes to Hollywood parties. Sometimes he sits and watches television chat shows. Sometimes he tries to track down the copyright on a lousy movie still so that he might use it as an illustration in his book (the still belongs to *Heathers*, and several phone calls to several different companies and Grey is still none the wiser). You see, *Sex, Stupidity and Greed* is as much about the absurdity of the nature of the beast — the protocol of movie-making today, the manipulation of the public, having a fourteen-screen multiplex and showing *Jurassic Park 2: The Lost World* on seven of its screens — as it is about shitty multi-million dollar box-office hits (although they do get a look-in). It investigates the frightening control that a handful of mega-corporations have over the entire media and entertainment industry, and how Blockbuster Video, after a film has already been rated by the MPAA, might enforce further cuts should they feel a title in its present form be unsuitable for rental from their stores. Grey speaks to Hollywood insiders — or at least those who agree to be interviewed for a book that isn't published by a subsidiary of their own company — and comes up with some startling information. For instance, hear about Roger Corman's *The Fantastic Four* and why a studio would finance a film they never intend to release; or, how about 'negative costs', which ensure even movies that bomb at the box office will still turn a profit.

One chapter is devoted to the fiasco that started out as Richard Stanley's dream project, *The Island of Dr Moreau* (though Stanley was promptly thrown off the set once shooting started). Grey claims that the end result — which the studios stopped touting as a horror picture and started to claim was campy good fun — is the only movie to have emerged from Hollywood in years that leaves any lasting impression. Why? Because it's a fuck-up on a monumental scale.

I went out and rented *The Island of Dr Moreau* after reading Grey's book, and *didn't* find it fun in a good bad-film way. (Though I did find the casting to be 'peculiar' — Marlon Brando, Val Kilmer, David Thewlis...) Similarly, I don't agree with Grey's dismissal of *Con Air*. If *Dr Moreau* can be said to be bad even by blockhead Hollywood standards, then Hollywood must, by the same token, be capable of getting its own formula right sometimes and producing cliché-driven, high-octane nuggets... of which *Con Air*, to date, is easily the biggest and the best.

But, like I said earlier, this isn't a book about the movies themselves, it's a book about the *system*. And

SUTURE

£14.95 / pb / 192pp / ISBN 1871592704 / Creation
1998 / www.creationbooks.com

TALES OF TIMES SQUARE

£9.99 / pb / 200pp / ISBN 0922915172 / Feral House
1993 / www.feralhouse.com

Grey would appear to have at least weeded out the problem that lies at the heart of it (it is after all the book's recurring motif and the central topic of more than one chapter). The problem with Hollywood, according to *Sex, Stupidity and Greed*, is breast implants. You heard me right, and I'm not joking: breast implants.

An eye-opening and entertaining book. [David Kerekes]

SUTURE
The Arts Journal Vol 1
Ed. Jack Sargeant

I really wanted to like this. The book looks great, with colour Trevor Brown illustrations on front and back, set against a matt black cover, and the first article I've seen on Suehiro Maruo, creator of *Mr Arashi's Amazing Freakshow* and Creation's indispensable *Ultra Gash Inferno*. It's a real shame, then, that it just doesn't live up to expectations.

The stated purpose of the collection is to "examine and explore (those) zones which have been ignored for far too long". A laudable aim, for sure, but I hardly think Lydia Lunch has been underexposed, or really Joe Coleman for that matter. Ironically one of the most interesting pieces is on John Hillcoat, director of *Ghosts... of the Civil Dead* and *To Have and to Hold* who, with two features to his name and probably a couple of *Sight & Sound* pieces, can hardly be considered 'underground'. He has some interesting things to say, though, and is allowed to say them by the interviewer, Billy Chainsaw, who fortunately employs a minimal interviewing technique far removed from that of editor Jack Sargeant. Jack seems to hold his own agenda to be more important than that of the interviewees. The other pieces are on Dame Darcy, Romain Slocombe, Marne Lucas/Jacob Pander, Mark Hejnar, Trevor Brown and James Havoc.

The book suffers from a lack of variety in terms of format, being with only minor exceptions a series of articles followed by interviews. Illustrations are minimal, and it would have been good to see more of them, and a colour section, especially for the price. This problem's exacerbated by the fact that most of the interviews are overlong and often repetitive, and some of the material is of severely limited interest. A tighter edit would have been very welcome. Of the illustrations, Lydia Lunch's recent photos look excellent. The Joe Coleman repros look a little murky, though, and the screen grabs used to illustrate the piece on Mark Hejnar, director of *Affliction*, are terrible.

The collection is, to its credit, exhaustively researched. You want a comprehensive listing of Romain Slocombe exhibitions? Works of Suehiro Maruo? It's all here.

However, some of the writing in the essays is, I'm afraid, difficult to like. It often reads as though Sargeant has swallowed a dictionary of critical theory and is bringing up what he can't digest. Almost all of them feature 'what the fuck?' passages such as the following:

> It does not seek to reproduce a mimesis of 'reality', rather it creates a phantasmagorical trope based on the bio-physical response of the body to stimulation. The film is an exegesis of fuck manifested via a thermophysiological cartography of the body.

Trevor Brown is the only person featured who draws attention to Sargeant's over-determined interpretations, and comes across all the better for it. Here the distance between the aims of interviewer and interviewee is most clearly defined, with Trevor Brown's disarming modesty and down-to-earth manner in violent contrast to Jack Sargeant's humourless, theory-ridden prose. Sargeant's footnote on the Chapman brothers made me laugh out loud and wonder if it's a piss take — after describing their work as "characterised by a morphogenic eruption in which bodies are distorted becoming twisted chimera", he writes: "These distortions are made all the more strange due to the fashionable sporting shoes the figures are wearing."

There's a telling quote during the Mark Hejnar piece, in which Sargeant states:

It seems to me that maybe that [sic] there is a 'trend' in the underground by people to document the underground, but the document is in itself part of an underground mode of expression. Maybe Adam Parfrey and Apocalypse Culture *started it.*

This collection clearly wants badly to be a document on the scale of Parfrey's book. Parfrey, however, drew attention to a whole host of unknowns — the truly marginalised — while here there are no surprises. It doesn't open any new doors. In a way it's a problem which dogs a lot of the underground (I hate the word, but it's a convenient shorthand) press — the same people, the same obsessions recycled again and again. Looking at this collection and at the material on display at a lot of underground outlets, you could be forgiven for thinking the underground more narrow-minded and conformist within its own ranks than any more dominant culture. You'd also be forgiven, looking at this, for believing that the underground is an almost exclusively North American domain. There are people doing interesting work in Britain who have been ignored by the underground press — who's seen a piece on film-maker Arthur Lager? — and a collection like this should be a forum for introducing them to a wider audience. It's a pity that it's not. [James Marriott]

Update Marriott: Looking back on this review now, my tone is a bit harsh, and what comes across as a personal attack on the editor unwarranted. I was disappointed that the book was not what it could have been, but any coverage of figures as marginal as Suehiro Maruo and Romain Slocombe deserves better. Still haven't seen anything on Arthur Lager, though…

TALES OF TIMES SQUARE
Josh Alan Friedman

Al Goldstein wanted to see if Larry Levenson could shoot off his pecker the way he could his mouth. Levenson retorted that he could cum eighteen times a day, easy. Goldstein put $500 down that Levenson couldn't cum *fifteen* times in one day. The bet was on. Butch Katz heard about the deal and put a further $10,000 on the table saying that Levenson couldn't do it. At 9PM on Friday night, in a back room at the Plato's Retreat swingers club, under strict superstition, Larry Levenson commenced to fuck.

Readers who recall Bill Landis' crack-fired puke-trawling zine *Sleazoid Express* will delight in *Tales of Times Square*. Where Landis left off, Josh Friedman takes up. Josh Friedman — brother of artist, Drew — spent several years as a journalist for *Screw*, during which time he had the foresight and enthusiasm to chronicle that area of New York known as Times Square, thirteen blocks constituting the porn capital of the world. The place has since been bought up, torn down and made 'respectable'. But here's how it used to be. History shows (courtesy of this book) that even from its earliest days, the streets of Times Square provided scuzzy little treats, such as Hubert's Museum and Flea Circus back in the 1940s, which exhibited side-show freakery and geeks in the basement. In the main, however, Friedman's odyssey covers the years 1978 to 1984 — porn's 'golden age' — detailing the nefarious day-to-day activities of its inhabitants. Decrepit doormen, fading burlesque stars, bums and cops, Friedman follows them all. Elsewhere, the reader is invited to accompany Josh in search of cheap thrills: stand in line at the Peep Show, sweating in nervous anticipation as the next available booth draws nearer. Once inside, an Eisenhower dollar bill buys a minute on the phone with the girl behind glass. The occasional stain of ejaculate mars the view.

A wonderfully grubby book.

But what of Larry Levenson?

Well, it's gone 1AM and Lev's just made his seventh orgasm. Alas, the referees claim this particular pop barely qualifies. "Just two tiny drops," they announce. Larry moans that he didn't pull out in time and the first spurt went in her cunt. Al and Butch are happy. They think

THAT'S SEXPLOITATION!
£14.99 / pb / 159pp / ISBN 1852868740 / Titan 1997 / titanpress@titanemail.com

A TASTE OF BLOOD
£16.95 / pb / 252pp / ISBN 1871592917 / Creation 1999 / www.creationbooks.com

TOTEM OF THE DEPRAVED
£12 / pb / 163pp / ISBN 1880985357 / 2 13 61 Publications / www.two1361.com

LOST HIGHWAYS
£14.95 / $19.95 / pb / 288pp / ISBN 1871592682 / Creation Books 2000 / www.creationbooks.com

the well is running dry. Still, Larry's got hours left to go and opts for another woman. Just like changing golf clubs. [David Kerekes]

THAT'S SEXPLOITATION!
The Forbidden World of "Adults Only" Cinema
Eddie Muller & Daniel Faris

Presumably Titan thought that the original US title for this book, *Grindhouse*, would be lost on Brit readers. Hence: *That's Sexploitation!* However, the original text inside remains unchanged, so you get the original running header throughout and constant references to a mysterious 'Grindhouse'. That's my petty grievance. Otherwise, this is a very welcome volume indeed. Covering sin, sex and sleaze movies from the 1930s to the arrival of 'porno chic' in the seventies, *That's Sexploitation!* is picture-heavy with a glorious selection of obscure posters, stills and ad mats for the likes of *The Orgy at Lil's Place*, *The Scissors Girl*, *The Big Snatch* and *Street of Shame*. Don't dismiss this as simply coffee-table fodder, though. Whistle-stop it might be, but Muller and Faris obviously relish their subject matter. So, as well as luminaries like Russ Meyer, Doris Wishman and Dave Friedman, the book also has time for the unsung heroes, such as 'visionary crackpot' Timothy Carey:

> When new friends, like the maverick actor/director John Cassavetes, came to Carey's house for the first time, he made them wear a bulky, padded suit. He then turned his attack dog loose on them. "It's not you," Carey would howl. "He just hates that suit."

[David Kerekes]

A TASTE OF BLOOD
The Films of H G Lewis
Christopher Wayne Curry

God bless Creation. Presumably richer than Midas due to a certain Mancunian rock band, they use their wealth wisely. This marvelous little outfit publishes interesting and erudite titles on overlooked cinematic talents, talents that Faber & Faber is unlikely to touch without asbestos gloves.

Talents like H G Lewis. Visceral auteur Lewis has been ripe for literary reappraisal for some time now. Despite and because of the nauseating trend towards retrokitsch culture, he has been both rediscovered and ridiculed afresh. What your average flares-wearing irony-enslaved twat doesn't realize, though, is that Lewis made great films. *2000 Maniacs*, *Wizard Of Gore*, *The Gore Gore Girls* will all stand the test of time long after *Independence Day* — and other such shite made with a million times Lewis' money but none of his charm and magic — has been discarded to the cinematic dustbin.

So it was with some eagerness that I started this tome — and with much disgust that I put it down. I had been hoping for an intelligent analysis of Lewis' movies, with a little cultural context thrown in *à la* Jack Stevenson (or at least Jack Sargeant). And what did I get? A fucking *fanzine*.

> I could have died. I never thought I would actually speak with him. Several million endorphins were suddenly released in my brain. I was euphoric...

Author Curry is too hopelessly infatuated with his subject to be able to produce a probing, objective book. Plus, he's a crap writer. In all fairness, he does admit as much at the start of the book (which is quite endearing), and his research is impressive [Not so impressive when one realises much of it is drawn from *The Amazing Herschell Gordon Lewis* by Daniel Krogh & John McCarty, the out-of-print status of which was the *inspiration* for Curry's own Lewis project!—Eds]. *A Taste of Blood* stands as a solid factual reference tome. If you found it as a B&W photocopied tipsheet and paid a few quid for it you'd be happy. But it's certainly not a book worth paying a disgraceful *seventeen quid* for. I've changed my mind about Creation — bollocks to them for such shameful money grubbing. If they want to charge this much they could have at least got someone in to write some actual *criticism* on top of Curry's collated facts (and filled in the many blank spaces while they were at it). But no. The author is so puppy doggish in his adoration of everybody that ever walked past a HGL set (check out the fawning interviews) that the book amounts to little more than *Hello!* with intestines.

There are some amazing ad mats, and the reader is left with sense of the here-today-gone-tomorrow/wing-and-a-prayer excitement of such filmmaking, but it's not nearly *enough*. What a frustrating book. A book I really wanted to like. There is no reason HGL shouldn't merit the sort of first-rate job recently done by Stephen Thrower on Fulci (*Beyond Terror*). When that Lewis book comes out I daresay it'll be courtesy of FAB, not Creation, and will probably cost less than this arse-kissing festival. [Anton Black]

Update Following the original publication of this review in *Headpress 20*, the Creation Books press dept notified us that they had no affiliation with Creation Records and weren't happy that some people kept on thinking they did.

TOTEM OF THE DEPRAVED
Nick Zedd

Big bad Nick. Love him or loathe him he does what he wants. This book of his is particularly ingratiating, however. Knowing Zedd's unfavourable view of the world, *Totem of the Depraved* could easily have come over like the angst-ridden bedroom meanderings of some rebellious adolescent. Angst-ridden it often is, but it's also witty with it (often at Zedd's own expense), rather personal and poignant, and thoroughly scathing. Zedd hasn't constructed his book to read particularly like an autobiography, he is often distracted, becomes infuriated while recalling an ill-experience and shoots off somewhere else.

At times like these, my mind wanders, pondering the misfortunes of even bigger fuckups than myself. It makes me feel better to think of how Tommy ruined his life.

People who he remembers fondly one minute are regarded as scum in the next. Zedd talks about his no-budget films, his no-hope friends, advises against using FedEx to try and send anything to Canada, spends a lot of time with insane people in Europe, and… wallows in the misery of being surrounded by bubble-headed nymphets:

I hated Dorota, but she was a beautiful Polish girl.

Love him or loathe him, it's a great book. [David Kerekes]

LOST HIGHWAYS
An Illustrated History of Road Movies
Ed. Jack Sargeant & Stephanie Watson

There are things about Monte Hellman's *Two-Lane Blacktop* that make repeated viewings eminently gratifying. It's a film that is outwardly sparse, containing very little dialogue, and sequences which take a long time to get to nowhere in particular (the end of the film arrives only because the film stock itself has physically slowed down and ignited under the heat of the projector lamp). The viewer must approach *Two-Lane Blacktop* like a painter might approach a blank canvas; repeated viewings are the application of more layers and depth. Of course, it was a disastrous flop on its release in 1971, particularly given that Dennis Wilson (of the Beach Boys) and James Taylor were its stars and Universal Pictures believed they had a sure-fire *won't-the-kids-just-dig-it* hit on their hands.

The story — such as it is — has Wilson and Taylor riding around the US, making their money by pitting their souped-up '55 Chevy against other vehicles in illegal road races. When they encounter another wanderer, Warren Oates in his flash-looking GTO, a cross-country race ensues in which the winner is the first to reach Washington DC, and the loser forfeits their vehicle. The paths of the racers constantly cross, and a young hitchhiker (Laurie Bird) who has drifted into the lives of the three men provides an unexpected distraction, before she suddenly drifts out again.

THE UNSEEN BRUCE LEE
£10.99 / pb / 104pp / ISBN 1852867787 / Titan Books / titanpress@titanemail.com

THE VOYEUR VIDEO GUIDE TO SPECIAL-INTEREST MALE EROTIC VIDEOS
£9.99 / pb / 150pp / ISBN 1889138053 / Companion Press 1997 / www.companionpress.com

WEIRDSVILLE USA
£12.99 / pb / 192pp / ISBN 0859652912 / Plexus 1997 / www.plexusbooks.com

Dennis Wilson as The Mechanic in Two-Lane Blacktop, *the defining road movie.* Lost Highways

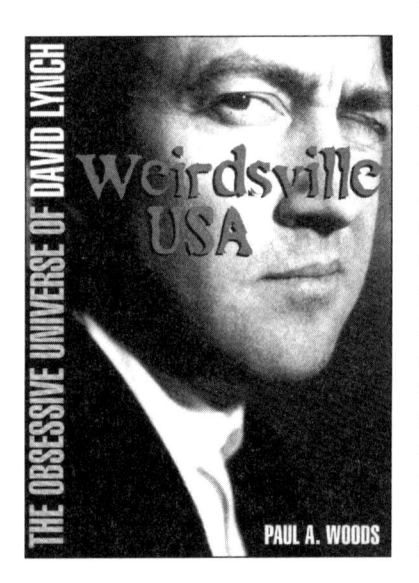

Other than Warren Oates (and a guy in a diner), none of the people in *Two-Lane Blacktop* are 'real' actors. But this fact isn't detrimental to the picture. Wilson (known only as The Mechanic; none of the characters have actual names) doesn't even appear to realise he's in a movie at times: he watches the other characters and listens to their dialogue as if he is genuinely hearing what they say for the first time. He is completely absorbed in the events unfolding around him. On more than one occasion he starts to laugh in the middle of a sentence, or when he's 'delivering' a line — these are moments of truthfulness that no amount of method acting could hope to emulate. He is caught in the moment. Something suddenly strikes him as funny; that happens to people sometimes.

Quite rightly, *Two-Lane Blacktop* gets a chapter to itself in *Lost Highways*. In a way it's the defining road movie; a road movie in its purest form. It's a film in which the viewer spends more time inside cars than he does outside of them; where The Driver (Taylor) turns the radio off while he's driving because "it gets in the way", and where he and The Mechanic only speak when there is something to say about the car. The only time The Driver appears comfortable speaking to anyone else is when he's ordering parts for the car from a guy in a motor spares store: reeling off the parts, the two men almost seem to be talking in an alien language. When he tries to make small talk with The Girl (Bird) she says "You bore me". Later, when the two men have a near-accident, the first thing The Mechanic does is check the car; when he checks the engine prior to a race, the car *really is* running at its peak and has the power to beat the other vehicle (so I've been expertly informed). It's not that these two men don't want to communicate, it's that they *can't* — they are bonded by their car and something that eludes them both. They have a common goal, and that is that neither knows what it is they're after. "It's best to keep the hunger on," The Driver says to his buddy at one point.

There are other chapters in *Lost Highways*, some with interesting takes on the road movie, such as the Vampire Road Movie, and The Road as River (incorporating *Aguirre, Wrath of God* and *Apocalypse Now*). But I'm particularly fond of the film *Two-Lane Blacktop*, and I like the fact that Adam Webb, the author of the *Two-Lane Blacktop* chapter, says that the film "was simply too dark for success". [David Kerekes]

THE UNSEEN BRUCE LEE
Louis Chunovic

Bruce Lee was the Cha Cha Champion of the Crown Colony of Hong Kong. On the ship emigrating to the United States, he was often called up from the lower quarters to show the ladies on board some champion-style dance moves. After which, according to Louis Chunovic's book, the young, handsome, head-strong, soon-to-be King of Kung Fu, went straight back down again below deck to sleep. No womanising for the notorious womaniser. Still, a book produced in co-operation with the great man's estate is hardly going to read like Albert Goldman.

Bruce Lee was born in 1940. By the time he was thirty-two he was dead. With but a handful of movies and TV appearances to his name, he was a star. Now he is a legend. According to the preface by Linda Lee Cadwell (Bruce's wife), *The Unseen Bruce Lee* sets out to correct the fallacy that Lee's skill and prowess were handed down to him in his genes. They weren't and Lee worked hard every day to hone himself to a physical peak, while devouring books on self-motivation and philosophy to get his head into gear. To be honest, the preface probably offers more of an insight into the workings of the man than the rest of the book put together — later chapters concentrate on the films, rather they offer blow-by-blow details of the big fight scenes in them.

The Unseen Bruce Lee is blessed with hundreds of rare and never before seen snapshots of Lee at work and with his family, sketches from his personal notebooks, and ephemera from his martial arts school. All in all, what could comfortably be described a 'crowd pleaser'. [David Kerekes]

THE VOYEUR VIDEO GUIDE TO SPECIAL-INTEREST MALE EROTIC VIDEOS
Ed. Steve Stewart

What you need from a good film and video guide — like all reference books — is plenty of information. The only reason to purchase such a book is to avoid disappointments in the video store. It should tell you what the video sleeves fail to reveal; criticise the crap and praise the good.

Dealing entirely in non-pornographic male nudity videos, many of which make up top-shelf gay fodder in the UK, the initial premise here is one of relevance and interest. However, once inside, *The Voyeur Video Guide* is a miserable failure in every respect: as a source of information, as a good read, as masturbatory material... Editor Stewart seems to think that thirty descriptive words make a good video review. I doubt if he has even sat and watched all the titles listed, but simply culled choice words from press material to compile this turgid example of vanity publishing. Anyone with a subscription to *Adult Video News* could put this turkey together.

Most stills consist of naked or semi-naked muscle men working out or posing in the great outdoors, taken from videos such as *Euroboy*, *Canadian Nude Oil Wrestling (volumes 1–5)* and *Uranus: Self Anal Massage* ("Everything you ever wanted to know about self-sodomy — but were afraid to ask!").

Mr Stewart also wrote *Full Frontal: Male Nudity Video Guide* and *Penis Puns, Jokes & One Liners: A Movie Quote Book*. With titles such as these under his belt, why am I not in the least surprised that his latest book sucks? [David Greenall]

WEIRDSVILLE USA
The Obsessive Universe of David Lynch
Paul A Woods

David Lynch is one of Hollywood's true auteurs. A director whose films fail to sit comfortably and succeed in dividing critics and audiences down the middle. A case in point is Lynch's recent feature, *Lost Highway*: while some judged it to be "the work of a thoughtless art school sophomore" (*Melody Maker*), others were beside themselves with joy. "Disturbing, intriguing, beautiful" said *Q* magazine. Paul Woods provides a blow-by-blow, scene-by-scene breakdown of the director's work, from early short films *The Alphabet* and *The Grandmother*, to unrealised projects like *Ronnie Rocket*, and a proposed adaptation of D M Thomas' novel *The White Hotel*. He traces the ill-fated *Dune* project, on which Lynch admits to "selling out" and which was beset with several directors and production companies prior to Lynch's arrival. Lynch's most resonant production, however, remains his 1976 debut, *Eraserhead*. Even today, over twenty years after its completion, *Eraserhead* instills in the viewer a sense of "this can't be happening", a sense of floating-nausea combined with jolting

WES CRAVEN'S THE LAST HOUSE ON THE LEFT
£14.99 / pb / 208pp / ISBN 1903254019 / FAB Press
1997 / www.fabpress.com

HEADPRESS 23
£8.99 $14.50 / pb / 160pp / ISBN 1900486180 /
Headpress 2002 / www.headpress.com

Roger Watkins, director of cult classic *Last House on Dead End Street* pays Peter Cushing a visit; England, early 1970s. *Headpress 23: Funhouse*

feet-on-the-ground realism. What started out as a proposed six-week shooting schedule, slowly ran on for several years. The American Film Institute could no longer fund the production and Lynch was forced to seek outside investors. One investor, upon viewing the sequence where Henry, the film's 'hero', sits at his girlfriend's dinner table, was compelled to rush out of the screening room yelling "People don't talk like that!... You people are crazy!" Well, what do you know? — people *do* talk like that, and life is a string of uncomfortable silences and compromises. Woods also notes that when *Eraserhead* made its debut, it ran for 110 minutes. Lynch, on account of the audience's total non-reaction, felt compelled to make three cuts and tighten the thing up a bit. Of the cuts, one involved a sequence where Henry hears a noise from down the hall and goes to investigate. Opening a door slightly, he sees two girls bound to a bed, with a man approaching them holding a black box with prongs. Another cut involved Henry looking out of his window to see a little boy digging in the dirt and discovering a line of dimes. Henry intends to get some dimes too, but his progress out of the building is hindered, no less because of his baby crying the moment he steps out the apartment. When Henry returns to the window, a crowd of people have arrived, also digging for dimes. A fight breaking out is all that remains in the film of the dime scenario. This kind of info ought to be reason enough to want to go out and pick up this book. If it isn't, how about the bungee-jumping success of *Twin Peaks*? Or those other, less commercial (!) TV shows of Lynch's — *On The Air* and *Hotel Room*? The latter Woods describes as having "the feel of an unpredictable talent marking time, almost condescending towards the mundane". Mundane in the Lynchian sense? That's something that doesn't sound half bad... [David Kerekes]

WES CRAVEN'S THE LAST HOUSE ON THE LEFT
The Making of a Cult Classic
David A Szulkin

Unlike *Night of the Living Dead* and *The Texas Chain Saw Massacre*, two other independent ground-breaking horror films, *Last House on the Left* — though not without its supporters — has failed to make quite the same critical impact. It's a financial success, but not a *great* financial success. One of the reasons for this, director Craven himself puts forward, is that the criminals at the heart of the film are so "utterly despicable"...

Two teenage girls, on their way to a rock concert, are kidnapped by a group of ex-cons. The gang take the girls to a secluded woods and subject them to torture and rape, before eventually murdering them. As fate would have it, the gang end up as the guests of one of the girls' unwitting parents. When the parents discover the truth, they take their revenge.

Wes Craven and Sean Cunningham were commissioned by Hallmark, a renegade distributing company, to make a horror film that pulled no punches. The result, shot over a period of five weeks and in the editing room for nigh on one year (on account of the fact the team knew nothing of 'continuity'), certainly pulled no punches — it made Hallmark sick! Jeramie Rain, who plays Sadie in the movie, says: "I apologise to my children for being in it…" The scenes with the two girls in the woods riled some audience members up so much, they felt they had to destroy the print itself, and projectionists were forced to barricade themselves in. In which case it's probably as well that several scripted scenes didn't actually make it into the film: these include an episode of necrophilia meted out on one of the girls' bodies. Also, the movie was originally intended to carry several hardcore sex cutaways, opening to one of the girl's masturbating in the shower (the filmmakers had met prior success with a pseudo-sex documentary called *Together*).

Author David Szulkin has managed to track down virtually everyone who took part in the production of LHOTL, and some of the people involved in distributing it. He has also been granted access to working scripts, dissected the many different prints of the movie in circulation, traced the wake of controversy that surrounded the movie on first release, and takes a look at the copycats and rip-offs that LHOTL has inspired. The result reads like a life's work for Szulkin; a bludgeoningly relentless investigation into what many regard as a classic and what many more will see as a blot on the cinematic landscape. Chapter after chapter throws out (sometimes conflicting) anecdotes and hitherto unknown details. Indeed, a *lot* of hitherto unknown details.

The film is a completist's nightmare. Szulkin reckons there are no less than five different versions of the film in circulation. Even a supposed 'restored' edition, released in 1986, was lacking scenes available elsewhere in other releases. It's little wonder LHOTL is in such a state, however, given the cavalier way it has been handled. Sean Cunningham, for instance, not appreciating the X-rating given to it by the MPAA, simply sliced the R-rating off another film, stuck it onto the beginning of LHOTL and sent it for duplicating! None of the versions currently available come anywhere near the fabled ninety-one minutes thought to be the original running time.

Another point of great interest (to this author at least) are the facts pertaining to the 'spin-off' movie, *Last House on Dead End Street*. Szulkin has probably gotten closer than anyone else to the origins of this near-legendary (supposedly unfinished) oddity. This book is recommend wholeheartedly. [David Kerekes]

Update The elusive director of *Last House on Dead End* Street finally emerged in 2001. Oblivious to the cult following that had built around his movie, Roger Watkins and several of the key players were interviewed extensively for *Headpress 23*.

HEADPRESS 23
Funhouse
Ed. David Kerekes

Headpress 23 turns its attention to the movie *Last House on Dead End Street*, with no less than seventy-six (of its 192) pages devoted to the cult 1973 obscurity. Editor and publisher David Kerekes tells of his long standing fascination with the film, and travels halfway around the world to New York to meet with the elusive director, Roger Watkins (who only recently discovered that three decades of interest had built up around his movie). Kerekes is driven almost entirely by gut instinct. He has no real assurance that Watkins is who he claims he is, never having made contact other than by email and a telephone answering machine.

Last House on Dead End Street is a disturbing low budget production that involves the making of "snuff" movies. The central character, a psychotic, frightening young man

THE X FACTORY
£14.99 / $19.95 / pb / 208pp / ISBN 1900486245 /
Critical Vision 1997 / www.headpress.com

ART OF DARKNESS
£29.99 / $39/99 / hb / 319pp / ISBN 1903254078 /
FAB Press 2002 / www.fabpress.com

THE HAUNTED WORLD OF MARIO BAVA
£24.99 / $34.99 / pb / 352pp / ISBN 1903254051 /
FAB Press 2002 / www.fabpress.com

BLOOD AND BLACK LACE
£19.99 / pb / 148pp / ISBN 095332611X / Stray Cat Publishing 1999 / PO Box 36, Liskeard, Cornwall, PL14 4YT / www.straycatpublishing.com

An alternate title for Lucio Fulci's western, Massacre Time. Beyond Terror

named Terry Hawkins, is Watkins himself. Kerekes speaks with him for the first time from his New York hotel room:

> "Hi, David," says the voice on the line. "This is Roger. Hey, I called you last night but the hotel said you'd checked out." "Well, I'm still here," I reply. It is only later, after I put the phone down, that I wonder who Roger might have spoken to the previous night. It certainly wasn't me, and besides, he had no idea where I was staying...

With its Kafka-esque backdrop, the subsequent meeting and interview doesn't disappoint. Neither do the interviews with other key people involved in the production. No mean feat, considering that the original distributors had effectively stolen the print and clouded the film in a heap of false credits and titles, leaving cast and crew in a smoke screen of ignorance and anonymity.

Headpress comes up trumps again, but this is one of their finest hours. [Sarah Turner]

THE X FACTORY
Inside the American Hardcore Film Industry
Anthony Petkovich

This expert compilation of interviews with actresses, directors and other luminaries from the strange world of US hardcore takes us on a fascinating and sinister journey, from directors' mansions in Malibu to backstage at Hollywood porn theatres, from third-rate film studios in downtown LA to in-between takes on the set of Gregory Dark's *Sex Freaks*. The lascivious Petkovich — himself no stranger to these seamy realms of sleaze — clearly laps up every minute of the interviews. Technical terms are explained in detail for the uninitiated (the different varieties of 'DP', for example), and the conversations with the author's favourite sluts grow increasingly wolfish, until the page feels virtually damp with drool. Like a hungry dog sniffing out scraps of meat, Petkovich tracks down the nastiest sluts, the freakiest anecdotes, and the sweatiest corners of the dirtiest lives.

And they are certainly dirty. Despite Petkovich's laudable attempts to personalise and dignify this cast of characters and the curious world they inhabit, the aftertaste that remains (and I read this book at one sitting) is not a pleasant one. One actress refers in passing to a recent nervous breakdown; another mentions her crack cocaine addiction; others discuss their fears of AIDS and the various indignities they have come to accept on set. One interviewee, Krysti Lynn, has since died in an accident. This seamy underside of an even seamier business is embodied by the current ubiquity of breast implants and the popularity of 'anal'. Most pitiful of all, perhaps, is the tragically short 'career' lifespan of any actress whose body happens to match the aesthetic preferences of the current hot director until everyone has had enough of her — a situation not unlike that of those bashful 'studs' lining up for their sheepish two minutes of third-rate glory in Petkovich's account of John T Bone's *The World's Biggest Gang Bang 2*, which provides the book with its appropriately anticlimactic finale. [Mikita Brottman]

Update The all-new *X Factory 2* is scheduled for publication by Headpress in the not-too-distant

ITALIAN HORROR

ART OF DARKNESS
The Cinema of Dario Argento
Ed. Chris Gallant

THE HAUNTED WORLD OF MARIO BAVA
Troy Howarth

The two latest titles in this Directors Series (the subjects to date all being Italian!) are again a joy to behold — big, fat lavish production jobs, a burden of illustrations and knowledgeable writers.

There can't be much to say about Dario Argento that hasn't been said, and while not much of the criticism here is actually critical, I defy anyone with any inkling of interest in the director to be able to resist *Art of Darkness*. Analysis of all the films and TV work, right up to *Sleepless* (courtesy of this 2001 updated edition), plus many scarce illustrations, make the book a necessary purchase.

Perhaps lacking the commercial clout of the Argento book is *The Haunted World of Mario Bava* — by no means a criticism. After all, Bava remains highly influential with directors who continue to draw on his ideas and keen sense of composition. He essentially set the benchmark for *giallo* thrillers with his 1964 movie *Blood and Black Lace* and another one for slasher movies with his 1971 *Twitch of the Death Nerve/A Bay of Blood*. Actor Cameron Mitchell regarded him as a film-making genius, but that wasn't an accolade that sat easily with Bava himself. In an interview conducted for *L'espresso* (1979), the director deliberated on twenty-five years in the film industry:

> BAVA In my entire career, I made only big bullshits, no doubt about that.
> INTERVIEWER Nowadays they are well regarded.
> BAVA Nowadays people lack culture.

Both books are tributes to their respective subjects. I think Bava deserves it more, but I prefer the work of Argento. There you go — Bava was right. [David Kerekes]

BLOOD AND BLACK LACE
The Definitive Guide To Italian Sex and Horror Movies
Adrian Luther-Smith

The second book in the 'Dark Side Presents' series, which fortunately stands head and shoulders above their preceding title, *Video Nasties!* This because it actually contains information to go with its pictures, penned with some authority by Adrian Luther-Smith. The subject here is *giallo* — the Italian mystery genre — but it encompasses just about any film with a murder in it.

Mario Bava is acknowledged as having started cinematic *giallo*, courtesy of his 1962 production, *The Evil Eye*. But following *Deep Red*, Argento's masterly redefining of the genre in 1975, the popularity of these films took a nose dive. (They came back with the US stalk and slash boom of the eighties.)

As well as cast and credit details, each entry in this book comes with a synopsis, informed critique and cache of factoids. Hear how the US distributor of Sergio Martino's *Torso* not only excised much of the film's gore, but was also responsible for the jarring guitar theme (that turns up again in Doris Wishman's *Deadly Weapons* and Leon Klimovsky's *Night of the Walking Dead*); or how different versions of the rape scene in Pasquale Festa Campanile's underrated *Hitch-hike* were shot for different markets.

A section entitled 'Hidden Treasures' compiles *giallo* material that remains elusive (or turned up too late for inclusion in the main text). Of these titles, *The Police Grope Around in the*

CANNIBAL HOLOCAUST AND THE SAVAGE CINEMA OF RUGGERO DEODATO
£13.99 / pb / 111pp / ISBN 0952926040 / FAB Press 1999 / www.fabpress.com

BEYOND TERROR
£24.95 / pb / 311pp / ISBN 0952926067 / FAB Press 1999 / www.fabpress.com

DELIRIUM
£10.95 / pb / 100pp / ISBN 1901759008 / Media Publications 1998

BACKSTAGE PASSES AND BACKSTABBING BASTARDS
$18.95 £13.95 / pb / 352pp / ISBN 0823082571 / Billboard Books 1999

Dark — directed by the aptly named Helia Colombo — sounds pretty fantastic, with a plot that includes murdered models and an invention that can photograph thoughts.

Blood and Black Lace is full-colour throughout and contains many rare images, but is a little steep at £20. [David Kerekes]

CANNIBAL HOLOCAUST AND THE SAVAGE CINEMA OF RUGGERO DEODATO
Fenton, Grainger and Castoldi

BEYOND TERROR
The Films of Lucio Fulci
Stephen Thrower

For those readers who require a breakneck discourse on how the 'small press' has advanced in recent years, take a look at these film books from FAB. In terms of quality, *Cannibal Holocaust* is the equal of anything being put out by the major presses, while *Beyond Terror* — an oversized hardback with dust-jacket and impeccable photo reproduction — puts most quality presses to shame. Of course, no major publishing house would devote so much time and care to subjects like Ruggero Deodato and Lucio Fulci, both of whom would be considered 'non-starters' on the scale of moveable units. But that's the leverage the small press has into the marketplace: Originality. Perhaps integrity. Now quality.

As to the books themselves: both Deodato and Fulci are legends amongst horror film fans — the former primarily for the eponymous *Cannibal Holocaust*, and the latter notably for his living dead trilogy of which *Zombie Flesh-eaters* is the most famous. The books are profusely illustrated with many rare illustrations (almost full-colour throughout, it's incredible that FAB managed to pull *Cannibal Holocaust* in for less than £14), with incisive commentary on each directors' work. Naturally, given the page count and the fact it's been several years in the making, *Beyond Terror* has the edge, with breakdowns of not only the films themselves but even the key characters who appear in them! Author Stephen Thrower dissects every aspect of Fulci's work, resulting in a satisfyingly intelligent, eminently readable book that is complemented by some truly great illustrations and a great look. [David Kerekes]

DELIRIUM
A Guide to Italian Exploitation Cinema, 1975–1979
Ed. Adrian Lusther-Smith

Four years may not seem an awfully long time, but in terms of Italian exploitation films of the mid seventies it's a frighteningly dense period, arguably Italy's golden age in which film-makers constantly pushed at the boundaries of taste and decency with nary a backward glance. There are literally hundreds of titles contained in this special book-sized edition of *Delirium*, with most accompanied by informative reviews, full credit details and rare illustrations. The primary motivating force in these films was money, and the easiest way to make that of course was to drown your movie in kinky sex and gratuitous violence. The result? A shameless and exciting era, wallowing in *Dirty Harry* rip-offs and *Omen* cash-ins. Nunsploitation, Nazi atrocity, Black Emanuelle, Mondo, hardcore, tacky comedies, they're all here. The only gripe with this book is the layout… and non-existent page numbers. [David Kerekes]

MUSIC

BACKSTAGE PASSES AND BACKSTABBING BASTARDS
Memoirs of a Rock'n'Roll Survivor
Al Kooper

If you're one of the people who don't assume this review is about Alice Cooper (the first thing Al points out in his introduction) you probably already know the big story about Al Kooper, how he slid into the empty bench behind the organ at the Highway 61 sessions, and how the licks he played on Like A Rolling Stone pleased Dylan so much they became the tune's signature. Of course, Al was a guitarist by trade, and had never really played the organ before ("your son will never be a good keyboard player," his piano teacher told his father). The French horn on the Rolling Stones' You Can't Always Get What You Want was Al again, and believe me, he wasn't classically trained. Al's tired of telling the Dylan story, in fact, he skips it with interviewers, but it's here in this book, and lest you think that Koop's nothing more than a rock'n'roll Zelig, showing up in the background of all the best album photos, think again. I've been a huge Kooper fan ever since the Blues Project days. When that group split up, Al started Blood, Sweat and Tears, and their first album, *Child is Father to the Man*, is still one of my all-time favourites. That group broke up ("We divided into factions," Al said in an interview. "There was me, and there was the rest of the band"). BS&T went on to chart-topping success, Al went on to Super Session, the original super-group jam session begun with Mike Bloomfield and finished with Steve Stills. He began producing, including a wonderful big band record (*Autumn*) with the Don Ellis orchestra. He discovered Lynyrd Skynyrd, for whatever that's worth. And he produced a series of solo albums throughout the seventies and early eighties that are a beguiling mix of the sublime and the ridiculous. He got into soundtracks, producing the noise for the late, great TV series *Crime Story*. And nowadays he's even teaching, at Boston's prestigious Berklee. Al's never been a commercial hit. Part of it is his voice ("like a soulful asthmatic" was one description), and part of it is his desire to make music to his own tastes: challenging and rarely formulaic, encompassing elements as diverse as classical strings and Hawaiian guitars, and often indulgent of his favourite influences. It's not a recipe for chart success, but it's a joy to listen to. It's partly that polyglot nature which helps make this memoir so entertaining. But there are two other factors. One is: Al can write. His songs were always full of literary allusions, bad puns, in-jokes, and sometimes striking metaphors. His albums usually featured outstanding concepts: the cover of *Child is Father to the Man* had each band member sitting with a child-sized dummy on his lap, each dummy had the player's adult face. His liner notes were a hoot. Two: Al's got a sense of humour. He just sees things as being funny, and he's never been afraid to toss humour into the mix. Having said all that, he's never been a very good self-editor! His delight in things spelled or played backwards is strange. He's had a fascination with country music ("there aren't many Jewish guys who play the mandolin") which hasn't always fit into his music. He's often been self-indulgent in extremis, but not in the overbearing way of most rock musicians, more in the way of an excited kid who wants to show you everything he can do that might be fun. This is probably why he was musical director for a band called the Rock-Bottom Remainders, put together by a bunch of best-selling writers and big-name columnists who really just want to be rock stars. Stephen King plays guitar in this band. He wrote the liner notes for the first album by Al's new band, The Rekooperators. I hope King plays guitar as well as Al writes. That's why this book is such a hoot. As a look at the early business of rock'n'roll, it's a revelation (Al was playing in bands in his early teens, and working in Tin Pan Alley while still in high school). His stories of the mid sixties scene in the Village are great — Bob Dylan, Eric Andersen, Judy Collins and the like — and of course, the saga of the personality clashes in the Project and BS&T, great bands both, are worth the price of admission in themselves. He's honest and amusing about his own personal life, and the weird sort of pulling and tugging rock exerts on the emotions of its stars. Plus, Al's worked with an editor this time (the book is actually a revision and update of a volume originally published in 1977, when Al was at the peak, shall we say, of self-indulgence) and it is a genuinely funny read. Get it. Michael Carlson]

Update Al Kooper had an op for a brain tumour not too long ago: but the music keeps on coming: a nice double CD called *Rare And Well Done*, which is out-takes and best-of, and a live performance with Mike Bloomfield and Johnny Winter at the

THE BEATLES UNCOVERED
£12.99 / pb / 160pp / ISBN 1902799046 / Helter Skelter Publishing 2000 / www.skelter.demon.co.uk

BOOK OF CHANGES
£10.99 / $14.95 / pb / 264pp / ISBN 1560974176 / Fantagraphics Books 2001 / www.fantagraphics.com

CRASH COURSE FOR THE RAVERS
£6.99 / pb / 136pp/ ISBN 1898927650 / ST Publishing 1997 / www.stpublishing.com

THE COVERT WAR AGAINST ROCK
£10.99 / $14.95 / pb / 280pp / ISBN 092291561X / Feral House 2000 / www.feralhouse.com

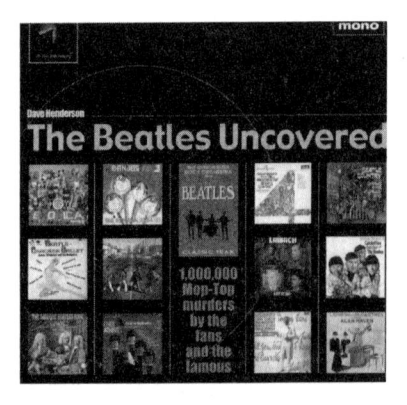

Fillmore. Now if we could just find that bootleg tape of Al and Mike at the Bottom Line in 1974!

THE BEATLES UNCOVERED
1,000,000 Mop-Top Murders by the Fans and the Famous
Dave Henderson

Dave Henderson is the publishing director of *Mojo* and *Kerrang!* With this book he takes a trawl through the weird, wonderful and frequently downright dull world of Beatles wannabes, cover-version artists and their recordings. If that doesn't sound like an awful lot to go on for a book, think of a number and then keep on doubling it — that's how many records are out there that fit into the oeuvre Henderson has devoted himself to pursuing.

Lots of colourful pictures and short, nothing too taxing, manageable bites of text give the book a somewhat inconsequential feel — which isn't necessarily a bad thing when all is considered. After all, we wouldn't want to delve *too* deeply into Liberace's Something or Val Doonican's All My Loving, would we? These are some of the more insipid exponents of the Beatles cover version; songs from those folk who are musically competent but about as creative as lint. Far more interesting and entertaining are those people who try to 'interpret' the Beatles, and manage to bring their own particular dynamic to the recording (Within You, Without You by Rainer Ptaceck and Howe Gelb, for instance). Alternatively, there are those artistes who make such a hash of the job that they hit a plane of relevance that is far, far higher (or removed) to anything they could have earnestly hoped to reach. Take, for instance, Marty Gold's *Moog Plays The Beatles*, an album recorded in 1970 which was intended to demonstrate the new, exciting and innovative instrument that was the Moog synthesiser — and what better way to do so than via some Fab standards. Unfortunately, Gold had no idea of the Moog's potential and simply banged out shrill twiddly fills and electronic sitar noises over a syrupy backdrop. In My Life, reconciles author Henderson, was a track "undoubtedly recorded on the Moon".

There are albums of Beatles covers done in a Latino style (*Tropical Tribute to the Beatles*), in a classical style, in a reggae style, in a soul style, in an indie-pop style, and — it goes almost without saying — plenty of marching bands have felt compelled to cover the Beatles over the years. One of these albums, *The Band of The Royal Military Academy, Sandhurst, Plays Lennon And McCartney*, features on its sleeve Major Fanshawe on his horse, Thor, riding up some rather grand-looking steps.

For those who remember *The Exotic Beatles* series of compilation albums featured in *Headpress 19*, here is the literary equivalent. With plenty of typos. [David Kerekes]

BOOK OF CHANGES
Kristine McKenna

Who the fuck is Kristine McKenna?

Yup, that's what I thought as well when I picked up the book. It seems she began as a journalist in the late seventies, writing about the punk scene, before moving on to more wholesome fare — art, film and music criticism — for rags like *Rolling Stone*, *Artforum*, *LA Times*. Shit, resumes like that almost write themselves these days and despite the wide range of interviewees featured, I couldn't help thinking "Here we fucking go" as I cracked the spine and dug in.

Well, I'm pleased to report that my initial doubts were unfounded. This is an excellent collection of (often short) interviews with a wide range of people, the names of most of which I'm sure will appeal to the average Headpresser. McKenna has a way of asking the right question (example: "What's been your biggest disappointment in life?"), the question you suspect many of the subjects are not used to hearing, and I was surprised to find that the people I knew least about had the most interesting things to say. Brian Eno, a man I had always suspected of being intimately familiar with the view of his own rectum, comes across as sharp, realistic and still excited about the creative possibilities in life. Leonard Cohen seems wiser and more positive about life than I'd expected from his music.

Meanwhile, some people only reinforce what you always suspected about them: Burroughs, the dour old curmudgeon, well-read and pissed off; Nick Cave, draped-in-black miserabilist, teetering on the edge of a psychotic episode and saved only by his art; George Clinton, off his tits.

And some are a disappointment: Iggy Pop hasn't got much to say that we couldn't figure out from the lyric sheets to *Funhouse* and *Raw Power*; Don Van Vliet (Captain Beefheart) has been in the desert too long; and Neil Young is just plain boring.

Each interview starts with a full page illustration, B&W linework from the likes of Robert Crumb, Los Bros Hernandez, Ivan Brunetti, Bill Griffith, Peter Kuper — everyone you'd expect to be associated with a Fanatagraphics book basically.

This isn't an expensive book and for the best of the illos and the interviews it's worth your cash and your time. [Rik Rawling]

CRASH COURSE FOR THE RAVERS
A Glam Odyssey
Philip Cato

This is an amiable and harmless little memoir of the early seventies Glam Rock era. Nothing much happens in the book apart from the author building up his record collection and putting together some tapes himself. Expect no insights into Glam, no inside information about the groups and not much in the way of analysis. You can also forget trying to relate what was happening in the music to what was going on in the wider world at the time. This is a twelve-year-old boy's view of the world, and it's relayed pleasantly enough in those terms and no more. What more can you say about a book where the most exciting thing that happens is that young Philip's dad gives him a haircut that goes horribly wrong? [Pan Pantziarka]

THE COVERT WAR AGAINST ROCK
Alex Constantine

In the wake of Alex Constantine's previous Feral House hardcore conspiracy-theory classics (*Psychic Dictatorship in the USA* and *Virtual Government*), this present volume may at first glance seem comparatively lightweight. After all, we've all heard the 'folk legend'-style rumours surrounding the mysterious deaths of Jim Morrison and Brian Jones, and read about the sinister ramifications behind the shooting of John Lennon. However, as we've come to expect from Constantine, *The Covert War Against Rock* sets these previously unsubstantiated rumours on more solid ground, the author supplying his usual meticulous and painstaking research in order to reveal a picture every bit as disturbing as any of his previous forays into the shadowy world of covert politics.

Constantine's basic premise — based on the research of the late Mae Brussell — is that various politically motivated rockstars (such as Jimi Hendrix, Bob Marley, Tupac Shakur, Michael Hutchence, and others) have suffered a strategic and concentrated campaign of intimidation and eventual assassination at the hands of a covert CIA-Mafia alliance code-named Operation Chaos, which is intent on eradicating those who speak-out on political issues in opposition to its own commercial and political ambitions. While this may seem rather far-fetched, Constantine backs up his thesis with a welter of chilling detail and voluminous references, all of which seem authentic, and… oh, *wait a minute, what's this?* Hold the presses! On page thirty-six I've spotted a reference to a 1970 'Process church bulletin' quoted verbatim by the author, and presented as genuine. The only problem with this is that it's a fake which was circulated in 1988 at the same time as *NOX* No 6: The Process special issue. Both items have the same electronic typewriter type-face. How do I know this? I was the editor of *NOX* magazine! How can I be sure the '1970 Bulletin' is a fake? I should know, of all people: I wrote it!

Just goes to show — no matter how good certain conspiracy books are, and Alex Constantine's *are* good, they should always be approached with extreme scepticism. Remember folks, this is the only field

CRUCIFY ME AGAIN
£8.95 / pb / 224pp / ISBN 1899598146 / Codex Books 1999 / PO Box 148, Hove, BN3 3DQ, UK / www.codexbooks.co.uk / codex@codexbooks.co.uk

where the author is more gullible than the reader. [Stephen Sennitt]

Update When *The Covert War Against Rock* was orignally given over to Stephen Sennitt for review in *Headpress 21*, the editor had no idea of Stephen's obtuse connections to the book. The editorial comment which appeared alongside the original review opened thusly: "For anyone who doesn't believe that we're all pawns in some big, premeditated plan, here's a cautionary tale..."

CRUCIFY ME AGAIN
Mark Manning
(aka Zodiac Mindwarp)

I've been waiting for this book for over thirteen years now, ever since I heard Zod's 1987 hit single Prime Mover and realised for the first time that in this howlingly-mad world I wasn't alone. It came with an accompanying video full of spacegod rock Stormtroopers, teenage slutvixens and exploding nun heads that was *so close* to my dreams that it was frightening. The lyrics, the Sven Hassel imagery, and the knowingly-adolescent celebration of the female sex's base appeal was a White Dwarf dense compression of every potent visual stimulant from my childhood. *Warlord* comics, Paul Raymond magazines and Motorhead album covers. It truly fucking blew my mind and came at a time when heavy metal (my only church) was daubed in mascara and spandex and needed a serious injection of the grease and hogsweat that *true* metal would always be lubricated by. Over the years I followed the band's breakneck decline into obscurity, trudging along to decrepit toilet venues like Rio's in Bradford to witness the very definition of desperation played out on stage. Zod, Cobalt Stargazer and the ever-changing line-up of under-mutants would pummel through the 'hits' and unleash the occasional blitzkrieg of new material from albums destined to only be released in Germany. They always looked up for it — perhaps driven less by enthusiasm than a brainstem compulsion to get the job done. Like soldiers in 'Nam they knew they were fucked but had only the combat to justify their existence. Little did I suspect that behind the façade of showmanship there was a fusion reactor of neuroses, electric snakes writhing in a pit of Freudian slurry.

Crucify Me Again is a submersible, complete with shit-caked windscreen, dropped into that pit. Nothing like an autobiography, this is a collection of Manning/Mindwarp anecdotes: his childhood in Leeds, his adventures in the Rock Wastelands and his Troubles with Women. I suppose the closest literary comparison would be Bukowski — the same world-weariness, the same sexual obsessions, the same alcoholic self-indulgence and the ever-enduring image of a damaged man hunched over a keyboard.

Behind a wildly inappropriate but amusing cover image of scowling Chinese Army Death Bitches are 190 pages of lies, madness and the often hard and unpalatable truth, loaded into chapters as short and no-nonsense as a Stanley Knife blade. With titles like 'Sympathy For The Paedophile', 'Fucked By Rock', 'Gobby Cunt', 'Sad Fuck' and 'Menstruating Nazi Fucker' the lazy and uninterested reviewer might think they could hawk up a quick slating of the book without actually reading it but they would be wrong, wrong, wrong. The label is not the contents, the map is not the territory and these

EX PISTOLS 1977 BY DENNIS MORRIS

ironic stabs at tabloid succinctness are designed to draw you in and then hammer their point home with ballpen accuracy.

Manning is more than comfortable with his chosen lexicon — an exuberant gutterspeak collision of Milton, Burroughs and Leeds boot boys — and revels in veering from one extreme to another across the pages. He eases the reader in with unsentimental tales of his youth: growing up in the shadow of Elland Road football ground and Armley Jail, schoolyard scraps, tap room initiations and mindless destruction — all numb responses to the grey monotony of life on a council estate in seventies England. As grim as these tales may be to some, to my eye they brought a dewy tear as I fondly remembered the 'old' Leeds before the yuppies descended on it like locusts and turned it into one huge café bar and hair salon. These experiences gave a solid foundation for the curious young Manning to build upon. At sixteen he went to Bradford Art College where his mind was raked open by extravagant homosexual lecturers who weaned him onto books by Reich and Burroughs. It was a short step from there to LSD psychosis and then he was ready for a bruising by the Great Beast itself: Rock!

The chapters covering his experiences in the music industry are perhaps the least interesting. He mentions a few noteworthy characters such as Joe (the giant black Nazi who wore a 'White Power' T-shirt) and Clive (lead singer of Dr & The Medics who had a magical ability with turds), but seems to have ditched a lot of that baggage in the scummy wake of endless tedious tours around Europe. There's no mention of any pleasure gained from being a rockstar, just a palpable sense of relief that it's all over and best put down to experience. He does point out that it's pretty rare for the actual culprits involved to write their own story — these days it's left to the hagiographers at *Mojo* and the roadies who remember which testicle Keef liked to shoot heroin into. The tone becomes less detached when he discusses the women he's collided with over the years: the three mothers of his three children and the dozens, hundreds, of others — some of who were nothing more than 'Road Gash', some who were teetering on the edge of sanity and some who, for one reason or another, managed to leave their crampons in his heart. He attributes his attitude to most of his 'conquests' (that some would knee-jerkingly react to with howls of 'misogynist') as the inevitable result of a life spent on the road in a rock band where the rules of consensus reality are skewed by unchecked indulgence, testosteronic overload and a gradual slide into an unreedemable state of psychological squalor. Here's an example of how bad it got:

I couldn't be arsed wanking myself, but I had this hard-on that just refused to go away. I got up and dragged this little blonde into my gruesome litter. I couldn't be arsed fucking her but I thought she'd be alright to just toss me off so I could get some sleep. Blondie started slurping around — she wasn't bad actually — I blobbed off onto her tonsils and went to sleep.

It seems cold but who's to say we wouldn't end up the same way in those same fucked circumstances? It's the beast in all of us, which is ultimately Manning's main point and his favourite subject, and it's the lifelong wrestle with this Tasmanian Devil that has left Manning emotionally napalmed and shuttered away from the outside world in his Clerkenwell hovel. With his days of howling at the moon on stage now consigned to the past, he's left to communicate his ideas via the medium that was always his best — as originally evinced in his lyrics. His casual mastery of language is not designed to impress *Guardian* reviewers and win Booker prizes — it's the peacock display of a man who dragged his intellect out of the gutter of diminished expectations and into the league of articulate deviants like de Sade and Burroughs. It delivers a punch of communication that intellectual (as opposed to intelligent) piffle merchants like Martin Amis would have to offer up a lifetime full of virgin sacrifices to Yahweh to match. Amidst the hilarious and breathtaking sexual metaphors ('cock snot', 'nad jam', 'fuck hammer') are genuinely profound declarations on the human condition, my favourite being

...language, custom, religion and culture are the thin paper that covers the cracks in the walls of a haunted universe

That pretty much sums it up for me.

In case you haven't figured it out, this is an important book. Mark Manning has nailed a portion of his soul to the masts for all to see. He's walked paths that many couldn't imagine, let alone dare to follow,

DESTROY
£19.95 / pb /155pp / ISBN 1871592747 / Creation books / www.creationbooks.com

DISSECTING MARILYN MANSON
£9.99 / pb / 176pp / ISBN 0859652831 / Plexus 2000 / www.plexusbooks.com

INVISIBLE REPUBLIC
£6.99 / pb / 297pp / ISBN 033033624X / Picador 1998 / www.panmacmillan.com

and is reporting back on the ruined state of the destination he's found. He did it so you don't have to. Now go read his book. [Rik Rawling]

DESTROY
Pictures of the Sex Pistols and the others
Dennis Morris

"Nostalgia for rejects to come"... Twenty years on and the nostalgia has well and truly arrived. No sooner have we recovered from the Sex Pistols' sad reformation, now we're getting regurgitated *NME*-type photos from the seventies and asked to pay £19.99 for the dubious pleasure.

Destroy, a book of paparazzi photos dealing with the Sex Pistols, that boat trip with Richard fucking Branson and gigs in Sweden, Coventry, Wolverhampton, Brunel University and Penzance. If you were at any of these gigs, or indeed, on that boat you may give a fuck about this book. I wasn't and I don't.

There are a couple of good pics: a nice one of Trojan looking fucked-up and the ever-beautiful Jordan (Amyl Nitrate) relaxing next to a friend; Nancy, doing impressions of that-dead-bloke-from-Nirvana's-widow. Also it proves that both Malcolm McLaren and Vivienne Westwood have always been pig ugly. Oh yes, and Sid's actually quite fuckable — anyone know where he's buried? [Rick Caveney]

DISSECTING MARILYN MANSON
Gavin Baddeley

Here are a few of the influences cited in *Dissecting Marilyn Manson*: Frederick Nietzsche, Kiss, *The Bible*, fascism, Queen, Sigmund Freud, absinthe, Alice Cooper, Aleister Crowley, *The Rocky Horror Show*, Charles Darwin, Kenneth Anger, the Church of Satan and... Dr Hook? Anomalies aside, it reads like a rolecall of the misanthropic male, and the male in question is Marilyn Manson, the USA's alternative rock ghoul of choice; a man whose success has allowed for experimentation with every available excess, and, on a sweeter note, allows him to shack up with that actress from *Scream* who got her tits caught in the garage door (semi-naked picture of her in here, flesh fans!).

Gavin Baddeley's book sets out to do just what the title suggests (although I'm sure quite a few people would enjoy a literal interpretation) and break down the influences from childhood onwards that have made this 'Antichrist Superstar' the person he is today. The trouble is that in attempting analysis, Baddeley also shows us how devastatingly unoriginal Marilyn Manson is. Admitting that the actual music is the least of his concerns, Baddeley creates — sometimes very tenuous — links between subject and influences and comes an embarrassing cropper more than once. Briefly touching on the subject of Manson Senior's role in the Vietnam war (as a helicopter pilot responsible for dropping Agent Orange), he rightly states how the hedonistic Paris of the 1890s was a result of the Franco-Prussian war, and that the same was true for WWI and 1920s Berlin, before cocking it all up with:

> *Could there be a link between American decadence — as personified by Marilyn Manson — and the humiliating defeat experienced by the US in Vietnam?*

For fuck's sake! We are, after all,

talking about a 'decadent' culture where Nietzsche can be paraphrased by the narrators of 'dangerous sports' videos; where Henry Rollins is thought of as a renaissance man; where a band like Slipknot are considered threatening because they wear masks... Throughout the book, Baddeley also attempts to draw parallels between events of the past and acts of the present, as undertaken by Marilyn Manson. It's a pretty wide chasm to leap across, and, unless you're a rabidly devoted fan (there's probably no other kind), you'll finish this book thinking all little Marilyn represents is a composite of Iggy Pop's self-hate, Throbbing Gristle's shock tactics, David Bowie's stage personas, and Alice Cooper's theatrics (strangely, the book's cover photo shows Manson to be the spitting image of Cooper). The last chapter even hints at a slide into messianic self-immolation, a route taken by so many others in rock history.

The best level on which *Dissecting Marilyn Manson* works is as a primer for less-obvious gothic culture. There are some dank alleys to go down, not just the usual ones populated by bats and shit. Here are a few: nineteenth-century decadent artists, Roald Dahl, *Lie*, Dr Seuss, J G Ballard, the Marquis de Sade, the White Album, classic gothic literature, David Lynch, Phillip K Dick, and Alejandro Jodorowsky. If this book does nothing else, I hope it leads Marilyn Manson fans on to somewhere else. Somewhere different. [Martin Jones]

INVISIBLE REPUBLIC
Greil Marcus

The American fantasy of public mastery contains a fantasy of public suicide

says Greil Marcus. He quotes D H Lawrence on the "alien" quality of American speech:

Why, if I say anything that displeases them, the free mob will lynch me, and there's my freedom.

When Bob Dylan walked onstage with Al Kooper, Mike Bloomfield, and most of the Butterfield Blues Band at the Newport Folk Festival in July 1965, he might have been lynched. The icon of folk music had sold his soul to the devil rock'n'roll. Pete Seeger tried to cut the cables bringing power to Dylan's heretical electric guitar. Later that summer at Forest Hills the crowd was even more hostile. Phil Ochs worried publicly that Dylan might be the next target of assassination. Kooper, a local boy, was so shook up at Forest Hills, he quit.

Dylan's new backup was a reassembled band known as The Hawks, and they began a monumental tour which ended in Britain in the spring of 1966. A bootleg CD of their performance in Manchester is easy to find: at one lull in an extraordinary set, someone in the crowd yells, "Judas!" at Dylan, who responds like a proto-McEnroe: "I don't believe you!" Dylan's electric records, *Highway 61 Revisited* and *Blonde On Blonde* were already huge sellers, but every night his integrity was being challenged. In July 1966, one year after Newport, Dylan broke his neck in a motorcycle crash. He retreated to pre-festival Woodstock, New York; the Hawks lived in a pink house nearby. In the basement of that house, Dylan began playing with the group that would become The Band: the tapes of those sessions became the stuff of rock mythology.

Marcus uses the music on the Basement Tapes to deal with myth on a larger scale. He made The Band an important part of *Mystery Train*, one of the classic books on rock'n'roll. *Invisible Republic* goes back deeper into the roots of the music; for Marcus this prequel is an extended riff linking itself to a lost vision of America. Bootleg copies of the Basement Tapes have been collectors' gold for thirty years. Playing only for themselves, Dylan and The Band transformed the dangerous impulses of American folk and blues into an exciting new drama of rock. They were chasing the authentic spirit of American music as if this were the last chance to catch it.

Marcus' genius is connecting the impulses that make that spirit live. He finds the murder that produced Stagger Lee. He may quote Lawrence on the "pitch of extreme consciousness" reached by nineteenth-century American writers "funked by Europe", but what Lawrence said of Melville is true too of Dock Boggs, a banjo-playing bluesman. "You get to the top of the mountain, it's easy to get down," Boggs sang. The top of the mountain for Dylan and The Band was this set of tapes.

In 1968 Dylan released *John Wesley Harding*, The Band debuted with *Music from the Big Pink*. But neither could mine this vein for long. By 1975, when a smattering of the Basement Tapes was released officially and *Mystery Train* appeared, The Band was history. Within five years Marcus, who was despairing of bland American rock, became enthralled by the dangerous aura of punk, and tried connect it to the European avant-garde. It never really worked. Back now in the dark pas-

I WAS ELVIS PRESLEY'S BASTARD LOVE-CHILD
£13.99 / pb / 224pp / ISBN 1900486172 / Critical Vision 2002 / www.headpress.com

LORDS OF CHAOS
$18.95 / pb / 378pp / ISBN 0922915946 / Feral House 1998 / www.feralhouse.com

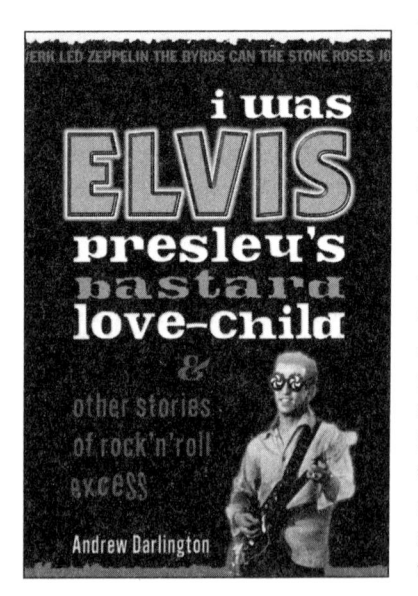

sages of American myth, "there were doors all around you, all you had to do was find the key". The key opens into the Basement Tapes. Enter at your own risk. [Michael Carlson]

Update Some Dylan bootlegs have since been released officially, including the Manchester Free Trade Hall "Judas" concert from 1966.

I WAS ELVIS PRESLEY'S BASTARD LOVE-CHILD
Andy Darlington

In 1980 I was becoming increasingly fed up with the whole post-punk scene. A mate named Dale who had a dead-end carpet cleaning job found an old magazine called *Planet* underneath a scruffy settee, a seemingly trivial incident which for a short time changed my life. The magazine in question comprised a special retrospective on the Fillmore scene of the late sixties, and I was galvanised by a sense of excitement I'd not felt for years.

Reading about the halcyon days of rock in such uncritical, glowing terms presented a viable alternative to that grey, cynical Joy Division scene which only days before had seemed impossible. The roster was certainly impressive by any standards: The Doors, *Anthem of the Sun*-period Grateful Dead, Iron Butterfly, Joplin, Hendrix, Quicksilver Messenger Service, Love, etc. etc.

But what grabbed my attention more than anything else was an atmospheric photo of Jefferson Airplane's Grace Slick — her crazy porcelain doll's face suggesting a strange and frightening sexuality. For the next year or so I ostentatiously rejected the contemporary music scene, in favour of collecting all the early Airplane albums, along with anything else I could lay my hands on from the pages of *Planet*. To say I lived in my own little world, scorning the current scene to the bemusement and irritation of my friends, is no understatement! But like all manufactured paradises my self-imposed exile (ha ha) came to an end with the realisation that if I kept banging on about 'ancient' groups nobody at the time was interested in, I would never get a girlfriend.

With the passing of time the follies of youth seem strange and difficult to fathom. Only a year or so later, I viewed my exclusionary pose as yet another example of a wilfully contrived and self-indulgent precocity — the unwanted ability to 'get up my own arse' that has haunted my plots and schemes ever since! What I realise now is that all this could have been avoided if there had been a book on the market like Andy Darlington's. Here we have a truly heterogonous mix of musical styles and artists reflecting the mature and considered tastes of a true enthusiast, never hidebound by obsolete questions of genre or category. Essays and interviews range between the manic oddity of Joe Meek, the cybernetic noodling of Kraftwerk and Cabaret Voltaire, the unmitigated pop of Mott The Hoople, the cool salaciousness of Robert Plant, to the manic oddity of Peter Green! Oh, and there's a nice piece on Grace Slick — twenty-two years ago the symbol of my objectless desire… Andy, where was your book when I needed it? Better late than never, I suppose. [Stephen Sennitt]

LORDS OF CHAOS
The Bloody Rise of the Satanic Metal Underground
Michael Moynihan & Didrik Soderlind

Off the infernal presses of Adam Parfrey's Feral House imprint (*Apocalypse Culture*, *Cult Rapture*, *The Satanic Witch* etc), comes this scorcher about rock'n'roll damnation in the frozen fjords of Norway. For those of you not up to speed on the events this book recounts, I'll briefly recap. In the late eighties and early nineties, a number of mostly well-educated middle-class young metalheads, mostly in Scandinavia and particularly in Norway (and why this should have been so is one of the most interesting questions exhaustively explored in *Lords of Chaos*) took the cod Satanism of such bands as Venom, Slayer and Mercyful [sic] Fate way, way too seriously. At first they were content to form bands — Burzum, Mayhem, Emperor and Bathory amongst others — that pushed the already-frenzied Black Metal sound to new extremes of intensity, unintelligibility, and unlistenability. But because the established Church of Norway failed to fall beneath this sonic onslaught, the frustrated headbangers hit on the idea of setting fire to churches. Mediaeval Norwegian 'stave' churches being of a unique (and beautiful) all-wooden construction, they burnt very well, and soon ancient monument arson became quite the fashion — nearly 100 churches were torched, warming up the icy Norwegian nights no end. Some of the more articulate Black Metal types saw this as a process of reclaiming their Viking heritage from the 'alien' creed of Christianity. The next logical step in this Satanic jihad would have been to start killing priests, but being crazy mixed-up kids they mostly turned instead, to killing (*a*) themselves, and (*b*) each other. Dead from Mayhem shot himself. Varg Vikernes aka Count Grishnackh, the whizkid behind Burzum, stabbed Oystein Aarseth aka Euronymous from Mayhem, apparently in a conflict over unpaid royalties (although a struggle for control of the Oslo scene seems also to have been a factor). And so on.

So you thought you were a bit of a rip in your so-called misspent youth? Well, sucker, read this and find out what real juvenile delinquents do. Gasp in wonder as picturesque churches explode in fiery homage to an atavistic retribution! Chuckle at the exquisite irony of a photo of a guy called Dead who's, well, fuckin' dead in the picture, having taken a shotgun to his head earlier in the evening! His homeboy Euronymous (later to die himself at the hands of Varg Vikernes), upon discovering the body, hastened out to buy a camera in order to take some album sleeve shots, informed the authorities, and then bustled around picking up skull and brain fragments to turn into necklaces for his friends and a nutritious stew — mmm, nice! Piss your pants (in mirth rather than fear) at the sight of hordes of skinny young lads made up to look like the living dead and waving medieval weaponry around, for *Lords of Chaos* is copiously and hilariously illustrated.

Most of the leading lights of the Scandinavian Black Metal scene are now either in Valhalla, Hades or some other afterlife-type situation, or else they are busy biro-ing pentagrams and inverted crosses on the walls of their cells. Varg Vikernes became a favourite media *bête noire* whilst standing trial for murder, due to his boyish good looks, his outspoken defence of his actions and his remarkable lack of remorse. He is now as much a national pariah in Norway as, say, Charlie Manson in the States or Myra Hindley in Britain, and, ever the trend-setter, has abandoned Satanism as passé, advocating instead both Fascism and an Odinic revival, signalling this shift by shaving his girlie locks off and cultivating a Manson/LaVey style goatee. 'Ásatrú' or Viking paganism is a rising force, and the combination of this religious atavism with a growing nationalism (bands singing only in Old Norse and rediscovering ancient instruments) forms a natural foundation for an interest in Nazi philosophies.

This book is as thorough, as well-researched and as well-written a look at this fascinating and sorry saga as it is possible to imagine. The authors, one American, one Norwegian, have talked to all the involved parties who are still alive, and not only dish up mounds of helpful background info on Heavy Metal, the Nazi occupation of Norway, the influence of Odinism on early Nazi thinking, but also delve into tangential issues like the resurgence of interest in Viking religion mentioned above, the international neo-Nazi scene, and Black Metal-inspired crimes in other countries — not only the USA and Britain, but also Russia, Poland, the former East Germany, France and many others.

This is a far more literate and serious book than the subject matter would lead you to expect. There are exhaustive footnotes, a bibliography, and several appendices on occultism in Scandinavia. Only the lack of an index mars its scholarly credentials. And it is better written than any book on rock music has a right to be. The authors maintain an admirably impartial tone — they are clearly not apologists for Satanism, but neither are they outraged moralists, nor pru-

**MAN ENOUGH TO BE
A WOMAN**
£11.99 / pb / 186pp / ISBN 1852423382 / Serpent's Tail 1995 / www.serpentstail.com

**THE MANSION ON
THE HILL**
£12.99 / pb / 431pp / ISBN 0224050621 / Jonathan Cape 1997 / www.randomhouse.co.uk

rient sensationalists. *Lords of Chaos* is one of the most important books on alternative/youth culture ever written, and the fact that it's about such a bizarre, marginal sub-cultural phenomenon does not alter this at all. Only *The Family* by Ed Sanders (admittedly a very different kind of book) rivals it as an account of youth culture-inspired crime. Anyone with any interest in Heavy Metal, occultism, Fascism, crime or Scandinavia will lap it up. I cannot praise *Lords of Chaos* highly enough, and may you burn in Hell if you fail to buy it! [Simon Collins]

Update Oh great, the biggest clanger I've ever dropped in a *Headpress* review and now they want to reprint it! As I wrote in a letter in the following issue of *Headpress* (No 19): "…I opined that the authors are 'clearly not apologists for Satanism'. It has since become apparent to me that Michael Moynihan is, in fact, a fairly major apologist for Satanism — a pal of Boyd Rice, a priest in Anton LaVey's Church of Satan, founder of the occult fascist band Blood Axis etc. I feel this is the sort of thing I should already have known. I'm still a great admirer of *Lords of Chaos*, however, and in fact I owe the authors my gratitude for a couple of things. The book turned me on to Scandinavian Black Metal, which now forms an important and fibre-rich part of my musical diet. It was also influential in my subsequent embrace of Germanic heathenism — a more mature and sustainable belief system than Satanism, in my opinion. I still haven't stabbed anyone or torched any churches, though."

According to Jack Sargeant, the updated 2003 edition of *Lords of Chaos* offers insight into new developments. Varg Vikernes, for example, still incarcerated, emerges as a believer in UFOs, which he somehow links to Odinism as well as racism via the belief that aliens tampered with evolution to create the master race.

**MAN ENOUGH TO BE
A WOMAN**
*Jayne County
with Rupert Smith*
In 1977, when I was in my last year at school, pupils of my age were allowed access during the dinner hour to a new building called the ROSLA. ROSLA stood for Raising Of the School Leaving Age. Allowing pupils to stay indoors unsupervised during dinner hour was a pretty radical move for the school. I imagine it was someone's idea of preparing us for the maturity of the outside world. We had our own canteen, which served a menu different to that of the rest of the school. Here I had my first unfulfilling taste of a hamburger. We didn't have to eat at tables either, but could sit in comfy chairs and eat with our plates on our laps. Fortunately there wasn't a TV set, otherwise we'd have been glued to it. But there *was* a record player.

Kids brought in their favourite records. It was always the same kids, too, so we heard the same records. (I didn't take any of mine in; I didn't want to get any of them scratched.) Punk rock was filtering into the mass media, and I had a copy of Gary Gilmore's Eyes by the Adverts at home. I would leave the arm of my record player up, so that the single would play over and over again. I didn't just simply listen to the lyrics — I *devoured* them. Lyrics *meant* something, and I never tired of pondering over their possible meanings.

Back in the ROSLA, one record

that got played a lot — by the same guy who played Iggy Pop's *The Idiot*, funnily enough — was Black Is Black, a disco record by a group I am reliably informed were called La Belle Epoque. You'll have probably heard it. It starts off with the softly spoken vocal: "We like the disco, we like the disco sound/Black is black is black is black." I disliked disco as much then as I do now, but I found this record intriguing. "Black is black, I want my baby back/Is grey is grey, since you went away…" What was the significance of the cyclic use of the lyrics? And was the record about someone who'd died?

One day, someone brought in a picture book about the punk phenomenon. I remember in it, near the back, was quoted a traditional Polish saying that went something like "Every man likes the smell of his own farts". There was also a full-page photograph of The Electric Chairs on stage, with transsexual frontman Wayne County on his knees, holding the mic between his legs like it was a dick. I remember this image particularly well, because it happened to be the day the school priest came in on one of his visits. As he wandered around the ROSLA, speaking to the kids, he picked up the punk rock book and flicked through it. I'm sure he saw the picture of Wayne County and the *faux* phallus, but he just put the book down again, said, "Very good, very good," and mooched off somewhere else.

That little scenario of a Catholic priest maybe seeing this guy on his knees pretending to masturbate is what I think of when I think of Wayne County.

Wayne County was just too *ugly* to achieve any kind of major punk success. His band had a record called Fuck Off (which remains the only record of theirs I've ever heard), he dressed like a woman, changed his name to Jayne, had the chop and *became* a woman. That's got to make for a pretty interesting autobiography… Indeed, *Man Enough to be a Woman* is such a colourful story that if it was a work of fiction it'd be toned down for credibility's sake. The punk rock years take up only a fraction of the book's page count — I was expecting more. Still, I was pleasantly surprised by County's fairy tale pre-punk history, associating with the likes of Holly Woodlawn, Andy Warhol, Patti Smith, Debbie Harry, the Kinks… Not forgetting the bum record deals, being harassed by both straights and gays, having an early backing band called the Backstreet Boys, meeting Brian Tilsey out of *Coronation Street*, driving across England in a transit van on tour with the Police as support ("The Police were the most boring people I have ever met," says County), playing the Reading Festival in 1977, going on between Hawkwind and the Doobie Brothers and being bottled off…

I don't know what kind of promotion and distribution this book originally got, but I assume not much; this is the only copy I've seen on sale and I bought it. After finishing reading it, I still had no inclination to hear another Electric Chairs record. And my story about the ROSLA and the priest is more interesting anyway. [David Kerekes]

THE MANSION ON THE HILL
Dylan, Young, Geffen, Springsteen and the Head-on Collision of Rock and Commerce
Fred Goodman

Bob Dylan and the Band feature in Fred Goodman's story of the growth of the rock business, but mostly in the ways they relate to their legendary manager Albert Grossman. Once again, Dylan is seen as the person breaking the mould, whether it's liberating the rock single with the added length of Like A Rolling Stone or taking over the studio process from the record label. Grossman was quick to realise that the new generation of rockers, unlike their predecessors in the fifties, weren't out to get rich through music, at least not solely. They thought of themselves as *artists*, and needed to be handled as such.

The Band, with their resolute failure to ever do anything commercial, might be the *ne plus ultra* illustration of this attitude. A lot of it, like the music Marcus traced, grew out of the folk background. Goodman is very good in centring much of his story on Boston. Although the Hub City isn't generally thought of as a key point in rock history — bands like Ultimate Spinach, the Remains, and the sadly neglected Earth Opera hardly blipped on the nation's hip Geiger counter — it was a major folk centre, built around Club 47, and later boasted the first rock FM station (WBCN), *two* weekly 'underground papers', and a thriving concert scene built around the Boston Tea Party.

Goodman shows how all these businesses grew around the original need to let the new music express itself, and how quickly they became embroiled in all the usual side-effects of the free enterprise system. The story of the *Boston Phoenix* newspaper was told, in simplified form, in a movie called *Between the Lines*, Goodman's fuller version is even more tragic and entertaining.

MONKEEMANIA!
£9.99 / pb / 144pp / ISBN 0859652920 / Plexus 1999 / www.plexusbooks.com

NEIGHBOURHOOD THREAT
£12.95 / pb / 144pp / ISBN 1899598170 / Codex Books 2000 / PO Box 148, Hove, BN3 3DQ, UK / www.codexbooks.co.uk

Micky Dolenz and Peter Tork get down to some serious music for the *Headquarters* sessions. *Monkeemania!*

The Boston scene also produced Jon Landau, who deserves billing in this book's subtitle alongside David Geffen. Landau went from record reviewer on the *Phoenix* to Bruce Springsteen's producer. Goodman tells the famous story of Landau's battle with Mike Appel for Springsteen's soul in great and telling detail.

He also traces much of the influence of Landau on Springsteen's songs, in that they are hugely derivative of the books and movies Landau instructed his pupil to absorb. His music may have grown more sophisticated in the *Born To Run* era, but the 1974 Boss was somehow more original, more touching.

Landau's record review protégé was Dave Marsh, Springsteen's hagiographer.

Writing biographies of a man when your mentor is his producer (and later manager) and your wife is on his management staff never conflicted with Marsh's ethics, so loudly expressed in his *Rock and Roll Confidential* newsletter.

As Landau took over the Springsteen business, the Boss himself turned Hollywood, moving to LA, marrying a supermodel, and hitting the gym. We all know the result of that.

In Hollywood, he might've bumped into David Geffen. If Landau was someone who fell in love with the music and charted his course to success through it, Geffen was someone who saw the success of the music, and decided to use it to propel him to success even greater than the music business. Goodman is at his best when he charts the slithery course up the ladder that Geffen took. Geffen was a lamprey attached to the conglomeration of the Warner Bros empire; one thing Goodman never explains is what hold Geffen had over Warner's chairman Steve Ross. CBS Records' chief Walter Yetnikoff once offered to give Geffen CBS if he'd only teach his wife how to give a blowjob. Perhaps Ross took instruction.

Geffen's legal battles with Robert (*Chinatown*) Towne over the movie *Personal Best*, or his lawsuit against Neil Young (whom he lured to Geffen Records with the promise of artistic freedom and then sued for delivering uncommercial records like *Trans*) are classic Hollywood, and of course today Geffen is a kazillionaire and part of Dreamworks with Steve Spielberg and the other guy who looks like Schwarzennegger playing Woody Allen playing a sperm.

"If you want to defeat your enemy, sing his song," Bob Dylan said in 1985, worrying that the good new music might never get heard again, since the businessmen had taken such complete control of rock, which was now an 'industry'. Goodman's book is exceptional in that he can move from an understanding of the spirit behind early Buffalo Springfield to an analysis of the corporate take-over of MCA. And show you how the two are related.

When Michael Moore was making *Roger and Me*, the film about the abandonment of his hometown of Flint, Michigan by General Motors, he went to his old friend Dave Marsh, as one underground journalist to another, to try to get the rights to use Springsteen's My Hometown in the movie. Marsh, offended by comments critical of Springsteen that a GM assembly-line worker had written in a column in a paper Moore edited, refused point-blank, saying the worker was his "ideological enemy".

In the end Moore's film was distributed by Warner Bros., who also controlled Springsteen's publishing company, so corporate synergy did what counter-culture contacts couldn't. Moore noted that "apparently, the largest media conglomerate in the world is no-one's 'ideological enemy'". As Pogo used to say in the funnies, "we have met the enemy and he is us". [Michael Carlson]

MONKEEMANIA!
The True Story of The Monkees
Glenn A Baker

If anyone picked up a copy of Micky Dolenz' *I'm a Believer*, expecting an exposé of one of the most successful musical groups in history, they would have surely been disappointed. That book was little more than a sliver of PR-nostalgia, lacking any real grit or insight. Those of you who want to investigate the Monkees phenomenon, dirty fingernails and all, ought to check out *Monkeemania!* instead. Don't be fooled into thinking that under its wacky cover lies some shallow Monkees reunion souvenir, because Glenn Baker has compiled a comprehensive and thoroughly fascinating investigation into the workings of the band. There's a chapter on *Head* which relates that the whole tone of the movie (which starts with the band committing suicide) was influenced by the fact three-quarters of the band had gone on *strike* the day shooting was supposed to start. The director and producer were not happy men. As part of the trippy ad campaign — or perhaps just sour grapes? — a minute-long TV commercial for the movie had no reference whatsoever to the Monkees.

The book also details how, by the latter part of the sixties, the band desperately wanted to be taken seriously as musicians. The organisers of the Monterey Pop festival had no intention of hiring the Monkees to play, but the Monkees wanted to be there nonetheless — or at least Mickey and Peter did, hopelessly striving for acceptance within the hippy community. Thus, Peter went to Monterey and got his picture taken with Brian Jones; Mickey went dressed as an American Indian (with full headgear) holding court and philosophising to pre-pubescent girls.

Perhaps the one downside with *Monkeemania!* is that since its first printing in 1986, no attempt has been made to update the thing. In a way this is good: I, for one, couldn't bear to trawl through countless reunion tour snaps. In a way it's bad: songs that are said to be unreleased or lost have since come to light in the last few years through official sources. All told, that's a minor quibble and this is a great book. [David Kerekes]

NEIGHBOURHOOD THREAT
On Tour With Iggy Pop
Alvin Gibbs

In 1988, sometime UK Subs bass player Alvin Gibbs got hired to play with Iggy Pop on his *Instinct* world tour. It's a mark of the precarious state of the jobbing musician when you consider Gibbs' substantial payrise: one day he's earning less that $300 for a couple of shows with his

NIGHTSHIFT
£5.95 / pb / 122pp / ISBN 1898927405 / ST Publishing 1996 / PO Box 12, Lockerbie, Dumfriesshire, DG11 3BW, UK / www.stpublishing.com

NOWHERE MAN
£14.99 / $22.50 / 221pp / ISBN 1887128468 / Soft Skull Press 2000 / www.softskull.com

OUR BAND COULD BE YOUR LIFE
£18.95 / hb / 522pp / ISBN 0316063797 / Little, Brown & Company / www.twbookmark.com

own band, the next he's contracted up and getting $1,500 a week. A friend mentions that the music business is either "feast or famine", and in *Neighbourhood Threat* Gibbs eats sensibly, for the most part. So does Iggy, now free of chemicals and alcohol (bar a *Scarface*-style coke incident in a Miami night-club), hanging out with a tanned Steve Jones and saving all his violence for the stage. Along with a potted Iggy history, Gibbs comes up with some snapshots from within the Big Rock Tour Machine: a member of The Jesus and Mary Chain gets floored by a roadie, Gibbs nearly gets off with the then-Sugarcubes singer Björk (he remains deliberately vague about his own shag quota throughout), fails to fathom the complex relationship between Iggy and David Bowie (although who wanted to know Bowie during his *Glass Spider* period?), trashes a hotel room because — of all things — Iggy was snubbed by Ryuichi Sakamoto, and watches smack-head guitarist Andy McCoy being verbally abused by one of the Everly Brothers. Absurdity and rock music walk hand in hand, and Gibbs is well aware of this.

Neigbourhood Threat isn't the greatest on-the-road memoir ever written, but it's an entertaining documentation of what it's like to be a well-paid hired hand on a major world tour, where the band will never meet the guy who drives the equipment truck. Such a disjointed sense of living has effects both on and off stage. What sort of effects? Here's Iggy telling Gibbs how he met his then-wife, Suchi:

"I did a show in Tokyo," he explained. "Saw her in the crowd from up on the stage and something just clicked, so I asked one of the road crew to invite her to the dressing room to talk, and we got on so well that we've been together ever since." The roadie in question later told me that Iggy had simply instructed him after the show to bring the Japanese girl in the glasses backstage. Having gone out into the auditorium, he noted at least a dozen optically-challenged daughters of the rising sun standing around. Not having a clue which one Iggy meant, he opted for the closest — Suchi. Whether she was in fact the woman that Iggy had clicked with from up on the stage, he, nor we, shall never know.

[Martin Jones]

NIGHTSHIFT
Pete McKenna
Predating punk rock by a couple of minutes, a youth culture erupted in the North of England that was every bit as intense in its devotion to an altogether different form of music. In this instance, the music was Soul and the movement became known as Northern Soul. Like punk, Northern Soul appeared to be more a reaction to the times than it was about liking music. It looked to have come from nowhere, but in fact has a history woven into street gangs, Mod and Ska revivals, and drugs. Clubs catering to the scene quickly sprang up — The Torch in Stoke and the Twisted Wheel in Manchester, for instance — but none captured the spirit and heart of the scene as much as the Casino Soul Club in Wigan.

Before we go any further, I'd like to point out that I'm not approaching this book as a fan of the music, or

— God forbid — someone who was once a part of the scene. Soul music does nothing for me. Despite Pete McKenna's enthusiasm throughout *Nightshift*, not for a minute did I ever feel I wanted to hear a single note of any of the records he was gushing over; I knew exactly how they'd sound, and that is just like every other soul record I've ever heard: *bad*. But, I am interested in 'movements', and I can appreciate the record collector mentality that leads hardcore fans to pay extortionate amounts of money for rare seven inch platters.

Wigan Casino ran regular Soul nights from September 1973 up until December 1981, at which time the organisers were unable to renegotiate their lease and the club was forced to close. (The club alternated between Soul nights and punk bands.) During this period, Wigan established itself as a Mecca for Northern Soul fans, who made the trip every weekend from all over the country to attend the Casino's All-Nighters. (Why All-Nighters should have become a requisite of the Northern Soul scene is never explained in the book.)

Needless to say, McKenna is a fan and writes about the ritualisation of his social life, how everything revolved around those eight-or-so hours spent in the Casino: The travelling from his hometown in Blackpool each Friday night (first by coach and then later by any means necessary), the drugs that were an integral part of the scene for most people, but which ultimately eroded it, and the 'coming down' and the void felt waiting for the next weekend.

McKenna relates many horror stories. Some of these are drug-related, but not all. As the book progresses, it seems that the bad times outweigh the good ones, but not once does McKenna's devotion to the scene falter. Ultimately, he gets Wigan-fever so bad that when one day he discovers his father lying on the stairs suffering from a stroke, he steps over him and goes to bed, hoping that someone else will deal with it — should it mess up his plans to get back to his beloved club.

Nightshift is not particularly well-written. It doesn't aspire to be a facts-and-figures historical chronicle, but rather a rites of passage recollection for McKenna. The blurb on the jacket says, rightly, that *Nightshift* is a fast-paced read. With some tighter editing (or any editing at all), it could have been a much faster one. [David Kerekes]

NOWHERE MAN
The Final Days of John Lennon
Robert Rosen

There are many books on the market which claim to offer some refreshing new slant on the man and legend that is John Lennon. I haven't read most of them so cannot say how this compares. However, I'm sure *Nowhere Man* has something which those other books do not — principally, the diaries of John Lennon. Rather, author Bob Rosen had the diaries but they were stolen.

Fred Seaman, Lennon's personal assistant and a close friend of Rosen, had been collaborating with Rosen on a book about Lennon for some months prior to the ex-Beatle's assassination. The idea to write a book came from Lennon himself apparently, who was sick of living a lie and wanted the world to know that his time at the Dakota was far removed from the official picture of happy house-husbandry, doting father and bread-baker, simply glad to let his wife Yoko Ono take care of business. In reality, Lennon was miserable and insecure, locked like a prisoner in his bedroom as servants tended to his every need. After Lennon's murder, Seaman was promoted to Yoko's executive assistant, and he took this opportunity to feed Rosen with the exclusive material now at his fingertips. Amongst the many photographs, slides, unreleased audio and videocassettes, random scribblings and notes, were Lennon's own journals. Rosen started transcribing these at the end of October 1981, spending long, amphetamine induced days deciphering the scrawl. For six months, Rosen claims to have "lived like a monk, confronting on a daily basis The Gospel According to John". But then Rosen says he was burgled and the whole lot was taken. Certain that Seaman himself was behind the deed, he went to see Yoko, who promptly had Seaman arrested.

Lennon's last days in *Nowhere Man* come courtesy of Rosen's memory of the journals and his interviews with the late-musician's friends, family and lovers. The concept of stolen diaries (now back in Yoko's possession) is an intriguing one (and reminiscent of *Paperback Writer*, a spoof alternate history of The Beatles). *Nowhere Man* engagingly depicts a life spiralling slowly into madness, with Lennon locked onto dietary fads, astrological charts and meaningless minutiae. Not many days are happy days here. [David Kerekes]

OUR BAND COULD BE YOUR LIFE
Scenes from the American Underground 1981–1991
Michael Azerrad

THE PORTABLE HENRY ROLLINS
£7.99 / pb / 324pp / ISBN 0753802112 / Phoenix House 1997 / www.orionbooks.co.uk

Whilst I heartily agree with Janeane Garofalo's blurb from the book jacket — "This book is essential for anyone who feels personally insulted by the Grammys, MTV, Top Forty radio, etc, etc" — I do think that many of the bands from this period (the 1980s) are championed a lot more than they actually deserve to be. Then again, the Yanks never did get the real eye-popping punk explosion that we Brits suffered, nor the subsequent fallout that resulted in a bleak decade of piss poor ballads, jangly guitar bollocks and the ultimate triumph of bubblegum pop. Their eighties was shaped largely by Reaganomics and much of the vital art was a reaction against such a stultifying spectacle as seeing a man once out-acted by a fucking chimpanzee sat in the White House. We had Thatcher, who, for the most part was feared or secretly admired rather than downright hated, which is why we got The Smiths when our wayward cousins had the likes of Black Flag, Sonic Youth and Butthole Surfers to contend with. With the benefit of hindsight I know where I would have rather grown up during that horror decade.

This book will immediately ruin any fantasies that still linger of teenage years in America being something like *Repo Man* or *Ferris Bueller's Day Off*. As much as it focuses on the bands it talks of the social forces that shaped them, often turning a potentially dull subject like 'new wave' also-ran's The Replacements into engaging figures on the edge of something vital and true. Before Nirvana and the subsequent mainstreaming of 'alternative rock' there was a vibrant and chaotic underground movement that raged against the lingering dominance of Jurassic Rock acts like REO Speedwagon and The fucking Eagles (who still to this day refuse to die), and author Azerrad has really tried to document the highs and lows of those times. Despite sometimes anally chronicling every 'significant' date and release, he does manage to get some juicy quotes and anecdotes from the right people. Greg Ginn (Black Flag) emerges as some kind of punk-Patton, a war-hungry General endlessly leading his gang of troops into battle with every venue a battlefield, every audience the enemy. Rollins mutates from Nietschze-quoting thrashpunk skater ball of suburban hatred into darkly enigmatic rock ubermensch. Steve Albini starts out as a twisted little fucker with a Bible-black sense of humour and coldly cynical disregard for Asylum Earth (the first Big Black EP *Lungs* was supposed to be called *Hey Nigger*!) and becomes reputable Kudos-cloaked producer for hire. Gibby Haynes and Butthole Surfers appear to be escaped lunatics who fell over some discarded instruments and any notions that they might ever have been 'faking it' are rapidly dispelled in a single chapter that is worth buying the book for on its own. Gibby & Co were dirt poor, living out of the back of a fucked up '71 Chevy Nova, painted in fluorescent colours with barbed wire on the front bumper and teeth painted on the grille. They went to the moon in it by all accounts and seemingly never came back, not mentally anyway. They were, albeit psychotic, light relief to much of the furrowed-brow macho-hardcore bullshit that repelled as many from the 'underground' as it attracted. Similarly, J Mascis and Dinosaur Jr provided a more dazed & confused — alright, stoned — approach to the proceedings for those too intimidated by shaven-headed moshers and meth-cranked human Rottweillers.

After reading the book you certainly come away with a renewed appreciation for what these bands were trying to do. Some failed, heroically, and some endured by sheer tenacity, and whilst I'd resist the temptation to rush out and get some Husker Du or Minutemen action it's worth playing *Locust Abortion Technician* again with slightly more of an insight as to where that fucking crazy shit came from in the first place. [Rik Rawling]

THE PORTABLE HENRY ROLLINS
Henry Rollins

Just what is it about Henry Rollins, the thinking man's Travis Bickle? On the face of it, his deficiencies are more obvious than his talents. He can't sing, he can't dance, he can't write poetry (his prose is more debatable, more on that later), and those of you unfortunate enough to have seen the dreadful *Johnny Mnemonic* will affirm that he absolutely can't act. He looks like a demented Action Man, he has some cheesy tattoos (and some great ones), and he admits to enjoying the music of Dave Lee Roth and Thin Lizzy. His first band, Black Flag, despite enjoying massive cult status now, were frankly mediocre, no better or worse than a hundred other hardcore bands; and whilst the Rollins Band have their moments, too often they sound like Black Sabbath with an even worse singer than Ozzy Osbourne. I know all these things, even if Rollins doesn't, and yet I have to confess to being a Rollins fan. And I'm not alone — his gigs and spoken-word performances now get respectful reviews in the quality press (well, *The Independent* and *The Guardian*, at least), and there is a growing opinion that Henry Rollins is, in some mysterious and indefinable way, cool.

This is largely a personality cult rather than an acclaim for his creative output. Rollins somehow manages to seem much more than the sum of his parts. Not that he's idle: in addition to extensive touring and recording, both solo and with his band, he's produced a dozen or so books, appeared in several films, and he runs the 2.13.61 publishing house, originally a self-publishing venture but now handling the work of many other authors as well. *The Portable Henry Rollins* is a sampler culled from his first eleven books ('Portable' is a bit of a stretch — this is a pretty weighty tome — but I'm sure it's easier to carry around than Rollins himself). The quality of the writing is wildly variable. Rollins is at his best writing travelogues, tour diaries, reminiscences (*Black Coffee Blues*, *Now Watch Him Die*, *Get In The Van*, *Do I Come Here Often?*), but he's embarrassingly bad writing 'poetry' about his various abortive relationships with women. This is some of the worst rock poetry penned since Jim Morrison and Jimi Hendrix gave it a rest (not that I wish to denigrate their respective excellent musical outputs). He lacks the subtlety, the sense of balance, and the empathy to get away with being 'sensitive', and I suspect these are personal failings as well as literary ones. Make no mistake, Rollins sustained some heavy duty damage from his evidently horrible upbringing, but instead of seeing a therapist and trying to rejoin the human race, he has founded his career on roaring like a wounded beast about how lonely he is. Check it out:

Close your eyes
Think of the filth
Think of the alienation
Become the isolation
Embody the alone
Use it as a weapon
Alienate others...

Henry, Henry, take it easy! Lighten up, dude! No man is an island, y'know. But of course Henry doesn't know.

It's also easy to read the rage Rollins feels against his mother behind this fear of women, just as his exaggerated hatred of the police is a transparent reaction to his bullying, militaristic father. Coupled with the hyper-masculine posturing, the obsessive bodybuilding, the boot-camp haircut, the view of life as an endless combat zone, a picture emerges of Rollins as a frightened little boy who wasn't taught how to love. I hate to think of the level of repression that has gone into the construction of Rollins' tough-guy façade. But this can make compelling reading. At its best, his writing is searingly honest, brutal, visceral and artless (which is why the poems don't work).

This collection is a good (and good value) introduction to all that's good and bad in Rollins' written output, and for the completist it also contains some work unavailable elsewhere, including transcripts of a spoken-word performance from LA in 1992. Just as with Lenny Bruce, a lot of Rollins' humour lies in the physical and vocal delivery, and the spoken word shows are often both funny and affecting, showing a self-deprecating irony which is nearly non-existent in the strident,

PSYCHOTIC REACTIONS AND CARBURETOR DUNG
£8.99 / pb / 390pp / ISBN 1852427485 / Serpent's Tail 2001 / www.serpentstail.com

SONGS IN THE KEY OF Z
£11.95 / pb / 271pp / ISBN 1901447111 / Cherry Red 2000 / www.cherryred.co.uk

STAIRWAY TO HEAVEN
£9.99 / pb / 384pp / ISBN 0060938374 / HarperEntertainment 2002 / www.harpercollins.com

Cover of Jandek album, *Six and Six*. *Songs in the Key of Z*

self-righteous written work. I still don't really know why I like Henry Rollins and buy his books and CDs. There's just something about the guy. Those of you who feel similarly indulgent, or are merely curious, could do worse than to buy this book. [Simon Collins]

PSYCHOTIC REACTIONS AND CARBURETOR DUNG
Lester Bangs
What's the point of music journalism? The impact of music precedes language, operating directly on the emotions; writing about it seems almost reductive, the sole apparently useful function to let a reader know what's out there. And perhaps what it's like, although reading reviews in a magazine like *The Wire* won't give you much of an idea what a record's 'like', or even whether the reviewer enjoys it or not; rather reviews show an overtly intellectual response, often fascinating but academic to a fault at times. And this is the best of a bad bunch — reviews in 'rock papers' like the NME seem to be written by poorly paid hacks keen to make a name for themselves by championing the next big thing, irrespective of its power or quality.

Music is today treated by journalists either as cultural curio or lifestyle accessory. Passion? Commitment? Not on the agenda. Not for some time, either, with self-consciously raddled egomaniacs like Nick Kent being lauded as the best music journalists of their generation…

So what does this have to do with Lester Bangs? Bangs' writing has the qualities I appreciate in other music writers in spades: passion, commitment, taste… But you shouldn't get the impression from this that *Psychotic Reactions* is po-faced or self-consciously worthy writing. Far from it: the best pieces here have a delirious energy, a kind of celebration of the rock'n'roll spirit at its most crass and moronic hand in hand with an appreciation of the cleansing properties of white noise. Bangs' writing is so conversational, drug-racy ranting veering off into endless *Tristram Shandy*-style asides, that it occasionally crosses over into sheer incomprehensibility:

boy at tidie ondine azza rule cquole kott, tax litza Obetrols in dan tux ubat uporih, zamdung woch a knaw gnitting eboit

And this from a book proposal he'd written…

Bands covered include Count Five, The Troggs, The Velvet Underground, The Stooges, Kraftwerk, The Clash, and for your money you also get excerpts from Bangs' novel fragments, tales of twisted love and wretched drug excess and an account of every New Year of his adult life. As editor Greil Marcus writes in his introduction:

What this book demands from a reader is a willingness to accept that the best writer in America could write almost nothing but record reviews.

Bangs died in 1982 aged thirty-three. This 'five star' edition of *Psychotic Reactions* was published to tie in with the film *Almost Famous*, which features Bangs as a role model for the central character. Untimely demise aside, I can't think of a better role model for an aspiring music hack. If you haven't read Bangs before, you're in for a treat. Highly recommended. [James Marriott]

SONGS IN THE KEY OF Z
The Curious Universe of Outsider Music
Irwin Chusid

During many years of working as a record producer, journalist and free-form radio DJ, the American Irwin Chusid collected huge amounts of information on obscure musicians. In this book he presents some of these 'outsider' artists, like the manic depressive Daniel Johnston (recently the subject of his own book *Hi, How Are You?*), who used to play all the instruments at the same time — and sing. Wesley Willis, a black, 350-pound paranoid schizophrenic, lives on the streets of Chicago and has around 400 nearly identical songs in circulation. He claims to have written 35,000, backed by his own Casio keyboard. The Swedish Eilert Pilarm is an Elvis imitator, but he knows less of the lyrics than me or you, and has absolutely no sense of rhythm. Harry Partch composed music only for instruments invented and built by himself. Since his death his music has rarely been performed, as the instruments are very difficult to play, tune and transport. The institutionalised Jack Mudurian gulps down ten cups of coffee and rants through 129 songs in forty-five minutes. Lucia Pamela believed that she had recorded some of her songs on the moon. The Wiggin sisters in the band The Shaggs were forced into the studio by their father, long before they had learned how to play, sing or write songs. The result was the legendary album *Philosophy of the World* (1969). Strangely, this was one of ultra-perfectionist Frank Zappa's favourite albums. The mythical hermit Jandek has put out twenty-eight albums since 1978, and nobody wants 'em. They're all filled with tuneless guitar strumming and depressing mumbling. There are also chapters on more well known eccentrics like Syd Barrett, Captain Beefheart and Wild Man Fischer. But for the most part this book goes through uncharted territories, and is very entertaining and well-written, without making too much fun of the sometimes mentally ill artists. Along with the book you should pick up the CD of the same name (also from Cherry Red) in order to listen to many of the artists you've been reading about. I think the CD is almost meaningless when separated from the book, and ideally the two should have come together as one package. Strongly recommended, anyway. [Jan Bruun]

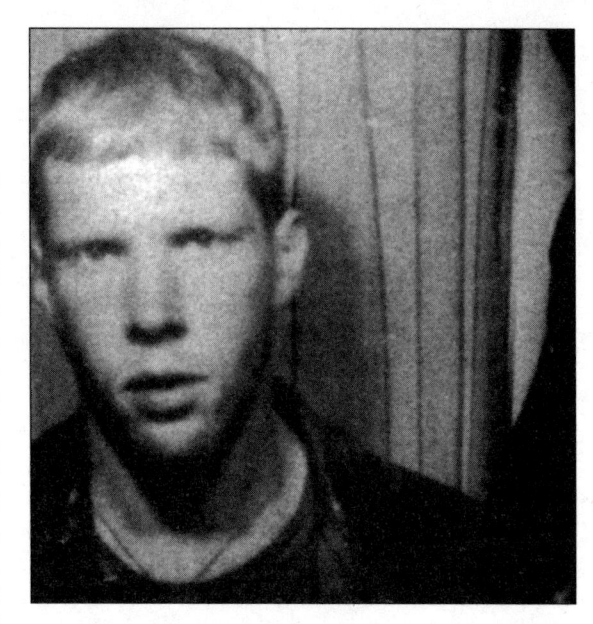

STAIRWAY TO HEAVEN
Led Zeppelin Uncensored
Richard Cole with Richard Trubo

Quite a responsibility being a tour manager: organising gigs, accommodation, ensuring equipment is in order, collecting money, keeping your charges happy and out of jail. "I was the only one to keep Led Zeppelin in line," writes Richard Cole, Led Zeppelin's tour manager for twelve years, "and I was usually just as possessed with alcohol — if not more so — than the rest of the band."

Yes, it's more unrivalled rock'n'roll mischief with the heaviest quartet in the annals of popular music — this time via the recollections of the snort-to-excess Cole.

Richard Cole's book opens with him in an Italian prison cell, hearing the news that his drummer buddy John Bonham is dead. The book closes back in that cell, after a rather scanty explanation as to how he got there (suspected of blowing up a train station in Bolognia) and 370 pages of Zeppelin overload.

And overload is the right word. I'm reminded of Frank Zappa's autobiography in which Frank relegates his on-the-road anecdotes to a single chapter. He seemed to think that was more than enough. After reading Cole's *Stairway To Heaven*, while Zappa's chapter still appears brief, I can see what he meant.

17% HENDRIX WAS NOT THE ONLY MUSICIAN
94pp / Slab-O-Concrete publications

ALEISTER CROWLEY
£9.99 / pb / 216pp / ISBN 1840182296 / Mainstream Publishing 1999 / www.mainstreampublishing.com

Stairway To Heaven just doesn't let up — every thing is in there, from groupies masturbating in a bath with an octopus, to Jimmy Page calling Jethro Tull "Jethro Dull" on account of them being so boring. The former is an interesting fact and needs to be known by you; the latter is just one of many flippant asides not deserving to be immortalised in print, and detracting from the impetus of the book… Impetus being the groupie stories, substance abuse, violence, and delusions brought on by the abject boredom of touring and believing yourself to be gods.

Robert Plant gets so drunk on a commercial flight that he has to call for assistance to go to the toilet, being led down the aisle by a stewardess and shouting, "Robert needs toilet!"

Members of the band stick a garden hose into John Paul Jones' apartment while he sleeps, filling his room with water.

The band book into the Grande Ballroom in Detroit only to find the floor covered in blood and a murder just having taken place.

These are just a random sample of the stories to be had, each page carries a couple more.

Like Peter Grant, Zeppelin's manager, Cole was not one to suffer fools lightly. In fact, the Zeppelin entourage had quite a reputation and Cole would readily attack and beat people up for merely *looking* suspicious when in company of the band. More than once, he and several of his crew pull a guy from an audience during a concert and pulverise him 'round the back'. One priceless instance, after fearing there might be a riot, Cole decides to secure himself beneath the stage and smashes with a hammer the kneecaps of any fans within swinging distance.

Alongside the mayhem, there is a genuine sense of wonder and excitement that what the band are doing is unique and timeless. Not that Cole particularly views each individual member with fondness — there are personality clashes, petty grievances and arguments). But while his offstage relationship with Robert Plant, Jimmy Page and John Paul Jones often fluctuates, with John Bonham he strikes a lasting friendship. It says a lot about Cole, however, that Bonzo comes over as something of a moron. His pranks go beyond mere rock'n'roll bravado, and in many instances are dumb and repetitive. Incessantly trashing hotel rooms, smashing things, buying lots of fast cars. Some of his pranks are also a little odd. For instance, Bonzo finds pleasure in taking a shit in female apparel — in separate instances in the book he deposits a turd in a woman's handbag and another in a woman's shoe. There's a spiteful reason behind one, no reason at all behind the other. He also derives pleasure in throwing fresh orange juice over guitarist Alvin Lee as Ten Years After play a live set before thousands of people, resulting in Lee's fingers becoming too sticky to proceed as normal. This he finds absolutely hilarious.

Inevitably things begin to slip down the slippery slope…

While Cole and Pagey's addiction to heroin certainly doesn't help things for the better, come the eighties, the band are in an era that they were never designed for. In a way, the death of John Bonham comes not a moment too soon, for with his demise Led Zeppelin call it quits. Sad but true. [David Kerekes]

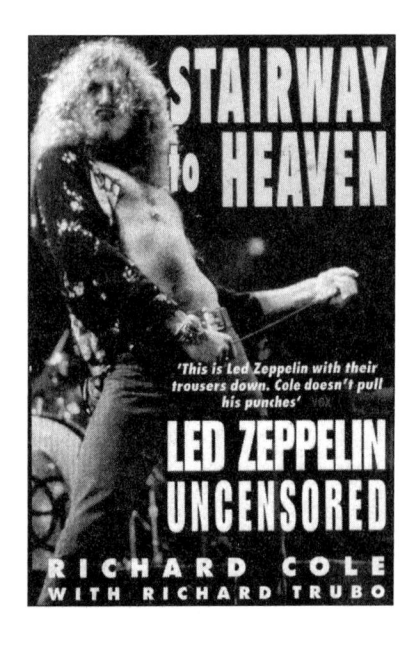

GRAB BAG NON FICTION

17% HENDRIX WAS NOT THE ONLY MUSICIAN
Billy Childish

Billy Childish comes across as a man on a mission. Now at thirty-nine years old, Billy has a full and creative life. Self-confessed punk poet, he also turns his skills to painting, literature, music and, believe it or not, woodcarving! All represented here in this book — a retrospective look over Mr Childish's career.

The journey begins with Billy's school report card, from whence the title for the book is taken — '17% Hendrix was not the only musician' is a comment made in 1972 by his obviously frustrated music teacher. It then moves on to a selection of his paintings, the topic for most of which, I guess, is himself. Most depict scenes of violence of some form, crudely painted and indeed quite childish. For example, his *Fight Snowman* shows a scene where a young man is strangling a snowman; *Sex Crime* shows a young man decapitating a young girl. These images remind me of the work of Salfordian artist, L S Lowry: stick-like, brightly coloured people doing what comes naturally.

After the paintings, we move on to 'Communications from Group Hangman,' a sort of artist's bible on how to approach the world of art and deal with the ramblings of the artistic elite. If that doesn't get you excited, quickly move on to the photo-booth pages, where you can reflect on Billy's life via the medium of photography (does this book have no end to its talents?). We see angry (but quite cute) Billy as a young teenager in 1979, with punk attitude and all. Marvel at the passing of time from one photograph to another, finally ending with his last photo taken in 1988. I guess the punk movement played a sick joke in that it made no provisions for reaching old age.

We then head for the land of poetry. Here is my favourite part. With titles like 'Dissection' and 'Strange Bravery', we see the real Billy Childish, and by far the most entertaining part of Billy's work.

At the back of the book is a compact disc with fourteen recordings on it, including a cover of Teenage Kicks by The Undertones, and Pinhead by The Ramones. This CD certainly has its moments, and takes us back to the heady days of punk rock. Together with his group, Thee Famous Headcoats, Billy has released a staggering eighty records in total.

I like this book. I enjoy artists stretching their limits and getting into new fields (unless it's David Bowie trying to revive his acting career). It's a journey through mixed feelings, like spending the afternoon in a mental hospital with a sick relative. An entertaining, multi-tasking book that I am sure will interest the most cynical punk rocker. [Will Youds]

Update Slab-O-Concrete folded a couple of years back but Codex Books might be able to help.

ALEISTER CROWLEY
The Beast Demystified
Roger Hutchinson

Far from merely demystifying Aleister Crowley, this book sets out to completely debunk the myth. Stripping away the layers of occult mysticism (and grandiose titles) with which Crowley clothed himself, it paints a picture of a man driven entirely by selfish and egotistical needs. The author doesn't paint a pretty picture, and the figure of Crowley which emerges is not only unlikeable but at times actively despicable. That's not to say that Crowley isn't given his due: his skills as chess player and mountaineer, for example, are clearly acknowledged. However even here Crowley's egomania over-shadow his achievements. When Crowley abandons a mountaineering expedition in a sulk, leaving behind dead and injured colleagues, it's not only the end of his career as a climber it's also an example of the petulance which stayed with him all his life. The contrast between this biography and Francis King's *The Magical World of Aleister Crowley* is remarkable, and in the final analysis it comes down to the authors' differing attitudes to 'magick'. Roger Hutchinson claims to be an agnostic on the matter, but it's clear that he's got no time for any occult nonsense. And where others might be tempted to apologise for Crowley's extreme hedonism and egomania as a reaction against his strict Plymouth Brethren upbringing, Hutchinson clearly shows that not only was that upbringing not as strict as would at first appear, but also that the arrogance Crowley displayed was firmly rooted in uncompromising Christian fundamentalism. By the end of the book Crowley is shown to be a sad and lonely old man, a heroin addict with delusions of grandeur, a pathetic figure in every sense of the word. And yet… There is nothing here to explain Crowley's continuing appeal.

AMOK FIFTH DISPATCH
$19.95 / pb / 620pp / ISBN 1878923129 / Amok Books 1999 / 1764 N. Vermont Ave, Los Angeles, CA 90027, USA / www.amokbooks.com

AN UNSEEMLY MAN
£6.99 / pb / 352pp / ISBN 0747533989 / Bloomsbury 1997 / www.bloomsbury.com

Mercenary, perverse, monstrously selfish, how is it that he attracted so many acolytes? There's nothing here to explain why a pathetic old druggy could attract so many young, attractive women into his orbit and into his bed. And why is it that all these years later Crowleyana shows no signs of abating? "Do what thou wilt shall be the whole of the law" may not strike many people as a particularly deep philosophy, but it continues to resonate. So while this book makes interesting reading, there's something clearly missing from it: Crowley's undeniable charisma. [Pan Pantziarka]

AMOK FIFTH DISPATCH
Sourcebook of the Extremes of Information
Ed. Stuart Swezey

Snowdomes — those tacky souvenir panoramas in Perspex bubbles which, at the flick of the wrist, become pretty snowy winterscapes. Except they aren't always that tacky and their history is often intriguing. Dating back to the 1800s, some snowdomes are intricate pieces of art, while some others (made in Hong Kong) were banned in the 1960s for having untreated, polluted water in their domes.

Snowdomes by Nancy McMichael is just one of the many fascinating books featured in *Amok Fifth Dispatch*. A random flick through this tome's pages reveals other esoteric delights, like *The Prisons* (a book of "grandly brooding etchings depicting imaginary prisons executed between 1743 and 1745 by the frustrated Italian architect Giovanni Battista Piranesi"), *Amputees and Devotees* ("scholarly study of female victims of lost limbs and the men who eroticize them"), and *Countering the Conspiracy to Destroy Black Boys* (which "describes how African-American boys are systematically programmed for failure").

Continuing where Amok's own *Fourth Dispatch* of some years ago left off — but ditching the pulp look for superior paper stock and a more pleasing layout — *Fifth Dispatch* still doesn't offer much by way of a critique for any of its entries. Many titles are represented with an extract from the book's own publicity blurb, and in some particularly vague instances no text at all other than title, author and publisher details. Although Amok no longer claim to be the mail order source for this material, *Fifth Dispatch* remains for all intent a sales catalogue, albeit one that has mutated out of all natural proportions. But I'm not really complaining, I haven't actually used it to source anything but have spent many a happy hour leafing though its pages, delighting in the sheer diversity and wealth of material covered… which is illustrated with plenty of contentious images. And if you turn the book upside down it snows. Only kidding. [Joe Scott Wilson]

AN UNSEEMLY MAN
My Life as Pornographer, Pundit and Social Outcast
Larry Flynt with Kenneth Ross

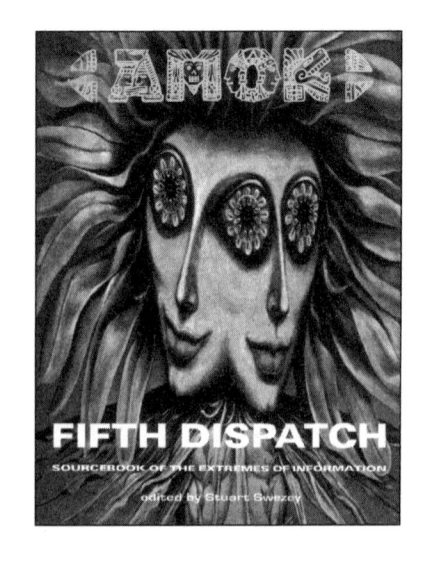

Available for a time in bargain bookshops (I think my copy cost £1.99), it would certainly be worth paying full price for this compulsive little page-turner. Arriving hot on the heels of Milos Forman's excellent film *The People vs. Larry Flynt* (superior, I thought, to the overrated *Boogie Nights*), this is the ghosted autobiography on which the film was based, and this edition contains no less than four forewords — from Oliver Stone (producer), Milos Forman (director), Woody Harrelson (star), and Al Goldstein of *Screw* magazine, all running along the lines of what a surprisingly affable fellow Larry Flynt is when you get to meet him, and why his story is required reading for all those interested in defending the First Amendment. The book's political and cultural credentials established, let's get down and dirty.

An Unseemly Man energetically recounts Flynt's dirt-poor Kentucky hillbilly upbringing, his early sexual experiences, with a 'neighbor girl' at seven, and with a chicken at nine (in his mad-tycoon phase, Flynt immortalised this episode by having a three-foot high replica chicken installed, with a mock-up of his shotgun shack childhood home, in the basement of his mansion), his careers in the armed forces (Army and Navy), his three failed marriages (or was it four? I lost count, and no doubt so did Larry) and sundry illegitimate offspring, before bringing us into more familiar territory — the founding of the Hustler go-go clubs in Ohio, and the subsequent launch of *Hustler* magazine. The latter half of the book is largely taken up with accounts of his bizarre conversion to born-again Christianity at the hands of President Carter's sister Ruth Carter Stapleton, the lengthy legal battles he fought on *Hustler*'s behalf, the white supremacist assassination attempt in Lawrenceville, Kansas that left him permanently wheelchair-bound and in constant pain for years (but at least it destroyed his religious faith), and the death from AIDS of his consort Althea (played with great bravura by Courtney Love in the film). There is plenty of entertaining incident along the way, and, as you'd expect, lashings of sex.

Flynt evidently possessed an overweening interest in making the beast with two backs long before he got into the skin trade. He recounts an incident in Cannes during his Navy days when, on shore leave, he hired the entire staff of a brothel — twenty girls — lined them up naked, and proceeded to play musical dick. He had to be carried back to his ship. Finding himself running a string of topless clubs in the late sixties, he was indeed a happy camper:

I was insatiable, sometimes having a different woman every four or five hours. There may have been someone who had more women than I did, but I seriously doubt it. It got to the point where I couldn't remember who I'd screwed.

Chance would be a fine thing! Nor did this behaviour diminish after he met the love of his life, Althea Leasure, an underage dancer who was swiftly promoted to managing the clubs whilst Flynt nursed his nascent magazine, and who eventually ran the magazine whilst Flynt spent all his time in court:

We recognized each other's proclivities. I slept with a lot of women; she slept with a lot of women. It worked. We were happy.

It is clear that Larry Flynt's astonishing rags-to-riches-via-rudeness story happened because Flynt possessed several invaluable personal qualities — a flair for publicity, a ruthless instinct for profitability, a pugnacious enthusiasm for baiting the bourgeoisie, and an uncanny sense for what would appeal to the blue-collar readership he courted (although he makes the interesting point that *Hustler* also proved popular with the intelligentsia, highly educated people evidently being "less hung up on conventional morality" than the amorphous middle-class masses who were his real bugbear). It is also clear that the fury and animosity that *Hustler* aroused had as much to do with its social and political outspokenness as it did its sexual explicitness. Flynt had a genius for making enemies, and a righteous unwillingness to back down. You have to admire a man who appears in court wearing a T-shirt emblazoned with the words "FUCK THIS COURT", and who screams at the Supreme Court of the United States of America, "You're nothing but eight assholes and a token cunt!" *Hustler*'s most protracted court case was fought over a Campari ad parody in which Flynt depicted TV evangelist Jerry Falwell reminiscing about screwing his drunken mother in the outhouse, but my personal favourite *Hustler* prank was the spoof ad they ran headed "Jesse Helms — Phone Sex — Blacks Preferred", and giving his home and office numbers.

First and foremost, though, all red-blooded men owe a profound debt to Larry Flynt for being the man who brought us the split-beaver shot, the man who had what seems in retrospect an obvious realisation:

To put it bluntly, if you got the models to spread their legs a little wider, you'd sell more magazines. I made a mental note of that.

Thanks, Larry. [Simon Collins]

APOCALYPSE CULTURE II
£11.99 / $18.95 / pb / 458pp / ISBN 0922915571 /
Feral House 2000 / www.feralhouse.com

ASK DR MUELLER
£9.99 / pb / 320pp / ISBN 1852423315 / Serpent's
Tail 1997 / www.serpentstail.com

Issei Sagawa, cannibal man. Colin Wilson's contribution to *Apocalypse Culture II*.

APOCALYPSE CULTURE II
Ed. Adam Parfrey

I know a few people who own a copy of *Apocalypse Culture*, and many of them don't know why. They rarely pick it off the shelf but when they do they usually find something in there that either strikes a resonant chord or makes them want to throw the loathsome tome into the trash. The unrelenting focus on the symptoms of despair and madness allows for no passive stance — the reader either senses its purpose or flinches in horror.

At the time of its publication the editor, Adam Parfrey, declared that there was no possibility of a sequel, which may be a reflection on just how far down the slide into madness the world has gone because now, thirteen years after the first edition, comes just such a volume.

In that intervening period there has been the rise of an entire 'underground' or 'alternative' culture (which is really just a small and grubby part of the ever-consuming mainstream behemoth) and a number of publications that have served to seemingly steal the thunder of this new book. Regular readers of *ANSWER Me!*, *Panik*, *Funeral Party*, *Headpress* and others may find some of the potential 'shock' factor of its contents reduced by regular exposures to weird shit. However, Parfrey has used his considerable resources to find the real signposts that point to the region described here as The Forbidden Zone. There are a couple of familiar names from the original *Apocalypse Culture* — Boyd Rice, James Shelby Downard and the now completely over-exposed Peter Sotos — but the majority of material comes from new writers with new perspectives. The subjects covered are everything from serial killer confessionals, paedophilic art, religious icons and 'conspiracy theories'. The astute assembly of the book and the often contradictory and jarring juxtaposition of the contents serves to add to the inevitable sensation of psychic overload that you get when reading the book in long sittings. For example: Colin Wilson displays his consummate skill and experience in the telling of the case of Issei Sagawa, a 'sexual cannibal' who killed and partially ate a Dutch student, went on to be found not guilty and is now a widely published author. This is followed by a list of recipes for meals like Stillborn Stew and Sudden Infant Death Stew.

The enigmatic series of incidents and co-incidences that surrounds the capture of Ted Kaczynski, The Unabomber, are covered by James Shelby Downard understudy, Michael A Hoffman II. Parfrey himself checks out the 'Slash' convention where women — "chronic suburban masturbators" — meet to share their obsession with gay porn fantasies featuring TV heroes like Starsky & Hutch and Kirk & Spock. Peter Sotos' increasingly shrill voice is applied to the JonBenet Ramsay case, where he seems to imply that the media coverage of the murder, and others like it, were a mass collective 'rape' of the dead girl's corpse. Quotes from Geraldo Riviera's show are interspersed with self-indulgent fantasies clearly written by Sotos while wanking himself silly.

Yes, Trevor Brown's in there too, and the cover art is by Joe Coleman but it never devolves into a roll-call of 'the usual suspects' (unlike the recent *Suture*) thanks to excellent articles by Dan Kelly, Parfrey himself (on Richard Green, lone member of the radical group 'Jews for Hitler') and, most surprisingly, Crispin Glover who lays into modern culture and dares to ask:

> Is it possible that the Columbine shootings would hot have occurred if Steven Spielberg had never wafted his putrid stench upon our culture, a culture he helped homogenize and propagandize.

Genesis P-Orridge describes this book as the New Testament. What it stands as a testament to is more than just the fact that the world is mad; the world has to be mad otherwise it wouldn't work. Meanwhile we can't seem to help ourselves, staring into the abyss, scribbling notes and making sketches. Are we trying to understand our condition? Are we making records for future generations? Are we mapping the outer edges of man's society?

If it wasn't such an excellent collection of fantastically weird shit then it would still be a valid document, even if only to stand as a significant lump of *Yang* to the *Yin* of *Ally McBeal*, Harry Potter and DreamWorks. Buy this book and save your soul. [Rik Rawling]

ASK DR MUELLER
The Writings of Cookie Mueller
Cookie Mueller

Cookie Mueller is probably most famous for her appearances in underground and independent movies by John Waters, Amos Poe, and Eric Mitchell, although — as this collection testifies — she was also a great writer. *Ask Dr Mueller* collects together a fair selection of Mueller's work: *Walking Through Clear Water In A Pool Painted Black* (previously published by Semiotext(e) as part of their Native Agents series), her Hanuman books, her 'Art and About' column from *Details* magazine, and her advice column from the *East Village Eye*, from which this edition gets its name (a column which John Waters' describes in his introduction as offering 'highly questionable medical advice'). Also included in this edition are nine previously unpublished stories.

The short autobiographical narratives, which make up much of this collection, detail Cookie's experiences, from runaway, to stripper, to nearly meeting Charles Manson in Haight Ashbury, to acting in *Pink Flamingos*, as well as wild, adventurous trips to Jamaica, Italy, and Berlin. The tales offer the reader a tantalising glimpse into a genuinely bohemian world, where rebellion meant enjoyment, and surviving the times without resorting to the-straight-gig was, in itself, an achievement. All are written in a style which catches the absurd pathos of the 'human condition' with insight and humour. As a writer, Mueller also had a unique ear for voices and accents, managing to capture the nuances of individual expressions — ranging from Jamaican patois to Edith Massey's drawl — without submitting her subject's speech to syntactic garbage.

Ask Dr Mueller is also a book haunted by the spectre of AIDS. At the end, in an article originally for *Details* magazine, dated August 1989, Mueller writes about her husband, the artist Vittorio Scarpati, who is in hospital with collapsed lungs, yet is still drawing: "Things are never so bleak and threatening as we believe. Vittorio is fortunate he has his incandescent wit and his work to keep him out of darkness. I hope he comes home soon." Turning the

BECHAMP OR PASTEUR?
$20 / pb / 298pp/ ISBN 0787311286 / Health Research Books 2003 / www.healthresearchbooks.com

BIZARRISM
£11.95 / pb / 157pp / ISBN 1900486067 / Critical Vision 1999 / www.headpress.com

BOB FLANAGAN
$16.99 / pb / 132pp / ISBN 0940642255 / Juno Books 2000 / www.junobooks.com

The story of Donald Crowhurst, or, How To Become A God, in *Bizarrism*.

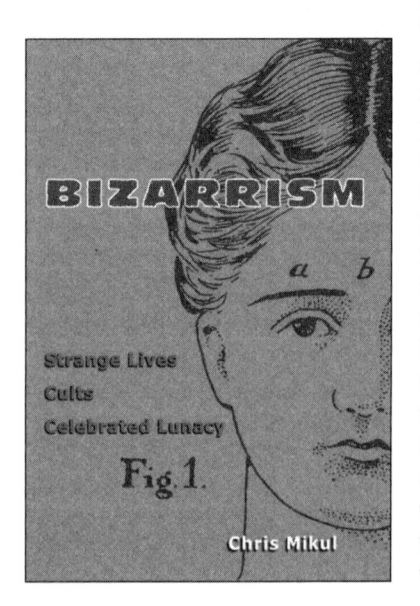

page the reader is confronted with the author's biography: "Cookie Mueller died of AIDS... on November 10, 1989, seven weeks after her husband died of the same cause." Reading it — and now re-reading it — still saddens me, as Mueller herself wrote, AIDS is a 'war' which has killed so many people working in the arts: "People who hated and scorned pettiness, intolerance, bigotry, mediocrity, ugliness, and spiritual myopia; the blindness that makes life hollow and insipid was unacceptable. They tried to make us see." Mueller writes to enable the reader to see, and at the same time attack this blindness. [Jack Sargeant]

BECHAMP OR PASTEUR?
A Lost Chapter in the History of Biology
Ethel Douglas Hume
This history of germ theory seeks to prove that Louis Pasteur was a plagiarist and "monumental charlatan" who actually stole his ideas from a fellow scientist and "ignored genius" named Pierre Jacques Antoine Bechamp. More significantly, according to the author, Pasteur actually got it all wrong. By taking Bechamp's discovery that homeopathy, acupuncture and holistic therapies can cure disease, and distorting it into the concept of vaccination, Pasteur has apparently caused the loss of millions of lives. This book claims that virtually every serious and minor ailment known to humanity has been linked to vaccine damage, and there's an "unaccountable" connection between the AIDS epidemic in Central Africa and the massive vaccination campaigns that occurred there. As a non-scientist, it's hard for me to comment on the evidence for this. And, whilst it's always nice to see idols being smashed, I think Hume would have a more convincing argument had she drawn Bechamp as less the humble savant, and Pasteur less the egomaniacal monster. [Mikita Brottman]

BIZARRISM
Strange Lives, Cults, Celebrated Lunacy
Chris Mikul
This is a bit of a departure for publisher Critical Vision. *Bizarrism* is an Australian zine covering mainly items of Forteana; it's one of the few zines stocked by Mark Pawson, which is something of a recommendation. This book is a collection of highlights from the zine; short articles, most no more than three pages long, about material like scientology, hollow earthers, lobster boys and Mormons — all the usual suspects. I'm not really big on Fortean stuff, and the problem with a lot of the material on display here is that it's been mined to death already — there aren't very many surprises. Mikul was inspired to start the zine — the subject matter of which is described by him as "beacons of shining if erratic brilliance in a world of sensible conformity" — after reading about Donald Crowhurst, and the collection opens with a piece about him. It's jokey and a little dismissive and really rubbed me up the wrong way, especially as I had read sensitive treatments of his life in Tacita Dean's book *Teignmouth Electron* and others. In a way this epitomises the whole Fortean take on its material: the reduction of complex personal lives and struggles into throwaway freakshow fodder.

It's not a bad book, though. On the plus side, Mikul's writing is extremely readable and concise, and held my interest throughout

— although most of the material is familiar, it is still fascinating, and Mikul does succeed in unearthing some truly weird nuggets. As it's an Australian zine there are a fair few pieces on Australian strangeness, and it's these pieces which are the highlight of the book for me, as they offer something totally new. I also really liked the postscript, a piece entitled 'Why I Love Cults', which offers a refreshing antidote to all the cult hysteria around at the moment. While I don't think it's one of the best Critical Vision books, it's a fun read and cheap to boot. [James Marriott]

BOB FLANAGAN
Supermasochist
Ed. Andrea Juno & V Vale

Some of you will have seen *Sick*, Kirby Dick's astonishing 1997 film about the life and times of the late Bob Flanagan (he died in 1996). For those who haven't, Bob Flanagan was an American performance and installation artist whose work focused on (a) his sexual masochism and (b) the cystic fibrosis he suffered from all his life. Cystic fibrosis is a hereditary disease of the pancreas, which is incurable and inevitably terminal — when he died at forty-three, Flanagan was exceptionally old for a CF sufferer. This in itself would make his life remarkable and dramatic enough.

What is really extraordinary and inspiring about Bob Flanagan, however, is his decision to, in his own words, 'fight sickness with sickness' and devote what little time he had left to him to sexual deviation of a really extreme nature. Progressing from solitary sickbed experimentation in childhood, through the Californian S&M scene to a 24/7 committed Mistress-slave relationship with his partner Sheree Rose, and ultimately to public performances and exhibitions documenting his sexual practices, Bob Flanagan disarmed moralistic objections to his work and lifestyle with a dry wit and total lack of coyness or guilt about what he was doing. The book *Bob Flanagan: Supermasochist* originally appeared in 1993 under the RE/Search imprint whilst Flanagan was still alive and can thus be seen as a major part of his project of total self-revelation. Flanagan also worked with rock groups Sonic Youth and Nine Inch Nails. He stars in the widely banned Happiness In Slavery video (stills from which appear in this book) and it is his screams which punctuate the track Screaming Slave.

In his work as a performance artist, Bob Flanagan bears obvious points of comparison with such people as Franko B, whose work also features feats of masochistic endurance and blood-letting related to a traumatic childhood full of religion and clinical interventions, and Ron Athey, who addresses themes of disease, religion and sexuality through grandiose Grand Guignol psychodramas. Both Franko B and Athey, incidentally, are homosexual, thereby providing another connection, via alternative sexualities, to Bob Flanagan. And of course, all these people owe a debt in common to the Viennese

BODY PROBE
£19.95 / pb / 192pp / ISBN 1840680040 / Creation 1999 / www.creationbooks.com

BROTHERHOODS OF FEAR
£18.99 / hb / 255pp / ISBN 0713726873 / Cassell Illustrated 1998 / www.orionbooks.com

Aktionists of the late sixties and early seventies, who set the trend for sexual and visceral extremity in performance art. Bob Flanagan's work, though, is remarkable for its lack of pretension, its frankness, and its humour. His lack of self-pity in the face of his afflictions was admirable, and his acceptance of his own sexuality remains deeply inspirational for the many people crushed with guilt about their own 'abnormal' urges.

The first thing to strike the casual reader of this book is the photographs. Oh God, the photographs! Don't leave this book lying around where normal people might see it. Page after leg-crossing page shows Bob in postures of a more or less excruciating nature. He is generally naked. His penis is often erect. In the course of *Bob Flanagan: Supermasochist* we see his cock and balls shaved; tightly bound with thongs; padlocked and chained; pierced and bleeding; nailed to boards; covered in wax or clothes pegs; distended with heavy weights; sewn up with surgical sutures; and tattooed with a crown of thorns in a nicely impious gesture reflecting his Catholic upbringing. Didn't his mother ever warn him that it'd be taken off him if he couldn't play nicely?

We see Bob's emaciated and disease-ravaged form suspended in bondage harnesses, tied in a closet (was a guy ever less in the closet?!), whipped, branded, covered in food and paint, cut, hanging upside-down from the ceiling of an art gallery in Santa Monica, in rubber hoods, in hospital gowns, and, above all, in pain. And what's more, he seems to be enjoying every minute of it. As he comments on the eye-watering sensation of hanging a ten pound weight on his scrotum:

I'm in seventh heaven, stroking my stump of a penis as this excruciating pendulum swings back and forth between my legs, my feet pressed deeply into the carpet, but I feel weightless, head in the clouds, as high as a kite on a drug called pain.

Most of us will never get very near experiencing these kinds of things, nor would we all want to, but it sure makes for compelling reading! The bulk of the book consists of six long interviews with Bob and one with Sheree Rose conducted by Andrea Juno and V Vale. The interviews range freely back and forth in time to discuss his childhood, medical and sexual history, writing, music and performance, and the big-hearted character and engaging personality of the man come over very clearly. I feel the book could have used a tighter edit, though — the discursive to-ing and fro-ing makes the chronological order of events hard to sort out, and the same stories crop up in several chapters. Couldn't these interviews have been conflated into one super-long interview covering everything in order?

A much more serious fault in the book is Juno and Vale's introduction, a truly tendentious piece of PC moralising and white liberal guilt about "Judeo-Christian brainwashing", "genociding [sic] indigenous peoples", mad assertions that "a third of all children have been sexually molested as children [sic]" and so on. How early nineties! A bit of this creeps into Interview Three as well, as Andrea Juno appears to encourage Bob Flanagan to join in with her critique of pioneering modern primitive Fakir Musafar — and this is from the people who published

Modern Primitives, in which he featured prominently! Talk about biting the hand that feeds you! Apparently Fakir Musafar is guilty of collusion in:

> the incredible ego and ethnocentricity of American white culture to actually think they have any deep understanding of what ancient cultures were about, and then to rip out of context "natural, pure, primitive" social practices — that's just another form of colonialisation.

According to this logic, then, Bob Flanagan is more ideologically sound because he references Porky Pig cartoons in talking about his performances rather than the Lakota Sioux! Well, sorry, but I believe we live in a more complex and multilayered world than this kind of callow judgementalism allows for. I'm also a bit disappointed that this reprint for 2000 hasn't been updated to include events since 1993, notably Flanagan's death in 1996 and the release of *Sick* the following year. It would be interesting to know what Sheree Rose is doing now, and whether Bob Flanagan's work has been exhibited anywhere since his death. (Incidentally, I read an article by Andreas Whittam-Smith, the erstwhile head of the BBFC, recently, in which he cited *Sick* as the kind of film which demands special consideration from the censor in spite of its explicit content, because it has other socially redeeming virtues.)

These reservations aside, however, *Bob Flanagan: Supermasochist* is a great book— interesting, funny and even (dare I say it?) life-affirming. You will be amazed by what a wholesome experience reading a book crammed with explicit images of genital torture can be! The world is slightly less lively and diverse with his passing:

> Mine is the bittersweet tale of a sick little boy who found solace in his penis at a time when all else conspired to snuff him out, or, at the very least, fill his miserably short life span with more than its share of pain, discomfort and humiliation... That first swat on the ass from the obstetrician's skilled hands not only started my diseased lungs sputtering to life, but it also sent a shock wave through my sphincter, up my tiny rectum, and straight into the shaft of my shiny new penis, which ever since then has had this crazy idea in its head that sex and pain were one and the same.

[Simon Collins]

BODY PROBE
Torture Garden
Ed. David Wood

This fascinating volume of essays and images offers a real primer of cutting-edge information about today's cyber-fetish scene; and in this context seems light-years ahead of it's obvious model, RE/Search 12: *Modern Primitives* (now amazingly over ten years old!) and more in keeping with Mark Dery's *Escape Velocity*. In fact there's only one tired-old tat article (Alex Binnie again...) amongst a disturbing morass of mutational manifestos; the most thought-provoking of which comes from the pen of Dr Rachel Armstrong, cyborg anatomist and 'Post-Futurologist' (the last phrase is mine!) who offers the provocative weirdisms, 'Sex in Space' and 'Alien Abduction and Fetishism'; some of the most disturbing ruminations on the outer limits of sex symbology you're likely to encounter in a long time. *Body Probe* is exciting, lively and extremely well designed — it also contains fifty colour plates, making it good value too! [Stephen Sennitt]

BROTHERHOODS OF FEAR
A History of Violent, Magical and Revolutionary Organisations
Paul Elliott

Brotherhoods of Fear is a book that promises much more than it delivers. In looking at such diverse groups as the KKK, the Red Army Faction, and others, one would hope that Elliott would apply some kind of theoretical or psychological framework to link the different groups together. Instead we get the sketchiest kind of definition imaginable, which boils down to the fact that these groups are (a) violent and (b) they don't give a toss what the rest of the world thinks of them. If that sounds like a Reader's Digest view of the world then you'd not be far off the mark. There's a bias here, of course. Given the author's hazy definition of what constitutes "a brotherhood of fear" (and hey, don't a lot of these groups have women in them?), it's no surprise that he doesn't include such vicious and violent brotherhoods as the SAS and the Metropolitan Police. But of course, they're alright because they're on the 'right' side of the law.

What this leads to is a survey of a number of different, unconnected groups and attempts to offer some degree of insight into their histories and motivations.

CAR CRASH CULTURE
$19.95 / pb / 356pp / ISBN 0312240368 / Palgrave 2002 / www.palgrave.com

COCKROACH PAPERS
£3.99 / pb / 232pp / ISBN 1568581378 / Four Walls Eight Windows 1999 / www.4w8w.com

CONCRETE JUNGLE
$24.99 / pb / 224pp / ISBN 0965104222 / Juno Books 1996 / 111 Third Ave, #11G, New York, NY10003, USA / ajuno@junobooks.com

Car wreck in Northern Cyprus, October 1993. *Car Crash Culture*

And it's a pretty mixed bag, starting with the Inquisition and the medieval witch-burnings and ending with Aum Shinrikyo's sarin attack on the Tokyo subway. Along the way we meet nineteenth-century anarchists, the Mafia, British neo-Nazis, Baader-Meinhof, the Klan and more. In each case we get a smattering of history, some facile analysis and then we're off onto the next group.

There's little depth here, and no understanding of the ideologies which underpin these disparate groups. For example the section on anarchists focuses on anarchists as lone assassins and ruthless bombers. There's no mention of anarchism as a mass movement or as a coherent ideology, no mention of the Russian Revolution or the Spanish Civil War. The author doesn't even mention the phrase "propaganda by deed", which even the most cursory research on nineteenth-century anarchism would have turned up.

The treatment of anarchists is indicative of the whole book, which is superficial, poorly researched and likely to appeal to people who find long words problematic. If you're interested in any of the groups included in *Brotherhoods of Fear* then take my advice and seek out something better, it shouldn't be too difficult to find. [Pan Pantziarka]

CAR CRASH CULTURE
Ed. Mikita Brottman
The arbitrary divide between the underground and the mainstream receives yet another dent here. A rather subversive concept for a mainstream book, *Car Crash Culture* comes complete with the lavish treatment an academic publisher can bestow on a limited-appeal job, including a joint hardback and paperback print-run.

A diverse cross-section of writers, tops of their respective fields and many familiar to *Headpress* readers, contribute articles on every facet of automobile accident. These range from the anecdotal and informal (such as first-hand smash-up stories and the Beatles' Paul Is Dead phenomena), the kind of writing that rarely has a place in 'serious' volumes, right through to detailed case studies (such as those concerning autoerotic fatalities and artist Jackson Pollock).

Some chapters traverse both styles, obsessive and informative at the same time. With regard to the latter, A Loudermilk's chapter 'Clutching Pearls' is a particular standout, in which the author ruminates over a suicide fatality photograph from *Life* magazine that has haunted him since high school. A woman, having thrown herself from the eighty-sixth floor of the Empire State Building, lies dead at the crumpled point of impact — which is a sedan on West 33rd Street. The body is dishevelled but its composure is more akin to someone daydreaming than dead, and shows no physical damage. She is holding onto a necklace around her neck — a force of habit it looks like, forcing itself from beyond the grave. "She fell as if she had an appointment to fall", writes Loudermilk (what a great opening line!). And the hub of his fascination with the photograph? "Passing which floor did she clutch her pearls and never let go?"

Car Crash Culture is a great book on a fascinating subject, one that is driven by the editor's own psychological demons. [David Kerekes]

COCKROACH PAPERS
A Compendium of History and Love

This is an absolute gem of a book. Even if — like me — you've got no particular affection for cockroaches this is a book that you have to read. Richard Schweid takes us on a grand tour of the cockroach world, and along the way we learn about the life and times of the cockroach, about pest exterminators, forensic pathologists dealing with cockroach infestation in dead bodies, the effects of globalisation in Mexico, the bead trade in sub-Saharan Morocco, entomologists and other scientists, cockroaches and asthma in working-class children and a whole lot more. Interspersed with straight reportage (and the piece on Ciudad Juarez is especially good), are anecdotes and extracts from cockroach appearances in literature.

Having worked in the catering trade, and having lived in a Mediterranean country for a while, I can tell you that unless you're up close to a cockroach you just can't imagine how alien the thing is. I remember working in the kitchens of a big Victorian hospital in South London, where there was all out war between the staff and the roaches. The stockpot in the centre of the kitchens was on day and night, home to left-over veg and always bubbling away with a nice thick vegetable stock. When the lights came on late at night the roaches used to scurry for cover. The extra protein probably never did anyone any harm, honest.

That pales into insignificance compared to some of the infestations listed in this book. Some of the stories are enough to make all but the most ardent animal-liberationist reach for the strongest insecticide to hand. But the fact that roaches were here before us — in fact they were here about 150 million years before the dinosaurs — suggests that we're the infestation, not them. Still, most of the thousands of cockroach species seem to do fine without any contact with us at all.

Skilfully written, the writing is matched by the excellent design of the book. While the B&W photographs of roaches aren't especially stunning, the flip book showing two roaches mating is a nice touch that's cleverly done. Having read this I'm more than eager to read more of Schweid's work.

CONCRETE JUNGLE
A Pop Media Investigation of Death and Survival in Urban Ecosystems
Ed. Mark Dion & Alexis Rockman

The final years of RE/Search were a sad affair, each publication only re-visiting previously explored territories — more angry women, more strange music, more tattoos. Now that V Vale and Andrea Juno have parted, things seem to on the up, with Vale's V/Search reprinting the Daniel P Mannix classic *Memoirs of a Sword Swallower* and now this from the Juno camp. *Concrete Jungle* is

I get to review a lot of different material, from Peter Sotos' books to S&M fiction to commercial software to weirdo music, and I have to say that nothing I've reviewed has ever caused such strong reactions. In the eyes of some people the fact that I raved about this book marked me down as a weirdo much more than confessing to a love of industrial white noise, fetishism or extreme politics. Hell, if you need an excuse to buy this book then get it for the 'yuck!' factor alone. [Pan Pantziarka]

very probably one of the finest and most interesting collection of essays I have encountered since the publication of *Apocalypse Culture*. It concentrates on the relationship between man and other forms of life in the urban landscape, from plants to parasites. Chapters include an appreciation of nasty parasitic beasts which live on and in our bodies, native plants in Nazi Germany, killing stray animals, public sanitation, feral cats… It's an eclectic bucket-load of terrors and treats, the type that can

THE CORPSE GARDEN
£5.99 / pb / 256pp / ISBN 1874358249 / True Crime Library 1998 / www.virginbooks.com

CRASH
£8.99 / pb / 112pp / ISBN 085170719X / BFI Publishing 1999 / www.bfi.org

DANCING QUEEN
$12 / pb / 138pp / ISBN 0805043926 / Henry Holt & Company Ltd 1996 / www.henryholt.com

be dipped into at random.

Some of the contents seem pretty gross but there is a mad logic behind it all. Take the road-kill chapter: would you scrape a squashed animal off the road and take it home for tea? Probably not. But writer James Eckle argues that if you are poor and hungry, then the road is a banquet. Even if you are neither poor nor starving, just how many times have you ordered an aged steak or Peking Duck from your local restaurant? When you think about what must go on in restaurant kitchens around the globe, 'Bambi in Guinness' and 'Couscous with Squirrel Squirrel' don't seem that revolting a menu after all (I'm not so sure about 'Rat with Olives' though).

On more serious matters, an interview with a New York pest exterminator will make your toes curl. Not only has this man encountered 3,000 roaches on one boat, he's also eaten mealworm and crickets at a New York Entomological Society dinner. However, the section on humans as a host for others is really disgusting, and a part of the food chain we'd prefer to view from afar. Photographs of bodies feasted upon by turtles, rats, vultures and maggots are prominent. If you ever discover small worms swimming around your eyeballs, the good news is that it's not fatal; the bad news is that the parasite is probably travelling through the entire mass of your body via lymph and blood vessels.

Bulging with information, *Concrete Jungle* not only reads great but looks fantastic. The stills are amazing, the design is excellent, all bound behind a wonderful cover painting by editor Rockman. Expensive, but worth its weight in tapeworm larvae! [David Greenall]

THE CORPSE GARDEN
The Crimes of
Fred and Rose West
Colin Wilson

There is a serial killer writer on the loose in Cornwall. He preys on tabloid accounts of grisly crimes, of grisly schlock purveyed by true crime writers, and disguises it under a veneer of psychological and historical background that gives it an air of respectability. At the same time, he cannot hide his fascination with the sexual detail, and he is adept at reporting it both salaciously and scientifically at the same time. "Stop me before I write again," ought to be at the end of Colin Wilson's author bio.

Actually, Wilson is a deft summariser of evidence, able to sift through varying accounts, point out contradictions, and resolve them. He's very convincing on the issue of Rose West's undoubted guilt. He's also very good at getting into the various points of views and agendas which earlier chroniclers have brought to the case. As you'd expect from someone who's been on the serial killer path for nearly forty years, Wilson brings a depth of knowledge and is able to make connections that most writers might miss.

Of course, many of these connections are old hat if you've read Wilson before. Maslow's theories of dominance, the divided brain, the sexual superman, all this has been rehashed many times before. And as Wilson drifts off into synopses of various serial killings from around the world, you feel sort of like you're listening to your grandad tell the same family story for the umpteenth time: "C'mon gramps, tell me again how Gerald Gallego sodomised his daughter."

DARK MOON

Apollo and the Whistle-Blowers

Life also seems to have passed him by. He remarks on the unusual sadistic cruelty Canadian serial killer Paul Bernardo showed when he forced his lover/accomplice Karla Homolka to write "I must never forget to record *The Simpsons*" a hundred times. For a guy who raped and murdered at least three women, including Karla's younger sister, this seems pretty mild. Especially when we recall that each episode of *The Simpsons* begins with Bart being punished by having to write some penance on the school blackboard. Post-modern irony from a serial killer. What'll they think of next?

Wilson's fascination has always been with the area where the sexual impulse and the violent impulse cross over. This makes his compendia both useful reading and quality schlock. Rest assured you'll get plenty of the good stuff here, and it might make you think as well. Or pretend you do. It just could've done with some pictures. But don't worry about this one. Somewhere out there there's a killer waiting to provide Wilson with another book. [Michael Carlson]

CRASH
Iain Sinclair

As Iain Sinclair makes clear in this slim but interesting little book, *Crash* exists not as a single work by Ballard, but as a sequence of projects that have mutated and evolved over time. *Crash* exists as a set of works by Ballard, as an exhibition piece, as a documentary, as a film by David Cronenberg and now as a series of essays by Sinclair. This abundance of works, over-lapping in terms of media, time and intent are ably uncovered by Sinclair, who exposes the secret histories, the hidden and the submerged. With an almost surgical precision he delves into *Crash* to reveal the different agendas at work in its various incarnations. Sinclair's critical intelligence posits Cronenberg's film a work that obscures Ballard's subversive fictions. He makes it clear that the film is a re-writing of Ballard. And, just as persuasively, he shows us that the film is a necessary step for Cronenberg, according him the critical respect that his earlier films did not garner. *Crash* was an inevitable and logical progression from *Naked Lunch*.

With this as a central thesis Sinclair also examines J G Ballard and James Ballard — the blurring of fact and fiction, author and fictional creation, is a central theme of Ballard's work. *Empire of the Sun* and *The Kindness of Women* are written as a means to an end, according to Sinclair. Ballard writes Ballard in order to recast himself, to control the picture of the man and the myth.

Anyone who seeks to understand Ballard needs to read this book. It is the most incisive and interesting commentary on Ballard to date. And, one has to ask, what of the hidden themes that underlie Sinclair's *Crash*? Just as Ballard and Cronenberg seek to change or control public perceptions, so too does Sinclair. This book is as much a part of the uncovering of London — in particular the relationship between the urban and the suburban — as it is about Cronenberg's not very interesting film.

I look forward to seeing where Sinclair takes us next. [Pan Pantziarka]

DANCING QUEEN
Lisa Carver

Of all the figures to emerge from the zine 'community', Lisa Carver is one of the few who has been able to actually create something new and worth reading. Her publication *Rollerderby* transcends the mediocrity of most zines via its genuinely perceptive stance, which is by turns funny, tragic, shocking and magical. Lisa has developed a literary style which remains unique via its presentation of extremely personal events, in a manner that retains their intimacy yet simultaneously recalls and evokes the feelings and experiences of her audience (a fact which is borne out by *Rollerderby*'s letters page).

Further, *Rollerderby* challenges the aesthetic amateurism of most zines by actually looking good, an important statement in an art-form in which the proponents are frequently proud of their sloppiness.

Dancing Queen is Carver's first book (save for a collected edition of the best of *Rollerderby*, published by Feral House and worthy of attention from anyone not familiar with the magazine) and focuses on the sheer pleasure of growing up and living in white-trash USA. *Dancing Queen* includes chapters on the joys of Lawrence Welk, and the sadistic pleasures of a hairdresser named Elba. The book also details Carver's sexual development, from her youthful fantasies of molestation by a bear to her dreams of being seduced by various Russian leaders. As well as essays on the erotic-trash-pulp literary-classics (such as Judith Krantz' *Scruples*), more details of her early sexual experiences, and her fondness for gynaecological examinations. Carver's skill is in her ability to describe — and more importantly *celebrate* — 'trash culture' with genuine feeling and style, retaining an obvious devotion to it, yet simultaneously able to maintain enough distance

DARK MOON

£16.99 / pb / 568pp / ISBN 1898541108 / Aulis Publishers 1999 / 25 Belsize Park, London, NW3 4DU, UK / www.aulis.com

DEATH SCENES

£13.99 / pb / 220pp / ISBN 0922915296 / Feral House 1996 / www.feralhouse.com

"The reflection in the visor (which does not have a camera positioned at eye level) cannot be that of the actual photographer of the image."
Dark Moon

to make the reader laugh. In this respect *Dancing Queen* is reminiscent of John Waters' *Crackpot*, or Richard Meltzer's *Gulcher*, and — like Waters and Meltzer — this book makes a fine addition to anyone's library of Americana. [Jack Sargeant]

DARK MOON
Apollo and the Whistle-Blowers
Mary D Bennett & David S Percy

The idea of the Apollo moon landings being nothing but an elaborate hoax — with supposed 'live' broadcasts of moonwalks actually taking place in secret locations here on earth — has been kicking around the public consciousness for some years now. It was certainly fuelled by the 1978 movie *Capricorn One* (the plot of which revolves around a mission to Mars being a hoax), and is insinuated as early as 1971 (not two years after the first manned landing on the moon) in another movie: *Diamonds are Forever*.

In their introduction to *Dark Moon*, authors Bennett and Percy claim they wish to put into "question the entire validity of the official record of mankind's exploration of the Moon especially the Apollo lunar landings themselves". It's not without some relish that they set about their task, and at times some pretty preposterous ground is covered (dressing down Santilli's alien autopsy footage is one thing, but analysing the 'flaws' in the *Independence Day* tie-in novel…?).

One of the most 'supportive' aspects of this conspiracy theory are the snaps supposedly taken by the astronauts themselves while on the Moon. Most everything else in the book can be held up as mere conjecture, but these pictures are consistently damning when presented in the context of a hoax. It starts with the innocuous point that each picture taken by Neil Armstrong is a rather beautiful composition, and then bangs in the fact that his camera had no viewfinder. (*None* of the cameras had viewfinders — they were fixed on the astronauts' chests.) A lot of the images suffer from 'unnatural' lighting, with shadows defying logic and falling in a variety of different directions; they lack consistency, too, with some shadows being long and dark while those adjacent are short and grey. With the sun clearly visible in the background, nearside images are inexplicably clearly lit when they should be in silhouette. Such anomalies seem to indicate the presence of more than the sun as a strong light source, but NASA didn't take any lighting equipment to the Moon. 'Hot spots' — or reflections — on objects also suggest the existence of secondary lighting.

Events supposedly caught simultaneously on still-camera and TV camera reveal curious anomalies — like they never happened at the same time at all. Stranger still are the markings evident on a rock and a nearby patch of the lunar surface, interpreted as an alphabetical placement guide for the 'set dresser' in the lunar hoax landscape…

Which brings us full circle: What to believe? The authors suggest the lettering mentioned above has been airbrushed out of the photograph on its publication elsewhere, while readily admitting that they themselves have enhanced the markings here "very slightly just for clarity". Well, one man's enhancement is another man's conspiracy theory. You'd need to be very gullible indeed to swallow everything *Dark Moon* puts forward as indicative of foul play. However, few people will come away from this book without some suspicion that NASA has something big to hide. [David Kerekes]

Update A 222-minute documentary based on Part One of *Dark Moon*, entitled *What Happened on the Moon?*, is also available from Aulis, the publisher.

DEATH SCENES
A Homicide Detective's Scrapbook
Ed. Sean Tejaratchi

A battered head with a gag in its mouth is propped up for the camera. Beneath it, shakily written in uppercase, is the caption "killed by bandit". Next to it sits a second picture, a man, again propped up, wearing a hat, eyes staring beyond the camera. The caption here reads. Elsewhere, the torso of Mrs Dorothy Lee Eggers, age forty-one, lies on a slab, her head and hands chopped off by her husband jealous of "Mrs Eggers asserted dalliance with other men". Miss Samuelson, cut-up by the "Arizona Tiger Woman" in order that her body may fit into a trunk, lies on the slab stitched back together like some macabre human tapestry. James P Watson, a hermaphrodite who "married twenty five wives and killed sixteen of them", displays his genitals for the camera. The Red Lipstick Murder Case has a forty-year-old victim naked and "stomped to death by a fiend who crudely printed an obscene phrase (fuck you) on her chest". A boy and girl are discovered literally blown to pieces after finding and playing with dynamite. Victor Whealand "fell a sleep in the bath tub and drowned". A man's brains spill from his opened skull, the victim of suicide. Several other suicide victims, dead through hanging, are held under the collective caption "just a little throat trouble..."

It'd be all too easy to crack a gag and suggest that *Death Scenes* is the book one might expect to find on the coffee table of the family Addams, but then again it wouldn't be a suggestion completely removed from the truth. OK, it has nothing whatsoever to do with Charles Addams. What it is, however, is a collection of photographs — bodies in the morgue, crime scenes, medical anomalies, shots of suicide victims and so forth — as collected by Jack Huddleston, a homicide detective with the LAPD from the 1930s to the 1950s. He pasted them into a huge scrapbook which ultimately measured in at eighteen by twenty-four by six inches thick. Feral House's *Death Scenes* reprints 230 of the photos in a more accessible volume, complete with captions originally furnished in Huddleston's handwritten scrawl, and with an added introduction by Katherine Dunn.

The public got their first taste of Huddleston's scrapbook in 1989, courtesy of Nick Bougas' film *Death Scenes*, in which the photographs were supplemented by a narrative by Anton LaVey. In *Death Scenes*' literary incarnation, Dunn's 'narrative' is not only more pertinent but thankfully kept separate from the main body of work — allowing the images, and Huddleston's own perfunctory captioning, to speak for themselves. This introductory essay is itself fascinating, offering compelling hypothesis on the man behind the collection. (Though they were approached on the subject of Huddleston, the LAPD wouldn't allow any "archaeological excavation" for the purpose of a mere book.) Painting in a backdrop of crime and era, against which the pictures take on greater perspective, Dunn (author of

DEEPENING WITCHCRAFT
$19.95 / pb / 359pp / ISBN 1550224956 / ECW Press 2002 / www.ecwpress.com

MAGICKAL WEDDINGS
$21.95 / pb / 185pp / ISBN 1550224611 / ECW Press 2001 / www.ecwpress.com

PHILOSOPHY OF WICCA
$19.95 / pb / 268pp / ISBN 1550224875 / ECW Press 2002 / www.ecwpress.com

WITCHCRAFT AND THE WEB
$16.95 / pb / 271pp / ISBN 1550224662 / ECW Press 2001/ www.ecwpress.com

DEVIANT
$14 / pb / 242pp / ISBN 0671025449 / Pocket Books 1998 / www.simonsays.com

DEVIANT DESIRES
£16.99 / $24.99 / pb / 252pp / ISBN 1890451037 / Juno Books 2000 / www.junobooks.com

Geek Love) also attempts to decipher the nature of the man who takes to assimilating such photographs in his spare time. For a hobby. "We can imagine him coming home from work with a manila envelope," writes Dunn, "tossing it on a dresser or desk. He would wait until after supper to open the envelope, to arrange and label his latest find. Did he share this hobby with his wife? Did he frighten his children with these images and the stories that went with them? Or was it his private pornography, locked away until he was alone in the house for a few hours?"

The detective wasn't compiling 'evidence' or case histories. Not all of the snaps in his scrapbook are from cases that Huddleston was working on, some aren't cases at all but feature the likes of shrunken heads from Borneo, Siamese cats, obese people, and victims of leprosy. Photographs that aren't of a professional capacity at all but simply of *interest* to Huddleston. It was a fascination no doubt fuelled by the job of homicide detective, and at the same time a job that exonerated the collection from merely being a morbid curiosity or a 'dangerous' hobby (imagine a post office worker or a centre-lathe turner compiling such a scrapbook without raising suspicion).

This is no easy book to cut through. It's compelling and horrible in a deep down way, touching upon human frailty and inhuman behaviour. Knife wounds are deep; gunshot blasts devastating; babies tossed into rivers. There are no clean and tidy deaths here; no TV-movie apology for a dead body — if Mrs Marple was to walk into any one of these true-life cases she'd throw up. The book also manages to hit the viewer in a way that Bougas' film could not — the cinematic medium managing to transpose Huddleston's dog-eared B&W photographs into a world a light-years from home.

Death Scenes is a landmark piece and will cause waves one way or another. Feral House haven't just pushed at the boundaries with this one, they've kicked in a couple of doors. Something has changed with the publication of this book — quite what that might be only time will tell. [David Kerekes]

Update A companion piece to *Death Scenes* is Feral House's *Muerte!*, edited by Harvey Bennett Stafford and published in 2000. An overview of "Death in Mexican Popular Culture", in many ways it pushes out the envelope even further with at least one dead child on the cover.

DEEPENING WITCHCRAFT
Grey Cat

MAGICKAL WEDDINGS
Joy Ferguson

PHILOSOPHY OF WICCA
Amber Laine Fisher

WITCHCRAFT AND THE WEB
M Macha Nightmare

I would like to be as kind as possible to ECW Press, after all we're not all cut out for descending into the underworld of the Tunnels of Set, or conjuring the malevolent automata inherent in Austin Spare's system of sentient sigils, are we? Even so, it's difficult to relate to the mind-numbing New Age quality of these books which are ostensibly about witchcraft and magick (spelled with a 'K', no less, as if in homage to the profound system devised by Aleister Crowley!) but seem so saccharine and homespun that it's mortally difficult not to discount them as twaddle, without even getting past the pastel shaded covers! That said (though I can't understand why anyone over ten years old would want to call themselves Grey Cat), *Deepening Witchcraft* is a fairly sensible read, in the present context, offering some reasonably well argued insights into the group structuring of Wicca. Similarly, Amber Fisher's shorter *Philosophy of Wicca* is basically sound, if far from inspired. The less said about the other two volumes, the better! All in all, though there seems to be a lack of good, balanced material on the occult these days, with more and more commercialised recycled rubbish filling the shelves, I can't in all honesty recommend these books from ECW as a viable alternative. [Stephen Sennitt]

DEVIANT
The Shocking True Story of Ed Gein, The Original 'Psycho'
Harold Schechter

About fifteen years ago, a colleague of mine was invited to a psychiatrists' party at the Mendota Mental Health Institute in Madison, Wisconsin, and at the end of the evening was surprised to learn that the small, grey-haired, docile man serving canapés was none other than Ed Gein, the Wisconsin Ghoul himself. Many 'fictionalisations' of the Gein case come over as simply absurd. I recently had the misfortune of watching a 'reconstruction' of the case on American television, which featured a middle-aged actor dressed in a rubbery 'woman skin' capering and gibbering ludicrously under a Hammer horror-style full moon. Fortunately, Schechter's book brings us none of this malarkey. Instead, it presents a meticulously researched account, a thorough and serious recreation of the Gein case, which surely stands as the 'locus classicus' of the middle American psychopath. Schechter is especially good at evoking the heart-sickening, isolating gloom down on the farm in Plainfield, Wisconsin, the unimaginable filthiness of the old Gein place, and the crazy incongruity of the mad little old man.

Deviant was originally published in 1989, so it does seem a little dated in places, especially since the interim years have seen something of a Gein revival, whose hallmarks include Schechter's own *Outcry*, a novelisation of the Gein case, and Paul Anthony Woods' *Ed Gein — Psycho*, the handbook of the card-carrying Gein-fiend, plus a number of movies. These more recent works make Schechter's small collection of photographs look rather tame. [*The more horrible pictures which appeared in the earlier print of the book have been removed for this one — Eds.*] Still, *Deviant* contains some classic descriptions of this "idiot savant" of the macabre, especially Gein's mixture of childish simplicity and monstrous criminality. Shechter even seems to reveal a kind of ghoulish respect for Weird Old Eddie, appearing to relish certain details of the case. At least he doesn't attempt to diagnose him as a transvestite or avant-garde gender transgressor. Instead, Schechter believes that Gein's grave-lootings and corpse-violations were simply the instincts of a sexually normal man whose latent Oedipus complex somehow ceased to be latent. This much may be true, but there's more to be said here about the cold comforts of pioneer history and the inherent violence of the rural shotgun culture. All of America went into the making of Eddie Gein. [Mikita Brottman]

DEVIANT DESIRES
Incredibly Strange Sex
Katherine Gates

Taking its cue from such RE/Search volumes as *Incredibly Strange Films* and *Incredibly Strange Music*, Katherine Gates' book takes the reader deep into some *extremely* uncharted territory on the map of human sexuality. *Deviant Desires* makes no attempt to be exhaustive in its coverage of sexual deviation, so there's none of your usual boring flagellation, necrophilia and bestiality — Gates obviously felt she'd be flogging a dead horse! Instead, there's lots of stuff you've never even *thought* of. Areas covered include balloon fetishism, body inflation and giant women fantasies, 'crush' videos, 'slash' fiction by sci-fi fans, *extreme* fat admiration, robot fetishism, sex with soft toys, mudlarking and fun with messy foodstuffs. If you believe your sex life to be pretty exotic and out there, prepare to think again. There's *no way* you can compete with some of the freaky people in *Deviant Desires*.

Examples are numerous, but here are a few of my personal favourites. Ducky DooLittle has found a niche performing as Knockers the naughty topless clown:

> *I hate cakes... if there's a cake anywhere, I have an overwhelming desire to sit in it... I got protested by birthday party clowns in portland because I show my breasts and I'm dirtying up the business for them. There's something wrong with these people.*

CALIGULA

£9.95 / $14.95 / 159pp / ISBN 1840680490 /
Creation Books 2001 / www.creationbooks.com

Image from "Death in the Afternoon", a Squish Productions video. *Deviant Desires*

Ron H produces *Black Giantess* magazine, which is full of his demented collages of black porn models pasted into, and towering over, scenes of urban destruction:

I remember being in jobs where I dealt with people who really really pissed me off... in my mind I would imagine these specific people getting destroyed by the giant woman... it's a kind of revenge.

Ponygirl Frisky gives a long interview about her fantasies of morphing into a pony and being ridden around, as well as discussing the burgeoning human pony scene in general:

Apparently there's a town in central Texas that's very into this. The whole town is supposedly a 24/7 training facility.

Supersize Betsy is a star model of the 'fat admiring' scene. She's got to the point, though, where she has to watch her weight carefully:

I get lots of offers from men who just want to fatten me up for a night or a weekend, but I'm 420 pounds already. If I were to do that, I could become immobile very easily and I'd still be single! That would be disastrous.

Supersize Betsy is one of the more unsettling interviewees in *Deviant Desires*, raising as she does awkward questions about exploitation and self-harm in pursuit of sexual gratification, although she seems very self-determined and forthright about her quest for obese immobility. Most people interviewed for the book, though, are doing basically harmless, if extremely weird, stuff.

The glaring and disgusting exception is Jeff 'The Bug' Vilencia, a noted producer of 'crush' videos, which feature barefoot and high-heeled women stomping on a variety of small creatures like bugs and worms, filmed in extreme close-up. Crush videos were recently declared to be obscene under British law in the first prosecution for their importation. Vilencia, incredibly, claims to be a vegan!

As with all RE/Search and Juno books, *Deviant Desires* is beautifully produced and copiously illustrated. I should have thought one or two of the photos in here run the risk of attracting unwelcome attention from the authorities, due to the presence of flagrant stiffies. Inevitably, given the marginal nature of the sexual micro-communities Gates is describing, a lot of the fetish material reproduced is amateur or home-made (though often surprisingly sophisticated), which only adds to the obsessive *frisson*. Gates generally approaches her subjects for interview with a warmth and empathy that encourages them to open up and wax lyrical on their bizarre fixations. And how many books can you think of where the author has posed naked with a gun for their author photograph? Respect is due.

One recurring theme in *Deviant Desires* is the way in which most of these people are locked into a very narrow groove, though many of them evince a degree of self-deprecating humour about it. For example, the balloon fetish community — a small enough group, you would have thought — is evidently radically divided between those who revel in the popping of balloons and those who get all anxious and tearful at the very thought of popping balloons! There are rival websites and chatrooms where the two groups diss one another.

Another point evident throughout *Deviant Desires* is the extent to which the Internet has revolutionised the lives of these people, creating thriving little subcultures, relationships and scenes where initially there could only have been isolation and frustration. And of course, a lot of the weirder fantasies described here — such as Roald Dahl-style body-inflation or giant women — are only realisable through computer-generated imagery and/or movie special effects. Much of the material covered is available online. Gratifyingly, *Deviant Desires* is peppered with website addresses for you to do some erotic window-shopping of your own.

On the back cover, veteran sexual adventuress Annie Sprinkle challenges you to read *Deviant Desires* and not get turned on. Whether you actually find any of this stuff exciting, however, seems to me beside the point. I feel enriched just by knowing that such possibilities exist. Though I must admit I'm pretty attracted to the idea of 'plushies' or 'furverts', people who have a sexual thing for funny cartoon animals like Bugs Bunny and who dress up in furry costumes (with strategically-placed holes) to act out their fantasies. Th-th-that's all folks! [Simon Collins]

CALIGULA
DIVINE CARNAGE
Atrocities of the Roman Emperors
Stephen Barber & Jeremy Reed

I hate to be brutal (after all, I'm no Caligula, am I?) but there's something half-baked about this book, and I can't figure out exactly what it is. On the surface, Barber & Reed's selective readings of the *Atrocities of the Roman Emperors* would seem to be perfectly sound. All the chapters are in order, so it's not that. Even the somewhat hysterical and empurpled prose in which the bulk of the book is written (with headings like 'Orgy of Death,' 'Blood,' 'Semen,' 'Death' and 'Black Sun Rising') should be excusable; after all, what other subject merits such excess? Not only that, the book is genuinely informative, quoting sources and references with academic judiciousness.

Perhaps there is something unwittingly camp about the book. It is undoubtedly ridiculously straight-faced in its lurid presentation of historical data as hyperventilated entertainment, in which the authors unconsciously emulate the subjects of their essays with their crazed outpourings. Perhaps, also, there is something bathetic at the outset in the introduction by the normally-intriguing James Havoc, which not only mentions Tinto Brass' film *Caligula* as an inspirational touchstone (without a trace of irony, I might add) but also makes the fatuous claim that *Divine Carnage* is the first non-academic book on the subject, thereby entirely ignoring Dan Mannix' far superior pulp classic, *Those About to Die* (first published in 1958

FEMALES, 18-35, wanted to step on bugs barefoot for short movie

and reprinted numerous times since). Perhaps, indeed, it is a combination of these steroid-inflated factors that makes Barber & Reed's book seem like the puzzling failure it is: in pulling out all the stops in order to seem 'cutting-edge shocking' and truly decadent, the effect has been to create one of the silliest and most undisciplined works of non-fiction you're ever likely to read. To top it all off, Havoc tips off the clueless by needlessly mentioning Ridley Scott's *Gladiator* as though *Divine Carnage* was some kind of unofficial movie tie-in. [Stephen Sennitt]

THE ENCYCLOPEDIA OF WESTERN GUNFIGHTERS
£12.50 / pb / 401pp / ISBN 0712666826 / Pimlico 1998 / www.randomhouse.com

THE END OF TIME
£16.99 / hb / 392pp / ISBN 0874518490 / University Press of New England 1997 / www.upne.com

END-TIME VISIONS
£13.99 / hb / 448pp / ISBN 0805417699 / Four Walls Eight Windows 1998 / www.4w8w.com

THE ENCYCLOPEDIA OF WESTERN GUNFIGHTERS
Bill O'Neal

Bill O'Neal is a quick draw when it comes to shooting down reputations. His encyclopedia describes Wyatt Earp as a "Farmer, section hand, buffalo hunter, horse thief, saloonkeeper, gambler, bunco artist, sportsman, law officer, and prospector". Roughly in that order, though not necessarily consecutively. O'Neal is one of those who considers the Gunfight at the OK Corral a case of premeditated murder by the Earps and Doc Holliday; he implies Earp's two other killings, revenging the assassination of his brother Morgan, were murder as well.

O'Neal doesn't suggest Earp was responsible for the mysterious death of Johnny Ringo, found under a tree with his boots off, shot through the head, but it's clear that debunking the mythology of western novels and movies is O'Neal's business, and business is booming. Thus America's West becomes a farce of drunken con men, petty thieves, and greedy ne'er-do-wells, skulking about dirty little towns occasionally shooting someone in the back if they got drunk enough or if the perceived insult was bad enough. You start to think the amazing thing is any civilization at all emerged from what appears to be absolute chaos. Then you realise what has emerged is a country filled with cities like Atlanta or Dallas. Indeed, the big difference is that the towns aren't quite so dirty, the demarcation lines for the bad sides of town are drawn even more sharply today, and of course, the weaponry is more sophisticated.

It's lucky for gunfighters that western firearms were nowhere near as accurate or reliable as portrayed in the movies. Even a direct hit from a pistol ball needed not be fatal. One of the best lines in this book refers to Billy Breakenridge: "In 1881 he shot Curly Bill Brocius in the mouth, thereby persuading Curly Bill to hang up his guns." Indeed, the quicksilver skills of gunmen turn out, inevitably, to be somewhat exaggerated. When John Armstrong arrested John Wesley Hardin, Armstrong was already walking with a cane because he'd shot himself by accident. Despite having Armstrong's gun levelled at him, Hardin drew his own and might have killed the lawman, only his pistol's hammer got caught in his braces.

Many of the West's leading figures, from Billy the Kid on down, actually hailed from the East. I discovered two gunmen from my home state of Connecticut, a long way from the West. One, Mysterious Dave Mather, was rumoured to be a descendant of Cotton Mather, the fiery fundamentalist preacher. His nickname was the most mysterious thing about Dave, but gunfighters did get good nicknames. Texas Jack Vermillion was called Texas Jack because he came from Virginia. In Britain, he'd have been called "Vermsy". Texas John Slaughter would be "Slaughters."

Henry Plummer deserved a colourful nickname, but never got one. He was a baker elected City Marshal, and in the final year of his term, a man named John Vedder caught Plummer in bed with Mrs Vedder. When he ordered Plummer to leave, the Marshal shot him dead. He was sentenced to ten years in prison, but was pardoned after a year. A year later he killed a man in a whorehouse fight. The next year he killed a man who made fun of his

Yankee accent. Eventually Plummer was shot in the arm while laying in wait with a shotgun to ambush a sheriff. The sheriff quit the West, while Plummer taught himself to shoot left-handed.

This is an invaluable book to anyone interested in the origins of modern American killers. You can argue a direct line, say, from Jesse James coming out of Quantrill's guerrillas in the Civil War, and the Bonnie & Clydes of the 1930s, and from there the line is easy to follow through the mythology which grows up around killers. Perhaps through O'Neal's eyes it all seems funny after a century has passed, but even the art of our greatest westerns, the films of John Ford, or Budd Boetticher, or Sergio Leone, or Sam Peckinpah, pales in the face of the black comedy of the West as it really was. [Michael Carlson]

THE END OF TIME
Faith and Fear in the Shadow of the Millennium
Damian Thompson

While many books have come out in the last few years attempting to chart some of the wilder excesses of human behaviour at the end of the second millennium, perhaps most notably Adam Parfrey's excellent *Apocalypse Culture*, none have before now given a systematic analysis of the millennial fervour crucial to an understanding of the cult practices and religious absurdities so widespread today.

This scholarly yet fascinating tome gives just that: it is divided into two parts, one dealing with pre-twentieth century apocalyptic expectations and the other specialising in contemporary deviant buffoonery, covering in painstaking detail the strange and terrible sagas of Waco, Aum Shinrikyo, and the Order of the Solar Temple, whose members all died in mysterious circumstances a few years ago. Most journalistic endeavours covering topics like this are written by tabloid journalists and as such are lurid drivel, pandering to the baser expectations of the 'true crime' set; this, however, is refreshingly well-written, meticulously researched and delivers more insightful analysis of any of the topics given above in a chapter than you'll find in most complete books.

The inherent readability of these parts (Aum Shinrikyo is the Tokyo nerve gas cult whose leader, as of writing, is currently on trial) should be readily apparent; other chapters deal with the range and weight of belief in an imminent cosmic showdown in the Christian church, the current vogue for apocalyptic New Age cults, and an extensive history of such beliefs, including accounts of Fortean drama at the end of the first millennium. The latter section is dry at times, but as the book is presenting itself as a definitive account, possibly for use by academics as well as the curious public, it's difficult to fault it for the overly scholarly tone it sometimes has. It also concentrates perhaps too explicitly on a Christian history, although this is arguably because the makeup of Christianity is simply more overtly apocalyptic than other religions, and Thompson's account of changing perceptions of time kept my interest up while wading through tale after tale of self-destructive cult behaviour.

It is the repetitive pattern of the lives and deaths of cults that is perhaps the most telling message to be drawn from the book. The template for the Waco disaster had been drawn up more than a thousand years before, even down to the harem-humping activities of its head man. As the author argues, if the authorities had consulted any relevant source for information prior to the siege, they would never have attacked the compound as they did: as it happens, the only people they did consult were criminal psychologists versed in drafting profiles of serial killers. It is clearly demonstrated here that only the thinnest line separating the beliefs of Koresh's followers and popular end-time beliefs all over the Christian world: the pervasive and straight-faced convictions of Satanic shenanigans as shown here are unwittingly hilarious until you consider the violence and prejudice that such beliefs invariably lead to, and Thompson deserves credit for drawing attention to this.

Highly recommended for its lucid and objective approach to usually hysteria-inducing material, this is surely the definitive text on apocalyptic belief. [James Mariott]

END-TIME VISIONS
The Road To Armageddon?
Richard Abanes

At some point in the near future our world will be destroyed... Throughout history, civilisations and cultures have been creating their own unique belief systems based upon the idea that the world would end and be born anew. Today's religions are no different, but it is the apocalyptic teachings of Christianity that have had the greatest influence on western society and around which Richard Abanes concentrates his book, *End-Time Visions*. As early as 150AD, prophets were foretelling the return to Earth of Jesus Christ and of the anguish that would befall sinners.

ESOTERRORIST
£11.99 / pb / 68pp / MediaKaos/Alecto 1994 / AK Distribution, PO Box 12766, Edinburgh, EH8 9YE, UK / www.akuk.com

Former traffic cop Serghei Torpo aka "Vissarion" claims to be the reincarnation of Christ. He seeks to establish his own kingdom in Siberia, and has attracted approximately 5,000 followers to his "City of the Sun", near to the isolated town of Minusinsk. If mankind does not believe in him, Vissarion threatens that nuclear power plants will explode and a new, catastrophic virus will be unleashed. *End-Time Visions*

Just as millions flocked to Jerusalem at the turn of this Millennium, so was there a mass exodus the last Millennium, when people gave up all their belongings and travelled to the Holy City in anticipation of the Second Coming. When the end didn't come, the dates were simply reshuffled.

And they're being reshuffled to this day — a plethora of end-time prophets, seers, and cults, all promising hellfire and damnation. For the Korean *Hyoo-go* movement, the end-time was scheduled to start on October 28, 1992; that was the day of Rapture, when all good Christians would be whisked up to Heaven in the blinking of an eye, leaving millions to suffer the Tribulation — seven years of unparalleled destruction — after which the world would be destroyed. Cult members prayed so loudly through the nights in the run-up to the big day, that spitting blood became a sign of salvation. Many believers quit their jobs or schools; sold their homes; abandoned their families. Pregnant women had abortions so that they wouldn't be too heavy to be lifted up to Heaven. Others simply committed suicide. Minutes after the deadline passed, the senior pastor of the cult announced, quite simply, "Nothing has happened. Sorry. Let's go home."

The Amazing Criswell, friend of B-movie director Ed Wood Jr, also gets a look-in, thanks to some strange end-time predictions: "pressure" from outer space, he wrote in *Criswell Predicts*, will "cause all solids to turn into a jellylike mass… the people who attempt to escape in wild panic will be unable to move through the gummy streets". (Criswell's career in predicting the future started quite by chance. He was a TV newscaster in New York when, one evening, he ran out of news fifteen minutes early and decided to fill the remaining air time with his thoughts on what *might* happen the next day.) Nostradamus gets a whole chapter to himself, as author Abanes takes to systematically debunking several of his most highly regarded prophesies. He claims that these have been badly translated from the French, juggled about, and in some instances even fabricated outright in order that Nostradamites — fans — can fit them to major events in world history. What's more, Abanes suggests they're not even prophesies, but 'contemporary political lampoons' of the day — an interesting explanation but not a wholly convincing one.

The murky ideology of Patriots and Militiamen are also discussed. These groups believe that barcodes, visa cards, and the death of Princess Diana all point to a New World Order and the rise of the Antichrist. Their message is reaching a wider audience, thanks in part to Bible-bashers like Pat Robertson who see only a shared fundamentalist vision. However, if Robertson bothered to check his sources, he'd probably be dismayed to discover that some of the literature he has been quoting was of neo-Nazi and anti-Semitic origin, and some of it just plain lies. (To add insult to injury, the very people Robertson looks to be supporting have turned around and accused him of being a part of the dreaded New World Order.)

Then there is the curious story of William Miller, and how "the great disappointment" of his prophesised world end in 1843 didn't deter followers from establishing their own apocalyptic cults. Out of the Millerites sprang the Adventists, and later the Jehovah's Witnesses — a group Abanes describes as "one of the most deceptive and dangerous of today's apocalyptic cults".

End-Times Visions covers a lot of ground in a thoroughly satisfying way (so long as you overlook the silly little typos). Written by a Catholic and former cult member, it applies logic, common-sense and hard research to a very mad subject. Excellent. [David Kerekes]

ESOTERRORIST
Selected Essays 1980–1988
Genesis P-Orridge

Genesis P-Orridge (or 'P'Orridge', as he is unaccountably referred to on the cover), the man behind COUM Transmissions, Throbbing Gristle, Thee Temple Ov Psychick Youth and Psychic TV, veteran provocateur, media terrorist and 'cultural engineer', has been going through something of a cultural rehabilitation process in the UK of late. Last summer's triumphal 'Time's Up' gig at the Royal Festival Hall (his first appearance in Britain for seven years, following his self-imposed exile in the USA) was merely part of a string of events including the publication of Simon Ford's *Wreckers of Civilisation*, the definitive history of COUM and TG, a spate of articles in the quality press, and an interview on Channel 4's *DisinfoNation* that seemed to signal Gen's readiness to come in from the cold (though by all accounts he's now very happy in the States), and/or the British establishment's willingness to have him back. The past year has also seen the release of the first two volumes of Psychic TV's *Origin of the Species* box sets, a retrospective look at the influential acid/hyperdelic phase of the band. What better time, then, to take a fresh look at some of his written output?

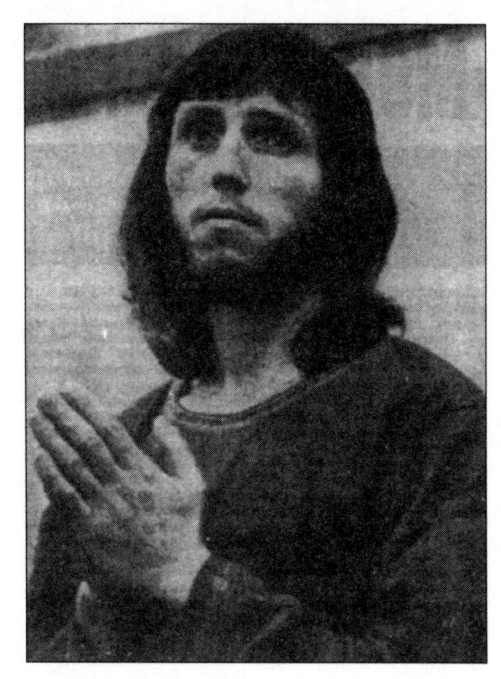

Esoterrorist was originally issued in America by ov-press in 1989, and this reprint is unrevised. What's gathered here are various short pieces that first saw the light of day as TOPY and PTV mailings, publications in anthologies and the like, nicely interspersed with photos and hermetic collages by Gen. Highlights include 'His Name Was Master', a moving eulogy to the late Brion Gysin, pieces on Muzak and 'German Order', and five linked essays on 'Behavioural Cut-Ups and Magick'. All the familiar P-Orridge preoccupations are present — control and authority in all its manifestations, the quest for alternatives to linearity and rational thought, a plea for reintegration of the human organism.

So, a top quality read, then? Well, *no*, actually — for twelve quid I was expecting something rather more substantial than this. The pieces in the book are interesting enough, but there are nowhere near enough of them for the money. Granted that Gen's writing is dense and aphoristic, it's still a *lot* of money for only sixty-eight pages, and the production, binding etc aren't marvellous either. A couple of the pages in my copy have smeared print on them.

It's a shame that no more up-to-date or exhaustive collection of Gen's work is available — a thinker and artist of his significance deserves better representation than this. In the meantime, you'd do better to trawl the Internet. Start at the official site [w] www.genesisp-orridge.com, which contains just as much interesting material as this book, free for the taking.

I ordered *Esoterrorist* sight unseen from a bookshop, and was sorely disappointed in what I got. Now you know more than I did, don't let the same happen to you! Avoid. [Simon Collins]

Update My plaintive cry for a 'more up-to-date [and] representative collection' of the works of Mr

THE ETHICAL SLUT
£11.99 / pb / 279pp / ISBN 1890159018 / Greenery Press 1997 / www.greenerypress.com

EXTREME ISLAM
$16 / pb / 317pp / ISBN 0922915784 / Feral House 2001 / PO Box 13067, Los Angeles, CA 90013 / www.feralhouse.com

FREAK LIKE ME
£6.99 / pb / 224pp / ISBN 0575400331 / Gollancz 1996 / www.orionbooks.com

P-Orridge has now been answered. *Painful but Pabulous: The Lives and Art of Genesis P-Orridge* was published by Soft Skull Press in March 2003. My review of it will be appearing in *Headpress 26*, but here's an exclusive preview — it's a lot better than *Esoterrorist*! [Indeed, the book cover illustration on p.170 is from *Painful but Fabulous* for no other reason than we didn't have *Esoterrorist* to hand! — Eds]

THE ETHICAL SLUT
A Guide to Infinite Sexual Possibilities
Dossie Easton & Catherine A Liszt

It's hard to take a book seriously that quotes praise from the pagan goddess 'Morning Glory Zell', and includes an acknowledgement to somebody by the name of 'Joy Wolfwomyn', but then, my suspicions were already aroused when I noticed this book is also published by Greenery Press, responsible for *The Sexually Dominant Woman*. A closer look, and my suspicions proved well-founded. Co-author 'Dossie Easton' turns out to be none other than 'Lady Green', author of that other tome.

This, however, is quite a different kind of book, and not only in that its print almost runs up to each margin. It's a serious look at the values and ethics of what the authors refer to — presumably so as not to be confused with the ageing Californian hippies they at one point confess to being — as 'slutdom'. This is the style of living that used to be known in the sixties as 'free love', or 'swinging'. In other words, the book gives moral and ethical advice to people of all genders and sexual orientations involved in all kinds of 'open relationships'.

The first part explains the fascinating dynamics of these kinds of relationships; the rest of it seems mostly dedicated to exploring and resolving the jealousies, conflicts, health risks and boundary debates they involve, many of which seem so traumatic and complicated that the authors' children are sure-fire future guests of Jerry Springer. I must admit, by the time I'd got to the end of the book, I wished I was still married. But if you're stuck for a Christmas present for your lesbian partner's co-dependent live-in lover, then this is definitely the book for you. [Mikita Brottman]

EXTREME ISLAM
Anti-American Propaganda of Muslim Fundamentalism
Ed. Adam Parfrey

It is the age of the virtual state, where a handful of demagogues can beam their incantations around the world, a magic of speed and fire with the power to command workers to jump from the summits of their cities. The impact on WTC Towers One and Two, like tuning forks of steel and glass, will echo for ages to come.

How did this happen? What brewed in the minds of the men who inspired these acts? This book now means that no English speaker has an excuse to be ignorant. Here is a window inside the Jihad: its justifications, its reasoning, its edicts and epistles, its replies to correspondents. And words direct from the mouths of those arch-nemeses of the moment: Bin Laden, Saddam, 'the one-eyed' Mullah Omar, Colonel Quadaffi, and the forbears who inspired them with their words, the first weapons of any spiritual war.

The concise extract from *The Neglected Duty*, 'The Book that

Killed Anwar Sadat and inspired Bin Laden's Holy War' makes its point. A list of restrictions imposed by the Taliban makes for grim reading. The axis is on the political tracts rather than the religious, so don't expect to be stupified by theological pinhead dancing. The meat of the book is arguments, cogently thought out and more often than not, expressed with grace.

The final section dealing with Al Queda is the most intense. Bin Laden's 1998 fatwa. Transcription of an interview with Mullah Omahar, pulled from the airwaves on the recommendation of the NSC, America's 'invisible' listening agency. How to make poison from Castor Beans, yum. How to survive an interrogation — what they'll do, how to use strategies such as pretending the pain is worse than it really is, no heroic posturings in this first-hand advice. And in the days leading up to the September hijackings, the actual mental disciplines the holy warrior must stay true to in order to fulfil the words of his masters. Recovered by the FBI, these letters were left by hijackers on three of the four September flights. Even until the moment the aircraft merges with nature, each second is proscribed in word, from protection-breathing spells, recitations, and points of main actions, until the hijacker will hear every creature in the universe singing sweet songs to his deeds. This song to suggestion is the Rosetta Stone of the mentality of those who did and would again go to a joyful death in the skies, with no word or thought spared for any other soul but their own. In Death's Comely Reward we see the delights awaiting the suicide bomber — a pornucopia of girls with transparent bodies. 'The marrow of her bones is visible like the interior lines of pearls and rubies.' She looks like 'red wine in a white glass' and her shin marrow is 'visible to the eyes, and whose large breasts 'are not inclined to dangle.' She does not perform any bodily function (other than fucking, we assume). And surprise, surprise, the girl does not have to wear a veil or be covered by anything other than transparent skin, which sounds less like the ultimate vision of carnal sport than something Herschell Gordon Lewis would cook up. Maybe the translator missed a few points.

For those not blessed with the creatures of paradise, the final section is an uproarious vision of The Infidel Hell, painted with a surrealist distortion of human bodies, scales, and demonically cunning torments. The blasphemers have their tongues stretched out for up to nine miles and on every inch dances a demon. In another banquet of torments the damned are hungry, so they are given *Zaqqum,* a thorny plant which would get stuck in their throats. Now crying for water, they are given boiling water from another level of Hell, thus being scalded to death, regenerated, then subjected to it all over again, ad infinitum. The boiling water is put to many good uses in other regions where an 'extreme sport' twist is added. 'In Hell,' we are told, 'the part between the shoulders of an infidel would be equal to a distance of three days' journey, by a horse rider. His jawbone would be as big as the mountains of Uhud and the thickness of his skin would come to a distance which can be covered in three days.' (One demon lord's plan to build a resort complex in this remote outpost is expected to provide a full range of facilities, including giant octopus-infested swimming pools. And yea!, it will have all the channels with full live coverage of all Hell's major events, such as "Terrorists explode 'dirty bomb' made of bibles" and "Shaitan declares one femtosecond relief from torment, instantly rescinds idea as 'too generous'".)

As well as the fascinating text, the pictures are worth mentioning. Eight pages of colour photographs showing anti-Zionist cartoons, stamps and posters, plus currency from Iran and Iraq which is printed large enough to permit forgery. Wait, is Feral House a CIA-affiliated company? Perish the thought! The B&W pictures show pages from a pro-Palestinian 'martyrs handbook', quality anti-superpowers cartoons, and loads of others including a raffish shot of Colonel Qaddafi and the Taliban execution of a woman. A four page final glossary contains dozens of Arabic words pertaining to sex, religion, and ritual.

Every page of this book contains interest. Parfrey has done another outstanding trawl of data, presented here in its bare face and without a distorting commentary. With *Extreme Islam*, Feral House maintains its reputation as the most courageous and incendiary publisher in the US. [Jerry Glover]

FREAK LIKE ME
Inside the Jim Rose
Circus Sideshow
Jim Rose with Melissa Rossi

Pincushion really got them when he poked the needle in his eye. That was a faint-jerker.

A faint, to Jim Rose, is a falling ovation. At the age of twenty-eight, Rose was selling cars and exterminating bugs for a living in

FUNERAL PARTY
£13.99 / pb / 128pp / ISBN 1890528005 / Rude Shape 1997 / www.rudeshape.com

A typical illustration from The Nooseletter. *Funeral Party Volume 2*

Phoenix, Arizona. Now Jim Rose is the head of a travelling circus freak troupe, resurrecting the old carny side-show tradition and delivering it to millions of people world-wide. A logical progression if you think about it. As a boy in junior high, Rose would hawk soft drinks at the local fair during the summer breaks. Day-in, day-out, he heard nothing but the repetitive, hypnotic banter of the barkers as they drew in their crowds. "Big Bertha, she's big, she's fat, she's happy — ha ha ha. Takes six guys to hug her and a box car to lug her. Big Bertha, she's big, she's fat, she's happy — ha ha ha. Takes six guys to hug her and a box car to lug her." On leaving school, stuck in jobs he didn't much care for, Rose got the notion that he would go to Europe to meet street entertainers and learn their trade.

Freak Like Me charts the fascinating and meteoric rise of the Jim Rose Circus, as told by the Ringmaster himself. It's no less the inside story of a cultural phenomenon (but don't let that put you off), with Rose coming over as a witty, likeable, down-to-earth, rock'n'roll kind of guy.

In 1990, fresh back from Paris with his new wife Bebe, armed with a bunch of eye-popping tricks, Rose got himself a patch on Venice Beach — knocking nails up his nose, breathing fire and having his head ground into broken glass for dimes and quarters collected in a hat.

So I was having a horrible time getting a crowd. My shows became only practice; even Bebe was bored being my sole fan as I ran through my routine over and over, waiting vainly for an audience to gather. By the afternoon Bebe looked dejected, fingering designs in the sand. I noticed they were arrows, all pointing down. She refused to stand on my head. "What's the point?" She asked. "Nobody's looking."

From Venice Beach, Jim and Bebe moved to Seattle — a city only months away from going into the stratosphere with the 'grunge' music thing. Out of desperation, Rose hit on the idea of performing his act in a friend's restaurant (!), itself in need of a boost. The show was a success. More restaurants followed and more and more people began turning up to watch. Out of these audiences emerged several of the key players who would later pack up their day jobs and join Jim on the road — Pincushion, Matt the Tube, Lifto. The Jim Rose Circus Sideshow was born. TV coverage followed, as did a slot on the Lollapalooza tour in 1992. Two years later, opening for Nine Inch Nails at Ball State University, the circus played to a crowd of 17,000.

The latter part of the book is taken up with the European tour, and the troupe's controversial visit to Britain (if Sooty and Sweep were Japanese, HM Customs would have trouble letting them in). Here, the tabloids had a field day and Tory MPs called for a ban after *The Word* screened Mr Lifto dangling irons from his penis. In Holland, a woman came backstage and blew fire between her legs, aided by a candle in her vagina. In France, suffering a fever, Jim hammered a nail up his nose… but badly. In Scandinavia, members of the audience thought the whole point of the show was to try and be more disgusting than the acts themselves.

Wanting to be a geek out of

design would seem a pretty strange desire. But how about wanting to be a *world-famous* geek — could that be classed as a more normal preoccupation? And while chugging down other people's vomit might not be everyone's idea of a groovy night out, the sheer, honest-to-goodness *feel-good* quota of *Freak Like Me* could make you consider it worth a try. At any rate, here goes! [David Kerekes]

**FUNERAL PARTY VOLUME 2
A Celebratory Excursion into Beautiful Extremes of Life, Lust & Death**
Ed. Shade Rupe
Not having seen the first volume of *Funeral Party* (and not knowing anyone who has), I can't say how this figures by comparison. However, volume two would have me believe it must have been very entertaining indeed. As the subtitle suggests, *Funeral Party 2* is a grab bag of the kind of things that give our days that little extra sparkle. That extra pizzazz. Which means exactly… Jack Stevenson disseminating 'The Sleaziest Fucking Tabloids in America', including in its itinerary *Transvestite Monthly* and *Interracial News* (and reproducing three illos from the latter's pages: the first, a naked black man with a big cock, saying "Hey White Boy — Look what I got for you [sic] wife!"; the second, a picture of blonde bimbette Beverly who wishes it known "I swallow nigger sperm!"; and third, a snapshot taken by John D Kirby, of his white wife being shafted by a black co-worker buddy of his. The accompanying caption reads, "Pig white woman… Doing what she does…"). Another chapter has Michael Kenmir discussing *The Nooseletter*, his hanging/execution newsletter for gay men (a typical contact ad in which, reads: "Like Electric Chairs? White male submissive, fantasizes about being strapped into and wired to an electric chair, being strapped up and noosed, or being put into some other execution machine…"). Also on the agenda is a survey of lesbian clubs in decadent Berlin, an interview with Ulli Lommel (director of *The Devonsville Terror*), an interview with Trevor Brown, a look at the paintings and comic art of George and Mike Kuchar, extreme seventies porn, New York City's Aboutface Theatre Company (who stage modern adaptations of the original Grand Guignol plays) and plenty more, all presented in a highly desirable quality package, with a heap of full-colour illustrations to boot. On a downside, there

GARBAGE PEOPLE
£10.99 / pb / 178pp / ISBN 1878923072 / Amok Books 1995 / www.amokbooks.com

THE GATES OF JANUS
$24.95 / £17.99 / hb / 305pp / ISBN 0922915733 / Feral House 2001 / www.feralhouse.com

GODS OF DEATH
£16.99 / hb / 320pp / ISBN 0684814455 / Pocket Books 1998 / www.simonsays.com

is way too much fiction. I've never believed short stories sit easily with non-fiction material, whoever's written it, however good it might be. Still, you'd have to be a pretty sick individual to let that put you off. [David Kerekes]

GARBAGE PEOPLE
John Gilmore with Ron Kenner

With this reissue, the big three of Charlie Manson books are all available: *Helter Skelter* by LA DA Vince Bugliosi is more about him than Manson, and *The Family* is Ed Sanders' attempt to place Charlie and his dune-buggy attack battalion somewhere off the peace love and tie-die map, over where Sgt Fury meets Jimi Hendrix playing Beatle records backwards.

Gilmore's book, originally published in 1971, places Manson firmly within the tradition of small time hoods who con their way in over their own and everybody else's heads. It's like a Jim Thompson character walking into a psychedelic movie. Because, in effect, when Charlie was released from his wonder years in prison, and out into the just-swinging 1960s, it was like setting a piranha loose in a pool filled with fat stoned sea bass. Guppy power, and all you need is love.

Check out the reactions of the Hollywood sleazos who encountered Manson, most of whom had just enough reptile response to keep him at a distance. These included Doris Day's son Terry Melcher and his Beach Boy buddies. Charlie made some music, but he also went to Hollywood parties where they looked at him like the ex-con creepo he was.

Sanders made much of the family aspect of Manson's family, but Gilmore is sharp enough to realise that for Charlie, families were there to be used, not to provide a source of love. Although there was plenty of the latter about.

Gilmore keeps the story moving better than he did in *Severed*, which was the story of the Black Dahlia killing, and provided an excellent theory for that case, though in hard-to-read fashion. Gilmore's original writing in this book, strangely enough, reads better than the revisions added for this edition.

Bobby Beausoleil, of Ken Anger movie fame, didn't like sharing the credit for his killings. How did Anger ever escape ritual murder, anyway? Beausoleil's gone Aryan Brotherhood in prison, and hates seeing Charlie get all the interviews from today's Hollywood reptiles, the Barbara Walters and Geraldo Riveras of the world. Squeaky Fromme missed killing Gerry Ford. Outside prison, the Family lives on. I'm surprised they're not selling souvenirs. The Spahn Ranch will someday be a theme park, just you wait. Helter Skelter City. Every time I see Charlie and his family I think of the local greasers in my childhood neighbourhood, with their DA haircuts and Harleys, and how fucked up they got when drugs lured them into a mainstream they desperately wanted to avoid. Their chicks were always big-titted and chubby and they probably wouldn't kill anyone if they were told to. Not even to bring on Helter Skelter. [Michael Carlson]

THE GATES OF JANUS
Serial Killing and its Analysis
Ian Brady

Here it is, then, 'The Evil Book They Tried to Ban' — at least, here it is for US readers, where serial killers are a dime a dozen, Ian Brady is virtually unknown, and defamation suits rarely prosper. Apparently, publication of the UK version will include a glued-in page disclaiming any responsibility on the part of Ashworth hospital and various other bits of legal malarkey.

The book was originally going to be published pseudonymously (by 'a serial killer'), and apart from one or two seductive asides, Brady says virtually nothing about the Moors Murders. In fact, the first hundred pages or so are a bit of a yawn, mainly due to Brady's florid, abstract and somewhat repetitive style. The fact that the author has spent the last thirty-five years in a prison cell is made obvious by the ponderousness of the writing and the absence of any references to popular culture or public life. He's very fond of lengthy philosophising, and often goes in for quoting pithy apothegms from Shakespeare, Montaigne, Schopenhauer and Nietzsche, which, however pertinent the quotes, eventually gets a bit tiresome.

Things perk up a lot in the second section, however, which is devoted to a study of various serial killers: Henry Lee Lucas, John Wayne Gacy, Dean Corll, Peter Sutcliffe, Richard Ramirez, Ted Bundy, The Green River Killer, Carl Panzram, and the scandalously neglected (at least, according to Brady) Mad Butcher of Kingsbury Run. Here, Brady really does come up with some engaging thoughts and insights. He brings up some new theories about the Mad Butcher, admits his admiration for Panzram and reveals that anti-psychotic medication has led Peter Sutcliffe to grow fat. Most interesting is his description of Graham Young, the St Albans Poisoner and Brady's one-time prison chess partner. We learn, for example, that the only two pieces of popular music that Young could bear to listen to were the double album of *War of the Worlds*, and the single Hit The Road, Jack.

But gems like this are sadly rare; the book is almost entirely humourless. Brady's main thesis is that the serial killer is a superior being, because he's brave enough to separate himself from the herd instincts of the rest of common humanity and really stand up for what he believes in. It's moral relativism taken to extremes, enhanced by a violent hatred for all journalists, politicians, and those involved in the penal system. It's also a view of himself — as Superhuman Monster — refracted through the funhouse mirror of tabloid journalism ('Ban This Evil Book'), without the moderating influence and more subtle nuances of everyday experience. The worst passages read like the rantings of a crazed supremacist — evangelism untempered by ordinary contact with daily life. You start to wonder who he's trying so hard to convince.

I think the key to the book can be found in the afterword by Peter Sotos. Sotos has cunningly filtered through Brady's dense writing and extracted the most critical and revealing passages, then weaves these deftly together into a pattern that shows us how Brady is actually exposing much more about himself than he has intended. What these passages reveal is that the 'timid spectators' Brady refers to — who love thinking about grisly crimes 'from the comfort of an easy-chair' but would find the real thing quite shocking and disturbing — are none other than Brady himself.

Sotos helps us to understand how the whole book is a PR job put on by Brady's unconscious mind to convince the conscious part of himself that serial killers are, in fact, ethically superior, intelligent, sophisticated alpha males courageous enough to take the law into their own hands. By refusing to discuss his crimes, he manages to keep his face turned away from the truth — that most murderers are pathetic incompetents, and their crimes — certainly those committed by Brady and Hindley — are awkward, unexciting, unpleasant, and often quite embarrassing. In the words of the 'Moors Murderer' himself:

> It is invariably the case that actions bright and exciting in the imagination are, unfortunately, often disappointing and farcical in practice, more so when it has not been thought through thoroughly. Deep thinking gives people a headache.

[Mikita Brottman]

Update Since this review was written, the controversy surrounding the expectant arrival of *The Gates of Janus* in Britain gave way to a much delayed, publicity-shy release.

GODS OF DEATH
Yaron Svoray with
Thomas Hughes
After infiltrating the neo-Nazi underground in Germany — the subject of an earlier book — ex-paratrooper and Israeli detective-turned-writer Yaron Svoray claims to have witnessed a film which has haunted him ever since. Screened to a select audience of the masturbating far-right, the film depicted the rape and murder of a little girl. Svoray had encountered a 'snuff' movie.

GREAT TALES OF JEWISH FANTASY AND THE OCCULT
$22.95 / £16.99 / pb / 724pp / ISBN 0879517824 / Overlook Press 1987 / www.penguin.com

Years later, still waking in the night to the terrible images in that film, Svoray concluded that the only way to exercise his demons was to prove to the world that snuff films do exist. *Gods of Death* is the result. It hasn't yet made *News at Ten*.

But then, Svoray's cause isn't helped any by the fact his platform is a book which reads like a two-bit hard-boiled detective novel, full of cliff-hanger prose, and a note at the beginning which informs the reader that "the story you are about to read is essentially a true one". That's a pretty telling statement for a work of non-fiction.

Svoray's investigation took place over a several-year period, but in order to provide a "cohesive narrative", as he puts it, the timescale has been compacted and some details have been changed. All of which is a shame for anyone who is less inclined towards a thrilling mystery and more interested in Svoray's proposed investigation of the 'truth'.

The first part of the investigation takes the author to Bangkok, where Svoray cashes in a favour with an old acquaintance and pays a visit to a dodgy geezer running a bar. That trail gets him nowhere, and Svoray returns to Israel where he meets a Russian arms dealer with a chain of porn shops. Then to Germany. Then to England. From one country to the next and back again, with little to show for his investigations but a string of empty promises, and a wife and family pleading for him to come back home.

But Danger is Yaron Svoray's middle name... To try and infiltrate the snuff underground, first he poses as a buyer of snuff movies and later as a dealer of them. Most everyone he speaks with claims to be able to get hold of such films, or put him in touch with someone who can. Svoray takes all of this at face value and affirmation that there is an industry out there peddling murder on tape for sexual gratification. Not for a moment does he stop to think that these 'low-lives', who he knows full well hustle for a living and will do anything to turn a quick buck, might say anything that he wants to hear if they think there might be something in it for them.

His luck seems to change for the better when he gets into a one-off screening of a snuff film. Made up of professional-looking people aged between thirty and fifty, Svoray pays the $1,500 entrance fee and watches as two men cut a woman's throat as she is being fucked. But Svoray needs hard evidence — he needs a copy of a snuff film himself.

The way the book is going so far, it would be a reasonable assumption to suggest that the story is more grounded in Svoray's fantasy than it is in hard reality. It has all the dynamic of a Hollywood movie adaptation and more than once Svoray talks of film rights, contemplating who might portray him on the big screen! People get murdered, Svoray does a hard-man act, there are gangsters and clandestine meetings, there is a sting on a Mr Big...

But when all seems like it might be plain bunkum, Svoray deals a hand there can be no arguing with (short of landing the publisher with a multi-million dollar lawsuit): he enlists the help of Robert De Niro.

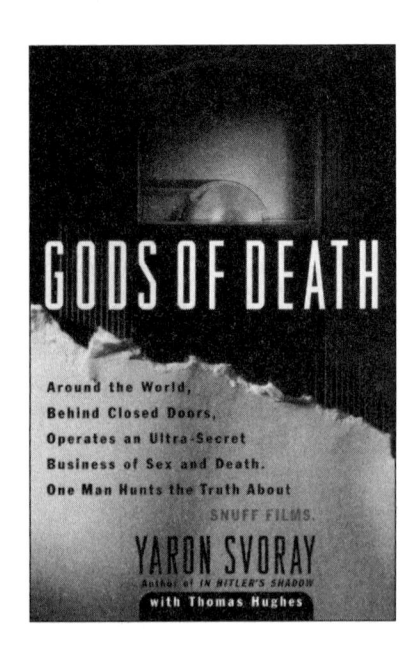

When the opportunity does arise and Svoray finds himself in a position to be able to buy snuff film, the $50,000 asking price shoots it completely out of his range. Through a fortuitous set of circumstances, and sheer determination on Svoray's part, however, he is able to interest megastar DeNiro into posing as a rich client for whom he is working — the deal being that DeNiro will see some of the film, announce to the dealer that he has seen it before and isn't interested in buying it, and then go on public record stating snuff films do exist. With DeNiro's name attached to it, the world's press couldn't fail to be interested.

Although the actor does attend the screening, things don't quite go according to plan. Consequently, DeNiro has never announced that he has seen a snuff film, and Svoray remains yet another frustrating hand-reach short of coming up with the hard goods.

Gods of Death milks its subject matter for every ounce of sensationalism. As snuff film detective stories go, you could do worse; then again, you'd do a whole lot better to pick up a copy of Robert Campbell's *In La-La Land We Trust*, which has no aspirations to get to the 'truth'. [David Kerekes]

GREAT TALES OF JEWISH FANTASY AND THE OCCULT
Ed. & Tr. Joachim Neugroschel

> Now, these good, wise and honest men who aspire to open people's eyes, so that they can tell the good and useful books from the bad, foolish, and harmful ones — these men are known as critics.
> (From 'The Gilgul or The Transmigration')

So that's what it's all about, eh? Well, I'll do my best. I'm not going to pretend to have read all of this hefty beast (oh c'mon, it's over 700 pages long! I do have a life outside of *Headpress* hackwork, y'know). But I hope I've read a representative enough sample of the thirty-one tales collected in this volume to be able to give you a reasonable idea of what to expect. All of these stories are translations from Yiddish, and the majority are by nineteenth- and early twentieth-century authors, although the earliest pieces are anonymous and come from *The Mayse-Book* (1602), a compilation of the fables, parables and folk tales typically told at a farbrengen, a social gathering of a rabbi and his followers (maysenen is Yiddish for storytelling). The stories originate largely from Central and Eastern Europe — the ghetto and stetl cultures of Germany, Poland, Czechoslovakia and Russia — and offer a fascinating glimpse of a largely vanished culture. Those who have studied Cabbalism and alchemy (and I'm sure there's some of you out there), or indeed read the juicier and more poetic parts of the Old Testament, will know how richly evocative Hebrew imagery and mythology can be. Recurrent themes in the collection include matrimonial quests (in classic folk-tale tradition), conversations with, and visitations from, the dead, the wrong-righting and culture-defending deeds of 'wonder-rabbis', and, especially, the fractious relations between the Jews of the Diaspora and their frequently hostile Christian host communities.

One of the more famous tales presented here, 'The Golem or The Miraculous Deeds of Rabbi Liva' by Yudl Rosenberg, was a Yiddish best-seller when first published in pamphlet form in 1909, and subsequently appeared in several other forms, including a stage play, a novel adaptation, and in 1914, as one of the earliest horror films. It recounts the exploits of Rabbi Liva in sixteenth-century Prague, and the Golem (a sort of Frankenstein's monster made from clay and animated by Cabbalistic invocation) he created to defend the Jewish community from the perennial threat of the Blood Libel, that is, the false accusation that Jews carried out ritual murders of Christian children at Passover to obtain blood for making unleavened bread. The Blood Libel has been aired again in this century, firstly in the notorious forgery *The Protocols of the Elders of Zion*, and later in low-rent Nazi propaganda sheets like Julius Streicher's *Der Stürmer*. As Norman Cohn and others have pointed out, the same accusations have been made throughout history against unpopular minority groups, from the early Christians of Imperial Rome, through the witches of the Middle Ages, to the 'Satanic abusers' of our own times.

The other well-known tale collected here is 'The Dybbuk' by Ber Horowitz (also filmed, in Poland in 1938, shortly before Hitler's troops set about removing Yiddish culture from the face of the earth), a story of a displaced evil soul, the eponymous Dybbuk, and its ousting from its host body by Rabbi Israel Baal Shem-Tov. Despite its subject matter, 'The Dybbuk' is more funny than scary (think *All Of Me*, not *The Exorcist*), and in fact, if I have any criticism of this collection, it is that I didn't find any genuinely creepy stories at all, in spite of there being demons, witches, evil spirits, ghosts and Jewish werewolves galore. The stories are too pious to dwell on the dark side for its own sake, and goodness and order inevitably prevail. What

GROSSED-OUT SURGEON VOMITS INSIDE PATIENT!
£9.99 / pb / 147pp / ISBN 0922915423 / Feral House 1997 / www.feralhouse.com

INAPPROPRIATE BEHAVIOUR
£10.99 / $15 / pb / 271pp / ISBN 1852426853 / Serpent's Tail 2002 / www.serpentstail.com

INDEX
£7.95 / pb / 164pp / ISBN 1840680008 / Velvet 1998 / www.creationbooks.com

Weekly World News, May 20, 1997. *Grossed-Out Surgeon Vomits Inside Patient!*

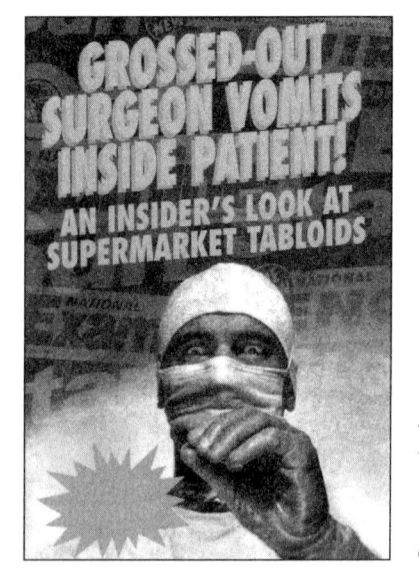

you will find here in abundance are quaint, charming vignettes of mittel-European life, a poignant blend of pathos and *joie de vivre*, and, above all, the abiding commingled sense of faith and perplexity felt by people who considered themselves the Chosen of God, but found themselves dispossessed and cast adrift in an alien and hostile culture:

The world is wondrous in its distances and its occurrences...
(From 'The Jewish Pope — a Historical Tale')

[Simon Collins]

GROSSED-OUT SURGEON VOMITS INSIDE PATIENT!
An Insider's Look at Supermarket Tabloids
Jim Hogshire

Grossed-Out Surgeon is quintessential Feral House. What starts out as a history of supermarket tabloids, by the end of the book has become a welt of intrigue, dodgy-dealings and brain-washing on a national scale! And in this instance, no one is better suited to the investigation than Jim Hogshire, himself a former tabloid journalist. Hogshire determines that supermarket tabs are the only real form of journalism left. This because mainstream journalists start their career at journalism school, use the same phraseology, toe the line, re-word press releases from official sources, while tab journalists *snoop*. "Supermarket tabloids," writes Hogshire, "can be very good sources of news in the truest sense of the word — information you haven't heard before." His argument in their defence is generally a good one. But while *Grossed-Out Surgeon* will certainly change some of your dismissive attitude towards the tabs, a browse through, say, *Weekly World News* or *National Enquiry* will stop you getting too carried away on such colourful notions of 'news in the truest sense'. No, the book is at its most engaging — and gets into really high gears — when deciphering the phenomena of the tabs (the US *Sun*, for instance, is "most popular among college students and bona fide insane people"), analysing the mechanics behind the layout and stories, detailing squabbles in-house and with competitors, and dissecting how the tabs control and influence the masses, i.e.

Police officers say they believe Satanists are at work, the news media hypes it, and soon the public perceives a problem without any evidence. If the deception is successful enough in cowing the public, people may begin to tolerate certain abuses of their rights to stave off the manufactured menace.

In the world of the tabs, everything is black and white. US troops are always seen as 'knights in shining armour', and while police may occasionally flounder, they are never seen as corrupt. Bob Hope is pretty infallible, too. When one editor uncovered information that Hope was having sex with Miss World, he nixed the story saying that to run it "would have been like setting fire to fuckin' Santa Claus". Such hot news doesn't sit easily with the tabloid-buying public, and the story could have lost the tab sales of 10,000 copies. While it's no big surprise to learn that not all of the stories carried by the tabs are true — these fake stories are known as 'wing-its'

— it's interesting that many of the more unlikely-sounding stories *do* have some loose basis in reality. So arbitrary is the dividing line between fact and fiction, however, many of the writers themselves can't remember which story they penned is fact and which is fiction. A good rule of thumb is to stay away from defaming living persons. With living persons, the story has to be true or reasonable steps towards verifying it have to be taken. (Still, I'm a little upset that a story on how Michael Jackson and Jack Nicholson were planning a trip to the moon together didn't make it into print.) Neglecting to adhere to these rules resulted in one of the biggest tabloid blunders to date for the *Sun*. A photo of one Nellie Mitchell, a bicycle-riding eighty-six-year-old from Arkansas, was found in the files. The paper wrongfully assumed Nellie was dead and assigned her picture to a fabricated story about an 101-year-old woman who had just given birth. Nellie took the *Sun* to court. The prosecution argued that faked news stories were a violation of 'journalistic ethics'. The defence testified that the paper hadn't violated any '"journalistic ethics" at all — since the *Sun* wasn't even journalism'. [David Kerekes]

INAPPROPRIATE BEHAVIOUR
Ed. Jessica Berens & Kerri Sharp

Who could resist a cover depicting sexy red devil girls licking ice creams in the bowels of Hell? Well, not me anyhow. After such a visual treat it's not exactly all down hill from here, but just about, as the texts comprising this anthology of mad scribblings by self-confessed Bad Grrrrls do on the whole tend to be too flippant to be as irreverent as they would like to be, and too insubstantial to really grab the attention fully. However, with a list of contents as diverse as this (Satanism, matricide, guns, anti-Jennifer Anniston beauty tips, etc) there's bound to be something to appeal, and for me it's Penny Birch's Lovecraft-inspired essay, "Squiddly Diddly" (honest) mentioning good old Cthulhu and his minions, and even the obscure booklets issued by occult group, the Esoteric Order of Dagon. Go on, give it a go! [Stephen Sennitt]

INDEX
Peter Sotos

My tastes run very similar to those of Ian Brady and I enjoy his work because it is 100% honest and self-concerned. Females are dogs whose only worth is as pawns for my pleasure. Almost exclusively, this involves physical violence.

Remember Peter Sotos? His interview with Paul Lemos, from which the above bons mots are taken, was one of the more startling inclusions in Adam Parfrey's seminal *Apocalypse Culture*. Sotos, an advocate for what may best be described as an 'alternative' morality, produced a zine in Chicago in the mid eighties called *Pure*, which extolled the virtues of child molestation and sexual murder. Its third and final issue landed Sotos in court on a kiddie porn possession charge — he had cut-and-pasted images from a magazine called *Incest IV* into *Pure*. Did being placed on probation cause him to mend his ways? Did he get therapy and find out what made him so fucked-up in the first place? Did he become a born-again Christian and devote his life to the service of others? Well, no, no and no — he has been far too busy with his other projects. Following *Pure*, he produced a short story collection, *Tool*, and a new magazine, *Parasite*. All three were collected (without the offending pictures, natch) in *Total Abuse*, an elusive 1995 volume published by Jim Goad, of *ANSWER Me!* notoriety. He has also become a permanent member of extreme electronic noise-terrorists Whitehouse, and samples of his prose have appeared in the excellent 1997 Velvet Books anthology *Heat*, and Rude Shape's *Funeral Party II*. 1998 has seen the publication of two more books by Sotos: *Index* and *Special*, another one from Rude Shape.

So what is *Index* like? Well, it's every bit as intensely nasty as you'd expect, given its pedigree. Sotos dwells on all kinds of exploitative sexual relations — peep shows, anonymous gay sex in toilets, gang

I WAS FOR SALE
£9.95 / $14.95 / pb / 192pp / ISBN 1840680539 / Velvet 2000 / www.creationbooks.com

JOE GOULD'S SECRET
£6.99 / pb / 192pp / ISBN 0099772310 / Vintage 1998 / www.randomhouse.com

JUICE
£9.99 / pb / 170pp / ISBN 1890159069 / Greenery Press 1998 / www.greenerypress.com

Frying tonight! *Juice*

bangs, porn videos etc. The paradigmatic act is the blow-job culminating in facial cum-shot — all take, no give, sexuality stripped back to a commercial transaction. This is the authentic voice of a man who's completely rejected the idea of any human interaction not predicated on either money or violence.

There's an audience out there who [sic] likes to look at your bloated busting pig meat and the holes you continue to offer.

The writing style is terse, arid, adapted like a predator to the harshness of the territory it inhabits. The only contemporary authors I know of who write stuff this bleak and despairing are Michael Gira of the Swans (who shares Sotos' fascination for peep shows), Henry Rollins in his more nihilistic moments, and the late Jesús Ignacio Aldapuerta, whose most disturbing collection *The Eyes* (pub: Critical Vision) was reviewed in *Headpress 13*. Sotos seasons his stew of misogyny, misanthropy and child-lust with a fat dose of racial hatred too. All in all, then, I wouldn't recommend you buy *Index* for your dear old mum this Christmas, unless you have a very scary mum. Like de Sade, Sotos situates himself at a terminal point of unwillingness to compromise his rage for the sake of an easier life. I really feel sorry for people who paint themselves into such a wretched corner of alienation — there just seems to be no way back in from the cold. The mind of Peter Sotos — an interesting place to visit, but I definitely wouldn't want to live there.

… I'm sorry to have had to add to this sort of noise, this sort of filth, this sort of demeaning consideration… I'm sorry, just truly sorry, for all of it.

Yeah right, Peter, I'm sure you are. [Simon Collins]

Update Peter Sotos has now parted company with Whitehouse — one hardly dares to imagine that the usual 'musical differences' could be to blame. In any case, the latest Whitehouse album, *Bird Seed*, proves them to be as noisy as ever.

I WAS FOR SALE
Confessions of a Bondage Model
Lisa B Falour
In endeavouring to bring something of the profundity which underlies the unremittingly squalid life of your typical bondage model, author Ms Falour has seen fit to quote from William Peter Blatty's *Exorcist* sequel, the almost incoherent and interminably rambling *Legion*. This should come as no surprise as, at the outset, Falour admits: "my spirit is broken, I am alcoholic and my bouts of depression are lasting years at a time." Prepared for the worst, we certainly get it — in spades — as the author reveals her hopeless confusion and misery via a series of anecdotal 'true confessions' which outline her seedy life in late seventies New York. Nothing remarkable here, except the almost bovine tolerance for self-inflicted deprivation, which the author secretly revels in — despite her protestations to the contrary. Pathetic — in the truest sense of the word. [Stephen Sennitt]

JOE GOULD'S SECRET
Joseph Mitchell
Joe Gould was a little man who hung around Greenwich Village panhan-

dling. He was a hairy geek in bum's clothes, doing what panhandlers do with a total lack of self-consciousness. Gould was also a Harvard man, from an old family (related, if I'm not mistaken to Robert Gould Shaw, whose fame was recalled in the movie *Glory*). He claimed to understand seagull language, and often tried to talk with them, which was one of the reasons he was known as Professor Seagull.

He was also working on a book, his *Oral History*, and if you paid him or bought him a meal he would read you sections of it. He worked feverishly in notebooks he carried around with him, writing his view of the world and its interaction with his small life. These were reputedly secreted around New York City, and he was so well-known around the Village, publishers even showed interest.

Joseph Mitchell wrote two profiles of Gould for *The New Yorker*. The first, in 1942, made Gould something of a friend, and Mitchell indulged Gould a little for about as long as he could take it. Gould's friendship could become obsessive. It was always one-sided, and it also withdrew whenever Mitchell got too close to something he didn't figure out for a long time.

He told Gould's story a second time, again in *The New Yorker*, seven years after Gould's death in 1964. Gould had bummed the streets of the Village from 1916 to 1953, when he was committed to Pilgrim State Hospital on Long Island.

Mitchell's wonderful portrait of Gould grows from his sensitivity to Gould's own self-understanding. He knew how much of a disappointment he was to his old Boston family. Mitchell quotes two episodes from his sessions with Gould. In one, Gould recounts how he caught his mother looking at him one day when he was young. Tears ran down her cheeks and she murmured "my poor son". Gould never forgot it. Nor did he forget his father taking him to the Boston rail yards to see a new locomotive, when he was nine or ten, before "he had given up on me", and introducing him to one of the other enthusiasts as "my son". Fifty years later it would still bring tears to Gould's eyes. Mitchell realised not only the crushing effect this pride and disappointment had on Joe, but also the heroic nature of his response. As he says:

He had declined to stay in Norwood and live out his life as Pee Wee Gould, the town fool. If he had to play the fool he would do it on a larger stage, before a friendlier audience.

This is the story of geeks through the ages, though few are as true to their adopted personae as Joe Gould. I wouldn't presume to give away his secret. Mitchell figured it out, and kept it to himself for years before, luckily, sharing it with us in this book. It is a memorial to a place that still exists, even if it comes from a time and milieu that are both long gone. The joke is on the people of style with no understanding. They still live in the Village. And elsewhere. [Michael Carlson]

Update Stanley Tucci made a wonderful film of *Joe Gould's Secret*, with Ian Holm delivering an Oscar-worthy performance. Tucci himself played Mitchell, who never wrote another word for the *New Yorker* after his second Gould story, though he continued to go into his office every day for twenty years. I recommend Mitchell's other writing unreservedly, particularly a marvellous collection called *The Bottom Of The Harbour*. The film was one of the highlights of the 2000 London Film Festival — nevertheless I interviewed Tucci the following spring for *The Financial Times*, simply because the editor thought him 'fab'.

JUICE
Electricity for Pleasure and Pain
Uncle Abdul

You don't get much more bizarre than this! Instructions on how to assemble (at home) sundry torture devices for use in the bedroom — or kitchen for that matter: The Violent Wand, "a high voltage toy that uses a Tesla Coil... when the bulbs are in close proximity to the bottom's skin, a spark can jump"; The Shock-

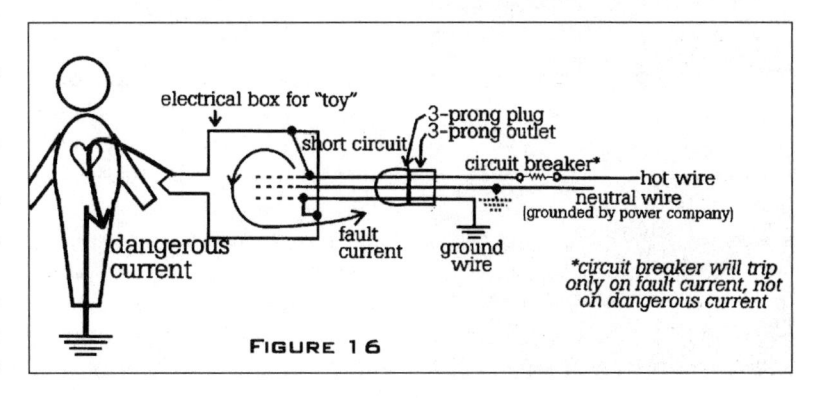

FIGURE 16

LUCIFER RISING
£12.99 / pb / 256pp / ISBN 0859652807 / Plexus 1999 / www.plexusbooks.com

LUSTMORD
£14.95 / pb / 228pp / ISBN 0691015902 / Princeton University Press 1995 / www.pup.princeton.edu

THE MAMMOTH BOOK OF WOMEN WHO KILL
£7.99 / pb / 558pp / ISBN 1841193887 Constable Robinson 2002 / www.constablerobinson.com

MEAT IS MURDER!
£14.95 / pb / 213pp / ISBN 1840680407 / Creation Books 1998 / www.creationbooks.com

ing Animal Collar, a "small electronic low-voltage shocking device is placed in a pet collar"; The Electric Fly Swatter, "may not be effective on flies, but it's very effective on body parts…"

Juice claims to be the first and only book (and I believe it, I really do!) about how to use electricity safely in S&M relationships. It is as exhaustive and in-depth as you would wish a book like this to be. For all his technical expertise and know-how, the author, 'Uncle Abdul', has created a brisk and fun-filled book which leaves your reviewer feeling bothered and bewildered — will folks actually buy this book and use it as the manual it's meant to be? Is the world really full of little would-be 'Uncle Abduls'? [Stephen Sennitt]

LUCIFER RISING
Sin, Devil Worship and Rock'n'roll
Gavin Baddeley

This is something of a departure for Plexus, a company which usually publishes books on relatively mainstream stars of popular culture. More surprisingly, it's an entirely sympathetic treatment, and an enormously entertaining read. Looking much like an old issue of *Headpress*, with a back-printed motif of a woodcut demon recurring throughout and a B&W illustration on virtually every page, the book is broken into three sections: the history of Satanism, Satanism in twentieth-century culture, and the Satanic millennium. The book's not really exhaustive enough to work as a general overview — hardly any films are mentioned, and there's not much of an account of Satan as a literary figure past Baudelaire. This is fair enough, insofar as each of these areas is worth a book in its own right. Where the author really has done his work, however, is with Satanic music, which it covers in a far broader sense than Moynihan/Soderlind's indispensable *Lords of Chaos*, although the two do intersect at times. I don't know much about the current state of 'black metal', but this seems to be a pretty solid account of Satanic imagery and beliefs in bands from the Stones and Black Sabbath through to Cradle of Filth, through back-masking scandals, Satanic ritual abuse hysteria and electronic industrial bands.

As you might expect, some bands see it as a gimmick, a marketing tool, while others are more grimly serious about their relationship to the Horned One. One thing all the bands have in common is the same cheesy gothic look. Surely if you've done a deal with the devil you can look better than that? But Baddeley doesn't raise the issue with his interviewees, probably realising that types like Count Grishnackh ("If I, for example, murdered a person, I could steal his aura and add it to mine, so I would get a more powerful aura") and Danzig ("If the situation happened right here where I had to cut your throat, I would do it") wouldn't take too kindly to comments about their sartorial elegance.

There's also an informative and entertaining history of Satanic organisations, from the Hellfire Club to the Order of the Nine Angles. LaVeyan Satanism is gone into in some detail, with lengthy interviews with LaVey himself and other pretenders to the throne. The interviews with contemporary groups (Baddeley covers some which are not explicitly Satanic) reveal a disturbing if well-documented trend in modern occultism — the celebration not only of the imagery of the Third Reich but also of its ideology. In a way this seems to be both a reaction against the cosiness of established organisations such as the Church of Satan or Michael Aquino's Temple of Set — they're just not evil enough — and a deliberate attempt to bait the liberal media. At the same time, for some it must provide a woolly, cod-mystical justification for their far-right beliefs, and a number of the interviewees give evasive answers when asked about ritual sacrifice. LaVey's take on all this? To advise his followers to become 'Jewish Nazis'. To his credit, Baddeley doesn't skirt round the issues involved here. He doesn't attempt to censor the voices of anyone involved, and nor does he justify or condemn. This kind of objective approach to such an emotive topic is rare and extremely welcome. While I would have welcomed more on the contemporary occult scene and less on black metal bands — a few of the interviewees in the latter category are virtually indistinguishable — I can't fault Baddeley's research or his approach. Highly recommended. [James Marriott]

THE MAMMOTH BOOK OF WOMEN WHO KILL
Ed. Richard Glyn Jones

Back at the dawn of recorded history, when I was at university studying literature, it became necessary for me to write a couple of dissertations. Being a *Headpress* kind of guy, I decided that one of my dissertations would be about the symbolism of dismemberment in western literature, and I spent a happy few weeks reading authors like Edgar Allan Poe, Alfred Jarry, Joe Orton and of course the Marquis de Sade. I also read, for comparative purposes, a lot of true crime accounts. Some of these were classics of the genre like Brian Masters' *Killing for Company* and Flora Rheta Schreiber's *The Shoemaker*, but others were, I must confess, just what I happened to find at charity shops and on market stalls. Thus, it came to pass that I became one of what must surely be a very select band of people to have cited *The Mammoth Book of Murder* in an academic paper. Amazingly, the university authorities let me graduate anyway. Years have passed and here I am, writing about *The Mammoth Book of Murder*'s sister volume. There are quite a number of these *Mammoth* books now, covering topics as diverse as chess, erotica, the SAS and UFOs, though disappointingly there doesn't seem to be a *Mammoth Book of Mammoths* yet.

The *Mammoth* books I've seen all follow a similar format — big doorstops of books, formed from many short chapters by many different authors, in the case of *Women Who Kill*, forty-nine chapters by thirty-four authors (including J Edgar Hoover, who writes about Ma Barker). All your old favourites are here — Myra, Lizzie, Rosemary — though at three to fifty pages a pop, many of the chapters are too short to really give you much insight into the often complex and fascinating cases they describe. What is surprising, given the number of different authors involved, is the uniformly terrible quality of the prose — a breathless tabloid style is favoured, which is often replete with howlers and inaccuracies. Consider this representative opening from Dorothy Dunbar's chapter on Lizzie Borden:

For sheer Alpine altitude in the illustrative peaks of crime, the blood-stained palm goes to Miss Lizzie Borden of Fall River, Massachusetts, and her inseparable symbol, the hatchet.

The author then goes on to inform us that "it was written literally in blood that Miss Emma and Miss Lizzie were inheritors of $175, 000 each." Really?! Literally? Miss Borden is eventually delivered to a truly Lovecraftian fate:

Did the bloodstained images of Second Street ever gibber idiotically at her memory? Did the wet footprints of the past walk through her mind?

There's a whole lot of idiotic gibbering going on, that's for sure. You can see that your chances of gleaning much information about any particular crime are pretty slim. Despite the size of this book, it's aimed at people with short attention spans — one of the shorter chapters might just about while away a visit to the loo or a bus ride. You'd do better to invest in a book covering just one of these cases in a lot more depth. [Simon Collins]

MEAT IS MURDER!
An Illustrated Guide to Cannibal Culture
Mikita Brottman

Our shared human fascination with cannibalism is connected to infantile needs and desires arising in the oral-sadistic phase of childhood development, by virtue of which it becomes a powerfully repressed element of the human unconscious.

Mikita Brottman obviously has

MUERTE!
$16.95 / pb / 93pp / ISBN 0922915598 / Feral House 2000 / www.feralhouse.com

MURDER BY NUMBERS
£17.99 / hb / 310pp / ISBN 0233991387 / Andre Deutsch 1998

Scary looking villains make the news. Muerte!

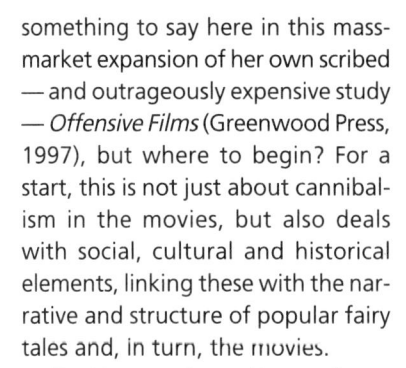

something to say here in this mass-market expansion of her own scribed — and outrageously expensive study — *Offensive Films* (Greenwood Press, 1997), but where to begin? For a start, this is not just about cannibalism in the movies, but also deals with social, cultural and historical elements, linking these with the narrative and structure of popular fairy tales and, in turn, the movies.

Brottman doesn't condemn exploitation cinema, in fact she's rather fond of the genre, but far too much space is taken up with synopsis. Unless you have never seen or read about the likes of *Cannibal Holocaust* and *The Texas Chain Saw Massacre*, the urge to skip pages of text is overwhelming. When she finally gets round to the dissection of such titles, the culmination becomes somewhat repetitive — although not entirely uninteresting — with elements originating in fairy-tale lore.

With the exception of Manoel de Olieira's *Os Cannibales* (1988) and Liliana Cavali's *I Cannibali* (1970), *Meat Is Murder* looks only at the popular examples of filmic cannibalism, and many worthy titles are all too briefly mentioned: Danny Lee's *Dr Lamb* (1992), for example, is restricted to a footnote condemning its "sickening scenes of depravity" condemned. This is such a shame. If Brottman had focused her energy and enthusiasm at such deeply disturbing and more recent, less well-known examples of the genre, then this could have been a great book.

As for being an 'illustrated guide', however, the reproduction of many stills is appalling, and I do wish Creation would up-date their unoriginal cover designs. And while I'm moaning, there's one more thing: Brottman feels the audience of Mondo films consists "chiefly of *that* group of thrill-seeking adolescent male voyeurs that comprises the main audience for the traditional horror film" (my emphasis). Now this may be true, but the tone of the sentence is certainly derogatory. Being female, Brottman is obviously outside of *that* group, but with words like 'explicit', 'transgressive', 'bodily extremes', 'murder' and 'mutilation' splashed across the back cover and Leatherface on the front, is it not precisely *that* group of people who will be drawn to buy this book? I don't see this as a case of the author biting the hand that feeds her, rather a clash of intention between writer and publisher.

Returning to the quote atop, I am fascinated with my own personal interest in cannibalism, but being adopted and deprived of the joys of mammary lactation as a child, I am still no closer to discovering the roots of my fascination, or my own penchant for cannibalism: eating cock and enjoying it! [David Greenall]

MUERTE!
Death in Mexican
Popular Culture
Ed. Harvey Bennett Stafford
Feral House's incredible *Death Scenes* is a much-thumbed tome in these parts — with an apparently endless stream of visitors wanting to gasp and then groan at the pictures of savaged flesh. This book, whilst not a sequel, certainly fulfils those with salacious desires to see 'more'. Edited by artist Harvey Stafford (some examples of his work are reproduced in the book), *Muerte!* explores the bizarre history and culture of Mexican murder and death tabloids. Through a series of essays by various authors, *Muerte!* locates these tabloids within a wider cultural

milieu that includes the work of the artist José Posada who was similarly interested in depicting the freaks, executions and murders for Mexican audiences. *Muerte!* is comprehensively illustrated with bloodied grisly images from the magazines — exploded heads, bullet wounds, decomposing corpses, and scary looking villains — all reproduced in the same insanely lurid colour as in the original magazines, as well as translations of several articles, written in a brutal style that accompanies the visceral images perfectly. This is a thoroughly entertaining, yet terrifyingly grim view of the unique relationship between the world of excessive violence fuelled by bludgeoning poverty, and that of Technicolor Mexican tabloid journalism. [Jack Sargeant]

MURDER BY NUMBERS
Anna Gekoski

If there's one thing the world needs more than another serial killer it's another serial killer book. Right? Someone ought to chart the rise of serial killings against the number of words the subject generates. What's the correlation? Not that I'm going to do a Colin Wilson and blame serial killing on pornography, or even on the pornography of true crime writing. It's just that with the death of religion we're no longer scared of Satan, Hell or eternal damnation. The supernatural, currently undergoing a bit of a revival, doesn't frighten most of us. Instead we like to scare ourselves with something of the here-and-now, and yet possessed of that quality of evil that separates it from the 'normal'. Is it any wonder that Robert Ressler, ex-FBI and the man who coined the phrase 'serial killer', entitles his books *I Have Lived In The Monster* and *Whoever Fights Monsters*. Demonisation is the name of the game; in this secular and confused age we'll invent devils to frighten ourselves with, and, just as importantly, to confirm to us the parameters of our 'normality'.

Which brings us in a round about way to Anna Gekoski's *Murder By Numbers*. This is a detailed look at the life and crimes of British serial sex killers. All of the usual demons are included here: Christie, Ian Brady, Myra Hindley, Dennis Nilson, Fred and Rose West. However this isn't just a case of going over the same old ground. There are chapters here on Robert Black and Colin Ireland, for example. The latter is interesting as there is practically nothing in print about the man who preyed on men from the gay S&M community.

The book looks closely at the childhoods of these deadly, twisted individuals. And even on the Nth reading, the crimes these people committed are frightening. If you're a sick fuck, of course, you'll even find these sickening crimes arousing. However, Gekoski takes her task seriously. What made these people commit crimes awful enough to cast them forever as demons? And in asking that simple question she steps away from the standard line. She does much more than make us shudder and check the locks on the door at night.

But looking at these people as people, by probing their young lives she gives us a picture of young souls that are seriously damaged, of personalities that are recognisably vulnerable and which elicit sympathy as much as their adult crimes evoke revulsion.

If you want to understand rather than sample a frisson of fear and disgust, then this book is highly recommended. [Pan Pantziarka]

NECROTOURIST

DOC. GORDON TRIPP LECTURES AGAIN

28pp / 12pp / Contact: Bella Basura, PO Box 5454, Leicester, LE2 0WP, UK / bella@pixie-inc.demon.co.uk

THE OKLAHOMA CITY BOMBING AND THE POLITICS OF TERROR

£12.99 / $18.95 / pb / 509pp / ISBN 0922915490 / Feral house 1998 / www.feralhouse.com

NECROTOURIST
Bella Basura

DOC. GORDON TRIPP LECTURES AGAIN
Bella Basura

The Internet may well be a carboot sale for any Joey's opinion, but getting something printed on paper still displays a desire to *make an effort*. Bella Basura's simple A5 booklets are prime examples of this ethos. *Doc. Gordon Tripp Lectures Again* is dry pastiche filtered through mock-scientific record: Dream Machine stuff. Much more interesting is *Necrotourist*, a collection of brief travelogues to places most year-out students will hopefully remain ignorant of. Like all the best adventures, the set plan of each journey inevitably becomes mislaid: exiting the Paris Catacombs, Basura finds herself lost in the city, perhaps miles from her bike; in Mexico, the Frieda Kahlo museum is undergoing repairs, which unwittingly sends Basura to the house where Leon Trotsky was assassinated; a motorcycle trip to Derek Jarman's bleak seaside cottage in Kent is cut short by a notice in the window from the present occupier dissuading visitors and photography:

> We slouched away, feeling slightly disappointed, slightly embarrassed to find ourselves nosing around in a complete stranger's garden.

Over all-too-quickly, there are five compelling journeys in *Necrotourist*. It's well worth a visit. [Martin Jones]

THE OKLAHOMA CITY BOMBING AND THE POLITICS OF TERROR
David Hoffman

T S Eliot once wrote that "April is the cruellest month". The nineties certainly seem to be vindicating him. In April 1999, connoisseurs of atrocity could take their pick from the ongoing bloodbath in the Balkans, nail bombs in London, and the Trenchcoat Mafia shootings in Littleton, Colorado. Earlier in the decade, April 19, 1993 saw the Mount Carmel compound of David Koresh and his Branch Davidian followers go up in flames in the culmination of a fifty-one-day siege which had been catastrophically mishandled by every government agency to get involved, especially the FBI, who had taken over from the ATF (Bureau of Alcohol, Tobacco and Firearms), who had provoked the standoff in the first place with an ill-conceived attempt to raid Mount Carmel in order to search for illegal weapons. Eighty-six people died in the blaze, including twenty-seven children. And on April 19, 1995, probably not coincidentally, the Alfred P Murrah Federal Building in Oklahoma City was destroyed by a huge explosion (or explosions? See below), causing the loss of 169 lives, including nineteen children, over 500 injuries, and hundreds of millions of dollars worth of damage.

Americans, unused to acts of domestic terrorism, reacted with outrage and disbelief. Almost everyone initially assumed that Islamic fundamentalists were responsible, as they had been for the bombing of the World Trade Centre in New York in February 1993, which, until the Oklahoma City bombing, had been the worst terrorist incident seen in the United States. But within three days, the FBI had made two arrests, Timothy McVeigh and Terry Nichols, white men with military backgrounds and connections to the libertarian rightist anti-governmental 'Militia' movements. They were tried separately in Federal courts and convicted by prosecution cases based on the premise that they had together built a large (4800 pound) truck bomb out of ammonium nitrate fertiliser and fuel oil and detonated it outside the Murrah Building (a protest against the government's actions at Waco and at Ruby Ridge, Idaho, in August 1992, where federal agents had shot and killed family members of white supremacist and gun-nut Randy Weaver). In some ways, the case against the two men was strong — forensic evidence showed they had been handling explosive substances, they were both known to hold violently anti-governmental views, they had been seen setting off bombs on Nichols' farmland before, and McVeigh was placed at the scene of the crime by many witnesses. Above all, McVeigh made little attempt to argue his innocence. On closer inspection, though, the government's case was full of holes, many of which are examined at great length in David Hoffman's fascinating book.

In some ways, the case against Tim McVeigh and Terry Nichols resembles that against Lee Harvey Oswald in the assassination of President Kennedy, the most salient difference being that McVeigh and Nichols survived to stand trial. The title of the first chapter of *The Oklahoma City Bombing*, 'The Mannlicher-Carcanno Bomb', explicitly makes this comparison. Like the Mannlicher-Carcanno Italian hunting rifle allegedly used to kill JFK, Hoffman convincingly argues that the size and type of bomb supposedly set by McVeigh simply could not have wreaked the havoc seen in Oklahoma, and he includes as an appendix an interesting bomb damage analysis report by explosives expert Benton Partin.

This is only the first in a long series of loose ends and lacunae in the Feds' case exhaustively explored by Hoffman. This is a serious and wide-ranging investigation (it took me a solid week to wade through it!), and I can only attempt to give a brief summary of the most important questions raised.

Who was 'John Doe 2', the suspect seen by many witnesses with McVeigh in the rented truck used for the bombing? An APB was initially issued for him, only to be hastily withdrawn as the authorities announced that he didn't exist after all. Suspicions remain that he was a government agent (provocateur?), who was ignored in order to protect his cover.

Why were the warnings given of the impending bombing by several different FBI informants within the Militia movement ignored? Or were they? No ATF agents were injured in the blast — they had been told not to turn up for work that morning.

What of the connections Terry Nichols had to various shady Middle Eastern people? He met some very dodgy characters on several mysterious trips to the Philippines.

A white supremacist named Wayne Snell was executed in Arkansas on the very day of the Oklahoma bombing. Snell, convicted of two racially-motivated killings, had been a member of a far-right Christian paramilitary group called the Covenant, Sword and the Arm of the Lord, which, remarkably, had plotted in 1983 to destroy the Murrah Building with a truck bomb. Why was this extraordinary coincidence never investigated?

Why did McVeigh behave so stupidly in the aftermath of the bombing? Stopped for speeding, he made no attempt to evade capture, despite having firearms in the car with him. Again, like Lee Harvey Oswald, his movements and behaviour in the weeks and months preceding the bombing seem erratic, to say the least. Admittedly, he could have been a 'lone nut', but that hardly explains how he existed with no visible means of support, apparently as an itinerant arms dealer living in the back of his car, having turned his back on a promising military career. In yet another Oswald parallel, McVeigh's time with the Marines seems to have brought him into contact with some very shadowy military intelligence operations. Was he released into civilian life only to act as an undercover agent in the Militia movement?

Ultimately, one is left not so much with a feeling that McVeigh and Nichols were innocent — they are clearly both deeply unpleasant and dangerous men — but that a much larger picture was wilfully ignored by the investigating agencies, who seemed to have an undue fervour and haste to insist that McVeigh and Nichols were the only conspirators, despite large amounts of evidence to the contrary. McVeigh in particular looks like a classic patsy.

The Oklahoma City Bombing suffers from the usual fault of conspiracy tomes of offering too many alternative suspects and explanations — at times, it seems there was hardly anyone in Oklahoma that fateful morning who *wasn't* trying to bomb the Murrah Building! And Hoffman's writing style doesn't really make the book a pleasure to read — earnest though it is, it's also

OSWALD TALKED
£21.99 / hb / 454pp / ISBN 1565540298 / Pelican Books 1996 / www.pelicanpub.com

PILLS-A-GO-GO
£11.99 / $16.95 / pb / 284pp / ISBN 0922915539 / Feral House 1999 / www.feralhouse.com

POLITICS OF THE IMAGINATION
£12.99 / $17.95 / pb / 206pp / ISBN 1900486202 / Critical Vision 2002 / www.headpress.com

tedious and dry, and the frequent heavy-handed sarcastic asides make it all too obvious where Hoffman is coming from, politically speaking. But like the JFK case, the bombing in Oklahoma refuses to go away — Russ Kick's invaluable *Psychotropedia* lists four other books and one video on the same topic, none of them anywhere near as substantial as this — and if you want to take a serious interest in the case, it's difficult to see how you can avoid reading this.

For those who just can't get enough (and God knows, after wading through this hefty sucker, you really should give it a rest — it's just not *healthy*!), I recommend Adam Parfrey's essay 'Finding Our Way Out Of Oklahoma', collected in his *Cult Rapture* volume. And for conspiracy buffs generally, *Prevailing Winds* is a well-researched and classy magazine covering a wildly eclectic range of topics — contact them at PO Box 23511, Santa Barbara, CA 93121, USA. Issue five contains several pieces relevant to this book, including an open letter from Oklahoma State Representative Charles Key, who also contributes a foreword to Hoffman's book, and an article by Hoffman himself on a train derailment in Arizona (this material is recycled in the book), as well as an interesting speech by Oliver Stone, himself the subject of conspiracy theories (see Feral House's *Secret and Suppressed* for improbable information regarding subliminal images use in Stone's film *JFK*).

As William Burroughs so wisely observed, "A paranoid is someone who knows what's going on". [Simon Collins]

Update Tim McVeigh was executed by lethal injection on June 11, 2001 — the first federal execution since 1963. His co-conspirator Terry Nichols was found guilty on December 23, 1997 on counts of conspiracy and manslaughter, but not guilty of using a weapon of mass destruction and of destruction by explosive. He was sentenced to life imprisonment, but is currently awaiting trial in Oklahoma on state murder charges, for which, if found guilty, he may also receive the death penalty. Although now somewhat overshadowed by the events of September 11, 2001 and subsequent genuine Islamic terrorism, there are still many unanswered questions about the Oklahoma bombing.

OSWALD TALKED
Ray & Mary LaFontaine
If you accept that Lee Oswald was indeed a 'patsy' in the Kennedy Assassination, and that there was indeed a conspiracy, the question of what exactly Oswald was doing, or thought he was doing, has prompted years of informed guesswork. This book ends all the guesswork. Working with Dallas police records released in 1992, in the wake of the furor surrounding the film *JFK*, the LaFontaines have reconstructed Oswald's stay in custody, and proven both the existence of a conspiracy and his status as its patsy.

Dallas Police kept no records of their interrogation of Oswald, but Mary LaFontaine discovered that he had actually shared his cell-block with two other prisoners. One of those men, John Elrod, testified that police brought a badly-battered prisoner into the cell for Oswald to identify, and that Oswald said he had met that man along with Jack Ruby.

Tracing the identity of that prisoner proved more difficult, but he turns out to be Lawrence Miller, arrested on November 18 after a high-speed chase involving a car laden with weaponry stolen from the US Army base at Fort Hood. Miller's partner was Donnell Whitter, a sometimes employee of Jack Ruby, and it was with Ruby that the two had earlier met Oswald. Why? The FBI, contrary to policy, destroyed the informant report that led to Miller's arrest, but the LaFontaines make a credible case, including testimony of an FBI file clerk, that Oswald was that informant.

Oswald would have been ratting out the mob-linked gunrunners and an anti-Castro Cuban organisation, the Student Revolutionary Directorate (DRE), both of which were linked directly to the CIA. The likelihood that Oswald blew his cover would make him a perfect candidate to serve as a patsy, and the fact that he was on the FBI payroll helped insure that J Edgar Hoover's G-Men showed no real interest in investigating the actual facts of the assassination on behalf of the Warren Commission.

This explanation resolves a lot of the contradictions in Oswald's pseudo-Marxist behaviour, and his multiple appearances within the Cuban exile movement in Texas and Louisiana. This is probably the single most important work on the Kennedy assassination to have appeared in the past decade, and demands far more attention than it has thus far received. [Michael Carlson]

Update Oswald Talked never did get much mainstream attention, though it created a stir within the assassination community. The authors came under a lot of pressure for (a) defending Jim Garrison and (b) suggesting Dallas cop Roscoe White's jaw and body may have been the rest of the famous faked Oswald 'revolutionary' photo. But these were diversions, and the basic thesis of the book remains compelling.

PILLS-A-GO-GO
Jim Hogshire

Pills-a-go-go is neither a guide to getting high nor a dreary, academic pharmacopoeia, but rather a history of pills written for unrepentant drug takers of all kinds. The concept for the book first emerged in a twenty-two issue zine devoted to "Which pills worked, which pills didn't, and how they could be hacked so as not to ruin one's internal organs". The best of this information, along with further high-dosage active ingredients, is collected here in *Pills-a-go-go*.

There is plenty of stuff on the ingestion of recreational drugs, and also genuine, registered pharmaceutical product — albeit not for the usages approved, i.e. extracting codeine from painkillers. Readers seeking new highs should find the book useful, though possibly a little too diverse, delving as it does into many other areas, like pharmaceutical-style drug marketing.

Nestling amongst the heavier articles on alternative uses for over-the-counter medicines and lists of controlled ingredients within prescribed drugs, are song lyrics about pills, lists of pill-popping celebrities, and overly cute marketing gimmicks. More radical are the sections on prescription forging, and on how to get your pharmacist to give you exactly the drugs you want.

Pills-a-go-go is well researched, detailed, stylishly laid-out and informative, with a large bibliography and a section on online reading. However, the lack of an index means the book seems stuck as a collection of writings and pictures, rather than the definitive reference work it could have been. Worse though, are the many errors which render entire sentences unreadable or illogical — consider "Getting pills that have aspirin instead much better" from page 223, or "She takes her attitude a step further when she exalts the pill to holy status she feels the drug is being profaned" from page ten. [Sarah Turner]

POLITICS OF THE IMAGINATION
The Life, Work and Ideas of Charles Fort
Colin Bennett
(Foreword John Keel)

This is one of the most compelling biographies you will read this year, or any year, for that matter. Despite a massive cultural and ontological presence which grows in stature at an exponential rate, Charles Fort (from whom we derive the word Fortean as a catch-all reference to all kinds of unexplained phenomena) has been the subject of only one previous full-length biographical study, Damon Knight's *Prophet of the Unexplained*, a sterling effort published in 1971, but which is now completely overshadowed by Colin Bennett's definitive and comprehensive overview.

Particularly compelling is Bennett's well-argued opinion that Fort's influence can be recognised to extend far beyond the paranormal/unexplained 'ghetto' with which he is usually exclusively associated, extending into more general culture to sit on a par with recognised cultural architects, such as Charles

PORNOCOPIA
£9.99 / pb / 416pp / ISBN 1852427205 / Serpent's Tail 1999 / www.serpentstail.com

THE PROFESSIONAL PARANOID
£9.99 / $12.95 / pb / 195pp / ISBN 0922915547 / Feral House 1999 / www.feralhouse.com

PSYCHEDELIA BRITANNICA
£9.99 / pb / 212pp / ISBN 1873262051 / Turnaround 1997 / www.turnaround-uk.com

Charles Fort aged nineteen.
Politics of the Imagination

Darwin, James Joyce, T S Eliot, Henry Ford and Stephen Hawking. In fact, despite my life-long interest in Fort and all sorts of related weirdisms, this was the first time I had been compelled to view Fort in his true light as a really serious major shaper of popular cultural perceptions. If only for this matter, *Politics of the Imagination* is a work that demands to be read. [Stephen Sennitt]

PORNOCOPIA
Porn, Sex, Technology and Desire
Laurence O'Toole

'Porning' is how Laurence O'Toole defines the growing trend of sexualising the look and content of many mainstream magazines — a trend which has increased dramatically these recent years. While this itself may not be a bad thing, the editorial hypocrisy concerning pornography evidenced in many of these same titles is. People may be more open with regard to matters of sex, but there remains a stigma attached to pornography and its use. Look across any newsagent rack and you'll be hard pushed to spot a magazine — regardless of its content — that doesn't feature a bikini-clad babe on the cover displaying her ample charms. Hardly in a position to deny that sex sells (or that they're selling it), look *too* hard however and you're liable to fall into the sad, raincoat category, so regularly vilified in those same pages. Where does the boundary of sexual 'coolness' and social acceptability finish, and where does the 'sad wanker' start? Is the boundary governed by the revenue sex generates for these publications?

An article in one mainstream publication proposed to be an investigation of video porn, conducted by a male and female journalist, enduring together a marathon hardcore video-viewing session. The result was obvious cock-a-snoop stuff and the marathon viewing session understandably not very arousing for the intrepid viewers. In the one instance when the journalists admit to the stirrings of arousal, they immediately pull themselves into check and laugh it off.

And that, in a nutshell, is the dilemma that is pornography: something that we don't want to be seen looking at or enjoying.

This updated edition of *Pornocopia* contains a new chapter, covering porn's many developments since the book was first published in 1998. With a refreshing British vantage point that also takes in the phenomena of softcore sex mags and the necessity of buying hardcore under the counter, *Pornocopia* comes highly recommended. [David Kerekes]

Update Laurence O'Toole was interviewed in *Headpress 19*. An exhaustive interview with John (Buttman) Stagliano appeared in *Headpress 24*, which was originally scheduled by O'Toole as a chapter in *Pornocopia* but pulled due to space limitations.

THE PROFESSIONAL PARANOID
How To Fight Back When Being Investigated, Surveilled, Stalked, Harassed or Targetted by any Agency, Organisation or Individual
H Michael Sweeney

Moving into territory usually dominated by the likes of Paladin and Loompanics, Sweeney's hugely technical book has blood ties with publications by Alex Constantine and Rex Feral. Mind control, law enforcement, listening-in, private mail boxes, surveillance and the like are all dissected in fanatical detail. It is at times fascinating but strangely distant, certainly the fact that Sweeney's perspective is solidly American will alienate UK readers; also its seventy-two page appendix of technical information will mean nothing unless you are familiar with electronic communication systems. This is not a book of dirty tricks or revenge tactics — you would have to be seriously paranoid or a contentious criminal to be in a position where such information could be put into practice. Despite its initial complexity, the book's central message is very clear: when targeted/harassed by an organisation or individual, identify your enemy and choose your allies with care. When this has been achieved, study the enemy and use the information to either assist protection or put to your own advantage (I say advantage, but self-defence is the primary motivation here).

You can look at volumes like this in two ways: fictions from a paranoid mind, or gospel. The former is certainly the least frightening of the two (only one loony out there instead of an entire network of belligerent individuals/organisations peeking in at your every move). Take all this seriously and delusions of persecution could make you unbearable! [David Greenall]

PSYCHEDELIA BRITANNICA
Hallucinogenic Drugs in Britain
Ed. Antonio Melechi

17 December, 1974
Dinner

A lady is yattering on and on
Natasha: Do you hear what you're saying
Lady: No (startled) Thank God! (giggle)
Natasha: (severely) If you wiggle your ear with every mind in you your chair might go up

R D Laing is a psychologist. An early book of his, *Conversations with Children*, published in 1978, consists of fragments of dialogue and off-the-cuff remarks made by children and collected by Laing over a period of several years. Some of this dialogue — as in the extract above — is rather abstract, some of it is funny and some of it is remarkably enlightened and astute. And of course, it can at times be poetical and read on many levels. Following *Conversations with Children*, I decided to track other works by Laing down and arrived at *Do You Love Me?* and *Knots*. The former takes human anxieties and emotions and puts them into a child-like verse. As poetry it's not very good. As psychology I suspect it might be 'cute'. The other book, *Knots*, is worse — the wordplay is even more cyclic and goes so far as to include schematic layouts and symbols (such as arrows) within the text.

It didn't cross my mind whilst reading these books in the late seventies and early eighties — though I

PSYCHEDELIC DECADENCE
£12.99 / pb / 175pp / ISBN 1900486148 / Critical Vision 2001 / www.headpress.com

PSYCHOPATHIA SEXUALS
£9.95 / pb / 256pp / ISBN 1871592550 / Velvet 1997 / www.creationbooks.com

Elton John eat your heart out! Robin Askwith in Confessions of a Pop Performer. Psychedelic Decadence

suppose it's rather obvious in retrospect — that R D Laing might have quite an audience amongst the drug underground. His radical views on schizophrenia made him unpopular with the medical fraternity in the sixties, while his controlled ingestations of LSD and magic mushrooms were a hit with the hippies. Timothy Leary regarded him as 'the most fascinating man on the planet'.

This information I procured from *Psychedelia Britannica*, not a volume which attempts to alphabetise drugs or their availability in the UK, but a thoroughly absorbing series of essays on hallucinogenic culture and changing attitudes towards drug use. Including its place in psychiatric history. Antonio Melechi submits the essay 'Drugs of Liberation', which takes in Laing and other mind physicians — some of whom wanted all mental health workers to take mescaline in order to understand what it was like to be mad.

A good portion of the book is naturally devoted to music, with three essays covering everything from the consciousness-altering sounds of The Byrds, Pink Floyd, and the like, right through to the rise of Ecstasy and Acid House in the nineties. Here, in 'Ecstasy Evangelists and Psychedelic Warriors', Stuart Metcalfe relates how E pretty much killed any experimentation in Dance music by changing it into exactly what Ecstasy-consumers wanted — no longer a stimulant to the music, the constant, seamless, unfaltering 4/4 beat became a stimulant to the drug.

Psychedelia Britannica refuses to tread common ground, and while the music chapters are essential to a history of hallucinogenics, it is perhaps with the stuff in between that the real gems are to be found. Michael Carmichael's 'Wonderland Revisited' offers a — ahem — potted history of the Reverend Charles Dodgson, more commonly known as Lewis Carroll. Carmichael reflects on the overt drug references in Carroll's most famous work, *Alice in Wonderland*, the Reverend's own interest and experimentation with opiates , his relationships with little girls (apparently, to paedophiles, Carroll is now regarded as something of a 'patron saint' of pornography and child sexual abuse) and how babies in nineteenth-century England were regularly dosed with soporific drugs. Fascinating. [David Kerekes]

PSYCHEDELIC DECADENCE
Sex Drugs Low-Art in Sixties & Seventies Britain
Martin Jones

Now you're talking! Tell me: who could possibly resist a book which claims its spooky tutelary spirit to be made up of components incorporating the music of the Stooges, the books of J G Ballard and the groovy living-dead killer from *Scream and Scream Again*...? That's one vicious homunculus I certainly wouldn't want to meet down a dark alley! Thankfully — and in the true spirit of psychedelic decadence — you don't have to. You can read all about it instead, experiencing the purely vicarious cheap thrill beloved of all culture vultures. And let me state in no uncertain terms: author Martin Jones is a scavenger of the first water (hey, calm down, that's meant to be a compliment!). In picking through the ossified relics of British pop culture circa 1967–77 Jones has revealed a strange gnostic homogeneity that brings these artifacts back to living, breathing life — something which only the most advanced adept is capable of achieving. Yes; Jones collects the bones, pieces them together again and breathes *life* into them, making them a part of *himself*. It's a combination of uncanny necromancy and slick appropriation which makes for great reading. With hardly an out-of-place paragraph, Jones conjures up a zeitgeist from apparently disparate elements including Linda Hayden, Basil Fawlty, Mike Raven, *Mayfair* magazine, Michael Reeves, *2000AD* comic, NEL biker paperbacks, Ingrid Pitt, Robin Askwith, and other lowbrow ne'er-do-wells, and creates a thick atmosphere of pseudo-nostalgia so pungent it smells even riper than the real thing. In summoning to visual appearance this spectrally 'unique time in British cultural history' he also throws penetrating insights into arguably 'higher'-brow elements as represented by J G Ballard, David Bowie, Peter Cook and the film *Performance*.

Somehow, it's all a perfect blend, but perhaps the crux of the book rests on a seemingly slight, short piece on Roxy Music which evokes the bizarre spirit of the times by contrasting singer Bryan Ferry's earlier alienated songs, which show distrust of the shallow glamorous lifestyle, to his later songs which celebrate it. In this, Ferry is like one of J G Ballard's characters, adapting to the sudden, 'catastrophic' change thrust upon him as his only means of survival. And like any classic Ballardian character, Ferry not only survives in this element, he *flourishes*. Similarly, *Psychedelic Decadence* as a whole has a bright and attractive surface hiding unsuspected depths. Martin Jones says he'll settle for the *image*: a circular bed sporting a couple of nubile *Mayfair* models, "Bowie on the stereo, *The Vampire Lovers* on the TV, Burroughs on your mind and… endless booze and drugs…" but I suspect this would only provoke yet deeper thought from him. [Stephen Sennitt]

**PSYCHOPATHIA SEXUALIS
The Case Histories
Baron Richard von Krafft-Ebing**
Psychopathia Sexualis was first published in 1872. Despite it being over 100 years old, and many of Krafft-Ebing's conclusions seen today as rather ludicrous, it is still regarded as the seminal work of its type. A Shakespeare of the psychiatric world, when it comes to sexual lovemaps, Krafft-Ebing covered every base and permutation thereof. His case history scenarios are also, given their age, exceptionally lucid, and Krafft-Ebing doesn't pull away from hard fact the way some of his contemporaries did. Here you will find true tales of bestiality, masochism, sadism, coprophilia and necrophilia, all delivered in a detached, clinical manner. (Funnily enough, much contemporary erotic fiction appears to mimic this style.) Some case studies run to several pages in length, some are only a paragraph.

Velvet have doctored the original *Psychopathia Sexualis* by cutting out all the 'medical psycho-babble' and reprinting just the case histories, all 238 of them. While it would have been nice to have had the whole lot together, in one piece, few of its readers are likely to miss Krafft-Ebing's pontificating.

The introduction to this collection is an interesting and astute piece provided by Terence Sellers, author of *The Correct Sadist*, and helps to form the ultimate irony of it all: this scholarly work is now directed at

PSYCHOTROPEDIA
£15.99 / pb / 576pp / ISBN 1900486032 / Critical Vision 1998 / www.headpress.com

RAPID EYE MOVEMENT
£17.95 / pb / 255pp / ISBN 1871592690 / Creation Books 2000 / www.creationbooks.com

THE REDNECK MANIFESTO
$13 / pb / 274pp / ISBN 0684838648 / Pocket Books 1998 / www.simonsays.com

exactly the kind of pervert it once aspired to analyse. [David Kerekes]

PSYCHOTROPEDIA
A Guide to Publications on the Periphery
Russ Kick

More than "a guide to publications on the periphery", *Psychotropedia* is your skeleton key to books most often sniffed at by your high street bookstore. From this book I have discovered the paintings of Judson Huss, and the essential British horror comic. I know why I get ratty when I chew too much sugar-free gum, and what Clinton's really saying when his speeches are played backwards. I know what Thomas Pynchon might look like. Oh, and I know where to get erotic furniture and what happens when bedbugs mate. So with all that, tell me, what else is there *worth* knowing?

Thanks to Russ Kick's diligent research (how I'd love his bookcase), I am no longer pissed off that I can't walk to the Compendium bookshop, because this book, with it's browse-by guides to well over a thousand *shade-culture* titles, is the next best thing. Fourteen sections covering sex, art, conspiracy, comix, drugs, the body, politics, etc, document a fair slice of some of the best and strangest titles out there, often with quoted extracts and bullet-point factoids from the books. Russ Kick writes crisply and without the taint of judgement, whether he's outlining a book on how to succeed in topping yourself, the conspiratorial writings of David Icke or Alex Constantine, or one of the many titles on taboo and marginalised sex. Too heavy for you? Then take *All I Needed To Know I Learned From My Golf-Playing Cats*. I kid you not, that book exists and you'll find it in here.

As publishers and their outlets roll together like blobs of mercury, increasing — so it would seem — the pressure on the survival skills of smaller publishers, the messengerial role of the peripheral presses is moving ever further towards front of stage, filling the vacuum created by the few who gratify what they assume to be the needs of the many, and in so doing deepen mass trance and restlessness. The worst sins of the mainstream, their blandisation of culture, feeds the fires of many of those writing and being written about in the books outlined here. So not all vicious circles are as savage as they seem, and I am not inordinately disappointed to see that the balance in *Psychotropedia* weighs down on the side of American titles. The United States' hyper-accelerated culture has created the hottest subcultural dynamo in these terminal years of the millennium. The author acknowledges the greater amount of US books. Perhaps future editions will see him look more towards redressing publishers from Europe and the East. An aspect of *Psychotropedia* shows that at the moment too few on this side of the Atlantic are choosing to take up the gauntlet thrown down by publishers such as Feral House and AK Press. The back pages contain full publisher's details and a complete index of titles.

Russ Kick's great achievement in crafting the close-on 600 pages of *Psychotropedia* is to prove — if proof were needed — that you're not as messed-up or marooned as the mainstream would have you believe. There's other ways of thinking, of being, and how inspiring it is to dip into this volume and be reminded so. As Russ Kick writes, "it's nice to know that some things will never be co-opted by the Spectacle". Or as someone else once had it: gravity doesn't work on mutants. The unwitting legacy of the mainstream's timid steps towards a cookie-cut society is the creation of more sovereign mutants. As long as there are more channels of looping, rolling, repeating television — as long the best-seller lists are stacked with tasteful tat — as long as there's magazines existing only to feed off everyone else's ideas — and even if the Internet becomes the boot system for Bill Gates' Xanadu 1.0, there will be enough jewels to fill a hundred *Psychotropedia*s.

A box of gold stars to *Headpress* for this addition to their range of provocative titles. *Psychotropedia* is both the Devil's library index and a stand-alone feast for your mind. [Jerry Glover]

Update Now out of print but check out [w] www.headpress.com for used copies. Russ Kick has samples from the book at his website [w] www.mindpollen.com/mp.htm

RAPID EYE MOVEMENT
Simon Dwyer

I can still remember the time I came across the first volume of *Rapid Eye Movement*, it felt incredible, like I'd just stumbled across something so wonderful that it couldn't be true. I grabbed the copy there and then, convinced that it was important. This was where I wanted to be, I realised. It wasn't just that the content covered areas I was already interested in: industrial music, conspiracy theories etc, it was also that it was well-written, extremely intelligent and obviously a labour of love.

Years later I can remember the launch party for the third and last volume of *Rapid Eye Movement*. It was some dingy art space near Clerkenwell, Mr Andy Weatherall was doing his stuff, Gilbert and George were there in a corner with a couple of prettyboy minders, Stewart Home was due to spout his stuff… And where was Simon Dwyer? I was looking forward to meeting him at last. I asked one of the Creation Books crew and was told that he was in hospital. With what? My answer came a little while later when Peter Colebrook took the stage to deliver a message from Simon, in hospital with AIDS. I was stunned. It seemed so unfair that he should be ill on a night like that.

I was never fortunate enough to meet Simon Dwyer. Jealously, selfishly, I had hoped that he would recover to continue with *Rapid Eye*. Where was volume four? I wanted so much to contribute, to add something back to a project that had given me so much. It was never to be, as Simon fell victim to the disease.

Creation Books have taken the best from those three volumes of REM and created a tribute edition, dedicated to Simon and his widow, Fiona. Reading back over some of those first articles I can still feel a sense of excitement, even though my interests have moved on. There is still much to be admired about it as a work. Simon's critical intelligence is clearly evident, and his passionate interest in art, creativity and the state of the world shines through. If you've never read REM then this must count as vital reading — primary material for anybody interested in 'industrial' culture, modern art and the state of the world. [Pan Pantziarka]

THE REDNECK MANIFESTO
Jim Goad

I never saw any of the original issues of *ANSWER Me!*, and only came across the writings of Jim and Debbie Goad in the AK Press *ANSWER Me! First Three* collection. For the uninitiated, their stock-in-trade is the furious, vitriolic debunking of myths surrounding taboo subjects. Not just your average, run-of-the-mill taboos, either — the Goads knew what kind of people would read their rants, and focused on the topics which produce knee-jerk reactions in the most 'liberal' and 'enlightened' of readers: racism, sexism, rape, suicide, etc. They were not only unafraid of attacking their audience, but positively delighted in it. Whoever you are, you're a target for indiscriminate but acute Goad rage and hatred — nobody escapes. Highlights of the *First Three* are 'top 100' pieces on murderers and suicides, written with a sharp wit and an angle unlike anything I've seen before. For such a degree of distilled anger shaping such ironic social comment, Jim Goad's writing recalls Swift circa *A Modest Proposal*, an infamous piece concerning a plan to deal with Irish hunger and overpopulation in one fell swoop, by eating babies — recipes included.

This is the first book-length project from Jim Goad, and kudos should go to Simon & Schuster, a mainstream publishing house, for putting it out. It's basically a polemic in defence of "the cultural clan variously referred to as rednecks, hillbillies, white trash, crackers and trailer trash", to quote from the back cover blurb. The book's obviously very US-centric, but a lot of its ideas are applicable in Britain too, and it's interesting to note how we've swallowed wholesale American cultural assumptions about class in the States. I don't think

SATAN SPEAKS!
£9.99 / $13 / pb / 179pp / ISBN 0922915660 / Feral House 1998 / www.feralhouse.com

SCUM MANIFESTO
£6 / pb / 60pp / ISBN 1873176449 / AK Press / www.akpress.org

SEARCHING FOR ROBERT JOHNSON
£7.99 / pb / 96pp / ISBN 0712666680 / Pimlico 1998 / www.randomhouse.com

the USA has a Ken Loach or a Mike Leigh, or much idea of class pride for the underprivileged, compared to the often inverse prejudice in the UK media. But this is getting off the point…

Goad's basic premise is that poor American whites are prejudiced against, both economically and in terms of media representation, and blamed for a range of sins they never committed. He argues convincingly that class and wealth distribution rather than race are the key dividing factors in American society, and that institutional racism was established by the ruling elite during slavery as a divide and rule tactic. Goad shows that the volume of European slaves imported into the country far outweighed that of African slaves, which is news to me, and that most 'rednecks' now are descendants of these slaves — not really 'the oppressor', or able to experience any of the much-vaunted white privilege. He debunks myths about the Civil War, specifically that it was a war to free black slaves, and offers an acute analysis of media representation of both poor whites as 'rednecks' and as militia members, exploring the extraordinarily biased reporting on militias and the legitimacy of their concerns. He also deals at length with inverse racism and white guilt, and the absurdity of a situation in which racial pride is encouraged in all groups except whites, pointing out that white racial pride is usually seen as a fascistic tendency. And it certainly can be a fascistic tendency, but that doesn't mean that Nation of Islam can't.

The first few chapters are taken up with a consideration of these issues, which can be a little dry at times — Goad is, after all, seeking to show that a number of historical assumptions are built on false premises, and backs up his argument with liberal quotations from contemporary documents. To offset this, though, Goad writes extensively about himself, 'a proud member of the White Trash Nation', his community, and 'trailer trash' culture. Goad's arguments are more convincing and credible than I can do credit to here, and as an added bonus you get some prospective reviews written by the author, such as the following:

This book is a psychotic, self-pitying, one-sided, historically revisionist screed. What an accomplishment — making people feel good about racism again.

Goad's sawn-off shotgun approach to the reader might not win him many new friends, and it is easy to see this book being misinterpreted. Only someone as angry as him would have the balls to write it, though, and it needed to be done. It killed a few assumptions of my own, and made me think about the situation here more clearly — it's refreshing to have someone cut through all the sensitive tiptoeing and be unafraid to offend everyone with a giant 'fuck you'. Angry? You should be. [James Marriott]

SATAN SPEAKS!
Anton Szandor LaVey
Foreword by Marilyn Manson

Anton LaVey's recent books have had neither the charm nor the relevance of *The Satanic Bible* — a timely tome indeed, which raised the status of popular occult paperbacks from their lowly 'pot boiler' position to one of 'best-seller' credibility. LaVey followed the *Bible* with *Satanic Ritu-*

als — a book which revealed what all those glossy Church of Satan photographs depicting pig-headed and dog-headed ritualists were all about!

Jump to the nineties and the release of the long-awaited *Devil's Notebook* (replete with Adam Parfrey's Feral House seal of approval) and now the current, albeit posthumous, *Satan Speaks!* What we have here are two books which are pithy, archly humorous and nihilistic but which lack the 'timely' feel of their predecessors. LaVey seems to be having to work that much harder to maintain his rancorous stance, sometimes merely exposing his own boredom without successfully identifying its legitimate source. In some ways this isn't helped by the subject matter he chooses to discuss in *Satan Speaks!* Though perhaps inanely humorous, LaVey ranting on about panty shields, fake snot and witch's shoes (yes, witch's shoes) is hardly inspiring; neither is his searing anger served well by turning it against stereo-recordings as opposed to good old mono-recordings! It's difficult to envisage anything more bathetic than this impressive-looking Satanic High Priest grouching like some ordinary old fart in an old folk's rest-home about things as mind-rottingly mundane as this… [Stephen Sennitt]

SCUM MANIFESTO
Valerie Solanas
Valerie Solanas shot and almost killed Andy Warhol at The Factory, in June 1968. That action assured media interest in the SCUM *Manifesto*, a booklet of esoteric ideas which Solanas had written and self-published the year before, selling it on the streets. Maurice Girodias, of the prestigious Olympia Press, was quick to re-release the *Manifesto* under his own imprint — he had shown an interest in it prior to the shooting, but had wanted Solanas to turn the concept into a novel before considering publishing it. Now SCUM *Manifesto* traverses the annals of Warholian weirdom — another Pop Art incident which, in retrospect, seems almost too good, and too exciting, to be true. It is with a little surprise, therefore, that we learn the *Manifesto* is only in its *eighth* printing incarnation — Solanas' self-published booklet being the first and AK's edition being the most recent.

SCUM is short for the 'Society for Cutting Up Men'. It argues that man is nothing but a biological accident ("… the Y [male] gene is an incomplete X [female] gene, that is, has an incomplete set of chromosomes") and the world must be rid of them — or, at the very least, favour the female of the species. With that as its springboard, the *Manifesto* picks out 'flaws' in the current social order, and offers radical alternatives. These sexual-sociological observations are quite interesting, if hardly earth-shattering, but the latter part — Solanas' SCUM initiative, which advocates the taking over of the airwaves and such like — is stoned idealism, pure and simple.

Prior to the shooting, Solanas believed that Girodias had screwed her over in a contract. She also believed that some kind of — here we go — conspiracy against her was going on between him and Warhol. When she got hold of the revolver which she ultimately fired on Warhol, it was Girodias she had originally intended to shoot, only she couldn't find him.

Valerie Solanas spent the seventies in and out of mental institutions. She had a drug problem and was turning tricks up until she died in April 1988, penniless and suffering from emphysema and pneumonia. The decade prior to her death, she was completely free from the public eye, except for a letter to *Playboy* in 1977, in which she accused the editor of being a Hit Man for The Mob. It was in this same year that Solanas 'came clean' with the SCUM *Manifesto*, telling a reporter that it was lust a 'literary device'. "I thought of it as a state of mind," she said. "Women who think a certain way are in SCUM. Men who think a certain way are in the men's auxiliary of SCUM." [David Kerekes]

SEARCHING FOR ROBERT JOHNSON
Peter Guralnick
They say Robert Johnson sold his soul to the devil, one midnight at a crossroads, and that was why he was able to play the blues the way he did, like no one else.

One night he just showed up at a roadhouse where Son House and Willie Brown were playing, and asked if he could play. Last time they'd seen him he was strumming around. Now he bent the strings like a man possessed.

Peter Guralnick wasn't able to track down the Devil and ask him for his side of the story, but otherwise, this slim volume is about as comprehensive as we are likely to get on the mysterious life of possibly the most brilliant bluesman ever.

Of course, part of Johnson's appeal is that he died young, poisoned by a jealous husband. The way he played and sang just drew the women, and Robert always wanted one to take care of him, as if he needed

SEEK!
£10.99 / pb / 364pp / ISBN 1568581386 / Four Walls Eight Windows 1999 / www.4w8w.com

SEVERED
$16.95 / £12.95 / pb / 230pp / ISBN 1878923102 / Amok Books 1998 / www.amokbooks.com

'The Black Dahlia.' *Severed*

protection. Husbands didn't always appreciate this. And because he died young, there was no success phase, nor decline to his music making. No fat Robert Johnson in spangles with backup singers playing Vegas or appearing on rock and roll hall of fame TV specials.

Guralnick comes to Johnson's music from the days of the fanatic: the fifties and sixties, before Clapton and the Stones made versions of Crossroads and Love In Vain popular, before Sweet Home Chicago and Walking Blues were covered by everyone. He has the tone of the true believer, one small step away from the anorak. You really think he'd be happier if the music were only available on 78s, or wax cylinders, still as mysterious as Johnson's life.

Yet he's right about his analysis of what makes Johnson's art so special.

Whatever the Devil promised Robert, he delivered. Even though all that is left are a limited number of songs, all primitive recordings, the sheer shuddering power of Johnson's blues reaches through in almost every song. Voice and guitar seem to meld to produce sounds that rise from some darker part of humanity, somewhere far deeper in the shadows than any of us can imagine. Stones In My Passway, Terraplane Blues, Hell Hound On My Trail, and Me And The Devil Blues have that perfect freedom of art without bounds.

The best part of Guralnick's tale is the way Johnson becomes something different to everyone who knew him. His contemporaries, Johnny Shines, Son House, Honeyboy Edwards, tell stories that contradict each other, then take on parts of the others' best. Sonny Boy Williamson used to claim Johnson died in his arms. Even Robert Junior Lockwood, as close to a son as Johnson had, seems at times to be recalling a dream when he talks about the man.

With the advent of CDs, it's easy to assemble Johnson's complete recorded oeuvre. And that raises the one fault with this book. Originally published in 1989, this should have been updated before it was reissued. First, to let us know if Mack McCormick's *Biography of a Phantom* was ever published (I don't think so, but I could be wrong) and more importantly, to update the discography to take account of the CD revolution. But that's a mere quibble. This is as good a look at the Devil as you're likely to get and still retain your own humanity, even have it enhanced. Until Mr Scratch makes his own CD, this one'll do for me. [Michael Carlson]

SEEK!
Selected Non-fiction
Rudy Rucker

This anthology of magazine, diary, and occasional pieces from the past decade-and-a-half suffers badly from the difficulty of collected writing on cutting-edge subjects. While they may have been hot several years ago, they have become either sidetracked or redundant as science and information technology makes near-weekly quantum leaps. Rucker is a professor of computer science and an award-winning writer of science-fiction novels, among them *Infinity and the Mind*, and the *Ware* series. He writes in a chatty, laid-back style, usually very smooth and readable, sometimes boring and self-absorbed. Mostly, though, quite good fun if, that is, your interest is piqued by things cybernetic and SF-related. The pieces are organised into three sections: Science, Life, and Art, and range from interesting musings on nanotechnology (remember that?), to past-their-sell-by-date musings on fractals and artificial life, to pointless musings on a dog called Arf. Rucker is writing all the time and about everything. Unfortunately, only sporadically does he have interesting observations to make, electing on publishing pieces that should have either remained as journal notes or stripped of their chaff. Articles written just a few years ago on what was then cutting-edge stuff often feel very dated, occasionally irrelevant. I'd question the point of reprinting such writing, which takes me back to my computer science lessons: hour after hour learning stupefyingly outdated facts about card-hole reading machines and ferrous-core memory drives. Rucker's pieces were written for magazines, consequently they don't have the fact-density that would make for absorbing reading. You find yourself snacking on odd paragraphs, wearied or amused on being reminded about datagloves and the struggles he had to create a virtual cube on old CAD software. The historical value is marginal, and a few minutes on the web shows me what's happening now. This book is a repository; don't go here to seek out where things are going. This is future past.

The anecdotal pieces work better. 'Drugs and Live Sex' is a beatnicky evening with strung-out New Yorkers. Funny. And the 'Jerry's Neighbours' chapter is very good on the paranoia that crept over Rucker after he'd pissed-off a right-winger. The interview chapters and reported conversations also engage. Rucker meets Ivan Stang (the man behind the Church of the SubGenius), nanotechnology proselytiser Eric Drexler, and Stephen Wolfram, the creator of Mathematica.

Also enjoyable are the pieces on silicon chip fabrication plants, trips to Japan and Hawaii, and the experience of making a movie on Portugal with Robert Anton Wilson (who is an ordinary mortal with ordinary mortal gripes and emotions as it turns out). What I do not like is paying to read about Rucker's dog (so many times I've tried and failed to read this chapter), his shopworn *Star Trek*-SF concepts, and his hopes of being remembered as an SF writer as great as Philip K Dick, a writer for whom Rucker sees purely in terms of ideas, grasping non of the late writer's anger and political awareness. I can't help feeling that things are just a little too comfortable in Rucker's tenured world for his ideas to be more than merely mildly interesting. Pages spent plugging concepts of robots and artificial life and how they are worked-up in his fiction had me flicking to other sections. This is and always will be one of the perils of writing about SF. While robots may well be where it's at out Rucker's way, to me they're about as interesting as those plastic tropical fish that bob around on magnets (how *do* they work?). A century of work into and speculation about robots, and where are we? Car assembly plants and substitute-pet automata. Follow-up pieces to these chapters wouldn't have been a bad idea.

For a writer with two Philip K Dick awards to his name, I find *Seek!* dejecting. [Jerry Glover]

SEVERED
The True Story of the Black Dahlia Murder
John Gilmore

Elizabeth Short, 'The Black Dahlia.' Ever heard of her? The nickname may ring a distant bell, but the chances are you're not sure why. Ever heard of Fatty Arbuckle or Marilyn Monroe? Short's death as much as theirs stands as an inspiration for the phrase 'Hollywood Babylon'. An aspirant actress and model, Short was found dead at the age of just twenty-two, her body hacked in half and dumped in an empty LA lot. She had been anally and vaginally violated and forced to eat human faeces: to ascertain her height, the coroner had to measure the two separate portions of her corpse separately.

Short was the archetypal small-town girl wanting to make it big in movies. With striking features and jet black hair, she stood out in

SEX AND ROCKETS
$24.99 / hb / 320pp / ISBN 0922915563 / Feral House 1999 / www.feralhouse.com

SEX CARNIVAL
£13.99 / $18.95 / pb / 250pp / ISBN 1550224158 / ECW Press 2000 / www.ecwpress.com

her hometown — but then as now, she was just one of thousands of lookers in LA. Never able to apply herself, never able to find the right job, the right man (except for one, her fiancée, tragically killed during the last days of World War Two), she drifted about sleazy bars, flophouses and shady characters before her untimely demise.

It is in this milieu that Gilmore's talents shine: he describes a world now long gone, a world both sleazy and glamorous, a world of cocktail dresses and heroin needles, B-movie actresses and abused prostitutes, lipstick and mascara and blood trickling into gutters. Hollywood will never again be as we perceive it to have been in those heady days. And Elizabeth is the perfect metaphor for how we might remember this time few of us actually experienced: happy and gay but with an otherworldly edge; friendly, vivacious, yet never really in the some place as everyone else. "Elizabeth was of the night. She was the dark..."

Gilmore (who has had a real Holly-Baby life himself) tells a fascinating story but one which can drag. The first 100 pages, in which various lowlife try to get into Short's pants, feel stretched — Short's character has been established and she doesn't change much, so why all the detail? What must be appreciated though is the author's devotion: he has spent twenty years cocooned within this story, so I suppose the least we can do is listen. And one must respect Gilmore: his obsessive research has added to the sum total of human knowledge. Many facts here have never been brought to light before and he does offer a convincing answer to the mystery of who killed Short. This mystery is the concern of the book's latter half, and fascinating, twisted reading it makes: hardboiled detectives suspicious of one another, innocent men's lives ruined by the same 'tecs desperate to convict somebody, anybody, of the murder, LA Confidential-style pondlife hacks digging for dirt, even William Randolph Hearst himself covering up any connection to the slaying of a wealthy heiress who may have fallen prey to the same killer. The inquiry is far more fascinating than the murder itself, just like classic film *noir* rules dictate it should be. Of the murder, the book contains some very grisly photos, though I feel it a shame that *Severed* might be bought by gorehound thrill-seekers in search of visual titillation. It has far more to after than that.

So who did kill her? I have no idea, but I'm prepared to believe Gilmore for now — he has certainly put the graft in. [Anton Black]

Update Gilmore's thesis has since been discredited by, amongst others, James Ellroy — see *Headpress 22*.

SEX AND ROCKETS
The Occult World of Jack Parsons
'John Carter'

'John Carter' is the Edgar Rice Burroughs-inspired pseudonym of American occult researcher, Paul Rydeen, who has a background in the more lightweight or popular end of this subject-matter via appearances in a multitude of small-press UFO/Fortean magazines and booklets. However, *Sex and Rockets* is light years away from the homemade atmosphere of such publications (just as one would expect from a publisher like Feral House) sporting a colour dust jacket wrapped over a nicely produced hardback, with sewn-in binding and quality paper. Pity, then, that the content of the book is still so amateurish and 'light' in tone, offering few real insights into a character as complex as Parsons. 'Carter' just seems happy to write-off this pioneering rocket scientist, poet, and Thelemic magician as a naïve, moody failure with a mother-fixation, and leaves all the more complex occult ramifications to 'hardcore' researchers such as Kenneth Grant and Michael Staley. This is a shame, because the author had a golden opportunity here to extend our understanding of Parsons who's still a relatively obscure figure in 'underground culture'. Instead, 'Carter' offers a rather bland, colourless account of Parson's dual career; touching all the bases, but only in the most desultory of fashions and totally lacking in any insightful arrangement of the obviously voluminous and painstaking research notes he must have assembled. [Stephen Sennitt]

SEX CARNIVAL
Bill Brownstein

Sex Carnival charts the erotic odyssey embarked upon by Bill Brownstein, a Canadian journalist with the *Montreal Gazette*, whose publisher gave him six months and an unspecified sum of money to explore the world of sex. Sounds like the plot of a porn movie — and maybe the dream assignment for any hot-blooded young writer.

Brownstein's *Sex Carnival* begins backstage at the Adult Video News Awards Show in Las Vegas, where he chats about the porn biz with luminaries John Leslie, Bill Margold, Bobby Slayton and Melissa Monet. Next, he takes a trek through the Playboy Mansion courtesy of Hef himself, and has lunch with Lou Paget, a lady who gives lessons in fellatio to the pampered wives of the rich and famous (she won't reveal her client list, but her dishwasher, Brownstein notes, is chock-full of assorted dildos). He then gets juicy in the Big Apple, where he drops into a fashionable S&M bar on Wall Street, turning down an offer to be whipped into shape by an especially nasty-sounding dominatrix who specialises in humiliating the yuppie clientele. Mee-ow!!

There isn't quite enough cash in the kitty to take him to the Far East, but he does manage to get as far as the sex hubs of Europe — Amsterdam and Paris. In Amsterdam, he joins a tour group for a visit to the red light district and drops in on a few live sex shows, as well as the infamous Bananenbar — a club whose waitresses perform various kinds of genital acrobatics with everybody's favorite fruit. In Paris, the places he visits are a little more refined — the Moulin Rouge, the Crazy Horse — but he does also manage to take a quick trip to the Place de la Pigalle. Finally, and in a rather unlikely twist, Brownstein's odyssey takes him right back to his home in Montreal (Montreal? Did he run out of cash?). Here, Brownstein checks out the local sex scene, visits Club Cream on Fetish Night, covers an afternoon porn shoot on a yacht, then attends the Salon d'Amour et Seduction, where booths exhibit all kinds of sex toys and marital aids, from the mildly titillating to the downright sleazy.

However unlikely it might seem, it turns out that Montreal is touted by connoiseurs of such matters as the new Sex Mecca — especially since, as of December 1999, lap dancing is no longer considered illegal or indecent, and many lap dancing clubs advertise 'legal contact' — that is, the you can touch the girls, though the girls aren't legally allowed to touch you. Brownstein hangs out with a couple of young Canadian punters who claim that the women in Montreal are the hottest in the world — and, even better, the price is right. "Two hundred bucks can go a long way in this town," says James. "Go to the Chicken Ranch in Las Vegas, and it will cost close to a thousand dollars, but the quality just isn't the same as here." Montreal, sex capital of the free world? That's what they're saying...

Actually, one of the difficulties I had with *Sex Carnival* is that Brownstein never really does come right out and say very much. He comes across as generous and likeable, his observations are full of amusing details, he has a great turn of phrase and the book is fun to read, but Brownstein is always very careful to distance himself from the people he meets and the places he visits. Occasionally he'll say things like "vodka has clouded my judgment", but throughout the whole of his six-month sex tour, we never learn if he samples the goods — Hell, we never learn if he has a single lap dance, or even if he cops a feel! What gives, Bill? Wife and kids at home? Inquiring minds want to know...

To do him a little more justice, however, Brownstein isn't writing a guide book or teaching us where we should go to get the best bang for our buck. Truth is, this isn't a 'sex carnival' so much as a series of descriptions of various sex 'scenes' around Europe and the US, and some friendly chats with the people who belong to them. It's all very gentle

THE SEXUAL CRIMINAL
£13.99 / pb / 448pp / ISBN 0965032426 / Bloat

SEXUALITY, MAGIC & PERVERSION
$16.95 / £12.99 / pb / 208pp / ISBN 0922915741 / Feral House 2002 / www.feralhouse.com

THE SEXUALLY DOMINANT WOMAN
£8.99 / pb / 96pp / ISBN 1890159115 / Greenery Press 1999 / www.greenerypress.com

and whimsical, and Brownstein has a real knack for describing people who could easily be made to appear quite ridiculous — suburban dentists and lawyers dressed in lederhosen, for example, cavorting with middle-aged women sporting skin-tight latex suits — while respecting their sexual preferences, and without making fun of them. And if there's any conclusion to be reached from Brownstein's *Sex Carnival*, this is it: that the world of sex has changed, and that everybody's doing it. The people Brownstein meets and talks to at the sex expos, fetish clubs and museums of erotica are everyday people from all walks of life — mothers and fathers, singles and couples, parents and grandparents, old and young, gay and straight. If Brownstein learns anything that surprises him about the sex scene, it's that there's no longer any stigma attached to the most unusual and eccentric fetishes.

Some readers might feel that Brownstein doesn't really get far enough beneath the surface — that he never gives us even so much as a glimpse of the sordid underbelly of the sex industry — the addictions, the boredom, the corruption. But *Sex Carnival* doesn't set out to be a behind-the-scenes exposé. Instead, Brownstein takes us on a family-friendly jaunt round a few sex-themed tourist sites in the US, Canada and Europe. It's all done in the best possible taste — and frankly, it's nice to read a book about the sex industry that doesn't leave you feeling like you need to take a shower. [Mikita Brottman]

THE SEXUAL CRIMINAL
A Psychoanalytical Study
J Paul de River

A sleazy-as-hell-epic of sexual degradation courtesy of J Paul de River, the founder — in 1937 — and director of the Sex Offense Bureau of the LAPD. In a lengthy biographical introduction Brian King offers a portrait of de River, who emerges as an archetypal *noir* figure, a man who wanted to examine every sex-freak, sicko, pervert, and deviant arrested in order to catalogue all the moral offences in LA, and create a kind of legitimate psychopathological *One Hundred and Twenty Days of Sodom*. Working with the LAPD, de River had exclusive access to the human cesspool he desired, and freedom to indulge in his psychological fascinations. In the end — like a character from a pulp novel — de River tried to 'fix' his 'theories' a little too much and got willingly dragged into the Black Dahlia mystery, from which he was unable to fully extricate himself. In the following scandal numerous untruths were exposed and de River's tenure at the Sex Offense Bureau was over. However, despite this, de River was able to write and publish his 'research' in *The Sexual Criminal* in 1949. de River's fascinations, as articulated in the book, reveal two basic elements. The first is a clear realisation of Foucault's nosological gaze as articulated in *The History of Sexuality* and *Power/Knowledge*. The second element de River's work reveals is that his fascination with the sexual abnormalities of criminals, and sexual crimes in particular, was particularly voyeuristic. To these ends *The Sexual Criminal* presents the reader with crime scene photos, descriptions of victims' wounds, descriptions of the criminal physiognomy, and reprinted Q&A sessions between Paul de River and criminal. This is an incredible book, reading it you enter a world where no one comes up smelling of roses — just rotting flesh and disinfectant. [Jack Sargeant]

SEXUALITY, MAGIC & PERVERSION
Francis King

Damn, with a title like this how can you go wrong? Those are three of my favourite things, right there. And when you open the book and find that Chapter One is called 'A Dildo for a Witch'… well, that doesn't hurt either.

In fact, I was particularly happy to get a review copy of this book — *Sexuality, Magic & Perversion* was originally published in 1971 and has been out of print for decades, with second-hand copies fetching silly money. I used to own a tatty old paperback copy, but I lent it to someone and never saw it again. Thank you, Feral House, for making this book available again! *Sexuality, Magic & Perversion*'s cult reputation rests on its status as a fairly innovative and ground-breaking work. The late Francis King was a well-respected authority on the occult and author of other works such as *Ritual Magic in England*, *The Magical World of Aleister Crowley* and *Satan and Swastika*. In the late sixties, he shrewdly judged that the British public was ready, indeed eager, to hear about the extensive links between sex, magic and the history of witchcraft.

Sexuality, Magic & Perversion is not a scholarly tome but a popular history, and it covers a lot of ground, from the pagan orgies of the ancient Greeks to the sacramental shagging of the Fraturnitas Saturni, a particularly dour-sounding German wing of the OTO (Ordo Templi Orientis) who swapped sexual positions according to the alignments of the zodiac. In between, we learn about such disparate topics as the supposed medieval witch-cult and the actual modern one, the Black Masses celebrated in seventeenth-century France by the Marquise de Montespan, mistress to Louis XIV, the Rosicrucians, the Knights of the Garter (was the Garter actually a sanitary towel?!), and the Knights Templar with their Baphomet worship and their *osculum infame*, eastern traditions such as the left-hand path of Tantra and Chinese sexual alchemy, Jayne Mansfield and Anton LaVey's Church of Satan, Wilhelm Reich's orgone energy and the Theosophist chicken-hawk Charles Leadbeater. And of course, there's plenty about the Old Crow himself, Aleister Crowley, who scandalised polite society during the first half of the twentieth-century and got lumbered with the sobriquet 'The Wickedest Man in the World' for generally carrying on like a moderately dissolute rock star seventy years before Led Zeppelin existed. Incidentally, I was amused recently to see that Crowley appeared in a list of one hundred Great Britons voted for by BBC viewers!

A panoply of rare photos and illustrations, as well as lengthy quotations from obscure volumes you and I are unlikely ever to see, increase the worth of this book to occult researchers. Inevitably though, it shows its age a little, not only in King's rather sniggering attitude, but also in what is not mentioned. There is nothing about Chaos Magic, TOPY or the satanic ritual abuse myth, for instance, though all of these have been important in the history of sex magic in recent years. Still, even with these limitations, *Sexuality, Magic & Perversion* is a minor classic. And it's hard to dislike an author who includes footnotes like this:

I, although not possessed by a spirit, not only insult my friends but smoke their cigarettes, filch their drink and even sell malicious stories about them to the editor of Private Eye.

I feel that after whetting your appetites for this book, it's only fair to provide an extract for your edification and delight. So here you go — this is from a speech made by the god Mercury during an invocation performed by Aleister Crowley and Victor Neuberg in Paris in 1914:

Every drop of semen which Hermes sheds is a world. The technical term for this semen is kratos… People upon the worlds are like maggots upon an apple, all forms of life bred by the worlds are in the nature of parasites. Pure worlds are flaming globes, each a conscious being… Ma is the name of the god who seduced the Phallus away from the Yoni; hence the physical universe. All worlds are excreta, they represent wasted semen. Therefore all is blasphemy. This explains why man made God in his own image.

Blood sugar, baby, sex magic! [Simon Collins]

THE SEXUALLY DOMINANT WOMAN
A Workbook for Nervous Beginners
Lady Green

This flimsy, nintey-page 'workbook' is devoted to giving advice and instruction to any woman who con-

THE SHINING ONES
£12.99 / pb / 303pp / ISBN 1904126006 Radikal Phase Publishing 2002 / www.radicalbooks.com

SNITCH CULTURE
£10.99 / $14.95 / pb / 235pp / ISBN 0922915636 / Feral House 2000 / www.feralhouse.com

siders herself 'sexually dominant' — that is,

> who enjoys giving her lover orders, tying him up and/or giving him strong sensations — but part of her enjoyment comes from the knowledge that her partner is enjoying these things, too.

Written by a middle-aged dominatrix and published by herself and her submissive male lover, it's one of those books with little hand-drawn cartoon illustrations and print that runs down the middle of the page only, so you can finish it in about fifteen minutes. Still, there are better ways of spending fifteen minutes. Most of the advice contained here seems pretty redundant, with tips along the lines of "check hands and feet often; if they feel cold to your touch, loosen the bondage". It strikes me that if you're enough into domination to want to buy a book about it, then you probably already know what you're doing. And if not, if you really are a 'nervous beginner', it's difficult to see how your pleasure's going to be greatly enhanced by ticking off little boxes on a checklist, as you remind yourself to do things like "gently remove the nipple clamps". [Mikita Brottman]

THE SHINING ONES
The World's Most Powerful Secret Society Revealed
Philip Gardiner

A startlingly 'new' hypothesis on the hidden meaning behind hermetic and esoteric symbolism which serves the hypnotic purpose of an all-powerful shadowy elite etc, etc. If this sounds all too familiar, it's because it has been the subject of any number of conspiracy tomes over the years, beginning in 1801 with John Robison's *Proof of a Conspiracy*, through the early part of the twentieth-century with Nesta Webster's *Secret Societies and Subversive Movements* (1924) and the pseudonymous *Inquire Within* (ex Golden Dawn cultist Christina Stoddart) with *Light Bearers of Darkness* and *The Trail of the Serpent* in the thirties. In more recent times we have seen a plethora of excellent books on the subject, for example Roberts and Gilbertson's *The Dark Gods* and Michael A Hoffman's exemplary *Secret Societies and Psychological Warfare*. Are any of these genre classics mentioned in the bibliography of Mr Gardiner's stultifyingly condescending book? Of course not! He would have us believe that the conclusions he has drawn from more exoteric works are the product of his own genius for discovering facts which we poor lost souls are unable to fathom!

A ready-made defence has been furnished via the author's assumption that any bad press he's likely to get will be the result of *The Shining Ones* tampering with the minds of zombified reviewers; which makes Yours Truly nothing less than an unwitting pawn of the Power Elite. Yeah, it's not just because this is the worst example of conceited so-called scholarship I've read for years! Couldn't be that, eh? No, if anyone thinks Mr Gardiner's book is a poorly written load of junk, they must be a zombie! Of course there *is* a shadowy Cryptocracy at the apex of the pyramid; everybody knows that. We don't dislike this book because we disagree with it; we dislike it because, despite the author's claims, he is not telling us anything new. [Stephen Sennitt]

SNITCH CULTURE
How Citizens are Turned into the Eyes and Ears of the State
Jim Redden

Although I'm not really a biker (well, I've got a bicycle — does that count?), I have, in the past few months, found myself at two events organised by the Outlaws Motorcycle Club, a large and influential gang in the Midlands, and at both these events (a tattoo show and a custom bike rally), the Outlaws had a merchandise stall for T-shirts and stuff — presumably to raise funds for beer, ammunition, lawyers and that kind of thing. I got a shirt saying 'Support Your Local Outlaws' with a picture of a gun in a fist, which has proved quite useful for intimidating shopkeepers and people at bus stops. But one of the other designs they had said 'Snitches are a Dying Breed'. Well, maybe they are in the Outlaws' sphere of influence, but according to Jim Redden, snitches have become endemic in American society. *Snitch Culture* deals with what Redden sees as the steady encroachment of the state upon every aspect of the lives of its citizens, though exclusively within an American context — too bad, as we subjects of the British Crown are no slouches in having our rights eroded either, and what's more we have no written constitution, no 'Don't Tread On Me' heritage of distrust of heavy-handed government and no right to bear arms with which to protect ourselves. We have more CCTV cameras per capita than any other country on earth, a domestic situation in Ulster that has led to the permanent adoption of the supposedly temporary provisions of the Prevention of Terrorism Act, and a Home Secretary, David Blunkett, whose contempt for 'airy-fairy' civil liberties is evident in everything he says and does. Following the events of September 11, both the American and British governments have shown themselves all too eager to introduce new powers to detain and interrogate suspects without trial, intercept communications and stifle dissent. But *Snitch Culture* does not cover such recent developments. Some comparisons with conditions in former Iron Curtain countries would have been instructive too.

The title is actually somewhat misleading, at least if you take 'snitch' to mean 'human informant'. Although the increasing use of informants by those in power at every level of society — from the schoolroom through the workplace to the military and penal systems — is thoroughly catalogued, there is also plenty of information about surveillance and technological intelligence-gathering generally. Conspiracy theory favourites like COINTELPRO, the JFK assassination, Watergate, Waco and the Oklahoma bombing are all revisited. There is a lengthy examination of McCarthyism, still one of the most shameful episodes in US history and an enduring source of bitterness more than half a century after the fact. Witness the furore in 1999 over the Lifetime Achievement Oscar awarded to Elia Kazan, acclaimed director of *A Streetcar Named Desire*, *On The Waterfront* and *The Searchers*, and infamous HUAC snitch. I found lots of new information too, though, about such things as the gung-ho asset-seizing activities of the DEA (Drugs Enforcement Agency) and BATF (Bureau of Alcohol, Tobacco and Firearms — responsible for the Waco debacle and the ostensible target of the Murrah building bomb), the appalling exceeding of bounds by ostensibly worthy civil rights watchdog organisations such as the Anti-Defamation League and the Southern Poverty Law Center, the FBI's Carnivore email-monitoring programme and the extent to which school students are cajoled into tattling on any of their little chums who express an interest in, say, listening to Marilyn Manson or buying a trenchcoat.

The chapter that struck closest to home for me deals with employers' surveillance of their hapless wage-slaves. Emails, phone calls and Internet usage are routinely monitored, and some poor guy called Wayne Hensley, a database manager and part-time journalist, was forced to resign after his employers accused him of looking at such 'pornographic' sites as feralhouse.com and gothic.net. Hensley unsuccessfully argued that there was nothing pornographic about these sites, but his employers were obdurate — the snitch software said they were porn, therefore they must be porn.

Hardcore conspiracy theorists among you will be disappointed to hear that I haven't gone through the book with a fine tooth comb looking for errors and inconsistencies — could it be that I'm part of the cover-up conspiracy myself? — but I did notice one or two careless slips. Graham Greene was not the author of *The Spy Who Came In From The Cold*! A more serious problem for real data buffs is that *Snitch Culture* lacks both a bibliography and an index — for such a footnote-festooned and evidently heavily researched book, this seems inexplicable. Such carpings aside, though, *Snitch Culture* is a worthy and substantial look at issues central

STRAIGHT FROM THE FRIDGE DAD
£9.99 / hb / 218pp / ISBN 1842430009 / No Exit Press 2000 / www.noexit.co.uk

TALES FROM THE CLIT
£7.99 / pb / 128pp / ISBN 1873176090 / AK Press 1996 / www.akpress.org

TEIGNMOUTH ELECTRON
£19.95 / hb / 72pp / ISBN 187069936X / Book Works 1999 / 19 Holywell Row, London, EC2A 4JB, UK / www.bookworks.org.uk

to the future of Western democracy. Like the dude in *Strange Days* says, "The issue is not whether you are paranoid… the issue is whether you are paranoid *enough*." [Simon Collins]

STRAIGHT FROM THE FRIDGE DAD
A Dictionary of Hipster Slang
Max Decharne

Dig this, daddy-o. It's a lot of fun simply leafing through the pages of this compendium of jive talk, and Decharne should be swelled up like a poisoned pup about it. But call me cubistic, because I'm not really gone on this volume, and let me blow the works about it, straight from the cookhouse. First, Decharne's hipster slang is really a combination of two things. The major one is beat talk from the fifties, which is largely derived from musical influences, primarily the blues and jazz records where, by and large, the beatniks found it. The other source is hard-boiled detective fiction, primarily from the thirties. What they have in common is that they *sound* cool to us today, but these two elements were not necessarily part of any one slang, not as anyone would define it or use it. Maynard G Krebs would be no more likely to tell someone to lamp a frail's gams than Sam Spade would be to talk about a no-goodnik from Creepsville.

Second, many of the citations here aren't really part of slang at all, but rather a single writer's invention. When Philip Marlowe says he "found a good bottle and went into executive session with it", does that mean 'executive session' was something people actually said when they meant drinking, or is it just Raymond Chandler coming up with another brilliant turn of phrase by using a business term as a metaphor? Donald Hamilton (the Matt Helm creator) is cited for "Let's brush it hard and see where the dandruff falls". Far from being slang, this is a takeoff on fifties ad-man speak: "Let's run it up the flagpole and see who salutes" of which there are as many different versions as there are issues of *Mad* magazine. And is "flat as a matzoh" really slang, or is flat (meaning broke) the slang, and 'as a matzoh' just a simile, replaceable by any nearly-two-dimensional noun?

There are older, standard terms here, like 'four-flusher', which surely goes back to the nineteenth-century, and others, like 'bobby-soxer', which are specific to an era and were part of general slang in America. Hipster or no, everyone knew what a four-flusher was. It would be nice if Decharne had investigated some derivations. Four-flusher, for example, refers to poker, and trying to pass off four good cards as a flush. Decharne defines 'straight, no chaser' as meaning the undiluted truth and attributes it to a jazz record by Art Taylor. Well, it's also a tune by Thelonius Monk, covered famously by Cannonball Adderly, and of course it refers to drinking whiskey neat, without a beer or water to chase it. This doesn't change the meaning, but it might be nice to know. Like 'dead presidents' being slang for cash money? Of course that's because presidents are on American bills. But they are dead presidents because American law prohibits anyone living from being represented on currency (or stamps).

And of course, no one really knows where 'eighty-six' — meaning to get rid of — comes from. It can be traced to restaurant use, but its origins are still debatable (rhyming slang for 'nix', perhaps?).

Decharne doesn't show much curiosity along those lines. You get the sense that he has simply done a lot of good reading and heard a lot of good music, and noted down the interesting phrases as he went. There's nothing wrong with that, and it makes for an entertaining book, but as a reference of any kind, it won't get your knowledge box hitting on all cylinders. [Michael Carlson]

TALES FROM THE CLIT
A Female Experience of Pornography
Ed. Cherie Matrix

As its subtitle would imply, this collection of pieces from Feminists Against Censorship features a wide range of women writing about their experiences of porn. That these experiences are as diverse as the contributors should be no surprise; what is a surprise is just how positive some of those experiences are. Reading Avedon Carol writing about how she came to terms with her, er, cunt, by looking at other women's bodies in porn mags is a revelation. Fuck it, she makes looking at porn sound sickeningly healthy.

Not all the experiences are as positive, or written with as much humour as Avedon Carol's piece. Annie Sprinkle, for example, is less than enthusiastic about porn, but even she comes out strongly against censorship. Not that this collection is all heavy about politics. People like Nettle Pollard, of Liberty, make valid political points, but for the most part this book is women talking about porn: what turns them on, what turns them off, how they discovered porn, the lies they discovered about porn etc.

The anti-porn feminist is a thing of the past. However, like *Daily Mail* readers, born-again zealots and conservative politicians, they've got a knack of hanging on to power. The intellectual arguments of the pro-censorship feminists have been blown to smithereens but they're still the ones presented as the real face of feminism, even though they've got more in common with misogynist religious nutters than anyone.

A book worth reading, especially for those who remain convinced that porn is still a boy's thing. [Pan Pantziarka]

TEIGNMOUTH ELECTRON
Tacita Dean

This is a remarkable book. Tacita Dean was shortlisted for the 1998 Turner prize with her exhibition of large-scale drawings and video installations dealing with Donald Crowhurst and the issues raised by his journey — how man copes with isolation, obsession with time, and the theme of being lost at sea. I went to the exhibition and have to admit I was less than impressed — I've never been a fan of video installation art, and I wasn't aware of the broader context of Dean's work. It looked a little dull, especially when seen alongside Cathy de Monchaux' eroticised metal mandalas. But this book makes me want to see it again.

The story of Donald Crowhurst has been well-documented in at least one non-fiction book, two films and a novel — Robert Stone's *Outerbridge Reach*. It has a resonance which continues to attract attention (a CD given away at part of Labradford's second Festival of Drifting was illustrated with one of the photos from this book). The Crowhurst saga is also cited as being the starting point for Chris Mikul's obsession in the Critical Vision book *Bizarrism*, so I won't recap the story itself here. *Teignmouth Electron* is, in Dean's words, "the culmination of a personal research and involvement with the voyage of Donald Crowhurst which has been part of my life now for over four years." It is a slim hardback volume which is profusely illustrated, principally with photos taken by Dean of Crowhurst's boat, derelict, stripped, bleached by the sun and surrounded by lush foliage in Cayman Brac. The photos are haunting and unusual, especially as juxtaposed with the other images in the book: film stills from Crowhurst's journey itself, stills from the films made about Crowhurst, and a postcard commemorating Crowhurst's departure.

This last item points to a staggering tale of petty-minded England. It is widely believed that Crowhurst realised that his boat would not survive the journey, but that he felt under so much pressure from his local community — the council of which was using the voyage to promote tourism in Teignmouth — that he didn't feel he could back out. One of the councillors is reported to have said, after Crowhurst's boat was found abandoned, that "the voyage has brought us more publicity than this committee has managed in fifty years. We have had this extremely cheaply, and I hope the town appreciates it". Dean's comments regarding this are worth quoting in full:

It is astounding with what ease they could pitch a man's life against the revenue brought into their seaside resort by tourism. The language they were speaking was wildly dispro-

THINKING OF ENGLAND
£6.99 / pb / 292pp / ISBN 0349108641 / Abacus 1996 / www.twbookmark.com

TIHKAL
£16.99 / pb / 800pp / ISBN 0963009699 / Transform Press 1997

portionate to the hugeness of Crowhurst's ordeal and human failing. You imagine that if you met Crowhurst in the Teignmouth Yachting Club, you might find him a bit arrogant, but as a human being, alone in an unremitting seascape trying to come to terms with his deteriorating psychological state and his monumental deception, his story is genuinely tragic and existential, and leaves the aspirations of Teignmouth Council and little England way, way behind.

Dean's angle on the Crowhurst tale, as portrayed here, reminded me of Alan Moore's epilogue to his superb psychogeographical Jack the Ripper work, *From Hell*. Moore's epilogue deals with the peripheral issues surrounding the case — it's a document about the documentation rather than the events themselves, and comes across as being all the more interesting for it. Dean's book, similarly, constructs a tangential framework around the journey itself, with short pieces on the current owner of the boat, time-madness and the works of Ballard, Antoine de Saint-Exupéry and the two films, along with very personal recollections of her own journey to Teignmouth to discover more about Crowhurst. It's a beautifully written and lavishly constructed work, with each short piece providing a novel yet relevant context for the rest. It's an art book, so doesn't come cheap, but is highly recommended all the same. [James Marriott]

THINKING OF ENGLAND
A Consumer Guide to Sex in a Cold Climate
Kitty Churchill

In 1994 or thereabouts, Kitty Churchill, freelance veteran of the women's magazine circuit, decided to immerse herself in the kinky depths of English sex culture, bringing back jaw-dropping revelations of suburban seediness for her prurient readership... but it didn't quite turn out that way. In fact, she barely got her toes wet. For, as participant-observation field studies go, this one contains a lot more observing and a lot less participating than most. Despite her early declaration that, "there were several fantasies I was keen to try out," when it comes down to shit-or-get-off-the-pot time, Kitty bottles out time and again. Thus, we accompany her to famous fetish clubs like the Torture Garden and Submission, to dodgy nudist clubs, to Westward Bound, a B&D B&B in Cornwall (no, really!), to private swingers' parties, to weird Tantric sex therapists, and... nothing happens! Or rather, she stands in the corner like a latex-clad wallflower, drinking too much and being bitchy about the physical shortcomings of the pathetic men who make advances to her. Her companion on most of these forays is Ben, a gay friend with whom she can pose as a couple, thus cravenly avoiding any possibility of interaction with the people she meets. I'm pleased to report that her solo visits to the Muir Reform Academy, a "real school for adult boys, girls, and 'boys who would be girls'" left her with a very sore bottom. But by the end of the book, I was feeling that Kitty Churchill actually wasn't that much into sex in the first place. In fact, she admits as much:

... in over six months, I amassed a grand total of two orgasms directly related to my research

and, as one of them was with my husband, I don't think that one really counts... Months and months of treating sex as a non-contact sport had rubbed off in my bedroom. I did say 'yes' to Dominic on occasion but only when he tipped my head forward first.

In addition, *Thinking of England* is written in a breezy you-don't-have-to-be-crazy-to-work-here-but-it-helps style that would be fine for a magazine article, but becomes arch and tedious over the course of the book. For a book about sex, this book is remarkably unsexy. I don't know why Kitty Churchill bothered, and you shouldn't bother reading this, even if you find it in a bargain bookshop, as I did. *Thinking of England* left me with a sour taste like a mouthful of cum, though evidently *Cosmo* and *The Daily Express* liked it. Which tells you a lot. [Simon Collins]

TIHKAL
Alexander Shulgin & Ann Shulgin

Due to one of those unexpected coincidences that make life interesting, a couple of days after I'd received *Tihkal* in the post, Alexander Shulgin's earlier opus *Pihkal* was plastered all over the Scottish news. It would appear that an off-duty police officer had been in a local branch of 'a major high street record shop' and had come upon a copy of the book. He picks it up, intrigued by the subtitle *A Chemical Love Story* and opens it.

Cue media hysteria, angry parents, misinformed officials, and a general lack of understanding bordering on the ignorant: as if it isn't enough that our teenagers consume more illicit drugs than anywhere else in Europe, now they can buy books which show how to make them! And now there's another one!

Well, yes and no. If you decide to buy either of these books expecting an A to Z of 'how to make drugs in your bathroom', forget it. *Tihkal* is a continuation of the earlier work, part autobiography, and part 'recipe book' (for want of a better phrase). Obviously, the recipes are what is going to sell this book. And there will be a lot of disappointed people.

Anyone familiar with the work of Alexander Shulgin will know that he is a 'man of science', a chemist. An alchemist, even. His recipes are, therefore, very much rooted in advanced chemistry and pharmacology, way over the heads of most people. The first book covered a number of the phenethylamines, such as MDMA, MDA, MDE, etc. This book concerns itself with the tryptamines: LSD, DMT, and suchlike.

Before I started writing this review, I asked several graduate chemists I'm acquainted with whether or not these recipes would 'work', and the general view was that the recipes were very complicated, and that a number of the required chemicals (e.g. benzene) are so carcinogenic and/or toxic that it simply would be too risky to use them. It took a professor of chemistry to tell me that they would indeed 'work', but anyone considering trying any of them would be better advised to use their, uh, usual outlet.

That said, for anyone seriously interested in the field of psychoactive substances, *Tihkal* is a must. The writing is eloquent, elegant and easy on the eyes, there is a good glossary for those unfamiliar terms, and Shulgin makes several timely and pertinent swipes at the prevailing 'War on Drugs', though I did feel that his comparisons between himself and Galileo are maybe a bit grandiose.

For all that, I found the book a pleasure to dip into, with lots of pearls of wisdom and psychedelic sixties anecdotes. Read it and enjoy, but there are two things to remember: First, in spite of the much vaunted *Freedom of Information Act*, it would appear that only certain kinds of information are acceptable in our new 'socialist utopia'. Second, and of far more importance, don't try this at home. Getting it wrong could be extremely hazardous to your health; getting it right could be extremely hazardous to your liberty. Don't say I didn't warn you. [Phil Dalgarno]

Update Since this review was written all those years ago, the impact of the Internet has radically transformed the face of communication and the exchange of information and ideas. As well as this, it's had a major effect on commerce. The whole idea of home shopping has been transformed, and product which would have been difficult, and in some instances impossible, to get hold of a few years ago is now available to anyone with access to the web. And a credit card.

I'm not suggesting you can buy drugs over the net. Or at least not the sort we're talking about here. However, most of the substances described in *Tihkal* have precursors in a whole range of different plants, fungi and even in animals (in particular, toads). These originated in the main in Central and South America and for a long time the only way something like Ayahuasca could be sampled by the eager psychonaut was via the prohibitively expensive drug tourism route. In his book *Pharmacotheon*, Jonathan

TOKYO SEX UNDERGROUND
£14.95 / $22.95 / pb / 99pp / ISBN 184068044X / Creation Books 2001 / www.creationbooks.com

TOO GOOD TO BE TRUE
£22 / $29.95 / hb / 480pp / ISBN 0393047342 / W W Norton 1999 / www.wwnorton.com

THE BIG BOOK OF URBAN LEGENDS
£9.99 / $14.95 / pb / 223pp / ISBN 1563891654 / Paradox Press 1994 / www.dccomics.com/paradox/

TRAVELS WITH DR DEATH
£12 / pb / 518pp / ISBN 0333750314 / Macmillan 1999 / www.panmacmillan.com

Too good to be true? The story of 'The Kentucky Fried Rat' in *The Big Book of Urban Legends*. Art: Glenn Barr

Ott writes how (in 1993) pre-mixed Ayahuasca preparations were allegedly changing hands for $800 a shot. Incidentally, if you're really serious about this subject and you've thirty quid to spend, then *Pharmacotheon* is another must-have.

In a respect, the Internet has changed all that, and there now exist numerous commercial sites, some domestic, selling dried leaves, fresh leaves, cuttings, live plants and varying strengths of extract of a whole range of these plants. The better of these sites also provide information regarding the preparation and (supposedly) safe use of their products.

As stated, approach with caution. Alexander Shulgin is a scientist and knows this stuff inside out. In the case of some of the material appearing on the web, the quality and in some cases the accuracy of the information is highly questionable. Unless you know what you're doing, you'd be best advised to leave well alone.

TOKYO SEX UNDERGROUND
Romain Slocombe

Not a man to repress his obsessions, Romain Slocombe. His unique photographs combine Japanese females and artefacts of medicine. *Tokyo Sex Underground*, however, offers a shift in emphasis. Now Slocombe trains his European lens on the faces and bodies of Tokyo's sex industry: frumpy club hostesses, rope-bound models, video actresses at work and play, party-goers, passers-by and, perhaps unintentionally, definitive 'westerner' takes on Oriental sexuality, courtesy of unreadable model Yuka (long straight black hair, make-up like a mask) and enthusiastic adult-video actress Hidemi (white briefs and ankle socks, worn during an act of masturbation). The Enigma and the Submissive — half-a-world-away exotica. Fittingly, Jack Sargeant writes in his introduction that *Tokyo Sex Underground* is

> Slocombe's testament to the enigmatic women of fin de siècle Tokyo, a city on the brink of cultural liberation — a liberation which now threatens to destroy the clandestine allure which has so compelled him since his youth.

This liberation may well intervene, but to many the sexual pre-conceptions of Japan's females remain as indelible as the beautiful tattoos spread over back-cover-girl Natsuki's body. [Martin Jones]

TOO GOOD TO BE TRUE
The Colossal Book of Urban Legends
Jan Harold Brunvand

THE BIG BOOK OF URBAN LEGENDS
Various artists

When I was nine years old I told the world that an Alsation dog had been discovered in the freezer compartment of a local Chinese takeaway with its legs cut off. How did I come to know this? My best friend had told me. He got the news off some other kid whose parents apparently knew someone who knew a health inspector. Or something. At nine years old it didn't really matter where the news came from — it was a gross story with something dead in it. But then, into my teenage years and beyond, I heard others recount the same tale anew, pertaining to some other suitably ambiguous eating establishment in the locality — occasionally 'foreign' but more and more of the fast-food restaurant variety. Sometimes, a patron of the restaurant had to be rushed into hospital after a chicken bone had become lodged in their throat — only, upon examination, it wasn't the bone of a chicken but that of a rat.

I found a vague familiarity in other stories I was hearing, too. Stories concerning disfigured escaped lunatics prowling lovers' lanes, and lick-and-stick tattoos for kids that had been impregnated with LSD (a café I once visited had a notice warning parents to be vigilant of innocent-looking Disney transfers that actually contained mind-altering chemicals). But it wasn't until I read Jan Harold Brunvand's *The Choking Doberman* did I realise how widespread these tales were, how so many of them had little or no factual basis, and how they keep on coming back. They are a social phenomenon known as the Apocryphal Tale, or the Urban Legend.

After twenty-odd years of collecting these stories and studying their origins, Brunvand is something of an authority on the subject, and his new book, *Too Good To Be True*, is a kind of Brunvand-greatest-hits package. Sweeping from the Kentucky Fried Rat and other old favourites through to kidney heists and "gerbilling", the tales are categorised and come complete with an analysis, often supplemented by comments sent to Brunvand by readers of his earlier books. There's a sense of perverse satisfaction in discovering that supposed 'news-breaking' stories you may have heard only a few weeks ago are in fact false and have been kicking around for fifty or more years — carried by word of mouth, or resurrected through the media (radio phone-ins are a prime source for the resurrection of an urban legend). Of course, tales of poisoned dresses, indecent exposure at the hair salon, secret cake recipes and such like, are related by people in all good faith — that's the nature of the beast. Probe beneath the surface of these stories, however, and everything is always suitably ambiguous: the tale has an indeterminate setting in which the participants are all someone somebody else knows, or friends of a friend. It's interesting to note how many of these legends turn up in motion pictures and advertising, often as plot devices or elaborate sight gags (dog in a high-rise chasing a ball out of the window, for example). Mondo documentary films also utilise urban legends — alligators in the sewers of New York, for instance, is one myth which *This Violent World* (1978) plays out as fact. Brunvand's approach is rarely haughty or overbearing, but constantly engaging and entertaining. *Too Good To Be True* is a fascinating, funny and fairly definitive collection.

A very good companion to the above is *The Big Book of Urban Legends*, part of the Factoid series of books, in which a chosen topic is adapted by various artists in comic form. (Other volumes have been devoted to Hoaxes, Conspiracies, Martyrs, Losers, Vice, Death and Scandal.) The stories — of which there are approximately 200 — are generally related to a page apiece, with the penmanship by many familiar artists being consistently high. The introduction is by Brunvand so it's no surprise that the stories and their categorisation are a lot like *Too Good To Be True*. There is no extraneous comment or analysis here, however. But then there really is no need — the comic strip form works well and most adaptations convey the humour and creepiness inherent in the tales without further embellishment. And let's face it, if you want insight you're not going to be on the look out for a series entitled *The Big Book of...* anyway. [David Kerekes]

TRAVELS WITH DR DEATH
Ron Rosenbaum

No, Ron Rosenbaum didn't have

TRICKS AND TREATS
£12.99 / pb / 202pp / ISBN 1560231629 Harrington Park Press / 10 Alice St, Binghampton, NY 13904, USA / www.haworthpress.com

UFO
£14.99 / pb / 317pp / ISBN 3980587630 / Goliath 1999 / www.goliathclub.com

A scratchy photo of a UFO. UFO

to share the back seat with David Owen on his way to partition yet another country or political party (how *do* you say "troubles" in Serbo-Croatian?). Nothing so horrible. *This Dr Death* is Dr James Grigson, a Texas psychiatrist who testifies as an expert witness during the penalty phase of murder trials. His judgement is always the same: the guilty party will inevitably kill again, unless the state puts him to death. Rosenbaum rode along with the Doc as he hit three separate murder trials in three towns in two days, testified against three men, and saw all three sentenced to die. 'Dr Death' was written originally for *Vanity Fair* in 1990, and as the title piece of this collection of intriguing journalism (from one of the best feature writers in America) it may be a little misleading. Although Rosenbaum has a nose for intriguing stories (his piece 'Dead Ringers', on the Marcus Brothers, was *not* the source for the movie of the same name, but his take on the identical twin gynaecologists is even sadder than the film's) and writes well about "clandestine cultures", like people in search of illegal cancer cures, or the staffers in nuclear missile silos, his most telling work is what he terms "investigations of investigations." The most entertaining, if least successful, of these is probably 'The Corpse As Big As The Ritz', an account of the murder of David Whiting, who was the business manager of actress Sarah Miles, and was found dead in her motel room during the filming of the movie *The Man Who Loved Cat Dancing*. Rosenbaum's account raises more questions than it answers, though the American judge's reaction to Miss Miles likely set the standard for Mary Archer's fragrant performance in the British courts a decade later.

In all his exegeses of questions which perplex others, Rosenbaum resembles nothing as much as a theologian. For he brings an almost religious sensibility to almost every question, as if looking for something to believe in, when the world has been made entirely relative by physics and philosophy. In this world journalists become sort of secular exorcists, investigating the strange beliefs of myriad cults, and revealing them as heresy. As Rosenbaum says while checking out Dealey Plaza with Penn Jones, he will drop down the manhole, but he won't pull the manhole cover over his head. If Rosenbaum isn't a theologian then he's a literary critic, and he analyses the literature of these cults like a book reviewer. Still, it becomes eerie when the characters lurking behind the cultic mysteries start popping up in each other's stories. Thus, the diary of Mary Pinchot Meyer, the JFK mistress found murdered on a towpath in Georgetown, was destroyed by James Jesus Angleton, head of counter-intelligence at the CIA. And Angleton himself is the star of Rosenbaum's best piece, about Angleton's CIA mole-hunt which nearly destroyed the Agency from within. When dealing with the levels of bluff and counterbluff, the 'they knew we knew they knew' paradoxes which drove Angleton to distraction (and was Kim Philby behind the entire game?), Rosenbaum becomes a high priest of ambiguity. His philosophy teacher at Yale, Josiah Thompson, himself became a leading Kennedy assassination critic. Maybe Yale prepares you for such things, because another of the best pieces in this book delves into the Yale secret society, Skull and

Bones, which has produced George Bush and just about all the CIA. Having grown up in the area myself, I can testify to the strangeness of the clubhouse where the Boners gather to exchange their sexual secrets, in echo of some Heidelberg fraternity, but Rosenbaum shrugs it off with as a joke. Maybe this is his role, to act as the sceptic for the people who read *Vanity Fair* or *Harpers*, and to de-mythologise and thus render safer the interpretations of our world advanced by those not as content with their Yale backgrounds. That's a cruel interpretation, but you do wish that at some point he'd let on he believes in *something* besides his deadline. But actually he does. The reason this book was given a reprint in the UK was because of the essay, 'Who Was Maria's Lover?' which investigates the old question of whether Adolf Hitler's father was fathered illegitimately by a Jew. It also appears to have been the jumping-off point for Rosenbaum's successful book, *Explaining Hitler*, which was his effort to try to come to terms with the idea of inhuman evil in human society. Perhaps all the essays in this volume were, in a way, his apprenticeship, paving the way for the big story where he might do more than debunk. For whatever reason, getting this exceptional collection of journalism into print was worth it by itself. [Michael Carlson]

TRICKS AND TREATS
Sex Workers Write About Their Clients
Ed. Matt Bernstein Sycamore

A collection of stories and recollections from people who act in porn movies, work in sex shops, hookers, outreach workers (who happen to be hookers), brothel errand boys and so on. These tales are interesting, and they do offer a glimpse into the sometimes unpleasant worlds occupied by some sex workers, but there's not enough meat on these bones, the stories are too piece meal. Anybody who is interested in sex work, pornography, sleaze, depravity and verboten pleasures has already either read bios or met enough sex workers to have heard dozens of stories. I would have been happier reading a volume about each of the occupations rather than this scattershot collection of what is essentially anecdotes. In fact, if I had to recommend anything it would be the strippers' fanzine *Danzine*, which contains better anecdotes and better advice. Plus this book has the worst cover I have ever seen. [Jack Sargeant]

UFO
Richard Brunswick

Richard Brunswick, we are told, has spent much of his life devoted to collecting photographs of UFOs as well as documents, films and newspaper cuttings. Here he presents us with 300 snaps of UFOs (and a distinct lack of text) sighted over various holiday spots around the globe. Although quite pleasing to the eye, the photographs look pretty much like every other UFO picture (which is perhaps the point) and there are one or two that are suspiciously a little *too* scratched and filthy.

For the most part, the 'craft' are of the saucer-shaped variety but towards the end of the book we come to the highly amusing 'eye witness' reports and 'corresponding photographs'. Amongst these

UNDERWORLD OF THE EAST
£9.99 / pb / 170pp / ISBN 0953663116 / Green Magic 2000 / www.greenmagicpublishers.com

THE VELVET UNDERGROUND
£18 / pb / 192pp / ISBN 1871592283 / Velvet 1997 / www.creationbooks.com

WHITMAN'S WILD CHILDREN
£12 / $18 / pb / 300pp / ISBN 1883642868 / Steerforth Press 1999 / www.steerforth.com

THE X-RATED BIBLE
£10.99 / $14.95 / pb / 245pp / ISBN 0922915555 / Feral House 1998 / www.feralhouse.com

we see a Chinese man with an antenna coming out of his head (for alien contact), bruised buttocks (the result of buggery by aliens), and perhaps most alarming of all a group of naked children wearing nought but sunglasses (preparing for a rocket trip to space)!

For someone who — we glean in the briefest of introductions — has not only studied air and space travel technology, but also devoted forty years of his life to collecting related photos and films, one would have expected to see a little more written information from the enigmatic Mr Brunswick. Further to his technical qualifications, he is said to be an abductee who supposedly remains in contact with aliens!

If nothing more, the book does provide a few laughs. And if you're not sure of where Brunswick is coming from, you should have a fair idea by the time you get to the final photograph of a rock formation that resembles an alien head.

This book might make you ask some big questions — but not about UFOs particularly. [Ben Blackshaw]

UNDERWORLD OF THE EAST
James S Lee

Described as a long lost classic of drug literature, this book was first published in 1935. As far as I know this is the first 'official' reprint, though a spiral bound 'pirate' copy was doing the rounds some years ago, complete with semi-defaced library stamps, etc. I wonder whether the extremely knowledgeable Mike Jay, who writes an otherwise first class Introduction, is unaware of this fact, or not... Simply, *Underworld of the East* is a much sought-after tome, the first edition of which often exchanges hands for extortionate prices; that is when it can be found at all. It recounts the first-hand experiences of the author's travels and drug use in the "underworlds, drug haunts and jungles of India, China and the Malay Archipelago". It is clearly written, as most books tend to be from this period, exciting, gruelling and not in the least bit dated. The final revelatory discovery and experiences with mysterious substances in the jungles of Sumatra makes for breathtaking reading. [Stephen Sennitt]

THE VELVET UNDERGROUND
Michael Leigh

Not a book of the band, more a book of the banned. Or rather, the practices which Michael Leigh, the compiler of this report into sexual corruption and depravity, might prefer to be banned. He writes of "an unquiet under world" of contact ads, depraved photographs and "moral decadence". He may have believed his research subjects were sick, but at least most were happy within their sickness. Despite this, Leigh flinches, claiming one would have to be a scientist or psychopath to relish the events of his investigation into the "diseased underbelly" of society. Yet unwittingly he provided the backdrop for the chaos years of the late sixties and the ethos behind the book's musical namesake.

There's little sexual detail here, so those expecting titillation will be disappointed. Kind of interesting for those with tastes for the swinging, swapping, sado-masochistic world of bygone years, but personally I couldn't lose images of Sociology classes. Like Leigh we watched and read and felt something (usually pity) for those unburdening themselves of such sins. Yet in contrast, our sheltered middle-class lives were the pitiable ones.

To readers of this book, even those attuned with the academic and historical, a word of advice — don't even *try* to read the introduction. The rest, clinically and dispassionately written, is a report; neither a condemnation or a love affair with the generally less acceptable pleasures of the flesh. [Sarah Turner]

WHITMAN'S WILD CHILDREN
Portraits of 12 Poets
Neeli Cherkowski

Walt Whitman is a good place to start any examination of the Beat poets. Ginsberg acknowledges his debt explicitly in his wonderful 'A Supermarket in California'. More than just the image of Whitman as gay icon, or the liberating flow of his American free verse influenced Ginsberg, but also the sense that Whitman was a man of the streets, constantly out among the public, writing about ordinary people, to the extent of visiting Civil War battlefields where he would comfort the wounded. Cherkowski's idea of 'man of the streets', may be more an image of a proto-hippie Walt cruising the docks for willing sailors, but love beads were never a part of Whitman's image, not even when his hair was long.

Actually, Whitman is a role model for Cherkowski himself, because this book might better be subtitled 'Song of Myself'. Neeli in Wonderland, as it were, and sometimes this preoccupation with self is downright hilarious. Ginsberg's first words on meeting Cherkowski were "You're fat". Neeli riposted "You're old". He then reports, deadpan, "Things were never smooth between us after that." Johnson shat on Boswell from greater heights than that without creating undue bumps in the relationship road! The high point of Neeli's life appears to be when his own poetry is praised by some youngsters who mistake him for Ginsberg in his beads and buttons, or when he beats the great man at Trivial Pursuit, which turns out to be one of Ginsberg's favourite pastimes.

That's appropriate, because this book is really a Beatnik Trivial Pursuit game between covers. We know the Beats have become an industry, and there is a lot of mileage in constantly recreating a neighbourhood tour of San Francisco in the late fifties, or the Village in the sixties. Hell, Michael McClure (one of the twelve poets discussed here), who was adept at riding the waves toward the next celebrity or grant, once wrote a book called *Scratching the Beat Surface*. That would seem deep by Neeli's standards.

Not that Neeli's standards are very demanding. He makes no bones in refusing to make critical distinctions about Harold Norse. He is overcome by the *faux* sentimentality of Jack Micheline, just gives up and lets it all wash over him. When he's asked to review John Wieners' *Selected Poems*, he's paralysed by 'feelings', yet actually his take on this unjustly neglected poet is probably the best in the book. And it's nice to see attention paid again to people like Philip Lamantia.

Otherwise, there is better stuff out there on the major subjects: Ginsberg, Ferlinghetti, Bukowski. Neeli says Buk "didn't buy the Eisenhower fifties, didn't buy the Kennedy sixties" but misses the point: that was when he did his best writing, and when he did buy into the Reagan eighties, he lurched into self-parody. Of course, self-parody is a staple of the Beats, and Gregory Corso's ever-inventive riffs are the other highlight here. As when Corso tells him: "I'm the elder now. A daddy. You who do so love the Gregory got the goodie gumdrops from me." Then Neeli, calling him a pied piper, marches off with Corso through the streets of North Beach, reminding me of nothing as much as a happy hamster munching them goody gumdrops.

The other link to Whitman, which Neeli ignores, is that Walt was a major-league mama's boy, sleeping at the foot of her bed long into adulthood. This is a theme that runs through the Beat poets, most notably Kerouac. And so with Neeli. When he takes 250mg of bad acid in 1978 what does he do? He calls mom, and she advises him to find Lawrence Ferlinghetti, who's sitting in a café reading the *New York Times*. Far out. Maybe Neeli's mom could have drawn us a better map, that would've got us to Ferlinghetti sometime before disco became king. [Michael Carlson]

THE X-RATED BIBLE
An Irreverent Survey of Sex in the Scriptures
Ben Edward Akerley

Under such chapter headings as 'Incest: Single, Double and Multiple' and 'Scatology, Bestiality & Castration', *The X-Rated Bible* offers short biblical passages followed by Akerley's sex-related interpretation. Yes, these interpretations may occasionally be irreverent, but I can't help feeling that exposing sexual malpractice in the bible is pretty obvious and

BARROOM TRANSCRIPTS
$11.95 / pb / 229pp / Craphouse Press 1999 / PO Box 2691, Lancaster, PA 17608, USA / www.craphousepress.com

MORE BARROOM TRANSCRIPTS
$13.95 / pb / Craphouse Press 2001 / PO Box 2691, Lancaster PA 17608, USA / www.craphousepress.com

ANAMORPHOSIS
£3.75 / pb / 48pp / ISBN 0951441795 / Sabotage Editions 2000 / BM Senior, London, WC1N 3XX

pretty cheap: the only people who might give this book the time of day will probably know what to expect and not be surprised or shocked by it. An altogether better book would have resulted if Akerley had set out to catalogue the same biblical passages but included multiple interpretations, as opposed to his singular definitions (that sex was as rampant back then as it is now). *The X-Rated Bible* could have been a useful and fascinating book of argument, but I fear it's more of a naughty Christmas present. [Sarah Turner]

BARROOM TRANSCRIPTS
Tony Straub & Rich Stewart

Who is Tony Straub? I had no idea until I picked this book up, and it was only well into the text itself that I began to have an inkling. The introduction gives little away, other than to call Straub "notorious". *Barroom Transcripts* comprises a bunch of true stories and snippets of conversations recorded in or around Lancaster, Pennsylvania, during 1999. Drinking and bar-hopping naturally predominate the tales, as does Straub. Other folk who have tales to tell include Old Joe Blow Crackhead, Jack Groovy, Buggy and JS. Raymond Carver made a career of writing stories in which nothing happens. Nothing much happens in Tony's stories either, but I doubt that he or his drinking buddies will pluck a career out of them — more the pity, for *Barroom Transcripts* is highly entertaining. In 'The Handgun', Tony relates how he once disarmed a man who pulled a revolver on him: he spat in his eyes.

> He will blink... the handgun's yours. It only takes a second, 'cause it shatters your eyes for a second or two.

In 'Takin' Care of Business', Tony speaks of his fondness for karaoke and how he came to fall out with Dancin' Dan. It all started in the bar, like this:

> Like Dancin' Dan that one night. He was terrorizin' me.
> He says, "Oh, are you gonna try to sing karaoke tonight?"
> Well that disturbed me, right? He did it about four times. "Are you gonna try to sing tonight?" I said, "Why don't you get up there and sing, guy? Let's see how good you are."

The tensions escalate when Tony next bumps into Dan. This time Dan chides Tony for wearing his "Indian stuff... a necklace made with a feather on it."

> So I said, "Don't you worry about what I'm wearin' guy. It's none of your business. don't make any comments on me and by the way, the next time I see ya, I'm gonna fuck ya up! Is that all right with you?" So the barman said, "Tony, you got to leave."
> I said to him, "You got me thrown out of this place and I didn't even get a beer yet."

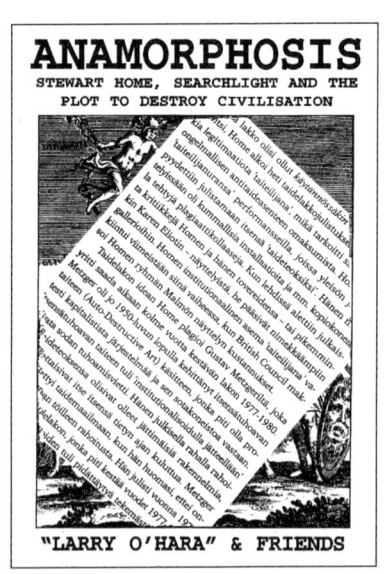

In another story, 'Tony Beats the Bartender', a fight ensues when Tony hits George the bartender for not serving him a beer. Four or five guys drag Tony outside and beat him up. The tale concludes with Tony being arrested: "…and I forgot what came out of it. Nothin' pro'bly."

Elsewhere conversations arise concerning the tape recorder that Rich Stewart uses, compiler of the book. Soon the conversation transmutes from the recorder into the subject of Don X, a man who wasn't quite normal and decided one day he wanted to make something out of tree stumps. BC recounts a tale of Don in the early seventies:

> I talked to him and he was normal. But he was a little out in left field. And we would have good conversations. But then I had a business up in Marion Court called 'Living Woods'. It was a shop. And one day he walked into the shop and he said to me that he was interested in tree stumps. He wanted to provide me with tree stumps because he wanted to take something that was socially negative and turn it into something that was socially positive. And he said, "What I would like to do is, I would like to have these stumps that people could put in their living rooms and grow watermelons out of them." OK? "And cantaloupes." Now I'm listening to him and I'm on the verge of breaking into hysterical laughter. Then I said to him, "Don, a stump to me is something that's this high off the ground, two or three feet off the ground or it could be something level with the ground."
>
> Then I said, "Which are you interested in?" He looked at me and he said, completely serious, "Let me assure you I do not want anything that has been defecated upon." So that ruled out those goddamn low stumps.

"Everybody's got their own sense of nonsense," is the revelatory deduction at the end of the tale.

But *Barroom Transcripts* isn't all fun and games. Later in the book Tony is taking Librium for the shakes and assorted pills to help him eat. He recalls how, having checked himself into a Substance Abuse Centre following a week-and-a-half drinking binge, he was asked to leave early. The reason being he was "running his own program". Do yourself a favour — buy this book and get pissed. [David Kerekes]

MORE BARROOM TRANSCRIPTS
Rich Stewart & Tony Straub

Ever notice that group of dodgy old drunks in the corner of your local, and wonder what they talk about all the time? Well, now you can find out — and without the disadvantage of having to sit and talk to them. Now you can pick up your very own copy of bar room blather — no spittle, no vomit, no old men's mucus-filled coughing, and, best of all, no having to shell out for yet another round of pints with whisky chasers. Touted as the story of 'a man who's escaped through the alcohol tunnel one too many times', this sequel to *Barroom Transcripts* — apparently 'the book that started it all' — is similarly a spiral-bound, 'kitchen-table' published compilation of transcribed conversations shared by a group of drunks in various bars in Lancaster, Pennsylvania. The stories are pretty much what you'd expect, rambling memories of drunken brawls, life in the VA hospital, heroin, prison, prostitutes and arrests for non-payment of child support. There are inconclusive, repetitive anecdotes about arguments, porno movies, laughing gas, orgies and suicides mixed with the usual drunken nostalgia about beautiful but crazy ex-wives. It's enough to drive anybody to drink. The mistake made by this little group of Bukowski wannabes is to assume that drunken tales of sordid exploits are interesting in themselves. But it's not enough just to live a sordid life and talk about it, you also have to have a sense of style, an ability to shape this material into some kind of literary form; otherwise, it's just pointless and dull. After all, there's a reason why those dodgy old drunks in the corner are always sitting on their own. [Mikita Brottman]

Update Both *Barroom* books are out of print. However they've been combined (with a few new stories) as *The Complete Barroom Transcripts*, $15.95, ISBN 0970431260, and available from the listed address and website.

ANAMORPHOSIS
Searchlight and the Plot to Destroy Civilisation
Stewart Home

There really isn't much to recom-

CONFUSION INCORPORATED
£7.95 / pb / 160pp / ISBN 1899598111 / Codex 1999 / www.codexbooks.com

OUT-TAKES
£3.75 / Sabotage Editions / www.stewarthomesociety.org

FLICKERS OF THE DREAMACHINE
£7.95 / pb / 129pp / ISBN 1899598030 / Codex 1996 / www.codexbooks.com

WHO RUNS MAY READ
$25 / pb / 76pp / ISBN 0934301336 / Inkblot 2000 / orders@aftermathbooks.com

CONFUSION INCORPORATED
A Collection of Lies, Hoaxes & Hidden Truths
Stewart Home

The cover and blurb of *Confusion Incorporated* centres around Stewart Home's piece in *The Big Issue* that suggested ex-KLFer Jimmy Cauty kept a comfortable arsenal of weapons at his Devon home. It's the most clear-cut hoax in the book. As I know cock-all about modern art, philosophy, or whiskey, articles related to those subjects meant nothing to me, unsure if they were genuine, or wind-ups aimed at some establishment or other.

But, for provincial bumpkins (such as myself), there's some great stuff amongst the interviews, travelogues and lecture notes collected here: 'How To Be An Art Tart' seems to be aimed specifically at *Guardian* readers; the 'Royal Watch' columns paint our favourite inbreds as drug-dealing occultists; 'Dennis Cooper Does Drugs' (from *Headpress 17*), in which Home attempts to guide the mend in Stewart Home's latest little tract, unless you're a 'fan'. *Anamorphosis* continues the ideological feud between Home and Larry O'Hara, Michel Prigent and others. It's no longer even entertaining, and to be honest Home doesn't come out of this particularly well. Come on, surely he's got something better to do with his time than this? The stories aren't especially funny, the pretend letters boring. The best of the collection is 'Death In June Not Mysterious', which has already been published on the Internet, but it does show that Home has interesting things to say when he can be bothered. [Pan Pantziarka]

CONFUSION INCORPORATED
A Collection of Lies, Hoaxes & Hidden Truths
Stewart Home

The cover and blurb of *Confusion Incorporated* centres around Stewart Home's piece in *The Big Issue* that suggested ex-KLFer Jimmy Cauty kept a comfortable arsenal of weapons at his Devon home. It's the most clear-cut hoax in the book. As I know cock-all about modern art, philosophy, or whiskey, articles related to those subjects meant nothing to me, unsure if they were genuine, or wind-ups aimed at some establishment or other.

But, for provincial bumpkins (such as myself), there's some great stuff amongst the interviews, travelogues and lecture notes collected here: 'How To Be An Art Tart' seems to be aimed specifically at *Guardian* readers; the 'Royal Watch' columns paint our favourite inbreds as drug-dealing occultists; 'Dennis Cooper Does Drugs' (from *Headpress 17*), in which Home attempts to guide the tripping cult novelist around Jack the Ripper murder sites, manages to be both depressing and hilarious. Of the interviews, the best are with ex-Art Attacks members Steve Spear and Edwin Pouncey ("we went all over the place to promote that *Streets* album, mostly Yorkshire"), and Laurence James — AKA Mick Norman — author of the classic NEL 'Hell's Angels' quartet from the early 1970s. James makes you nostalgic for the days when it was possible to knock out a novel in a couple of weeks in order to pay the rent. The working methods of 'hacks' such as himself (165 books in twenty years!) and Peter Cave put today's 600-page-plus bloated 'serious' novelists to shame. The excellent interview is the highlight of a book where some articles (hoaxes?) went so far over my head they carried passports. However, if I ever happen to find myself at an art premier, literary event, or, God forbid, dinner party, then Stewart Home — a self-confessed worshipper at the shrine of his own image — is exactly the kind of gatecrasher I'd want around in my defence. [Martin Jones]

OUT-TAKES
Stewart Home & 'Friends'

I read this, but I don't really feel qualified to comment... It's a collection of pieces largely by or about Stewart Home — some previously published, some not — and consists mainly of people slagging other people off for not having the right critical attitude to some nineteenth-century text or other. Contemporary anarchist thought, from the evidence on display here, seems to resemble Christianity in its fractures and factions and in-fighting over what appear to be cosmetic differences...

Seems like a lot of wasted energy to me, and a distraction from what these people could be doing. If you're interested, topics of debate include the Art Strike of the early nineties, the K Foundation (who thankfully aren't as humourless as most of this bunch), and odds and sods too numerous/uninteresting to mention.

There's what might be construed as a veiled warning at the end of this collection during an interview with Home:

If a critic wishes to write about 'my' texts and/or activities, then they cannot assume that they are equipped a priori to do so. It is not my responsibility if having applied the wrong theoretical tools to the task, a critic makes a series of category errors and is thus transformed into a laughing stock.

Not a laughing stock — please, anything but that! To be fair, this is, as the title 'suggests', out-takes, and is probably not a good introduction to Home. Actually, I quite like the tactics of disinformation and confusion on display in what I've seen of Home's works. Perhaps 'Stewart Home' doesn't exist at all except on paper, and is simply a 'multiple name' like those others described here. Whatever the case, this is still for Home completists and pamphlet addicts only. [James Marriott]

FLICKERS OF THE DREAMACHINE
Ed. Paul Cecil
A 'headbook' of collected essays detailing one of the most interesting — and neglected — developments in 'modern art': the dreamachine. Devised by William S Burroughs associates Brion Gysin and Ian Sommerville, the dreamachine is a device which creates a hallucinatory/visionary state based on the stimulating effect of the repetition of a flicker of light on the closed eyes of the 'viewer'. Utilising the book *The Living Brain* by Grey Walter (extracts from which are included here), the experimenters were able to calculate the correct speed of flicker necessary to trigger visionary effects. The dreamachine has been a source of fascination ever since, and, for the uninitiated, there are plans for the device included with the book. *Flickers* contains essays by both Gysin and Sommerville, both of whom attempt to detail their invention, although an explanation and conceptualisation of the dreamachine is best provided by Ian MacFadyen's contribution 'Machine Dreams: Optical Toys & Mechanical Boys'. Genesis P-Orridge and Ira Cohen both contribute personal visions and reminiscences of Gysin and the dreamachine, while Terry Wilson recounts a dreamachine session. Cecil's own contributions ('Inside Out: The Mysticism of Dream Machines' and 'Nothing Is True —Everything Is Permuted') are far more esoteric, dancing across a combination of occult and spiritual philosophies to re-interpret the dreamachine within the larger processes with which Gysin's work engaged: the cut-ups and the permutations (of language). Against all this seriousness author Simon Strong contributes 'Starflicker', an hilarious essay which deliberately fails to detail the link between Kurt Cobain's suicide, Nirvana conspiracy theories, and dreamachines with an absurd and self-promotional style reminiscent of Stewart Home in non-fiction mode.

Flickers is a long overdue account of the dreamachine and is a necessity for any bibliophile's Beat shelf. [Jack Sargeant]

WHO RUNS MAY READ
Brion Gysin
To anybody interested in William Burroughs' Beat Hotel days the name Brion Gysin should be familiar. For those less versed in Beat genealogies, Gysin was the experimenter/visionary/magician/thinker behind the cut-up and the permutation methods.

Gysin wanted to 'free the word', he was the figure who understood the way in which language and image controlled reality, and who sought to rewire and/or sabotage this form of control. Gysin also visualised the dreammachine, and inspired many of the experiments engaged within the films of Antony Balch (*The Cut-Ups, Bill & Tony* etc). He worked on the numerous tape-recorder experiments with Ian Sommerville and Burroughs, contributing to the sonic explorations that would influence Cabaret Voltaire and Throbbing Gristle, amongst others. He was a calligraphic artist whose figures and paintings appear as a cross between hallucinatory space, abstract expressionism, and an organic visual language part-based on Arabic writing and part-based on Japanese texts. As a painter/visual artist he frequently worked with methods such as the grid, which attempted to do the same to visual

BUKOWSKI
£12.99 / pb / 357pp / ISBN 1883642299 / Steelforth Press 1997 / www.steerforth.com

BUKOWSKI UNLEASHED!
£9.99 / pb / 160pp / ISBN 095352311X / Little Lagoon 1998 / www.akuk.com

LOCKED IN THE ARMS OF A CRAZY LIFE
£10 / pb / 304pp / ISBN 0862419069 / Rebel Inc 1998 / www.canongate.net

media as the permutation did to the written word.

Who Runs May Read collects unpublished and long out of print Gysin. Included is *No Name Hotel* (Gysin's original book proposal, paid for, but eventually turned down, by Doubleday), as well as a lengthy travelogue which sees Gysin searching through Iran for Hassan i Sabbah's assassins' castle at Alamut. For all his interests in radical stylistic practices, the writing is easy to read and accessible — essays and notes rather than the radical poetry that many know Gysin for.

Also included is a selection of interviews with Gysin from the seventies, which provide some bibliographic details and also allow Gysin to expound on his ideas of literature, music and art, the role of which is 'to provide extreme experience'.

One of the key figures of modern art, largely neglected and excluded from the art histories of the academy, hopefully the publication of this book will go someway towards redressing the balance, and, one hopes, open Gysin up to a new audience. [Jack Sargeant]

BUKOWSKI

BUKOWSKI
Neeli Cherkovski
This fine-looking life of the underground poet Bukowski currently being pushed in the "cult writing" sections of most major bookshop chains is in fact a revised version of Cherkovski's 1991 biography of the original "dirty old man" of American letters. When Cherkovski first began the project, his friend and mentor, Bukowski, apparently asked him to keep a certain distance from certain incidents; when Bukowski read the finished book, however, he apparently regretted asking Cherkovski to keep out the "wilder stories". This revised edition, published after Bukowski's death, is hence touted as an unexpurgated life of the legendary foul-mouthed, grizzle-faced, beer-guzzling postman.

But if you're hoping for wild tales of public drunkenness, vomiting at poetry readings and punch-ups in the sorting office, forget it. Cherkovski is too close to his mentor and far too reverent to see the old man's sordid life for what it really was — a miserable, compulsive *folie de grandeur* in which an indulgent drunkard proclaimed himself the natural heir to Hemingway and Whitman, and fooled a generation of disillusioned ex-beatniks into thinking the same thing.

Instead, this arse-kissing neophyte continues to praise the Emperor Bukowski's new clothes, giving us a portrait no more revealing than that of the old man breaking a couple of windows on a dare, puking discreetly from nerves before a poetry-reading, and — on one occasion — drunkenly exposing himself in a fast-food restaurant, incidents all portrayed by Cherkovski as moments of feverish and uncharacteristic madness in the life of an otherwise warm-hearted, hard-working, unacknowledged literary genius. And anyway, Cherkovski seems to be implying, wouldn't twelve years in the sorting office make even the mildest of us want to go postal?

To be fair to Cherkovski, he's on firmer ground when it comes to discussing the poetry itself, and locating it within a particular American tradition, and alongside the work of some of Bukowski's contemporaries. But if you're looking to flesh out the bones of the poet's life, forget Cherkovski — read about the hard-living Henry Chinaski in Bukowski's *Ham on Rye*, or *Post Office*, or — even better — *Notes of a Dirty Old Man*. In his prose works, at least Bukowski can get up enough steam to spin out a decent story — which is more than can be said for Cherkovski, whose writing stinks of the terminal Creative Writing Program, with sentences like "the bare branches of the trees reached into the approaching darkness of early evening. What a bad time he had suffered in that office." Ironically, Cherkovski claims in his introduction that Bukowski's prose style has influenced his own way of writing. If this is true, it must have been the old man's last grim joke on us all. [Mikita Brottman]

BUKOWSKI UNLEASHED!
Essays on a Dirty Old Man
Bukowski Journal Vol 1
Ed. Rikki Hollywood

Volume One (and to date the only volume) of Rikki Hollywood's *Bukowski Unleashed!* picks up where his own *Bukowski Zine* left off, but in a nice compact book format, and at an increased price. A venue for Bukowski-related ideas, suggestions, reviews and artwork, this is pretty much territory for the pre-initiated; neophytes, of course, should start with the real thing. For international aficionados of the dirty old postman, this is probably a very useful resource for reviews, contacts, info, and all things Bukowski-based. The current issue contains pieces on the archetypal Buk kook, Bukowski-themed comic strips, reviews of Bukowski-based films and other, non-Bukowski-related writing. The fact that this is a nicely-produced and well-illustrated journal isn't the only place where *Bukowski Unleashed!* has the upper hand over similar publications, however — it also has a ban on "Bukowski-influenced poetry and stories". I'll drink to that. [Mikita Brottman]

LOCKED IN THE ARMS OF A CRAZY LIFE
Howard Sounes

Although Charles Bukowski achieved a cult status in America — which seems to be growing all the time — for most of his career he was actually more popular in Germany. Perhaps this was because he had been born there, though father soon moved him to the USA. More likely it was because Bukowski's autobiographical stories, poems, and novels struck a chord with Germans:

> Bukowski was a man who wrote bildungsromans all his life. There is an adolescent quality which his work never loses, and it seems to appeal to the adolescent which lies buried under many adult selves.

Charles Bukowski was ugly. He drank. Boy, did he drink. He sorted letters in a post office. He went to the track and played the horses. He chased easy women. He got into fights. All that made him different from thousands of other wasted souls in flop houses and skid rows across America was that he wrote about it.

Fuelled with a sort of hard-boiled romanticism, he wrote in a bare, straightforward style which gave an air of reality to his tales, and turned much of their adolescent worldview into self-deprecating humour. It was his way of coming out on top, of maintaining faith in a romantic view of the world (maybe *that's* why the Germans love him!), even when seen through a haze of smoke, drink, and rejection. It is not that the life Bukowski presents to us is false, it is that it is presented through eyes that are never as bloodshot as they seem, a sensibility never as lost or cynical as it appears on the surface.

Through the unlikely avenue of two small-press publishers, Bukowski became famous in a fashion, and through his fictional alter-ego of Henry Chinaski, his bottled dreams came true. All the booze he could drink, pretty women throwing themselves at him, and his work being taken seriously.

Writing a biography of someone who has constructed such a vibrant existence through fiction is a challenge which Howard Sounes meets head-on, and battles at least to a draw. He is particularly good on the realities of Bukowski's childhood, and on his progression to loser status. Detailing the nature of his relationships, and seeing in particular the three women who made up the bulk of his life, before his writing became successful, rounds out the more romantic picture Bukowski draws in his work.

Strangely enough, Sounes is less revealing about how it was that Bukowski's work eventually caught the public's eye. Although he turned against most of the small-press people who aided him in the early days, it is not a common thing for someone to move from the mimeographed magazines where he began his career, to financial success. It can be argued that Bukowski made

666 WAYS TO GET INTO HEAVEN
$9.99 / pb / 184pp / ISBN 0970267304 / Stuck Pig Productions 2000 / www.stuckpigproductions.com

A GOOD CUNT BOY IS HARD TO FIND
£5 / pb / 76pp / ISBN 1886988080 / Cyber-Psychos AOD 1998 / available from BBR Distribution, PO Box 625, Sheffield, S1 3GY, UK / distribution@bbr-online.com

ALL ABOUT EVIL
£7.99 / pb / 176pp / ISBN 0953936708 / Apple Pie 2000 / publishers@apple-pie.fsnet.co.uk

BECAUSE SHE THOUGHT SHE LOVED ME
£7 / pb / 181pp / ISBN 1899344276 / Do-Not Press 1997 / 16 The Woodlands, London SE13 6TY / www.thedonotpress.com

Black Sparrow Press, but there isn't a good sense of just how that came to happen, of whether Bukowski's ultimate popularity 'just happened' or whether John Martin or someone else played the Buk card deftly. He's also not very interested or adept at analysing what it is that makes Bukowski's stuff work, or not. What are the differences between the poetry and the stories, if any?

Given all that, this biography cries out for more space and more salacious detail. Perhaps not surprisingly, Sounes is also one of the many writers to produce books on the West killings. His *Fred and Rose* is one of the most reticent of the genre, unwilling to dwell on prurient gore. This is understandable, perhaps, when dealing with murder. But when you're relating the life of a man who tossed the intimate details of his own life onto the page with a seemingly casual disregard, it's more surprising. Sounes pointed out that severe head trauma may have helped transform Fred West into a sex fiend and sadistic killer. Bukowski's cranium certainly absorbed its share of poundings, which might help explain the sex part.

Bukowski was a classic drunken fuck-up, crying in his beer the next day. In classic juicer behaviour, he turned against many of the people who loved him or helped him. Becoming successful gave him more opportunity to indulge, and to screw-up more spectacularly. As the situations get more and more bizarre, you long for more detail. I wish Amber O'Neil's 'Blowing My Hero', an account of being sickened by having sex with Bukowski, could have been reprinted as an appendix. The recollections of the various women who now found Bukowski-the-successful-writer attractive and romantic stand in sharp contrast to his early life; yet almost all the stories seem cut off before they get to the gut-wrench stage. The tension between Bukowski the romantic, and Bukowski the cynical love machine, lies underneath almost all of them, and needs to be brought to the surface. Even the potential absurd hilarity of Hollywood tough-guy types like Sean Penn paying homage to a small-press poet doesn't get played out for all it is worth.

In the end, Bukowski got to indulge his adolescent fantasies of priapic power, not just in the pages of little magazines, but in life. No matter how bad the night before, Bukowski was back at the typewriter the next day. Few of us can literally work and make our dreams come true, but he was able to. In that sense, Bukowski's life was far less crazy, and less tragic, than people think. Was he, in the end, heroic, or were the readers who believed in Henry Chinaski simply taken for a giant con, and wound up buying the drinks for the guy telling funny stories at the bar? That's the question Sounes doesn't ask, and it stops this engrossing biography just short of the final hurdle. [Michael Carlson]

FICTION

666 WAYS TO GET INTO HEAVEN
Jamie Hill

Not really sure what the point of this is — perhaps the literary equivalent of a novelty record — but apparently intended mainly as a vehicle by which the author can refer to and name-drop his many friends and drinking companions. Perhaps he could give it to some of them for Christmas; I'm really not sure who else is going to be buying it. The book consists of — yes — 666 ways to get into heaven, each listed in spacious paper-wasting capital letters on the page, with occasional addenda. Reasons include #404 Buy Beer, #368 Put Gas in God's Car, and #888 Get a Note from your Mother ("an idea of Jacqueline's", apparently). Illustrated with two pictures of the author and some of his drinking buddies in a bar, this is a vanity publication by some pathetic soul who's been hanging around with people foolish enough to make him believe he's some kind of a wit. So sad and pathetic I could hardly bear to read it. [Mikita Brottman]

A GOOD CUNT BOY IS HARD TO FIND
Doug Rice

Doug Rice is an English professor at Kent State University, Salem, and the author of the autobiographical fragment, *Blood of Mugwump*. This is a collection of his short stories — tales of sexual excess and degradation, virtually non-stop sex scenes detailed in high postmodernist fashion. This means that most of the stories are virtually unreadable, full of nonsense like this, from 'The Fire Sermon':

She and her demonic flesh gone dyslexic on me. All over my body. She rudely forced her body before my eyes. Perceived my desires. Her belly wrecked by the sound of our parents screaming. Frozen syllables from the dark languages of our ancestral past. Words loitering in the dull corridors of my hollow, sterile cut. Throbbing for tongue.

If this isn't bad enough, Rice also likes to play games with footnotes, gender, typography and identity, so we have stories about the desire of a boy to be raped by a girl, a boy-girl "suffering at the surface of mouth, cunt, word and skin", an offal girl living in a male body, characters with "mutable or nomadic gender", "pornology", sado-masochism and transsexuality. Influences — or so the introduction claims — are Artaud, The Marquis de Sade, Jean Genet, Giles [sic] Deleuze, George [sic] Bataille, William Faulker, William Burroughs, and, rather less impressively, Kathy Acker and Courtney Love. Basically, this is the kind of thing that Peter Sotos does far better, and without all the bullshit.

In her introduction, the brown-nosed Lidia Yuknavitch claims that "small bands of nomads will read the book, eat the book, fuck the book". Others, less easily excited, will simply toss it away. [Mikita Brottman]

ALL ABOUT EVIL
Philip Davenport

Poet, novelist, journalist, advertising copywriter and film director, this Philip Davenport sounds like a busy man. *All About Evil* is a collection of other-worldly, surrealistic 'contemporary fairytales' in the style — or so the jacket claims — of Poe, Angela Carter, and Brett Easton Ellis. This is already a telling indictment, since these three writers have almost nothing in common. They may all deal very broadly with 'horror', but horror can manifest itself in a whole multitude of themes, forms and styles. Davenport has none of Poe's lyricism, none of Carter's fascination with the sublime and grotesque, and none of Easton Ellis' sense of abstraction or alienation. *All About Evil* is structured like a futuristic *Thousand and One Nights* and touted as being 'nasty as a barrel of Rottweilers', but don't believe the hype. This is adolescent, self-involved, and unreadable — and the Rottweiler, by the way, is actually a very sweet dog. [Mikita Brottman]

BECAUSE SHE THOUGHT SHE LOVED ME
Maxim Jakubowski

Maxim Jakubowski has perfected the art of networking to a degree us mere mortals can never hope to emulate. As editor, publisher, anthologist, bookshop owner, columnist, reviewer and author, he's got all bases covered. And, despite the fact that his writing's never been top-rank, he's very much a central figure in the crime writing establishment of this country. Given that he's 'the king of the erotic crime thriller' according to *CrimeTime* magazine (hey, doesn't his bookshop advertise big time in *CrimeTime*?), his latest, *Because She Thought She Loved Me*, ought to be something to look forward to.

Unfortunately this reads like a long list of crime fiction clichés sea-

BILE
£6.99 / pb / 232pp / ISBN 0754400603 / Citron Press

THE BLACK ROSE
£7.95 / pb / 122pp / ISBN 1871592798 / Velvet Publications 1997 / www.creationbooks.com

BURGER DUDE
$9.95 / pb / 47pp / ISBN 0741404354 / buybooksontheweb.com 2000 / info@buybooksontheweb.com / Jon Stone, PO Box 5121, Kinchelow, MI 49788, USA / payable Jon Stone, incl p&p

BUTCHERSHOP IN THE SKY
£11.95 $19.95 / pb / 208pp / ISBN 1871592666 / Creation 1999 / www.creationbooks.com

Art from Burger Dude.

soned with a sprinkling of erotica-by-numbers sex scenes to pad it out. Take your pick of cardboard cut-out characters straight from a 'how to write hard boiled crime fiction' manual. There's the stripper with the PhD, the serious book-collecting habit and the tendency to orgasm spontaneously when asked to murder someone (OK, we've all had phone calls that have excited us but come on!). Or the married woman whose sexuality, once awakened, leads inevitably to desire, death and destruction. Or the tragic male lead whose flawed desire means that his obsession with the latter femme fatale ensures he winds up collecting bullets in the chest.

Aside from the clichéd characters there's an unconvincing story, which would be forgivable if it were not for the pretensions behind every sentence in the book. Every action is imbued with a significance which is sadly lacking, every scene attempts a gritty realism which reminds the reader that there's nothing realistic going on here.

The book moves ponderously from A to B, with no detours. And if you think I'm being overly harsh, here's a taster of some of the 'breathless' prose that convinces me once and for all that this book's not worth seeking out except for its comedy value (and believe me, the last scene had me rolling on the floor).

Her taste was electric as her hot breath moved inside me like a strong peppermint-flavoured Gulf Stream of unchecked desire and reached every extremity of my body with its velvet caress.

The Do-Not Press are publishing some interesting books, but this isn't one of them. [Pan Pantziarka]

BILE
Mark Brand
It's fifteen minutes into the future, when Helmut Kohl runs the Euro super-state that invades poor old Blighty. Of course the spooks in our intelligence services engage in all kinds of black ops, especially in the Anti-Hygiene Underground (the Krauts being world class hygienists of course). Somehow everybody talks in a nasal estuary whine, which is transcribed phonetically for our reading pleasure — it took me ages to figure out who the "Ow Biw" are. And I won't even mention the massed ranks of rubber-suited gimps. Does it sound a mess? It is. An absolute mess of shifting tenses, points of view and writing styles. It shifts in and out at random, switching character and tense mid-paragraph and then back again. But, despite its myriad faults, there's a real page-turning quality about it. For the first hundred pages I wanted to jack it in, but after a while I was hooked, like "a kant" and had to keep going. And it's funny too, in a warped sort of way. The book is so obviously after cult status that it won't get it. It's a shame. This would have been a much better book. [Pan Pantziarka]

Update Citron Press went bust in 2000.

THE BLACK ROSE
Josephine Jarmaine
Here we have a woman, Rosamund, countenancing the destruction of her identity as anything but a collection of three holes (CF *The Story of O*) in an isolated environment of random and unending perversion (CF *Salò*), and in the company of characters

with names like Diamanthus, Firebird and Spear (CF Finbarr Saunders). Unlike Pauline Reage's heroine though, Rosamund relinquishes her ID not for one man but rather to facilitate the growth (in her vagina) of the story's eponymous flower which will, in the words of the scheme's instigator, "make impotent men as lions… sworn to the gods of love and venery" — or at least it will once this gent infiltrates the world's water supplies with its essence. While the plot may sound like an odd cross-pollination of Russ Meyer and Abbie Hoffman, Jarmaine's writing is affectedly dreamy and florid; the chapter detailing 'The Filling' reads like the tripped-out shooting script for one of the iffier sequences in *Girl on a Motorcycle*. All the purple prose in the world can't hide the fact that this is a fairly superficial affair, but it's a readable one and the well-rendered catalogue of perversion should have any discerning deviant's wanger waggling in appreciation. And it all comes up roses in the end. [Anton Black]

BURGER DUDE
Jonathon Stone

Somewhere in North America, 1971. Hippie Ray wants cash fast to buy some wheels so he and his pal Richie can cruise off down the highway: "It'll be like *Easy Rider* — except with a car." Ray gets his hair chopped and takes a temporary job at McBurger's flipping cow chunks. Fourteen years later, he's still there. Richie, however, has become a corporate cock-rack. Two decades-plus of the same job, same apartment, lousy cars, lousy sex, lousy money all take their toll, and, after hallucinatory visits from giant talking burgers, Ray turns up at work one day with a loaded rifle, ready to deal it out to employers and former friends…

Burger Dude isn't particularly well-written, reading more like a screenplay that hasn't been cut into scenes yet. It's also fairly monotonous and predictable, but maybe that's the author's intention, as Ray's life is just the same tedious shit all day every day. *Burger Dude* works best as a depressing realisation of non-skilled working life: where you're always going to get another job next week, where the plank between 'paying the bills' and 'eviction' is supported only by a pittance wage, where employers' demands become increasingly tiresome, where all you find yourself doing after each shift is getting drunk in front of the TV… Millions of kids being trained to say "Enjoy your meal" *and* easy access to firearms? Why hasn't the apocalypse arrived yet? [Martin Jones]

BUTCHERSHOP IN THE SKY
Premature Ejaculations 1989–1999
James Havoc

> *If his ludicrous 'anti-novel'* RAISM *had not existed, there would have been no reason, no inspiration to form Creation press, which I did (with the invaluable collaboration with Alan McGee) solely in order to inflict this atrocity upon an unsuspecting world.*

Thus writes James Williamson in his forward to this remarkable collection of writings.

James Havoc has evidently been around since the late eighties, creating literary havoc and knocking about as a Primal Scream groupie, persuading Bobby Gillespie to frock up as the Gilles de Rais for a Super-8 film, and recording his own LP, *Church of Raism*. His writings — or rather, outpourings — are a pungent mixture of extreme sex and violence, set in an unspecified 'time of legends'; places packed to the skies with viscera and monsters. But for the super-concentrated nature of pieces such as *Satanskin*, *Third Eye Butterfly* and *White Skull*, this book could be classed as erotica, yet Havoc's incredible facility for imagery and language, and his relative lack of narrative interest puts these works in quite another league — too elaborate to be nightmares, too overwrought to be invested with more than mere curiousness.

And here lies Havoc's strengths and his weaknesses. In contrast to regular erotic writing, there is no variation of tone, no boring bits of 'proper' story between the good juicy bits. No characters to engage with, no story to speak of, just atmosphere and a barrage of violent sexual events. Everything is pitched at the same level of screaming intensity. This is not a criticism as these are not your usual one-handed erotic writings. Havoc shoots for short and intense, the language equivalent of sequences from a Jerry Bruckheimer movie, or a series of MTV-market commercials extolling the sights of Hell. His feel for language is extraordinary, if untamed; plenty of gems cumulating in over-decoration, simple stories festooned to a point where they read like cut-ups. Take this example:

> *They construct a spiralling garrison from carnage, a folly of pubic pelts and sawn scalps, the juice of exploded sexes, succulent stools speckled with tapeworms, spine rippled by*

CHARLIEUNCLENORFOLK TANGO
£7.95 / pb / 160pp / ISBN 1899598138 / Codex 1999 / www.codexbooks.co.uk

CAMDEN PARASITES
pb / 227pp / ISBN 1871593212 / Unpopular Books 1999 / www.unpopular.org.uk

COBRALINGUS
£9.95 / $14.95 / pb / 121pp / ISBN 1899598162 / Codex 2001 / www.codexbooks.co.uk

CRIME WAVE
£6.99 / pb / 303pp / ISBN 0099279991 / Arrow 1999 / www.randomhouse.co.uk

the hand of rabies, crab-like in patterns, nipples punctuated by greedy flowers, all rigged tight with gelatinous hawsers of head integument and packed in ice.

I cannot in my heart of hearts get excited about this stuff because the hyper-baroque stylings make for a tiring and obscure read. Leaving out the 'children's' 'Gingerworld' fragment and a couple of other pieces which should have gone in the bin, Havoc's often haphazard, sometimes unreadable gifts are a rare and strong meat, like being trapped in an oubliette with a crazed adolescent who badly needs a Valentine's card. Taboo after taboo is thrust into one's eyes, every repulsive and necrotic act that de Sade didn't get round to describing. It would all be a bit of harmless fun, but Williamson's foreword over-selfconsciously builds Havoc up as some kind of legendary literary 'character'. And Jack Sargeant's next introduction, hailing Havoc's 'importance' as a libertarian crusader (and bizarrely citing his colloquial use of language), alternates between the insightful and the pretentious, even more gratuitous than Havoc's pieces.

With so much polite, good taste, crap on the shelves, this book deserves to be out there if only to give people with unfossilised reading habits the chance to expose themselves to something decidedly unmainstream. How widely it is distributed is another question. Many bookshops will still behave in a scandalised fashion if you enquire whether they carry Crowley's *White Stains*. If words had the power to replace drugs, *Butchershop in the Sky* would be whipped-up by the tabloids into a national moral panic.

That isn't going to happen, of course, but the analogy goes some way to expressing my feelings towards both the strengths and the absurdities of this work. Fine for it to have been published. But then, if it wasn't, if it stayed in Havoc's bottom drawer, it wouldn't matter that much.

The two illustrative strips by Mike Philbin are imaginative, let down by school-magazine draughtsmanship and for being uncoloured. I keep returning to look at them: comedy and evil pouring from every scratch of his nib, strong hints of Goya's influence.

Havoc is supposed to have 'disappeared' after an eleven-day binge in Tokyo on Millennium Eve. The scrupulous logging of the details of this binge by James Williamson (even down to the label of beer Havoc was on), and the seemingly intimate knowledge of Havoc's life in the years before that makes me wonder if Williamson is none other than the real-life incarnation of the shadowy Havoc. It would be Havoc's best story yet, if true. [Jerry Glover]

CHARLIEUNCLENORFOLK TANGO
Tony White

"Lissen yew cunts," begins our tale — with one single phrase printed in the middle of each page — "Coz yore problee wundrin wot we woz do-inn there in the ferss place & ow we cum ter be juss dryvin aroun din the fuckin dark myles & myles from fuckin enny ware…" As the opening of *CharlieUncleNorfolkTango* makes clear, this is hardly your traditional roman policier. Three officers — Lockie, Blakie and The Sarge — are driving around at night in a police van. After they've been abducted by aliens from "a soddin spay ship or summink", we find out that one of the trio isn't exactly human. But which one...? Not quite the "lode a bollux" it might sound, *CharlieUncle...* basically presents us with a stream of consciousness from the perspective of the narrator, Lockie, whose musings cover subjects as diverse as mad killers prowling the streets, "blokes and birds", the anatomy of *Charlie's Angels*, and the lights of the city streets. Lockie's thoughts are interspersed with various atrocities and acts of corruption which make the police seem as trapped in their alienation as the criminals they're out to get — or even the "free-fingerd fuckers" who abduct them. Starsky and Hutch it surely ain't. *CharlieUncle...* works if you read it as a long poem. The problem with reading it as a novel, however, is that there isn't really much of a plot. In the case of the best writers to use this kind of experimental, phonetic prose — Anthony Burgess, for example, or Hubert Selby Jr — the idiosyncrasies of the style quickly fade into the background as matters of character and plot become more and more absorbing. Here, though, there seems to be little more than the style itself, which never becomes unobtrusive, and the narrative voice is foregrounded to such an extent that in the end the whole thing sounds a bit like a pathological Frank Butcher. Still, if you can handle it, you'll find a lot here that's brutal, poignant, penetrating, even funny. And if you like stories of "fuckin coppers" being abducted by aliens, you're going to eat this up. Ain chew mate? [Mikita Brottman]

CAMDEN PARASITES
Daniel Lux

This apparently autobiographical book charts the rise and fall of the author, a small-time thief and junkie, from humble origins through a flirting with pop stardom to a brief stint in a mental hospital and beyond. There's no fictional framework placed around the events, and nor is there much comment made about them — just endless ups and downs, various addictions and brushes with the law. Danny's an interesting character, though, and a fairly complex picture of him is built up throughout the book, albeit more by what he leaves out than anything else. He constantly ridicules his richer peers for lacking in street smarts, and attempts to justify his stealing from them through badly digested Class War ideas — there's a quotation from a Stewart Home review on the back which refers to the book as "A savage indictment of bourgeois society". Trouble is, he rips off everyone he knows — all of his friends, who unsurprisingly eventually reject him, his long-suffering girlfriends, his parents — and the only relationship he can have with people seems to be one of exploitation. When Danny's on form he's also almost intolerably arrogant and full of himself, spraying his ego over all and sundry, and for this reason I was more taken with him when things weren't going so well — when he's institutionalised, friendless and bloated he seems somehow more human (not sure what that says about me!). In a postscript it is revealed that the author died of a heroin overdose when the final proofs were being prepared. While saddening, it's not entirely surprising, considering the full-throttle self-destruction Danny embarks upon whenever he has any cash. The book is very readable — despite the absence of 'plot' — and makes for a far more compelling and convincing picture of this kind of London life than most novels I've come across. [James Marriott]

Update A note from Danny's flatmate and buddy that accompanied the review copy of this book suggested that Danny was also responsible for the much publicised smashing of the *Blue Peter* garden in the seventies. See Phil Tonge's Cak-Watch in *Headpress 18* for details.

COBRALINGUS
Jeff Noon

Despite its appearance, *Cobralingus* is not a paperback book but an "engine" which "allows language to partake of a future liquid state of consciousness". Jeff Noon, apparently, "uses the Metafiction process to apply the techniques of electronic dance music to the production of words, dissolving language". *Cobralingus* appears to be a collection of illustrations, concrete poems, word games, extracts from literature and other kinds of 'samples' and 'dubs'...

I read the introduction, but I'm still not sure what I was supposed to do with it (nothing so old-fashioned as reading, that's for sure). Sections have titles like 'exploding horse generator unit', 'decay sample', 'organic pleasure engine' and 'inlet texts'. A graphical device, a pure experiment, a 'word snake' or just a pile of wank? You be the judge. [Mikita Brottman]

CRIME WAVE
James Ellroy

It's a problem that Joseph Heller's struggled with since *Catch 22* — how do you top something that's monumental, seminal and so fucking

CUNT
£7.50 / pb / 192pp / ISBN 1899344454 / The Do-Not Press 1999 / www.thedonotpress.com

DIGITAL LEATHERETTE
£8.95 / pb / 256pp / ISBN 189959812X / Codex 1999 / PO Box 148, Hove, East Sussex BN3 3DQ, UK / www.codexbooks.co.uk

DIRTY MONEY AND OTHER STORIES
£7.99 / $11.95 / pb / 142pp / ISBN 0916397610 / Manic D Press 1999 / www.manicdpress.com

THE DUNGEONMASTER'S APPRENTICE
£7.99 / pb / 216pp / ISBN 1852426233 / Serpent's Tail 1999 / www.serpentstail.com

brilliant it redefines an entire genre? Let's face it, the likes of you and I are never going to have to grapple with this one, but it's one that James Ellroy seems to be having trouble with right now. Having produced the nightmarish, twisted vision that is the LA Quartet, he's now faced with the task of writing something to match it. And, like Joseph Heller before him, he's having trouble hitting his game. After the detour that was *American Tabloid*, *My Dark Places* was a return to the scene of the crime in many senses. The LA of the fifties that he evoked as memory echoed the fictional alternative reality that he had crafted to perfection in books like the *Black Dahlia*. In moving from fiction to memoir he managed to produce a compelling insight into the long journey from 'kid whose mum was murdered' to maladjusted schoolboy Nazi to druggie panty sniffer to Mr James Ellroy-crime-writer-par-excellence. However, good as *My Dark Places* is, it still left me with the feeling that he's stuck, looking back at what he's done and struggling to find somewhere to move to next. On the evidence of *Crime Wave* the answer is that he's not moved anywhere yet, and that he still shows no sign of knowing where to go.

Crime Wave is a collection of reportage and fiction culled from the American edition of *GQ* magazine with a couple of new short stories thrown in for good measure. The non-fiction mostly reprises material from *My Dark Places*, which is no surprise because that book grew out of a feature from *GQ* in the first place. Aside from his mother's case, he looks at another unsolved homicide in the same area and with a similar MO. He looks at the O J Simpson case; he spends time with cops; he meets people with whom he went to school. It's all mildly interesting stuff but that's it, perfect magazine fodder but somehow lacking when collected together in book form. The short stories are, if anything, even more disappointing than the reportage. All the Ellroy trademarks are here: alliteration; short, sharp sentences; plot changes aplenty. Unfortunately it reads like a caricature of Ellroy. The alliteration is taken to excess, so that a couple of pages into the story 'Hush Hush' you want to scream. And there's a plot change every sentence, as though he feels compelled to produce fiction that's ever more complex. I like James Ellroy and consider the LA Quartet to be amongst the best works of American literature this century. He illuminates a nether world of cops and corruption, racism and homophobia, paranoia and violence that has been air-brushed out of history. If his relationship to the 'big bad white men' who have the power is at times ambiguous, it's no matter because he pulls no punches. I just hope that he can get it together to write better books than this one. If you want a recommendation then check out the *Black Dahlia*, *The Big Nowhere*, *LA Confidential* and *White Jazz*. [Pan Pantziarka]

CUNT
Stewart Home
Hey kids, dig those crazy London novelists! Could you really give a dog's 'nad about them, or anything they write? Dead parents, emotionally-retarded men, lonely alcoholic women, gay librarians, blocked writers. Boo-fucking-hoo. *Cunt* is a novel about a London novelist. Sort of. Thankfully, author Home dogs

the heels of Sinclair and Moorcock more than Amis and Self, and so this book is a long way away from queeny literary tiffs...

The girl sat down on the toilet bowl and I licked her clit while she took a shit. She stood up again and said I could fuck her up the arse. We didn't need a lubricant, her lunch hadn't agreed with her and she'd just had a very loose crap.

Meet David Kelso. A cunt is what he is, cunt is what he's after, and *Cunt* is his journal; it charts the final stages of his attempt to re-fuck the first thousand women he ever had. As protagonists go, Kelso is somewhere between *Complicity*'s Cameron Colley and *American Psycho*'s Patrick Bateman, but without the morals of the former or the social etiquette of the latter. Travelling through the bleak landscapes of East Anglia, Finland and Scotland, Kelso translates his mission onto hard disk, give or take a few distractions — as he also happens to be a money-burning, whiskey-devouring, teen-shagging superman. We discover this in chapter one — in which our hero fellates a she-male — and there's no let up thereafter. *Cunt* is so over the top it reads like nothing more than a novelist's megalomaniacal wet dream: Miller, Bukowski and Crews all jacked off into the gene pool and out popped David Kelso — one hand holding a bottle of fine malt, the other up a fifteen-year-old's skirt. Home has injected every clichéd vice into one character and let him plough his own course, as well as adding some genuine pranks — such as Kelso inventing a Dead Young Poet and secreting his 'work' on the shelves of charity shops, then sitting back and watching a cult of nothing emerge. OTT, yes, but give me Home's book over 'I don't think you really realise what it's like to be a thirty-five-year-old single man' record shop shelf-fillers any day.

Buy it for the female English literature student in your life. [Martin Jones]

DIGITAL LEATHERETTE
Steve Beard
Praised by William Gibson as "an exuberant, neurologically-specific neo-Blakean riff-collage", this piece of "ambient hyperfiction" fuses fictive text samples from internet websites, court transcripts from a complex espionage case, briefing documents, screenplay excerpts and some *faux* Elizabethan drama. A writer for the "style press", Beard uses his journalistic experience to add some authentic details to the dense, abstract, metaphor-laden prose of this tightly-knit conceptual "anti-novel". Significant themes include MI6, Morrissey, drugs, raves, the millennium and something about Battersea Power Station; psychogeography is a futuristic London as reflected through the eyes of William Blake, Iain Sinclair and J G Ballard. Fragmented, convoluted and ultimately highly irritating, this is strictly a book for boys. [Mikita Brottman]

DIRTY MONEY AND OTHER STORIES
Ayn Imperato
As with Jeri Cain Rossi's *Red Wine Moan* [below], these "strange tales of bizarre employment and punk rock hijinx" form another terribly inconsistent collection from another 'writer and musician' who maybe needs to make up her mind which art she's going to focus on. As with *Red Wine Moan*, the unevenness of this collection suggests that Imperato doesn't have enough material for a full-length novel, and is seldom willing to stray too far from the realms of personal experience. What struck me most about this collection of scenes from the writer's early life as a drop-out Goth is how ordinary it all is. Reading *Dirty Money* is more like reading somebody's personal journal than reading a sustained collection of stories — which might be interesting if the writer was leading a particularly fascinating life, or had an especially profound capacity for self-reflection — neither of which are the case here. Moreover, *entire pages* are taken up with banal and disconnected scenes, like this one:

Walking to the Philly train, snow coming down. Big flakes like tiny ghosts, almost scaring me. The tracks laid out. a young girl runs to catch it as it runs away. The train moves on through the haunting.

This kind of thing really confirms all the clichés about small press fiction. [Mikita Brottman]

THE DUNGEONMASTER'S APPRENTICE
Mark Ramsden
Don't let the garish cover or stereotypical title put you off, *The Dungeonmaster's Apprentice* isn't just another granite-faced exercise in S&M literature. Fleeing New York in the wake of some vaguely outlined murders, Matt and diminutive dominatrix Sasha plan to blend into the London fetish scene, only to have the mysterious Apprentice of

EXTRATERRESTRIAL SEX FETISH

$15 / pb / 216pp / ISBN 0970497105 / Supervert 32C 2001 / www.supervert.com

FLOOZY

£5 / pb / 100pp / Slab-O-Concrete Publications / www.codexbooks.co.uk

Its wings and claws tighten in *Floozy*. Art: Xtina Lamb

the title start leaving them presents involving bits of dead cat. Things go from bad to worse as one of Sasha's clients has an unfortunate asphyxiation accident, and they subsequently get wrapped up in the mechanics of neo-Nazi occultism that also involves a high-kicking Hong Kong tattooist, a Cruella de Vil-style hag, and a longhaired old ponce with Crowleyite aspirations…

There's not a lot of sex, plenty of casual drug ingestion, and splatters of violence, but what makes this novel stand out is the supreme debunking of the lifestyle it describes, with Matt as its cynical narrator. Here, everyone is trying to out-transgress everyone else, and nobody wants to break their 'been-there-done-that' stance for fear of looking uncool. True to the consumerist nature of the late twentieth-century, if these freaks feel they want something, they demand to have it. This scene is pretentious, expensive, cliquey and so far up its own arse it's probably considered another sexual peccadillo. And, as written by ex-*Fetish Times* editor Mark Ramsden, it's also very, very, very funny.

What I find amusing about people who carp on about sexual activities that are considered 'alternative' is how they either (a) try to portray themselves as just your average working bod, or (b) think that an open relationship, a few bolts through the genitals and a maze of Celtic tattoos sufficiently distances them from the world's wage slaves and *Sun* readers. *The Dungeonmaster's Apprentice* shows that the rules and regulations of such lifestyles are not a million miles away from the *Art of the Barbecue* or *Proper Caravanning Techniques*; there are the usual lines you don't step over, and political correctness rears its freshly scrubbed head at the oddest of times. Some of the scenarios Matt and Sasha strike a pose through are disturbingly akin to Real Ale festivals.

This is an excellent novel, and deserves a much wider readership than it might initially attract; I can imagine *The Dungeonmaster's Apprentice* being ritualistically burned in cabalistic murder ceremonies in some of London's more humourless fetish clubs. I hope Ramsden doesn't feel he has to confine himself to this particular rubber-room of delights in future books. [Martin Jones]

EXTRATERRESTRIAL SEX FETISH
Supervert 32C

Supervert 32C Inc is "a media company that utilises the techniques of vanguard aesthetics to research the pathology of novel perversions". Devoted to exploring the notion of exophilia — an abnormal attraction for beings from worlds beyond earth — *Extraterrestrial Sex Fetish* consists of a series of interrelated short texts (narrative fragments, philosophical speculations, diary excerpts, parodies, snippets of computer code) written in the style of a Space Age Marquis de Sade. It's not quite as intimidating as it sounds, however, since the book's format allows you to dig in and out at will. You can follow the narrative of Mercury de Sade and his frustrated attempts to satisfy his fetish for alien sex, or you can get acquainted with philosophical speculations about otherworldly life from Descartes to Roland Barthes and back again. Personally, I found it difficult to get a foothold on the book's stylised, slightly robotic prose, though sci-fi aficionados and *Star Trek* fans may find a rare treat in the descriptions of exophiliac copulation. If it's beach reading you're after, however, I'd recommend something a little more down to earth. [Mikita Brottman]

FLOOZY
Jane Graham
Illustrated by Xtina Lamb

Jane Graham is 'Jane S Stamp', creator of *Shag Stamp* zine (reviewed *Headpress 17*). *Floozy*, her first book, is a picaresque autobiographical jaunt through strip shows, lap dancing, life modelling, hitching, and generally skirting the fringes of the demimonde, doing whatever it takes to avoid getting a 'proper' job. Jane is evidently what the Victorians called an 'adventuress' — not really a committed tart, not really respectable, living for kicks. It has to be said, though, that the relentless shabbiness of her surroundings, and of the uniformly revolting male punters she comes into contact with, leave her more jaundiced than full of the 'up-for-it' quality she starts the book with. Although there is little coherence or connecting narrative to the vignettes which make up the text, *Floozy* charts a consistent trajectory of increasing weariness and disillusionment that make the latter part of this little book rather more poetic and interesting than the first. There are moments of real pathos:

> ... I can't write more than a couple of lines about them anymore. Where's the variation? I put my make-up on, do my hair nice, and you push me down, shove it in, come and leave.

Whilst the likes of Peter Sotos may get off on this kind of thing, most people, most men, even, will see it as pitiful. One's sympathy for Jane, however, is tempered by the knowledge that she has the intelligence and resources to leave this life whenever she likes. What about her co-workers who don't have her advantages, who really don't have a choice? Jennifer Blowdryer's introduction compares Jane Graham to Kerouac, but I think better comparisons can be made with the William Burroughs of the *Junkie* and *Queer* period, Orwell's *Down and Out in Paris and London*, or Jack London's *The People of the Abyss*. Like these, *Floozy* is a report from the shady side of the street by someone who's been there, but isn't actually from there. This is not to say that Jane Graham is as good a writer as Burroughs, Orwell, or London. She's a perfectly adequate one, though. My favourite chapter is 'The Tattooed Lady', in which she describes getting a large tattoo, and then having sex wearing the new design, with tenderness and verve:

> ... as she watches his cock teasing at the entrance she watches the dragon also, its wings and claws tightening as she lures his cock into its lair, watches them unfurl as her belly lets out small spasms of ecstasy.

This is the only point in the book at which the sex act is described in pleasurable terms. It is also one of only two chapters written in the third person — make of that what you will.

Jane's stories are nicely set off by Xtina ('Christina', presumably) Lamb's clean-limbed pen and ink illustrations, some of domestic details (keys, bags, photos), and some of people doing rude things. Add to this a nifty square format, and the modest price tag, and *Floozy* is a recommended product. [Simon Collins]

FLOWERS FROM HELL
£11.95 / $19.95 / pb / 285pp / ISBN 1840680245 /
Creation 2001 / www.creationbooks.com

THE GRAY'S ANATOMY
£10 / $15 / pb / 240pp / ISBN 1852426357 /
Serpent's Tail 2001 / www.serpentstail.com

HARRIET STAUNTON
£5 / pb / ISBN 0952813599 / Visual Associations 1999 / 3 Queen Adelaide Court, Queen Adelaide Road, Penge, London, SE20 7DZ, UK / available direct from publisher, payable Visual Associations, incl p&p

I'D RATHER YOU LIED
£9.95 / pb / 219pp / ISBN 1899598103 / Codex / www.codexbooks.co.uk

THE IMAGE OF THE BEAST/ BLOWN
£9.95 / $15.95 / pb / 319pp / ISBN 1840680288 / Creation 2001 / www.creationbooks.com

JUNK DNA
£7.95 / $12.95 / pb / 189pp / ISBN 1899598197 / Codex 2001 / www.codexbooks.co.uk

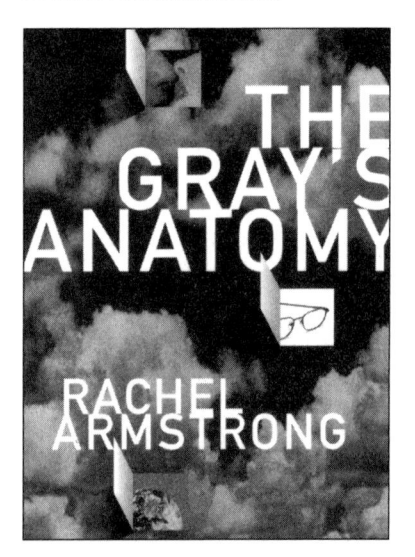

Update Slab-O-Concrete Publications is no more, but sister publisher Codex may be able to point you in the right direction for a second-hand copy [w] www.codexbooks.com

FLOWERS FROM HELL
A Satanic Reader
Ed. Nikolas Schreck

What a good idea! A Satanic Reader which samples some of the major infernal texts from the renaissance to the present, along the way taking in Gothic literature (Beckford, Lewis and Maturin) epic poetry (Danté and Milton), decadence (Poe, Baudelaire and Huysmans), modernist wit (Max Beerbohm's delightful 'Enoch Soames' is rightfully included) and 'inspired' occult texts from Aleister Crowley and Temple of Set alumnus, Michael Aquino. The illustrations, though mostly a little over familiar (Rops, Beardsley, Doré, Von Stück) are appropriate and plentiful. But the most outstanding aspect of this timely volume is editor Schreck's thirty page introduction, which is a model of precise, assured scholarship without an ounce of excess verbiage, or the type of woolly circumlocution of which the typical Left-Hand Path occultist is so fond. In wake of Schreck's previous book from Creation (*The Satanic Screen*) this comes as further confirmation that Nikolas Schreck is without doubt the clearest and most cogent commentator working in the 'satanic underground' at present. [Stephen Sennitt]

THE GRAY'S ANATOMY
Rachel Armstrong

This bizarre and curiously disinterested novel by Dr Armstrong at first takes the form of a 'future history' on the scale of Olaf Stapledon's classic *First And Last Men*. However, this exciting premise is only there to set up a background to the main plot, in which a Gray alien anatomist named The Chronicler psychically and physically probes a vapid Earth female named Candy. The rest of the novel explores the complex results and ramifications arising from their ensuing relationship and its effect on the society of Grays which inhabit the unlikely-named planet Rune 66. The Grays scientific and social hierarchy is explored in immense detail by Armstrong, and every component of their lifestyle and culture is examined exhaustively. This is good in parts, but the whole is strangely bereft of any engaging philosophy and the book is therefore for the most part 'flat' and (most surprisingly) not particularly thought provoking. The backcover blurb describes *The Gray's Anatomy* as a 'cunning satire' both 'intoxicating' and 'outlandish'. It certainly is outlandish, but not, I think, intoxicating at all; certainly not in comparison to other intellectual/satirical sci-fi I've read by the likes of Sladek, Disch, Vonnegut, P K Dick and Gibson, which despite their knowing irony still retain something of the essential sci-fi ingredients of cosmic wonder and excitement. [Stephen Sennitt]

HARRIET STAUNTON
A Victorian murder ballad
M J Weller

On Friday 13, 1877, the body of thirty-six-year-old Harriet Staunton was found at a house at Penge, in South East London, apparently a victim of "cerebral disease and apoplexy". A few days earlier, her baby son Tommy had also died. At a widely-publicised trial, Harriet's husband and young in-laws were accused of murdering her by starvation. Author M J Weller takes what has the potential to be a really fascinating story, and instead of analysing details of the case, re-enacts the story in the style of a 'Victorian murder ballad' — though thankfully not in verse — which leads to a lot of tedious and ham-fisted attempts to reproduce Victorian diction and courtroom style. Section titles include 'Go Back, Missus Harriet', and 'Is She Keeping the Food Down, Clara?'. Yet another reason to steer clear of small press fiction. [Mikita Brottman]

I'D RATHER YOU LIED
Selected poems 1980–1998
Billy Childish

From the wood-carved naked image
Her womb is washed and stained
From flowing tears of Billy Childish
Published on page two.

How quickly two decades have raced away
And how quickly our little Billy has grown
The result: the angry young man
Shot paradoxically across the universe
Determined verse to undermine
Overthrow his inner demon
To rehabilitate the soul and create fever
Throughout his existentialist university.

We salute you one hundred and thirty eight
Page compendium.
A guide light through our night
A template to daylight that promises
Bliss.

This I give to you, an inspirational high
A proposal of beauty and truth.
Or would you rather I'd lied.

[Will Youds]

THE IMAGE OF THE BEAST/ BLOWN
Philip Jose Farmer

Two groundbreaking horror-sci-fi-porn novels in one book by Farmer which rocked the staid world of sci-fi when they appeared in the late sixties from sleaze paperback outfit Essex House (incidentally, a copy of the Essex edition of *Image* recently sold for $180 in a LA book auction!). Really graphic, full-on, horrifying stuff which seems as shocking today as it did originally, *Image* is without doubt the better of the two because *Blown* suffers from being too retrospectively kind to the mildly irritating Forest J Ackerman for its own good. The new cover by John Coulthart is mind-blowingly great, making this item an essential purchase. [Stephen Sennitt]

JUNK DNA
Tania Glyde

I was a little wary of this novel at first, since I'm not a fan of science fiction, and *Junk DNA* is set in a strange, future London peopled by malicious children, sexually-frustrated housewives, Heritage Counsellors, postmodern performance art and capitalism gone horribly askew. Things start to look up, however, when we are introduced to the main character, Regina Voss, a forty-something feminist who makes her living as an unconventional sex therapist, and performs erotic performance art on the side. The real emphasis here is on 'unconventional' — one of her favorite techniques, for example, is to masturbate her female clients to orgasm by hand, and she's a great fan of bringing sex toys into the therapeutic relationship. Her services suddenly become increasingly popular when she starts to incorporate stolen pharmaceuticals into her work — drugs devised by men to make women into perfect sexual partners (that's right — no sagging breasts, no chubby hips) which have the additional effect of making children appear disgusting and repellent (the perfect female partner: firm tits and no interest in children?).

On the subject of children, we next meet Lucy, Regina's upstairs neighbour — a bizarre, precocious brat obsessed with the colour white, despised by her parents and rejected by her schoolfellows. When the two women get together after murdering Lucy's mother and father (mother's corpse is tucked away in the deep-freeze), they embark on a series of grotesque and witchy genetic experiments, starting with mice and working their way up to minor celebrities.

Junk DNA is the second novel from provocative writer and sardonic performance artist Tania Glyde. A strange, erotic morality tale set in a dystopian, post-Thatcherite England gone to the dogs, it reads like a sexy and accessible fusion of Angela Carter and William Burroughs. The book is at its weakest when there's too much going on — a transvestite in peach silk camiknickers, a sexually obsessed ex-boyfriend, pregnant women, writhing worm-like creatures, pools of menstrual blood, psychedelic drugs, ravaging genetic diseases, animal experiments, performance art. In such places, the urban landscape is hard to visualise

KILLER FICTION
$14.95 / pb / 308pp / ISBN 0922915431 / Feral House 1997 / PO Box 13067, Los Angeles, CA 90013, USA / www.feralhouse.com

MANCHESTER SLINGBACK
£5.99 / pb / 272pp / ISBN 033036927X / Picador 1999 / www.panmacmillan.com

and the plot sometimes difficult to follow. Characters appear and disappear almost at random, and — since this is a world in which people seem simply to follow their sexual instincts, without judgement or restraint — motivations are sometimes rather difficult to discern.

But if you read the book as a kind of erotic, feminist magic realism, it really works. Dialogue is terrifically rendered, images are horribly unexpected, sex is hard and dirty, and the tone is consistently dark and warped. After two or three chapters I found myself totally engaged, not engrossed in the plot, necessarily, which is jumpy and sporadic, but dying to find out what black and twisted image I'd come across next — like the description of the mussels Regina is served in a restaurant, "soft, crumbly yet strangely greasy primrose-coloured things, like the tongues of diseased dwarves". A horrid, bizarre treat. [Mikita Brottman]

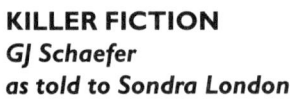

KILLER FICTION
GJ Schaefer
as told to Sondra London

Gerard John Schaefer's brutal, repellent short stories were one of the highlights (or low points) of the excellent 1996 Bloat Books compilation of the writings and artefacts of murderers, *Lustmord*, though I was already aware of his work from the 1993 book *Knockin' on Joe: Voices from Death Row* (Nemesis Books, edited by Sondra London). Schaefer was, until his death in prison in 1995, serving time for the 1972 murders of two young women in Florida. A serving policeman until his arrest, Schaefer was convicted partly on the evidence of writings found by the police in his room — writings that dwelt obsessively on fantasies of torturing, hanging and strangling women, and on the mechanical details of committing crimes and disposing of the bodies and weapons. These stories, under the heading 'Actual Fantasies', are included in *Killer Fiction*. Schaefer protested that these were merely 'realistic horror fiction', but the courts didn't believe him, and neither should you. Following his conviction, Schaefer continued to write, and in 1989, Sondra London's Media Queen company published the original edition of *Killer Fiction*, following a correspondence between Schaefer and herself in which he sent her manuscripts. It's fair to say that Ms London had a special interest in Schaefer's work — not only had she lost her virginity to him whilst they were (briefly) high school sweethearts, but she wound up marrying another serial killer doing time with Schaefer, Danny Rolling. The relationship between London and Schaefer is exhaustively, even boringly, documented in the present volume — from their first kiss to the death threats and paranoid rants he started to send her after their Media Queen arrangement turned bad. In America, Sondra London has been roundly (and rightly) excoriated for her grandstanding celebrity-killer-chasing groupie antics, but the original printing of *Killer Fiction* swiftly became an impossible-to-find-but-must-have collector's item for murder junkies everywhere. With this greatly-expanded reissue from Feral House, owning a copy is now within everyone's grasp. But do you really want it? Well…

Schaefer never copped to being a serial killer, nor indeed a killer of any sort, although the authorities believe that he may have killed up to thirty-four more people than the two he was convicted for. Instead, he adopted a teasing Ted Bundy-like attitude: whereas Bundy would ruminate hypothetically in the third person on his crimes, Schaefer would write about his own depredations in the most intimate, visceral, first-person reportage style, and then claim it was all fiction. No one reading these hellish documents, however, will doubt that Schaefer was as guilty as sin — his evil mindset drips off the pages. In story after story, young women are stalked, kidnapped, humiliated, tortured, executed and dismembered. And why must they die? Because they're *whores*, dammit! The little minxes have the temerity to reject poor Gerald's fumbling advances, and for this crime they deserve to be hung by the neck until they poo in their pretty pink panties (this physiological phenomenon is dwelt on at gloating length in *Killer Fiction*, and appears to have been the chief motive behind Schaefer's modus operandi). The titles of the stories — 'Whores: What to *do* About Them', 'Gator Bait', 'Blonde on a Stick', 'Flies in Her Eyes' — offer a fair indication of their contents, but don't even begin to hint at the awesome hatred, misogyny and rage of Schaefer's prose. Check it out:

I approached her, kicked her smartly in the ribs, and listened to the suppressed scream behind the gag. It hardened my cock. I unbuckled my pants... then slickened her cunt and anus with a handful of spit... I arose and returned to the trunk of my car. Flung the plastic-wrapped corpse of the blonde out onto the earth and removed it from the bags. I could feel Betsy's eyes following me... I severed the blonde's head, carried it to a steel spike and mashed her head down upon it. There was a curious squish as the rod went up into her brain, and goo began to drip on the ground.
I returned to Betsy. 'I want some ass, whore, or your head will be on the other stick.' Betsy made love like a dream.

Equally unpleasant are the 'Starke Stories', tales of doing hard time in Florida State Prison at Starke. The worst of these, 'Nigger Jack', serves up a potent brew of racial hatred, gloating misogyny, necrophilia and nihilistic terror, as Schaefer regales the hapless reader with every minute detail of the electrocution of a female prisoner and the subsequent sodomising of her corpse by the black orderly assigned to prepare the body for burial. This story caused a permanent rupture in the relations between Schaefer and his editor, London.

It is relatively rare for serial killers to meditate in print on their horrid deeds at such length, and this in itself makes *Killer Fiction* essential reading for true crime buffs and shameless gorehounds alike. Be warned, though, this is a seriously fuckin' unpleasant book — the only items I've come across that rival it in intensity are Carl Panzram's memoirs (also extensively extracted in *Lustmord*), and *Final Truth: Autobiography of a Serial Killer* by Donald 'Pee Wee' Gaskins (Mondo Books, 1993; reviewed in *Headpress 9*). Schaefer's literary career has been cut short by a prison shiv making little holes all over him in his cell in 1995 — it couldn't have happened to a nicer guy — but it seems unlikely that he would have produced anything startlingly different to the fifty or so pieces collected in this volume. His writing is way too obsessional and fixated for that. Schaefer fancied himself to be a great realist crime writer, telling it the way it really went down (or the way he wished it did).

My own books make no compromise in the presentation. I give you bloody murder in such a way that you recoil from it. My reader is not given a cheap thrill, but an emotional whipping... This book will give you sleepless nights.

This is no idle boast — reading *Killer Fiction* gave me bad dreams. Seriously. More risible are Schaefer's claims to be serving both God and mankind by writing as he does. I for one have no doubt that the composition of these grim little tales gave Schaefer endless hours of spunky-fingered joy, as he relived his crimes and imagined others he'd have gotten around to if only he'd had a little longer in which to prey upon co-eds and hitchhikers. And his claims to being a great writer are bullshit. In fact he totally lacks the kind of objectivity and critical distancing that makes for good art. They are raw, brutal, crude, unpolished and as intense as hell. Reading *Killer Fiction* is as close as I ever want to come to being at a murder scene, and Schaefer's peers agree — the back cover carries praise from John Wayne Gacy and Lawrence 'Pliers' Bittaker. If you didn't have it before, reading *Killer Fiction* will give you the thousand-yard stare for keeps. [Simon Collins]

MANCHESTER SLINGBACK
Nicholas Blincoe

MONKEY GIRL
$11.95 / pb / 128pp / ISBN 0916397491 / Manic D Press 1997 / Box 410804, San Francisco CA 94141, USA / www.manicdpress.com

THE MUSE-TRAP
136pp / Bella Basura, PO Box 5454, Leicester, LE2 0WP, UK / bella@pixie-inc.demon.co.uk

NEVER HIT THE GROUND
£10 / pb / 228pp / ISBN 190107207X / Pulp Books 1997 / PO Box 12171, London N193HB, UK / www.pulpfact.demon.co.uk

In a particularly apposite instance of synchronicity, I came across a copy of the biography of James Anderton (the religious zealot who used to run Manchester's police force), whilst reading Nicholas Blincoe's latest — *Manchester Slingback*, published by Picador. Not that I'm saying you need to read *God's Cop* (Michael Prince, New English Library) to enjoy or understand Blincoe's book, but rather that it serves to remind us of the real mania of the man who had been at the helm of Britain's second biggest police force. Anderton is the man who launched a crusade against filth, pornography and political subversion, which meant raids on gay bars, bookshops and publishers (like Savoy Books for example) and collusion with the National Front. Blincoe's book is set in that same era, though thanks to our libel laws *God's Cop* is here transformed into an acolyte of John Anderton — one John Pascal to be exact. And although the names have changed, the atmosphere comes across as depressingly authentic, the routine harassment of gays and pornographers a reminder of those days back in the eighties. And, just as it was then, while Pascal/Anderton see Sodom and Gomorrah in the grimy streets of Manchester, the real horrors are taking place in the children's homes outside the city.

Rent-boys, outrageous queens, Bowie clones and kids running away from institutionalised abuse; Blincoe paints a vivid picture of life in the dark underbelly of our second city. The story is all the more harrowing at times because Blincoe doesn't make a big deal of what was going on in the kids' homes. He doesn't revel in the horror to the detriment of his story or its characters, and the book's stronger because of it. The abuse is just another fact of life, just like police raids on queer bars and porn shops.

Like all of Blincoe's books, this one is shot through with a humour so black it almost makes you choke. This doesn't have the same edge of weird inventiveness that featured so strongly in *Jello Salad* (I for one will never forget how one of the characters is tied to a wooden beam), but somehow this is a stronger book. If you really want darkness, then this is the place to find it. It's everything that crime fiction ought to be. [Pan Pantziarka]

MONKEY GIRL
Beth Lisick

Sassy — that's how Beth Lisick comes across in this collection of short pieces and odd bits of poetry. Lisick is described as a "spoken word artist", and I can well imagine her on stage reading her stuff; it'd probably work better than it does written down like this. This is an easy book to read, it doesn't require too much thinking, it doesn't ask too many questions and it doesn't really stretch you too much. I read a big chunk of it in a hospital waiting-room and it was perfect. Hell, it even kept my hands off the stack of *Reader's Digest*s stacked up in the corner.

Lisick's observations of daily life are described as "wry", and that's as good a word as any. It can make you smile but don't expect to bust a gut laughing. And, just in case the longer bits (about five minutes a piece) get too much, the text is interspersed with speech bubble humourisms:

The day you are tempted to clip out a comic strip and post it on a bulletin board is the day you need to quit your job.

It's when she talks about her suburban upbringing that you get flashes of something interesting, but that alone's not enough to elevate this to the 'buy me' category. [Pan Pantziarka]

THE MUSE-TRAP
Bella Basura

In the nineteenth-century, a biologist whose name I can't recall became noted for ripping the guts out of cockroaches, replacing said organs with cotton wool: the roaches would continue on their merry way, none the wiser. I want to do a similar thing to *The Muse-Trap*. There's nothing malicious in this desire, just a sense of frustration over what this novel *could have been*. The frame of an interesting story is here, but the operation is necessary.

Through an autobiographical viewpoint, Bella Basura — mooching around on the dole — rejects the Gregorian calendar and replaces it with a lunar update, then launches on a search for the mythological Muses. She also attempts to make sense of 'The Muse-Trap', an orange pamphlet (included here) by the (fictional) Dr Gordon Tripp. Because of my own occasional visits to the wasteland of the unemployed, I like things that deal with that particular life: the despair, ennui and microcosmic needs that see you retreating further and further, physically and mentally. On the plus side, when else could you reverse your sleeping habits, for example, or spend all week in the library? This might have been the book to tackle such feelings, but Basura — a good writer, as her previous non-fiction work *Necrotourist* has proved — chooses to cloud her prose with ineffective novelties (The Cult Of St Giro being the starting point), repetitive style, cut-ups, and an assortment of possibly-existing supporting characters who carry with them the foetid aroma of ex-ravers (her boyfriend plays the bongos, for fuck's sake!). A pity, as there are glimpses of what *The Muse-Trap* could have been, stripped of its guts:

I spent the day in distracted disappointment, mainly gazing out of the window, watching the traffic, cars storming up and down. The occasional harebrained cyclist, cold to the bone.

But such places are few and far between. *The Muse-Trap* reads like it was written for the eyes of friends only, hence the hand-bound limited edition of twenty-three. I've probably got someone's copy here — they're welcome to have it back.

If ever a book deserved to be grabbed by a publisher, updated, expanded and pitted with illustrations, then *Necrotourist* — travelogues to places of the dead — is that book. I'm afraid I can't say the same for this one. Here's hoping Basura gets her walking boots back on soon. [Martin Jones]

NEVER HIT THE GROUND
Kirk Lake

Ray Gardner is a petty crook looking for a grubstake so that he and Lisa can quit the urban wasteland of South London for sunnier climes. Unfortunately, Ray is not only broke, he's also in the shit with Rudi, an altogether more heavy duty crook, for selling bad drugs in Rudi's club, Hades (it's supposed to be called Shades, but the neon sign's bust). Rudi is not a nice man. Rudi has an ashtray made out of a hand on his desk. That's the kind of man Rudi is. Ray finds himself coerced into taking Rudi's prize Siamese fighting fish over to Amsterdam for an important bout, and he decides to try to turn the situation to his own advantage after his old mucker Loose Joints tells him about a bloke he knows who's looking for someone to mule Es back to London. Even though the whole deal stinks worse than a dead fighting fish, Ray gets on the ferry. Lisa goes along for the ride. Loose Joints goes along to effect introductions. Harry and Rootboy, two other companions-in-villainy of Ray's, are flown over by Rudi to keep an eye on his fish (which, natch, turns out to be no fish at all). Meanwhile, Absolutely Sweet Marie and Queen Jane Approximately, a pair of transsexual drag queens financing their hormones and operations via shoplifting and prostitution, see a big break coming their way when Queen Jane is offered a plum part in a porn flick. The location? Yup, ol' Sin City, Amsterdam.

So far, so noir, so good, eh? Well, I thought so, too, but there are serious problems with this debut novel from Kirk Lake. Ray's incessant attempts to play both ends against the middle make him a less than sympathetic protagonist, and when he and Lisa come to a sticky end, I was neither surprised nor saddened. Lisa is never sufficiently developed as a character, though there are some intriguing touches (the collage of eyes she constructs above her bed, her sudden ability to bottle a guy to death). Queen Jane and Sweet Marie seem entirely dispensable — I was expecting their parallel story line to converge with the main plot

NINETEEN SEVENTY SEVEN
£6.99 / $14 / pb / 341pp / ISBN 1852427442 / Serpent's Tail 2000 / www.serpentstail.com

NOIROTICA 3
$16 / pb / 269pp / ISBN 1892723034 / Black Books 2001 / www.blackbooks.com

PENNY IN HARNESS
£5.99 / pb / 256pp / ISBN 035233651X / Nexus 1998 / Thames Wharf Studios, Rainville Road, London W6 9HT, UK / www.virginbooks.com

PRETTY THINGS
£8.99 $16.95 / pb / 208pp / ISBN 1891241125 / Verse Chorus 2001 / www.versechorus.com

in some ingenious manner, but it never happens, and I'm not very convinced by the notion of Dylan-worshipping drag queens anyway. I mean, Bob Dylan?! He's not exactly gay icon material, is he? Structurally, the book divides very neatly in half — London/Amsterdam — the latter half being considerably pacier than the former, which is slow to get going. But then the resolution is a mess — lifelike, maybe, but not aesthetically satisfying.

The urbane, streetwise style of *Never Hit The Ground* places it in the modern crime fiction territory previously staked out by Elmore Leonard (*Get Shorty*, *Rum Punch* et al), Robert Campbell (*In La-La Land We Trust*), and, especially, James Hawes (the excellent *A White Merc With Fins*, the less excellent *Rancid Aluminium*), but Kirk Lake has some ground to cover before he's as good as any of these authors. I don't enjoy being negative about people's work, still less when it's their first novel, but I just couldn't get much satisfaction from this — sorry. But then, the book jacket is adorned with praise from *NME* and *Dazed and Confused*, so why should Kirk Lake pay attention to what I think? [Simon Collins]

NINETEEN SEVENTY SEVEN
David Peace

The second in Peace's Yorkshire Noir trilogy (*Nineteen Seventy Four* was the first) follows alcoholic true crime journo Jack Whitehead and not-completely-corrupt cop Bob Fraser as they search through the whore houses, red light districts, porno scum, police corruption, lies, racism and human degradation for the Yorkshire Ripper. Like James Ellroy, Peace uses actual historical events as a springboard for his own explorations of the outer fringes of the human psyche, in this case the Ripper murders. Indeed if there is any comparison here it is with Ellroy's LA Quartet, and especially with *Black Dahlia*, which also uses the extreme violence enacted on supposedly fallen women as a way into the neither regions of the soul.

Stylistically, Peace writes in a stripped down, barren language that uses few words and relies on moments of punctuating repetition, in such a way as to make the whole page reflect the scream of his protagonists.

'Course, nothing Peace has done reaches the staccato brutality of Ellroy's *White Jazz*, but it took Ellroy ten-plus volumes to get there, and Peace already has an understanding of the genre that shows he's well on the way to becoming a master.

English *noir* is an understated genre — its true master remains Derek Raymond — but Peace has written a page-turner, and I'm already looking forward to the next volume of Yorkshire Noir. [Jack Sargeant]

Update I liked this book at the time, and was enthused by the notion of Yorkshire Noir, although reading this back I clearly used the word/phrase too often, and didn't really explain what I meant. Thus are all hasty reviews written.

NOIROTICA 3
Stolen Kisses
Ed. Thomas S Roche

Now here's a concept to toy with: an anthology that links *noir* crime narratives and erotica. *Noirotica 3* is a curate's egg, but I'll give it good marks for effort. As the editor points out in his well-crafted introduction, sex is a force that strains against the bounds of civilised behaviour and leads us to do, ooh, terrible things. Along with avarice, desire remains the chief motivating factor for crime. So then, these stories should make sense as a literary cross-pollination; after all, the writers are simply making explicit the undertones present in any detective novel.

Much as this may make theoretical sense, the formal and structural requirements of the *noir* thriller do not fit easily into the short story format, especially when they are jostling for space with passages of pervy prose. Tales such as 'Night Of A Thousand Fishes' prove that there is simply not enough room for any sort of narrative complexity in this form without the need for a writer to curtail the investigative details and end the story somewhat cursorily. Better, then, are the likes of 'Syndromes' (an amusing anecdotal piece, like a scene from a particularly smutty Quentin Tarantino film) or 'The Ghost Of Her' (which opts for freeform bleakness, emphasising the lovelessness of the genre). 'Hollwood Black' takes the latter's approach to some sort of logical conclusion, ignoring any sort of plot mechanics in favour of impressionistic prose; it ends with a rather nasty assisted suicide.

Whilst 'The Crush' serves as a reminder that *noir* stories are usually erotic even without any explicit sexual content, overtly pornographic contributions don't make for especially good stories. 'Faithful' demonstrates this, as does 'Private Dick', which also bores the reader with tired queer jokes and poor impersonations of Jim Thompson ('sheets of rain so ugly that K-Mart wouldn't stock them').

'Stone Cold Perfect' is perhaps the best melding of the two threads, using idioms of both whilst retaining its own identity; on the other hand, 'Girls Are A Nuisance' is simply crime with S&M trappings — or vice versa — with no feel for the actual subject matter.

Tighter editing could make this series a worthwhile prospect for the future. [Anton Black]

PENNY IN HARNESS
Penny Birch

From the wine label style 'Adults Only' warning to the tasteful B&W cover shot of the pouting blonde in PVC (looking like she's dressed for a Roxy Music album cover without realising that boat long since left the island), this wants to be sophisticated smut. Art Porn. It wants that title so bad that you can almost smell the *need* coming off of the pages. And, from the first line — "There are few things more embarrassing than getting caught short in the middle of nowhere" — to its promise of an insight into the "bizarre world of whips and harnesses, of crops and restraints", you would think it's pulled it off with ease.

But, this is a plain and simple fuck book. Admittedly there's more imagination and eloquence on display than in your average top-shelf mag's space-between-the-twats filler, but when our heroine has a corn cob up her arse by page eight you just know it's going to go all the way.

Employing a polite prose style, generously peppered with plenty of "wonderful" and lines like "after what seemed an eternity", Penny takes us through the initiation of a curious girl into the world of 'unusual' sex. From her first tentative fumblings in the woods through to her training as a 'Pony Girl' and ultimately to her graduation as a fully fledged 'mistress', our heroine never quite manages to satiate her appetite or, more appropriately, "Relieve the burning ache in her pussy."

For your money you get at least one major and one minor sex scene per chapter — ranging from eagerly delivered blow jobs to spankings, restraints, horsy rides, butt-plugs, dildos-a-plenty, blistering dyke action and some exquisitely detailed, well-lubricated, safe-sex buggery. And all performed behind the lace curtains and on the private acres of toffs in Wiltshire. Posh birds going at it like you were always told in school they did, and I just couldn't help but picture Liz Hurley as 'Penny', particularly during her description of, "her boyfriend's cock against my anus, pushing, breaking into me and then sliding up my bottom with what must be the rudest feeling of all." Come to think of it, if this was 'Our Liz' then surely Hugh Grant wouldn't have had to trawl in the gutter for a horror like Divine Brown with which to experience the seamier side of life. Just a thought. [Rik Rawling]

PRETTY THINGS
Susan Compo

Verse Chorus is an Oregon-based small press specialising in Rock music writing, so it seems fitting that Susan Compo's tale of agents, groupies and wannabes is part of their fiction imprint. *Pretty Things* is Compo's first novel after two short story collections, and is set on the fringes of the LA showbiz industry. Giselle Entwhistle is a talent agent with an unlikely roster of archetypes for her clients: country singer Len Tingle, teen idol Adon, child star Frances Culligan and her feckless mother, Rock impresario Hedda Hophead, Tupperware maverick Troy Harder,

RED WINE MOAN
£7.99 / $11.95 / pb / 138pp / ISBN 0916397629 / Manic D Press 2000 / www.manicdpress.com

SATAN! SATAN! SATAN!
£6.99 / pb / 128pp / ISBN 184068030X / Attack Books 1999

TITS-OUT TEENAGE TERROR TOTTY
£6.99 / pb / 260pp / ISBN 1840680326 / Attack Books 1999 / www.creationbooks.com

and a host of others.

Compo has a light, breezy style to match this frothy tale; the dialogue is unconvincing and the characters one-dimensional, but hey, this is LA, and that seems to be part of the point. What's more difficult to swallow is her endless repertoire of terrible puns; apparently, Compo's narrative voice has been compared to Dorothy Parker's, but Dorothy Parker doesn't makes you flinch the way Compo does. As the novel progresses, this punning seems to get almost pathological, and you have to work harder and harder to untangle passages like the following:

> Now that Tammy is officially out of Glee Club and her answer-song has some kind of legs, even if only in a nose-thumbing sense (she pictures the contortions), her former band is combusting like the dud log cabin in a five-dollar box of old fireworks. Glee Club's recent effort Outskirts featured a raucous cover of 'Johnny Get Angry', but it still got lost in a jukebox shuffle of platters.

Equally convoluted is the novel's structure. No sooner has the story got going than we're caught in the middle of a book-within-a-book; there are so many characters that it's hard to keep them apart; an apparent murder turns out to be a red herring, and little comic vignettes take the place of a coherent plot line. There are some good things in the book — some moments that seem real, psychologically — but they're few and far between. You end up wishing the author concentrated more on things like plot and character, instead of trying quite so hard to be hip and funny. [Mikita Brottman]

RED WINE MOAN
Jeri Cain Rossi

Jeri Cain Rossi is an author (*Angel With a Criminal Kiss*), a musician (she's opened for Sonic Youth, The Birthday Party, and Nick Cave and The Bad Seeds) and a filmmaker (*Black Hearts Bleed Red*). Perhaps she's spreading herself a bit thin, because this collection doesn't really hang together. The theme of the book seems to be boho life in the sultry and exotic underworld of New Orleans, but the overriding vision is inconsistent. The first seven short stories are brief nihilistic vignettes of drunken bums and elderly strippers who inhabit a world like that of Hubert Selby Jr's *Last Exit to Brooklyn*, but less poignantly detailed. This is a promising start, but what follows is a 100-page story of a rather monotonous unrequited love affair — all flaming hearts and wine-fuelled passion — recounted in a naïvely humourless and romantic tone quite at odds with the bleak realism of the opening stories. Iris falls in love with Jack. Jack is kind and then cruel, leaves then returns, is devoted then heartless. Iris finds solace in red wine. A very uneven collection. [Mikita Brottman]

SATAN! SATAN! SATAN!
Tony White

TITS-OUT TENNAGE TERROR TOTTY
Steven Wells

Attack! is a new imprint from Creation Books dedicated to pulpy wannabe-cult fiction, or, as they themselves style it, 'avant-pulp' or 'literary punk rock'. These are two of the three titles currently available. With a distinctive graphic style and lots of manifesto-like propaganda at the back of the books, and even a club to join, just like the *Beano*, Attack! is evidently concerned with fostering a strong brand identity and reader loyalty, though I must admit being buttonholed with 'Oi! Reader!' and addressed in horrible sub-*Loaded* wideboy street talk

in your face, down your trousers and up your arse like a shit-eating rabbit on speed...

does not make me feel inclined to join in the fun. As all this is accompanied by a lot of vituperation directed at the literary 'establishment' ("the self-perpetuating ponce-mafia oligarchy of effete bourgeois wankers who run the 'literary scene'..."), it suddenly becomes clear that Attack! is the hellish mutant offspring of Stewart Home's attempts to update seventies New English Library 'yoof' fiction for the nineties. Be afraid, be very afraid... But what of the books themselves?

Satan! Satan! Satan! is by Tony White, author of *Road Rage*, which was (pretty unfavourably) reviewed in *Headpress 18*. The plot concerns a group of Goth girls in Leeds and their visit to the 'Festival of the Night' in Whitby to see a load of bands dressed in black. Bilko, a pathetic small-time speed dealer who has the hots for Debs, one of the Goth chicks, has his entire body tattooed with designs by occult visionary artist Austin Osman Spare in a misguided attempt to impress her. When this fails, he hares off round the country, indulging in a little ritual murder to attain his desires. Meanwhile, Vlad Vargstrom, asthmatic lead singer of mad Swedish Death Metal band The Dogs of Thor, is making elaborate plans for a memorable entrance to the festival at Whitby, and Jeremiah Jones, a demented evangelical Christian cult leader, is rallying his followers to picket the event. Little do they know that he has become possessed by the spirit of Jim Jones, and is planning to restage Jonestown in the seaside town...

I didn't like this book much at all. The plot was silly, the characters unengaging, and the whole thing culminates in an unholy mess at Whitby, which is doubtless meant to seem apocalyptic, but just reads like a mess. Even apocalypses need choreographing, if they are to read plausibly. The style is off-putting, too:

The magic words 'Access all areas' were printed across the front... They were dead cool, and Deb was gobsmacked.

Words like 'ace', 'sound', 'wicked' and 'brilliant' litter the narrative, not as part of reported speech, but as the authentic authorial voice. It's very hard to do this kind of writing in slang and get away with it. Mark Twain could do it. Iceberg Slim could do it. Irvine Welsh can do it. Tony White can't do it. I can see that it's meant to give a street feel to the text, but all it does is make the language dull and impoverished. Even more misjudged is the near-exact repetition of entire sentences and paragraphs throughout the text. Whenever there is a sex scene involving Debs (and there are many), it is described in nearly the same words. Why? If this book was by Martin Amis or Will Self or one of those clever fellers, I'd guess they were having a bit of a laugh about the predictability of life or the cyclical nature of narrative or something, but *Satan! Satan! Satan!* is nowhere near being a serious enough book to sustain these pretensions, and the device just seems bizarre and irritating. I also found the extensive quoting from Jim Jones' suicide speech a bit distasteful — taking a real-life tragedy like Jonestown and recycling it into pulp entertainment this flimsy and inconsequential seems like pure exploitation, and not exploitation of the enjoyable sort. If you're a dim teenage Goth from oop North who doesn't like reading, you might enjoy this novel. Otherwise, avoid.

Tits-Out Teenage Terror Totty is a rather more substantial piece of work, though I still didn't really like it. Steven Wells is perhaps better known as Seething Wells, the rant poet who achieved some notoriety in the early eighties alongside Attila the Stockbroker and John Cooper Clarke, and he has also worked on the *NME* and the excellent comedy show *The Day Today*. He is also the general series editor for Attack!, and thus has to shoulder some of the blame for *Satan! Satan! Satan!*

It's pretty impossible to attempt to summarise the plot of *TOTTT*, or even to quote an extract, as all the sentences in it are about three pages long, but it's set in a dystopian near-future UK featuring evil Tory vampires, a girl-power terrorist group led by Justine Justice, Margaret Thatcher sex-golems, weekly resurrections and ritualistic re-killings of Princess Diana, a rock band called Helen Keller's Iron Lung and assorted other highly-coloured but still recognisable exaggerations of the country we live in. The text

SISTERS OF SEVERCY
£5.99 / pb / 256pp / ISBN 0352332395 / Nexus 1998 / www.virginbooks.com

SLAVE OF PASSION
£9.99 / pb / 156pp / ISBN 1901838013 / Blue Sky Books 1998 / PO Box 79, Blackburn, Lancs, BB1 9GF, UK

SNAKE
£6.99/ pb / 213pp / ISBN 1852427183 / Serpent's Tail 2000 / www.serpentstail.com

SUBCULTURE
£9.95 / pb / 252pp / ISBN 0953795306 / Palmprint Publications 2000 / PO Box 1775, Salisbury, SP1 2XF, UK / www.palmprint.fsbusiness.co.uk

is almost impenetrably dense, the narrative careers along at a blink-and-you'll-miss-it pace, and there are frequent strange sound effects in large type. The whole thing comes across as a nightmarish circle-jerk involving William Burroughs, Terry Pratchett, Tom Sharpe and Douglas Adams, but this is not a compliment! I found it indigestible and annoying after a while — it's just so bloody noisy and hectic. Reading this book is like having a speed-freak yelling in your ear non-stop for hours. Or maybe I'm just getting old. *TOTTT* is certainly OTT, but it ain't really my cup o' tea! Whatever, I'm prepared to believe that some people will think this is brilliant, and will thus give it a cautious thumbs-up. You know better than I do if this sounds like something you want to read. According to the front cover, Irvine Welsh says this is 'Fucking brilliant', but the front cover of *Satan! Satan! Satan!* features Jesus Christ imploring us to 'Ban this evil book', so why should I believe one cover than the other?

Attack! books were the subject of an incomprehensibly reverential piece in the *Guardian Saturday Review* ("We're Brutal But Brilliant"), although the author, Elizabeth Young, protests too much in stating:

Only the most mean-spirited could deny the sheer energy and animation of the... books.

However, Creation are going to have to do better than this before they convince me that the future of British fiction lies in big block letters and exclamation marks. I just get the feeling that these authors would all rather be getting tanked up and pinching traffic cones than writing fiction, and since the yobs they're pitching their product at think that reading anything more than the sports pages and a Haynes car manual is for girls, it's difficult to see who's going to buy these books. [Simon Collins]

SISTERS OF SEVERCY
Jean Aveline

Like other forms of genre fiction — no, like all forms of information — erotica suffers from a serious noise problem. Gone are the days when you'd have to work hard to find a source of pornographic writing; these days every bookshop has an erotica section. In fact even my local corner shop regularly stocks between ten to twenty porn novels. That's part of the problem of course. There's just too much smut out there. And looking at those smut-laden shelves, the books all merge into one glossy mass. You want S&M? Tons of it. You want gay? Stacks of it. You want bitter and twisted; sweet and straight; bawdy romps? You name it and it's there on the shelves. Unfortunately most of it is utter dross. Clichéd, unadventurous, poorly written and taking up too much space. You see what I mean? Noise.

However, it's with some pleasure that I can point to at least one recent title worth the effort. *Sisters of Severcy*, by the pseudonymous Jean Aveline, is a real find; one of the best books from Nexus in a long while. Featuring an excellent cover by Christophe Mourthe, this is the story of a virgin, who, by the end of the book, remains exactly that — technically. One of the problems with much pornographic writing is that the emphasis is on the sexual acts themselves; characterisation, plot, location and narrative are too often sacrificed to the need to excite.

There are no such problems here. The writing is spare, the descriptions of place are vivid and atmospheric and it creates its own unique environment in which the characters grow and develop.

In many ways the book reminded me of the film, *Forbidden Planet*, itself based on Shakespeare's *The Tempest*. The character Alain takes on the mantle of Prospero, though sadly in this case the logical, incestuous relationship he has with his daughter Isabelle is not taken to its conclusion. Sadly Nexus guidelines forbid father-daughter incest, though the book goes a long way towards it. The book does have some faults: there are two strands to the book, one based on Isabelle and the other based on Charlotte, the wife of Robert (whom Isabelle is in love with), and the stories revolving around Charlotte have a different atmosphere about them, and they do nothing to move the story forward. They do provide, however, more of the S&M sex which is at the heart of this story.

Recommended to all fans of S&M, erotica and good writing in general. [Pan Pantziarka]

SLAVE OF PASSION
Xantia

"I am Xantia — Recorder of the Written Word."

There are photos of 'Xantia' at the back of this book — she's a middle-aged fetishist with the writing style of a filthy-minded adolescent who spends too long playing Dungeons and Dragons. And uses phrases like 'sex milk' and 'fuck cavern'. Anyway, this is the second book in her Thorean Master series, which is set on the planet Thor "where women are slaves and men are masters". The men have square dicks that, during coitus, grow a sort of sucker that attaches onto the woman's clit. Some Thorean nobles like Baal (eldest son of Titan) can deposit sex-dew inside a womb, which leads to powerful orgasms. There's also a race of yeti-type things called the Umar — they're the baddies. See what I mean about Dungeons and Dragons? It's a little puerile to ridicule this nonsense, since its author states that she writes solely to verbalise her sexual fantasies (which are extremely masochistic by all appearances) so good luck to her, I suppose — on that level if no other, the book is a success. Her first book sold 2,000 copies, a fair amount for this sort of thing, so she must be doing something right; however, her audience clearly values graphic torture sequences over graceful, fluid prose. I wish she wouldn't use bold print for S&M audio effects — **Wack! Wack!** (not much use for the letter 'h' on Thor) — and get shot of her artist, who cannot draw for toffee. Her 2,000 fans will he pleased to learn that she will be writing another book under her real name, Zephyr Beau-Bradley. Yeah, I'm so fuckin' sure.

Women are slaves and men are masters, eh? I know a planet a bit like that. [Anton Black]

SNAKE
Mary Woronov

Cult film star Mary Woronov (*Eating Raoul*, *Rock and Roll High School*) is perhaps best known for her associations with Andy Warhol's Factory (see her interview with Jack Sargeant in *Headpress 22*), but is also a talented writer. Her debut novel, *Snake*, is the story of Cassandra, a girl whose strange affinities with nature give way to sexual and emotional abandon as she drifts aimlessly through the LA Punk scene. Trapped in an abusive marriage to a wealthy business tycoon and S&M aficionado, she dreams of freedom, finally discovering an escape route in the arms of Luke, a handsome young hitman hired to kill her husband. Hunted by both the cops and the mob, Luke takes Cassandra with him to his cabin in Idaho, where, surrounded by rednecks and survivalists, she rediscovers her connection with the natural world. But Cassandra is haunted by strange fits during which she hallucinates a series of strange scenes set in an ominous Californian clinic. Are they prophecies of the future, like those experienced by Cassandra's mythical namesake, or flashbacks caused by too much LSD? Lyrical, surreal and unsettling, *Snake* works on a number of different levels. Sometimes Cassandra's passivity can get a bit annoying — despite her many displays of prodigious inner strength, she seems drawn to hollow relationships with destructive men — but, in a way, this is all part of her mysterious complexity. Like the snake of its title, this story twists and turns back on itself ambiguously, driven by a secret inner logic, then finally, when you're least expecting it, reveals the poisonous twist in its tail. [Mikita Brottman]

SUBCULTURE
Sarah Veitch

My first impression of this book was that the Nexus Classics imprint had had a make-over, and that they'd commissioned the extremely talented Lynn Paula Russell to do a cover. In point of fact this isn't a

TICK
£9.95 / $16.95 / pb / 224pp / ISBN 1840680482 / Creation 1999 / www.creationbooks.com

THE TORTURE GARDEN
£9.99 / $12.99 / pb / 128pp / ISBN 0965104265 / Juno Books 2000 / www.junobooks.com

Art from *Slave of Passion*.

Nexus book at all, though the delivery is close enough to fool the casual observer. However the name Sarah Veitch should be known to most Nexus readers, especially given the recent batch of classics which have been re-issued. To the uninitiated Ms Veitch specialises in Corporal Punishment (CP) fiction, with females on the receiving end of all manner of stern punishments. In addition to the Nexus novels and short story collection, she is also a regular in magazines like *Kane*, *Forum* and *Desire*.

Subculture is both Sarah Veitch's latest novel and also the launch title for a new CP press called Palmprint. The story involves a private Health Clinic in Malta, run by the enigmatic Dr Landers and his team of young, female staff. Arriving to work with Dr Landers is Lisa, the archetypal innocent abroad. What she discovers is that Dr Landers, a self-confessed disciplinarian, has no compunction in putting her across his lap. Here's an extract:

> "Glad to hear it," Michael said, "The rest of the staff are just beginning to enjoy your squirming." He watched the colour spread over the back of her neck and knew that her face was a similar shame-filled shade. "Time I put that nice plump cushion under your belly," he added softly, "so that your bum sticks even more fully out." He picked up the satin-clad square, "After all, an arse that's being punished should be a fully raised target. And we want the owner of that bottom to know that she can't escape."

Of course the story sounds familiar, much CP writing involves variations on a theme. Whether you go for it or not depends largely on whether spanking and CP are your thing. Palmprint are unashamedly targeting the CP aficionado, and with Ms Veitch kicking things off they can hardly go wrong. [Pan Pantziarka]

TICK
Peter Sotos

Peter Sotos, perhaps best known as frontman of the extreme noise band Whitehouse, describes himself as a 'pornographer', but *Tick* isn't easily recognisable as the pornography most of us are familiar with, and those compelled by this particular vision of lust, sadism and child-murder have probably already discovered Sotos' work long ago. For the rest, his work remains difficult, perhaps frightening; as a result, his writing tends to be either coarsely mocked or nervously shunned. Those who do review Sotos' books generally find his fascination with child abuse an easy target for ridicule and scorn. But Sotos is a talented writer with a loyal following, and his work deserves to be taken very seriously. *Tick* has no central narrative in the traditional sense, but is composed of a series of subtly interlinked and darkly contrasting vignettes. Questions posed to child-murderers in real criminal trials are juxtaposed with apparent first-person reminiscences, scenes from pornographic films, and incidents from actual sex murder cases reported in the press, or in crime literature (Polly Klaas, Nicole Brown Simpson, Matthew Shepherd, JonBenet Ramsey). This fusion of the factual and biographical is especially powerful, lifting the veil on the bleak truths of human sexuality and sexual relationships, and revealing some of the ways in which mediated depictions of and reactions to sex murder are one of the primary factors in the incitement to child abuse. Description takes the place of commentary, and the sordid violence of this psychosexual landscape is left to speak for itself. Sotos is most articulate when he allows his own pathology to speak through his art. When he does so, his own criminality becomes an adversarial gesture, as in the writing of Genet, which gives the finger to bourgeois society in a very similar way. Also like Genet, Sotos never seems to care very much about his market, or what others may think of him. Consequently, regardless of commercial concerns, he allows himself to pursue his deviant compulsion until it exposes the void beneath all 'legitimate' sexual acts. In brief, this is a very cruel book, but one that tells the truth about human nature, and the sordid extremes to which it leads us. [Mikita Brottman]

THE TORTURE GARDEN
Octave Mirbeau

This is a reprint of RE/Search books' 1989 edition of Mirbeau's notorious *fin-de-siècle* novel of passion and pain in imperial China. Opening with a framing device reminiscent of Conrad's *Heart of Darkness*, the narrator recounts his flight from France in the wake of a political scandal. Voyaging to Ceylon at the head of a trumped-up scientific expedition, he meets a certain Miss Clara on the ship, a hot-blooded young Englishwoman who, we are told, "was given to strange lapses, flights of fancy, incomprehensible caprices and terrible desires", and who possesses "teeth which so often have bitten into the bleeding fruits of sin". Crikey! Does her dentist know?

Clara, is in fact a dominatrix figure, a *belle dame sans merci* cut from the same cloth as de Sade's Juliette or Sacher-Masoch's Wanda. She says things like, "I promise you'll descend with me to the very depths of the mystery of love... and death!" It's always nice to see a French character getting instructed in the arts of love by an English one — the other example that springs to mind is Sir Stephen in *The Story of O.* Hey, if you want to learn to be a pervert, ask the English! Small wonder that our hero follows her to China rather than posing as an 'embryologist' (this must have meant something very different a hundred years ago!), dredging the pelagic ooze of the oceanic gulfs of Ceylon.

Once in China, the narrator's personal heart of darkness is attained in the torture garden of the title, an exquisitely decadent anti-Xanadu, a walled compound filled with temples, gardens palaces, pavilions, and, er, torture. Lots of torture. Torture of a fiendish, oriental and minutely described variety, judicial punishment of trivial offences raised to the level of an art form. This, it transpires, is Miss Clara's favourite place in all the world, and the narrator is simultaneously disgusted and fascinated as their tainted love spirals out of control towards an apocalyptic climax (I use the term advisedly!).

The Torture Garden is very much a book of its time. Its oriental exoticism, sexual perversity and preoccupation with sin and guilt are paralleled in the works of Mirbeau's contemporaries Beardsley, Wilde, Huysmans, Swinburne and indeed the young Aleister Crowley. An unflinching willingness to question the basis of all morality aligns Mirbeau with Nietzsche, who died in 1900, just a year after the first publication of *The Torture Garden*. Mirbeau's anarchist and republican sympathies are evident right from the dedication page: *"To Priests, Soldiers, Judges — to men who rear, lead or govern men I dedicate these pages of murder and blood."*

The opening sequence, featuring an assembly of emblematic worthies (a lawyer, a scientist, a writer, a philosopher etc) discussing the nature of murder, is highly reminiscent of de Sade's writings, in particular the *One Hundred and Twenty Days of Sodom*. A number of topical references throughout the book — to the Dreyfus affair that divided France at the time, to European colonialism — reinforce the authentically *fin-de-siècle* tone of world-weary disgust:

In China life is free, joyous, complete, unconventional, unprejudiced, lawless... at least for us... Europe and its hypocritical, barbaric civilisation is a lie.

This strand of thought connects *The Torture Garden* to the misanthropic French literary tradition of the twentieth-century, extending through Céline, Camus and Sartre to Genet. Whilst on the evidence of this book I would hesitate to place Mirbeau in the same class as these writers, this novel is still highly readable, reasonably short, and filled with enough kink and gore to titillate the jaded palates of *Headpress* readers.

There is, though, a fundamental contradiction at the core of Mirbeau's book. On the one hand, he seems determined to produce a politically engaged indictment of social institutions, a blazing denunciation of colonial and imperial power structures, but this seemingly righteous and noble aim is fatally undermined

BAPTISED IN THE BLOOD OF MILLIONS
£20 / hb / 254pp / Savoy 2001 / 446 Wilmslow Road, Withington, Manchester, M20 3BW / office@savoy.abel.co.uk / www.savoy.abel.co.uk

by the slavering enthusiasm and intricately bejewelled prose with which he delineates all the torture and violence. As de Sade could have told him, condemning sin whilst simultaneously revelling in it is a very tricky balancing act to pull off, and in my view Mirbeau doesn't succeed. This makes *The Torture Garden* a curio rather than a classic, though it's still worth reading.

As always with RE/Search and Juno books, this edition is well produced, although I would question the appropriateness of the oversized coffee-table book format for a novel — long double columns of text don't make for the easiest reading. And I must admit that the copious photographic illustrations by Bobby Neel Adams — stagy soft-focus tableaux of people in indeterminate period dress with their heads averted — didn't really add to my appreciation of the text. I would have preferred to see some appropriate Symbolist pictures by Mirbeau's contemporaries.

The best reason to read *The Torture Garden* is the brilliant central conceit of the garden itself, which not only lent its name to the famous fetish club, but also stands in a noble tradition of walled gardens of more or less corrupt pleasures extending back for centuries, including Coleridge's *Kubla Khan*, of course, along with the *One Thousand and One Nights*, the tales of Hassan-I-Sabbah, the Old Man of the Mountains and his *hashishin*, and Coleridge's source materials in the journals of Marco Polo. Did you know that the word 'paradise' is derived from the Persian for 'hunting park'? I was also reminded of Blofeld's Japanese suicide garden in the James Bond novel *You Only Live Twice*.

Ah, yes! The Torture Garden! Passions, appetites, greed, hatred and lies; laws, social institutions, justice, love, glory, heroism and religion: these are its monstrous flowers and its hideous instruments of eternal human suffering. What I saw today, and what I heard, exists and cries and howls beyond this garden, which is no more than a symbol to me of the entire earth.

[Simon Collins]

SAVOY

BAPTISED IN THE BLOOD OF MILLIONS
A Novel of
Fucking Holocaust Terror
David Britton

Is literature dangerous?

Big glow-worms, red as cinders, made entrance from his stretched bowels, walking *right* out, onion-stenched, the colour of niggers dropped smooth on their heads. How could I see this in the flame? I do not know, but answer carefully that all that can be viewed is *never* the full canvas; and stood foursquare before that blaze-topped being resembling (as I have stated) Azazel, the goat shamen, that reviled pig of the Jew.

Hanged boys, their cocks spurting as their necks snap, can be found in branches of Waterstones up and down the country: check the fiction section, under B for Burroughs. The excesses of fashionable shock merchants like Brett Easton Ellis and Dennis Cooper nestle alongside bloated Jilly Cooper novels; even works explicitly detailing the fine points of the greatest bugbear of the day, child sexuality and abuse, have found a home here. A distinction is made, a line drawn. This is literature. Where one burns books, one finally burns people. And Savoy?

I want a better England. Who could not want a better England? Not just a return to empire and expansion, but *real* pride expressed in old Albion, in our national achievements, which is superior to all countries excepting Germany. We rode unseeingly into the valley of cursed blood, and to our detriment we allowed foreign blood to pollute our sacred heritage. England has become a mongrel circus. The rejects, the spastics, the bent, the mental cripples of the world have gleefully mounted our motherland, in the process fucking her down to her knees, without clemency. Handouts to every sub-continent of ethnic wasters on earth have weakened our divinity. What is England now but the laughing stock of the earth? So unsure of our worth that under the guise of liberal moralising, we throw away our greatest asset — the pureness of English blood.

It is perhaps unfair to start any review of a Savoy product referring to censorship. Savoy have been around for such a long time, and have published such a wide variety of books, that to be considered solely as the victims of a tyrannical state's efforts to silence the subversive must be galling for them. And yet it is keenly pertinent here. The first Lord Horror novel, *Lord Horror*, published in 1990, was the first book to be banned in England since Hubert Selby Jr's *Last Exit to Brooklyn* in 1968; the ban was overturned on appeal in 1992. The Lord Horror comics have similarly come under fire, with some still banned to this day. Lord Horror's strong stuff, make no mistake.

So what's so contentious? Books dealing with the Holocaust, anti-Semitism and fascism are hardly new. The Holocaust has indeed attained iconic status as the ultimate display of man's inhumanity to man — a nightmarish other-world of pure evil, the kind of thing that could never happen in England. The industry surrounding the revisiting of the Holocaust today, from high-budget Hollywood recreations to tourist trips to Auschwitz, an inverse Disneyland, strengthens the iconography by ensuring that the Holocaust and Nazi Germany occupy bogeymen position in our minds — a kind of fairytale grimness hangs over these revisited scenes. But allowing the imagination free rein to play with the established iconography is strongly taboo; any divergence is often punished by law, demonstrating not only a panicked reaction to the spectre of neo-Nazism but also a keen desire to keep the boundaries clearly marked. We are good. They are bad. We could not do this. We are not responsible. It's a similar dichotomy to that found in the phenomenon of 'true crime', and the press coverage of paedophiles and child killers: a demonising which serves to distance 'us' from 'them', a reassurance that this is what 'pure evil' is like. Inhuman, bestial — these people couldn't possibly be like us.

Such passionate hatred is only seen elsewhere on these shores in the reaction of some parts of the British population to immigration — newsgroup postings with titles like 'send them back or string them up' are not uncommon. Immigrants (a distinction is occasionally but not often made between illegal immigrants and asylum seekers) are filthy, lazy and greedy; not a million miles from the projected face of Jews in Nazi Germany. But of course *that* could never happen here — although there were English sympathisers to the Nazi cause. It blurs the boundaries a little, so they're not discussed much nowadays. One was William Joyce, who broadcast Nazi propaganda from Germany to Britain; he was better known as Lord Haw-Haw, whose doppelgänger here is Lord Horror.

The world of Lord Horror is one which takes the constituent elements of the Holocaust and the culture surrounding it — along with liberal dashes of absurdist humour, modernist literature and full-bore rock'n'roll — and forces them together in ways which simultaneously don't fit and perversely shed more light on the psychology of fascism than any number of more straight-laced tomes. The world of Lord Horror is one of irreducible weirdness. There's no discernible plot development, either here or in the Lord Horror comics; just a cycle of horrific atrocities peppered with grotesque comedy. Burning Jews rain from the sky, confectionery spilling from every orifice; new extremes of slaughter are matched blow for blow with new extremes of absurdity. It's not only the content which jars, either; the style is a similarly bizarre mix of register, arcane dialogue mixing with wartime slang and a continual use of asides — Horror's thoughts on life, the universe, buggery and the judicious use of a straight razor.

THE EXPLOITS OF ENGELBRECHT

£20 / hb / 194pp / ISBN 0861301072 / Savoy 2000 / 446 Wilmslow Road, Withington, Manchester, M20 3BW / office@savoy.abel.co.uk / www.savoy.abel.co.uk

THE GAS

£10 / pb / 180pp / ISBN 0861300238 / Savoy 1980 / 446 Wilmslow Road, Withington, Manchester, M20 3BW / office@savoy.abel.co.uk / www.savoy.abel.co.uk

MONSIEUR ZENITH THE ALBINO

£20 / hb / 250pp / ISBN 0861301099 / Savoy 2001 / 446 Wilmslow Road, Withington, Manchester, M20 3BW / office@savoy.abel.co.uk / www.savoy.abel.co.uk

"…Our frail human forwards are too light…" from 'The day we played Mars', *The Exploits of Engelbrecht*. Art: James Boswell

It's important to see *Baptised in the Blood of Millions* as the latest instalment of an ongoing project, dovetailing neatly into the space left by the first Lord Horror novel and the Lord Horror comics, which have been published at an astonishingly slow rate — about one a year at present — since 1989. The text in the Lord Horror comics is more impenetrable than that on offer here, some issues being made entirely of cut-ups from works like *The Waste Land* and *Ulysses*; but the fact that the series features some of artist John Coulthart's most impressive illustrations makes it an essential read, if not the only British comic around worth reading. *Baptised in the Blood of Millions* presents the Horror universe in a different light altogether; while the comics present a sense of fracture and discontinuity, all fragmented quotations and looping atrocities, this is presented in the style of an autobiography, with Horror concomitantly awarding himself the airs and graces of a turn-of-the-century dandy, proud as a peacock. The style and content here are moreover absurdist rather than modernist, and Horror's egotism reveals his fallibility and weakness — a far cry from the superheroic character of the comics.

As tasters for the Lord Horror universe, either will do — you'll want to investigate more, even if neither the comics nor the book can truly be said to entertain. Britton's vision is too dark, his take both too bizarre and too perfectly fitting for this to be an easy read — but you can be sure, at a time when popular fiction has all the verve of a limbless whippet, that it'll be like nothing you've ever seen before. [James Marriott]

THE EXPLOITS OF ENGELBRECHT
Maurice Richardson

This is the first in a series of fantasy classics from Savoy — other books in the series include *Zenith the Albino* by Anthony Skene and *The Killer* by Colin Wilson. As the good people of Savoy are keen to point out, these are no ordinary reprints. Unlike Millennium's current Fantasy Masterworks series, these are not set from old galleys, but are exquisitely produced, limited edition hardbacks with a good deal of supplementary material — in this case artwork from John Coulthart, Kris Guidio and James Cawthorn, a further Richardson story, an introduction by Cawthorn and an epilogue by Michael Moorcock. This last casts Richardson as a boozy chancer, as quick with his fists as his wit and ever keen to trade a story for a drink — a writer who'd fit seamlessly into any Iain Sinclair book — but for me the defining reference point is a photo of him in late middle age, looking like a cross between J G Ballard and Terry-Thomas. The style of prose here isn't far off such a cross, either: English Surrealism with the psycho-sexual seriousness replaced by a sense of theatrical fun.

Unlike most other Savoy products, and to the inevitable disappointment of the Greater Manchester authorities, *Engelbrecht* is a book which contains no graphic bloodletting, no sexual deviancy (unless you count the pugilist dwarf's date with a Giant Sundew) and nothing to make it inaccessible or dull to, say, a nine-year-old who liked Harry Potter books. And mescaline. What it does contain is a series of extracts from the Surrealist Sportsman's Club Chronicles, in which the titular boxer, a gentleman of short stature and simian aspect, is pitted against an assortment of foes and obstacles, from villainous octopi to Butlin's Redcoats. That the dwarf should prevail each time is the only thing to be expected — otherwise there's a gleeful sense of play at work here, unlikely juxtapositions carried by a lean, pacy prose style and offset by perfect comic timing. You can imagine Richardson honing the stories on bleary-eyed cronies in favoured drinking dens — they're made to be listened to — and a *Sir Henry at Rawlinson's End* musical treatment would work perfectly. It's criminal that *Engelbrecht* hasn't enjoyed the same degree of exposure as *Sir Henry* — both are true classics of English Surrealism — and hopefully this Savoy edition will go some way towards restoring the balance. [James Marriott]

THE GAS
Charles Platt

> "I love you," she was wailing, embracing him, pressing her tear-stained cheek to his chest, rubbing her crotch against his stomach. "I love you, daddy!"

Although *The Gas* was first published in the States in 1970, it remained unpublished in Britain until 1980, when those naughty boys at Savoy (*Meng & Ecker*, *Lord Horror*, *Reverbstorm* etc) unleashed it as part of their campaign to aggravate the forces of law and order in the person of James Anderton of the Greater Manchester Police (see the *Headpress* anthology *Critical Vision* for further details). The novel has remained an underground classic of sorts, and copies of the 1980 printing are still available, albeit at a somewhat revised price.

The Gas relates the story of Vincent, a research scientist at a secret lab in the West Country, who witnesses an accident which releases an experimental gas into the atmosphere above Britain, a gas which provokes uncontrollable lust and aggression in those exposed to it. As Vincent tries to reach London, where his wife and children are waiting to flee to the hills with him, the country falls into increasing social disorder. Vincent, reunited with his family and travelling with a young hitchhiker, Cathy, and a renegade priest, drives from London to Cambridge, where the book's Bacchanalian climax ensues in King's College chapel.

Whilst *The Gas* is not very well written, and is easily outclassed by the tales to which it may most easily be compared — *The Day of the Triffids* by John Wyndham, J G Ballard's *High Rise* and *Concrete Island*, David Cronenberg's film *Shivers* — Platt does score heavily in the visceral gross-out stakes, and there are several set pieces that linger nastily in the mind: the exploding Cambridge landlady, for instance, the panorama of perversion found in the engineering and medical labs, the incestuous orgy in which Vincent and his gas-happy family indulge, the demented coprophagous sci-fi fan and the dog-masturbating policeman. Philip José Farmer, in his not very illuminating introduction, also mentions the parachute sex and the postie shagging the letter-box, and indeed these and many other lurid interludes are both funny and lively, but I think Farmer is altogether too generous to the book's rather ham-fisted attempts at satire. Sure, there are orgiastic nuns, randy vicars, mad scientists, and so on, but this does not make *The Gas* the equal of *Gulliver's Travels*. It is a scurrilous, scatological, puerile, silly book — and perfectly enjoyable on that level! The hilariously bad cover art is a fair indication of the unsubtle delights within. [Simon Collins]

Note For years, *The Gas* was the book that critics steadfastly refuse to review. To our knowledge, the above, as it appeared in *Headpress 18*, was the first review of *The Gas* to appear in print in Britain in almost two decades.

MONSIEUR ZENITH THE ALBINO
Anthony Skene

This is the second in Savoy's series of classic reprints, and while it isn't

MOTHERFUCKERS
£20 / hb / 250pp / ISBN 086130098X / Savoy 1996 / 446 Wilmslow Road, Withington, Manchester, M20 3BW / office@savoy.abel.co.uk / www.savoy.abel.co.uk

as essential a publication as the first (*The Exploits of Engelbrecht*), it's still well worth a look. Skene was a pulp writer working principally with 'the sleuth of the second-rate', Sexton Blake, from 1916 to 1948. Zenith was conceived originally as one of Blake's more colourful villains, jockeying for position with 'reincarnated High Priests of Ancient Egypt' and 'avenging toffs', and became from his first appearance one of the most popular adversaries in the Blake universe. Readers just couldn't get enough of the albino's deathly pallor, immaculate grooming and death-defying opium habit, and Skene wrote almost sixty novellas along with fifteen full-length novels featuring the dapper yet freakish master criminal. Here Zenith appears without Blake, and is pitted instead against examples of the more crassly criminal element, as well as two typically hapless policemen.

Notwithstanding Sexton Blake's reputation as 'the office boy's Sherlock Holmes', Monsieur Zenith has more than a little of Conan Doyle's creation himself, being, as already mentioned, a prodigious user of opiates, a master of disguise and a virtuoso violinist. Although Zenith operates on the wrong side of the law, he is morally on the side of justice, for all his amoral posturing — when a lady's welfare is at stake Zenith knows just what to do.

Despite Skene's punchy, highly readable style, this isn't a forgotten masterpiece. But as a criticism this misses the point. Zenith is a character delirious enough to deserve to live on — equal parts Holmes, Fantomas and Diabolik, as well as having been a formative influence on Moorcock's Elric — and Savoy's presentation here makes the volume nothing less than a paean to weird pulp in all its crazed glory. Not only is the original text incredibly obscure — the publishers are aware of only three extant copies — but Savoy have also included original Zenith illustrations, including a number of covers from the likes of *Detective Weekly* and *Union Jack*, as well as new illustrations from Savoy stalwarts Kris Guidio and John Coulthart, an exhaustively researched foreword by Jack Adrian and a fascinating reminiscence on the contemporary pulp scene by Moorcock. This is about as far as it gets from cynical hack publishing — but then Savoy sets higher standards than most. Recommended. [James Marriott]

MOTHERFUCKERS
The Aushwitz of Oz
David Britton

How shocking is 'shocking'? It's pretty wishy-washy if half the novels heralded as such are anything to go by. The entire book-reading world would, by now, be a mass of gibbering idiots with all the supposedly 'shocking' fiction out there. It's utter rot. There should be a separate language for critics. They call a book 'disturbing' and 'dangerous' and it means poop. There are exceptions, of course. Here's one. Police seized David Britton's novel *Lord Horror* in 1989 and wanted it destroyed. Forget 'dangerous' in context of the Booker Prize for Fiction. That is dangerous with an official *real-world* stamp. Now Britton has a new novel, *Motherfuckers* — every bit as worrying.

Cast your mind back to the Nazi Death Camps. According to 'The Thirteenth Law of Faerie', every camp shall have its twins. Ub and Sub in Buchenwald, Amos and Andy in Ravensbrück, Fudge and Speck in Sobibor, Weary Willie and Tired Tim in Maidanek, Tweedle Dee and Tweedle Dum in Chelmno, and in Auschwitz, Meng and Ecker. The latter pair were rescued for 'research' purposes by Dr Mengele, who in turn gave them to the ubiquitous Lord Horror as a gift. If it's necessary to pin *Motherfuckers* to a plot, let's say that the 'creep boys' Meng & Ecker are in search of their master. But that's almost beside the point. (Particularly as Horror's location is divulged to Meng at the opening of the novel, but he forgets.) The book is a surrealist fantasy, folding in upon itself one moment and erupting the next to offer a myriad vile avenues down which the reader may be taken. Here Herbie Schopenhauer is a little red Volkswagen surreptitiously coaxed into the shower rooms of Dachau, holding philosophical conversations with Elvis; Mr Toad (of Toad Hall) is hunting down leftover body parts in order to sell them off again; Bruce Springsteen has lost his arsehole in New Orleans; and, Bismarck, a stall holder on the market near Tib Street makes his living selling dodgy fruit, because his customers like the danger.

Manchester is the microcosm for this pre-decimalisation, *Radio Fun* universe. Sights familiar on that fair city's streets can be found in abundance here, in *Motherfuckers*, but — in typical dream fashion — they're askew. Piccadilly Station has become Toon Town. Mickey Mouse is shopping in the Arndale. Dead men reminisce with the living and ponder the nature of their own demise. It might be Heaven, more likely Hell. It's a world which sticks to the feet when the chase is on.

Prior to this book, Meng & Ecker featured regularly in the comic book series of the same name (also published by Savoy, issue one of which is still down as obscene by law). But with *Motherfuckers*, the mad characters, mad backdrops and mad situations shimmer to life with a spark that the comic medium fails to provide. Britton's prose is a delight. The manner of the book is outwardly genial, hopeful and optimistic, but there's a couple of loose wires which keep shorting out the system. A big muddy boot stomping on the clean carpet transmission.

"Caps off! Caps on!" The ritualistic call from the two SS men duetted with a frivolity incomprehensible to a normal human brain. The twin scratched his head. Bestial cruelties, unimaginable vileness and damnable occurrences were so commonplace here, it was pointless writing a letter home.
The dying man stopped before Ecker, staring wordlessly. Maggots were already acrawl in his nostrils.
"Put your face straight," cautioned Ecker.
The man crumbled. Ecker dodged his vainly fluttering stick-like arms. The man seemed to melt all over the clay. Suddenly his body burst open. Parts of his intestines lay smoking, coiling on the outside of his stomach.
Bite marks were visible on the spilled organs.
Now here was a mystery new to Ecker — another conundrum offered to him for inspection by the killing grounds of Bikenau.

Lord Horror, David Britton's previous novel, was accused of being anti-Semitic. It was cleared. Maybe the case — which ended with Britton going to prison anyway — burst a vessel in the author's brain, for *Motherfuckers* is far more liberal with its ethnic abuse and slurs than that earlier book. But the Jews aren't the sole target here; everybody gets a shout. One early chapter has Meng, a superstar, with a following of underage groupies, getting up to perform his world famous comedy routine. Of course, as it's blatantly modelled on the controversial Mancunian comic, Bernard Manning (even down to using some of his material), the police can hardly be seen to come down too heavily on Britton this time. After all, it was the Manchester police who were recently taken to task for having hired Manning to perform at one of their official functions. The chapter in question pounds relentlessly, with one sick joke after another. It is groan-inducingly humorous to begin with, pitiful, embarrassing, then, after about the hundredth gag, numbing. But Britton isn't simply going through the motions, nor is he burning his bridges with the Manning/Manchester Police metaphor, there's a point to be made.

The book is a moral one without preaching morals. But it does occasionally open itself — like a sore might under pressure — and allows the reader to peek within. The real *within*. One such break in the surface manifests on page eighty-six:

A work of fiction that would do justice to the Holocaust must take as its first principle the shattering of chronology.

Dangerous. Like recreating rational thought from scratch. A very powerful book indeed. [David Kerekes]

CONTRIBUTOR NOTES

K A BEER Tall, broad shouldered, inevitably dressed in black, his contrasting long grey hair in a pony-tail, he looks gothic, possibly a master of some black art. He is however mild mannered, courteous and thoughtful, a carpenter by trade. His interest in the unusual, the bizarre, even the grotesque sets him apart. He likes reading books of the darker side, even the perverted. He enjoys art, films, music, and sex. He is bisexual, embracing all things transgender, dressing as Kay occasionally. You may unknowingly have read one of his essays on some morbid theme or bondage.

ANTON BLACK was born in London in 1973. After doing an interesting yet vocationally useless degree, he returned. He would love to move out, if only he had somewhere to go. He works as a freelance script analyst for The Film Council, writes for *Headpress* and *Adverse Effect*, has DJed at the Horse Hospital, and, posing fraudulently as film director Hal Hartley, once published a libellous article in *The Guardian*. His interests include Northern Soul and finding aesthetic transcendence in Italian gore movies. He is a good cook.

BEN BLACKSHAW doesn't write much and doesn't like what he does write. He contributes to this book begrudgingly, and refuses to work for anyone else. He lives in Manchester, England.

TOM BRINKMANN Born 1955 in Manchester, New Hampshire, USA, Tom Brinkmann is an avid collector of underground and counterculture comix, newspapers and magazines. He worked as a printer while being peripherally involved in self published (*Pure Sex 1–3*, *Tattooed Paper*, *Science Friction*, etc) and alternative comix, with Clay Geerdes' *Comix World* and others from 1979–85. His artwork has appeared in *Hair To Stay*, *Assertive Women* and *Leg Tease* magazines, and he has contributed material to Headpress since 1998. He currently lives on Long Island, New York. His book *Bad Mags* is scheduled for publication by Headpress/Critical Vision in 2005.

MIKITA BROTTMAN is a longtime contributor to *Headpress*. She writes for a number of different publications, both mainstream and alternative, and is professor of language and literature at the Maryland Institute College of Art in Baltimore. She is the editor of *Car Crash Culture* (NY: Palgrave, 2002), and the author, most recently, of *Funny Peculiar: Gershon Legman and the Psychopathology of Humor* (NY: Analytic Press, 2004).

JAN R BRUUN Born 1966 in Norway, Jan Bruun has been writing reviews and articles for a variety of zines, newspapers and journals in Europe and the USA since 1984. Subjects: obscure music, cult movies, true crime, conspiracies, freak shows... His first contribution to *Headpress* was a photo in No 16. [w] http://home.online.no/~janbruun/

MICHAEL CARLSON Michael Carlson has written studies of Sergio Leone, Clint Eastwood, and Oliver Stone in the *Pocket Essentials* series, eight collections of poetry, and the Channel 5 Guide to Baseball. He is the film editor of *Crime Time* magazine, and has written for the *Spectator*, *Guardian*, *Telegraph*, *Financial Times*, *TLS*, *Petrolhead*, *Xtreme*, and many others. As Mike Carlson he presents sports programmes for Channel 5, Sky Sports, and Showtime Sport. Born in New Haven Connecticut, educated at Wesleyan and McGill, he has lived in London since 1977, and has worked for a television news agency, an American TV network, and Major League Baseball. He's married with a son born on Halloween, 2003.

JOHN CARTER Aging (fifty+) grumpy old man. Been a member of the British Fantasy Society since the mid seventies and got hooked into the *Headpress* vibe some years later. Tried his hand at short stories (and had a number of them publsihed in the 'small press'), but found his niche in reviews, which he enjoys far more. Also known as Mad John or Whisperin' John Carter.

RICK CAVENEY is a proletariat poof with a passion for porn.

SIMON COLLINS was in utero in the Haight-Ashbury during the Summer of Love. He was given a fine education and every chance in life, but has been merrily skipping down the highway to hell hand-in-hand with Headpress since 1993, when he was delighted to discover there was a media outlet for twisted slackers like himself. His work has also appeared in *Chaotic Order*, *Judas Kiss*, *ByPass*, *h2so4*, *Piercing World* and *Desire Direct*. Current obsessions include heathenism and European folklore, shamanism, runes and ogham, fetish culture, tattoos and piercings, absinthe, espresso and industrial music. Some day, he hopes to be able to make a living from this hodgepodge of unhealthy interests, but that day is long in coming…

MARK FARRELLY [All attempts to track Mark Farrelly down have proven fruitless. We have included the one review he submitted to *Headpress* in this book — a review of *Ghastly Terror!* which originally appeared in *Headpress 20* — and hope that he forgives us for it.]

DAVID GREENALL Adopted at birth in 1968, spoilt rotten and allowed to watch horror films from an early age, David Greenall dressed up in his Grandma's clothes to re-enact scenes from Hammer productions, fuelling rumours of sexual perversion and bloodlust among worried family and friends... Video entertainment pre 1984 VRA fed his addiction, and violent Goth music shaped his appearance resulting in suspension from school. Eventually gained a first class BA(Hons)Degree in Photographic Studies (his Degree show screening prompted a visit from the Boys In Blue), leading to specialist work at Kino Film Club, Cornerhouse, It's Queer Up North (Manchester), Jyvaskyla Arts Festival (Finland) and Bolton Institute. Currently trying to hold down "proper" jobs with an income enough to fuel his passion for deep house music and associated stimuli!

MARTIN JONES is the author of *Psychedelic Decadence: Sex Drugs Low-Art in 60s & 70s Britain* and the editor of *Lovers, Buggers & Thieves: Garage Rock, Monster Rock, Psychedelic Rock, Progressive Rock*, both published by Headpress/Critical Vision. With the artist Oliver Tomlinson he runs Omnium Gatherum Press, creators of *Careful*, a comic so sinister one would normally shun it. [w] www.omniumgatherumpress.com

DAVID KEREKES Born in Manchester, England, David Kerekes is editor, publisher and co-founder of Headpress. He is author of the book *Sex Murder Art: The Films of Jörg Buttgereit*, co-author of *Killing for Culture* and *See No Evil*, and has contributed to the studies *Punk Rock: So What?*, *Car Crash Culture* and *Modern Death*. He has written for many periodicals in the mainstream and alternative press. [w] www.headpress.com

JAMES MARRIOTT lives in Bristol and has written two true crime books, *Danger Down Under* and *Tourist Trap*, under his pseudonym Patrick Blackden. He is currently working on a book about tourist misbehaviour and an encyclopaedia of the supernatural. He can be contacted at [e] jmarriott78@hotmail.com

PHIL DALGARNO has contributed one review to this book

and doesn't know what to say in a bio. However, if anyone wishes to contact him about *TIHKAL*, his review, he may be reached at [e] dimethyltryptamine777@hotmail.com

TEMPLE DRAKE A turbulent upbringing in the American south has given Temple Drake an acute knowledge of sex, religion and death, making her eminently qualified to select reviews from the last ten years of *Headpress Journal* for this *Guide to the Counter Culture*. Little more is known about her other than wherever she is, whiskey and mischief are sure to follow.

PAN PANTZIARKA Author of *House of Pain* and *Lone Wolf* (and a dozen other books he prefers not to mention), Pan is busily re-inventing himself as an academic. He is also the editor of Black Star Review [w] www.blackstarreview.com, and continues to write for a number of magazines.

RIK RAWLING Exiled from Yorkshire for not beating his wife and reading books without pictures, Rawling ekes out a living in Bristol selling pegs. His numerous artistic ventures have gained him neither fame nor notoriety — but he's not bitter, just twisted. Those intrigued should visit [w] www.rikrawling.co.uk

ROBERT ROSEN is the author of the critically acclaimed biography *Nowhere Man: The Final Days of John Lennon*, an international bestseller available in the US from Quick American Archives [w] www.quickamerican.com, and in the UK from Fusion Press. He is currently working on a memoir, *Beaver Street: An Insider's History of Modern Pornography*.

JACK SARGEANT Born in 1968, Jack Sargeant's earliest memory is of knocking on the neighbour's door at the age of three in the hope of seeing their newborn baby, which he was told had six fingers on each hand. A pivotal event in his life, his interests haven't changed since then. He is the author of several works on underground film (*Deathtripping: The Cinema of Transgression* and *Naked Lens: Beat Cinema*), and has written and edited various true crime books (*Born Bad* and *Death Cults*). He has had work published in various book collections and magazines, including *Car Crash Culture*, *Underground USA*, *Headpress*, *BBGun*, *Panik*, and others. When not writing, he curates various film and arts festivals, and lectures widely.

STEPHEN SENNITT edited and published the highly controversial and respected occult journal *NOX* from 1986–90. He is the author of four books; *Xenos* (1989) and *Monstrous Cults* (1992); and *Ghastly Terror!* (1999) and *Creatures of Clay* (2003) — the last pair from Headpress/Critical Vision. His articles and reviews have appeared in publications such as *Rapid Eye*, *Esoterra*, *Kaos*, *The Book of Ebon*, *Dark Doctrines*, *Cthulhu Codex*, *Red Stains*, *Headpress* and *Creeping Flesh*. He likes Highbrow and Lowbrow culture and despises everything in between.

SARAH TURNER Having recently found herself a house in the country, the reviews Sarah Turner wrote for *Headpress* may well prove the last reviews she ever decides to write.

JOE SCOTT WILSON was born in the north of England and is lame. His passion for life is equalled only by his love for great music. He shuns publicity and doesn't care much for modern things (except computers and the television). He is a contributor to *Headpress* and the forthcoming Headpress/Critical Vision book, *Lovers Buggers & Thieves*.

WILL YOUDS has been contributing to *Headpress* for the a good few years with reviews, interviews and features with artists on the proverbial edge. He is keen on performance poetry and also play writing. Currently involved with a new avant-garde act for performance involving the Theremin.

THE ALTERNATIVE FORTEAN TIMES

(beware imitations of this monthly magazine)

http://www.combat-diaries.thewhyfiles.co.uk

Google registers 2.5 million hits for thewhyfiles!

Contributions welcome, drop a line to: **sharkley1@panzerben1.fsworld.co.uk**

No skeptics please, we are all elvish.
Dedicated to all those insane enough for Last Thoughts in these Last Days.

---

www.headpress.com

Headpress/Critical Vision, PO Box 26, Manchester, M26 1PQ, UK

INDEX

101 Best Graphic Novels, The 43
17% Hendrix Was Not The Only Musician 149
2024 43
666 Ways to Get Into Heaven 225
79 Reasons Why Hitchhiking Sucks 6
Adventures of Meng & Ecker, The 43
Aleister Crowley: The Beast Demystified 149
All About Evil 225
All About Fuckin' 20
All I Need To Know About Filmmaking... 89
Alternative Cinema 6
American Splendor Presents... 86
Amok Fifth Dispatch 150
Anamorphosis 219
Angels in Distress 29
Animal Man 44
AntiCristo 89
An Unseemly Man 150
Apocalypse Culture II 152
Art at the Turn of the Millenium 44
Art of Darkness 127
Art of the Nasty, The 90
Ask Dr Mueller 153
Avengers Companion, The 92
Azrael Project Newsletter 7
Babylon Blue 93
Baby Doll 44
Backstage Passes and Backstabbing... 129
Bad Pills 7
bAnal Probe 7
Baptised in the Blood of Millions 248
Barroom Transcripts 218
Batman: Other Realms 45
Beatles Uncovered, The 130
Because She Thought She Loved Me 225
Bechamp or Pasteur? 154
Beef Torpedo 7
Best of American Girlie Magazines, The 46
Beyond Terror 128
Big Book of Urban Legends, The 212
Bile 226
Bizarrism 8, 154
Black Rose, The 226
Bloodsongs 9
Blood and Black Lace 127
Blown 235
Blue Blood 9
Bob Flanagan Supermasochist 155
Body Probe 157
Bomba Movies 9
Book Happy 9
Book of Changes 130
Book of Mr Natural, The 86
Brotherhoods of Fear 157
Brutarian 10
Bukowski 222
Bukowski Unleashed! 223
Bukowski Zine 11
Burger Dude 227
Butchershop in the Sky 227
Caligula Divine Carnage 167
Camden Parasites 229
Cannibal Holocaust 128
Careful 11
Caricature 81

Carpe Noctem 11
Car Crash Culture 158
Chaotic Order 12
CharlieUncleNorfolkTango 228
Cheesecake! 46
Christopher Walken: Movie Top Ten 93
Chuckling Whatsits, The 47
Cinema Contra Cinema 95
Cine East 94
City of the Broken Dolls 47
Cobralingus 229
Cockroach Papers 159
Collected Checkered Demon, The 48
Collected Palestine 48
Completely Mad 49
Complete Cannon, The 49
Complete Crumb Comics, The 87
Complete Frankie Howerd, The 95
Concrete Jungle 159
Confusion Incorporated 220
Cop Porn 12
Corpse Garden, The 160
Crash 161
Crime Wave 229
Cunt 230
Dainty Viscera 13
Dancing Queen 161
Dark Moon 162
DC vs Marvel 50
Dead Walk, The 95
Death Scenes 163
Deepening Witchcraft 164
Delirium 13, 128
Derriere 13
Desire Direct 15
Desperate Visions 95
Deviant 165
Deviant Desires 165
Diabolik 15
Digital Beauties 51
Digital Leatherette 231
Dirty Money and Other Stories 231
Doc. Gordon Tripp Lectures Again 188
Draculina 15
Duh 51
Dungeonmaster's Apprentice, The 231
DVD Delirium 96
Encyclopaedia Anatomica 51
Encyclopedia of Western Gunfighters, The 168
End-Time Visions 169
End of Time, The 169
Eros in Hell 97
Erotic Review, The 15
Esoterrorist 171
Essential Monster Movie Guide, The 97
Ethical Slut, The 172
Exit Collection, The 52
Exploits of Engelbrecht, The 250
Exquisite Mayhem 53
Extraterrestrial Sex Fetish 232
Extreme Islam 172
Fantasy Worlds 54
Fear and Loathing 16
Fear of Comics 54
February 24 17
Fetish 55
Filmbook Reference Guide 98
Fleshpot 99
Flesh & Blood 17
Flickers of the Dreamachine 221
Floozy 233
Flowers From Hell 234

Former Child Star 100
Fragments of Fear 101
Freak Like Me 173
Fuck 18
Fucked Up & Photocopied 58
Funeral Party Vol 2 175
Garbage People 176
Gas, The 251
Gates of Janus, The 176
Gauntlet 19
Generation Fetish 56
Ghastly Terror! 57
Ghost World 82
Global Tapestry Journal 20
Gods of Death 177
God Is Happy! 20
Good Cunt Boy is Hard to Find, A 225
Gray's Anatomy, The 234
Great Tales of Jewish Fantasy 179
Grossed-Out Surgeon Vomits Inside Patient 180
Hair to Stay 21
Hammer Story, The 102
Happyland 21
Hard Boiled 57
Harriet Staunton 234
Haunted World of Mario Bava, The 127
Headpress 125
Head Magazine 22
Healter Skelter 22
High Art 58
Hip Pocket Sleaze 32
Hog 23
Hollywood Hex 103
Hollywood Rat Race 104
Hoover Hog 23
Hôpital Brut 59
Horrorgasmo 60
Horror of the 20th Century 61
How to Draw and Sell Comic Strips 63
I'd Rather You Lied 235
Icon 64
If I'm So Famous, How Come Nobody's...? 104
Ilsa Chronicles 105
Image Of The Beast, The 235
Implosion 24
Inappropriate Behaviour 181
Index 181
Infiltration 25
Is it... Uncut? 25
It Came from Bob's Basement 106
I Was For Sale 182
Jack Cole and Plastic Man 65
James Bidgood 106
Jimmy Corrigan 65
Joel Peter Witkin 67
Joe Gould's Secret 182
Judge Dredd: Goodnight Kiss 68
Judge Dredd: Helter Skelter 68
Juice 183
Junk DNA 235
Justice League of America: The Nail 70
Keeping the British End Up 107
Killer Fiction 236
L'Horreur est humaine 24
Legs That Dance To Elmer's Tune 71
Life and Times of R Crumb, The 87
Life Sucks Die 25
Like a Velvet Glove Cast in Iron 83
Locked in the Arms of a Crazy Life 223
Lost Highways 121

Lucifer Rising 184
Magickal Weddings 164
Malefact 26
Malicious Resplendence 71
Mama Snake 29
Mammoth Book of Women Who Kill, The 185
Manchester Slingback 237
Mansplat 26
Mars Attacks! 107
Mattress 71
Maxon's Poe 88
Meat is Murder! 185
Monkey Girl 238
Monsieur Zenith the Albino 251
Moonchild 108
Morbid Curiosities 27
More Barroom Transcripts 219
Motherfuckers 252
Muerte! 186
Murder By Numbers 187
Muse-Trap, The 239
Naked Lens 109
Nameless Aeons 27
Nasty Tales 71
Necrotourist 188
Network News 28
Never Hit the Ground 239
Nineteen Seventy Seven 240
Noirotica 3 240
Nox 28
Offensive Films 110
Oklahoma City Bombing and the Politics of Terror 188
One Summer Day 29
Ongaku Otaku 29
Oswald Talked 190
Out-takes 220
Paperback Dungeon 30
Pass The Marmalade 110
Penny in Harness 241
Philosophy of Wicca 164
Pills-a-go-go 191
Planet of the Apes 111
Planet of the Apes Chronicles, The 111
Politics of the Imagination 191
Porco Mondo 30
Pornocopia 192
Porn King 111
Pretty Things 241
Professional Paranoid, The 192
Prohibited Matter 31
Psychedelia Britannica 193
Psychedelic Decadence 194
Psychedelic Nazis 32
Psychopathia Sexualis 195
Psychotronic Video Guide, The 113
Psychotropedia 196
Pulp Art 64
Punk Strips 72
Pussey! 83
Rag 32
Randy Reviewer, The 32
Rapid Eye Movement 197
Raw Creation 73
Redneck Manifesto, The 197
Red Wine Moan 242
Reel Wild Cinema 32
Roy Stuart 85
Roy Stuart Vol II 85
Satan! Satan! Satan! 242
Satanic Screen, The 113
Satan Speaks! 198
Scary! 73
Screams & Nightmares 114
SCUM Manifesto 199

Searching for Robert Johnson 199
Seek! 200
See No Evil 115
Severed 201
Sex, Stupidity and Greed 117
Sexuality, Magic & Perversion 205
Sexually Dominant Woman, The 205
Sexual Criminal, The 204
Sex and Rockets 202
Sex Carnival 203
Sex Murder Art 116
Shag Stamp 33
Shining Ones, The 206
Shock Cinema 33
Sick Puppy Comix 33
Sisters of Severcy 244
Slave of Passion 245
Snake 245
Snitch Culture 207
Something Weird Video Blue-Book 34
Straight From the Fridge Dad 208
Struggle 73
Struwwelpeter 75
Subculture 245
Supergirl 77
Superman: Whatever Happened to the...? 77
Suture 118
Sweet Smell of Sick Sex 35
Tales from the Clit 209
Tales From The Idiot Box 35
Tales of Terror! 77
Tales of Times Square 119
Taste of Blood, A 120
Teignmouth Electron 209
Temple of Blasphemy 78
That's Sexploitation! 120
Thinking of England 210
Third Eye 36
Tick 246
Tihkal 211
Tits-out Teenage Terror Totty 242
Tokyo Sex Underground 212
Too Good To Be True 212
Torture Garden, The 247
Totem of the Depraved 121
Trash City 36
Travels with Dr Death 213
Tricks And Treats 215
TwoBlue Couples 37
UFO 215
Ugly Cunt Fuck 20
Ultra-Gash Inferno 79
Ultra Flesh 37
Ultra Violent 37
Underworld of the East 216
Unrated 37
Unseen Bruce Lee, The 122
Velvet Underground, The 216
Vex 38
Vixxxen 38
Voluptuous 39
Voyeur Video Guide To Special-Interest Male... 123
Weirdsville USA 123
Weird Zines 39
Wes Craven's The Last House on the Left 124
Whitman's Wild Children 217
Who Runs May Read 221
Witchcraft and the Web 164
X-Rated Bible, The 217
X: The Unknown 39
XXXOOO 80
X Factory, The 126
Yankee Clipper 40